The Jews in the Soviet Union since 1917

Paradox of Survival

Volume II

The Jews in the
Soviet Union since 1917

Paradox of Survival

Volume II

Nora Levin

NEW YORK UNIVERSITY PRESS
New York and London

Library of Congress Cataloging-in-Publication Data
Levin, Nora.
  The Jews in the Soviet Union since 1917
  Bibliography: p.
  includes index.
    1. Jews—Soviet Union—History—1917–
2. Soviet Union—Ethnic relations.   I. Title.
DS135.R92L48   1987   947'.004924   87-21951
ISBN 0-8147-5018-4 (set)
ISBN 0-8147-5034-6 (v. 1)
ISBN 0-8147-5035-4 (v. 2)

Book design by Ken Venezio

Dedicated to the many thousands of men and women in the Soviet Union who have suffered and perished struggling to maintain personal honor, integrity, and freedom for the sake of Jewish survival, despite terror, wasting exile, and the breakdown of trust.

Contents

Photographs

Maps

Tables

24

Intensified Persecution: Anti-Semitism Becomes Official Policy, 1952–54

They are never to be forgotten, those Elgen children. I'm not saying that there is any comparison between them and, say, the Jewish children in Hitler's empire. . . . And yet when one calls to mind Elgen's gray, featureless landscape, shrouded in the melancholy of non-existence, the most fantastic, the most satanic invention of all seems to be those huts with signs saying "Infants' Group," "Toddlers' Group," and "Senior Group."

EUGENIA GINZBURG, *Within the Whirlwind*

Just ask my contemporaries:
Camp women, prison women, martyrs,
And we will tell you of numb terror,
Of raising children for execution
At the block, or back to the wall,
Of raising children for the prisons.

AKHMATOVA

THE writers Markish, Feffer, Bergelson, Kvitko, Hofshteyn, and Halkin, who had been arrested in 1948–49, languished in prison until the summer of 1952 and were among the twenty-five Jews brought to trial on July 11, after going through Beria's inquisition cells. They were charged with being enemies of the USSR, agents of American imperialism, guilty of bourgeois national Zionism, and trying to sever the Crimea from the Soviet Union. It is believed that there was a secret trial from July 11 to 18, at which twenty-five Yiddish writers, actors, and cultural activists were tried, including Bergelson, Feffer, Hofshteyn, Kvitko, Lozovsky, Markish, Nusinov, Persov, Spivak, and Zuskin. Esther Markish also mentions two women who were tried: Mira

Zheleznova, Feffer's secretary, and a woman named "Chaika," "a journalist and one-time American citizen who had worked as a translator
in the committee [JAC]."[1] The names of the remaining twelve persons
are not known. Dr. Lina Shtern, a gifted scientist, was also among the
twenty-five defendants, and the only one among them who survived.
The others were executed on August 12, 1952, in the cellar of Moscow's
Lubyanka prison.[2] Dr. Shtern was sentenced to life imprisonment, a
sentence later commuted. She was released and exonerated in the course
of the de-Stalinization of the mid-fifties. To this day, the circumstances
under which these executions took place have never been revealed by
the government, nor is it known where the individuals are buried.
Among those murdered were the intellectural elite of Soviet Jewish life,
its most creative elements, leaving no doubt that Stalin intended to
destroy the possibilities of a future Jewish culture for good.

After her "rehabilitation," Dr. Shtern,[3] who had emigrated to the
Soviet Union from America in the late thirties, told Mrs. Markish that
early in 1949 she was told the Minister of State Security Abakumov
wanted to have a "chat" with her. As soon as she stepped into his
office, he began shouting: "We know everything! Come clean! You're
a Zionist, you were bent on detaching the Crimea from Russia and
establishing a Jewish state there!" "That's the first I've heard of it,"
she replied. "Why, you old whore!" Abakumov roared back. Until May
1952, the only person she saw of the group arrested was Feffer, who
looked "sick, pitiful, demoralized." He apparently wanted her to say,
in the presence of an interrogator, that she was involved in a "Zionist
underground"—a shocking notion, which she rejected outright. "With
her own eyes," as recounted to Mrs. Markish, she later saw "the
bloodied [Dr. Boris] Shimelovich, [a former director of the Botkin Hospital in Moscow] and Zuskin, half-crazed, and Bergelson, who had grown
old and feeble." And she saw Markish, too, who "delivered an eloquent and devastating speech at the trial . . . [in which] he lashed out
against his tormentors and their mentors with all the power of his creative genius. While Lina Shtern could not recollect his exact words, she
remembered that he spoke not as defendant but as a prosecutor." None
of the defendants, according to her, pleaded guilty except Feffer.

In the Soviet Union itself, Jews, and other Soviet citizens, of course,
knew that a great many leading figures and less known ones had disappeared, but officials refused to release any information about their
fate, or the fate of thousands of others who had been exiled, shot, or

sent to far off prison camps (see Map 24.1).[4] There were rumors and whisperings and great apprehensiveness but no hard facts. Moreover, between 1949 and 1955, there were frequent attempts by Western Jewish institutions and personalities, and occasionally by non-Jews, to obtain authoritative information about the rumored liquidation of Jewish culture. Inquiries were addressed to Moscow, and to the Soviet officials at the UN, and to the Soviet ambassador, and questions were asked of Ehrenburg and Fadeyev (who had come to America in the spring of 1949). But they were answered evasively, shrugged off, or denied as insults (see Chapter 25). Yet the complete severance of contacts and the marked silence of Soviet Jewish writers spoke more compellingly than these unconvincing mutterings. In 1951, Hayim Greenberg, the fearless and eloquent editor of the *Jewish Frontier*, wrote a bitterly sarcastic open letter to the Soviet ambassador in America:

> I am told that the entertainment columns of the Moscow newspapers no longer mention the existence of the Yiddish theater. Yet only a few years ago the dramatic art in Yiddish had been highly praised. These are not military secrets which the government is justified in concealing.
> And what happened to the Yiddish press in the Soviet Union? Has it committed suicide or has it been murdered? . . .
> And what happened to the Yiddish writers? . . . . We in the United States do not know whether these vanished Yiddish authors have been kidnapped, executed, exiled to forced labor, or whether they have committed suicide. . . .
> But what about other Yiddish authors, the ones not exiled or liquidated? . . . .
> Have all the Yiddish authors in the Soviet Union been found guilty without exception? Has the Yiddish press proved to be counter-revolutionary in its entirety.[5]

This letter, too, remained unanswered. It was only in 1956 that the American Jewish journalist Leon Crystal first publicly disclosed the fact that twenty to thirty Soviet Jewish writers had been executed on August 12, 1952. Later it was confirmed that twenty-four writers and others had been executed, "and reportedly six Jewish engineers from the Stalin Vehicle Assembly Plant in Moscow"[6] (see Chapter 25).

The onslaught against Jews charged ahead. Just two days after the Prague trial ended (November 27, 1952), a wave of cases against Jewish "swindlers and embezzlers" swept over the Soviet Union, involving managers of factories, administrators in ministries, employees in banks, educational and scientific institutions, cooperatives, theatrical studios, railroads, lawyers, and engineers. Their alleged crimes involved profiteering, stealing state property, wasting funds and materials, bribery,

MAP 24.1
Prison Camps and Places of Exile

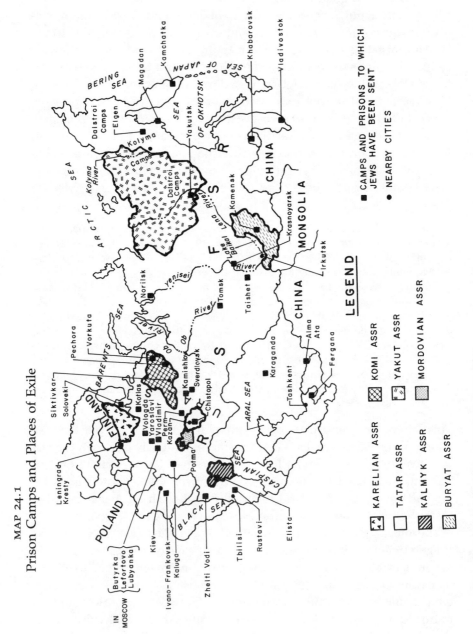

LEGEND

■ CAMPS AND PRISONS TO WHICH JEWS HAVE BEEN SENT

● NEARBY CITIES

KARELIAN ASSR

KOMI ASSR

TATAR ASSR

YAKUT ASSR

KALMYK ASSR

MORDOVIAN ASSR

BURYAT ASSR

Adapted from Martin Gilbert, Soviet History Atlas,

and fraud. Few highly placed Jews still held positions, but there were some in supply and distribution jobs and in retail trade.

Newspapers and periodicals were full of exposures of "criminals" with conspicuously Jewish names, defrauding Soviet society of varied consumer goods: clothing, shoes, building materials, foodstuffs, watches, and private vehicles at a time when there were shortages.[7] Old but effective clichés reminded readers that most of the criminals were indeed Jewish because they were described as "pushy," had "fat, cozy jobs," "covered up" for each other, and were "greedy."[8] Many were described as having Zionist connections, or as being Zionist agents serving foreign enemies. The non-Jews named were generally "accomplices" or minor partners, drawn into deals by crafty Jews.

Fear gripped the Jewish population as these accusations hailed down. Many grew despondent, feeling helpless against the barrage of propaganda, and stricken by the hostility of the press, institutions, officials, and neighbors. Jews also faced economic downgrading as well as social ostracism and were eliminated from certain categories of work. For example, during the war, there had been a fairly high proportion of Jews in the supreme command, but nothing was heard of them in the late forties. Between 1948 and 1953, 63 Jewish generals, 111 colonels, and 159 lieutenant-colonels were retired.[9] By 1953, there wasn't a single Jew among the hundred or so top-ranking officers. In 1948–49, Jewish military and administrative personnel in the Soviet Union were purged, and military academies were barred to Jews.[10] Milovan Djilas, who visited the Soviet Union with a Yugoslav delegation in 1948, was informed by a central party official, that when the deputy chief of staff General Aleksei Antonov was discovered to be a Jew, it meant the end of his career.[11]

In the thirties, there was only one Jewish member of the Politburo, Lazar Kaganovich, but there were nine Jews in the party's Central Committee of seventy-one members in 1939. Of these, only Kaganovich was re-elected at the Party Congress in 1952. Nor were there any Jews in the Secretariat of the Central Committee or among the first party secretaries of the republics. Jewish membership in the Supreme Soviet, consisting of the Soviet of the Union and the Soviet of Nationalities, also dwindled. In the former, there were only five Jews in 1946; no statistics are available for the latter, but it has been estimated that Jews ranked twenty-sixth in 1946, from eleventh place in 1937, among all nationalities.[12]

A large number of Jews were also expelled from leading positions in planning, economic, and industrial agencies. Because "security" concerns affected virtually every economic and service activity, Jews lost their jobs in trade unions, propaganda, and informational agencies and journalism. One of the very few journalists who had survived, David Zaslavsky, was removed from his position on *Pravda* in 1953 after one of his colleagues reportedly claimed that he could not work together with a man who belonged to a race of traitors and poisoners.[13] Jewish radio announcers and commentators were charged with having Western sympathies and insufficient knowledge of the Russian language.

There were conspicious dismissals of Jewish students from technical institutes in 1950–51 and mass dismissals following the Nineteenth Party Congress in October 1952.[14] For example, in Leningrad, scores of Jews were discharged from the Institute of Sanitation and Hygiene, and at the Institute for the Advanced Training of Doctors, there was a thorough purge.[15] At the Institute of Pediatrics, the Jewish woman director named Mendeleva, an old Bolshevik who had known Lenin well, was dismissed and arrested; her successor named Shutova expelled all Jews.[16] A witness to these purges reports that those who were dismissed were not re-engaged even after Stalin's death. Most went into the provinces. University professors and researchers were also dismissed. Jewish jurists and legal experts were accused of ideological deviations and nepotism. Even Mark Gallai, perhaps the most famous test pilot in the Soviet Union, lost his job because he was Jewish.[17]

A young Jewish economist, who had graduated from the Moscow State Economic Institute in 1949, could not do creative scholarly work in the early 1950s, and worked part-time at a "College of Book Distribution".[18] He also worked as a volunteer speaker for the Moscow Komsomol Committee and was able to visit many enterprises, enabling him to write a book in 1952 on interrelations between forms of organization of production and wages in Soviet industry. He was subsequently charged with trying to "blow up [subvert] the plant from within" by suggesting that the functions of machine operators and adjusters be combined and by highlighting a gap in wages between foremen and highly qualified workers—in favor of the latter—thus discouraging workers from going into foremen's jobs. Unknown to the young economist, soon after the war Stalin had signed a secret circular prohibiting increases in wages and wage-rates. Later he also learned that the man who instigated the charge—Valery Belkin—had done so because "in order to succeed you have to learn how to 'sell out' those who need you to those whom you need." Belkin had "sold him out" during the period of raging anti-Semitism.[19]

In 1950, in one Institute of Technology, almost one hundred Jews were dismissed within three days. No reason was given. A list of those dismissed was posted and some students stopped talking to those listed, "as if they had the plague." A few managed to find positions in other scientific institutes; others went to factories. Many went to the provinces. At the time the KGB carried on sudden, grueling interrogations in which the victims were not allowed to sleep or have any food. Informers were cultivated and accusations concocted.[20]

Some of the dismissals were brutally direct and swift. In other cases, Jews were instructed to apply for discharge on the grounds of health, or agree to demotion "to relieve pressure of work."[21] Trivial mistakes were inflated and used punitively. Whereas, before the war, Jews had accounted for 40 percent of students in the department of philology in the University of Moscow, in 1951, only three Jewish applicants out of a total of 250, were admitted. Jews began to seek unobtrusive positions and openings in those fields still available to them: Russian literature, painting, sculpture, music, ballet, the exact sciences, and technology. Many began to refer to themselves as "fifth-rate invalids"—a reference to the fifth entry on the Soviet internal passport which indicated the bearer's nationality.[22] The designation *Evrei* punctured the shield of assimilation of many Soviet Jews.

The re-writing of Jewish history, which heretofore had been viewed through the restrictive screen of Marxism, but which, at least, had been acknowledged as a valid field of human experience, was now contracted to virtual nonexistence. In 1952, the year of the Slansky Trial in Czechoslovakia, a new edition of the *Bolshaya sovetskaya entsiklopediya* (Great Soviet Encyclopedia) began to appear. Volume 15 (1953) contains the article on Jews. The brevity of material—just four columns—is in shocking contrast to the entries in the first edition, which began appearing in 1932. In the first edition, the entry under "Evrei" ran to 108 columns, or fifty-four pages. In addition, there were entries under Jewish literature, the Jewish Problem, the Yiddish language, the Jewish religion, Jewish music, art, and the theater as well as Jewish parties, newspapers, institutions, and important events in Jewish history. These entries in Volume 24 ran to another forty-five columns in the first edition.[23]

In the second edition, Jewish content is virtually nonexistent, or skewed. Stalin's essay *Marxism and the National Question* is used to deny that Jews are a nation. They are defined as "different peoples, having a common origin in the ancient Hebrews. . . . Their economic, political and cultural life they share in common with the peoples around them." As to Yiddish, the editors grant that the Jews of Russia spoke Yiddish "in the past," as if the language and literature were already dead. Mendele Mokher Seforim and Sholem Aleikhem are included, but none of the other great Yiddish and Hebrew writers is mentioned. Most striking is the total omission of all Soviet Jewish writers. There is no reference to the great Habimah Theater. Nor is there anything on Jewish history in Russia before the Revolution, on the role of Jews in the Revolution, or their achievements afterward, to say nothing of Jewish life elsewhere in the world, and four millennia of history.[24] There are four columns under "Jewish Autonomous Province" (Birobidzhan), three of which are devoted to a geographical survey of the region.

Thus, the Black Years were not only a period of physical destruction of Jewish lives and cultural expressions, but a period of rewriting Jewish history to the point of erasing it, making it disappear so that the Jewish presence would become a mere vestige, indeed a fossil.

Yet, paradoxically, while Jewish secular culture, which the regime had encouraged, was being obliterated, there was a somewhat less harsh attitude toward religious activity. Some synagogues were allowed to exist, although in wretched condition, and a few rabbis conducted services—possibly as window dressing for the outside world, and to appease visitors and others asking questions. The rabbis, of course, had to be excessively wary and circumspect and were mainly used to refute reports that the government was suppressing Jewish religious life. But they were also used for political ends, this time to praise the great Stalin's foreign policy, based on peace and friendship, and declaim the duty of Jews to join in the struggle against warmongers. These were the messages of Rabbi Solomon Shlieffer of Moscow and Rabbi Itsko (Yitzhak) Shekhtman of Kiev at a peace rally held in Zagorsk in May 1952.[25] These last vestiges of Judaism, in any case, were regarded as a "dwindling substance" that had lost all vitality and would "shrivel of itself very soon." By keeping it under strict surveillance, "it could still be allowed to exist as a kind of fossilized museum exhibit." The limits were still severe: no rabbis were being trained, religious literature was out of bounds, and devotional articles were very difficult to obtain. Moreover, less compromising rabbis who laid particular emphasis on Zion and Jerusalem in the prayers were still being punished. In 1950 Rabbi Shmuel Lev of Kharkov was sentenced to ten years' confinement in a "rigid discipline" camp, and later, groups of non-Ashkenazi worshippers and rabbis, including the Sephardic rabbi of Tashkent, began arriving in the labor camps.[26]

However, to keep up the facade that Jewish religious life was still viable, an official invitation was sent at the time to the New York Board of Rabbis to visit the Soviet Union.

The period of the early fifties was also marked by a secret trial of eight arrested Birobidzhan leaders, a process which throws further light on the methods and purposes of the widespread anti-Jewish persecution.

The trial, which took place in Moscow, lasted from November 1951 to the end of February 1952, and has been described in great detail by Khaim Maltinsky,[27] one of the survivors of the process, who later emigrated to Israel. (He died February 7, 1986.) Maltinsky had gone to Birobidzhan from Minsk and became an editor of a Yiddish children's newspaper *(Young Leninist)*. He was also editor of the *Birobidzhan Almanac* in 1949, from which he was fired at the end of 1950. The trial was hidden from the world at the time and, although rumors and unverified reports spread, Maltinsky's account is apparently the only one in which the source is both victim and witness.

His ordeal began on May 17, 1951, when he was arrested and taken to an MGB prison in Khabarovsk, where he was kept in solitary confinement under brutal conditions. Sometime in September or October he was taken to a common prison and learned that seven others from Birobidzhan were also being held there and that all eight were bound up together in "the Birobidzhan Affair." They were Bakhmutsky, secretary of the Regional Party Committee; Levitin, chairman of the Provisional Executive of the JAR and a prosecuting attorney in Birobidzhan (he had published an article in *Einikayt* of July 22, 1948, summing up prospects of renewed emigration to the region); Moshe Zilbershtain, former chairman of the Regional Executive Committee, who was arrested in Moscow; Brakhin, in charge of propaganda in Birobidzhan and Maltinsky's boss; Abrashe Rutenberg, longtime secretary of the

Regional Executive Committee, whom Maltinsky had met in Minsk[28] while working in a Pioneer youth organization; Fradkin, editor of the Birobidzhan *zvezda* (Star); and Nachum Friedman, editor of the *Birobidzhaner shtern* and one of the earliest settlers in the region. Friedman was a fine journalist and critic who had survived the terror of 1937–38. Maltinsky had met him in 1947 and found him extremely helpful in his work with the *Almanac*. For a time they lived in the same place, but when Maltinsky was removed from the *Almanac*, he felt himself under suspicion and tried to avoid Friedman. Both men were arrested on the same night.

Maltinsky's investigation began the day of his arrest, May 15, 1951. He was told that his case was prepared by a special court or consultation, called the ASA, under a procedure referred to as the "troika." This system actually disposed of cases quickly. But the accused had no inkling of the way his case would be handled and had to wait blindly. Mostly in solitary confinement, Maltinsky was watched day and night by guards peering through a cell peephole in the door, "how I sit, how I stand, provoking me while I sleep." He lost all sense of time, except that on Sundays there were no interrogations. Often he lay or squatted in a corner of his cell like an animal or banged the iron door with his fists. When frost piled up on the floor, he knew it was winter.

One day a prison official came into his cell and said, "Your case goes to the highest jurisdiction; you don't have to wait for the ASA. You will be tried by the Military Collegium of the Supreme Court in the Soviet Union." Maltinsky judged that sometime toward the end of January 1952, he was awakened one night and taken in the "Black Raven," a prison bus to Moscow, over 5,000 miles away. During the bitterly cold ride his only protection was a tattered army short coat he had been given in a military hospital, where one leg had been amputated as a result of war wounds. He was taken to the notorious Lefortovo prison in Moscow and once again placed in solitary confinement. Here he was stripped naked and searched for anything he might try to use to kill himself. The day before the trial, which started on February 20, he was forced to sign a seven-page document in which he was accused of espionage and treason and threatened with the death penalty. Being a disabled veteran apparently did nothing to mitigate the charges.

The court hall contained the seven other prisoners, three judges, and sixteen guards. The court met for three days, and it was in the courtroom that Maltinsky saw the other prisoners for the first time. Bakhmutsky, Levitin, Brakhin, and Rutenberg had been at a regional party conference in 1949, but Maltinsky did not know when or in what city they were arrested. Fradkin and Friedman worked until they were arrested and were not expelled from the party until their arrest in May 1951.

Bakhmutsky,[29] together with his closest co-workers Fradkin, Zilbershtain, Levitin, and Brakhin, were accused of deceiving Stalin and the executive of the Central Committee by "artificially trying to establish a Jewish state in the Far East with the help of the spying Jewish Antifascist Committee in Moscow and a group of Jewish writers in Moscow, who were linked with the principal organs of the American espionage service." The indictment also stated that as early as 1949, Malenkov, Beria, Ponomarenko and Gaglidze, at a session of the Central Committee of the party, reproached Bakhmutsky and Zilbershtain for exploiting certain Jewish party activists, such as Lozovsky, Molotov's wife Paulina Zhemchuzhina, and prominent Jewish generals in the Soviet army, in carrying on their criminal purpose and making contact with American imperialists with the aim of detaching the Jewish republic and selling it to the Americans or Japanese. "Now, years later," Maltinsky later reflected, "the mind does not grasp the senselessness and insanity of such a brutal travesty."

Again and again, words were hurled at the defendants out of context—something Lozovsky said, a line from Feffer, a phrase from a telephone conversation, a letter from an American Jewish leader to "prove" the espionage and treason charge. For example, when Bakhmutsky or Levitin said that he had visited the JAC in Moscow, Feffer had said, "The Americans do not give anything free." Whereupon, the judge said, "It is clear as the day that you were in collusion with agents of the CIA, who masked themselves under the protection of a Soviet institution . . . the Jewish Antifascist Committee . . . and that for the pay which you received and hoped to receive, you paid and would pay with counter-revolutionary activity, and through the intermediary Feffer, transmitted government secrets regarding the Jewish Autonomous Region." Much was made of an article Bakhmutsky published in *Einikayt,* which mentioned numbers of Jews in the Red Army who came from Birobidzhan and had fought in the war. According to Maltinsky, Bakhmutsky and Brakhin, grasping at straws, confessed that they "had lost their political vigilance. Like blind people, we didn't understand what the Jewish Antifascist Committee really was." But the judge maliciously interrupted: "Do not pretend to be children . . . to be little sheep. Who will believe you?"

In his memoir of the trial, Maltinsky cited a long list of pro-Soviet and pro-government activities of the defendants, all of whom were deeply assimilated, who faithfully carried out every Stalinist order and practice. But he reflected bitterly, "one must not dare to move a little stone from one place to another without the consent of the highest party institution, especially in the delicate matter of the national question. . . . Suddenly, in less than a year everything that was white became black. . . . The wolf should be sated so that the goat may be spared." The defendants had done everything that was required. Moreover, he emphasized that there were plenty of non-Jews in the Birobidzhan administration who would promptly have called Moscow's attention to anything out of line. Significantly, no non-Jews were accused, even those who openly preached that "it was no shame," with the help of the JAC, to receive clothes, typewriters, and other things from the United States. "For the grotesque fabrication" of the accusations, "Jews alone were needed, even assimilated Jews." When the defendants specifically cited directives from regional and central committees, they were told to stop trying to implicate others.

There were many volumes of "evidence" produced for the court and much irrelevant material on the parallel activities of the Jewish writers in Moscow, Minsk, and Kiev—gathered by the MGB "to impress the court with their thoroughness . . . in the hope of earning another decoration or a higher position." Maltinsky also believed that "all understood from earlier experience that the party chiefs together with the refined anti-Semitism of Malenkov, Ponomarenko, and Beria had prepared everything as a gift to Stalin for Army Day, February 23, 1952," with the help of the Military Collegium. He was also certain that the regional Birobidzhan conference in the summer of 1949 (see Chapter 22) had been used to entrap the defendants and lay the groundwork for their eventual prosecution. "The whole time," Maltinsky recalled, "they kept pouring out sewer stuff against the condemned leaders, guilty of kneeling and scraping to American imperialism, having traitorous links to the arrested Jewish writers in Moscow and Birobidzhan, and neglecting the work of the region." (The writers Buzi Miller, Israel Emiot, and Herschel Rabinkov in Birobidzhan had already been arrested.) After the conference, Bakhmutsky, Brakhin, Levitin, and Rutenberg "must have left the region," but Maltinsky didn't know where they had gone. Only Fradkin and Friedman remained in responsible positions on the regional press. When Bakhmutzky and Levitin returned to Birobidzhan, meetings were organized at which the "nationalism" of the Jewish leaders was exposed.

The defendants were charged with counterrevolution, disclosure of military secrets, treason and espionage, and anti-Soviet activity. Hoping to escape death, they "confessed" to "anti-Soviet nationalist activity" and were forced to read their own indictments, although none had signed confessions or confessed to treason or espionage. At the end of each day's session, when Maltinsky was returned to his cell in Lefortovo prison, his crutches, cane, and eye glasses were taken away so that he became "a caged, creeping creature between his cot and the latrine."

On the third day, the defendants were allowed to make statements but were sharply rebuked if they mentioned Stalin's name. All made "obsequious protestations" of loyalty: Fradkin said that he had named his daughter Stalina. Bakhmutsky, Brakhin, and Fradkin hinted that their Russian wives were proof of their devotion to the great Russian people and Russian culture. They also emphasized that their mother tongue and that of their children was Russian, as if to say, "how can we conceivably have any connection with Jewish nationalism?"

Late at night on February 22, sentence was pronounced. Bakhmutsky and Zilbershtain were sentenced to be executed; Levitin and Brakhin, to twenty-five years of strictest regime in a camp "in distant places"; Maltinsky, Rutenberg, and Fradkin, to ten years in a prison camp and five in exile; and Friedman, to ten years in prison. Maltinsky asked no pardon or moderating sentence. He did, however, mention his service to the nation in the war and the fact that he was seriously wounded in the Battle of Berlin. (Later charges of treason and espionage were removed from Friedman and Fradkin.) Within twenty-four hours Maltinsky was taken to Butyrka prison in Moscow, where he stayed for several months until he was sent to Siberia. For the next twenty-six years, he saw none of the accused.

In November 1955, he was released from a camp in Vologda and went to distant Namangan in Uzbekistan to rejoin his wife and surviving children. Rumors had reached him that Bakhmutsky's and Zilbershtain's sentences had been commuted. This news was later confirmed. Later, when he arrived in Minsk from Namangan, he heard that Levitin had been killed by criminals in camp. Brakhin went to live in Khabarovsk and Rutenberg, near Gorky.

Israel Emiot, a Jewish writer from Poland who joined the ranks of Soviet Yiddish writers in Bialystok in 1940 and later became Birobidzhan correspondent for the JAC, has also left a vivid account of his arrest and imprisonment beginning in 1948.[30] He was interrogated without respite and accused of having engaged in "bourgeois nationalist activity," for writing poems about Jewish partisans during the war, and for "implanting Jewish culture artificially" in the JAR at the time when there was no need for it.[31] The investigation revealed that he had been closely involved with Mikhoels, who, it was charged, had been employed by a foreign espionage agency. He was also accused of negating the preeminence of Russian literature. He was told, "whether you confess or you don't confess makes little difference. You won't leave here a free man. . . . If you do confess, however, they may go easier on you at the end."[32] The same particularly sadistic interrogator Ozirsky kept him from sleeping and frequently punished Emiot by throwing him into a pit for four or five days at a stretch. He had collected all of Emiot's dispatches and letters to the JAC in Yiddish—"evidence" (which he couldn't read) that he was an imperialist spy. The investigation also charged that Emiot had defamed the Soviet Union by alleging that anti-Semitism still existed there.[33] At one time, when he tried to logically argue with his interrogators and referred to Kalinin's endorsement of Jewish national consciousness, he was told: "Everything has its special time. In our country, policies change frequently. Our dialectical approach is dictated by life itself. What was correct yesterday may be incorrect—even criminal today."[34]

While in his cell, he was handed a slip of paper which said he was sentenced under sections 10 and 11, article 58 of the Criminal Code to ten years at hard labor. He was "tried" in Moscow by a special MGB military court and thus had no trial at all. At the Taishet camp where he was sent, he found many Jews who had been arrested in Birobidzhan, "Golda's prisoners"—those who had cheered Golda Meyerson in Moscow—Yiddish "nationalistic" writers, including Moshe Broderzon, old-time Jewish Communists imprisoned for Trotskyism and re-arrested, Sephardic Jews from Samarkand, and Lubavitcher Hasidim.

They worked digging ditches, laying pipes, cutting and carrying logs, often suffering from hunger and beatings.[35]

Emiot was released in March 1953.[36] His sentence was never completely annulled but the charge of participating in an anti-Soviet movement was removed. His sentence was thus shortened to five years, but he had already served seven.

In some respects, the year 1952 was the blackest of the Black Years, punctuated by mass arrests, mysterious disappearances, venomous attacks on Jews and Zionism, and dozens of trials, many concealed from public view. However, a new terror opened the year 1953, one of the grimmest and most frightening of all the events—the so-called "plot" of "murderers in white gowns," the "doctors' plot." On January 13, the official communiqué stated that

Sometime ago agencies of State security discovered a terrorist group of doctors who had made it their aim to cut short the lives of active public figures of the Soviet Union through sabotage medical treatment. . . .[37]

The doctors named were Professors M.S. Vovsi, V.N. Vinogradov, M.B. Kogan, B.B. Kogan, P.I. Yegorov, A.I. Feldman, Y.G. Etinger, A.M. Grinshtein, G.I. Maiorov, six of whom were Jewish. They were charged with making incorrect diagnoses, dooming their patients by wrong treatment, causing the death of Andrei Zhdanov and General Alexander Shcherbakov, and undermining the health of "leading Soviet military personnel." The communiqué also stated that "most of the participants in the terrorist group (M.S. Vovsi, B.B. Kogan, A.I. Feldman, A.M. Grinshtein, Y.G. Etinger, and others) were connected with the international Jewish bourgeois nationalist organization 'Joint' [Joint Distribution Committee] established by American intelligence for the alleged purpose of providing material aid to Jews in other countries. In actual fact, this organization, under direction of American intelligence, conducts extensive espionage, terrorist and other subversive work in many countries, including the Soviet Union."[38]

According to the announcement, Dr. Vovsi told investigators that he had received orders "to wipe out the leading cadres of the USSR." These orders allegedly had been received from JDC by way of the noted Jewish doctor Shimelovich [director of the Botkin Hospital in Moscow] and the "well-known Jewish bourgeois nationalist Mikhoels." (This is a reference to the Yiddish actor Shlomo Mikhoels, Vovsi's cousin, who had been killed in 1948.) Special praise was given a Dr. Lydia Timashuk "for assistance rendered to the Government in exposing the murderer-doctors."

There was no specific charge against any individual doctor or the names of patients treated by them, or even those treating Zhdanov and Shcherbakov. Shcherbakov's death certificate was published without any signatures, while the medical report on Zhdanov, which was published in *Pravda* on September 1, 1948, was signed by Yegorov, Vinogradov, Maiorov, Fedorov, and Vassilenko, but only the first three named were among the accused.[39]

A furious press and radio campaign was set in motion, lasting for two and a half months, "during which hardly a day passed without bitter charges against persons with clearly identifiable Jewish names." Newspapers in Moscow and the capitals of the Soviet republics with Jewish populations and medical organs carried accounts of alleged crimes. "While the word *Yevrei* never was mentioned in this flood . . . the items dealt predominantly, if not exclusively, with Jewish names. . . . Whenever the Jewish origin of the bearer was not suggested by his family name, the person's given name and his father's name would be added." In the case of women, Jewish maiden names were added.[40]

Typical was an editorial in *Pravda Ukrainy* of January 16, entitled "Guard Public Property as the Apple of Our Eye" with the following items:

Information has already appeared concerning the wrecker band of Khain, Yaroshetsky and others, which operated for a long time at the Kiev textile base of the Chief Light Industry Marketing Administration and which has been sternly punished by the Soviet court. . . .

All these Khains and Yaroshetskys, Grinshteins . . . Perses and . . . Kaplans and Polyakovs . . . arouse the profound loathing of the people. . . .[41]

In an article in the humorous weekly *Krokodil*, called "The Poisoners", January 30,

. . .Vovsi, B. Kogan and M. Kogan, Grinshtein, Vinogradov, Yegorov, knew how to change the expression of their eyes, let their wolves' souls assume a human appearance. . . . They had passed through a certain school in this respect under the hypocrite Mikhoels, for whom nothing was holy, who for thirty silver coins sold his soul to "the country of the yellow devil" [the United States] which he had selected as his homeland. The poisoners also took lessons in disguise from their medical colleague—the criminal Shimeliovich. . . .

[The arrested doctors] will remain the personification of baseness and infamy. The born creations of that same Judas. A devastating blow has been dealt to the Judas gang.[42]

The Moscow papers commended provincial youth newspapers for implementing official directives to be vigilant by exposing delinquents with typically Jewish names. Representative titles of articles during January and February were: "Zionist Agents of the American Secret Service," "Zionist Agency of the Dollar," "Zionism in the Service of American Imperialism." Features luridly described "the dirty face of this Zionist espionage," "despised degenerates from among men of science," and "despised hirelings who sold themselves for dollars and pounds sterling." References were made to earlier medical murders, for example, "the machinations in the guise of doctors . . . who killed the great Russian writer A.M. Gorky and the outstanding Soviet statesmen V.V. Kuibyshev and V.R. Menzhinsky."[43] One of the doctors mentioned was Professor Lev Levin who had been a defendant at the trial of the "bloc of rightists and Trotskyites" of March 2–13, 1938. Levin had been asked to tell about his contacts with Yagoda, his patient, who succeeded Menzhinsky as head of the Soviet Secret Police, and who ordered the murder of Gorky's son and Menzhinsky. Levin then explained that he had prescribed "wrong doses" to all four of his "weakened" victims, all of whom had been very ill before they died. On March 11, 1938, Levin was sentenced to death and he was executed a few days later.[44] (Similar accusations of medical murder were made during the purge trials of 1936–38, including the case of Dr. Ernest Aschner, a German refugee, who worked in the Soviet German Republic and "confessed" to spreading plague germs in his district on order from the Gestapo.)

Suspicion and hostility began to infect the daily life of Jews. In a document written between 1952 and 1955 which reached the newspaper *Davar* in Israel, the writer vividly describes the texture of everyday life during the doctors' trial, which made "every Jew . . . fair game." In the ubiquitous queues, "a Jew . . . looks carefully about him. . . . Christian women who share kitchen facilities with Jews have begun to make the lives of the latter miserable; Christian children direct vulgar, insolent remarks at Jewish adults." Many doctors are being dismissed from their jobs; others are resigning, fearing sudden arrest on trumped-up charges. Many Jews who are not doctors are also losing their jobs. A caricature in *Krokodil* shows a man with a long hooked nose (Dr.

Vovsi) poking his fingers into the throat of his victim. Jews grasp what the call to "vigilance" means; the people of the Soviet Union understand very well to whom the phrase "people of uncertain origin, who possess no fatherland" alludes.[45]

Cases of alleged medical fraud, negligence of medical duties, forged medical certificates, malingering, worshipping "things foreign," "preaching views alien to Marxism," opportunism, taking of bribes, publishing "unscientific and harmful books," and fraud were publicized, all linking doctors with characteristically Jewish names to the crimes. A Professor Frankshtein of the Institute of General and Experimental Pathology of the Soviet Academy of Medicine was charged with having an "idealistic conception." Jewish physicians at the Central Clinic for Legal Psychiatry were accused of having failed to apply the methods of "patriotic Russian psychiatry." Some doctors were even accused of being "child murderers."[46] Whole clinics in Moscow were denuded to the extent that some of them had to merge because of a shortage of teachers.[47] It was said that in a particular chemist's pharmacy they arrested a Jew who had been dispensing poison instead of medicine. A medical school student at the time has said that it was rumored that there was no meat in shops because some Jews had poisoned the cattle which then had to be killed. He recalled "simple women in the polyclinic asking to be assigned to a doctor who was not Jewish. Nothing was done to stop the rumors. In communal apartments, "there were many cases of non-Jewish residents holding meetings and demanding that Jews be forbidden to use the common kitchen so that they couldn't put poison in the food."[48]

Panic gripped Soviet Jews during the early months of 1953. Earlier such campaigns and show trials had led to massive arrests and purges. Would they be repeated? Jews were insulted and attacked on trams, and many were afraid to travel. The newspapers were full of accusations and complaints against Jewish doctors. Copies of the *Pravda* article of January 13 were translated into all the languages used in the Soviet Union to make sure every Soviet citizen became informed. Arrests and purges of Jewish doctors occurred as far as Novosibirsk.

As in the thirties, Soviet workers were expected to express their anger and indignation against the base "murderers." Meetings were organized for this purpose, and those in hospitals had a special significance.[49] Several faculty members at various institutes refused to condemn Vovsi, who had been very well regarded, but others vilified him, as the party expected them to.[50] Scientific journals stopped publishing articles by Jews. The press and radio barrage was incessant and the publicity given the monstrous crimes of Jewish doctors was accorded fearful credibility by many citizens. There were many Jewish doctors in the country and they touched the lives of many families, not only those who needed treatment but those who needed medical certificates permitting workers to get work releases and rest slips.

The campaign against Jewish doctors was accompanied by a simultaneous campaign against alleged economic crimes of which Jews were guilty: squandering supplies and funds, nepotism, embezzling, fraud, falsification of records, speculation, and theft of state property. But it was the "murderer-doctors" who were most prominently exposed and publicized. The suggestion that there would be a trial was merely a smokescreen. An editorial in *Pravda* on January 13—the day of the arrests and presumably before the investigations were completed—already indicted the doctors in its headline: "Foul Spies and Murderers in the Mask of Doctors and Professors," as well as in its substance. "Exposure of the band of poisoner-doctors is a blow at the international Jewish Zionist organization," it said. There were also veiled threats, of much significance later, against state security agencies, which "did not discover the doctors' wrecking, terrorist organization in time."[51]

What did these seemingly unrelated elements signify, and what was the motivation behind this bizarre as well as sinister campaign? There has never been a full explanation—later Khrushchev blamed Stalin—but two theories have been suggested. One sees the attack on the doctors as part of a master-plan of Stalin to once more exploit anti-Semitism for political ends. In this interpretation, Stalin staged the "doctors' plot" as a prelude for a subsequent purge and demanded charges of criminal guilt. According to later revelations in 1956 by Khrushchev, Stalin himself had given the order for their arrest, told the interrogators to beat some, and even to chain Dr. V. N. Vinogradov, one of those arrested. He also threatened the State Security Minister: "If you do not obtain confessions from the doctors, we will shorten you by a head." The investigating judge was told to "beat, beat, and, once again, beat."[52] Two of the doctors died under torture.

The doctors would thus be sacrificial victims in another projected massive purge or reorganization of the old Politburo that would destroy the political ambitions of Stalin's would-be successors (see Chapter 23). As the British historian Trevor-Roper has observed:

No one would murmur when they were tried, sentenced, executed. By then, they would have fulfilled their function. That function, now as before, was to create evidence against their patrons. And who could doubt who those patrons would be shown to be? They would be the members of the old Politburo, who would then, on this evidence, be tried, sentenced, executed.[53]

The death of Zhdanov, which had never been explained, was now said to have been caused by a "murder"—lifting all responsibility from either Stalin or Malenkov who may have had him eliminated. General Alexander Shcherbakov had been chief of the main political adminstration of the Soviet army, the first Russian to serve as chief political commissar of the army. He had died on May 10, 1945. However, he was "indifferent to party doctrine" and "opposed any war that involved fighting beyond the borders of the Holy Russian Fatherland."[54] Shcherbakov was very likely murdered at Stalin's order as a troublesome opponent of Stalin's thinking. The tale of a Jewish plot against a Russian general would have wide appeal in the army. There is also evidence that Shcherbakov opposed emphasizing anti-Jewish atrocities of the Nazis and acts of Jewish heroism, thus giving further weight to the vengeful, murderous plans of the Jewish doctors. The prosecution was thus at last bringing his assassins to justice. "Those in the Kremlin who extorted the confessions were making a bid to the Red Army,"[55] whose leaders were generally the most loved and respected in the Soviet Union. The fact that Shcherbakov was now "revealed" to have been the victim of a "Zionist plot" implied that the enemies of the Red Army were Jews. Malenkov had much to gain in this.

Malenkov came to power briefly after Stalin's death, but earlier had been frustrated in his bid for supreme power by a coalition of Beria, Bulganin, and Molotov, after Zhdanov's death. While Stalin still lived, Malenkov had reason to fear that his fate might be like that of Kirov and Zhdanov. Stalin seemed to favor Malenkov as his successor, but he had also helped the Beria-Molotov faction edge Malenkov out after Zhdanov's death. Pitting rivals against each other was a favorite weapon of Stalin's—it has even been suggested that *his* power was threatened from time to time by ambitious, contending comrades. He may have, at this time, encouraged or ordered Malenkov to make an open appeal for army support by framing the "doctors' plot." Press outpourings meanwhile exposed security agencies for being "not sufficiently vigilant, and for being "infected with gullibility"—charges aimed at Beria and Molotov. The "doctors' plot" thus became an unseen arena for a savage struggle for political power, possibly set in motion by Stalin, who could watch each faction devouring the other while the country was being distracted by rampant anti-Semitism.

The second theory holds that Malenkov himself may have framed the "plot"[56] at a time when Stalin was ailing or incapacitated, or even when Stalin was the targeted victim of a power struggle. If so, the frenzied campaign against the doctors was a "move to eliminate the medical staff that had in the past so faithfully liquidated troublesome Politburo members on Stalin's orders all the while it had guarded his own health." Three of the doctors named in the "plot"—Yegorov, Vinogradov, and Maiorov—non-Jews—had signed most of the death certificates of Soviet leaders who had died (or were murdered) in the past. (The first two were known to be Stalin's personal physicians, but the signatures on the official bulletins dealing with the progress of Stalin's last illness were those of doctors entirely new to the Kremlin.[57] On the other hand, since it is known that Stalin was extremely paranoid in the last years of his life, he may have believed that his own physicians were planning to poison him.

Meanwhile Jews were suffering, and most Russians accepted the accusations as true. One document reveals a writer who was horrified at the gullibility of people, including some Jews, mainly women. His own son, an intellectual, assumed that "there must be some truth in the accusation." His daughter-in-law, a non-Jew, accepted, without questioning, everything the party did. The poet Evgeny Evtushenko told not only of the glee with which the news was greeted among some of his friends, but admitted that he himself believed the report. The widespread gullibility was attributed to blind faith in Stalin's authority and power, and to the very astonishing dimensions of the accusation.[58] How could it have been fabricated?

Stalin's cunning has actually been described as "a new technique of governing through systematic alternation between terror and relaxation," requiring the creation of a "cast-iron apparatus totally dependent on the dictator, and the determination to make permanent purge a calculated instrument of statecraft.[59] The disciplined and secretive professionals in the widespread police and intelligence network had replaced the ardent, fully committed party men as the central apparatus of the Stalinist system. "Just as technicians in the infamous Special Section of the Ministry of the Interior found that one of the simplest ways to 'break' a reluctant prisoner was by a blinking alternation of total light and total darkness, so the servants of Stalin sought to disorient and subdue the outside world with an incessant and bewildering alternation between smiles and scowls, amity and threat."[60] So skillfully did Stalin manipulate these shifts that even the victims tended to speak of a new terror "as the creation of an underling: *Yezhovshchina* in the thirties, *Zhdanovshchina* in the forties."[61]

During the two months that the "doctors' plot" riveted the country's attention, several of the many rumors which raced through the country were of terrifying literalness to Jews. One was that they would be sent to exile in Siberia. Another, that Stalin was planning a public execution of the Jewish doctors at the Lobnoye Place in Moscow, to be followed by a prearranged pogrom.[62] Another rumor turned around a staged Zionist attempt on the life of Molotov, after which there would be a deportation of Jews from the large cities.[63] The alleged plan to deport Jews is said to have been announced by Stalin at a Politburo session on March 1, 1953. The existence of such a plan was reported by the Yiddish journalist Ben Zion Goldberg,[64] and Solzhenitsyn, in his *The Gulag Archipelago*, repeated the report that in 1953 Stalin planned a forced resettlement of Soviet Jews in eastern Siberia, to follow the death of the doctors on Red Square. Roy Medvedev also wrote in a 1970 samizdat article that

the organs of the NKVD hastily prepared for a massive expulsion of the Jews from all the main cities of the USSR. . . . In several districts of Kazakhstan, barracks for Jews were urgently erected. A text of an appeal to the Jewish people, which several distinguished scientists and cultural leaders of Jewish nationality had to sign "requesting" resettlement, was prepared; several large factories passed resolutions for the eviction of Jews [and] in several regions of the country pogroms and slaughters of Jews were carried out.[65]

Soviet Jewish emigrés have talked of an atmosphere in terms of "preparing for pogroms."[66] Leaflets and posters in small villages bore inflammatory phrases such as "Beat the Jews." Officially inspired anti-Semitism throughout the whole postwar period is generally described as worse than the spontaneous popular anti-Semitism. "Without the bad example of the government," one Soviet Jew has put it, "the situation wouldn't have been so bad."[67] Police and militia guards often stood by or aggravated the situation during anti-Jewish attacks, physical as well as verbal.

Many Soviet Jewish emigrés to Israel and the United States have spoken of these fears of a wholesale deportation had not Stalin died. A further Stalinist fillip was added in the form of a "rationalization." As reported by the well-known Soviet specialist in international finance, Professor I. A. Trakhtenberg, after the "doctors' plot" had been announced, the editor in chief of *Pravda* brought together a large group of prominent Soviet Jews, himself included. The editor

suggested that they sign an appeal to the Soviet Jewish population, convincing them of the necessity to move to Siberia . . . rationalized as follows: as the experience of the postwar years had shown, there were many Jewish renegades, saboteurs and the like, who had sold out to the Joint and other Western intelligence organizations. According to Marxist-Leninist doctrine, the objective causes of this phenomenon were that the Jews lacked their own working-class and collectivized peasantry. The Soviet Government wished to help the Jews correct their mistakes and create the appropriate conditions for them to build their own working class and collectivized peasantry in Siberia.[68]

There are numerous confirmations of this planned deportation[69] and many individuals who claim to have stopped it. In a version leaked in 1957 by the then Soviet Ambassador to Poland, Panteleimon Ponomarenko, to French journalists, it was Marshal Voroshilov who openly defied Stalin. (After Stalin's death Voroshilov tried to clear himself of personal anti-Semitism and admitted that he had to overcome the inherited anti-Semitism of his environment.) In another version, told by Ehrenburg to Jean-Paul Sartre, the "revolt" of the Politburo members was led by Kaganovich, who tore up his party card at that session in a rage. Later, in 1956, during an official visit to Warsaw, Khrushchev claimed that he was personally responsible for the intervention.[70]

The political analyst Franz Borkenau, who made a penetrating analysis of the reasons for thinking that Malenkov was indeed the prime mover in the anti-Semitic campaign that raged in the Soviet Union before Stalin's death, also made an astounding prediction in January 1953 in a West German weekly, namely that Stalin's life was in immediate danger. Seven weeks later, his death was announced. Borkenau's prediction was based mainly on the strength of a resolution passed on January 4, 1953, by the Central Committee of the German Socialist Unity Party that dealt with the "teachings of the Slansky case" and revealed "an extreme anti-Semitic tendency." Borkenau noted that "Malenkov was quoted at inordinate length, and so identified with the anti-Semitic campaign that had just reached its first climax in the Prague trials. . . .

Stalin *was quoted with a mere half-sentence dating from 1910*. Such a deliberate affront could have been offered only by people sure of the tryant's approaching downfall, or else out of reach of his retribution. Otherwise it was sure suicide."[71]

The trial of the "doctor assassins" was scheduled to open in the Hall of Columns of the House of the Trade Unions, but on March 4, Stalin suffered a massive stroke and died the next day. It is quite possible that Malenkov hastened or caused his death. We are not certain of the actual events leading to his death and may never know them.

Thus a quarter of a century of personal dictatorship marked by bloody purges, vast human suffering and terror, cynical abuse of power, and bureaucratic nightmares had come to an end. Malenkov was thought of as the heir-apparent, but a ruthless struggle among the hierarchs followed. For Jews, Stalin's death removed the threats of deportation and the venomous anti-Semitism that was poisoning their lives. There were still fear and anxieties, but they were intermixed with relief and hope.

25

The Heirs of Stalin, 1953–56:
Restricted Thaw

To double
    To triple
        The guard at this slab
      So that Stalin may not rise,
      And with Stalin
          The past . . .
    We rooted him
      Out of the Mausoleum
      But how to root Stalin
        Out of Stalin's heirs?

EVGENY EVTUSHENKO

THE threatened deportations did not come, but in the last convulsions of the power struggle, Stalin himself may have exceeded his own manipulative cunning and been murdered. Beria controlled the vast police apparatus and the prisons, and Malenkov, the government and party machine, with their respective supporters. But the alliances at the top were precarious and short-lived.[1]

After Stalin's death, more and more evidence began to point to struggles within interest groups in the Soviet Union, indicating that "the Soviet system, was far from being 'conflictless' and that behind the facade of the monolithic party a genuine struggle was taking place among rival groups."[2] The concept of "totalitarianism," involving the absorption of all power by Stalin or the Communist party and the destruction of every channel of autonomous behavior, gave way to a more complex view. One scholar spoke of a "continuing battle between powerful and entrenched elements in the party's higher echelons," and referred to these as "constraints built into the Soviet system of power," limiting the complete freedom of the top leaders.[3] Another interpreted the struggle as a mere personal struggle for power among the party apparatus, the state bureaucracy, the army, and the police, largely divorced from questions of policy or ideology.[4] Other studies suggested that the struggle was linked with major issues of policy and was related to more narrowly defined groups, such as central or peripheral party organizations, central or local economic management, the intelligentsia, special interests (heavy industry, agriculture, arms production), the nationalities, peasants, etc.

The sprawling nation which Stalin had brutally forged into an industrial and military colossus was rent with dissatisfaction, waste, and suffering. Stalin's power had been tyrannical, and his chief weapons had become savage persecution and destruction of all creative forces. The men around him were building up their own power blocs while maintaining a common front against him and flattering him at the same time. As for Stalin, during the last three years of his life, "his main objects . . . were to curb Malenkov while nevertheless presenting him as his most obvious successor . . . and also to reduce the enormous personal power wielded by Beria, without wrecking his indispensable police apparatus."[5]

At the Nineteenth Party Congress in October 1952, he had allowed Malenkov to dominate the event, while Nikita Khrushchev, the sly and ambitious rising party leader from the Ukraine, lashed out against the party Malenkov controlled. But at the end, it was Stalin himself who destroyed the fantasies of victory of any and all of the men at the old center. He suddenly and drastically changed the old power structure through which he had ruled. The small Politburo was renamed the Party Presidium and enlarged from a total of eleven to twenty-five full members and eleven candidates, while the Secretariat was increased from five to ten members.[6] Many of the new members were unknown, untried men—now equal to the old veterans. A new power order of some fundamental kind was in the making.

Throughout 1952, there were waves of arrests, trials—many of them secret, threats by Stalin against old comrades, including the one-time Commander in Chief of the Red Army Kliment Voroshilov, and innuendos that security measures were faulty.

It is not clear exactly what Stalin intended, whom he meant to win out, or if, like other tyrants, he wished for a deluge. In any case, in reducing the value of the old members of the supreme party bodies and in bringing in outsiders, a new bloody purge was foreshadowed that would destroy former chiefs and deprive large cadres of their followers. In the scrambling to survive to find cover, new allegiances, and scapegoats, anti-Semitism was to prove once more an invaluable weapon, culminating in the sinister "doctors' plot" in January 1953, to produce the ultimate "cleansing."

Upon his death, Stalin's swollen hierarchy was quickly reduced and a new power command appeared, leading many Russians to believe that Stalin had been murdered. Although a facade of collective leadership was presented, there were four principal figures maneuvering to succeed Stalin: Malenkov, Beria, Molotov, and Khrushchev. Malenkov's and Beria's positions at first seemed to be the strongest, but their claims were short-lived. On March 10, 1953, Malenkov, who became first secretary of the party and chairman of the Council of Ministers, (a post Stalin had held since 1941), was apparently overeager to pose as Stalin's rightful heir, and reproduced an altered photograph in *Pravda*, which had originally included many Soviet and Chinese dignitaries, but which in the doctored version included only Stalin, Mao-Tse-tung, and Malenkov. Apparently the collective leadership did not appreciate the elimination of their photographs and a few days later, Malenkov "requested" that he be freed from duties, including secretary of the Central Committee of the party. The post went to Khrushchev, who thus became de facto boss of the party machine.

With Stalin's death, anti-Jewish incitations vanished from the press for the moment. If Malenkov was indeed the prime engineer of its exploitation, it did not avail him success in winning over the army or secret service. In April came the official repudiation of the "doctors' plot" and the arrest of the prosecutor. A hectic peace campaign ushered in the immediate post-Stalin period, with Malenkov's name receiving less and less prominence.

After Stalin's death, there was a general desire among his associates to refurbish their images in the eyes of their own people and of the West. Beria was among the first to try to dissociate himself from Stalin's policies and crimes as well as his own. He began to present himself as "the patron of some of his own victims, keen to help persecuted intellectuals, especially members of national minorities."[7] These included the great Ukrainian film director Aleksander Dovzhenko, whose life as an artist was destroyed by Stalinist suppression, and, posthumously, the Jewish actor Shlomo Mikhoels, possibly one of Beria's own victims.[8] He appeared as a champion of "national rights," and during his brief ascent, the first secretary of every non-Russian republic had to be a local "national," not someone sent from Moscow. "This policy ploy on Beria's part apparently was an attempt to use the divisive nationalities issue as a prime means to wrestle supreme power in the immediate post-Stalinist hierarchical struggle."[9]

This turnabout in Beria's self-promotion, however, was short-lived. He, too, was brought down in June 1953. After his downfall, during interrogations of imprisoned Yiddish writers petitioning for release, their reference to him in connection with Mikhoels' rehabilitation was brushed off:

When a writer tried to prove that he was innocent because Mikhoels had been rehabilitated and with Mikhoels' rehabilitation all the Jewish writers were cleared of any guilt anyway, the "objective interrogator" . . . used to cut him short and say: "I would advise you not to bring Mikhoels as an argument". "Why?" "The rehabilitation of Mikhoels is Beria's doing."[10]

On April 4, 1953, came the astounding news that all charges against the accused physicians had been invented and the confessions obtained by torture. Seven of the original nine who survived were released and exonerated. Two had died of torture. (The April 4 statement mentioned fifteen doctors, but it is not clear when or why they were added to the original nine. It has been suggested that "some fair-minded Russian doctors had attempted to forestall the slanderous accusation"; or, that, for the sake of foreign consumption, the addition of non-Jews would offset the charge of Soviet anti-Semitism.[11])

After this announcement, several of Beria's subordinates were arrested and Beria himself was arrested on June 26, 1953, and denounced as a "hireling of foreign imperialist forces," an "enemy of the people," guilty of "criminal anti-party and anti-state work," and aiding "the activity of bourgeois nationalist elements." He was shot on December 17. Subscribers to the Great Soviet Encyclopaedia were asked to remove his photo and the account of his life with a razor, and replace it with an article on the Bering Sea.[12]

Khrushchev's fortunes now picked up. He overhauled the party machinery, putting his own men in key positions, and with the help of his appointees became first secretary of the party, the position Stalin had used to become absolute dictator. Tirelessly, he traveled throughout the country creating the image of the effective and powerful successor to Stalin. Yet the appearance of "collective leadership" was being cultivated in the process of downgrading Stalin, or "de-Stalinization," "carefully timed, masterfully controlled, and doled out in tolerable . . . doses."[13] Controls on writers and intellectuals were gradually loosened and they began to raise their voices after a long silence. But the men in this leadership were Stalin's men, and Khrushchev, who eventually won out, rose in and was tutored politically by the Stalin dictatorship. In the years of Stalin's rise to power, 1929 to 1939, Khrushchev also rose—"at a time when success could be obtained only by atrocious methods and over the dead or broken bodies of innumerable comrades."[14]

Unlike most other Soviet officials, Khrushchev was a hearty, joking, sociable, accessible leader, described as a "true man of the people," whose ancestors had been serfs, and whose father had been a peasant, then a miner. Khrushchev was the first member of his family to be schooled. He joined the Bolshevik party in 1918 and fought in the Civil War. In the twenties he became regional party secretary in the Ukraine, served for several years as first party secretary in the Moscow region, and then returned to the Ukraine as first party secretary in 1939–41. In 1930 he became First Secretary of the Moscow city and regional party organizations and quickly showed skills combining cunning, boundless energy, organizing ability, brutality, and a certain courage, "which distinguished him from many of his contemporaries."[15] Brash, noisy, and overbearing at times, he could also be calculating and devious. When, in 1932, he became Kaganovich's deputy in Moscow, he shot into national significance in party matters. He was involved in bloody purges, the cruel collectivization process, and forced industrialization under the Five Year Plan, serving Stalin obediently all the while. His rapid rise is generally attributed to his cunning, strong sense of realism, and flexibility. After he assumed the formal title of First Secretary, Khrushchev began to outbid and outmaneuver Malenkov, purging the party of his supporters and putting his own men in key positions all over the land. In 1955, Malenkov had to resign the premiership after confessing to his "guilt and responsibility for the unsatisfactory state of affairs in agriculture" and "incompetence in local work"; a few months later, Molotov confessed that he had misled the party by failing to recognize socialism when he saw it! Khrushchev then began to quickly fill the presidium, secretariat, and party secretaryships in the republics with his own men. Forty-four percent of the Central Committee elected at the Nineteenth Party Congress were purged. The power struggle raged on until June 1957 when Khrushchev finally emerged as the new dictator and Malenkov was expelled from the party. The wheel of political life and death momentarily stopped its spinning.

The great war hero Marshal Zhukov, an arch opponent of Malenkov, became Minister of Defense, and Marshal Bulganin, a "political general" became Prime Minister. Military support for Khrushchev was impressive, but by 1957, when he reached a position of unchallenged authority, Khrushchev himself realized that his erstwhile allies had assumed "an unprecedented political role," and that their military appetites were showing "a dangerous intensity." He then set about re-establishing party dominance in the military and everywhere else. Zhukov was removed and party units within military commands became supreme. The party henceforth defined military theory, doctrine, and strategy. There was further resistance and alienation from the military when Khrushchev ordered vast manpower and budget cuts in the defense establishment.[16]

Visitors to the Soviet Union during the period following Stalin's death found the general public mood in the country more relaxed and less constrained than under Stalin, but Jews were still haunted by fear and anxiety despite some signs of a milder atmosphere. Many had first heard the thrilling news annulling the charges against the doctors on April 4 on the radio, when the announcer Levitan said: "The people guilty of perverting the inquiry have been arrested and summoned to trial to bear the responsibility for their criminal guilt." He then identified the case by referring to the chief prosecution witness Dr. Lydia Timashuk, whose Order of Lenin was withdrawn.[17] Jews were overwhelmed by this miracle—the government admitting that the charges against the doctors had been false and libelous. Did this mean a change in official Soviet policy toward Jews? April 4 marked the third day of Passover, a contemporary celebration of a liberation, as well as a historical one. Jews celebrated together in small parties; some waited patiently for the "Voice of Zion" from Israel and heard the good tidings in Hebrew. The use of Jewish names and references to persons of "Jewish origin" in the newspapers suddenly stopped.[18] A *Pravda* editorial said that "Ryumin's clique" in the Ministry of State Security, had slandered Mikhoels, "who was an upright communal worker."[19] If Mikhoels was thus exonerated, there seemed reasonable hope that other imprisoned or exiled Jewish cultural figures would be released. Some Jews also celebrated Israel Independence Day on May 16 at quiet parties.

But economic discrimination and anti-Jewish policies were to continue, although applied with more circumspection.[20] Beria by now had become the scapegoat for all past injustices, but for Jews the lingering taste of the Stalin period persisted after his death. Harrison Salisbury, who was in Moscow in April 1953, found a number of Russians who still believed the doctors were guilty. A taxidriver talked about "those rascals. They got away this time. But their day will come. We will get those yids!" To Salisbury, these reactions indicated "the terrible, terrible need of Russia for a scapegoat . . . on whom to pile the blame and guilt for the horrors of the Stalin epoch."[21] As late as 1959, a Soviet Jew told a visitor: "The 'doctors' plot' and the deportation menace in your mind were but dramatic episodes of recent history, whereas their impact is still haunting *our* minds."[22] The feeling of self-confidence and of belonging to Soviet society, of sharing equally with other citizens, was shattered for Jews during the Black Years, and was not healed during the Khrushchev years. Moreover, the new regime did not unequivocally condemn anti-Semitism. Some of its decisions, indeed, were deeply troubling to Jews (see Chapters 26 and 28).

The amnesty for the doctors was also accompanied by an amnesty for those sentenced for terms of less than five years. Some Jews were released in this amnesty, but most were unaffected, having been imprisoned for "counterrevolutionary activity"—large numbers who formed a large part of the prison population. Beria had been eliminated, but Semyon Ignatiev, minister of state security at the time, had prepared the case against the doctors and was held officially responsible for extorting false confessions, was not punished. He was transferred out of his security post but rehabilitated after Beria's fall and then elected to the Supreme Soviet.[23]

There were many other contradictions to grapple with. For example, Soviet diplomatic relations with Israel were resumed in July 1953, but attacks on Zionism continued to be vehement. Jewish communities in the West were prematurely relieved by restored relations and the partial amnesty, but thousands of Jews arrested and exiled in 1948–53 continued to languish in prison and exile. Zionism continued to be a criminal offense. Many people still considered Jews a dangerous, hostile group. The charges against those accused in the Slansky Trial were not retracted and another wave of Moscow-inspired trials swept over Czechoslovakia, Hungary, and Romania, with non-Jews as well as Jews accused of failing to check Zionist activities and failing to punish subversive elements, described as "Jewish capitalist smugglers," "Jewish Gestapo agents," and "agents of the Joint."[24] After the trial in Bratislava in April 1954, the European press noted the "revival in full strength of the anti-Semitic *leitmotiv* of the Slansky trial. . . . The punishing of non-Jewish defendants for allegedly protecting Jews is new. . . ."[25]

Most plaguing and painful was the silence surrounding the fate of the Jewish writers and cultural figures who had been seized during 1948–49, about whom nothing at all was known or revealed (see pp. 559–67 of present chapter).

The campaign against "cosmopolitans" had given some inkling of what was happening to Jews in the Soviet Union between 1949 and 1953, but it took almost three years following Stalin's death to know the full truth. Walter Z. Laqueur, writing in 1956, believed that it was only Ehrenburg's *The Thaw*, published in 1954, that gave the West a "real glimpse . . . of what ordinary Soviet citizens of Jewish birth went through during the last years of Stalin's rule,"[26] but that the full shock of their plight came much later.

Zyame Telesin, a well-known Soviet Yiddish writer who had been exiled, then allowed to emigrate to Israel, said that he had written

about pogroms and about those Yiddish writers who were murdered by the Soviet regime in '52. None of this was allowed for publication. One poem about the murdered Yiddish writers, I sent abroad, to Poland, and it was published there. This was after the fall of Stalin, in the more liberal times of Khrushchev. Anyway, even in those so-called 'liberal times,' I was reported . . . [by] that scoundrel, Aron Vergelis, chief editor of *Sovetish Heymland* [see Chapter 28], who reported me. So, I ended up by being called before the Union of Soviet Writers, and I was accused of publishing anti-Soviet literature abroad.[27]

Yosef Kerler was able to get some of his poems about those times through the censor by using symbolic language: "like the language of Aesop's fables . . . I was able to write about my years in the Soviet forced labor camp by using the language of anti-fascism, speaking of the camp as 'my ghetto'. . . . [But] much of my poetry never got published and remained as 'drawer poems.' In the case of some of it, it was passed from hand to hand in . . . Vilna and Riga."[28]

There had been continuing inquiries about the fate of the writers, more so after Stalin's death, but Moscow was deadly silent, and Soviet officials in Washington claimed they had no knowledge of those arrested. The rumors were mere anti-Soviet propaganda, they said. Communists in the United States and Western Europe, as well as Jews and non-Jews who had any interest in the future of Jewish culture and the fate of those who had disappeared, sought information from every possible source but were balked. The families of the assassinated writers were no better off—in fact, they still believed their men were alive. Mrs. Markish and her son David, who had been exiled to remote Kyzl-Orde, Kazakh SSR, kept up a continous stream of letters to the Central Committee of the CPSU, but received no information or release even after the exposure of the "doctors' plot" as a fraud.

Only in July 1955 did the first official word come, in Geneva, when the press representative of the Soviet delegation, Leonid Ilyichev, told inquiring reporters that "something unclean" had gone on at the JAC, suggesting that the committee had been closed for good reason. But he insisted that he had seen Markish "in the street only recently."[29]

Two months later, the Jewish Labor Committee in New York sent a memorandum to Molotov, who was attending a session of the UN, requesting information on the fate of sixty-eight listed persons. Ambassador Zarubin suggested that representatives of the Committee visit him in the presence of Molotov, and Molotov then suggested that they go to the the Soviet Union and see for themselves.[30] In August 1955, a delegation of Soviet writers headed by Boris Polevoy, second secretary of the Writers' Union, visited the United States and Polevoy, in answer to the inevitable questions, admitted that Bergelson was dead. A writer named N. Gribachev then admitted that Markish was dead. Later, at a meeting with American Communist writers, Polevoy denied all rumors about the execution of the Yiddish writers.[31] On September 16, 1955, the Congress of Jewish Culture in New York sent a detailed memorandum to the Soviet ambassador in Washington, Georgi Zarubin, asking for information about the Jewish writers and intellectuals who had disappeared and about the status of Yiddish literature. There was no answer.

Their tragic end was uncovered, not through official Soviet sources, but by Leon Crystal of the *Jewish Daily Forward*,[32] who went to the Soviet Union in the winter of 1955–56 and came out with a partial verification of the rumors. He saw some of the wives and children of those who had been executed, some of whom had fragments of the truth.

Boris Polevoy promised to help him, but in the end proved evasive. Crystal also phoned Professor Vovsi, one of the accused doctors, but could not see him. He returned, however, with some facts, setting the date of execution as August 12, 1952, and naming six of those killed: Markish, Bergelson, Kvitko, Hofshteyn, and Lozovsky.

This revelation was confirmed, not officially in the subsequent exposé of Stalin's crimes at the Twentieth Party Congress late in February (see Chapter 26) but five weeks later on April 4, 1956, in the Polish Communist Yiddish daily, *Folkshtimme* (People's Voice), published in Warsaw, but barred in the Soviet Union. Its editor was Hirsh Smoliar, who had received a numbered copy of Khrushchev's speech and was shocked to find no reference to Stalin's destruction of Jewish life among the other crimes described. Smoliar, still a doggedly loyal Communist, was the author of the article, "Unzer veytik un unzer treyst" (Our pain and our consolation).[33] Still equivocal about the full extent of the shattering of Jewish culture and Stalin's crimes, the article was the "first authentic statement from a socialist source concerning the fate of Jewish writers and institutions in the Soviet Union." The title reveals the mixed tone of the analysis. The full truth is still not faced, yet the writer, in great anguish, asks how it happened that "the spokesmen of the Jewish community, who in the most terrible, fateful hours, succeeded in cementing the unity of Jewish resistance—how could it happen that these representatives . . . the Jewish Anti-Fascist Committee . . . were liquidated and its leaders condemned to death?" The "destructive activity of the Beria Gang" and "the general destructiveness of the personality cult" are the only culprits named, but "the 20th Congress of the CPSU [see below], which gave the signal to eradicate the cult of the individual—the source of these distortions—justified the deep hopes and convictions of the Jewish masses in the victory of Leninist truth."[34]

dividual, there arose a certain distortion of nationality policy in the Soviet Union," making it possible for the Beria gang "to provoke friction among the nationalities," and bring about "a certain growth of nationalism and anti-Semitism." The statement then extols the "Leninist national policy" which brought about "political and social equality for Jews," and the development of a "Soviet Jewish culture which attained a height unprecedented in Jewish history."[35] The earlier victims of "infamous Beriaism" are named: Dimanshtain, Frumkin, Veinshtain, Levin, Merezhin, Litvakov, Levitan, Kharik, Kulbak, Erik, Bronshteyn, and Dunets. But, the statement goes on, "despite the many losses, the creative activity of the Soviet Jewish community continued."[36] The flowering of the work of the JAC, the rescue of millions of Jews from Hitler's grasp, and Jewish resisistance "under the leadership of the CPSU" are then extravagantly lauded. The insistent question is asked: ". . . how could it happen that these representatives [of the Jewish community], among whom were the best sons and daughters of the Soviet Jewish masses—the Jewish Anti-Fascist Committee—suddenly, and without a why or wherefore, were liquidated and its leaders condemned to death?" But the answer is hedged: the reason lay in "the entire destructive activity of the Beria Gang," exposed at the Twentieth Congress, which "brought countless victims to the peoples of the Soviet Union," with the "chief victim" the Communist party itself. The evil has now been torn out "by the roots" at the Twentieth Congress, and "in this victory . . . we find our consolation, our hope and our certainty of the future."[37]

The statement, still twisting to find an adjustment to painful truths, then lashes out against those Jews who have been asking "Why are you silent?": "For many years the united chorus of the Jewish enemies of the Soviet Union and the communist movement has bombarded us with 'questions' and 'interventions,' trying in various ways to misuse our tragedy. . . ." The silence is explained: ". . . we believed that only the party of Lenin could—and finally would—untangle the tragic knot. . . . Our faith and conviction has been fully justified!"[38] The chief victim, according to *Folkshtimme*, has been the Communist party, a victim of the "Beria Gang," now unmasked! A further "consolation" was that "today more than 60 Yiddish Soviet writers are again active and preparing publication of their work," and that the Jewish State Theater was re-established. For many readers, this was a tendentious accounting. Yet, the worst fears and rumors were now confirmed.

Many Jewish Communists in the West now began to raise their voices against Soviet silence, and they could not be so easily condemned as "enemies." Quite typical were the reactions of Max Rosenfeld, a well-known translator from Yiddish, who spoke of the "emotional shock" arising from a "crippling combination of naiveté, priggery and unquestioning faith which many progressives have accumulated over the years." A refusal to recognize the facts had resulted in "a certain type of dishonesty, which led to a glossing over of those things which marred our pretty, schematic picture . . . our first responsibility is to keep on asking questions and demanding answers . . . not merely searching for the 'right way' to handle the whole business." A number of acute questions are then posed: was Zionism used to cover anti-Semitism? Why was it necessary to outlaw Hebrew? What exactly were the executed Jews accused of? What is the nature of the Soviet judicial system? Why should a socialist country deny the right of emigration to those who want to leave? Was it true that, as Milovan Djilas has said, the present Hungarian regime is "the most anti-Semitic of all satellites because the "Kremlin disliked having that country's government in the hands of Jews?"[39]

The questions came pouring down. There were also many resignations in Western Communist party ranks, which caused consternation in Moscow. How could such "secret" news have reached a Yiddish newspaper in Warsaw? An investigation was ordered, leading to the source of the leakage—Polish diplomats—the same channel through which Khrushchev's "secret" speech at the Twentieth Party Congress was allegedly made known.[40] However, interviews by the *National Guardian* with two Soviet spokesmen, in June and September,[41] revealed not only the continuing evasiveness of officials but blatant contradictions when they had to confront Western journalists. Shortly after Smoliar's article appeared, Ekaterina Furtseva, Minister of Culture, was interviewed and

denied emphatically that there had ever been any suppression of Jewish culture or repression of the Jewish people. She acknowledged that she had not read the article in . . . *Folkshtimme*, detailing the shutting down of Jewish cultural institutions in the Soviet Union, the arrest and execution of Jewish leaders, and therefore could not express a positive opinion concerning these allegations. But she declared flatly that if there had been any drive against the Jewish people or Jewish culture, "we would have published it ourselves and would not need to have it published in the Polish press."

Ilyichev, also interviewed by the *National Guardian*, admitted "the tragic fate of the Jewish writers in the latter years of the Stalin regime," but claimed that it was "not the result of an isolated anti-Semitic drive, but rather a part of an anti-intellectual campaign which brought a similar fate to many nationalities—Russian, Ukrainian, Georgian, Belorussian and Armenian." When asked about the article in *Folkshtimme*, however, Ilyichev characterized it as "slanderous and anti-Soviet," in which the author "had picked up the facts and distorted them according to a certain tendency." The "true facts," he said "concern those

Jewish writers who were charged and condemned unjustifiably. But the conclusions this article draws as to the persecution of the Jewish people and their culture [are] a slanderous one." He added that the "good names" of the Jewish writers have been restored and their works republished.

Smoliar did not receive a direct reply from Ilyichev and wrote to him requesting details of the executions and a retraction of the attack on the newspaper. But Ilyichev remained silent. Finally on November 3, 1956, *Folkshtimme* published an "Open Letter to Comrade Leonid Ilyichev" in which it bitterly exposed the disillusionment of Jewish Communists and accused Ilyichev of continuing the injustices against Jews in the spirit of Stalin:

> Can you really answer the tragic question which we discussed in our article by merely declaring that it was "anti-Soviet slander"? Whom will such a declaration really convince? No one! . . . Is it not true that in the years 1948 and 1949 there took place in Russia the wholesale destruction, without exception, of all Jewish social and cultural institutions, including the Jewish Anti-Fascist Committee . . . the Jewish publishing house . . . the newspaper *Einikayt*, and the Jewish State Theatre in Moscow? All these institutions were liquidated because they were Jewish institutions.[42]

Ilyichev ignored this letter, too. He is reported to have described the protest as a "voice from the Warsaw ghetto." The Soviet government likewise ignored the letter and the substance of the grievances described.

During these months rabbinical delegations, journalists, and private individuals visited the Soviet Union, and news and commentary came from diplomatic and political sources. The historian Walter Laqueur wrote:

> The picture that has finally emerged is a very somber one, shocking even the most hardened Communists and fellow travelers and exceeding the wildest fears of anti-Communists. The most rabid of the latter would not have expected Stalin to execute the *majority* of Yiddish writers in the USSR (all of whom were good Stalinists moreover). Since these things have been revealed some Communist leaders in the West have been asking for explanations. But Stalin's heirs, while ready to make certain amends, have refused to make any explanations on this score.[43]

The "amends" were so meagre as to be barely palpable. Only toward the end of 1954 were some of the imprisoned and exiled Jews who had survived released for "insufficient" evidence against them. But for many months when wives asked about the fate of their husbands, they were told: "We don't know where they are. The documents have become lost."[44] The experience of Mrs. Markish[45] in her efforts to pierce the fog of official evasion, and downright lying about her husband's fate reveal the very limited thaw Jews were living through.

It will be recalled that after Markish's arrest, Mrs. Markish, who was no longer allowed to work as a translator, started a knitting class, in which one of the students was the wife of the Deputy Minister of State Security Yevstafyeva. She told the woman who she was, and was shocked to find that the deputy's wife was herself frightened. When she told her husband, he was apparently relieved to know that the lessons were being given in a neighbor's apartment—not his own—but the lessons were discontinued. The chief of the MGB Investigation Branch, M.D. Ryumin, told Yevstafyeva that he had completed a "serious, difficult investigation" of the JAC, that it had been "infiltrated by spies and traitors of the motherland"[46] and that the families of the traitors would be arrested and sent into exile. Feffer's wife was taken shortly after his arrest.

Soon after Markish's arrest on January 27, 1949, Mrs. Markish went to the MGB reception bureau in Moscow. "No news," said the uncommunicative major. "The investigation is under way." Parcels were not permitted, and information about sending money would have to be determined at Lefortovo. A long line of people was already there ahead of her. The queue buzzed with rumors about the possible fate of those arrested and reports of the terrible conditions in Lefortovo. To maintain the fiction that her husband was alive, Mrs. Markish received receipts of money sent to him until February 1, 1953.

One by one old acquaintances drifted away, but she was able to get a job as secretary to the All-Union Society of Microbiologists by using her maiden name. Socially, she wrote, "we lived like people in a leper colony." Toward the end of 1952, the net began to close more tightly around them, and there were more arrests and interrogations. On December 16, her son Simon was called to the MGB district office. The interrogator wanted to know the names of his father's and mother's friends. He and later his mother were required to sign a form pledging that they would not leave Moscow. On the interrogator's desk was a form called "Questionnaire Concerning Members of the Family of a

Traitor to the Motherland." Although Markish had already been dead five months, the family was not officially informed, but the caption on the questionnaire was ominously informative.

On January 13, 1953, the newspapers announced that tireless security investigators had uncovered a "doctors' plot" involving "agents of Zionism and American imperialism, whose purpose was to murder top party officials and patients in Soviet hospitals." Because of the tense, pogrom-like atmosphere, Simon, who was in his last year at Moscow University, decided to apply for permission to defend his thesis immediately, instead of waiting. He received permission and passed, but was extremely vulnerable. A classmate's father offered to adopt him, but such a gesture would have exposed the family. A younger son David had already been sent to Baku to stay with relatives. On January 31, Bergelson's family and Zuskin's and Kvitko's wives were arrested. On February 1, the Markishes received their summons to report the next day to the MGB district branch. A decision had already been made: the family was to be exiled for ten years to the remote region of Kazakhstan. Seals were placed on their apartment, their cat was heartlessly immured in the airless rooms, and a loyal housekeeper was made homeless. A bread van took Mrs. Markish and her son and nephew Yura to a prison train.

After several prison stops, they arrived in Kyzl-Orda, a city in west Kazakhstan, where they expected to remain, but from here, too, they were shipped to a small village called Karmakchi, 110 miles to the north. Here they were under the surveillance of the local *komendatura* (commandant's office, responsible to the district branch of the Ministry of State Security) and confined to a three-mile area. No housing or employment was provided. All of the inhabitants were exiles: Volga Germans, Chechens, Ingushes, and Greeks as well as some Russians. Simon finally found work apprenticed to a planer and Yura nailed crates in the main factory of the town. Mrs. Markish began knitting sweaters and hats again. David meanwhile had gone back to Moscow, but was picked up and sent to join the family in exile.

On March 6 came the news that Stalin had died, but no one seemed to be sure whether things would now be better or worse. About this time, Mrs. Markish began to receive letters from the Procurator's Office in response to her numerous inquiries about her husband. She was not told that he had been executed, but that "he had been condemned . . . for having perpetrated grievous crimes against the State."[47] This left her dangling between hope and despair. On April 4, there came the sensational news that the "doctor-assassins" had been rehabilitated—news that stirred her to believe she could save Markish. A number of desperate letters were sent to party and government officials. Rumors of a thaw in the political climate, a de-Stalinization, filtered into Karmakchi, of people being freed or being moved from a labor camp to exile. In August, the Markishes received permission to move to Kyzl-Orda—a civilized oasis after the barren wastes of Karmakchi.

The family spent a year here, where the local residents, many of them Bessarabian and Ukrainian "bourgeois" Jews and Koreans who had been exiled, took turns giving hospitality to strangers. The beginning of 1954 still did not bring news about Markish's fate. In March, however, Yura was told that he was now a free man. The Supreme Court had upheld his claim that he had never been a member of the Markish household. Simon was given permission to go to Moscow to take the State university exams. Some of the surviving wives and children of the condemned intellectuals returned from exile. In August 1954, the Markish family also returned, but Markish's fate still could not be determined. The Office of Military Procurator merely said that "his case is under investigation." Within a few days, the passports of all the arrested men were withdrawn from their wives and children. Residence in Moscow and Leningrad was forbidden. Another exile was feared.

Among other writers she sought for help was Ehrenburg, already old and declining. He, too, was defensive and evasive, spending a lot of time telling her about events in February 1953, when the editor of *Pravda* allegedly asked him to cosign a letter dealing with the "doctor-assassins in white coats"[48] and pointing up the collective responsibility of Jewry for the "crime." The letter presumably had been signed by others in the field of Jewish culture. Ehrenburg asked for some time. He apparently wanted to know if Stalin was acquainted with the letter. The editor showed him a copy which bore certain revisions which Ehrenburg recognized as Stalin's handwriting. He refused to sign it, and according to his account, thinking he might be arrested, he asked his wife to get his things together. The letter was not published. Ehrenburg was not arrested—another "throw of the dice," he might have said, but an accident of survival for which he was and would continue to be bitterly attacked.

On November 27, 1955, Mrs. Markish was summoned to the Military

Collegium of the Supreme Court. In the waiting room she met the wives of Bergelson, Kvitko, Hofshteyn, Lozovsky, and Shimelovich. Dr. Lina Shtern was also there. Mrs. Markish went into the office of General Borisoglebsky who told her that her husband had been "rehabilitated." "Where is he?" she asked. The general replied, handing her a glass of water: "Your husband was shot by enemies of the people." After insisting on knowing the date of his death, she was told it was August 12, 1952. But when she asked where his grave was, the general said, "He doesn't have a grave." Later she was told she could have the gold crowns that had been taken from his teeth.[49]

In a beautiful letter of condolence, Pasternak added a rueful confession:

That the years of our life have been filled with monstrous and terrible and countless examples of martyrdom, that is something suspected long ago, and my incapacity to reconcile myself to such a state of affairs, as far back as forty years, was the decisive factor in my life and tied my hands.[50]

Between 1953 and 1956, party and state offices were swamped by appeals from victims of the Stalin terror still in camps or exile, or from their relatives. Many, like Yelena Vladimirova, Mikhail Baitalsky, Pavel Shabalkin, Eugenia Ginzburg, Varlam Shalamov, and Pyotr Yakir had been imprisoned in the 1930s and spent much of their mature years in prison camps. Writing was generally forbidden, but their need to bear witness was intense, and they strained to memorize images and lines, to write snatches on cigarette paper and bury the paper in a tin can or bucket. Some of this work later appeared in samizdat. In Vorkuta, meanwhile, prisoners who had spent almost twenty years in prison camps, welcomed news of the amnesty after Stalin's death, but soon learned that it affected only criminals, that is, nonpolitical prisoners. The politicals remained, waiting for a review of their cases. While waiting, a prisoner transport of many thousands came in from the Karaganda camps with the promise of an immediate review. However, the review did not materialize and the prisoners decided to strike, causing the shutdown of two mines. Guards and soldiers killed a number of the prisoners during the ten-day strike until finally a former Soviet army pilot who had spent twenty-five years at hard labor was taken to Moscow and returned "rehabilitated." Mass liberation of the camps did not occur until after the Twentieth Congress in 1956.

In Magadan in the Kolyma, Eugenia Ginzburg and the other prisoners dared not talk of "rehabilitation" at first, but only of amnesty. On the radio, they heard that there had been "illegal methods of investigation" of the "doctors' plot." There were rumors of mutinies around Vorkuta and Igarka. No one was thrown into punishment cells, but here, too, the first to be amnestied were criminals. Then, slowly, passports were returned to the politicals, questionnaires were distributed to specially trained prisoners so that they could apply for specialized work. Feelings of vengeance swept the camps, but prisoners no more than masters could be sure of the next changes. When the stories of the first rehabilitations spread, Ginzburg wrote that they

were like the English children's tale about the small princess Sarah Crewe, who after all the horrors of growing up an orphan had inherited a rich diamond mine. . . . Meanwhile, events kept moving. Neither malice nor stupidity, neither obscurantism nor inertia could arrest the melting, in the hidden depths, of the age-old ice.[51]

Late in 1954 deportation was commuted to resettlement, which meant the end of the commandants' offices, freer movement and bursting hopes for a new life. Eventually, throughout 1955 and 1956, prisoners endured emotional shocks and jolts that they could only share with other prisoners. The sight of nightingales, olives, zipper fastenings, and a clean bed became miracles of another planet. For those whose homes had been Moscow, 41 Kirov Street, the address of the General Prosecutor's office, was the first stop in the rehabilitation process. Here many thousands of haggard, prematurely aged and exhausted men and women talked among themselves, victims of years of wasting life, fearful of being forever outcasts. More waiting followed, sometimes for days, then queuing up at the Supreme Court building for the yearned for rehabilitation certificate. There were two formulations on the certificates: "The case is closed in the absence of any corpus delicti," or "since the charges are not proven."

The dead also had to be "rehabilitated." Soon after his death, close relatives of Stalin's victims who had died began to flood the Military Prosecution Office with requests to clear their names. Most received a uniformly styled certificate saying that the person had been innocently sentenced and executed. A number of the victims had been arrested and executed in 1936–1937, including Baruch Huberman, who had been a leader of the Evsektsiya in the Kiev region and an enthusiast for Birobidzhan, and Professor Joseph Liberberg, the first chairman of the executive committee of Birobidzhan (JAR). Only in 1956 did their families learn what had happened to them.[52]

Rehabilitation of the dead by a military court, however, did not automatically restore party membership. Relatives had to apply to the highest party organs for posthumous reinstatement and rehabilitation by the party, mostly for the sake of the victims' children who otherwise would suffer socially and economically. When the long-awaited rehabilitation finally came, families sat down to mourn the dead.

For those who survived the camps and prisons, the party restored membership, though not easily or immediately.[53] Among them were the Yiddish writers Nathan Zabara, Riva Baliasne, Chaim Loytsker, Motl Talalayevsky, and Hersh Polyanker, all of whom had belonged to the Kiev group of Yiddish writers. It took some time to restore their undermined health so that they could begin to earn a living. Until then, they were dependent on the earnings of relatives. Some of the writers ultimately found work as typists and translators. A few renewed their contacts with publishing houses, but many remained idle and unemployed and led a lonely and monotonous life. "Stay where you are and have a rest," was a frequent answer of party leaders to requests for work. Apparently afraid that former deportees would arouse embarrassing questions, the party tried to keep many from work. Their dreary, futureless life has been described:

And so now they sit around for hours in the specially provided so-called "dietary bars" for old Bolsheviks, not knowing what to do with their vacant days and empty weeks. They talk little; and if they do it is about the weather, about their rheumatic pains. As to the rest, it is better not talked about. One cannot be sure of one's former friends. . . .[54]

This isolation is relaxed for two occasions: May Day eve and March 8, when they are paraded and exhibited on a platform and presented with flowers by young pioneers.

Some who survived were no longer able to pick up the threads of family life and went back to the icy wastes and vast taigas of the east.[55] Life there, they decide, will be quieter and simpler, where everything is familiar. Once back, they marry local Siberian women and establish new families. In other cases, there were Jews expelled from the party but not arrested or deported, who were *ordered* to apply for readmission, or risk endangering themselves and their families. Those in mental institutions could not re-apply, of course, but the others made their re-applications with self-contempt, shame, or cynicism. A few did not want to see their illusions completely crushed and waited anxiously for new party cards. The commission which ruled on these matters, however, perversely rejected a number of applications—especially from Jews—even where the official reasons for expulsion were no longer valid: for instance, when someone was expelled because he had been in contact with someone who had been deported but was now rehabilitated.[56]

Some of the younger Soviet Jews who now ascribed all of the past evils to Stalin waited expectantly for official denunciations of the special persecution of Jews, but they did not come. They also hoped for explanations from the older generation of Jews who had devoted themselves to communism, and answers to tormenting questions from those who returned from prison camps. One such youth recalled:

> They seemed to me strangers from another planet who had not only been through the most harrowing ordeals but . . . had acquired some special unearthly wisdom and were in possession of extraordinary qualities of character. Once a friend of father's, who had been in a camp for seventeen years, came to see us. How many hours—day and night—were spent talking, how many subjects and problems were sorted through! We not only listened to his hypnotising camp stories but also told him how we had lived here, "Outside." And it turned out that "outside" anti-semitism had at times surpassed camp anti-semitism.[57]

But neither the returnees nor events could explain what had happened or give prescriptions for the future. "For," the young Jew continued, "to tell the truth, how could we comprehend anything, when, for us, Soviet people, human history was presented to us—and assimilated by us—only in the form of events predetermining the October Revolution . . . when all the wealth of human thought was reduced for us to a dozen primitive slogans, duplicated in millions of copies and inscribed even on communal toilets. . . ."[58]

Among those released was the remarkable Hebrew poet Zvi Preygerzon, who had been arrested in March 1949, and sentenced to ten years' imprisonment, but was released at the end of 1955, under the terms of a law of September 3, 1955, which released certain invalids. His diary (*Yoman Ha-Zikhronot*), which he kept to help save his sanity, describes the pressures, tortures, investigations, and occasional acts of kindness in several prison camps. "Above all else, we are reminded time and time again of the diary-keeper's amazing dedication to the Hebrew language, which may be described as his secret companion throughout his trials."[59]

He was released from Vorkuta and met in Moscow by his wife, daughter, and son-in-law:

The meeting was a festive one. . . . We were waiting by the station for a taxi. All of a sudden, we were approached by a man of about 40: "Who said you could meet here, you bloody kikes!" the man said.[60]

Pyotr Yakir, the son of a famous Soviet Jewish general, was also released after Stalin's death in 1954. His father had been Iona Yakir, an army commander and member of the Central Committee of the party, who was murdered in June 1937 during the bloody purges. His son, then fifteen, and wife were also arrested. The wife's fate is unknown; she, too, may have been shot. Pyotr spent seventeen years in Soviet prisons and camps.[61] After his release he became a historian at the Institute of History, then, alarmed by the repression at the time of the Sinyavsky-Daniel Trial (see Chapter 29), he became an activist and was re-arrested in June 1972.

After Stalin's death, life in the labor camps became less harsh. Letters from home became more frequent and "contained words of hope."[62] According to some reports, there had been uprisings in the camps at Kolyma, Norilsk, Vorkuta and Karaganda, causing officials to loosen the camp regimes.[63] Traveling "artists' brigades" brought musicians and actors—themselves prisoners—to the camps. One Latvian violinist loaned his cherished copy of Sholem Aleikhem's story "Song of Songs" to the Yiddish writer Moshe Broderzon to copy in the camp at Lena, the first Yiddish book the Jewish prisoners had seen in years. The copy passed from hand to hand, bringing great joy to many readers.[64] In 1955, a number of works by Broderzon himself and other Yiddish writers recently released from camps appeared in Yiddish papers in Poland. There were at the time Soviet announcements that commissions had been appointed to publish the literary remains of some of the Yiddish writers, but the works were to be published in Poland, not the Soviet Union.

The first glimmer of news about the darkness enveloping Birobidzhan came from Harrison Salisbury, correspondent of the *New York Times*, who visited the province in June 1954, but found little to identify it as a *Jewish* autonomous region. Salisbury quoted Lev Vinkevich, the administrative head of the region, who admitted that "from the factual viewpoint, the Jewish Autonomous Region might as well be called the

'Soviet Autonomous Region.' Except for older, insignificant elements, all Jews read and use the Russian language." At the library, Salisbury was shown a 1938 edition of Mark Twain's *The Prince and the Pauper* and a novel by Flaubert, in Yiddish. Vinkevich explained that "Jews were a matured nationality," and did not need "the kind of helping hand the Soviet extends to less developed nations."[65]

When the poet Emiot[66] was released from labor camp, he returned to Birobidzhan in 1954 and observed that the four-page Birobidzhan *Shtern* was printing Yiddish translations from the work of a young poet of the Far Eastern Nanei people, who wrote mostly about fish that his people caught. At the government bookstore, the manager, a Russian woman, asked Emiot "Have all the Yiddish writers stopped writing?"

With the removal of Malenkov and Molotov, Stalin's closest lieutenants, Khrushchev tried to break the image and reality of Stalin's ghostly grip on the Presidium, but it still largely consisted of Stalin's men. Voroshilov, Kaganovich, Mikoyan Bulganin, and Khrushchev himself were Stalin's men who "owe[d] their place to him," who "made the purges, and were made by them. In a time when it took service to the cult, bloody activity, special luck, and an unusual talent for survival, these are the ones that survived." Moreover, "the new top appointees come almost entirely from the old Moscow apparatus previously headed by Khrushchev . . . and from the Central Committee's administrative apparatus headed by Khrushchev.[67] However, the ghost of Stalin could not be ultimately exorcised, even though a great number of significant changes under Khrushchev sent waves of relief through the country and outside it. Mass arrests, bloody purges, and the atmosphere of deadly terror disappeared. The paranoic excesses of Stalinism had ended. For Jews, the inflamed anti-Semitism of the "doctors' plot" had eased, and persecution of individuals had stopped. The exiled and imprisoned were returning home. For the world, there was détente with the West and China, reconciliation with Tito, cultural exchanges, a more "human" face to Soviet communism as some concessions were granted to consumers and as Khrushchev bounded all over the country and mixed amiably with people. A de-Stalinization was set in motion, accompanied by attacks on "the cult of the individual" and lavish praise for "Leninist socialism." Stalin's name and picture soon disappeared.

Soviet and party history were rewritten and the annual award of Stalin Prizes was discontinued.

These preliminaries were climaxed by the extraordinary "secret" speech by Khrushchev on the night of February 24–25, 1956, at the Twentieth Congress of the Communist Party, the first party congress after the death of Stalin, in which Khrushchev denounced in graphic detail most of Stalin's crimes but not those against Soviet Jews.

26

"We Have No Intention of Reviving a Dead Culture": Jewish Policy under Khrushchev in the 1950s

KHRUSHCHEV'S speech at the Twentieth Party Congress is often but mistakenly considered a damning indictment of communism, representing a fundamental break with all past Soviet history, and providing a new beginning because of his unflinching attacks on Stalin and Stalin's crimes. However, his real thrust was against the Stalin cult and Stalin's deviations from true Leninist-Marxist guidelines. That emphasis can already be seen in the Central Committee report Khrushchev made, as First Secretary, to the Congress, a report which was published in *Pravda* on February 15, 1956. (Khrushchev's speech to the Congress took place February 24–25.) There the party is presented as the hero of Soviet history and the Central Committee as being guided by Lenin's teachings and resolutely rejecting the personality cult. The creative role of the infallible party had been usurped by Stalin, but is and will be restored.

Khrushchev's motives in exposing Stalin are not altogether clear. In his memoirs he describes himself as virtually alone in fighting the opposition of the Politburo members who were obviously worried about their own complicity in Stalin's crimes.[1] He needed to carve out political terrain for himself and had to project himself as a leader in command while fighting off opponents. Yet, in less than a year, he pulled back and defended Stalin for defending the gains of the Revolution and the cause of socialism in a partial rehabilitation of him, only to hit back once more in 1961. Then he tried to destroy the memory of Stalin and removed his remains beside Lenin from the mausoleum in Red Square while placating old Stalinists by putting them in the Presidium. These retreats, attacks, and compromises involved intricate political balancing acts enabling Khrushchev to gain and keep power in the struggle for succession.

His "secret" speech[2] was heard by a carefully selected audience of 1,436 high party functionaries upon whom a strict discipline was imposed: no one could leave while the speech was read, no questions or interjections were permitted, and no one was allowed to take notes. The charges against Stalin were sweeping: practicing brutal violence, demanding absolute submission, inaugurating a reign of cruel repression, ignoring all norms of "revolutionary legality" and Leninist guidelines, killing off 70 percent of party members between 1934 and 1938, forcing confessions through torture and mass terror, ignoring warnings of the German invasion in 1941, ordering mass deportations of Soviet minorities, and creating and promoting a cult of self-glorification. As part of his attack, Khrushchev quoted from Lenin's famous testament, in which he had warned his comrades against Stalin. Khrushchev spoke as if this document had just come to light (it had been well-known in the West for many years), but, in fact, it had been suppressed by Stalin and his supporters, including Khrushchev, who had voted to remove it from the Party Congress record in 1927. Much else was omitted or distorted, including Khrushchev's failure to condemn the collectivization traumas and tragedy, and the rigged show trials and confessions of Stalin's ideological opponents—Bukharin, Zinoviev, Rykov, and others—and the deaths of millions of unnamed ordinary citizens who were wantonly killed.

The audience is reported to have responded to the speech with animation and applause, but it has never been published in the Soviet Union. However, it was read in closed party meetings at factories, institutes, and collective farms. Summaries were given to university and secondary school students. Copies were provided to the Eastern European Communist parties and it was apparently through the Polish Communist party that it was obtained by the CIA and then released by the American State Department in June 1956.[3] Despite efforts to contain dissemination, the speech leaked out and stunned millions of Communists and non-Communists alike. Within months the world Communist movement was in disarray and inside Russia there were large hopes and expectations of change, quickly checked and quenched by the party concern for control and order, and a limited short-term thaw.

Jews especially waited expectantly for some signal that Khrushchev would acknowledge Stalin's specific crimes against them, but they waited in vain. Not a word about such crimes appeared in his speech, nor afterward. A witness to the events surrounding Khrushchev's speech, Jewish party activist Esther Rozenthal-Shneiderman, was in Kiev at the time and has recalled the shock waves the speech created. The Twentieth Party Congress had lasted for a full twelve days, from February 14 to 25, 1956. Subsequently, the speech was read at certain party meetings in various parts of the Soviet Union. Any party member could come and listen—an unprecedented invitation. In Kiev, Khrushchev's speech was even read to Komsomol members in secondary schools, but notes were not permitted. Mrs. Shneiderman attended one such meeting of 14- and 15-year-old members in Ukrainian High School Number 7, where the speech was read by a teacher of Russian. The young Esther felt "a nerve-wracking tension." The nationality of many tortured heroes was mentioned, but not Jews. There was a similar silence about the identity of many of the Jews implicated in the "doctors' plot." "I wait in vain," she wrote. "There is not the slightest hint of the sufferings and the physical destruction which the pogrom era . . . has brought to my people."[4]

But hope did not die. There was, after all, the release of thousands of prisoners and the end of mass arrests, purges, and deadly terror. The "doctors' plot" had been exposed as a hoax. Many Jews still hoped for a genuine change in Soviet Jewish policy, for a restoration of Jewish cultural institutions, and for a more benign official position generally. Khrushchev was more approachable and more sociable than Stalin. He seemed to genuinely like people; he had Jewish friends, it was said. However, Jewish illusions about Khrushchev and a more sympathetic policy following Stalin's death did not receive any nourishment after the Twentieth Congress. On the contrary, new evidence was disappointing and embittering. At no point did Khrushchev or any other official concede that the "doctors' plot" had been an anti-Semitic machination for political ends, whether concocted by Stalin or someone else. Nor did he identify the anti-Jewish dynamic behind the numerous purges and trials in the satellite countries. Especially painful was the evasion of and refusal to answer the tormenting questions about the anti-Semitic persecutions of 1948–53 and the deaths of so many leading Soviet Jews.

The murder of the Jewish intellectuals was not acknowledged then, or since, by any official Soviet source. The Soviet people have never been told about their end. Subsequent repudiation of these crimes by Khrushchev or any Soviet leader might not only have been self-incriminating, but would require an explanation for the liquidation of Jewish culture and the reasons why it has never been restored. Such an action would also clear the tainted name of the JDC and Zionism, which had become whipping boys. It also would deprive Soviet leaders of a policy that has produced so many quick and easy political boons both inside and outside the country.

For the post-Stalin period the policy decision against reviving Jewish culture was formulated by a leading Politburo member and Communist theoretician, Mikhail Suslov, who, in 1956 stated it very simply: "We have no intention of reviving a dead culture."[5] These attitudes had already been set. Intermixed with Khrushchev's own strain of anti-Semitism, they would not be budged. Full-scale assimilation of Jews would remain official policy.

Khrushchev's origins and experiences in the Ukraine as well as his tutelage under Stalin in using popular anti-Semitism to achieve certain policy goals gave shape to a crudely anti-Semitic man, with enough cunning to occasionally evade or deny his express hatred of Jews. He was surely much less venomous in his feelings toward Jews than Stalin had been—there were even some Soviet Jews who were prepared to defend him against charges of anti-Semitism—but because of his outspokenness and inability to mask his true feelings, he often expressed his frank opinions of Jews, and they were blunt and harsh. Shortly before his death, Ehrenburg told Alexander Werth, the correspondent, that Khrushchev "had lived too long in my—though not his—native Ukraine, and had been infected with the kind of visceral anti-Semitism that is still very far from having been stamped out there."[6] He was born in Yuzovka, in the Kursk region bordering the Ukraine, and was raised by a religious mother in the traditional Russian Orthodox faith. As a turner's mate in Mariupol, a small port in the Ukraine with a large Jewish population, Khruschev lived as a boarder in a Jewish home. He seems to have had a warm lifelong feeling toward the family and helped Jews in Mariupol fight off pogromists in 1913. He also had a number of friends among Jewish Communists, including Lazar Kaganovich who had helped him in his political career. His own son was married to a Jewish girl, a fact which he often brought up to prove that he was not an anti-Semite.

Yet, there is another Khrushchev Jews remember. He maintained the policy of ignoring Jewish victimization during the war. During all of his rule and even after, Kiev was a forbidden city; the only foreigners allowed in were a few UNRRA officials. When the British historian Edward Crankshaw was finally allowed to go there in 1955, and asked to go to Babi Yar, the local director of Intourist at first pretended he had never heard of Babi Yar. But when Crankshaw insisted, he said, "Why do you want to go and look at a lot of dead Jews? If you're interested in Jews you'll see more than enough live ones in the streets."[7]

During the war, in addressing partisans and local people at Sarny in Volynia after the Germans had been driven out, he thanked the partisans for their heroic efforts and paid tribute to "many nationalities," citing them by name, but made no reference to Jews. To the Jewish fighters present, this was "a bitter shock and humiliating demonstration of Khrushchev's anti-Semitism,"[8] the more so since the meeting was held not far from a mass grave of 16,000 Jews who had been murdered. Jews also recall that toward the end of the war, numerous anti-Jewish disturbances broke out in Kiev. Khrushchev was then in charge of the Ukraine, but he did nothing to stop them.[9]

In his speech to the Twentieth Congress as well as in talks with foreign visitors, when he dealt with the "doctors' plot," he refused to acknowledge its anti-Jewish dimensions, even to the point of saying that "the majority were Russians and Ukrainians, like Vinogradov, Vasilenko, Yegorov, all honest people who have been rehabilitated. The whole affair was given a Zionist, Jewish coloring."[10] Khrushchev also insisted to Ehrenburg that there was no anti-Semitism in the Soviet Union. "But he added that it was better for Jews not to hold high posts in government, saying that in his opinion the unrest in Poland and Hungary in 1956 had been caused by the large number of Jews in high places."[11]

Like Stalin, Khrushchev had to mask or deny any personal anti-Semitism and attack those who expressed it openly. In an episode in which Jews were referred to as *"zhidi"* (yids), a crude word Khrushchev had known from his youth in Yuzovka, he scolded a Polish comrade for using it, but in moments of uncontrolled anger he used it himself.[12] "Because of sensitivity to accusations about his anti-Semitic tendencies, he was always eager to point to his 'Jewish friends' "[13] when *his* regime was being discussed. After Stalin came to power, he wrote, "instead of setting an example of how to liquidate anti-Semitism, he helped spread it. Anti-Semitism grew like a growth inside Stalin's own brain."[14]

He admitted that "after Stalin's death, we arrested the spread [of anti-Semitism] a bit, but only arrested it. Unfortunately, the germs of anti-Semitism remained in our system, and apparently there still isn't the necessary discouragement of it and resistance to it."[15]

Yet once he came to power, he reacted vehemently to any question or implied suggestion that anti-Semitism existed in the Soviet Union. In this connection, it has been suggested that a special definition of anti-Semitism, which a diplomat once offered, may apply. He believed that in Russia, it meant the "killing, beating, jailing, and ghettoization of Jews, not the milder forms of public and private discrimination and contempt," a difference which was the basis of Khrushchev's anger at the "bourgeois Western press raising the problem of so-called anti-Semitism in the Soviet Union."[16]

The perception that he had negative feelings toward Jews was reinforced in his visits, in 1956, to England, and in 1959, to the United States. When Jewish organizations tried to meet with him, he consistently refused. Not even the personal intervention of President Eisenhower could change his mind. Yet in August 1955, he met with a delegation of the Canadian Communist Party and spoke frankly about the "Jewish problem." J.B. Salzberg, a leading Canadian Communist in the delegation, had gone to the Soviet Union to look into the status of Jews and Jewish culture. He raised the question of Stalin's opposition to the settlement of Jews in the Crimea, and said that he (Khrushchev) agreed with him, that it "should not become a centre of Jewish colonisation, as in case of war it would have been transformed into a *place d'armes* against the Soviet Union."[17] He said he was sorry that Lozovsky (whose committee, the JAC, had drafted the proposal to create a Jewish Soviet Republic in the Crimea) had been executed, but he did not express any regret for what had happened to Jews during the war, or for the destruction of Jewish culture and so many Jewish lives during the Black Years. Neither Khrushchev nor any other Soviet leader made any deliberate effort to defuse the anti-Semitic atmosphere or to call for an educational campaign to expose it.

The political exploitation of Jews in the Soviet satellites followed by vehement scapegoating was another Stalin-type cycle Khrushchev pursued. Stalin had used many Jews to provide him with elements for the new army and new party in Poland after the war, and central policy-making roles there were filled by Jews until 1956. The Soviet leadership apparently thought the Jews "a necessity and a great help," but most

Poles were hostile to the government, which they felt was an occupation government set up by the Russians, and to the Jews serving in it.[18] As in Russia, Jews in Poland were to do important preparatory work and then be pushed off the scene. In 1955, the "Jewish question" began to assume importance as the severe economic situation and political crises spread dissatisfaction. Khrushchev attended the Congress of the Polish Party called to name a new party secretary. The Central Committee favored Roman Zambrowski, a Jew who had been in charge of party affairs since 1945, but Khrushchev vetoed him on grounds that no Jew could be head of the party. His choice was selected,[19] but his tenure was very brief. Immediately thereafter the Poznan riots and strikes erupted and numerous reforms were demanded. One party faction, the Natolin group, believed that Jews must suffer for the "sins of the past." Khrushchev agreed. During the summer of 1956 Soviet officials in Poland told various Polish secretaries of party committees that "the actual power in the country should be in the hands of provincial Party secretaries who are 'real Poles and patriots' and not weaklings like members of the government—who are not only influenced by Jews and cosmopolitans but are even themselves Jews." To save Poland and socialism, they said, all Jews must be removed from all important political and administrative positions, the press, and radio.[20] Meanwhile, Wladyslaw Gomulka, whom Stalin had purged in 1949, re-emerged as a political force and again became general secretary of the party in October 1956.

The network of Soviet agents operating in Poland in 1956 spread the idea that the Polish security apparatus was directed solely by Jews and that Jews were responsible for all the crimes of Stalinism and for economic failures. Khrushchev also openly made demands for a swift purge of Jews from state and party positions.[21] During 1956 in the Polish Communist party and in the country at large, a wave of anti-Semitism was rising. Michael Checinski, a Jewish member in one part of the secret service called "Military Information," tried to publish a letter documenting Soviet control and plans to impose a Soviet-type system on Poland, but it was rejected by Gomulka. However, he pledged Polish support for Soviet foreign policy and allowed Soviet troops to be stationed in Poland. Meanwhile, during 1956, there were eruptions of anti-Semitism throughout Poland. In some towns, Jews were beaten up and murdered, and in party and government posts, there were large-scale dismissals. By the end of the 1950s, anti-Semitism began to permeate the party and Mieczyslaw Moczar began to form his "partisan" group with the intention of taking over the most important posts in the party and discrediting Jews as unreliable and treasonable.[22]

Meanwhile, reports of anti-Jewish discrimination and anti-Semitism inside the Soviet Union challenged the new regime. Khrushchev fobbed them off, talked about Jews in political positions and his half-Jewish grandson, or made bluntly negative remarks about Jews generally. For example, he dealt with questions about alleged quota restrictions for Jews on May 5, 1956, when he met with a French parliamentary delegation of French socialists. After admitting, this time, to remnants of anti-Semitism in some of the republics, he added:

This is a complicated problem because of the position of Jews and their relations with other peoples. At the outset of the Revolution, we had many Jews in the leadership of the party and state. . . . In due course we have created new cadres.[23]

When asked to explain "new cadres," he said:

Our own intelligentsia. . . . Should the Jews want to occupy the foremost positions in our republics now, it would naturally be taken amiss by the indigenous inhabitants. The latter would ill receive these pretensions. . . . Or, for instance, when a Jew in the Ukraine is appointed to an important post and he surrounds himself with Jewish collaborators, it is understandable that this should create jealousy and hostility towards Jews.[24]

According to Roy Medvedev, even after Stalin died, Jews were denied "access to positions in the higher Party apparatus, in the provincial and regional branches of the Party, in . . . central ideological institutions, in the higher organs of the military leadership, in the diplomatic service, in the organs of the KGB, and in the procuratorship."[25] Khrushchev continued quotas for Jews for many higher educational institutions, military academies, and certain scientific and cultural sectors.

The practice of maintaining government-set restrictive quotas on Jews was confirmed in an interview of June 25, 1956, in the *National Guardian* with Yekaterina Furtseva, member of the Secretariat of the Central Committee of the Communist Party. Mrs. Furtseva explained that "the government had found a heavy concentration of Jews in some of its departments"—50 percent or more, and "steps were taken to transfer them to other enterprises, giving them equally good positions . . . without jeopardizing their rights."

In a series of articles published in November–December 1956, a staff writer for the New York Yiddish daily *Der tog*, on a visit to the chief Jewish population centers in the Soviet Union, reported the existence of persistent anti-Jewish discrimination. Jewish medical students complained that it was hard for them to obtain internships in hospitals in the metropolitan area. One woman doctor said, "It is so difficult to perform well in an environment electric with hatred for you." Some Jews were told, "Jew, go to Palestine!"[26]

After Stalin's death, Soviet economic science continued to play a leading role in Soviet ideology, and although Jews were less conspicuous, some continued to play a role as teachers of economics, while a few became pioneers of new trends in economic science: Nobel Prize winner L.V. Kantorovich, who is associated with introducing mathematical methods and computers into Soviet planning; E.G. Lieberman, who emphasized the importance of the role of profits; and A.M. Birman, E.L. Manevich, and G. Khanin, among others.[27] There were numerous Jewish professors at the Plekhanov Institute of National Economy in Moscow until the late sixties, when a vicious anti-Jewish purge was started by the head of the institute B.M. Mochalov.[28] (In recent years, a number of young and middle-aged economists and specialists in mathematical economics and a few older ones, such as Birman, have emigrated from the USSR, as the field becomes increasingly restricted for Jews.)

Officially, diplomatic relations with Israel were restored, but, as under Stalin, basic policy toward the Jewish state and toward Jews who expressed interest in it remained harsh. After relations had been severed in February 1953, Soviet media continued to devote considerable attention to the Zionist-Jewish-Israeli network, the alleged infiltration of JDC, and Zionist intentions to "divert the Jewish proletarian masses." After Stalin's death and the exposé of the "doctors' plot," relations were resumed and a small number of Jews re-established contact with the Israeli legation which reopened in the fall of 1953. The Chairman of the Presidium Voroshilov even went so far as to greet "the Jewish people of the State of Israel and its Government," and expressed the hope that Soviet-Jewish relations would be based on the same "understanding" that had prevailed in 1948–49.[29]

Commercial relations assumed special importance at this time and

Israel sent exports of bananas and citrus fruits to the Soviet Union in exchange for Soviet oil. The movement toward normalization was also expected to embrace the principle of "unification of families." Israel hoped for significant steps toward emigration, but Gromyko was "unequivocally negative," expressing surprise that Israel was raising an issue without any realistic foundation.[30] However, he made a distinction between emigration and individual cases of family reunification which could be handled on a consular level. Some elderly parents of Israeli citizens were permitted to leave, but there was no substantive change in policy.[31] In May 1953, an Israeli team took part in the European basketball championship in Moscow and Soviet media praised the high level of Israeli playing in the team's victory over Czechoslovakia.

In June 1954, the level of diplomatic missions was raised to embassy level; official Soviet participation in Israeli diplomatic receptions seemed to portend a new era of goodwill and relaxation of tensions. However, the Soviet attitude toward the Jewish state had not really basically changed, but its manifestations were different. Whereas at the end of the Stalin period, Israel was attacked for its ties with the alleged forces of world reaction, in 1953–54, the Soviet anti-Israel orientation "resulted directly from its [Soviet] rapprochement with the Third World . . . and the Arab countries," enabling the Soviet Union to reinforce its "struggle against imperialism," and penetrate the Arab world by way of commercial and technical deals with Egypt and allying in their common goal of ousting Britain from Egypt.[32] In the Security Council, the Soviet Union supported the Arab cause in several Arab-Israel conflicts during 1953, involving herself in the Middle East as an interested and influential factor. It now desired a leading role in the region and "saw in the Arab-Israel conflict a principal and unchanging means of acquiring influence in the Arab East."[33]

The Israeli embassy in Moscow, meanwhile, became increasingly out of bounds for Soviet Jews. When an American Jew in 1959 asked the militiamen who stood guard at the entrance if many people visit the embassy, one of them said, "Oh no. Only foreigners come in from time to time. . . . Our Soviet Jews stay away."[34] Except for some Jewish youngsters, Soviet Jews were reluctant to take Israeli postcards, coins, or stamps brought by visitors as souvenirs. But this inhibition did not mean lack of interest or curiosity, but rather deep anxiety and fear.

During the Youth Festival in 1957, however, thousands of Jews from all over the country came to Moscow to see the Israeli delegates. They cheered them at meetings, invited them to their homes, and asked for Israeli mementos. The retribution was heavy. One hundred and twenty Jews were sent to the forced labor camp of Vorkuta after this event—more than half were Moscow Jews who had entertained members of the Israeli delegation; the rest were Jews who had come to Moscow for the festival. Several thousand other Jews guilty of "fraternization" were reportedly removed from their jobs, on various pretexts. People were arrested for trying to obtain information from the Israeli embassy.[35] Those Soviet Jews who dared to ask questions of Jewish visitors revealed an extremely limited, confused, and often romanticized view of Israel.

The Soviet press published only the most negative and often maliciously slanted articles and letters about Israel. *Komsomolskaya pravda* was directed at Jewish youth, the trade union paper *Trud*, at Jewish workers, and the *Literaturnaya gazeta*, at Jewish intellectuals. *Krasnaya zvezda*, the organ of the Red Army, also had its specialized readers.[36] Letters were published allegedly signed by Soviet Jews who had gone to Israel (some after repatriation to Poland) and found life so miserable that they begged to be allowed to return to the Soviet Union. There was considerable skepticism among Soviet Jews about these reports, but also tentative, uncertain surmise. Facts were not available. A Ukrainian daily in December 1959 reproduced a confession by a certain P.Y. Teper that he had been "poisoned by the Zionist fumes" after the war; S.M. Tabak said that he had been "entangled in the Zionist web"; G. Livshits complained that "tens of thousands of Jews, deceived by rabbis, had left for the 'Promised Land' " and were "trapped in the yoke of cruel capitalist exploitation."[37]

Radio as well as the press carried anti-Israel programs and the Soviet theater produced didactic plays with a shrill anti-Israel message. The Sinai crisis of October–November 1956 intensified the hostility. The Soviet ambassador was recalled from Israel, threatening notes were dispatched, Israel was denounced, and prominent Soviet Jews were pressured to publish anti-Israel letters. Officially inspired and commissioned books also appeared, further blackening Israel's image and reality, and further shadowing the lives of many Soviet Jews, shaking their earlier natural interest and feelings about the country, and troubling their sense of self as Jew and citizen.

On the question of Jewish emigration, Khrushchev was inconsistent, actually contradictory. For example, when he met with French socialists in May 1956, he said that the government did not approve of visits or emigration of Soviet Jews to Israel: "We don't favor the trips to Israel. We are against it. . . ." In 1957, the pacifist leader Jerome Davis asked whether it was true that "Jews are not permitted to go freely to Israel." Khrushchev replied: "It is true to some extent and to some extent not true," explaining that the Soviet Union had permitted Polish Jews to return to Poland as part of a Russo-Polish repatriation agreement, even though "we knew that many of them would go on to Israel from there."[38] This agreement was concluded on March 25, 1957 (and extended until September 30, 1957 and then again until March 31, 1959), under which about 200,000 Poles were repatriated to Poland, of whom about 7 or 8 percent were Jews (about 14,000). Most of these were people who had lived in the parts of Poland annexed in 1939 (see Photos 26.1 and 26.2). Khrushchev pointedly avoided the question regarding emigration from the Soviet Union. In May 1959 he again refused to respond to a similar question posed by a group of American Jewish veterans.[39]

The matter of emigration rights which assumed dramatic importance in the following two decades was already in the late 1950s becoming a perplexing problem for Soviet officials. In the autumn of 1959, Foreign Minister Gromyko told Vice President Nixon in a telegraphed letter that "requests" aimed at permitting Soviet citizens to obtain passports in order to be united with their families in the United States "will be considered with proper attention." Nixon had addressed a letter to Khrushchev asking that, in the interest of improving relations, "matters such as this involving principles of non-separation of families which we both support should not persist as irritants to larger solutions."[40] Gromyko's letter was in response to this.

On July 13, 1959, a resolution of the inconsistency took the form of denying that Soviet Jews wanted to leave the Soviet Union, although at the time, it was known that 9,236 Soviet Jews had asked for documents enabling them to obtain exit visas.[41] In July also the Cairo newspaper *Al Ahram* printed an exchange of messages between Khrushchev and the Imam of Yemen, in which Khrushchev assured the Imam that no Soviet Jews had ever applied to leave for Israel.[42] The Cairo story was carried in the *Manchester Guardian* on July 14. On July 8, 1960, at a press conference in Vienna, Khrushchev was again questioned about the right of persons to leave for the purpose of reuniting families and he hedged by saying that Soviet Jews were reluctant to go to Israel and

26.1-26.2 Jewish women and children who had been deported from Eastern Poland to the Soviet Union and were repatriated in 1957–59 to Poland. The children are in schools and the women in ORT training classes, learning trades, in Warsaw, on the periphery of the Warsaw Ghetto, in preparation for transfer to Israel. Courtesy Rebecca Segal.

that there were "no requests of persons of Jewish nationality or of any nationalities wishing to go to Israel."[43]

During this period, about 1,000 Soviet citizens had been allowed to leave quietly to rejoin their families in Australia, England, Canada, Sweden, and Argentina.[44] Certain Spanish nationals, most of whom had been youngsters who had been sent to the Soviet Union in the late 1930s by the Spanish Republican government, were also repatriated (1,899 between 1956 and 1959).[45] While the subject is "shrouded in mystery," it is known that many Greeks who had been living in Russia from tsarist times have been permitted to leave the Soviet Union to rejoin their relatives elsewhere. Although the policy regarding Jewish emigration would be revolutionized in the late sixties (see Chapter 30), only a small trickle of Jews was permitted to leave before 1966[46] (see Table 26.1).

The Malenkov-Khrushchev years were also harsh ones for newly-forming Zionist groups (see Chapter 27) and for Jewish religious activity. A wave of arrests swept through Zionist groups in 1956 in Moscow, Leningrad, Kiev, Minsk, Riga, and Vilnius, probably exceeding the number of Prisoners of Zion arrested in the seventies, according to one source,[47] but they did not stop the movement's growth. The basic Soviet hostility toward Judaism was also reinforced. In the 1954 edition

TABLE 26.1

National Minority Emigration from the USSR, 1954–64

Year	Jews	Germans	Armenians	Poles	Spaniards	Greeks	Koreans	Total
1954	53	18						
1955	105	608						
1956	454	800	1956	1956	1956			
1957	149	1,221						
1958	12	4,681						
1959	3	5,960		1959		1959		
1960	60	3,460			1960			
1961	202	451						
1962	184	927						
1963	305	242					1963	
1964	537	262	1964			1964	1964	
Totals	2,064	18,630	6,000*	200,000*	6,000*	500*	100*	223,294

Source: B. Pinkus, "The Emigration of National Minorities from the USSR in the Post-Stalin Era," Soviet Jewish Affairs, Vol. 13, No. 1, 1983, p. 27.

Note: *The totals for these groups cover the years indicated in each column.

of the *Short Philosophical Dictionary*, the definition of Judaism is especially vitriolic:

The Bible and the Talmud are widely used by the rabbis and the Jewish bourgeoisie to dull the consciousness of Jewish toilers. Judaism developed its system of religious prohibitions and customs to enable it to strengthen religious fanaticism, to conserve darkness and ignorance. . . . Like any other religion, Judaism is uncompromisingly hostile to science and preaches anti-scientific views on nature and society. . . . Judaism sanctifies social inequality and private ownership; it deifies the rule of kings and exploiters. . . .

These traits of Judaism are extensively used by the Jewish bourgeois Zionist nationalists to stupefy the Jewish toilers with nationalism. . . . After World War II Zionism entered completely into the service and under the control of the American claimants to world domination. . . . [It] appears in the role of agent of American-British monopolists . . . and enemy of the USSR and the lands of People's Democracy.[48]

Yet simultaneously as the regime denounced Judaism and made it the focus of intensified attacks, it was making it into a nonexistent civilization, as if it never had or currently has any historic reality. In an edict called "On the Strengthening of Anti-Religious Activities," issued by the party in July 1954, the Jewish religion was not listed among the important religious faiths.[49]

Synagogues were permitted to hold services and became the only "Jewish address in the Soviet Union," but attendance was problematic for any Jew under sixty. Some synagogues were refurbished and in good repair and the worshipers were quite well-dressed. Some still clung to the synagogue, but the atmosphere as experienced by visitors was doleful. In September and October 1954, a group of editors of American college magazines toured the Soviet Union. Among them was Andrew Meisels,[50] who spoke briefly to the rabbi of the Minsk Synagogue. The rabbi was studying and chanting at a small wooden table in the tiny synagogue with two other old men. The Intourist guide said a few words to him and after introducing himself, Meisels asked if this were the only synagogue in Minsk. "This is all," the rabbi answered. "Before the war there were ninety synagogues in Minsk. But now this is all. There is no need for another synagogue," he continued sadly, "Unfortunately there is no need. Sometimes, during the High Holy Days, we could use another synagogue. . . . But—the next Saturday, the people are gone and there is no need."

"Is it because of the Germans?" Meisels asked.

"The Germans," he nodded. "Before the war there were 90,000 Jews in Minsk. Now there are only 7,000. But there are other things. . . . The government felt there was no need for these things any more."

Nevertheless, there were repeated requests for a new edition of the prayerbook—from Soviet Jews as well as from those abroad, repeated almost ritually every year. After innumerable petitions and many delays, Rabbi Shlieffer of the Central Moscow Synagogue finally succeeded in 1956 in obtaining permission to publish 3,000 copies of the old prayer book in a photo-offset reproduction.[51]

There was also the problem of imposed fragmentation of those synagogues that were permitted. Under the new pattern of church-state relations created during the war, about 450 congregations (synagogues and minyans), were placed with other religious groups (except the Russian Orthodox Church, which had a separate body) under the central government's Council for the Affairs of Religious Cults, but unlike most other "recognized" denominations, Judaism was left without a central body, or even regional bodies.[52] Since 1945, this Council has included delegates of the Greek Orthodox, Moslem, and Baptist communities. Whenever Jewish religious communities have applied for admission, officials have argued that Jews have no supreme central body and are not organized along hierarchic lines. Thus they rejected the application and continue to do so. There has been no way out of this circular reasoning, in which only one party determines ideological assumptions, definitions, processes, and conclusions.

The absence of a central Jewish religious body rendered each synagogue a separate unit, "forced to wage its battle for survival all alone," in contrast to other religious cults and in contrast to the situation prevailing in other Communist bloc countries.[53] The Russian Orthodox Church, a few Protestant denominations, and Moslem communities are permitted to have statewide organizations of congregations, to operate seminaries, publish their own periodicals, send delegations abroad, convene meetings, and be represented at official Soviet functions. However, Jews have had none of these, not even a religious bulletin.

In 1957, a renewed frontal attack against religion generally and Judaism in particular began. After this date, new elements were added to Soviet hatefulness of Judaism. It was (and is) attacked because, according to Soviet propaganda, it promotes the idea that Jews are a "chosen people" who have developed a "hatred" of other people. It was also "particularly immoral" because it has made a god of money.

Besides, Judaism advocated allegiance to another state, the State of Israel, and to the "reactionary, pro-imperialist movement of Zionism. Zionism was further equated with fascism.[54] So, by this time, distinctions between "Jews" and "Zionists" in Communist doctrine and propaganda disappeared, and the two were fused.

Among the more frightening cases of popular anti-Semitism during this period was an incident in Malakhovka, a town near Moscow, which began on October 4, 1959, when a group calling itself *Komitet bei zhidov*—"Beat the Jews and save Russia" (the slogan of the tsarist Black Hundreds) posted anti-Semitic leaflets on buildings and set the synagogue and adjoining home of the cemetery warden on fire. As a result, the warden's wife died. At first Soviet officials denied the facts, but later had to acknowledge them and reported that "a judicial investigation is currently being carried out."[55]

All Jews suffered from such popular and official denunciations regardless of their religious belief or unbelief, for the word "Jew" and "Judaism" blanketed all. Yet, in the less tense atmosphere of the post-Stalinist period, many hoped at least for a reconstruction of their cultural institutions, press, and literature. There had been a marked easing of restrictions in Soviet cultural life generally, and especially in literature, a cultural thaw (see Chapter 28) which had aroused Jewish expectations. American Jewish organizations made several attempts to intervene with Malenkov on behalf of Soviet Jewry, but these efforts were unavailing. Moreover, even after Khrushchev gained more power in 1955, nothing essentially changed. Not a single important Jewish cultural institution was restored. Small crumbs were offered to deflect foreign pressure and criticism that anti-Semitism still existed, and in 1956, there were a few gestures. A woman who had worked for Emes, the Yiddish publishing house, was summoned by the former director and offered her old job back. He himself had been called in and asked to re-open Emes and was organizing a staff of workers. Before his suicide in May of the same year, Alexander Fadeyev, secretary general of the Writer's Union, promised Jews a Yiddish newspaper, a Yiddish publishing house, a Yiddish bi-monthly and a Yiddish theater, and plans were made to re-open all of these. Applications were duly filed, but nothing materialized. Between 1949 and 1958, not a single Yiddish book or journal was published. In the mid-fifties, Russian translations of

Markish and Feffer began appearing, and in 1954, occasional "evenings of Jewish song" or "Jewish humor" were reported from Leningrad to Tashkent, but only in 1958 did the first book in Yiddish appear in ten years. It was a "magnificent edition of Sholem Aleikhem's story *The Bewitched Tailor* . . . with twenty-six lithographic illustrations, reproduced on cardboard in the finest printing tradition, by the noted artist Tanhum Bar Levi Yitzhak Kaplan."[56] But it appeared in a very small edition of 500 copies. In the following year, another small edition of 600 copies was printed. For wider distribution, a 200-page anthology of Sholem Aleikhem's collected stories was published in 1959 in an edition of 30,000 copies, but only a few thousand were kept in the Soviet Union. The rest were sent abroad patently to impress foreign public opinion with the notion that Yiddish culture was not being suppressed.[57] Long queues formed outside bookshops in the big cities of the Soviet Union and the small stock was quickly sold out. Before the end of the year, selected works of Mendele Mokher Seforim and Peretz were also published. In 1960–61, there was a volume devoted to Birobidzhan, and selected works by Bergelson and Osher Shvartsman.[58] In 1961, apparently to appease foreign queries, a Yiddish bi-monthly *Sovetish heymland* was started (see Chapter 28).

In 1956, the authorities permitted the establishment in Vilnius (Vilna) of a Yiddish dramatic amateur ensemble, but it was not allowed to give performances outside the Lithuanian SSR, not even in nearby Riga. A similar ensemble was established in Kaunas (Kovno) the following year. Individual performers such as Anna Guzik, Nehama Lifshits, Saul Lubimov, and Marc Broide occasionally gave song recitals and dramatic recitations to largely older audiences, but the repertoire was extremely limited, even trite, drawn from old nostalgic stand-bys. "Yiddish can be heard but not read," a Yiddish author confided to an American visitor. Even posters announcing Yiddish concerts were not allowed to use Yiddish, but had to be printed in Cyrillic-Russian characters—also the case in record inscriptions. Both the Yiddish singers in concert and on records had to include songs in Russian or other languages.[59] Some records of Yiddish songs became available in 1956, when a number of Yiddish musical artists who had been imprisoned earlier were released.

Much was also made of the opening of *Yeshiva Kol Yaacov* (Yeshiva Voice of Jacob) in the Moscow Synagogue in 1956, hailed as a major departure in Soviet policy. Rabbi Solomon Shlieffer wrote enthusiastically about the opening to the World Jewish Congress:

The festivity was attended by hundreds of our pious brethren headed by rabbis and communal workers. All took part in the great celebration, and with a song in their hearts they joyfully thanked the Creator . . . for . . . [being] privileged again to open a house for God's Torah. . . .[60]

But these optimistic hopes were not realized. Most of the new applicants—enough to fill three large schools, according to the rabbi—were rejected because officials opposed expansion. There was particular interest in Riga, but students there were turned down. Nineteen students were enrolled in 1959, about half of them from Bokhara, Tashkent, and Georgia, and most, apparently having been influenced by *Habad* Hasidim. Jews throughout the country as well as in Moscow contributed to the support of the yeshivah. Students were provided with free lodgings, kosher meals, and a stipend. But the attrition soon began. The head of the faculty, Rabbi Shimon Trebnik, was attacked for "overburdening the minds of his listeners," and thus should not be a member of a Soviet trade union. The student body diminished from nineteen in 1959, to eleven in the fall of 1961, and six a year later. Officials had seen to it that in the spring of 1961, nine of the students, who had come from Georgia, were instructed to return home to vote in elections there. When they returned to Moscow, however, they were denied residence permits.[61] Then, persons connected with the yeshivah were pressured to resign. By the end of 1963, there were only five students and it seemed that the yeshivah would be closed. Money had been raised for a new building, but permission to build was refused. The dwindling groups of students were shunted to a small room in the synagogue. Subsequent inquiries were and have been ambiguously treated.[62] The cynically motivated gesture of permitting a yeshivah to open served a Soviet purpose, namely in providing the regime with "a propaganda shield," while at the same time rejecting the needs of the Jewish religious community for training rabbis.

Another tantalizing crumb came on the eve of Rosh Hashana in 1958, when Rabbi Levin, who had succeeded Shlieffer, was permitted to exchange messages with rabbis in Israel and Great Britain. It seemed a small but hopeful breach in the wall of isolation encasing synagogues in the Soviet Union. But later, when the World Jewish Congress sent invitations to ten Soviet synagogue communities to send representatives to its forthcoming Stockholm Assembly, permission was refused on the grounds that the Assembly would deal with "secular affairs."[63]

Early in 1959, another gesture was made officially when it was decided to celebrate Sholem Aleikhem's centennial birthdate. A series of evenings devoted to his works was organized in the major cities, crowned by the appearance of Paul Robeson in Kolonnyi Zal, Moscow's famous colonnaded hall. The program was presented under the auspices of the Writers' Union and on the stage were leaders of the Union including Boris Polevoy. Robeson was greeted with wild applause and spoke with great feeling about the common suffering of Negroes and Jews, his delight in the productions of Mikhoels, and his love of Yiddish lullabies which he used to sing to his grandchildren, who were half-Jewish. To the great embarrassment of his translator and Polevoy, he also spoke about the great cultural and educational institutions of American Jewry. He then sang many favorite Yiddish folksongs and tunes, and lastly the famous "Song of the Jewish Partisans." These words, too, were translated as the crowd "froze in their seats, stunned" and then applauded thunderously. Polevoy, "pale with fury, got up and . . . asked him, demanded of him: 'Will you please now sing a Russian folksong . . . one which we love so much, Broad and Wide is My Homeland?" The song ends with the line, "For like ours, there is no other where man draws his breath so proud and free." When Robeson finished the last stanza, Polevoy asked him to repeat it, and Polevoy repeated it for emphasis. Then pointing a finger threateningly to the audience, he said: "For like ours, there is no other where man draws his breath so proud and free." [64] The audience undoubtedly understood the inference.

In the meantime, some of the Yiddish writers who had survived the Black Years and the prison camps were making a grim effort to put a hopeful face on their cultural future. Twenty of them met in Moscow in 1958 together with a few sympathetic guests including the French leftist Jewish writer Hayim Sloves who prepared a document [65] of the meeting. The only surviving writer of those arrested in 1952 was Shmuel Halkin. He had been in prison and a prison hospital in Siberia, was released in 1954, and was asked to be chairman. "Now you are the father," a poet called out. "Sit at the head." There were many empty chairs at the table. But, as Sloves insisted, "This was not a memorial evening for the dead. This meeting was for the living writers. . . . When [those] great artists were killed, the impression was created that all of Soviet-Yiddish literature had died. . . . Wonderful oaks did fall," but Sloves believed that Yiddish literature had not died. Seventeen poets read their work at the meeting—poems dealing with the war, the Vilna Ghetto, partisans, Mikhoels, loves, and fears. The discussions turned on the official negative arguments against the proof of need and high interest in a Yiddish cultural future: the attendance of very large audiences at Yiddish concert performances (according to information from the Vice Minister of Cultural Affairs); the constant requests from cities throughout the country for Yiddish books from the Moscow Lenin Library; the pledges of Jewish workers in White Russian and Ukrainian cities to buy and distribute Yiddish books; evidence that young Jews go to the concerts and read Yiddish periodicals in the libraries; the papers from abroad being "read to shreds" and reserved weeks in advance. One writer reported on a trip to farm collectives where he met hundreds of Jewish farmers in collectives who yearned for Yiddish literature.

At the meeting it was noted that there were eighty Yiddish writers in the Writers' Union and another twenty young writers with promise. Lately they viewed the future less and less confidently; a number tried to conceal "the hopelessness, the ceaseless and silent sorrow." Yet they had "never stopped putting the question of Yiddish literature" before the Writers' Union. A special commission was presumably set up, but nothing materialized. Sloves himself believed that "among large sections of Soviet Jewish youth a deep spiritual upheaval has taken place in recent years." They have awakened and are now "concerned with Jewish history, literature, art, etc. A new world has suddenly opened for them. . . ." He concluded that "not only is the official integration theory in . . . absolute contradiction to the facts of Soviet-Jewish reality, but that this theory, just as the policy which is based upon it, has led to results diametrically opposed to those they were intended to achieve."

The pressures for Yiddish in the 1950s were also deflected by a new strategy, of locking Yiddish out of the Soviet cultural scene by making some original works available in Russian translation. This trend was anticipated by a statement made by Nahum Oyslander at the meeting, who said that Yiddish literature in the USSR was part of the "great ocean of Russian literature." Oyslander's views were energetically protested by the other writers present. The poetess Rachel Boymvohl, for example, said: "In order that a river should flow into a sea, it must be a flowing river itself. You cannot make it part of the ocean by the use of a spoon only."[66] Jewish literature in the Soviet Union could not be revived merely by making it an adjunct to the greater and more powerful Russian literature, the writers asserted. However, the Soviet Ministry of Culture said it would "encourage more and more Russian translations of . . . Yiddish writings."[67] This shift, in fact, has occurred to some extent and may represent the only realistic hope for any future Jewish culture.

Very much in the spirit of the Warsaw *Folkshtimme* in its assessment of Khrushchev's speech, Sloves differentiated between criticism of Soviet Jewish policy from the right and left and excoriated those who were getting "a horrible satisfaction" out of the great tragedy. Mainly, however, he acknowledged the falsity of Soviet theory on Jewish culture as it was being practiced. He also found the silence in Left Jewish movements "an unforgivable mistake" and called upon them to speak out to "overcome the crisis" in Soviet Jewish culture. However, as months and years went by, the Jewish Left, disbelieving and traumatized, remained largely silent or apologetic. In Sloves' own words, "As far as the Jewish progressive movement is concerned, the old Yiddish folksaying may be substantiated: 'Until the consolation arrives, the soul can die.' "

For the most part, it was left to the Jewish establishment anti-Soviet or anti-Communist organizations, or non-Jewish liberals and intellectuals to ask the pertinent questions and make the necessary protests. But these efforts at the time were themselves unsuccessful as well as limited. For example, on January 18, 1958, the Congress for Jewish Culture organized a meeting in New York commemorating the death of Shlomo Mikhoels. Over a thousand persons attended, calling attention to the extinction of Jewish culture in the Soviet Union and "demanding an accounting from Soviet authorities for their actions." The gathering "sought to present to the world a record of the havoc wreaked on Jewish cultural life by Soviet terror and to re-establish identity with three million Jews in the Soviet Union."[68] Among the figures who attended were the well-known Yiddish poets H. Leivick and Chaim Grade, Reinhold Niebuhr the distinguished Protestant theologian, and Governor Averell Harriman of New York. A resolution was adopted declaring that "the voice of three million Jews in the Soviet Union has been muted. . . . We demand that the Soviet Union grant to Soviet Jews the freedom to live creatively, that it be given the right to develop its own literature, schools and theaters in the Yiddish language . . . and that Soviet Jews be given the right to contact Jews throughout the world."[69]

Nothing changed. There was no response from Soviet authorities.

Western visitors could only guess at the realities of Soviet Jewish life in the late fifties. A shadowy darkness underlay or alternated with an undefined, crepuscular sense of Jewishness for those who had not fully accepted Russification.

Ben Zion Goldberg, the Yiddish journalist who made another visit to the Soviet Union in 1959, wrote about his strong sense of this darkness. "I always felt shadows around me," he wrote, "when I came into contact with Jews—shadows of the dark past, shadows of the beclouded present and the uncertain future."[70] Since there were no longer any Jewish institutions or spokesmen for Jews except the synagogues and their dispersed, vulnerable rabbis, he had to rely on chance meetings with individuals who were willing to speak to him. Many simply wanted to be left alone in a society that was isolating them and making them feel different, as though they did not belong with the others. The general atmosphere had become poisoned. An elderly Jew who knew Hebrew did not complain about his lot or the social system—he was accepting them stoically, but he was agitated by the lies being spread about Soviet Jews and Israel and kept a secret account of these charges and his refutations on long pages in tiny handwritten Russian which he gave to Goldberg. "It was a pathetic document," Goldberg thought, "of an intelligent and educated man, living in absolute spiritual isolation and engaged in an interminable one-sided polemic with Communist writers."[71]

In sharp contrast was a retired Jewish professor of medicine in Leningrad who felt self-conscious about the proportionately large number of Jews on his faculty and said that Soviet Jews should not become a "nation of professors," that they should go "into the pits, into the foundries"—although his son was already a professor and his daughter a professional musician.[72]

Other Jews were deeply troubled by the rising social and occupational as well as official anti-Semitism. The word "*Zhid*" was being heard more and more and was bruising the lives of Jewish children in school. Maurice Hindus, a sympathetic observer of Russian life, recounted talks with assimilated intellectuals whose children were being beaten and told they weren't wanted at school.[73] Another observer, Walter Laqueur, found the spreading anti-Semitism creating a new "Jewish consciousness," which he described as "a vague feeling of common origin, of somehow belonging together, of sharing certain 'relics of the past'—such as a few Hebrew words, a few Jewish tunes—in other words, it is a kind of 'collective memory,' fragmentary though it be." Yet, in the main, he believed, "the new 'Jewish consciousness' of Soviet Jews must be defined as a response, sheerly, to social and—sometimes—political anti-Semitism."[74] One must add to this vague mixture the profound impact of the Holocaust and the creation of the State of Israel. Yet the new regime did nothing significant to respond to the post-Stalin Jewish yearning for healing, reconciliation, acceptance, and cultural renewal.

In the late fifties and early sixties, in small but significant circles, these vague feelings began to take on new forms and expressions of Jewish self-awareness, both astonishing and, in a certain sense, inevitable (see Chapter 27). Deprived of Jewish cultural expression, yet subject to anti-Semitism and ever reminded of their Jewishness, some Jews insisted on their right to know something about their history and religion, their origins in the land of Israel and the current life of that country.

The regime balked, making threats and arrests, continuing its anti-Zionist, anti-Jewish propaganda campaigns in waves, alternating its attacks on synagogues and trials for "economic crimes" with meagre opportunistic concessions, largely for foreign consumption. There was, however, one unprecedented concession, which was to have momentous consequences, namely, the granting of the right of Jews to emigrate. During this period there were also increasing visits by Western Jews to the Soviet Union and greater awareness of the Soviet Jewish predicament in certain Western circles. Eventually, this led to an understanding of the possibilities of Western leverage on Soviet policy and organizational action directed toward changing it (see Chapter 29).

The late fifties and early sixties also marked the emergence of a very small movement of dissidents who dared to openly protest against the suffocating repression, injustice, and hypocrisy of the regime (see Chapter 29). This was to become the first human rights movement in Soviet history, the first to speak out, petition, and protest the denial of rights guaranteed by the Soviet Constitution. They circulated the first samizdat materials in limited circles. There were Jews in this budding movement, some of whom eventually shifted their main activity to the Jewish groups, as well as others who remained within the human rights movement, which in time embraced the specific demands of the Jewish national movement.

These groups, at first, diverged on approaches and goals, then coalesced on fundamental principles, and ultimately divided to reveal a remarkably pluralistic underground political culture in the Soviet Union. However, in the beginning, the human rights movement and the Jewish national movement strengthened and influenced each other. Each helped to breach the walls of silence, fear, and ignorance that had imprisoned Soviet society for two generations. The fundamental nature of Soviet society has not been changed by them, and most of the population has remained indifferent or passive, but the thinking of uncounted numbers has been affected. As in the past in Russian history, the first great fissures were made in literature.

27

The Literary "Thaw," 1956–62, and the First Jewish National Stirrings, 1958–63

Τ H E critical changes in Soviet literature and literary criticism came in the post-Stalin period, but there were a few rumblings even before Stalin's death. By 1952, it had become clear even to certain party leaders that a regimented literature designed to result in ideological orthodoxy had turned Russians into eager readers of nineteenth-century Russian classics or wholly apathetic non-readers. A *Pravda* editorial of April 7, 1952, castigated those critics who condemned authors for depicting negative aspects of Soviet life and attacked works "whose heroes were described as entirely absorbed in production problems."[1] But the floodgates opened after Stalin's death in 1953. His death was greeted with much relief by a number of writers in the Writers' Union, and in October 1953, at a plenum, the Board of the Union called for frank discussions in literary matters. In the same month, in *Znamya* (The Banner), Ehrenburg declared that the "writer's proper domain is man's inner world and spiritual life and not simply descriptions of the external conditions of existence."[2] The composer Aram Khachaturian declared that "creative problems cannot be solved by bureaucratic methods."[3] A great stir was caused by Vladimir Pomerantsev's article in *Novy mir* (New World) of December 1953, in which he said flatly that Soviet literature lacked honesty, and that most works resembled gramophone records and worn-out slogans.

The revisionist campaign continued in 1954, resulting in violent clashes with the old entrenched commissars. The dissenters were reprimanded at an All-Union Writers' Congress in December 1954—the first in twenty years—but a number, including Ehrenburg, spoke out freely. Ten poems from Pasternak's great epic of the "other Russia," *Doctor Zhivago*, also appeared in 1954. The full novel was completed in 1955 and circulated among various Soviet magazines and publishing houses, but it was rejected and had to be published abroad, in Italy. But the influence of Pasternak's life as a creative, independent artist and of his work was and has been incalculable. There were also refreshing new plays in 1954 and the first part of Ehrenburg's important short novel, *Ottepel (The Thaw)*, the title of which served to describe the whole period. *The Thaw* is not considered an original piece of literature, but it deals with personal problems and emotions instead of the "communal apartments painted in gold, workshops in factories looking like laboratories, and kolkhoz clubs resembling palatial mansions,"[4] which Ehrenburg deplored in contemporary Soviet writing. Moreover, the novel also deals with topical problems of special interest to Jews: the notorious "doctors' plot," prisoners returning from the camps, and spreading anti-Semitism.

In 1955, some writers were rehabilitated posthumously, including Babel. This news and the "de-Stalinization" process begun by Khrushchev at the Twentieth Congress had a liberating effect on writers. Not all of the evils of the Stalin era were made known, but many details were, including letters from tortured writers in prison cells, and they provided further encouragement and a sense of release, sufficient to produce a genuine thaw.[5] The slashing attack on the dead hand and soul of the Writers' Union on literature made by Mikhail Sholokhov at the Congress, which was published in *Pravda* on February 21, 1956, had a special, cleansing impact. Moreover, the journal *Novy mir* was particularly open to writers striving to unshackle themselves from party constraints and dogmas. Among the works it serialized was the popular much-debated and much-translated novel *Not By Bread Alone*, by Vladimir Dudintsev, which pits an idealistic inventor against a party machine functionary.

By June 1957, the leading Stalinists—Malenkov, Kaganovich, Voroshilov, and Molotov—were removed from power and despite Khrushchev's own ambivalent wavering about Stalin's achievements, there was "guarded public discussion of past Stalinist abuses." "Anti-Stalinist themes continued to appear mutedly in belles-lettres between 1957 and 1961," especially the camp theme—the experiences of ex-prisoners freed after 1956.[6]

It was in this partially free atmosphere that the first stirrings of a postwar Jewish national movement began. Survivors of the prison camps speak of a "national-Zionist ideology" predominant among Jewish prisoners in the forties and fifties.[7] After the first amnesty in 1955, groups of returnees and some Jewish youths formed in Moscow, Leningrad, Odessa, Kiev, Georgia, Lithuania, Latvia, and in special settlement cities in Karaganda, Norilsk, Omsk, and Vorkuta.[8] Dr. Abram Kaufman, leader of the Jewish community in China, met with some of these youths in several Soviet labor camps.[9] These groups as well as small independent youth groups disseminated information about Israel and Jewish history, supplied by the magazine *Ariel*, the journal *Shalom*, published by immigrants from China who settled in Israel, and old editions of books by Herzl, Dubnow, Pinsker, Jabotinsky, Hess, and others discovered in private libraries. Some radio broadcasts from Israel could be heard in Vilnius.[10] Moreover, the first Jewish samizdat material began appearing in the fifties.[11] In 1956, Yakov Edelman disseminated dozens of copies of his article "A and B," a translation of Hannah Senesch's diary, and a translation of a book about Trumpeldor,[12] the hero of Tel Khai.

The ex-prisoners had been in a world apart, scarcely communicable to others, but for some there was enough energy and spirit left to be group leaders and teachers. The new, young members had to undergo emotional and intellectual transformations of a generation that had at first accepted Marxist ideology, Russian culture, and the idea of collective life and had felt a strong pro-Soviet attachment. This process was driven by knowledge of the Nazi mass murder of Jews, the experience of Soviet anti-Semitism, and the distant glow of Israel, creating fundamental changes and redefinitions of the youths as Jews. Some have spoken of the strangeness of the concept of the development of an individual personality, in the Western sense, of the conscious effort needed to unravel Soviet conditioning to find the individual self, and then the Jewish self; others, of the difficulty of overcoming their faith in Marxism, their conflicts with parents, their interior withdrawal from conventional Soviet values, beliefs, and behavior.[13] The passage to heightened Jewish national consciousness was especially difficult for assimilated Jewish intellectuals in the large Russian cities and seems to have been largely a reaction against the Soviet system in general and Soviet anti-Semitism in particular. In the Baltic republics, the familiarity with Jewish and Zionist traditions made the passage to Jewish consciousness somewhat easier. As in all transformations of this order, there were insistent questions, frustrations, arguments, and dilemmas.

The absence of a body of Jewish history and literature and a Jewish cultural leadership combined with the harsh anti-Jewish line of the regime made these inner changes fraught with risk and hardship. These early pioneering spirits were creating new lives in a cultural and ideological desert.

The earliest manifestations of national feeling combined with action were asserted in the late fifties and early sixties in Riga,[14] one of the great Jewish cultural centers in pre-Bolshevik Eastern Europe, the "Paris of the Baltic," but with a diminished Jewish population of only 30,000. Survivors of the Holocaust remembered the old traditions—whether religious or secular—but few remained after the war. Those who did, however, whenever they were not too crushed or afraid, helped to nourish the new generation of Riga Jews who had become fully assimilated, but then began to feel alienated from Soviet mainstream culture. Activities developed around samizdat publications; meetings at Rumbuli, the site of mass executions of Jews near Riga; visits to homes where family hospitality and eagerness to share Jewish experiences combined to create informal communities where young Jews could discuss Jewish matters, Israel, their own sense of Jewishness, and where they could sing Israeli songs and dance the hora; informal gatherings at the synagogue on Saturday mornings and holidays; showing and exchanging Israeli postcards and slides; records, lectures, and Hebrew lessons to further strengthen a sense of community and a core of Jewish knowledge.

Older survivors in Riga probably had graduated from schools where Hebrew or Yiddish was spoken, and in whose homes Yiddish was certainly the primary language. They were very likely affiliated with a part of an ideologically varied Zionist movement. Before the war and under the Nazi occupation, Socialist Zionism predominated and some members were able to flee to Palestine. After the war, however, it was Jabotinsky-inspired revisionist Zionism which had more influence among Riga Jews and inculcated a militant national position. Even in the distant reaches of Siberia, Latvian Jews made their impress. Boris Slovin, the son of a prosperous Riga family, founded what was probably the first Zionist student underground circle in Siberia, soon after Stalin's death, while he was a student at Tomsk University. After the 1956 Sinai War, Slovin made his way back to Riga and became an important activist leader. In Siberia, to which many Latvian Jews had been deported in 1940, some contacts were made with Jews from Belorussia and the Ukraine, who had no Jewish background at all. Some of these contacts were revived after the war. (Some of the Jewish male deportees from Belorussia and the Ukraine were released from prison or exile in Siberia in 1946–47 and then returned to exile to be reunited with their families; the Baltic Jews were released in 1956–57.)

The Israeli campaign in the Sinai in 1956 stimulated groups in Riga to create small Zionist circles, led by the activists Leah Bliner, David Garber, Dov Shperling, Iosif Yankelvich, and Iosif Shneider. In 1957 they issued their first samizdat publication, which dealt with the Warsaw Ghetto revolt. Later, they included material on Ben-Gurion's speeches dealing with the Sinai campaign, Dubnow's *History of the Jews*, and a summation of the Eichmann Trial.[15] Uris's book *Exodus* became their bible. The groups were "deeply underground," as one of the later activists described them. In the late fifties, "no one knows more than his small piece of truth. . . . I knew of five to ten people in those days. Someone else knew five or so. I don't know what they were doing exactly. We learned not to ask. We didn't want to know too much."[16]

In small Georgian towns, which had generally been free of anti-Semitism, and where Jews could practice their religion, the atmosphere surrounding the "doctors' plot" drove a wedge in Jewish/non-Jewish relations and turned some Jewish youths inward. In Tskhinvali, for example, Christians burst into Jewish homes, the last remaining synagogue was closed down, and matzo had to be baked in private homes.[17] The creation of Israel had already had an electrifying effect on many Jews. In 1959, one such youth, Gershon Tsitsuashvili, started his oriental studies at the university in Tbilisi and within a year started to teach Hebrew to a few others. They asked him to produce a Hebrew textbook and the project was launched. A typewriter was borrowed and photographic paper bought. The Georgian text was typed, but the Hebrew was handwritten. A photographer in Surami printed it and an old bookbinder was found to bind it. The few dozen copies were snapped up and then people began copying the book by hand. "These studies," Tsitsuashvili said, "stimulated them to think about Jewish problems."[18] Samizdat was also produced, largely from material sent by friends in Moscow, Leningrad, and Riga. In Georgia, too, the great influence of Uris' *Exodus* is emphasized by the early Jewish activists.

In faraway Taganrog on the Sea of Azov, the Rusinek family from Riga, who had been in exile in Siberia, received essays by Jabotinsky and a copy of *Exodus* in German. When they returned to Riga in 1963, they painstakingly and secretly had the book translated into Russian, two pages in two hours, with "Sarah" the typist typing on a blanket to muffle the noise. Every week the diligent Boris would call Sarah for a cup of tea, which meant that the next portion of the translation was ready. The most difficult problem was securing carbon paper. The quality of Russian carbon paper is not good and Polish carbon is very rare. Small quantities had to be purchased so as not to arouse suspicion.[19]

It took a whole exhausting year to finish the translation and typing. Two copies were kept in Riga and three sent to trusted friends elsewhere in the Soviet Union. Young people were given first reading privilege, and each copy had to be returned to the person who gave it to him. The Rusineks were "deluged by pleas from those who wanted to read the books" and *Exodus* began its dramatic journey among Soviet Jews. Before long, they heard of an abridged translation of the book in Russian, indicating that at least one other group had also begun its samizdat.

The struggle to maintain a Jewish choir and drama group in Riga in the late fifties also had its reverberations.[20] There had been a few Jewish concerts in Riga by professional singers such as Anna Guzik and Nehama Lifshits and a small amateur group from Daugavpils (Dvinsk) performed after Khrushchev's speech in 1956. But something more immediate and local was needed. In May 1957, a group of five people, led by a young lawyer David Garber, decided to organize an amateur Jewish choir and drama group. Officials allowed them to use the trades club in the center of the city, and within a week after notices were posted, 200 applied. When the town party committee heard of developing plans, they called the organizers to a meeting and told them that the party would not tolerate the development of culture in any language other than Russian or Latvian, and that Jewish culture could be developed only in Birobidzhan. The secretary Viktor Krumin went so far as to say that "You [Jewish art] will cause more harm than good." When asked what he meant, he said, "You will artificially slow down the natural assimilation of Jewish children."

The group argued and protested, and tried to invoke "Leninist nationalist policy" and various Soviet laws protecting the development of national cultures. Finally, Krumin gave permission to organize only the choir, forbidding a drama group or orchestra. At the same time the club manager was given a secret order to disband the choir.

The group evaded the order by holding rehearsals outside the club, in secret, in a shoemaker's workshop and sometimes in a cold base-ment room. The club manager could then say that the choir had been disbanded, and officials could say that "the Jews themselves do not want Jewish culture." But the 100–110 choir members were determined to salvage their small project and sang together and rehearsed for a concert under the conductor Israel Abramis, the son of a cantor. By February 1958, the choir was ready for a concert. A hall was arranged and several music critics and party representatives were invited to a program consisting of Jewish and non-Jewish songs. The audience was astonished at the professional level of the performance and officials agreed to allow the choir to continue, but under severely restricted conditions. The choir was not permitted to call itself a "Jewish choir," and the programs must never include more than half Jewish songs. The group was infuriated by these demands but relented in order to continue their work. They succeeded in giving thirty-eight concerts from 1958 to 1962. Every concert was held in a large hall and tickets were always sold out to enthusiastic audiences.

The famous singer Nehama Lifshits, who later emigrated to Israel, took part in several of the concerts and some songs were recorded by the local radio station. The repertoire included many popular Jewish songs, ghetto songs, classical works, and even new Yiddish composi-tions by Maks Goldin, Mendel Bash, and Sara Feygin. An official at-tended every concert and counted the number of Jewish songs per-formed to make sure the required ration was adhered to.

The group persisted in its efforts to set up a drama group and per-mission was grudgingly given, but with a set of conditions: the drama group could not cooperate with the choir, but must belong to the "club for workers in commerce"; every play had to be translated into Russian and pass the censors; at every performance several seats had to be provided with earphones so that the play could be simultaneously heard in Latvian and Russian. A group of 20 amateurs formed under the for-mer Yiddish actor Yosif Garfunkel and in March–April, 1962, gave eight performances of two plays by Sholem Aleikhem. Again, the audiences were very enthusiastic and the group chose another play about Baruch Spinoza, written by Haim Sloves, for its next production. It was trans-lated into Russian, and permission was granted. Rehearsals went on for several months when suddenly, in September, Garfunkel was called to the Central Committee of the Latvian Communist party and told that the drama group had to be abolished. "Jewish is not needed," an official said. "It is old, backward, you Jews must assimilate and not look back to Jewish culture."

Performances of the play were cancelled, but choir concerts continued. However, in March 1963, concerts which had been approved were cancelled. Latvian Communist officials said the choir, too, would have to be disbanded. Choir members petitioned the town authorities, the Latvian party Central Committee and the CPSU Central Committee in Moscow, but to no avail. In later years, letters were sent to Brezhnev and *Pravda* and a leading American Jewish Communist Paul Novick, editor of *Morgen freiheit*, who tried to intercede and have the decision changed, but without success. However, "the existence and abolition of the drama group and choir played an important role in the growth of national consciousness among Latvian Jews. The groups aroused new interest and love for Jewish culture and encouraged Jews to overcome the fear which Stalinism had implanted. . . . They also created a basis on which Jews could meet each other legally, after many years of keeping apart. . . ."[21]

Riga also was among the first cities in the early sixties to hold popular celebrations of Simchat Torah in the synagogue, and Riga Jews began to publicly wear the shield of David and other Israeli insignia. These reactions and memorial meetings in the Rumbuli woods in 1962–63, Riga's Babi Yar, were undoubtedly stimulated by the seizure of Adolf Eichmann in May 1960 in Buenos Aires by Israeli agents and his subsequent trial.

The news of Eichmann's capture and trial filtered into the Soviet press and revealed details of Nazi anti-Jewish atrocities that had been suppressed in the Soviet Union and new horrors as well. Lidia Zhdanova, a poetess in Riga, was inspired at the time to write a poem, "The Stars Gunned Down," lamenting the catastrophe that befell Jews, but it was subjected to severe criticism by officials and had to be published in samizdat form in 1964.

The response of Soviet authorities to the Eichmann Trial was an open-air antifascist meeting in October 1962 in the Bikernieki woods, near Riga. There, during the Nazi occupation, Russian prisoners of war and thousands of Jews were executed by a firing squad, but not a word of Jewish losses was mentioned at the meeting. It was at that point that Jews present decided to go to the Rumbuli forest where the Jews of Riga had been killed.[22] A primitive inscription was made on an old board, reading: "Here were silenced the voices of 38 thousand Jews of

Riga, on November 29–30, and on December 8–9, 1941." The board was nailed to a fir tree in the forest and twenty Jews assembled there in the winter of 1962 for the first open-air memorial meeting. This was done apparently in defiance of Soviet law which forbids the display of public signs by private persons without official authorization. The board hung there until 1964. At the same meeting, a wreath was placed on the grave of the great Jewish historian Simon Dubnow, who perished with the Jews of Riga at the age of eighty-one.

In the spring of 1963, the group observed the twentieth anniversary of the Warsaw Ghetto Uprising. A black wooden obelisk featuring a glass-covered photograph of Joseph Kuzkovsky's painting *On the Last Road*, was placed over the mass grave, which was being despoiled from time to time by Latvian grave robbers looking for gold and platinum teeth and crowns. Scattered bones, ashes, and the remains of children's shoes were gathered into bags. The obelisk remained for about a year and a half. The silence at Rumbuli had at last been broken.

Efforts were then made to erect a memorial. A modest stone slab, inscribed in Yiddish: "To the victims of Fascism, 1941," was proposed but rejected because there was no inscription in Russian and Latvian. A triply-inscribed slab was then made, with a hammer and sickle added. Jews gather at this site three times a year, on the anniversary of the Warsaw Ghetto Uprising, on the traditional Sunday between Rosh Hashanah and Yom Kippur, and on the anniversary of the Rumbuli massacres.[23] On these days, there is a Jewish guard of honor at the monument, changing every two hours, day and night. Many Jews from other cities join Riga Jews in these services. Once a year, non-Jews also gather to pay their respects to the memory of non-Jewish victims.

The Riga activists, meanwhile, produced some samizdat materials for internal use and for friends in Leningrad, Minsk, and Moscow, some of whom returned from prison in 1963. They were, however, plagued by a lack of funds and resource materials and by what they felt was the indifference of world Jewry and the seeming coolness of Israeli embassy officials whom they tried to contact for funds and materials. (For their part, the Israelis were apparently being extremely cautious and anxious about possible repercussions on Soviet Jews if there was conspicuous contact.) An occasional copy of *Ariel*, an Israeli cultural journal, could be had, or a Bible might be left in the synagogue, but "no sustained or meaningful effort was made to provide literature, so they could create samizdat, for which they were risking freedom."[24] The

Riga activists wanted Israeli officials to speak out on the right of Soviet Jews to obtain exit visas, but were told to be patient.

Feeling desperate and frustrated, they decided to do something to arouse outside protests. They prepared a collective petition signed by five people in Riga and four in Leningrad.[25] It was hoped that the Israeli embassy would carry out the message. Leah Slovin met the Israeli cultural attaché in Minsk in December 1964 and told him about the petition but he resisted any action: "You will be sent to prison. This will be a provocation and give the Soviet authorities the opportunity to make wholesale arrests and thus jeopardize all Soviet Jews."[26] The Israelis promised that quiet diplomacy was being explored that would result in emigration. But the petition was never sent, and no secret agreement was ever reached through quiet diplomacy so far as is known.

Meanwhile, the general cultural thaw dilated and contracted unpredictably, hardening and softening in spurts, often reflecting the domestic power struggle and events in Communist satellites. A new tough campaign against liberal thinking and writing began after the crushing of the Hungarian revolt in October 1956 and Khrushchev, not yet in full command, began to emphasize some of the positive achievements of Stalin. By early 1958 he had eliminated Malenkov, Kaganovich, Voroshilov and Molotov, but his efforts at domestic reform and the threat of implicating large cadres of officials in Stalin's crimes aroused great fear and hostility among old-line party members and Stalinist critics. Khrushchev himself admitted that the thaw might unleash a flood, which "we wouldn't be able to control and which could drown us,"[27] In 1957 he bluntly warned writers not to deviate from the general principles of socialist realism and to spread a positive image of communism. A refreeze, or cold rough spring with late frosts and cold winds set in. But the debates and clashing views did not stop. Nor did the publication of vigorous stories, novels, and poems, some underground.

Despite Khrushchev's warning, Ehrenburg, for example, published an article in 1957 called "The Lessons of Stendhal," in which *he* warned against any illusions that may be cultivated under the new leadership by quoting Stendhal:

What counts is not the personality of the tyrant but the essence of tyranny. A tyrant may be intelligent or stupid, good or evil—but whatever the case, he is both all-powerful and powerless, he is frightened by conspiracies, he is flattered, he is deceived. The prisons fill, the cowardly hypocrites whisper, and the silence becomes so complete that the heart almost stops.[28]

In partial explanation and confession of his own past silences and compromises, he again quoted Stendhal: "At fault is the society which demands hypocrisy, punishes for truth, and stifles large feelings on behalf of a multitude of conventions." Having kept silent at crucial times, Ehrenburg's plea to learn the greatest lesson in Stendhal—his "exceptional truthfulness"—may have been the final fruit of a turbulent odyssey in a totalitarian society or a kind of atonement in his old age. The same process also led him to acknowledge himself, after a long interval, as a *Jewish* writer, whose consciousness had been aroused not only by blood flowing in Jewish veins, but by the "river of blood" that had flowed out of them.

The late fifties and early sixties also witnessed the rise of a new generation of poets, including Evgeny Evtushenko, Yosif Brodsky, and Andrei Voznesensky, and excited poetry readings of their own work and long-condemned work by Akhmatova, Gumilev, Esenin and Tsvetayeva. For several years, thousands crowded Mayakovsky Square and the Luzhniki Sports Palace in Moscow in a near-religious reverence and passion for the work of the great poets of Russia and for the art of poetry itself. Organizers of these readings were attacked as "parasites" and arrested or exiled from time to time, but others took their place. Sons and daughters among the intelligentsia were in deep rebellion against their fathers and mothers in these readings. Evtushenko's call to freedom in his poem "The Promise" struck a responsive chord:

> Long live travel and scorching heat . . .
> I want to roam to my heart's content around London,
> To talk to everyone . . .

Small samizdat collections of the verse were assembled by Alexander Ginzburg, Vladimir Osipov, and Vladimir Bukovsky, all of whom were involved in the readings, but they soon came under police harassment and arrest and the readings were officially banned.[29]

Esenin's son Alexander Esenin-Volpin, who under Stalin had already been confined to a psychiatric hospital and then exiled to Karaganda in Siberia for reading a collection of poems to friends, was also part of this activist group. He was arrested several times and again sent to a mental hospital in the late fifties and released in February 1961. When several of his friends were arrested in February 1962 and charged with "anti-Soviet agitation"—i.e. readings in Mayakovsky Square—he decided to test the promise of the new Soviet leaders that trials would be open to the public and be in accordance with "socialist legality."

The trial of his friends was formally open to the public, but friends and relatives were not allowed in the courtroom. Undaunted, Volpin showed a copy of the criminal code to guards. They relented and allowed the public in. Another threshhold was breached as Bukovsky later was to write:

Little did we realize that this absurd incident, with the comical Alik Volpin brandishing his Criminal Code like a magic wand to melt the doors of the court, was the beginning of our civil-rights movement and the movement for human rights in the USSR.[30]

Toward the end of 1961, during the Twenty-Second Party Congress, Khrushchev again attacked Stalin and publicly described his crimes in greater detail. In the midst of the Congress, Stalin's body was removed from the mausoleum on Red Square and reburied in the Kremlin wall. Once more the liberal intelligentsia took heart, and most especially after Khrushchev authorized the publication of Alexander Solzhenitsyn's stark story, *One Day in the Life of Ivan Denisovich* to further unmask Stalinism—the system as well as the man. Solzhenitsyn's story was published in November 1962 in *Novy mir*, the first legally published exposé of life in a Stalinist concentration camp. Written in the form of a novel, this work touched numberless men and women in the Soviet Union, whose lives had been filled with personal memories of the dread camps, or reports of those who had perished there. A vast public silence had shrouded these degrading camps with their physical brutality, monstrous suffering, bureaucratic cruelty, and cynicism, even though every one in the Soviet Union talked privately about them, or lived in dread of the unspoken horror. Solzhenitsyn, himself a sufferer, broke open these horrors and seems, finally, to have created a work that restores some of the healing and humanity of traditional Russian literature.[31]

Hundreds of poems, stories, and reminiscences of the Stalinist camps began to pour into Soviet journals and publishing houses. But only for a brief time. Within a month Leonid Ilyichev, chief of the Central Commission's Ideological Commission, complained that writers were swamping the journals with manuscripts on the camp theme, that this was "impermissible," and threatened to "impoverish the life of the Soviet people, its history, its great achievements and splendid aspirations."[32] Other conservative and neo-Stalinist critics followed suit. Solzhenitsyn was found to lack the necessary Soviet "vision of historical truth" and "essence" central to socialist realism. The torrent was stopped and manuscripts were returned. Solzhenitsyn himself was curbed and all of his later works were officially suppressed.

It was during this second very short-lived thaw that Evtushenko's "Babi Yar" and Shostakovich's Thirteenth Symphony were also approved—both dealing with the mass executions of Jews at Babi Yar, the ravine outside Kiev on September 29–30, 1941 and later. These works, like Solzhenitsyn's, were at first hailed enthusiastically and then attacked and blocked. The rise and fall of Evtushenko's poem was of intense interest to Soviet Jews. Over the years the mass murder of Jews at the site and the refusal of the regime to memorialize this tragedy have symbolized the Holocaust in Soviet Russia and the erasure of this history by the regime.

The Babi Yar of history as well as the Babi Yar of the struggle for a memorial have had profound meaning for the Jewish national movement.

According to official German reports, 33,771 Jews were murdered at Babi Yar on September 29–30, 1941, in 36 hours. The massacres continued for several weeks and months. Estimates vary, but as many as 90,000 Jews may have been slaughtered, altogether a much larger number than Russians and Ukrainians—mostly partisans, prisoners of war, and Communists—who were also murdered here during the war. For Jews, Babi Yar was and has been the most piercing example of Jewish martyrdom on Soviet soil, but it has never received any official acknowledgment as such. Soon after the war ended, Jewish workers who had been evacuated from Kiev and Red Army men who returned to the city joined other Jews in a pilgrimage to the Babi Yar site. The official report on the massacres, published six months after Kiev's liberation, spoke of Nazi crimes at Babi Yar against Soviet citizens generally.

Soviet citizens learned something of what happened at Babi Yar from Ehrenburg's The Storm (1947), and from a poem by the Ukrainian Jewish writer Savva Golovanivsky. Plans were developed for a public monument at the site, but in March 1949, Golovanivsky's poem was attacked for "defamation of the Soviet nation," and plans for a memorial were shelved. Then, in the post-Stalin "thaw", another Soviet writer Viktor Nekrasov, after hearing that Babi Yar was to be flooded and filled in, wrote a letter to the journal *Literaturnaya gazeta*, protesting the desecration of the "site of such a colossal tragedy." Further appeals followed requesting the erection of a monument. In the fall of 1961, Evtushenko visited the site and wrote his famous poem, in which he indicts Russian anti-Semitism and reminds his readers that "No monument stands over Babi Yar." Thousands of students flocked to his readings, in which he had to read the poem over and over again, but the party grew anxious and balked. In one exchange, Khrushchev told Evtushenko that anti-Semitism "is not a problem," and that "this poem has no place here," to which the poet replied that it has: "It cannot be denied and it cannot be suppressed. . . . I myself was witness to such things. Moreover, it came from people who occupy official posts. . . . We cannot go forward to Communism with such a heavy load as Judophobia."[33]

The poet was also attacked in literary journals, his patriotism was questioned, and he was criticized for singling out Jews. At a conference of writers and artists in March 1963, Khrushchev gave a typical Soviet class analysis of anti-Semitism and provocatively brought up an instance of alleged treachery by a Jew named Moisei Kogan during World War II, in contrast with a loyal Jew General Jacob Kreiser. (The charge was later (1966) found to have had no foundation in fact.)[34] Characteristically, however, he denied the existence of anti-Semitism:

Who and what purpose needed the presentation which makes it seem that the population of Jewish nationality is restricted by somebody in our country? This is untrue. . . . No Jewish question exists here and those who invent it are singing a foreign tune.[35]

Evtushenko yielded to the pressures to the extent of changing the spirit of his poem by adding the lines "Here together with Russian and Ukrainians lie Jews," and "I am proud of the Russia which stood in the path of the bandits." As if to keep the immense gaping wound of Babi Yar open, a huge dam which had been built over the site collapsed. After the area was cleared and bodies dug up, Jews continued to meet there for memorial services, with special services on the twenty-fifth anniversary of the first executions, on September 29, 1966. The meeting was quite spontaneous; all publicity was suppressed. However, among the comments which have survived is a remarkable address by a Ukrainian literary critic and Ukrainian nationalist Ivan Dzyuba. He spoke of Babi Yar as "our common tragedy, a tragedy for both the

Jewish and the Ukrainian nation." He condemned the "open and flagrant attempts to use prejudice as a means of playing off Ukrainians
and Jews against each other . . . campaigns [which] wrought damage
on both nationalities . . . [and] only added one more sad memory to
the harsh history of both nations." He deplored and expressed shame
over anti-Semitism and urged greater mutual respect and understanding, partly blocked by a "conspiracy of silence" surrounding the nationalities question. Dzyuba called upon both Jews and Ukrainians to
take the road "to true and honest brotherhood": "The Jews," he said,
"have a right to be Jews and the Ukrainians have a right to be Ukrainians in the full and profound, not merely formal, sense of the word.
. . . Let them know each other's history and culture. . . ."[36] A plaque
subsequently appeared at the ravine, announcing that a monument
would be erected. This was done in 1976, but the inscription makes no
reference to the Jewish dead.

In the case of Evtushenko, the greater literary freedom which many
writers craved clashed with those opposed to exposing anti-Semitism
and the Jewish experience of the Holocaust, themes which some Russian intellectuals felt were an important touchstone of diminished party
control. Similar reactions were provoked by works of the great composer Shostakovich and a young Soviet writer Anatoly Kuznetsov.
Shostakovich composed his Thirteenth Symphony in the form of a musical and choral setting of five poems by Evtushenko, including "Babi
Yar." The symphony was premiered on December 18, 1962, the day
after Khrushchev had met with certain Soviet writers and intellectuals
to discuss art and literature. The symphony was given a tumultuous
reception, but no review appeared in the major papers or journals. The
day before, Shostakovich was criticized for choosing an undesirable
theme and thus failing to serve the true interests of the people. Public
performances thereafter temporarily ceased until certain revisions were
made.

That same year, beginning in August, Yunost, a literary monthly,
began a three-part serialization of a powerful documentary novel Babi
Yar by Kuznetsov, who had accompanied Evtushenko to the ravine
in 1961. Kuznetsov, a non-Jew who was born in Kiev, was only a child
of twelve when the mass executions began, but he had accumulated a
large file of material, including eyewitness accounts and the gruesome
experience of the one Jewish survivor, Dina Pronicheva. The two days'
slaughter of Jews, the complicity of some Ukrainians and Russians,

then the subsequent killing of many Jews, Russians, and Ukrainians— the whole ghastly record of 778 days of Nazi atrocities—is recorded. This work, too, became highly controversial,[37] with critics at first praising it as a "passionate and skillfully written work of art," and a work "vitally necessary both here and abroad," and then retreating. The early reviews were eventually attacked, as was the book itself, in 1967. When the book was published, substantial sections were censored out—specific references to Jews were kept to a minimum. Kiev's lack of preparation for the German attack and references to Ukrainian anti-Semitism were also left out. Kuznetsov himself defected and was granted asylum in England in 1969, where he found himself in new predicaments and the subject of further controversy because of a reviewer's challenge of the veracity of the new version, but the impact of his book has been powerful and lasting.

Discussion about Babi Yar disappeared from the public arena until the summer of 1966, when Jewish groups began to militantly demand some acknowledgment of the Jewish tragedy at Babi Yar. By then, both the human rights movement and Jewish national movement were strengthened and became openly demonstrative. By then, too, Western involvement in the cause of Soviet Jewry had grown and was publicly proclaimed (see Chapter 31).

Meanwhile, most Jews, removed from the intense intellectual analyses, studies, and probings of the groups of young Jews searching for individual spiritual fulfillment as Jews, were experiencing a continuing barrage of anti-Jewish and anti-Israel policies under Khrushchev and his successors.

28

The Sixties: Renewed Attacks on Jews and Judaism and a Few Concessions

T H E sixties marked a strengthening of the human rights and Jewish national movements, but also a targeting of Jews for alleged anti-social and anti-Soviet acts and toughening of anti-Jewish measures. One very threatening policy involved so-called "economic crimes." For several years, beginning May 1961, a massive campaign was waged in the Soviet Union against widespread corruption and various economic abuses. Jews were prominently cited, once again used to channel off resentment that would normally have been directed against the government. They were particularly vulnerable because of their role as middlemen in the Soviet structure of government trade activity and in the organization of supplies. The pivotal figure in this complex network is the *bukhgalter* (literally, a bookkeeper),[1] an expert on Soviet red tape and paper work, to whom managers of all shops, factories, and cooperatives turn in voluminous reports of inventory, prices, income, expenses, sales, and so on. In the Alice-in-Wonderland vagaries of Soviet economic life, the *bukhgalter* is often used in order to disguise infractions, stealing, and black market activity, which the manager himself may insist on, or be engaged in. He is generally a much disliked figure because he knows too much about the so-called parallel economy. Frequently, the bukhgalter is a Jew.

One reason why Soviet planning is less than successful is that a huge unofficial economy thrives in the country beyond the reach of official planners and watchers. It has been estimated that this unofficial economy may amount to 20 or more percent of the official one, consisting of private repairmen, private manufacturers, salespeople, underground traders of all sorts, and doctors who practice *nalevo*, "on the left," in the Russian phrase.[2] This is a vast network of bribetakers and givers— covering virtually the whole Soviet population. For example, gasoline is siphoned off government cars at pre-arranged garages to private owners at no charge; lumber or cement can be bought quietly from a government trucker of building supplies; a refrigerator inspector can be paid nalevo to make a repair on the spot—for a consideration; goods, parts, and foodstuffs are stolen from government stores on the principle that they are "nobody's property."[3]

The scope of this countereconomy is immense, with its own lore, channels, connections, and conventions, but in an economy of chronic shortages and carefully parceled out privileges, the practices that have been developed seem a necessary lubricant of daily life. The Soviet press is constantly attacking this illegal system, and *Krokodil,* the humor magazine, lampoons it. But the authorities, some of whom benefit from it themselves, cannot stem it.[4] The situation became very much aggravated in the 1950s and new laws and campaigns against "parasitism" appeared in 1956–57. In 1961, another set of laws against "economic crimes" was passed, for which the death penalty was added. Pilferage, bribery, currency speculation, and embezzlement of state funds were stressed. All the major newspapers and communications media, the party apparatus, the volunteer militia, and secret police were flung into massive campaigns against "economic crimes" from 1961 to 1964, and the courts were later brought into the crusade as mass trials, arrests, and death sentences ensued.[5]

In 1961 the press carried information on nine trials, in which eleven people were sentenced to death, five or six of them with Jewish names. During the next few years, over one hundred people were condemned to death, more than 40 percent of whom were Jews.[6] There were apparently many more trials throughout the country, involving only a small percentage of Jews, but " 'Jewish cases' were singled out—by editors or the authorities—for publication, either in order to make Jews the scapegoat for the 'sins' of society, or for the purpose of spreading anti-Jewish ideas."[7] The campaigns exploited anti-Semitic stereotypes of Jews and their love for money and resumed the practice of the 1948–52 period of printing the Jewish patronymic in parenthesis after a typically Russian name. The Jewish offender was also often associated with a synagogue, where the alleged offenses were plotted. In a Vilnius case, for example, eight persons were said to have engaged in foreign currency deals with the rabbi acting as "arbitrator" in their disputes. In Lvov, the local press called the case "Prayer and Speculation" and de-

scribed how "crooks and speculators of all types gather in the synagogue . . . and conclude all sorts of transactions."[8]

The campaign reached a very provocative level in October 1963, when
an *Izvestia* editor Paupanov said he was deliberately mentioning the
"Jewish family names of the accused [Roifman and Shakerman] because we pay no attention to the malicious slander . . . in the Western
press."[9] This was a reference to Bertrand Russell who had strongly
criticized the manner in which the Soviet economic crimes campaign
was being conducted. Russell had said that he was "deeply perturbed
at the death sentence passed on Jews in the Soviet Union and the official encouragement of anti-Semitism which apparently takes place. . . .
You of course know that I am a friend of your country. . . . I appeal
to you for an amnesty, proceeding from humane considerations and
our joint interests. . . ."[10]

Khrushchev wrote back, saying that Russell's criticism "derives from
a profound delusion," and that the clamor of the "Western bourgeois
press" was a "crude concoction, a vicious slander on the Soviet people,
on our country. . . . There never has been and there is not any policy
of anti-Semitism in the Soviet Union, since the very nature of our multinational socialist state precludes the possibility of such a policy."[11]

Lord Russell was not satisfied and wrote again, this time a two-page
letter stressing the disproportionate number of Jews accused, and once
more, in April 1963, deploring the death penalty for economic crimes
and making a broad appeal urging the "granting of full rights for Jews
as a national group."[12]

In January 1964, nine persons, six of them Jews, were sentenced to
death, including two who were said to be "ringleaders." The *New York
Times* (February 27, 1964) reported that "plans for the show trial were
shelved, presumably because of the involvement of bribe-taking Soviet
officials." Furthermore, Western newsmen and visitors were barred from
the courtroom "because the bribe-takers were to be identified during
testimony."

A careful investigation in 1964 by the highly respected International
Commission of Jurists showed that anti-Semitism was indeed closely
linked with the economic crimes campaign, and that the number of
Jews accused was "greatly disproportionate."[13] In the Ukraine, where
Jews constituted only 2 percent of the population, the percentage exe-
cuted was 80 percent. Particularly disturbing, the commission con-

cluded, was "an insidious and sometimes subtle propaganda campaign" against Jews that dominated the press campaign.

The intensity of the campaign against economic crimes reached a pitch in 1963. In that year an official from the Soviet Ukraine told the United Nations that "there are no instances of racial prejudice or of national and religious intolerance either *de jure* or *de facto*" within its territory— a bitterly ironic comment in the light of the publication that same year of Trofim Kichko's *Judaism Without Embellishment* by the Ukrainian Academy of Sciences, which appeared in the midst of a fierce campaign against the Jewish religion. Kichko had already published a Ukrainian-language textbook called *The Jewish Religion, its Origins and Character* (1957), which charged that "Judaism has always served, by the nature of its creed, the plundering policy of capitalism. . . . [It] has pitched the Jews against other nations . . . Zionist leaders were collaborators with Hitler in his crimes against the world." In another work published in 1962, Kichko had told his readers that Judaism is "permeated by a hatred toward work and scorn of the working man . . . its religious teachings are filled . . . with a narrow practicality . . . how to make profit, love of money, and the spirit of egotism." [14] *Judaism Without Embellishment* was more of the same, "illustrated" with caricatures resembling the coarse and brutal drawings of the Nazi period, and building on the old "Protocols of the Elders of Zion" fabrication, linking Judaism with Zionism, Israel, Jewish bankers, and Western capitalists in a crudely concocted worldwide conspiracy (see Photos 28.1 and 28.2). The book purports to prove the hostile attitude of Judaism toward the "revolutionary transformation of society," the anti-scientific nature of Judaism's dogmas and laws, and the immoral behavior of Judaism's spiritual leaders. Kichko points to the close relationship between "reactionary" Zionism and Judaism and the alleged support of Judaism for the "exploiting" classes.

So vulgar and repellent were the language and illustrations in the book, that waves of protest came from many parts of the world, especially from Communist parties in the West. In some ways, the "most significant reaction to the Kichko book was that of the French [Communist] party (PCF), because of its outstanding record of loyalty to the Soviet regime." [15] *L'Humanité* published protests by the Yiddish Communist daily *Naye prese*, and on May 5, 1964, Secretary-General Maurice Thorez wrote a critical letter to the party weekly *France Nouvelle*. Thorez also intervened personally, according to one source, and after

28.1 "During the years of the Nazi occupation, Zionist leaders served the Fascists." From Trofim K. Kichko's book, *Judaism Without Embellishment*, 1963. Courtesy Center for Research and Documentation of East European Jewry, Hebrew University.

his death, his successor likewise urged the leadership of the Soviet Communist party to put an end to anti-Semitism and to examine the problem of the rights of the Jews, as a community.[16] Neither man ever received a reply from Soviet leaders.

The reaction of the Italian Communist party (PCI) was even more direct. An editorial in *L'Unità* of April 1, 1964, denounced Kichko's book as "an antisemitic libel," and anti-Semitism as a "brake" on the growth of socialist society.[17] In London, the party secretary declared that the book's illustrations "shocked all those . . . who have consistently campaigned against antisemitism." The Dutch party deplored

28.2 "I recommend it as an excellent weapon! It was checked and tested at Auschwitz and the Warsaw Ghetto!" A Soviet cartoon published in *Izvestia*, November 12, 1964, after a West German-Israeli agreement. Drawing by V. Fomichev. Courtesy Center for Research and Documentation of East European Jewry, Hebrew University.

the reality that "the ideological activity of the Soviet Communist Party is lacking in a systematic struggle against antisemitism."[18]

Soviet officials were somewhat embarrassed,[19] but at first observed through the Novosti Press agency that Kichko was merely engaged in antireligious propaganda; neither he nor the book was charged with anti-Semitism. Later, on April 14, 1964, the Ideological Commission of the Central Committee of the Communist Party partially repudiated the book as possibly insulting the feelings of believers, conceding that it "might even be interpreted in the spirit of anti-Semitism," but also noting that it "merely serves as one tool in the nation's continued campaign against all religions."[20]

The first somewhat muffled Soviet criticism of the book appeared in March in a Ukrainian-language organ[21] published by the Ukrainian Ministry of Culture, excerpts of which were given worldwide circulation by Tass. "The chief shortcoming," according to this review "lies in the question of the survival of Judaism in our times [which] is not elaborated on." Unnecessary quotations from the Bible and Talmud are overemphasized, "rather than demonstrating the unsoundness of religion by the facts of contemporary life." The critic also allows that not "all strata of the Jewish population" were "enveloped" by Zionism. However, the book "merits on the whole a positive evaluation as a thorough examination of the reactionary nature of the Judaic religion." There is no reference at all to the offensive drawings, the falsity of the accusations, or the unvarnished anti-Jewish bigotry. Government spokesmen said apologetically that the book was never sold outside the Ukraine, and then, under continued criticism, withdrew it.

One leading Soviet journal *Literaturnaya gazeta* described Kichko as a "scoundrel"—there was evidence, apparently, that he had collaborated with the Nazis in the Ukraine. He was expelled from the party, but was not punished. Instead, he became a holder of the Order of Lenin and in January 1968 he was awarded the highly prized "Certificate of Honor" by the Supreme Soviet of the Ukraine. In the same year, the "Znamya Society" of the Ukrainian SSR published another of his viciously anti-Jewish books, *Judaism and Zionism*. This book was extensively serialized and printed in 60,000 copies; an opening statement admits that the work "is intended for a wide circle of readers."[22] Published after the Six-Day War, the book not only attacks Zionism but Judaism and world Jewry. Judaism as a whole is likened to Nazism, teaching contempt and hatred for other peoples, even to the point of destruction. Jews are described as people filled with ideas for ruling the whole world, as a result of their "God-chosenness". This work, with its vehement anti-Zionist content, inspired a deluge of articles, editorials, and letters in the Soviet press portraying Zionism as antisocialist, anti-Soviet, and imperialist, in which Soviet Jews are urged (and warned) not to go to Israel.

These works and others published in the Ukraine, officially dissociated from the central party, have been quietly encouraged and may indicate the appeasement of strongly nationalistic Ukrainian elements at the expense of tolerating anti-Semitism.[23] The unwillingness of central authorities to forthrightly expose and condemn anti-Jewish writing was clearly demonstrated in the Ideological Commission's *recommendation* of a book called *Catechism Without Embellishment*, also published in 1963 by a colleague of Kichko, A. Osipov. This work, which the Commission called "a useful publication," refers to God as "the principal bloodsucker where Jews are concerned. . . . The first thing we come across is the preaching of 'intolerance,' the bloody extermination of peoples of other faiths."[24]

This tract and others, it was said, would foster atheism among Jews. However, they were written not in Russian or Yiddish, but in Ukrainian and Moldavian, regarded by only a tiny percentage of Jews as their native language. Thus, it seems these materials were directed at the general populations of the two republics "and can only stimulate or reinforce strong traditional currents of anti-Semitism" there.[25]

Institutionally, Judaism remained and remains as it had been—condemned, vilified, scarcely surviving. Without a center, it has no official standing; rabbis have no official contact with the government or outside religious bodies and cannot attend religious congresses or meetings of other Jews. It cannot issue publications or devotional literature or articles such as *talisim* (prayer shawls) or *tefilin* (phylacteries). Study abroad of seminarians is permitted to other religious groups, as detailed in a Soviet report to the UN in 1963, but not to Jews.[26]

Soviet authorities exercise complete control over the synagogues and other religious institutions through laws, decrees, arbitrary decisions, and control of the religious and lay leadership. When it is expedient, rabbis are pressured to publicly denounce religion before a synagogue is closed, to affirm the rightness and justice of Soviet policy, and to attack the West, Zionism, and Israel.[27] Executive boards can be dissolved and accommodating replacements appointed. All synagogues in the Soviet Union are of equal rank, no matter what the size. None has the status of a "central synagogue," although the Moscow Synagogue on Arkhipov Street is frequently described as the Central Synagogue, and its rabbi is often referred to as the Chief Rabbi. In Moscow, besides the Central Synagogue, there are two small synagogues in Marina Roshcha and in Malakhovka, just outside the city, and one each in Leningrad, Riga, Odessa, and Kiev (see Photo 28.3). Each congregation

28.3 Leningrad Jews at prayer in the Choral Synagogue on Rosh Hashanah, the Jewish New Year. Courtesy of Dr. Abraham I. Katsh.

is completely separate from the other. There are no regular meetings of the rabbis or lay leaders.

Although there is no evidence that the persecution of the Black Years brought about a large-scale closing of synagogues, many Jews were undoubtedly too frightened to attend and their synagogues deteriorated or were taken over by the government. Many were also destroyed during the war. There was also a very severe crackdown on synagogues and churches, beginning in 1959, and many were closed, but Soviet authorities camouflaged what was happening by dressing up the statistics. In 1959, the Soviet Union informed the United Nations that the number of synagogues in the Soviet Union was 450,[28] then a short time later, *The Soviet Union Today*, published by the Soviet Embassy in Vienna, stated that "Jewish religious services are being held in 150 synagogues." In 1965, ninety-seven were reported. All of these figures, however, are considered very inflated. One reasonable estimate is that by 1966, there remained only sixty-two operating syn-

agogues, thirty of which were in the Caucasian and Central Asian Soviet Republics, which have only 10 percent of the Jewish population.[29]
Another estimate, as of 1968, was only twenty-six.[30]

Jews themselves have been frequently coerced by officials—a common Soviet practise—into "instigating" an antireligious action. For example, in the August 5, 1960 issue of *Sovetskaya Moldavia*, a statement
appeared which had been sent to the newspaper by seven Jews: "We
consider that the time has come to tell all Jewish believers that the
synagogue brings nothing to people but harm. We do not want to cheat
workers and ourselves any longer, and have consequently come to the
conclusion that the existence of the synagogue serves no purpose."[31]

The relentless drum beat of antireligious propaganda and the defamation of Judaism make attendance a harsh test of religious commitment. The future of the synagogue is thus uncertain. Once a synagogue is closed, it is not reopened—certainly not in recent years—and
the technique used in closing a synagogue is impossible to challenge.
In the 1960s, this technique was used frequently. For example, in Lvov,
a typical campaign was mobilized, which the community was powerless to stop. About 30 or 40,000 Jews had gravitated to Lvov, which
had been a great Jewish center, after the war. A *dvadtsatka* (the twenty
members needed to constitute a legally acceptable congregation) was
organized and Jews were permitted to open one small synagogue in a
square behind the Opera House. Suddenly in 1962, a series of articles
appeared in a local paper, describing synagogue ritual and activities in
a sarcastic and contemptuous way: "Does anyone really believe that
people only busy themselves with prayer when they go there? Of course
not. What do they really do? They deal in the black market. Foreign
exchange is bought and sold; gold roubles are changed into dollars."
Then the congregation was charged with drunkenness, because of a
rite involving drinking wine. Later articles accused American tourists
of visiting to tell the congregation "fairy tales" about the "Israeli paradise." These were followed by accounts of how terrible life in Israel
really is, how the country is nothing but an armed camp and base for
imperialism. The Jews of the Lvov synagogue waited apprehensively
for the next blows. Letters to the editor soon appeared, written by Jews,
"impelled" to write because of the scandals being exposed. They demand that this site of iniquity be closed. What can officials do but close
it down?[32]

The Lvov Synagogue was closed on November 5, 1962, following a show trial which involved two members of the *dvadtsatka*. A similar process was followed in Kharkov, Chernovtsy, Bobruisk, Smolensk, and other towns.

There is also persecution of the "gathering for purposes of prayer" of ten or more Jews (a *minyan*) in rooms and apartments in towns and cities where there are no synagogues. This is especially true during the High Holidays and after the death of a family member when *yiskor* (a traditional prayer said at memorial services for the dead) is said. Such a small gathering is illegal and fraught with great danger, housing conditions being what they are in the Soviet Union, with several families sharing the same apartment and informers lurking about.

In 1959, the Great Synagogue of Chernovtsy (Czernowitz) in the Ukraine was closed on the charge that it was being used for "nonreligious and illegal purposes" and housed "hooliganism and alcoholism." In 1964, in Minsk, in the middle of a prayer service, workmen began removing the roof of the synagogue. There was a sharp reaction in Western circles, and the community was permitted to purchase a former private home.[33] This, however, could accommodate only one hundred persons whereas the Minsk Synagogue had seated thousands.

The early sixties were also marked by ritual murder charges in Tashkent and the city of Margelan in the Uzbek republic, and in Buinaksk in the Daghestan Autonomous Republic, with the not yet exorcised accusation that Jews had allegedly murdered children for ritual purposes. Jews were assaulted and their homes looted, with police standing by or participating. The perpetrators remained immune from prosecution.

In the late fifties and early sixties, Jews were also prevented from securing *matzos*, or unleavened bread for Passover. Baking matzos requires the use of state bakeries by the synagogues or permission to make them in the home or receive packages. For several years, the bans were applied to cities off the tourist path such as Lutsk, Stalino, Rostov, and Saratov, but in 1959, they were applied to Kharkov, and in 1960, to Lvov, Chernovsty, and Kiev. In 1961, the ban spread to all areas of the Soviet Union, with the exception of Moscow, Leningrad, Central Asia, and the Caucasus. In 1962, virtually the entire country, with the exception of certain Oriental Jewish communities, was included in the ban.[34] Just before Passover in that year, Rabbi Levin of the Moscow Synagogue announced that Moscow's state baking facilities had broken down, and that, despite promises of repairs, he finally had to ask his congregation to eat peas as a substitute. In 1963 officials said that it was "unconstitutional and illegal for state bakeries to bake matzos and for state stores to sell them, because matzos are a religious article," despite a 1956 official statement registered with the UN to the contrary.[35] Baking matzos at home became dangerous, but some Jews did it and are known to have been arrested and sent to prison. At the same time, a campaign against receiving matzo parcels from abroad was started, with the press railing against the senders with insults such as "Take your rags back," and "Eat your matzos yourself, gentlemen, and leave us alone."[36]

Apparently eager to defend these actions and counter foreign criticism, Soviet officials said that a similar policy existed regarding the baking of *kulichi*, or Easter cakes used in communion. Slowly, however, the restrictions were eased. On February 25, 1965, the *New York Times* reported that the Moscow synagogue could bake matzos in rented facilities on the outskirts of the city. In 1966, the bans were lifted in some capitals of the Soviet republics and in Oriental Jewish communities. Rabbi Levin, in an "unprecedented telephone interview with the *Jewish Chronicle* in London," reported that "all Moscow Jews who will bring their own flour will be able to bake matzos in the special bakeries in the synagogues."

In 1969, Rabbi Levin also denied that there was any matzo shortage and told an American journalist that "our matzos are tastier than yours." The occasion was a conference of representatives of various religious groups in the USSR of July 1–4, 1969, called to discuss "Cooperation and Peace Among Nations" at the St. Sergius Monastery of the Trinity in Zagorsk. Many religious communities, including the Armenian Church, the Georgian Orthodox Church, the Russian Orthodox Church, various Evangelical Lutheran churches, Muslims, and Buddhists participated in the preparatory planning, but Jewish religious leaders had not. Many of the reports and messages denounced "aggressive acts by the USA and Israel," and among the conference documents was one which urged religious leaders of the world to increase "cooperation between believers and all the forces of peace in support of the people of the Arab countries and to step up this support."[37]

Religious books were and remain not only inadequately supplied but those that are available are very old, often disintegrating, and outmoded. The last Haggadahs for Passover were published in 1928; the

Makhzor (prayerbook for the High Holidays), in 1926; the last calendar was printed privately from movable type in 1930.[38] No Bibles or editions of the Talmud were ever published in the Soviet Union nor were they permitted to be imported until 1987. When an American Jew contacted Radio Moscow and asked when the last Torah was published in the Soviet Union, he received a very strange reply: "The Torah is written by hand, we do not publish it."[39]

During the twenties a few Hebrew prayer books, calendars, and three rabbinic books were published. A rabbinic journal called *Yagdil Torah* was banned in 1928 after two issues had appeared. A reprint of an old prayer book appeared in 1956, called *The Peace Prayer Book*,[40] but there was nothing new which might reveal the inner life of observant Jews until 1965. With Khrushchev's sudden ouster in October 1964, the militant antireligious campaign came to an end, as did the linkage between the synagogue and the campaign against economic "crimes."[41] In 1965, Soviet rabbis were permitted to publish, not in the Soviet Union, but in Israel, a collection of rabbinical *Responsa* and studies on homiletics called *Shomrei ha-Gahelet* (Guardians of the Glowing Coals) by several rabbis still living in the Soviet Union, including Rabbis Shlieffer and Levin, several who had emigrated to Israel, and a few from Communist countries in the Eastern bloc.[42]

In 1970, there appeared a book (also published in Israel) made up of sermons delivered by the Deputy Chief Rabbi of Moscow, Zalman Nathan Kiselgof, during the years 1960–1969.[43] The sermons were delivered in Yiddish but were written down in Hebrew, following a rabbinic tradition. They reflect the suffering, fears, and hopes of a withering synagogue-going culture, at least of the Jews in Moscow. Rabbi Kiselgof, who died in 1972, was not considered an erudite rabbi, but his words of encouragement, advice, and warnings unveil the silent and shadowed life he knew. Not the unleavened bread—the matzo—is redemption, he says, "but the bitter herb is the true redemption"; and, although it is easy for saints to be saintly in an age of saintliness, "to be a saint in a place where there is a lot of immorality, no worshipping of God, and [where] those who worship are mocked at like monkeys, this act of worship is a deed of martyrdom."[44]

Harsh words are addressed by Rabbi Kiselgof to informers, the curse of Soviet life and the greatest danger facing Soviet Jews, in the rabbi's view. In the presence of such Jews, inside and outside of the synagogue, the rabbi dares to say: "And now there is the plague of such people who base their living on the troubles of their friends." These people "desecrate God's image"; they are compared to a "hidden pit" into which a man falls. Because of "evil tongues" large numbers of Jews have been exiled to forced labor camps. The rabbi urges his listeners "to have the informers branded on their foreheads with the sign of Cain, so that future generations should know how we despise these blasphemers and desecrators of the Jewish people." His counsel to those who cannot carry out the commandments publicly is to "become united in life for each other and then the crisis will pass." His comfort is for Jews to contemplate "the soil of Israel, the soil of the prophets and the holy Talmudic sages."

During the heaviest assault on religion in the years 1959–64, tourists and Israeli diplomats were attacked for trying to distribute prayer books and prayer shawls and in the spring of 1960, packages containing religious items were returned to senders. The Jewish calendar was attacked as being "hostile to the Soviet people" for not mentioning the October Revolution or May Day. Anyone caught distributing such a calendar was charged with spreading anti-Soviet propaganda.

The number of Western visitors to the Soviet Union increased considerably during the 1960s, providing us with vignettes of Soviet Jewish life and an occasional deeper look. There was still extreme wariness, verging on fear, about meeting visiting Jews, coupled with curiosity, when it was expressed, about life in the United States and Israel. Fear and anxiety still gripped congregants:

A strong emotion overtakes you when you enter a synagogue in Russia—a sad, mysterious stillness descends upon you. One communicates with another with the help of a prayer or just a sigh. The prayer links the person not only with God and his fellow Jews, but also with Jews the world over. . . . Young people also attend the synagogue. They stand still. They cannot read the prayers, but in this place they become united, as it were, with other Jews. . . . Where else can they do this?

The atmosphere overwhelmed me, too. . . . When I saw the timid, helpless Jews, their anxiety took hold of me. . . .[45]

This anxiety was and is not exaggerated. Informers and agents—some recognizable, others not—abound, and congregants are painfully aware of them. Some have been seen to strike Jews for asking for a prayer shawl and *siddur* (prayer book). Any internal strife is seized upon to undermine the foundation of the synagogue and is sometimes the first stage of a process of closing the synagogue. There is no synagogue autonomy or religious community affiliated with the synagogue in the Western sense. The rabbi is not the spokesman for the congregants unless he is required by the authorities to make certain statements for foreign consumption.

The twenty members who sign the lease agreement of the synagogue premises are individually responsible for the property and conduct of affairs in the synagogue. An executive body administers the synagogue and must answer for any "anti-Soviet acts and anti-Soviet propaganda"—arbitrarily interpreted and difficult to predict.[46] Speaking to a foreigner, or passing a gift of a prayer book among the congregation may be an anti-Soviet act. In the larger synagogues, the rabbi, cantor, and sexton are paid employees; smaller ones have to search for part-time functionaries, and as the official line is to make war on belief and expose it as superstition, there are few candidates.

The decline in the number of synagogues and the advancing age of the few rabbis left has raised profound questions about the future of the synagogue in the Soviet Union, which has served not only as a place of worship but as the only place where Jews can gather. In 1965, the "Appeal to Conscience" was formed by Rabbi Arthur Schneier of New York largely in response to this problem. Its first fact-finding mission to the Soviet Union took place the following year, after which the government was urged to soften its stand and allow students to study for the rabbinate. In an unprecedented decision by the Council on Religious Cults, permission was given to two young men in 1979 to come to the Yeshiva University Theological Seminary in New York City for a three-year "crash course" in rabbinical studies. They returned to the Soviet Union each summer.[47]

The Oriental communities of Bukharan Jews in Central Asia, the Mountain Jews, and Georgian Jews in the Caucasus were still somewhat immune from the antireligious campaign in European Russia and have enjoyed greater freedom to practice religious rituals and observances without harm, although such freedom has been repressed from time to time. The Jews of these areas use vernaculars of their own, including the Judaeo-Persian spoken by the Jews of Bukhara, the Tati of Daghestan, the Turkish-Tataric dialect spoken by the Krimchak Jews, and the Georgian patois spoken by the Jews of Georgia.[48] Soviet scholars have apparently been somewhat interested in the linguistic varia-

tions and past history of these groups, but much less so in their contemporary life.[49] Many of the Jews who have remained in these distant
regions have a very ancient history, including descent from Jewish exiles who left Palestine after the destruction of the First and Second
Temples, and have been deeply influenced by the cultures of the non-
European peoples among whom they have lived. Despite changes introduced by the Soviet regime and contact with Ashkenazi Jewish refugees during the war, many old customs and values remain: large
patriarchal families, festive Jewish weddings, synagogue attendance,
rituals such as circumcision and the bar mitzvah, and celebration of
Jewish holidays, especially Passover and a high emotional fervor over
the promised redemption in Israel. Many Georgian Jews formed the
first wave of emigration in the late sixties (see Chapter 30).

A perceptive visitor who visited Tbilisi and Kutaisi in Georgia, Baku
in the Caucasus, and Tashkent, Bukhara, and Samarkand in Ukbeki-
stan in the late fifties[50] found substantial preservation of family and
religious traditions, but increasing tension between Jews and Uzbeks,
which he attributed to the influx of Russians and Ukrainians. Non-Jews
regarded Jews "as competitors for positions of power and influence,
particularly in the areas of commerce and culture."[51] In Georgian towns,
relations were much friendlier.

Religious traditions and the study of Hebrew wherever it exists are
passed from generation to generation. Some Jews are known to listen
to Hebrew broadcasts from Israel on short-wave radio, and adherents
of the Habad Hasidic movement continue their work with small groups
of children studying Hebrew and the Bible with commentaries. It is
said, "they wander from community to community," reminding Jews
of old traditions and not letting them forget.[52]

Politically, Khrushchev, the engineer of the harsh antireligious crackdown in Soviet Russia, was not destined for a long tenure. His attempts to combine "peaceful existence" with the United States, Soviet
control over Poland and Hungary, Communist world leadership in a
contest with China, and a hard line on Berlin created erratic policies.
He was forced to back down during the 1962 Cuban missile crisis. At
home, he lost the support of the military by reducing forces and was
unable to solve agricultural and industrial stagnation. For Jews, as for
others, there was a more relaxed climate in the country under Khrushchev. Many prisoners and exiles were allowed to return. But, funda-

mentally, he shared Stalinist attitudes toward Jews, Jewish culture, Israel, Zionism, and Judaism. Under him, the value of Jews as "bearers of Communist ideas," in providing valuable intellectual and economic roles, and in supplying leadership positions in the satellite countries was disappearing.[53] Russians, Ukrainians, Belorussians, and other national groups were filling up these old positions. Under so much attrition, the regime believed that the Jews would soon disappear. Meanwhile, they could still be used to draw the fire of anti-Semitic and anti-Israel invective to please the Arab world and give vent to Soviet frustrations over not having any control over the Arab-Israel conflict. Stalin's old formulation that Jews serve "foreign nations" found echoes in Khrushchev's hints that Soviet Jews were not loyal. He made very occasional concessions in the field of religion, mostly to appease Western opinion, calculating that there was less to fear from Jewish religious traditions than from Jewish secular culture. However, one potentially important exception was made when permission was given to launch a Yiddish journal, *Sovetish heymland* in 1961 (see pp. 632–37 this chapter). This was a very tiny crack in the heavy armor-plated refusal to revive Jewish culture, and it may not prove to be of any substantive value in Jewish cultural survival, but the question remains open. The magazine cannot be discounted, and even if the regime decided to create it as a concession to Western complaints and pressures, as seems likely, the consequences may be more significant than the regime calculated. Moreover, the decision may also reflect some uncertainty, some vacillation, in policy-making circles as to precisely what to do about the intractable "Jewish question" in the Soviet Union.

In answer to numerous inquiries and requests for a resumption of Jewish cultural institutions, Soviet authorities have steadfastly maintained that Jews had become fully assimilated, and that there was no need for reviving a "dead culture" (an expression used by Politburo member Mikhail A. Suslov in 1956, in a conversation with a delegation from the Canadian Communist party.) One person who frequently found himself in an awkward position because of these questions was the Soviet writer Boris Polevoy. In a secret memorandum[54] written in 1957, which came to light much later, Polevoy complained about the barrage of "letters and questions" on "the so-called 'Jewish question' in the Soviet Union," which he found increasingly difficult to answer, and which only played into the hands of "anti-Soviet publicists." There were also foreign Communists such as the French poet Louis Aragon and the American writer Howard Fast, who found it difficult to understand why Soviet officials were so adamant and rigid. "Wouldn't it be wiser," asked Polevoy, "to establish a Yiddish paper, a Jewish almanac, or a library of works by Jewish writers," and thus put an end to such obnoxious queries?

To quiet these insistent questions and appease foreign critics, *Sovetish heymland* was launched in August 1961, the first Yiddish periodical to appear since 1948. It came out as a bi-monthly of over one hundred pages until 1965, after which it appeared as a monthly. The first issue, however, did not admit that the journal was of special interest to Jews, but said that the "immediate goals" of the journal were to "reflect most of the important problems of our time"—the problems of "socialist reconstruction," and the problems of "the multi-language Soviet literature." The many dilemmas and paradoxes of having such a journal, however, have created unforeseen difficulties for the editors, and its basic concept has changed.

The editor was and is Aron Vergelis, the only surviving member of the old *Heymland*, who was selected to advance the theory that Soviet Jews are assimilating quickly into "Soviet national culture," but who may be helping to counter such assimilation by the mere existence of his journal. Vergelis was educated in Soviet Yiddish schools and for a time lived in Birobidzhan where he graduated from the Yiddish high school. In 1947, he was appointed director of Yiddish programs for Radio Moscow, succeeding Peretz Markish, and served the regime by attacking expressions of Jewish national feeling and ideas about the unity of the Jewish people. There have been frequent charges that he was implicated in the accusations against the murdered Yiddish writers, but they cannot be verified. "However, there is much evidence of the ignoble role he played in covering up the crime with denials of 'rumors' about the imprisonment and execution of the writers. When Jewish Communist leaders in the West expressed concern over the fate of the Yiddish writers who suddenly disappeared in 1948–49 . . . they were assured by Vergelis that there was no foundation to reports that the writers had been arrested. He repeated the official statement that they had all gone to the Crimea to continue their work. This cover-story, often attributed to Vergelis, was still circulating . . . in the West in late 1954."[55]

Some Jews felt heartened by the appearance of a Yiddish journal after so many years, but many saw the politically annointed Vergelis as an ominous sign. Outside the Soviet Union among Jewish writers and Yiddish readers he is regarded as a renegade Jew who serves Soviet and Communist party interests against the interests of Soviet Jews. His former comrades who emigrated to Israel speak of him with great scorn, and during his travels abroad, he is treated with suspicion and hostility, or, most often, ostracized entirely. He has zealously covered up Soviet crimes against Jewish culture and his abusive tirades against Zionism are in the current Soviet vituperative style.[56]

The first issue of *Sovetish heymland* featured an excerpt from the program of the Soviet Communist party and asserted that it would be a voice in the Soviet Union's "multinational literature." The first poems and pieces were contributed by thirty writers, most of whom had survived long years of suffering and persecution in labor camps. There was scarcely a hint of their tragic past, or that of the writers who perished. The first issue also listed 110 "creative" Yiddish writers who would be among future contributors, but most of these were not professional writers or critics, but engineers, teachers, farmers, etc. for whom writing was an avocation. The second issue published the names of more than forty Yiddish writers who fell during World War II, together with a bibliography of their works. In subsequent issues, the works generally conform to party dogma, but occasionally, "in Aesopean language, novels and poems lay bare deep and unhealed wounds left by Stalin's terror. . . . The finest prose writing deals with Jewish life in pre-revolutionary Russia."[57] Outstanding is Elie Shekhtman's *Erev* (On the Eve), dealing with a Jewish family in the years before the revolution of 1905.[58]

Special prominence is also given to writers from Birobidzhan of the 1930s. There have been many reminiscences of World War II and memoirs dealing with the pre-World War I Jewish cultural and literary life in Russia and Poland. There are also many recollections and emotional tributes to the murdered Yiddish writers and some of their work, but no acknowledgment of the circumstances of their death. They are described as victims of the "cult of personality." The editors have consistently refused to publish the novels of Solzhenitsyn, the poetry of Evtushenko, or Ehrenburg's memoirs.[59] There is a pronounced nostalgic tone in many of the issues and the absence of any analysis of the present condition of Soviet Jewry, but the journal has not stood still. Some of the recent material represents a great change from the first issues (see chapter 33).

Over a hundred Yiddish writers have contributed their work to the magazine—poetry, reminiscences, stories, sketches, reportage—many of whom have suffered in Soviet labor camps. One critic has said that

Much of the work . . . is competent . . . , and from time to time of surprising high literary value. Some of the writing displays talent, mastery of form, a genuine expression of Jewish life, and an authentic appreciation of Jewish values. Writers now describe Jewish life of the pre-Revolutionary period with more sympathy and understanding than their colleagues of the thirties. . . .[60]

Since 1969, moreover, Biblical phrases and idioms used in Yiddish literary works and criticism have appeared and are discussed in correspondence. Aron Raskin and Layzer Podriadtchik (until the former's application to go to Israel and the latter's emigration) have commented on Hebrew books published in Israel and some poetry that has been translated from Hebrew into Yiddish. There have been articles on Georgian Jews and on the translations of Hebrew poetry into Georgian by the phenomenally gifted Isaac Davitashvili.

Although it carries staple Soviet vehemence against Zionism and Israel, *Sovetish heymland* is primarily a literary journal, somewhat similar to the Russian *Novy mir*. Paradoxically, it sometimes conveys the sense of the existence of a pulsating, full-bodied Jewish culture in the Soviet Union while authorities keep speaking of the complete assimilation of Soviet Jews and absence of any need for revitalizing Yiddish. In August 1961, when the magazine was started, the editors told an American scholar that they had no intention of stimulating interest in Yiddish literature, but only of "satisfy[ing] the lingering needs of that small percentage of Jews that still spoke Yiddish." Vergelis chimed in with official policy, yet as editor of *Sovetish heymland*, he "counteracts, rather than encourages the process of assimilation."[61] Jewish themes and content have increased over the past years, and since 1969, every issue (except for 1972) has carried Yiddish lessons in Russian—for the benefit of Jewish youth, it is said.

This is a curious observation, since so many Soviet Jewish youths are assimilated into Russian culture, and since those who are interested in Jewish culture are known to favor Hebrew. Yet, apparently, some Jewish youths in the smaller towns, according to the reviewer of Shmuel Gordon's series on contemporary shtetlach, "show an increasing interest in Yiddish culture, Yiddish literature. This applies both to those who read and understand Yiddish and to those who do not . . . but who satisfy their demand in an extraordinary fashion: the small group of the knowledgeable ones must either read or translate for the much larger group of the unknowledgeable ones. . . ."[62] These pieces of Gordon's published in 1966, are nostalgic journeys through Russian shtetlach, of contemporary reality as well as memory. One of his travel pieces begins with a poignant rollcall of little towns as they appear on a bus schedule: "Pogrebishtshe, Tetiev, Polone, Bratslav, Ostropole, Lubar, Shpole. . . ." Some, of course, have declined or changed beyond recognition. But to others, some Jewish Holocaust survivors returned, even to their own houses. Now they are mostly old pensioners, but some still work in local factories or stores or on the railroads. In Derazhna, Gordon met an eighty-five-year-old man, Alexander Zevin, who learned bookbinding so that he could keep the last remaining Yiddish books from falling apart. Gordon also describes traditional weddings with klezmorim (musicians) and badkhonim (jesters) entertaining the guests, and the more common memorial services, often over the mass graves of Jews murdered by Nazis, which "attract pilgrims from every part of the Soviet Union."[63] In Medzibosh, he was taken to the grave sites of the practical jokester Hershel Ostropoler and the great Hasidic rebbe Baal Shem Tov, where pilgrims left candles and little notes.

Obviously, *some* young Jews feel drawn to this rendering of Jewish experience, and if they can obtain copies of *Sovetish heymland* and find older Jews to help them with Yiddish, they will be able to read Gordon's stories with pleasure, but these convergences are probably not too frequent. Most Jews, after all, live in the large urban centers of the Soviet Union. There is also the matter of availability of the journal. One cannot find accurate figures on circulation. Some observers say that out of the 25,000 copies issued, most are sent overseas for foreign consumption—and a better image of Soviet policy on Jewish culture. Others claim 17,000 to 18,000 copies are sold in the USSR and the rest abroad.[64] However, copies of those sold inside the country are undoubtedly made.

Before the large exodus of Jews in 1971–74 to Israel from the western border areas—Lithuania, Latvia, the Ukraine, White Russia, and Bessarabia—*Sovetish heymland* was read there eagerly, and the few copies passed from hand to hand. Many more copies are undoubtedly needed, for the evidence shows that Yiddish is still very much alive, if with a diminished flame. In the 1970 census more than 17 percent of Soviet

Jews (381,078) declared that Yiddish was their mother tongue and 166,566 declared Yiddish to be their second language—another 9 percent.[65] Thus at least over a half million Jews (26.4 percent) knew Yiddish well. In the 1979 census, 257,000, or 14.2 percent, declared Yiddish as their first language, and 135,000, or 7.5 percent, their second.

Sovetish heymland has been the butt of considerable criticism in the West and the source of occasional ferocious debate, while Vergelis himself has been embroiled in political as well as literary controversies inside and outside the pages of the journal. He has consistently denied the existence of anti-Semitism in the Soviet Union, but has attacked virulent anti-Zionists who use old inflammatory anti-Jewish canards. Occasionally, moreover, there are murmurings of discontent among the Yiddish writers. For example, in the December 1964 issue, there was an unusual discussion in the editorial offices of *Sovetish heymland*[66] involving several critics and the literary historian Professor Hillel Alexander, who had survived the notorious Kolyma camp regime in Siberia. Most of the participants asked for a revision of the negative attitude toward Yiddish literature outside the Soviet Union and toward non-Communist Hebrew literature.[67] The essays of the noted critics Aron Raskin, Oyzer Holdes, and Hersh Remenik that appeared following this discussion challenged Vergelis and the dogmatism of Soviet Yiddish literature.[68] They urged acceptance of Hebrew, and Holdes wrote emotionally of the importance of using the Russian language as well as Yiddish as a vehicle for Jewish themes.

Before the Six-Day War, Vergelis apparently made efforts to contact Jewish writers and journalists in the West, and it was revealed that a special issue of *Sovetish heymland* was contemplated, devoted to Hebrew literature. But the effort was stopped after the war when the government embarked on its rabid anti-Zionist campaign in which *Sovetish heymland* was a zealous participant.

Bertrand Russell dealt harshly with Vergelis' credibility in an exchange of letters in 1964, when Russell raised the whole question of discrimination against Jews in the Soviet Union. Vergelis published only his reply, saying that "the real needs of Soviet Jews are fully satisfied." Russell wrote back that his reply was "lacking in scruple," that concern for Soviet Jews had been expressed by Communist parties in many countries of the West over anti-Semitic literature and degradation of Jewish culture. Vergelis has enraged even left-wing Jews for referring to himself as a "Soviet writer of Jewish descent."[69]

Yet is this the "real" Vergelis? Some of his poems and reactions reveal a strong nostalgic tug when the past Jewish life in the shtetlach is described or evoked. In 1965, he visited Auschwitz and met survivors of the death camps and wrote with great feeling about his experience.[70] There was also a curious statement he made to a correspondent of the Israeli paper *Maariv* in 1966: "It was not in vain that the Jewish people underwent thousands of years of dispersion, and suffered terribly from the banishment from Spain until the establishment of the State of Israel. The heritage should be kept as most sacred."[71] Vergelis is also known to have tried to reverse the decision to close down the Yiddish theater and choir of Riga.[72] Moreover, he has tried to broaden the scope of his activities by cooperating with painters, sculptors, and composers. He has also established links with several amateur Jewish theaters, the Moscow Dramatic Ensemble, and with individual Jewish performers (see Chapter 30). The offices of the journal house a permanent exhibition of works by Jewish painters and sculptors, including some young Jews who are part of an artistic, dissident underground, and reproductions of some of this work appear in the magazine. Since there is no center of any kind for Jews in the Soviet Union, *Sovetish heymland* provides a mini forum and place for contacts with individuals interested in Yiddish and, therefore, Jewish culture. Yiddish writers who contribute to the journal visit towns with Jewish communities through subscription campaigns and other activities.

Vergelis himself perhaps embodies the ambiguities and contradictions of other Soviet Jews as well as the journal, and, indeed, expresses the unresolved conflicts and dilemmas inherent in the Soviet Jewish condition. If he is a tool of the regime, he has widened the wedge originally given him. Besides, if the regime cynically permits the gradual widening as a sop to foreign opinion, the effects domestically cannot be dismissed. *Some* Jews in the Soviet Union are reading Yiddish.

World Jewish opinion, however, scarcely gave any thought to Yiddish or *Sovetish heymland* in the middle and late sixties. Nor did the regime. Instead, there were fresh, new forces which it had to confront: a slowly growing involvement of Western individuals and organizations in the cause of Soviet Jewry and a strengthening of the human rights and Jewish national movements, epitomized in the Sinyavsky-Daniel Trial in 1966. A Soviet counterculture was emerging.

29

The West, Dissidents, and the "Jews of Silence" Protest Soviet Repression, 1960–68

"You keep talking about the Constitution and the laws," the doctors would explain to Bukovsky, "but what normal man takes Soviet laws seriously? You are living in an unreal world of your own invention, you react inadequately to the world around you." To which Bukovsky remarked, "We were born to make Kafka live."

WESTERN concern over the problems facing many Soviet Jews has profoundly affected the Jewish activist struggle and, at least in terms of emigration, Soviet policy toward Jews. However, the momentum to put the predicament of Soviet Jewry on the agenda of Western Jewry and international circles, was very slow in building.[1] Dr. Nahum Goldmann, the late president of the World Zionist Organization and the World Jewish Congress, had been especially concerned about Soviet Jewry and was perhaps the one Jewish leader who kept the issue alive for the longest time. In 1957 he said that the hoped for liberalization had not followed de-Stalinization, and that "the time has come when the Jewish people . . . must raise the question of Russian Jewry. . . . We must change our tactics." His call met with mixed reactions. "Deep anxiety," the demand for minority rights, and the right to emigrate to Israel were put into a Zionist Council resolution, but there was no appeal for a mobilizing action on an international scale. Individuals made contact with Soviet diplomats in the middle and late fifties, but nothing of importance was accomplished. Khrushchev refused to meet with American Jews during his visits to the United States in 1958 and 1959, but in 1959 the presidents of seventeen major Jewish organizations drew up a statement asking the Soviet government to grant full cultural and religious rights to Soviet Jews, permission to emigrate, and permission to resume contact with Jews outside the Soviet Union. Fourteen American labor leaders and liberals, including Walter Reuther and Senator Paul Douglas, issued a five-point statement making certain demands, but nothing came of that either.[2]

On the initiative of Dr. Goldmann, fifty political and intellectual leaders from fourteen countries, including Martin Buber, Arthur Miller, and Pierre Mendes-France, who were considered "friends of the Soviet Union," "or, at least hostile to the Cold War," were convened in Paris on September 15, 1960, to participate in the Conference on the Problem of Soviet Jewry. Only half attended, and some observers were critical of the soft tone that was set. But a small step forward was made in escalating the importance of the Soviet Jewry issue. A resolution was passed urging the Soviet Union to grant Jews full cultural and national rights, thereby improving Soviet prestige and strengthening the cause of peaceful coexistence. The resolution also reminded Soviet officials that anti-Semitism was a flagrant departure from Marxist-Leninist doctrine. Before adjourning, the Conference resolved to convene again to establish a permanent committee.

In the late fifties, Moshe Decter, a vigorous advocate of public action on behalf of Soviet Jewry, conceived the idea for a Conference on the Status of Soviet Jews. He had earlier written long, comprehensive essays on the subject for *The New Leader* and for *Foreign Affairs*.[3] The Jewish Labor Committee and the Orthodox Jewish community had also been concerned with the crisis facing Soviet Jewry—though from very different perspectives—before the major establishment organizations began a coordinated effort. The Conference was held in October 1963 and expressed general, not specifically Jewish support. Among the distinguished sponsors were Dr. Martin Luther King, Jr., Senator Herbert H. Lehman, Bishop James A. Pike, Norman Thomas, Supreme Court Justice William O. Douglas, United Automobile Workers President Walter Reuther, and the poet Robert Penn Warren. The Conference issued an "Appeal to Conscience," addressing seven specific grievances to the Soviet government, but there was no ongoing action.[4]

Meanwhile, grass-roots activity was mounting. In the same month as the Conference, the Cleveland Committee on Soviet Anti-Semitism was founded, "the precursor of the most militant anti-establishment group, the Union of Councils for Soviet Jews," a movement which maintained pressure on the major organizations and developed the "tools, techniques, and tactics to educate and motivate the Jewish public."[5] Trofim Kichko's *Judaism Without Embellishment*, published in 1963, (see Chapter 28) also provided a rallying flashpoint. Foreign expressions of protest and outrage filled newspapers. The major American Jewish organizations then decided to establish a new, roof organization to "marshal resources for public action and education."[6] A program was developed leading to the convening of the American Jewish Conference on Soviet Jewry on April 5–6, 1964, representing twenty-four Jewish organizations. A more militant approach was taken by the Student Struggle for Soviet Jewry, which was formed after a May Day demonstration a few weeks later at the Soviet Mission to the United Nations—the first group to take to the streets in support of Soviet Jewry. Jacob Birnbaum and Glenn Richter began working full time without salaries, organizing weekly, sometimes daily events, and providing a steady flow of press releases to the media and information to other groups.[7] Later the Union of Councils for Soviet Jews and other groups worked independently of mainstream Jewish organizations and prodded them to make the issue of Soviet Jewry a major item on the American Jewish agenda.

In 1965, a mammoth rally at Madison Square Garden in New York was addressed by Senators Jacob K. Javits and Robert F. Kennedy, who called on the Soviet government to grant Jews the rights guaranteed them by the Soviet Constitution.[8] The American government then officially joined in the appeal. Both houses of Congress passed a resolution containing the same principle. About the same time, the editor of the Jesuit weekly *America* visited the Soviet Union and on his return urged Catholics to pray for the survival of Soviet Jewry. Labor leaders, clergymen, and other public figures expressed their concern.

The Soviet government seems to have reacted to these criticisms: the ban on *matzos*, which had been in effect since 1958 through deliberate obstruction of requests and official delaying tactics, was lifted and the campaign against "economic crimes," in which Jews figured conspicuously as victims, came to an end. In 1963, a Hebrew-Russian dictionary was published in Moscow, the first in two generations (see this Chapter, p. 646). Interestingly, the introduction by Professor B. M. Grande stressed the historical continuity between the biblical language and the living Hebrew of modern Israel. A few more Yiddish books were published[9] and some Jews were allowed to emigrate.[10] In 1965, Rabbi

Israel Miller of New York led a delegation of American Orthodox rabbis to the Soviet Union, and in an unprecedented event, spoke in Yiddish from the pulpit of the Moscow Synagogue. In August 1966, twenty-two rabbis of the Central Conference of American Rabbis visited the Soviet Union and found the usual difficulties of communicating with the "invisible millions" and circumventing watchers and informers. The group was especially stirred by the excited wonder of the congregation of old worshippers in the Moscow Synagogue when one of the teenage visitors, Rabbi George Lieberman's son David, was called for an *aliyah*, to recite the Torah blessing. The congregation was noisy until the young boy was noticed. A hush fell over the synagogue and many old men came forward and crowded around the pulpit. Women hung over the balcony, trying to get a glimpse of the youngster with a red velvet *kipah* (skullcap). This was the first time in forty years that a young boy had participated in a synagogue service in Moscow. David later said:

As I turned around, the men started to close in on me; most of them were crying, and for a while I thought I'd be crushed. I noticed the tears in their eyes as they pressed forward. They just wanted to touch me and kiss my hand. After the service the women came down, and many kissed me. It was very moving, but also quite upsetting and depressing.[11]

The growing contacts and organizational interest opened a new channel of information, but it was soon observed that Western visitors "were frequently used as innocent messengers to bear tidings of Soviet promises for future improvement in the religious or cultural conditions" of Soviet Jews.[12] The Ministry of Cults promised that by the end of July 1966 there would be 5,000 new prayer books, and another 5,000 a month later. But when Rabbi Yehuda Leib Levin of the Moscow Synagogue spoke to the group, he said the plates were ready but that permission for paper had not yet been received. Later it was explained that paper could not be spared since it would be needed for the fiftieth anniversary of the Bolshevik Revolution. Then Rabbi Levin learned that some of the old plates had been damaged. In June 1968, when he came to the United States, he stated that 10,000 prayer books had been printed from the old and reconstructed 1956 plates, but this figure has never been confirmed and seems highly exaggerated (Moscow and Odessa had copies of the book, at very high prices, but Leningrad and other cities did not).[13]

When the journalist S. L. Shneiderman visited Moscow in 1969,[14] he found some worshipers in the synagogue with copies of prayer books from the United States or Israel, but none of the new official printing, called the *Peace Prayer Book*. He spoke to the sexton about the absence of books and was shown "a large closet crammed with the books," priced at ten roubles, or about ten dollars, very costly for a Soviet citizen. The book contains all the prayers for the entire year and the full text of the Passover Haggadah, even including the ancient hope: "Next year in Jerusalem!" Also included was a religious calendar covering the years 1966 to 1971, and the imprint bearing the year 1965.

A remarkable feature of the new version is the Hebrew alphabet in a table with equivalent sounds in Russian, and an explanation of the accents of spoken Hebrew. There are two special prayers for the government composed by the book's editor, Rabbi Levin, including a prayer for peace that begins with a description of the Soviet government as the "Protector of peace in the whole world."[15] According to Shneiderman, most sales of the book are made to foreign tourists because the price is beyond the means of the average congregant. The officially listed publisher of the prayer book and of an annual calendar bearing a picture of Rabbi Levin is the Moscow Jewish Religious Community (*Moskovskaya Yevreskaya Religioznaia Obschina*). The publication of the book has been described as "a landmark in Jewish religious life in the Soviet Union as well as a personal triumph" for Rabbi Levin, but also reveals the "special kind of discrimination" against Judaism within the antireligious campaign generally.[16]

For a number of years prior to his visit, Rabbi Levin had been invited by the Synagogue Council of America and other mainstream rabbinical bodies in the United States. He failed to respond to them, and came finally under the auspices of the American Council for Judaism and Neturei Karta, two of the most extreme anti-Zionist groups in existence. It might well be asked why he came under "soiled sponsorship" and consistently refused to meet with the major American Jewish organizations that asked to meet with him.[17] The answer lies in a Soviet pattern of response that was evolving to meet the charges of anti-Semitism and suppression of Jewish life: the Rabbi, answering for the government, not himself, said that such accusations were part of the Cold War. When asked why so many synagogues had been closed, he answered that "Jews prefer to worship in private." His figures were also doctored to suit Soviet purposes, in saying there were 110 synagogues (the best figure for that time was sixty-five, maximum) and eighty-five functioning rabbis, whereas fewer than ten were known to be functioning at the time.[18]

Some Jews in America were heartened by Rabbi Levin's visit and believed it signified a turnabout in Soviet policy, but more sophisticated people understood that his visit was staged, guided, and aimed at stilling questions and curtailing protests.

Western visitors to the Soviet Union during this time found many Jewish youths vaguely groping for some meaning in their Jewishness. They attended readings and skits and musical programs in Yiddish without understanding the language. At the high holidays some went to the synagogue and watched their fathers and grandfathers pray without understanding what the prayers meant. Jewish calendars, an El Al traveling bag, a *mezuzah* (a device mounted on a doorpost containing passages from Deuteronomy) or Jewish star drew an unwonted, often highly emotional response. More and more, small groups of young people followed visitors, plying them with questions about America and Jewish life there. Many were strong in their attachment to the Soviet Union and communism but also seemed to be struggling to find some other dimension in their life. For a few, the search led them to want to learn Hebrew.

At the Lenin Library in Moscow, the Hebrew daily of the Communist party in Israel, *Kol Ha-Am* (Voice of the People) could be read in the world press reading room. Copies virtually crumbled in one's hands from so much use. Visitors occasionally found young Soviet Jews reading *Kol Ha-Am* with a dictionary.[19] In the reading room for Oriental literature, there are many books in Hebrew, but because a careful check is made of all users, potential borrowers are deterred. One student who borrowed a book called *Hebrew-Russian Conversation* was surprised when the librarian took a copy right out of her desk drawer. She explained that the book was very much in demand so that it wasn't worth the effort to shelve it. A number of pensioners had been borrowing the book and some were teaching young Jews.[20]

A young Jewish father from a provincial town who had taught himself some elementary Hebrew tried a novel way of getting Hebrew texts for his daughter. He had no addresses in Israel and wrote to School

Principal of School Number 1(A), Tel Aviv. In a primitive but understandable Hebrew he asked for "books, some stories, books poetry, history Hebrew people."[21]

Other Jews, however, were becoming less inhibited about their feelings of Jewishness and were openly expressing and professing their identity. Expecting to find "the Jews of Silence," Elie Wiesel, in his visit in 1966,[22] found several thousand young Jews inside and outside the Moscow Synagogue, happy, dazed, and excited by the joyous atmosphere of Simchat Torah and being together with other Jews. Two gigantic floodlights had been installed and everyone entering the synagogue was photographed. Nevertheless, they came and danced and sang and marched in several processions to honor the Torah. Old men lifted their grandchildren on their shoulders, and the children looked on in wonder. The Israeli guests and Wiesel were touched and blessed; fragments of prayers, names of relatives in Israel, and endless murmurings of thanks were whispered by some, but spoken more forthrightly by many.

Outside the synagogue, thousands more filled the street and courtyards singing and dancing with fearless energy. "They were borne along on a crest that seemed incapable of breaking," Wiesel wrote, "[and] their faces reflected a special radiance. . . ."[23] Some had come without telling their wives or children; many admitted suffering because they were Jews; few of the youths knew Yiddish or Hebrew. "We are Jews for spite," one student said, reflecting the feeling of those who were reacting primarily to anti-Semitism, and turning shame into pride.

The Israeli presence in the Soviet Union, until the diplomatic rupture following the Six-Day War, also meant occasional events that thrilled Soviet Jews. For example, in 1965, when a visiting Israeli women's basketball team touring the Soviet Union visited Riga, the activists stood in line all night to secure tickets. They proudly sang "Hatikvah" as well as the Soviet national anthem; hundreds of Jews mobbed the bus on which the team was traveling.[24] In 1966, the popular Israeli singer Geulah gave a concert in Riga. Three thousand Jews greeted her with stormy applause, flowers, Israeli songs, and a feverish mass appeal to go to Israel. Soviet police frustrated the crowd and caused a near-riot. There were arrests and trials, a compilation of details of events, and frustrated efforts to have these documents published abroad. Many of the activists "speculate[d] that the documents were taken to Israeli officials who were at the time following a policy of silence about Soviet

Jewry."[25] Immediately after the incident, the Central Committee of the Latvian Communist party met and ordered a news blackout. Foreign correspondents who learned of the affair and tried to reach Riga were denied travel permits.[26]

In Kiev, the atmosphere was quite hostile toward Jews, but one young Jew, a locksmith named Iosip Chornobilsky, dared to talk to a woman from Detroit who attended Yom Kippur services in the synagogue in September 1964. Their encounter had important consequences later. Chornobilsky told her that he regretted not being able to teach himself or his children Yiddish and Hebrew, because of government restrictions, and then asked her if she would carry to the West a statement he had written, which was later translated and printed in the Detroit *Jewish News*. The statement expressed Jewish pride in Israel's restored existence and noted that virtually every country in the world permitted Jews to emigrate there, except the Soviet Union: "Where is your humanity?" he asked. No government practising democracy and socialism has a right "to forbid people of the Jewish nation to emigrate. . . . [It is] "because you hate us with a wild, anti-Semitic hatred . . . [that you] torture and shoot . . . hundreds of thousands of our brothers . . . [and forbid us] to erect one modest memorial . . . at Babi Yar and other places . . . and crush the rights of Jews in their education and work."[27]

Later, in February 1966, Chornobilsky tried to collect signatures petitioning for the re-establishment of a Jewish national theater in Kiev. The Ukrainian Communist party rejected the petition on the grounds that there were no premises or experienced Jewish actors available. Chornobilsky and a group of other Kiev Jews refuted this argument and were arrested. Although the precise charge is unknown, he was evidently accused of "slandering" the Soviet Union. He had been under surveillance for a long time; the KGB had copies of the article in the Detroit *Jewish News* and letters he wrote to a sister in Israel. He had also met with tourists and accepted books about Israel. A Ukrainian paper said that he had "fallen into the web of Zionist propaganda" and had been "pushed into the ravine of treason."[28]

In Moscow, one of the earliest groups clustered around the figure of a woman whose name became legendary in the 1960s and 1970s—Rachel Margolina Ratner.[29] Born in Vilna before the Revolution, Mrs. Ratner was the daughter of the editor of the Hebrew daily *Ha-Z'man*. Bialik, Sholem Aleikhem, Bergelson, and Kulbak were often in their home and the general atmosphere contributed to a lasting impress of the Jewish national idea on Rachel. She went to Moscow to study philology and history and taught history in Soviet high schools for many years. The spreading anti-Semitism during and after the war and the establishment of the State of Israel re-ignited latent national feelings and Rachel's apartment became a center for Jewish youths at this early time. She herself decided to apply to emigrate to Israel during the time of the "doctors' plot," and after six stormy years was allowed to leave in 1963.

It was her persistent struggle for the right to leave and then, after 1963, her letters, telephone calls, and packages from Israel that had deep meaning for the early Jewish activists in the Soviet Union and created strong bonds. One young Jew at the time who was deeply influenced by her was Michael Zand,[30] who had first met Mrs. Ratner in 1958 at the dacha of Professor Felix Shapiro, a distinguished philologist. It was she who established "a live connection with Israel for us," Zand reminisced, receiving souvenirs and packages, and setting an example of full Jewish commitment. She worked for many years on the Hebrew-Russian dictionary that Shapiro compiled and edited, and both she and Shapiro led small classes in Hebrew. After many requests, Shapiro finally received permission to compile such a dictionary and after eight years of collaborative work, it was published in 1963, two years after Shapiro's death. A very large printing was planned, but was restricted to 25,000 copies. (In recent years, activists and others who had copies or photostats of the dictionary have had them confiscated.)

This 700-page dictionary, hand-written and xeroxed copies, and copies of excerpts were to provide basic nourishment for those eager to learn Hebrew and became the main resource for many hundreds of young Jews. Some were also heartened, if they heard of it, by the glowing report of the revival of Hebrew in Israel by the non-Jewish Professor Vasily Struve at the 1964 International Congress of Oriental Studies in Moscow.[31] The work of several Jewish professors in the field, including Isaak Vinnikov, who taught at Leningrad University, was acknowledged by their non-Jewish colleagues[32]—another strange example of Soviet mystification, namely praise for work in an illicit language.

In Leningrad, in the early sixties, some young Jews were also heartened by older Zionists, such as Gedalia Pechersky, who, as chairman of the Central Synagogue, tried to expand Jewish religious rights and teach Hebrew.[33] Pechersky had been arrested in 1961 on "spying" charges but was released in 1968, when the charges were proved false. Natan Tsirulnikov was another group leader, who was arrested and convicted for receiving Hebrew textbooks from abroad. A young Jew from Leningrad, Hillel Butman, began studying Hebrew on his own in 1960 and soon began teaching it to others. In 1965, together with Grigory Vertlib, Zev Mogilever, and Solomon Dreizner, Butman formed the nucleus of one of the first emigration movements.[34] They made tapes of Jewish music and reproduced Hebrew grammars and works in Jewish history. In their discussions with Aron Shpilberg of Riga, the question of involvement in so-called "democratic activities" came up. This was the period of the Daniel-Sinyavsky arrests (see pp. 648–52 this chapter) and the deep interest of some Jews in the need for general internal reforms. Shpilberg, however, insisted that Jewish groups concentrate on Jewish educational programs and emigration, and ask for nothing that was opposed to, or outside, the framework of Soviet ideology, constitution, and law, or that smacked of Cold War polemics.[35] Such a position, which has to this day characterized certain activist elements in the Soviet Union and all the supportive movements in the West and in Israel, was to ask for nothing more than was already granted to other national and religious groups, together with a plea for the reunification of broken Jewish families.

Meanwhile, in the larger Soviet political and cultural spheres, during the early 1960s the intermittent liberalizing spurts were sputtering to a stop. The Cuban missile crisis and Sino-Soviet disputes in 1962 were foreign policy failures for Khrushchev, and their impact was reinforced by serious economic problems at home. Sharp price increases for consumer goods caused outbreaks of violence in several parts of the country. Any more revelations about the Stalin era would have been dangerous and certain to infuriate the growing number of Khrushchev's hard-line enemies. Besides, there were increasing pressures from Stalinist party men and literary commissars who wanted more "ideological purity." Besides the attacks on Evtushenko and Shostakovich, there were declarations of war against modernist art and Western influences on Soviet culture. In March 1963, Leonid Ilyichev, Chairman of the Ideological Commission of the Central Committee, led the attack on many writers, especially Ehrenburg. (In his memoirs, published in the Soviet Union in 1960–61, Ehrenburg had argued that he and many others had known of the terror under Stalin, but were compelled to remain silent, living with "clenched teeth." Ilyichev, in turn, accused

Ehrenburg of having openly and frequently praised Stalin hypocritically, thus enjoying special privileges and protection under Stalin, while he himself and others had flattered him out of conviction.)

Khrushchev then delivered a devastating speech which partially rehabilitated Stalin's tastes in art and literature, and to a degree rehabilitated Stalin himself.[36] Further de-Stalinization would have led to embarrassing questions, such as, "What were you doing during Stalin's criminal actions?" One of the main accomplices in these actions had been Khrushchev himself. In a defensive reflex, he put the threatening cultural ferment under a sudden freeze.

Writing for the "desk drawer," or painting for "the closet" continued as before. Literary works in increasing number passed from hand to hand in manuscript copies. In the phrase of one historian, "an organized Soviet counter-culture began to emerge," and *samizdat* as well as *tamizdat* (materials published abroad and smuggled into the Soviet Union) began to circulate.[37] Thus an unofficial literature, not subject to Soviet censors, spread underground.

In the stifling cultural "real world," two young writers, Andrei Sinyavsky and Yuli Daniel, sought to evade party controls by sending their work abroad under pseudonyms, beginning in 1956. They escaped detection until 1965. Their trial in the following year and subsequent harsh sentences shocked the Soviet intellectual community and brought to the surface a genuine movement of dissent, involving a number of Jews. A small but influential protest movement within the Soviet Union against the verdicts and sentences contributed to the birth of the human rights movement in the Soviet Union, which included a number of Jews, and did much to fortify the still fragile Jewish national movement.

Andrei Sinyavsky[38] was a forty-year-old Russian scholar and critic at the time, a professor at the University of Moscow and a contributor of reviews and critical studies to the literary journal *Novy mir*. Until his arrest in September 1965, he had gained a modest reputation in Moscow literary and academic circles, and just three months before his arrest, the censors had passed on the publication of a selection of Pasternak's poetry, with a long and illuminating introduction by Sinyavsky. A member of the Komsomol and the son of a loyal Communist, Sinyavsky had been jolted by the arbitrary arrest of his father in 1951 on a trumped-up charge. His father was released in 1953 but died soon afterward. Khushchev's speech at the Twentieth Congress demolished any residual belief Sinyavsky may have had in the post-Leninist Soviet system. In the corrosive disillusionment that other liberal intellectuals felt, he turned for spiritual support to Pasternak, who persisted in refusing to surrender to official blandishments, threats, and inquisitions. He read Pasternak's drafts of *Doctor Zhivago* (which was published in Italy), and his religious poetry and often visited the poet at his home in the writer's colony at Peredelkino. Inspired by Pasternak's example, Sinyavsky asked Hélène Pelletier Zamoyska, the daughter of a French diplomat he had met, to arrange for the appearance of his own work abroad. He chose the pen name "Abram Tertz," the hero of an underworld ballad in the tradition of the Jewish freebooters of Odessa, immortalized in the early stories of Isaac Babel. These were a special order of men among whom there existed a special code of honor and loyalty, in contrast with the rest of society.

The first "Abram Tertz" manuscripts were printed in France; translations followed, and through the early sixties readers in the West speculated about the identity of a writer who was "humorous, terrifying, phantasmorgic, satiric, devout."[39] The Soviet press fostered the view that Tertz must be a "White emigré bandit of the pen," but he was very much inside the Soviet Union, writing in the precarious secrecy of his Moscow apartment about the hollowness of "realism," shattering the familiar surface of everyday life to convey the "otherwise unimaginable quality of life" in Soviet Russia, the leaden oppressiveness of the Stalin years and the mental disorders rife in a population ruled for decades by fear and mutual distrust.[40]

Although some of his writing is beyond social criticism and deals with the fundamental self-divisions in man and the frailty of consciousness and beliefs, his work as well as Daniel's, also evokes the tragic predicament of Soviet Jews, the inability of even the most assimilated to forget they are Jews because of official and "spontaneous" anti-Semitism. In Sinyavsky's *The Makepeace Experiment*, the irremovable core pain of the Jew, no matter how assimilated, is described:

I once had a Jewess in my life—I won't forget her to my dying day . . . She spoke Russian like a Russian—you couldn't tell the difference—and the only Jewish word she knew was *tsores*, which in their language means sorrow or trouble, or a kind of prickly sadness littering the heart. There was a grain of this *tsores* buried in her like a raisin you could never dig out—immured in her as it were, mixed into the very composition of her soul.[41]

There are also two living Soviet writers among the protagonists in the novel, "both unreconstructed Stalinists" depicted exchanging anti-Semitic remarks.

Sinyavsky's friend Yuli Daniel, who used the pseudonym Nikolai Arzhak, is the son of Meyerivich, a Yiddish writer and veteran of the civil war, who died in 1940, probably in prison. Yuli fought in World War II, was wounded and discharged, and also became a writer. Outwardly assimilated, he wrote in Russian rather than Yiddish, but was far more alienated from his society than his father, and deeply aware of his Jewishness through the experience of anti-Semitism during and after the war. He was also inspired by Pasternak's courage and independence and together with Sinyavsky served as a pallbearer at Pasternak's funeral. His manuscripts were smuggled out of the country in the same way as Sinyavsky's.

Both were arrested in September 1965 and held in virtual solitary confinement, "seeing no one but their interrogators, stool pigeons put in the same cells with them, and material witnesses occasionally brought in for a 'confrontation.' "[42] Neither repented nor yielded. Details of their arrest were published in a major samizdat monthly journal called *Political Diary*,[43] started in 1964 by Roy Medvedev, historian and political dissident. Moreover, the activists Esenin-Volpin and Bukovsky, who had been released from a mental hospital early in 1965, organized a demonstration of about 200 people in Pushkin Square on December 5, Soviet Constitution Day.[44] A few carried signs that read "Respect the Constitution." The demonstration and numerous letters of protest at first caught officials off guard, but on January 13, *Izvestiya* attacked both writers and on February 10, they were brought to trial.

Rumors of the arrests began to reach the West quite soon; inquiries were made of Soviet officials, but were met with silence. The first official word came in the *Izvestiya* article, depicting the men as double-faced agents of anti-Soviet propaganda, having "hatred for our system, vile mockery of everything dear to our Motherland and people," amounting to an accusation of "sacrilege," which is punishable under the Criminal Code.[45] Another article appeared in the same month in the *Literaturnaya gazeta* by a literary critic, Zoya Kedrina, who also appeared as witness for the prosecution at the trial. Mrs. Kedrina accused Sinyavsky of a "revolting duplicity," whose writing has "a persistent odor of anti-Semitism" because anti-Semitic thoughts and actions are attributed to certain of his characters and because he uses the pseudonym Abram Tertz.[46] The attack was clearly aimed to "alienate the sympathies of Soviet writers who know Sinyavsky as a critic of distinction but have no access to his published works published abroad under his pseudonym."[47]

As was customary in such cases, the accused were convicted in the press. Technically, they were charged under Article 70 of the Soviet Criminal Code with disseminating "slanderous" and "defamatory" inventions about the Soviet system. What was unusual was that instead of pleading guilty, both defendants defended themselves boldly and eloquently. But sentencing was inevitable and harsh: Sinyavsky to seven, and Daniel to five years of hard labor.

This trial was unprecedented in several other ways: the contents of literature formed a substantial part of the proceeding, and the reactions that followed defined the first strong public protest movement in Soviet society.[48] The distinguished translator and critic Max Hayward believed that the Sinyavsky-Daniel case had "shaken Soviet society more profoundly than anything since the revelations about Stalin at the Twentieth Party Congress in 1956."[49] Sinyavsky's wife and several friends put together their notes—no one was allowed to attend all of the sessions of the court—and the transcript was smuggled out to the West and published in English as *On Trial*.[50]

The liberal intelligentsia inside the Soviet Union reacted with a great show of solidarity in support of the accused. They were shocked by the sentence and beset by the sudden fear that a Stalinist repression of literature and purge trials were returning. Many letters and petitions descended on officials expressing the energy of a new movement. Samizdat materials multiplied and dissident ranks grew. The trial was a milestone in the ongoing struggle for intellectual freedom. Very few writers of any stature except Mikhail Sholokhov could be found to approve the condemnation of Sinyavsky and Daniel. One class of students is known to have walked out of the class of a professor who had signed a letter approving the sentence. Several Western Communist leaders also criticized the trial. But a wave of new repressions followed.[51]

An official campaign was started against anti-Stalinist historians and a number of anti-Stalinists in the party were removed. Four young writer-activists: Alexander Ginzburg, Yuri Galanskov, Alexei Dobovolsky, and Vera Lashkova were arrested. They had collected materials on the Sinyavsky-Daniel Trial aimed at persuading officials to reopen the case.

The material was sent to the KGB and to deputies of the Supreme Soviet. The four were tried in January 1968 and convicted under Article 70. More than a thousand people protested this new trial, followed by further persecutions. Pavel Litvinov, grandson of the former foreign minister of the Soviet Union, began compiling transcripts of cases and letters of protest[52] and making appeals which were broadcast over BBC. A petition signed by 170 persons protested the violation of legal norms. The cycle of protest and repression intensified.

The atmosphere created by these events helped to nourish the budding Jewish national movement, "an atmosphere . . . prepared by the selfless struggle of a handful of the intelligentsia and the best writers of contemporary Russia,[53] without which the Jewish movement would have been completely isolated and too fragile to contend with the remorseless tests and trials individuals in the movement were subjected to. By the same token, when the early Jewish movement gained more strength, it had an enormous influence on many elements in Soviet society and helped to reinforce the human rights (or democratic) movement. Both movements emphasized the defense of legality and basic human rights guaranteed by the Soviet Constitution itself and the Universal Declaration on Human Rights. Premier Kosygin gave an additional spurt to the Jewish emigration movement when, at a press conference in Paris on December 3, 1966, he upheld the principle of reunification of families: ". . . as far as the reunification of families is concerned, if some families wish to meet or if they want to leave the Soviet Union, the road is open to them and there is no problem in this. . . ."[54]

The catalyst that caused the Jewish national movement to burst on the Soviet scene in a coherent, organized, and goal-directed form was the Six-Day War of June 1967 between Israel and the Arab countries. After that war, considerable numbers of Jews became involved in a full-fledged protest-and-emigration movement. The first days of anxiety, then the excited flush of victory after less than a week of fighting gave friends of Israel and Jews throughout the world incomparable relief and then exhilaration. For Soviet Jews, the feelings were much more complex because of the Soviet government's support of the Arab cause and hostility toward Israel. The vituperative, abusive attacks on the Jewish state, Zionism, and world Jewry reached new intensities of hatred and inevitably spilled over to Soviet Jews. They, for their part, were secretly or overtly joyous about Israel's victory, but those feelings clashed with the reaction of the regime, one set driving the other to irreconcilable positions. While Soviet Jews had shared the fears of other Jews that a new Holocaust was about to destroy another part of Jewry, Soviet dialectic made the near-victims into Nazis. *Izvestiya* on June 15 said that Israeli "invaders are killing prisoners of war and defenseless peasants, driving the inhabitants from their homes and publicly executing men, women, and children," and compared such "crimes" to those of the Nazis.[55] Newspapers and magazines again began to resort to Streicher-like cartoons and images. A massive anti-Israel and anti-Zionist campaign was also unleashed at the United Nations and relations between Israel and the Soviet Union were once more broken off.

Jewish and Israeli leaders in "ruling circles" were described as Nazi collaborators, and Israel was said to be intent on "establishing an empire from the Nile to the Euphrates in which Israelis will be a kind of Herrenvolk." Judaism was described as a "religion that calls for genocide and enslavement of all other peoples by the Jews." The fury of these accusations reflected the bitter Soviet disappointment with their Arab clients and the errors of their own diplomacy as well as the strong ideological reflex against the Jewish state. Soviet Jews were to suffer harshly from these reactions. A wave of arrests followed. An Asian student reported:

It is only natural that some of the Jewish students were secretly celebrating the victory of the Israelis. . . . When the authorities learned about the celebrations, they made a large-scale search of the participants. . . . In Moscow, there were rumors of pressure brought on Jewish personalities to sign a public condemnation of Israel, backed up by threats and arrests; but some well-known Soviet Jews were reported to have refused to sign it.[56]

Israel's victory has been described by one observer as a "psychological breakthrough for a large part of Soviet Jewry, particularly the younger generation, which has freed itself of apathy and fear, and has begun to make known its grievances. The valor of the Israelis has stirred feelings of pride even in the long subdued and silent older generation, awakening in many of them a spirit of resistance that was once completely atrophied."[57] Many non-Jews as well are known to have been secretly admiring of the Israelis and to have shed some of this respect on Soviet Jews. In street brawls, spectators are known to have cheered the victim of an attack by shouting "Beat him up the way the Jews do!" instead of the old cry, "Beat the Jews and save Russia!"

One young Jew had been brooding over these changes within and without and took a step to a new level of activity. On June 13, a few days after the Israeli embassy was ordered to close its doors in Moscow, twenty-one-year-old Yasha Kazakov wrote a letter to the Supreme Soviet, asking to be freed from the humiliation of being considered a citizen of the Soviet Union, renouncing his citizenship, and demanding what he called his right to go to Israel. In taking this dangerous unprecedented step, Kazakov became the first Jew to dare to personally challenge the Soviet state, demand the right to emigrate, and persist in the demand while at the same time striving to publicize his case in the West.

Kazakov had a typical background[58] for a young Jew in the Soviet Union: upbringing in a completely Russified home, some exposure to anti-Semitism as a child, shame, and then driving curiosity about his Jewishness, which led him finally to find some books dealing with Jewish history. On June 13, from his parents' apartment in Moscow, he decided that if the Soviet Union could sever relations with Israel, he could sever his connection with the Soviet Union. No reply came to his first letter, so he wrote a second copy to U Thant, Secretary-General of the United Nations, which he hand-delivered to the American embassy. As he walked out of the embassy door, he was arrested and expected to be put on trial. He was interrogated for many hours and told, "You do not have the right to leave the country. You will never receive an exit visa. You were born in Russia and you will die in Russia."[59] Unaccountably, he was released, but was never left alone. In November, he received a formal notification from the Ministry of the Interior that his request for an exit visa had been denied. He continued writing letters and was threatened with induction in the army and placement in a mental hospital. But the threats were never carried out. At the end of December, he went again to the Ministry of the Interior for another grueling interrogation, but no further threats. Meanwhile, he was careful to let friends know of his presence so that they would know if he suddenly disappeared.

On May 20, 1968, he wrote again to the Supreme Soviet, saying that he was applying once more and

shall continue to apply until my request is granted. I demand what is mine by right, and any negative reply . . . is unlawful and contrary both to the Constitution of the USSR and to the Declaration of the Rights of Man, which the Soviet Union has undertaken to observe and respect. . . .

I am a Jew, I was born a Jew, and I want to live out my life as a Jew. With all my respect for the Russian people, I do not consider my people in any way inferior to the Russian, or to any other people, and I do not want to be assimilated by any people. . . .

I do not wish to be a citizen of the USSR, of a country that refuses to the Jews (and to other nations, too) the right of self-determination.

I do not wish to be a citizen of a country where Jews are subjected to forced assimilation, where my people are deprived of its national image and its cultural treasures . . . of a country that conducts a policy of genocide toward the Jewish people. . . .[60]

This letter circulated in samizdat form in Moscow and other cities. No reply came from the Supreme Soviet, but Kazakov continued to be called in for questioning. Puzzled and made increasingly nervous by the uncertainty and tension, he made copies of his letter to the Supreme Soviet and took them to the British embassy where he asked that they be sent to the *New York Times*, the London *Times*, and the Israeli daily *Davar*. He tried to give several other copies to English-speaking tourists, but they drew away. Finally, he succeeded in giving them to a young German. Only one of the letters reached the West— eight months later. In the meantime, his studies at the Correspondent Institute of Economics were terminated. Kazakov found a job, but continued to press for an exit visa and held his ground with a Colonel Smirnov of OVIR (Visa and Registration Office), who advised him to go to a kolkhoz and live among the peasants and forget his "dangerous nonsense." Ironically, one of Kazakov's letters had reached Israel where his request posed an unprecedented dilemma. Some officials believed it was a Soviet trap, to provoke Israel into granting citizenship, thus giving the Soviet government a pretext for new show trials and Jewish victimization. Others believed that granting him citizenship would harm him and hurt chances for renewed Soviet-Israel relations. The best policy they all believed was to remain silent—just the reverse of what Kazakov wanted. Moreover, they refused to publish his letter.

However, a report on the letter was eventually published in the *Washington Post* on December 19, 1968. Kazakov himself learned the news that night while he listened to the Voice of America. Not a word about the letter was published in the Soviet press, but on December 28, it was published in *Davar* and carried on Kol Israel (the Voice of Israel). A large reading audience throughout the world now knew about the young Jew who was pitting himself against the great Soviet state. The climax came the following month at OVIR when Kazakov was told casually, "It took us time to get around to your request. You see, you have no relatives in Israel and we felt it might be difficult for you to manage on your own. . . . . We have a responsibility. When can you leave?" He obtained his passport and visa quickly and was warned not to engage in any "anti-Soviet activity or participate in any demonstrations abroad."[61]

This surreal dénouement, so momentous in its consequences, so full of historic drama, was an arbitrary act, not part of any pattern, but rather a form of Russian roulette, which all future Jewish activists would live under. One Jew could live unscathed while simultaneously another could be sent to prison for a long time, in solitary confinement, for the same action.

It has been suggested that local OVIR officials differ greatly in their decisions and that Kazakov had a stroke of luck, but we cannot be sure why he was allowed to leave at this moment, while a Jew from Kiev, Boris Kochubievsky, also asking for permission to emigrate to Israel, was in prison awaiting trial (see Chapter 30). Kazakov seems to have caught the authorities off guard; his audacity in directly and personally confronting the Soviet state and then publicizing his act in the Western press had no precedents. (Twenty Jewish intellectuals from Vilnius had written *their* letter on February 15, 1968. It had reached the West before Kazakov's, but was unsigned [see Chapter 30]). The Soviet image had become badly tarnished over the recent Soviet invasion of Czechoslovakia and needed burnishing. Soviet Jews in Israel later believed that Soviet officials had miscalculated the intensity of the gathering new movement and believed they could easily get rid of a few troublemakers, or "mad" ones. There was also the early exploration of détente and Kosygin's remarks in 1966 promising that Jews could leave the Soviet Union.

The new wave of Jewish national consciousness *was* growing, and demands for recognition of rights linked to that consciousness would grow stronger in the next decade, but the regime was arbitrary and capricious in dealing with specific requests. The inconsistent handling of Kochubievsky's case following on the heels of Kazakov's was to become an all too familiar unpredictable zigzag.

30

The Jewish National Movement:
Trials, Tests, and Affirmations, 1968–71

THE period 1968–69 surrounding the Kochubievsky case was one not only of Soviet capriciousness in dealing with activists, non-Jewish as well as Jewish, but one which marked the convergences and divergences existing between the Jewish national and general dissident movements. The period also witnessed the Soviet invasion of Czechoslovakia, the growing involvement of privileged, officially honored citizens such as Andrei Sakharov in the human rights movement, and dramatic, highly publicized trials which were reported in samizdat and the Western press. All of these events created new shocks and jolts for the regime, but no fundamental trauma that threatened it. It had, however, to deal with them, and in the process the lives of many thousands of Soviet citizens were greatly changed: some were allowed to emigrate; some found a heightened sense of inner freedom which enabled them to suffer shattering blows, including exile and prison; some were intellectually refreshed and enriched by underground literature; others broke relations with their families because of their new outlook and exposed situation. The vast majority remained ostensibly indifferent or unaffected by the protests of the human rights activists, but most non-Jews, it can be assumed, looked with suspicion, hostility, or worse, upon those Jews now announcing their desire to leave the Soviet Union.

The life of young engineer Boris Kochubievsky was profoundly affected, and his trial was the first to be widely known in the West.[1] Kochubievsky's father, a Red Army officer, had been killed by the Nazis at Babi Yar, and his grandparents, by Ukrainian nationalists in the early days of the war, after Soviet troops had retreated, but Boris' sense of his own Jewishness was almost extinct. He identified himself as a Russian on his documents and had married a non-Jewish woman. But during the early sixties he was influenced by the brief cultural thaw, then the swift repression, and the inability of Kiev Jews to memorialize the mass murder of Jews at Babi Yar. The very existence of the State of Israel was also becoming important—a surrogate spiritual and emotional presence to fill the bleak void Soviet Jews felt in an increasingly hostile environment. During and after the Six-Day War, the atmosphere became particularly ominous and ugly. Not only the press and radio, but factory meetings denounced Israel in the most abusive terms. One such meeting was held in June 1967 at the Kiev factory where Kochubievsky worked.

A resolution attacking Israeli "aggression" was expected to pass unanimously, but Kochubievsky disagreed. The other workers were stunned when he said: "I want the record to show that I disagree. . . . This was a necessary measure of protection of the Jewish people from total physical annihilation." In the subsequent months, he was abused, isolated, and taunted to resign, which he did, finally, in May 1968. At about the same time, he wrote an essay called "Why I Am a Zionist," which was circulated in samizdat form and later smuggled out to the West. In it, Kochubievsky charged that the regime and its policy reek of "the stench of narrow-minded anti-Semitism—in the highest bureaucratic elite of our government"—a phrase he had borrowed from another samizdat essay by the distinguished Soviet nuclear physicist and a founder of the Soviet Human Rights Committee, Andrei Sakharov.[2] He minced no words. Why do Jewish youths in the Soviet Union still retain a feeling of Jewish national identity? Because of the new brand of anti-Semitism, anti-Zionism—as well as the old, according to Kochubievsky. "Silence is equivalent to death. . . . If we remain silent today, tomorrow will be too late."[3]

That summer, Kochubievsky and his wife (whose father was employed by the KGB) applied for an exit permit to leave for Israel, but they were refused. On September 29, the anniversary of the slaughter at Babi Yar, official meetings and services replaced the usual intimate ones. Israel was subjected to abusive condemnation and officials made no reference to the large numbers of Jews who had been murdered there. A woman was heard to say that the Germans killed 100,000 Jews, to which a man answered, "Not enough." Kochubievsky became very angry, argued with the man, and said, "In this country, no one considers me as one of them. I want to go to a place where people will regard me as being one of them."[4] After the official portion, Jewish mourners remained and Kochubievsky spoke with great feeling: "Here lies a part of the Jewish people," he said solemnly.

In November, Boris and his wife were told that they had been granted an exit visa and could pick up their papers at OVIR on November 28. While they were at the office, their apartment was searched and ransacked. Incensed, Boris wrote an open letter to Soviet Party Secretary Brezhnev, to the Ukrainian Party Secretary, and to the investigator who was in charge of the apartment raid. This letter, too, was disseminated in samizdat form and expressed the main themes of the Jewish emigration movement that was to develop:

I am a Jew. I want to live in the Jewish state. That is my right, just as it is the right of a Ukrainian to live in the Ukraine, the right of a Russian to live in Russia, the right of a Georgian to live in Georgia. I want to live in Israel. That is my dream, that is the goal not only of my life but also of the lives of hundreds of generations that preceded me. . . .

I want my children to study in the Hebrew language. I want to read Jewish papers, I want to attend a Jewish theater. What's wrong with that? What is my crime? . . .

I have repeatedly turned with this request to various authorities and achieved only . . . dismissal from my job, my wife's expulsion from her institute, and . . . a criminal charge of slandering Soviet reality. What is this slander? . . . I don't want to be involved in the national affairs of a state in which I consider myself an alien. . . . I want to live in Israel. My wish does not contradict Soviet law. . . .

Listen to the voice of reason. Let me go! As long as I live . . . I shall devote all my strength to obtain an exit permit for Israel. . . .[5]

Within less than a week, Boris was arrested and charged under Article 187-1 of the Ukrainian Criminal Code with disseminating "slanderous fabrications, defaming the state and social system of the USSR . . . alleging that the Soviet state oppresses and keeps down Jews."[6] During May 13–16, 1969, he was tried, found guilty, and sentenced to three years in a forced labor camp. Leonid Plyusch, a dissident activist in Kiev, brought news of Kochubievsky's trial to Moscow to the editors of *Khronika tekushchikh sobytiy* (*A Chronicle of Current Events*), a samizdat publication which was started in April 1968 to document violations of human rights[7] (see below p. 662–63). By June 5, the *New York Times* carried a report of his sentence, datelined Moscow, June 4.

A number of cases now came to Western attention. In Ryazan 125 miles south of Moscow, six Jews who had applied to emigrate to Israel were arrested in August 1969, and their books and records seized. In the subsequent trial, they were charged with "participation in anti-Soviet organizations" and four were sentenced to prison terms.[8] In Bendery two Jewish schoolteachers sent letters to Brezhnev criticizing Soviet policy in Czechoslovakia and taped international broadcasts, including the Voice of Israel. Their materials were also confiscated, and they were charged with "anti-Soviet agitation" and sentenced to terms in a labor camp.

In Moscow, an older figure of great influence on Jewish youths was David Khavkin, who taught and counselled them after his release from prison for earlier Zionist activity. He stressed recourse to Soviet law and the right to emigrate under the Soviet Constitution and international law.[9] It was he who took the initiative in calling together a joint meeting of delegates from Moscow, Riga, Leningrad, Kiev, Minsk, Kharkov, and Tbilisi in August 1969 in Moscow, where details of activities of the embryonic movement were hammered out, including efforts to secure exit visas, disseminate samizdat materials, and petitions and letters.[10] The Khavkins themselves were given permission to leave on September 29 and hundreds of friends and well-wishers came to see them off but customs examination turned out to be a nightmare. Mrs. Khavkin was subjected to a gynecological examination and the family missed their plane. Nevertheless, a few days later they were allowed to leave. After their departure, the Moscow movement tended to gravitate around the figure of Vitaly Svechinsky, an architect, who had tried to escape to Israel in 1948 and had been arrested and sent to Kolyma.[11] By 1968, he had become a central figure in the repatriation movement, as it was sometimes called, but he also worked with the human rights dissidents such as Litvinov, Natalya Gorbanevskaya, Viktor Krasin, and Pyotr Yakir. By 1969, an industrial engineer specializing in spectroscopy, David Drabkin, who was dramatically affected by the Six-Day War, also became an influential figure. He requested permission to emigrate, but was refused in April 1969 through a call from OVIR with the words, "There are too many of you Jews. We shall not let you out, we shall finish you off here."[12]

In Vilnius, on February 15, 1968, appeared the first collective letter of Jewish protest demanding, not the right to emigrate, but the right to live as Jews, free of anti-Semitism. The writers deplore propaganda and cartoons which had "revived anti-Semitic passions . . . [and] local judeo-phobia." Specific government figures are accused of promoting anti-Semitism; facts are cited as evidence that there is discrimination against Jews in schools, universities, and official positions. The writers decry punishment of those who "dared to teach a group of young Jews the alphabet of their native tongue" and boldly state that "if the frontiers were opened today for emigration, approximately 80 percent of the Jews would emigrate to Israel."[13] The dilemma of being a Jew in the Soviet Union is then posed:

We are confronted with a paradox here. We are not wanted here, we are completely oppressed, forcibly denationalized, and even publicly insulted in the press—while at the same time we are forcibly kept here. As the Lithuanian proverb goes, "He beats and he screams at the same time."[14]

The group did not sign their names, observing that "we know well how people who protested against flourishing anti-Semitism in the Soviet Union . . . were dealt with summarily." This letter eventually reached the West.

Many individual and signed group letters and petitions followed. Among the most remarkable of this early period is the petition of eighteen Georgian Jewish families, dated August 6, 1969, addressed to U Thant, asking his support for their long-delayed application to emigrate to Israel. (The letter was sent to the Prime Minister of Israel, Mrs. Golda Meir, with a request that it be forwarded.) Georgian Jews have been a closely knit community with a long historic memory going back to identification with the ten lost tribes of Israel. Most Jews in Georgia have retained their religious traditions and feel strong bonds with the ancient Land of Israel. For them, it was not religious or racial discrimination that impelled them to want to leave, but because "the prophecy has come true: Israel has risen from the ashes . . . and needs our hands." These Georgian Jews also spoke for the "hundreds of millions who did not live to see this day, who were tortured to death . . . those who handed down to us the traditions of struggle and faith. . . . It is incomprehensible that in the 20th century people can be prohibited from living where they wish to live. . . . We will wait months and years, we will wait all our lives, if necessary, but we will not renounce our faith or our hopes."[15]

This letter stirred a swelling tide of letters, petitions, and declarations from varied individuals and groups of Jews in scattered parts of the Soviet Union in 1969 and 1970: Moscow, Leningrad, Minsk, Riga, Georgia, Vilnius, Odessa, Kiev, and Yurmala (Latvian SSR). They were addressed to the UN Committee on Human Rights, to U-Thant, to the

the USSR Ministry of Foreign Affairs, to Premier Kosygin, to the Presidium of the Supreme Soviet of the USSR, and to Zalman Shazar, the President of Israel. These were unprecedented, open expressions, wrung out of deeply felt humiliations, bitterness, and desire for a new life. Many who had signed such documents were immediately arrested and imprisoned.

Details of this Jewish movement of dissent began to appear in the 1969[16] issues of *Khronika*. *Khronika* was and is a bimonthly Russian samizdat publication devoted to the struggle for religious, national, and individual human rights and the defense of the guarantees in the Soviet Constitution. The movement had been building, especially in Moscow, after the Sinyavsky-Daniel Trial, and gained support from a number of developments: the Ginzburg-Galanskov Trial; Litvinov's transcripts and radio broadcasts; Solzhenitsyn's struggle; the demonstrations and petitions of the late 1960s; Sakharov's increasing involvement leading to the samizdat publication of "Memorandum," his breakthrough critique of Soviet society, published abroad as *Progress, Coexistence, and Intellectual Freedom* (1968); Roy Medvedev's study of Stalin's tyranny, *Let History Judge* (in samizdat circulation in 1969); and the reports of harassment and protest pouring into Moscow from distant points.

Khronika was begun in April 1968 by the poet Natalya Gorbanevskaya, who had been a student of Sinyavsky and had helped Ginzburg copy transcripts of the Sinyavsky-Daniel Trial. Litvinov among others organized and distributed the journal. On the title page of every issue there appears the text of Article 19 of the Universal Declaration of Human Rights, which calls for universal freedom of opinion and expression, and the statement, "The authors are guided by the principle that such universal guarantees [and those in domestic law] . . . should be firmly adhered to in their own country and elsewhere.[17] At the signing of the so-called Helsinki Accords on August 1, 1975, the Soviet Union pledged itself to act "in conformity" with the 1948 Declaration.

In the issues of *Khronika* one finds an extraordinary range of dissent and details of persecution: unpublicized trials in centers and distant parts of Russia; the activity of Buddhists, Jehovah's Witnesses, Lithuanian Catholics, Seventh Day Adventists, Ukrainian Catholics, and other religious groups under attack; arbitrary dismissals from work; politically motivated incarceration in psychiatric hospitals; accounts of hunger strikes; texts of letters, petitions, and declarations; news of raids on apartments, interrogations, and arrests; emigration requests, refusals, and permissions; excerpts from other samizdat; information about and from prison camps; the struggle of Ukrainian nationalists, Crimean Tatars, and other national minorities. With issue Number 18 (March 1971), a new section called "The Jewish Movement for Emigration to Israel" acknowledged the Jewish national struggle. (*Khronika* will be referred to as *Chronicle* hereafter.)

As has been noted, certain Jews were drawn into both the democratic movement for human rights and the Jewish movement for full national rights and the right to emigrate,[18] but differences in emphasis and splits were inevitable. Some identified themselves within the Jewish movement after activity in the human rights movement; others tried to bridge both in activity as well as thinking, believing they were truly indivisible. The government of Israel, very slow to engage in these issues at all, was consistently careful about avoiding any connection with the "democratic" movement or any suggestion of criticism of the Soviet government, in time lent support and gave publicity only to those who had a Zionist goal, that of *aliya* to Israel.[19] This was a distinction which many Jewish activists deplored both before and after their emigration to Israel. In early 1970, the first articulate albeit modest differentiation between the two movements appeared in the form of two publications in Riga, expressing the movement for aliya—*Iton Alef* (Newspaper A) and *Iton Bet* (B), published in February and May respectively. "Published anonymously, in a tiny number of copies and on mediocre paper, they represented the *first* attempt to speak out loud to Soviet Jews *from the inside.*"[20]

These issues (in Russian) were suffused with the Zionist dream: they contained an interview with Golda Meir, the text of the Israeli Declaration of Independence, a proud story about the Israeli army, reportage on the Six-Day War, texts of the first open letters requesting or demanding emigration rights, and an extract from a book on the Warsaw Ghetto Uprising. One writer has said that just as the young boys and girls "were called to battle by pride in the Jewish people" at the time of the ghetto uprising, so it might have been said of the first editors of the magazine, which "became the symbol of the incipient Jewish national movement."[21]

Extremely risky though it was, the journal was a joint effort of activists in Moscow, Leningrad, and Riga, who met during the fall of 1969 and early winter of 1970 and decided that collective letters should be initiated and published—a decision to move to an open struggle. In September 1969, such a letter appeared from ten Moscow Jews addressed to world Jewry, then another from the "Moscow 25" to U Thant, and another from the "Riga 22," indicating linkages.[22] The man who drafted the letter of the "Moscow 25" was Viktor Fedoseyev, a non-Jew. He did not sign it, however, thinking that it was inappropriate for a non-Jew to do so. However, he became a leading figure in the Jewish samizdat movement.

Fedoseyev[23] grew up in Shanghai where his father, a railroad engineer, had been sent by the Soviet government. Viktor decided to become a seaman after the war and made extended visits to the West. When he finally returned to the Soviet Union, he was horrified by Stalinist repression, the silence and fear, and the prison camps. In Sverdlovsk he met Rachel Koliaditskaya, a Jewess, who had also grown up in China, whom he later married. Rachel's father went to Palestine after the war; Rachel's mother, driven by a fierce idealism, took her to the Soviet Union, a country neither had known, but the nation that had defeated the Nazis. They were taken straight to a camp at Nakhodka, south of Vladivostok. After a month in the camp, they were shipped together with many other prisoners, including a number of Jews, in wagons to a small village in the Urals. For a year they were given no documents and lived largely by selling clothes. Eventually they were able to go to Sverdlovsk, about the time when the State of Israel was created. After their marriage, Rachel and Viktor moved to Riga where they became caught up in the democratic movement there. Meanwhile, Rachel's mother moved to Moscow, tried to emigrate to Israel to join her husband, and became involved in the Jewish national movement. Viktor and Rachel followed in 1968, when young Moscow Jews were trying to find copies of *Exodus* and enjoying the exhilaration of Israel's victory in the Six-Day War.

Viktor and Rachel argued that "it was perfectly legal, under the Soviet Constitution, for Jews to say openly and in unity that they wanted to leave Russia for Israel," that it was not a presumptuous idea. The letter of the "Moscow 25" and others followed.

In the meantime, *Chronicle* Numbers 8 and 9 (June and August, 1969) reported on the trial of Boris Kochubievsky, and protest letters appeared in Number 10 (October 1969) and thereafter. Some of the most active Zionists had left for Israel early in 1969, and in September, OVIR again began accepting applications, most for the first time, but there were also many refusals, frustrated expectations, and "the severing of any last traces of emotional identification with the social system of a country where the Jews felt they were strangers."[24] Meanwhile, *Iton Gimmel* was prepared but never circulated because of a sweep of arrests of Jews in June 1970. Most of its compilers were arrested and placed on trial in May 1971. But other samizdat materials were being disseminated, including the influential *Iskhod* (Exodus) that first appeared in April 1970 and was edited by Fedoseyev.

"It was important to publish *Exodus*," said Fedoseyev, "because the main achievement of the Soviet regime against Jews was that they were deprived of the WORD. You can't buy a Bible nor can you read and learn about Jewish culture and life. A people deprived of a voice faces assimilation; to stop assimilation, to recreate a nation, a people must communicate. What if the exodus from Egypt had never been reported? What if the Jews had been denied knowledge of their heritage? . . . Today, too, we need to record every word. . . ."[25]

Iskhod (subsequently referred to as *Exodus*) was patterned after *Chronicle* and reflected the influence of the democratic movement, but it clearly differentiated itself by dealing specifically with the Jewish struggle. Four issues appeared in 1970–71, bearing the subtitle "Collection of Documents" and included the texts of letters, documents, and Soviet laws bearing on the legality of civil rights. The first issue carried the text of the historic August 1969 letter of the eighteen Georgian families. The second appeared after the arrests in June 1970 and included names of those arrested, and strongly worded letters to Soviet authorities protesting the arrests. For example, a letter from Leningrad dated June 28, speaks about "humiliating searches, lasting many hours," and of the Jewish population in Leningrad waiting "in a torment of uncertainty" while "a trial of eight arrested Leningrad Jews is being prepared."[26] These Jews had applied for permission to leave the USSR according to the rules governing the reunification of families. The writers affirm that those arrested "never intended to commit any actions contravening the law or harming the Soviet people." They ask if "the Soviet government wants to frighten those Jews who wish to leave for Israel?" Will the coming trial be reminiscent of the infamous Dreyfus and Beilis trials, the "doctors' plot"?[27]

One letter signed by seventy-five Jews in Moscow, dated June 10, 1970,[28] and addressed to U Thant, who was in Moscow that month, was widely commented upon in the world press and was broadcast by a number of radio stations. The text of the "Letter of the 75" was also published in *Exodus* Number 2. Later in the month, the apartments of three of the signers—Vladimir Slepak, David Drabkin, and Vitaly Svechinsky—were searched under Article 64 of the Criminal Code ("betrayal of the motherland"). In general, the tone of this issue is open, direct, and even militant. Anonymity has been superseded. Addresses, ages, and professions of more than 60 signers are revealed. *Exodus* Number 3 (November 1970) continues this tone and includes the complete documentation of the case of Ruta Aleksandrovich, a 23-year-old nurse and one of the "Riga Four" arrested in June 1970, after house searches and almost daily interrogations by the KGB. The trial of the four began on May 24, 1971, and drew much attention in the West (see below, pp. 687–89). *Exodus* Number 4 (February 1971) is devoted wholly to the First Leningrad Trial of December 15–24, 1970 (see below pp. 672–80) and includes an annotated transcript of four reports from the court based on recordings, shorthand notes, and memorized portions, plus comments of observers inside and outside the courtroom.

Fedoseyev, the chief editor of *Exodus,* was helped by Svechinsky, Dr. Meir Gelfand, and Alexander Balabanov, all Zionist activists from Moscow and closely associated with the democratic movement, and Isai Averbukh, a young Odessa poet who stayed in Moscow and Riga at times[29] and married the Riga activist Ruta Aleksandrovich. *Exodus,* in contrast with *Iton Alef* and *Iton Bet,* was a straight reportorial journal; it carried no commentary and "sought to stay within the narrow, permissible line of dissidence that had been worked out through the experience of half a decade of democratic activity."[30] Fedoseyev and his wife received permission to leave the Soviet Union in March, 1971. Before he left, Fedoseyev had prepared sufficient materials for subsequent issues of *Exodus,* to be called *Vestnik Iskhoda* (Herald of the Exodus) and edited by Roman Rutman. Three issues appeared between 1971 and 1972. At great risk, they were smuggled out to Israel, but like *Exodus* One and Three, they were not published in the West.[31] Later, in 1972, mainly in preparation for President Nixon's visit, a 54-page samizdat document containing many appeals, court actions, and commentary, called *Belaya kniga iskhoda* (The White Book of Exodus), was circulated and reached the West.

For people used to freely available literature, the ordeals and official

and unofficial menace surrounding the preparation and distribution of
samizdat are scarcely imaginable. Leonard Schroeter, a historian of the
Jewish movement, has described some of the tensions and risks:

The production of *samizdat* in the Soviet Union involves a constant struggle
with the ever watchful authorities. First, the information must be gathered.
This is done by word of mouth, by surreptitious meetings and clandestine
reportorial techniques. To reproduce it, there must be a typewriter, paper, and
carbon paper.

In the Soviet Union, one cannot buy a new typewriter without showing one's
internal passport, and second-hand typewriters are difficult to come by. Type-
face (traceable by the KGB) must be periodically destroyed, disposed of, and
replaced. A 200-page document is prepared with 12 to 15 copies. This requires
3,000 sheets of paper. But . . . stores usually sell only thick paper which can
make only three or four copies. When thin onion-skin paper is available, the
KGB keeps a watch on stores that sell it. . . .[32]

It is impossible to know how many readers of early Jewish samizdat
there were, but meetings among people from different cities, encoun-
ters at synagogues, and, increasingly, at OVIR offices, created ever-
broadening networks. Publicity in the West, the revelation of names in
collective and individual letters, and the greater openness of demands
in the development of samizdat, combined with the fact that some Jews
were being granted permission to leave, heartened the activists. In the
last half of 1969, about 100 permits were granted per month, a rate
which lasted throughout 1970.[33] In March, it leaped to about 1,000 per
month. Letters also began to come from former friends in Israel, encouraging others to identify themselves with the Jewish national movement.

All of this unprecedented activity provoked an angry official response in editorials and letters to the press, some of them by Jews,
officially inspired and directed. For example, on December 14, 1969,
Izvestiya published a letter entitled "To Whose Tune Do the Zionists
Dance," signed by two Jews, in which the charge of Soviet anti-Semitism is denounced, and the idea that Soviet Jews want to live elsewhere, rejected. This "shameful and hypocritical anti-Soviet campaign
is to divert attention from Israel's acute problems . . . to convince the
credulous that Israel is a promised land." Israel, the letter alleged, only
wants cheap labor and "cannon fodder" for its army. Those who have
gone to Israel lead lives of misery and exploitation. The letter warned

Jews not to "forget the tenacity of the enemy, how he has recourse to the lowest methods in order to incline his 'brothers' to treachery, to the betrayal of their real motherland. . . ."[34]

There were many replies, but they were never printed in *Izvestiya*. However, they did appear in samizdat. The emigration campaign doubtless provoked resentment and anti-Jewish feeling, but also, according to some scholars, "brought the very concept of rights to the consciousness of a vast number of people in the Soviet Union who had never before thought about rights.[35] They occasionally spoke out in samizdat, but could scarcely offset or openly challenge the outpouring of official anti-Jewish material in all the Soviet media. An important theoretical analysis of the Jewish question in the USSR circulated widely and anonymously in samizdat in the early seventies and addressed this reality head-on. It was called "The Jewish Question in the USSR (Theses)"[36] and was written by someone who later identified himself as Michael Zand, a leading intellectual in the Jewish movement, who emigrated to Israel in 1971. His is a closely reasoned, well-structured exposition of the Jewish condition in the USSR, setting forth in great detail the forms of official and unofficial anti-Semitism and discrimination Jews were subjected to. The indictment is sweeping:

All sections of Soviet society are infected with anti-Semitism in everyday life. Every Jew living in the USSR could tell of humiliations personally suffered . . . in communal housing or in the street, on public transport, in shop queues, in the army barracks or the municipal hospital. . . . The revival of antisemitism is in no small degree facilitated by regular reproduction in the Soviet press of items from Arab sources on "the atrocities of the Israeli invaders".[37]

The campaign against Jews, Zand charges, "is directed from above," because "nothing happens in the Soviet Union without the consent of the leading Party and government organs. Discrimination, he believes, "is not an aim in itself," but "merely the tool used by the authorities in their assimilatory policy." But the intensity of anti-Semitism is so strong and the assimilationist goal so apparent that even children of mixed marriages who proclaim themselves as Jews are not so registered in their passports. Zand then summarizes the relentless destruction of Jewish culture throughout the Stalin and post-Stalin period, concluding that there exists in the Soviet Union "only one Jewish culture—that of the Mountain Jews in the Tat language,[38] and this only because the bearers of this culture are denied the right to consider themselves Jews! The crucial dilemma for those Jews searching for a

Jewish identity is then sharply juxtaposed: the synagogue has become "the center of Jewish spiritual life" but is unable to answer basic questions and needs, because "the active hostility of the state has reduced the synagogue to a slavish degradation . . . [and] fear of repressions. . . ." An assimilated Jew goes to synagogue "like a blind man," because he knows nothing of religious tradition. Thus, gravitation toward the synagogue "has not so much a religious as a national character," and since national expression is barred for Jews, it can be found only by repatriation to Israel. Those who wish to assimilate themselves can choose that alternative. The rest must decide between those two choices.[39]

In the course of his analysis, Zand mentioned two works which formed part of the intensified anti-Israel and anti-Jewish propaganda campaign after the Six-Day War: K. Ivanov's *The State of Israel* (Ivanov was the pseudonym of V. S. Semyonov, deputy minister of foreign affairs), and Yury Ivanov's *Beware: Zionism!* These were only two of the vituperative works in a massive, relentless drive to portray Israel as a worldwide evil bent on control of the world and a center of international espionage, and Jews as disloyal, subversive agents of this conspiracy. These books and others were highly praised in many Soviet newspapers and magazines, and in broadcasts by Tass in numerous foreign languages. On May 31, 1969, Belorussia's leading newspaper *Sovetskaya Byelorussiya* "discovered" that a secret meeting of Zionists had taken place in London in 1968, at which it was decided to take over the entire Arab world. To prove this, a quotation under a map is cited, saying that "Jesus Christ will soon return in order to rule over the whole world from Jerusalem." But the reference to Christ is described as a "witticism—who is going to believe this today? But as to world mastery, this is a fact. . . ."[40]

The themes so reminiscent of the *Protocols of the Elders of Zion* continued into 1970, with the added twist of involving Soviet Jews in a campaign not only to denounce Zionism and Israel, but "against the Zionist conception of Jewish history and . . . Zionist achievement [and] also as a massive defence of the way in which Russian Communism has solved 'the Jewish Question' both ideologically and in practice."[41]

On January 13, 1970, *Pravda* published eleven more letters from Jews, all of whom "indignantly rejected any idea that they or any other sane Soviet citizen might want to emigrate." In their introduction, the editors accused Golda Meir of creating "an openly anti-Soviet diversion," a reference to her appeal, during a debate in the Knesset, to permit all those Jews who wanted to emigrate to Israel to do so.[42] In February, three well-known Jews made "appropriate" statements: Rabbi Levin said that "Zionism has never had anything in common with honest Jews," and that Soviet Jews "do not need protection from the outside."[43] Vergelis, editor of *Sovetish heymland*, introduced the ugly equation of Zionism with fascism, accusing Zionists of entering into contact with the followers of Hitler, a reference to the negotiations in 1944 over the possible ransom of Hungarian Jewry.[44] The third personality was Lieutenant-General David (sometimes identified as Dimitry) Dragunsky, the only Jewish member of a party secretariat (Armenian) and one of the few Jews among top Soviet commanders. His association with the Jewish Antifascist Committee was also intended to give special weight to his statement. He repeated some of the usual anti-Zionist tirades and dwelt on the great blessings of his Soviet homeland.[45]

March 2 was declared "a world day for condemnation of Israeli aggression," and prominent Jews were called upon to give press conferences in Moscow, Riga, Kishinev, and Tbilisi. Hundreds of letters from Soviet Jews were published in the central and local press and statements were issued by Jews in the party, factories, at the universities, and by a group of "believing Jews in Kiev."[46] The peak of the campaign was reached in a press conference in Moscow, at which fifty-two Jews issued a statement denouncing Israel and Zionism and repudiating all charges of discrimination against Jews in the Soviet Union. The individuals who signed included several generals and figures in Soviet science, academic life, and literature—but almost none associated with Soviet Jewish interests. One analyst has concluded that by and large, "Yiddish and Russian liberal writers, Jews and non-Jews, have tried to avoid adding their names to these documents, and probably did so only when they had absolutely no alternative."[47]

Jewish activists, powerless to cope with such an onslaught and unable to have access to the media, had to rage among themselves in frustration and circulate counterarguments in samizdat form. For example, a group of forty Jews in Moscow, in a letter circulated on March 8, disputed the right of participants in the March 4 press conference in Moscow to represent all Soviet Jews and demanded the right to hold their own press conference to present their views, but their letter was not published in the Soviet press.[48]

The sorry spectacle of Jews fighting and denouncing each other was extremely painful to many Soviet Jews. One activist Ilya Zilberberg expressed this pain in *Exodus No. 1*: ". . . the newspaper columns are again strewn with the words 'Jew' and 'Jewish' and the eye aches from the profusion of Jewish names, some unknown, some world famous."[49]

The torrent of anti-Jewish and anti-Israel propaganda in the Soviet Union has poisoned the atmosphere and created fear among the many Jews who have remained uninvolved in the dissident or Jewish national movement, who have no strong spiritual or national-cultural convictions to give them the inner freedom or strength the dissidents feel. However, the ambiguities and contradictions in Soviet policy toward its Jews have created dilemmas and problems for the regime. The Jewish protest movement dramatized these contradictions and exposed them to the world. The appeals of activists, protests, arrests, and trials were being publicized in the West and news about them was transmitted back to the Soviet Union. It has been said that "a small sound left Russia but a loud echo was thrown back."[50] Western correspondents were now also linked in the "anti-Soviet fabrications" and were also viewed as representing "international Zionism." Clearly, the Jewish activists were going beyond all previous levels of challenge to the regime. Repression at home was one thing, but Soviet officials now found themselves with something they could not control: they were answerable to public opinion abroad and "the uncomfortable necessity of justifying their treatment of the Jews before a world opinion that was increasingly aware." Moreover, as the Jewish movement became more militant and daring, it was providing "an example to other aggrieved sections of Soviet society,"[51] and threatened to spread the infection of discontent and dissent to other segments of the population that had suffered national and religious repression and/or long pent-up frustrations and discontents.[52]

This was—and is—also the danger of exploiting traditional anti-Jewish prejudices and at the same time trying to sustain the image of the Soviet Union as the embodiment and carrier of socialist justice and internationalism. If, as has been suggested, the anti-Jewish campaign was aligned with the Soviet pro-Arab line, there is also a clear inconsistency in giving some Jews the right to emigrate and, from time to time, seeming to yield to Western pressures. An internal crisis of some sort was being partly defused, but also confounded, for the contradictions have not been resolved.

The hostility of the anti-Zionist onslaught may also be seen as a reflex of the insoluble dilemma the Jewish movement had created. A certain defensiveness in Soviet counterarguments can be discerned. For example, it was claimed that it was not the Zionist leadership that saved the Jews in Palestine from Hitler, but the Soviet Army victory at Stalingrad. Moreover, the great advantages given to Jews in Soviet society were recounted: higher education, professional opportunities, accounts of aid rendered Jews by non-Jews. There was also the unusual innovation of publicizing in the Soviet daily press, for the first time since 1948, the role played by Jews in the Red Army during World War II, including the number of military awards granted. But these arguments did not meet the central issues.[53] The failure to develop a self-consistent overall policy in dealing with the "Jewish problem" was becoming more, not less, apparent, and the tide of official rationalizations and unspontaneous statements by some Jews, many of whom were never associated with Jewish affairs, neither intimidated those who wanted to leave, nor smothered the dilemmas facing the regime.

A further aggravation of the Soviet Jewish question was added by the events of the so-called "Leningrad hijacking" and subsequent trial which moved the issue of Jewish emigration to the international stage and resulted in extremely strong condemnations of the Soviet Union—the strongest since the Soviet invasion of Czechoslovakia. The issues that emerged also presented the regime with unprecedented forms of dissent.

On June 15, 1970, at 8:30 A.M., twelve persons, including nine Jews from Riga, were apprehended at Leningrad's Smolny Airport, as they were walking from the terminal to an airplane. The evening paper in Leningrad, *Vecherny Leningrad,* and the next morning's *Leningradskaya pravda* briefly reported that "On June 15, a group of criminals trying to seize a scheduled airplane was arrested at Smolny Airport. Investigations are in progress."[54] At about the same time as the arrests, eight Leningrad Jews were arrested at scattered places—at work, at home, and even on vacation in Odessa. A few hours later, house searches were conducted by the KGB in dozens of Jewish homes in Moscow, Riga, Leningrad, and Kharkov, and a number of Jews were detained for questioning.

The arrests were made the day after thirty-seven Leningrad Jews had signed an appeal to U Thant, requesting him to intercede with the Soviet authorities on the question of emigration to Israel during his impending visit to Moscow. Among the arrested were six signatories to the letter, who had also signed numerous other letters. The house searches spread to Kiev, Odessa, Sukhumi, and Kishinev. Four of those arrested—Leib and Meri Khnokh, Silva Zalmanson, and Boris Penson—had been harassed at 4 A.M. in the forest near Priozersk, about forty miles from the Finnish border, before the arrests at the airport, and were charged with planning to join the others to hijack a plane and take it to Israel. Meri Khnokh later said that twenty men began shooting into the air in the darkness and "squirting gas into our eyes." The four were bound to each other, pushed into a truck, and taken to the Leningrad KGB. The conjunction of the arrests and confiscations strongly suggest a well-coordinated, preplanned police action, all the more so because of the quick reporting of the arrests at the airport. Normally, the Soviet press rarely publishes news about crimes, or, if it does, it is a long time after the event. In the late spring of 1970, Jewish dissident activity had spread and a policy decision was undoubtedly reached to organize a crackdown.

As to the events at the airport, there was no actual hijacking; the accused were arrested before they boarded the plane, but at their trial in December, they were accused of "betrayal of the fatherland," "responsibility for the preparation of a crime," "anti-Soviet agitation and propaganda," and "participation in anti-Soviet organization." In addition to the four arrested near Priozersk, the following were detained at the airport and arrested: Israel and Wulf Zalmanson, Edward Kuznetsov (Silva Zalmanson's husband), Yosif Mendelevich, Anatoly Altman, Mendel Bodnya, Mark Dymshits, his wife Alevtina and their two daughters, Yury Fedorov and Alexei Murzhenko. Mrs. Khnokh, who was pregnant, and Mrs. Dymshits and the two children were soon released and were not mentioned in the indictment. The others have become known as the "Leningrad Eleven," charged with planning to seize the plane and later tried in the first of many mass political trials involving Jewish activists.

As described by one historian,

the accused emerge as a mixed bunch of ardent young idealists, who had become burningly conscious of their Jewish heritage and wanted only to get to Israel and begin a new life. With them were one or two disgruntled hangers-on (one of whom may possibly have been a provocateur in the employ of the

KGB). They were led and organized by an older man, Major Mark Dymshits, who was a member of the Communist party until he was expelled when arrested. . . . [He] had served as a pilot in the Soviet armed forces. It was he who dreamed up the plot, recruited and organized the little group, and was to fly the machine to Sweden.[55]

The flight in fact never occurred, and Dymshit's role was subsequently viewed differently, but the indictment proceeded as if the whole plan had been successfully carried out. However, the trial did not commence until December 15. After the first brief announcement in June, there was a complete official silence surrounding the episode, but searches of Jewish homes in several cities—41 in Leningrad alone—and arrests continued. It seemed clear to many activists that the widespread arrests and confiscations had nothing to do with the attempted hijacking but were part of a deliberate plan to smash the Jewish national movement. Three letters focused on the arrest of eight Jews in the leadership of the Leningrad group and appeared in *Exodus* Number 2. One letter written by Viktor Boguslavsky to the Soviet Procurator General pointed out that "the searches were made with the object of 'removal of instruments of crime.' " Yet the "instruments" were merely letters and texts dealing with Jewish life. Invitations from relatives in Israel were also removed. The "evidence" of their "crime" had nothing to do with the airport incident. "What is their crime?" he asked. "My friends dreamed of hearing their own Jewish language from the mouths of their children. Is that a crime? No."[56] For his pains, Boguslavsky was arrested on July 9, and throughout the summer of 1970 activists in Riga, and Kishinev as well as Leningrad continued to be arrested.

The regime, however, was still twisting in a quandary it could not resolve. The momentum for emigration had quickened, but there was no consistent policy. Some applicants were refused permits; others were granted them. In sifting through official reactions and decisions, it was impossible to find a coherent pattern or underlying principle. The hijack attempt was to provide a convenient pretext for a wholesale attack on the Jewish movement, but it did not stop emigration. The regime could use all the powerful resources of press, radio, and control of opinion, but dissenting Jews were circulating samizdat, sending copies abroad, and applying for permission to emigrate.

At the time, a very strong statement attacking the official confusion was included in a petition to the USSR Supreme Court, in which the signers questioned what the court proposed to do about the "nonexistent Jewish question" that had become an "unhealing sore on the body" of the USSR. The question of emigration, it stated, is under constant attention by Soviet authorities and, indeed, the whole world. Does applying for permission to emigrate and efforts to "widen our knowledge of Israel" mean "furthering racial . . . hostility"? The slippery slope of Soviet law was then criticized. No one can be sure what precisely is "criminal." Proceedings are often started, it is charged, when "competent powers choose a given moment and some given people to frighten and [to] edify others." Only two alternatives are possible: "either let us depart in peace, or enter into the well-trodden path of mass reprisals. Because as long as we exist, we will demand the freedom to depart—and we will raise our voice louder every day and our voice will become intolerable for you." [57]

The voices of the activists were undoubtedly becoming "intolerable" to a regime that had never had to face such a bold, even defiant, challenge to its absolute authority. It could not allow the Leningrad episode to pass by without a clear, unmistakable message. [58] Very likely Stalinist hard-liners in the regime now began to speak out more stridently in official deliberations, aimed at inducing the masses—"first of all . . . the Jews"—into giving vocal support to the new Soviet military stance in the Middle East; equating Zionists with Nazis, and using trials and threats against Zionist dissidents instead of more measured ideological arguments. [59]

There was also a re-assertion of Zhdanovism in cultural and ideological matters. Certain party members and military leaders condemned the slackening of discipline and an "unhealthy independence of spirit among youth and intellectuals." [60] Zhdanov's ideas on politics and culture re-emerged in some circles and a generally repressive wave affected literature. In 1970, for example, there was a purge of the *Novi mir* staff and Alexander Tvardovsky, the liberal editor, resigned. The internal party debate over political and cultural policies very probably created the shifting, unresolved, and often inconsistent decisions regarding the Jewish activists. Intimidation and punishing harassment alternated with concessions. On the matter of the attempted Leningrad hijacking, however, the very harsh-liners prevailed—for the time being.

Meanwhile, throughout the fall of 1970, there was increasing anxiety among Western Jews about the fate of the Leningrad group awaiting trial and others who had been arrested. The issue of Soviet Jewry became more prominent on the agendas of Jewish organizations. [61] Those arrested became known as "prisoners of conscience"—a term borrowed from Amnesty International. Finally, on December 15, 1970, the case of the plane hijacking began in "open court," in the Leningrad City Court.[62] Many people—mostly Jews—came out in the cold and tried to gain admittance, but were told, "Go away. Don't disturb. Admission only on passes." Mainly party and KGB officials filled the 200 seats available, but some relatives were admitted. No Western observer or correspondent, however, was allowed in court. Eleven of the sixteen apprehended at the airport and at Priozersk were put on trial.[63] (Wulf Zalmanson was later tried and convicted by a military court.) Of the eleven, nine were Jews who had planned to flee to Israel. The two non-Jews, Murzhenko and Fedorov, apparently hoped to seek asylum in Sweden. What had motivated them to take such an extreme and illegal course? Except for Dymshits and Israel Zalmanson, all had applied for exit visas and had been refused. The result was a profound frustration and despair. Israel had not applied because he feared expulsion from the Riga Polytechnical Institute. Dymshits was motivated by personal experience of Soviet anti-Semitism, which prevented him from finding work in Leningrad as an airline pilot. He refused to go through the time-consuming procedures involved in applying for an exit visa and began to concoct schemes for escaping. A mysterious, unidentified person called "Venya," who was mentioned at the trial, introduced Dymshits to the leader of the Leningrad group, Hillel Butman, sometime in 1969, and Butman then introduced Dymshits to the Riga activists. "Venya," whose real name was never known, was summoned by a defense counsel as a witness, but the request was turned down by the court. Was "Venya" an agent provocateur who created the "indispensable link between a purely latent 'criminal' idea and the core of the Jewish national movement," thus discrediting and smearing it? The fact that the government has shielded "Venya's" identity lends credence to this hypothesis.[64]

Additional testimony at the Second Leningrad Trial in May 1971 (see below) and later information from released defendants and their families in Israel seem to confirm the belief that the crackdown was a KGB provocation. Conditions in the USSR militated against legal emigration; Leib Khnokh had been told, "You'll never get out until you grow old," while Mendelevich had been warned, "You'll rot here."[65] Moreover, it was reported that six months before their arrest, the Leningrad party boss told a group of party leaders not to worry about the Zionist organization: "At a suitable time and place soon, we will strike and destroy them."

A so-called "Testament," written by Mendelevich[66] and signed by the others, described the motivation of the group and was to have been released if the group were killed. It vividly describes the forlorn hopes of the group, their sense of desperation because of the "monstrous hypocrisy" of Soviet and international authorities, "the endless tragic situation of Jews in the USSR," and stresses that no harm will come to anyone if the hijacking succeeds.

However, the Leningrad group were convinced that the hijack plan would be harmful to their cause and tried to persuade Dymshits to give it up. They also found out that Israel was adamantly opposed to the scheme. But Dymshits would not be diverted, and the Riga group, despite certain misgivings, were pulled along by the dream of finally going to Israel. As Silva Zalmanson expressed it in her final statement to the court: "Some of us did not believe in the success of the escape or believed in it very slightly. Already at the Finland Station, we noticed that we were being followed, but we could no longer go back . . . to the past, to the senseless waiting, to life with our luggage packed. Our dream of living in Israel was incomparably stronger than the fear of suffering we might be made to endure. . . ."[67]

There is no Soviet law that specifically covers hijacking, but the defendants could have been charged under Article 83 of the Criminal Code, which deals with "illegal departure abroad" and carries a relatively mild penalty. Instead, they were charged with "betrayal of the fatherland" (treason), under Article 64a, which is subject to very heavy penalties, including death. They were also tried under Article 15, which deals with the "preparation of a crime," and Article 93 (1) dealing with "misappropriation of state or public property on a large scale."

The trial lasted until December 24. The Jewish defendants pleaded that they had no intention of harming the Soviet Union, that their only purpose was to reach Israel. Silva Zalmanson delineated the inconsistencies in the prosecution case: "I don't think that Soviet law can consider anyone's intention to live in another country 'treason' . . . . Let the court take into consideration that *if we were allowed to leave*, there would be no 'criminal collusion' which has caused so much suffering. . . . By going away we would not have harmed anybody. . . ."

A number of the defendants complained about distortions in pretrial interrogations and exhausting struggles with interrogators to produce accurate transcripts.[68] Much of the testimony was forthright and eloquent. The courage and solidarity of the defendants and their mutual concern for each other were in sharp contrast with the trials of Stalin's time. Dymshits, for example, said: "Our group . . . is made up of different kinds of people. Many of us had not met until the last days. And yet, it is good to see that even here, in the dock, we have not lost our human face. And we have not started biting one another like spiders in a jar."[69] Kuznetsov was sharp during the political questioning, but said that he was "extremely sorry that I agreed to take part in this affair. I appeal to the court to show understanding . . . of my wife Silva Zalmanson, and I ask for a just verdict. One lives only once."[70]

The prosecution summation devoted much time to the "intrigues of international Zionism" and the absence of a Jewish question in the USSR. It held that all but one of the defendants (Bodnya) were "unrepentenant" and had been prompted by anti-Soviet motives. The death penalty was demanded for Dymshits and Kuznetsov, and sentences from five to fifteen years for the others. Defense counsel asked for reduced sentences, emphasizing Jewish cultural motives and the absence of anti-Soviet intent.

The harshness of the sentences caused an immediate, unprecedented outcry in the West, including protests from Communist parties. Suddenly aware that the anti-Jewish nature of the trial was being exposed, the Soviet-managed press focused on "Zionist circles abroad whipping up anti-Soviet propaganda" and slander and alleged plans to use violence.[71] But the Kremlin was deluged with protests from political and religious leaders throughout the world, as well as from Jewish activists and the Soviet Human Rights Committee, headed by Andrei Sakharov. There were also mass demonstrations in many foreign cities and a National Emergency Conference on Soviet Jewry in Washington on December 30. Stunned by the intensity of world reaction, the government hastily arranged for an appeal of the verdict by the Supreme Court on December 29—just five days after the verdict was rendered. The government then found itself in a further embarrassing situation: on December 30, Franco had commuted the death sentences of Basque nationalists, whose trial the Soviet Union had steadily denounced. On the following day, the Supreme Court announced its decision: the death sentences were commuted to fifteen years, and several of the other sentences were reduced. The "specially strict regime" imposed on Kuznetsov, Federov, and Murzhenko, meant solitary confinement in a prison cell consisting of a plank bed, barred windows, and a "slop tank" (no plumbing). These prisoners were allowed one visit per year, but were not allowed any packages. Their daily food intake was about 800 calories. The "strict regime" imposed on Dymshits, Mendelevich, Khnokh, Altman, Silva and Israel Zalmanson, and Penson meant housing in a prison dormitory, one short and one long visit per year, one package per year, and permission to send one letter per month. The "enforced regime" for Bodnya was somewhat milder (see Photos 30.1, 30.2, and Map 24.1).[72]

By all measures, the sentences were very harsh, yet in reducing them,

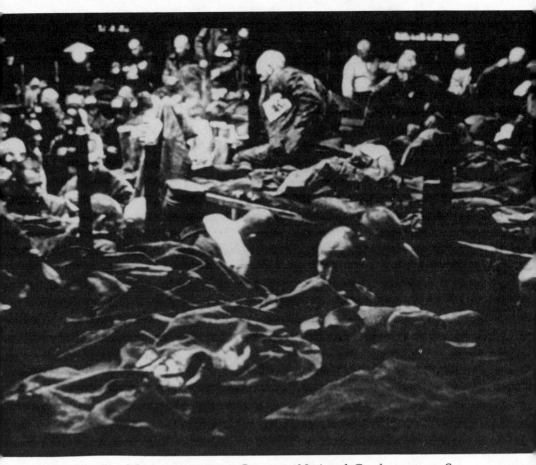

30.1 Siberian labor camp scene. Courtesy National Conference on Soviet Jewry, New York.

30.2 Siberian labor camp scene. Courtesy National Conference on Soviet Jewry, New York.

the Soviet regime had apparently bowed to world public opinion, and the trial, instead of intimidating and crushing the Jewish national movement, gave it greater vigor and spirit. The official secrecy of the trial had been dramatically exploded by the communications network the activists had developed, including contacts with Western correspondents. The Soviet Jewry struggle was now on the front pages of major newspapers around the world and the stage was set for the historic World Conference of Jewish Communities on Soviet Jewry—the Brussels Conference of February 23–25, 1971 (see Chapter 31).

Meanwhile, despite the waves of arrests, emigration, application rejections, sudden raids on apartments, and KGB harassment, a total of 14,300 Jews left the Soviet Union for Israel in 1971, as compared with 4,300 in the two-year period 1968–70. A marked upturn started in March 1971 and has been attributed by Mikhail Zand to a "victory won by the 'liberals' among the leadership over the so-called 'neo-Stalinist' leadership faction. . . . [T]he 'Jewish policy' advocated by the 'neo-Stalinists' had prevailed earlier, but was discredited when the Leningrad trial . . . failed to produce the desired result, i.e., intimidation of Soviet 'Zionists.' "[73] Moreover, in this view, Soviet leaders had not anticipated the magnitude of the adverse international reaction to the trial and harsh internal Soviet policies, thus giving the "liberals" more leverage in pressing for greater emigration quotas. If this interpretation is correct, then for several years thereafter, during which emigration figures ran a jerky course, there must have been serious internal conflict over the Jewish question. Moreover, continual Soviet interest in the Middle East and in gaining a role in the settlement of the Arab-Israel conflict could make use of increased emigration as a carrot to induce Israel to give the USSR that role. Conversely, it could serve to "overload the Israeli domestic budget" and add anti-Communist rightest Jews "to distort Israel's domestic political balance."[74] (The impression of many observers has been that, despite their immense gifts and talents, the absorption of Soviet emigrants in Israel has been costly and difficult.) The periodic reduction in emigration, in this context, may be a reassuring Soviet signal to the Arab states.

The heroic aura which is sometimes cast over the struggle of the activists often obscures the extreme emotional and economic toll exacted. The official emigration process, which would-be applicants have tried to understand and master, has been in itself an unfathomable, often capricious round of procedures which leaves the applicant exhausted, frustrated, and apprehensive. Regulations governing exit from the Soviet Union were passed in 1959 and amended on September 22, 1970 (effective January 1, 1971). An exit visa and passport for travel abroad are granted by stipulated ministries and republics on the basis of a written petition. For Jews who wish to go to Israel, a *vyzov*, or affidavit of invitation, must be secured from a relative in Israel. The vyzov must be notarized in Israel and taken to the Finnish embassy in Tel Aviv (which represents the USSR in Israel) for certification. It is then sent to the applicant in the USSR, who takes it to the local Office of Visas and Registration (Otdel Vizy I Registratsii—OVIR), where a detailed form has to be filled out and supporting documentation provided. What kind of documentation is required? It is here that a grinding, exasperating collision with the bureaucracy and Soviet system is experienced. A *karakteristika*, or character reference is required—from the head of one's factory or office, from a representative of the Communist party, and the appropriate trade union representative. If the applicant has not already lost his job, requesting the character reference may automatically cause him to be fired or demoted and labeled a traitor, or deserter, or worse. References for children in school or university are also needed and they, too, are often the targets of abuse and discrimination. All members of the applicant's family, including parents, must consent to the emigration; one refusal in a number of cases has blocked emigration. Approval is also required from the local committee supervising the apartment in which the applicant lives.[75] But assuming all of these details have been completed, they are only the beginning.

Under the 1970 amendments, Jews seeking to leave the Soviet Union had to surrender their citizenship, thus becoming stateless persons and requiring substitute travel documents bearing a valid exit visa instead of an official passport. There is also a payment of 500 roubles (about U.S. $560) for renunciation of citizenship[76] and an additional 400 roubles levied on stateless persons who wish to reside in countries other than those considered socialist. There was also a 30 rouble (later 40) filing fee. Then comes the wait for a call from OVIR—often lasting six months, then getting a rejection, an appeal, and another long wait of a year if there is another refusal.[77] Some Jews have applied a dozen times, suspended in life by a Kafka-like administrative machinery that is faceless, arbitrary, and inscrutable. Exit visas are supposedly issued by various government ministries, but for stateless persons, procedures have been set by the Ministries of Internal Affairs of the USSR and the republics and the internal affairs departments of local governments—in other words, the police, who are not generally known to identify with principles of human rights (see Photo 30.3).

Most infuriating and finally numbing is the absence of clear guidelines for acceptance or rejection. The 1970 directive

30.3 Emigration document, given to Mikhail Davidovitch on November 4, 1971, after years of waiting. Courtesy National Conference on Soviet Jewry, New York.

failed to shed the slightest light either on the practical details of how individuals seeking an exit visa could initiate and pursue their quest for the necessary authorization or what substantive criteria would guide the competent agencies in deciding whether to approve or reject such petitions. . . .[78]

Rejections can be explained on the grounds that certain jobs are "sensitive" or of military importance, that individuals constitute "security risks," or live in "closed areas," or because of concern for "the State interest," but these terms have never been precisely defined. If an application has been approved, many documents must be completed and fees paid and job, apartment, and school matters cleared up to official satisfaction within 10 to 25 days, sometimes within 24 hours. Then, in Moscow, at the Dutch embassy, there is a triple personal search and check by Soviet officials and a check of all goods leaving. Because a Jewish emigrant to Israel is neither a tourist nor a Soviet citizen, and has given up his apartment, he is unable to get a hotel room. If the family has no friends who can put them up, they may have to sleep on park benches for several nights. If the deadline is missed, the whole process[79] has to be started again.

Sometimes there is great suffering at the very end of the departure process, as in the case of Ulrikh Gait and his family from Chernovtsy.[80] Gait and his wife and child had received an exit permit on February 2, 1971. They had completed all of the documents, given up their apartment, paid the necessary fees, and received the exit and transit visas. All that remained was to buy railroad tickets. But just before the departure date, Gait was called in by OVIR and told to return his visas, without any explanation. Meanwhile, all of their belongings were packed and they could not earn any money. OVIR at first tried to persuade Gait to remain, but when he refused, they advised him to leave alone and presumably have a better chance to fight for his wife and child. He agreed reluctantly, and for months made appeals without avail. In other cases, parents have been arbitrarily prevented from joining children and vice versa. Others have been given a body-search until it is too late to embark. Yet the regime maintains that Soviet emigration procedures operate "in strict accordance" with Soviet laws and pertinent international agreements, including the 1966 UN International Covenant on Civil and Political Rights, and that the vast majority of persons applying to emigrate have been allowed to do so.[81] This has been the stock Soviet position but may change under Gorbachev.

While Jews who wanted to emigrate wrestled with unpredictable OVIR decisions, on May 11, 1971, the Second Leningrad Trial opened[82] involving the elite of the Leningrad Jewish movement, which had existed since 1966 and was the most highly developed in the country: Hillel Butman, Lev Korenblit, Solomon Dreizner, Lassal Kaminsky, Vladimir Mogilever, Viktor Boguslavsky, and Viktor Shtilbans, all highly educated men in various scientific fields and quite sophisticated in their organization of a full-fledged program of Jewish and Hebrew studies. They had been arrested for eleven months and had suffered relentless interrogation. At the trial, the prosecution stressed the involvement of the group with the hijacking scheme (although most had been vehemently opposed to the idea from the beginning, and all, by April 1970) and Israel intelligence, including efforts to recruit Soviet scientists. They were also accused of stealing a duplicating machine, and of distributing Zionist anti-Soviet literature. Zionist centers were also linked with events in Hungary in 1956 and with "counterrevolutionary forces in Poland and Czechoslovakia in 1968." It is generally assumed that the accused were under enormous pressure and duress to "confess" their guilt before the actual trial, during which the KGB had amassed a forty-volume protocol![83] Moreover, in the course of the trial, the defendants understood that the official definition of "anti-Soviet" literature had narrowed to anything not officially approved. Korenblit, a mature, philosophically oriented man, acknowledged this in his ironic admission of "guilt":

As has been dinned into me . . . since my arrest, 'anti-Soviet' is any suggestion that differs from the official Soviet line, anything that does not coincide with, or is contrary to, the letter of Soviet newspaper articles. In this sense, those articles that expressed sympathy for Israel and support for its struggle for existence are really 'anti-Soviet,' even though the Soviet Union might not even be mentioned in them. . . ."[84]

The defendants argued that their aims were never to harm the Soviet Union, only to fight against assimilation and obtain permission to go to Israel. However, their guilt was predetermined under Soviet interpretation of Articles 70 and 72 of the Russian Criminal Code. Sentences ranged from one to ten years' imprisonment—"lesser penalties", according to Tass, because of the "sincere repentance" of the defendants (see Photo 30.4).

30.4 "Prisoners of Conscience" in the early 1970s. Courtesy National Conference on Soviet Jewry, New York.

After the arrests of the Leningrad activists, there was confusion, shock, and sober re-assessment of the Leningrad movement's activity. Perhaps those arrested had been "brave but not careful," too "emotional" as compared to the cooler, more experienced approach in Moscow and Riga, too bold in wanting to do both open and underground work and to link up the work of many cities.[85] Mistakes in judgment were mulled over. Few leaders were left. Yet the movement recovered and new young people joined the activist struggle in Leningrad.

The next group trial, the trial of the "Riga Four"[86] took place from May 24 to 27, 1971. Again, the prosecution attempted to link their activity with that of the Leningrad hijack plan, although they knew nothing about it, and could not have had any involvement whatsoever. Four young, well-educated activists were accused: Ruta Aleksandrovich, the niece of Leah Slovin, a twenty-three-year-old nurse of strong will and delicate health; Mikhail Shepshelovich, a mathematician and physicist; Arkady Shpilberg, a design engineer and leading figure in the Riga movement since 1967; and Boris Maftser, a young engineer, who ultimately cooperated with the prosecution. Their ordeal began with the widespread arrests and searches of June 15, 1970, followed by intense interrogations and the accumulation of twenty-one volumes of "evidence." Maftser was kept incommunicado for ten months, one month longer than is legally permitted, and Ruta was grilled almost daily by the KGB. Ruta strenuously refused to cooperate and at the end of September wrote an open letter, "In the Expectation of Arrest," which began:

One after another of my friends are arrested and, evidently, it will soon be my turn. Of what am I guilty? I don't know how the charge will be formulated and what statute will come to the minds of my accusers. I only know that my conscience is clear. . . . I shall be put on trial only because I am a Jewess and, as a Jewess, cannot imagine life for myself without Israel. . . .[87]

Early in the morning on October 7, five KGB men entered the family apartment and ordered Ruta to come with them. In reply to the family's questioning, they were told she would be back home in a few hours. She was taken away by two men; the remaining three had the order for arrest and house search. One of the men said that she was accused of anti-Soviet agitation and propaganda. Maftser, who did admit his guilt (". . . Zionism is opposed to the Soviet national policy . . . to the political line of the party and government . . .") and gave details of his activities, later explained that he believed the government's whole case rested on the samizdat literature which the Riga movement prepared and distributed. After the arrests and searches the KGB had all of this literature. "They were particularly angry about *Iton*," he said. "They told me *Iton* could not be forgiven and they would find an occasion to punish us for it. It was not the book itself but the fact that Jews were publishing a periodical." Maftser's resistance was also weakened by the violent physical attack on his younger brother, his wife's loss of job after his arrest, his mother's death, the ceaseless interrogation, and isolation in jail. He wished, he said plaintively, that he could have been "more brave."[88]

The others, however, refused to confess. Thus, the authorities wanted to avoid publicity of the trial and tried to isolate it from the public. It was held far from the center of Riga, at "Fisherman's House," a large workers' building, with admission to the courtroom highly restricted. The Soviet press darkly hinted at an anti-Soviet conspiracy and tried to link the Riga Four with the hijacking attempt. The vital issue was the so-called slanderous literature, which the prosecutor said constituted "concrete punishable crimes," but which were never explicitly spelled out. The Hebrew words *Alef* and *Bet* after *Iton* apparently were highly suspicious. A leaflet called "Your Native Tongue," which urged readers to tell the census taker (in the January 1970 Census) they still spoke Yiddish to stop the forced assimilation, had also been prepared and was produced as evidence.[89] Much was also made of a questionnaire on anti-Semitism in the Soviet Union, drawn up by Mendelevich in May 1969, and discussed with Maftser but not seen by him or the other defendants, and discarded altogether.

Once more, during this trial there was immense interest in the West and widespread protests, including a suggestion from the BBC that student groups form "Free Ruth Aleksandrovich" committees, as they had done for Angela Davis, an American Communist who was being tried at about the same time in the U.S. In Riga, itself, sixty-seven Jews sent an open letter to the KGB and the local authorities, announcing their intention to hold a peaceful demonstration on the day the trial opened and asking them to provide a meeting place. Needless to say, this was not granted.

Noteworthy was the courage and sense of fairness of Shpilberg's counsel, A. I. Rozhansky, who demonstrated that there was an absence of intent on the part of the defendants, and lack of evidence on the part of the prosecution. But, in the end, all were sentenced to prison terms of from one to three years, which were considered relatively mild, possibly due to western public opinion.[90]

The last of the trials[91] linked to the hijacking attempt took place in Kishinev, once the capital of tsarist Bessarabia, the city of a horrible slaughter of Jews in 1903, and now (since 1940) the capital of the Moldavian SSR. There were about 130,000 Jews in Soviet Moldavia in the early 1970s, of whom about 55,000 lived in Kishinev, which had strong Yiddish and Zionist traditions. Moreover, many Moldavian Jews had relatives in Israel and the Six-Day War had an intoxicating effect on many young Jews. Jewish national consciousness had also been raised by the activity of two Moldavian high school teachers, Yakov Suslensky and Yosef Mishener (who was a member of the party for a time), who wrote open letters condemning the Soviet invasion of Czechoslovakia in 1968. Mishener was expelled from the party and both were sent to prison where they were later joined by activists from the Leningrad and Riga trials. There they renounced Soviet citizenship and went on hunger strikes in support of the Jewish movement.

In order to prove collusion between Leningrad and Kishinev, three Leningrad Jews were among the nine defendants: David Chernoglaz, Anatoly Goldfeld, and Hillel Shur. The six arrested youths from Kishinev were: Alexander Halperin, Semyon Levit, Khary Kizhner, Lazar Trakhtenberg, David Rabinovich, and Arkady Voloshin. They, too, were linked to the attempted Leningrad hijacking, the theft of a government-owned duplicating machine, and the preparation and dissemination of "anti-Soviet" literature. According to the brief account of the trial in *Chronicle of Current Events (Khronika)* Number 20, this literature included Leon Uris' novel *Exodus*, Howard Fast's *My Glorious Brothers*, and an unidentified item called "The Six-Day War." The prosecutor also stressed the *ulpan* (Hebrew language class) in Kishinev as a cover for an anti-Soviet organization and referred to the ulpan as "a school for future anti-Soviets."

In this case, too, the defendants told the court that "they never had any intention of weakening or undermining the Soviet regime, and that their involvement with the Leningrad group and . . . distribution of books and articles had solely an educational and cultural purpose." Apparently, all of the defendants except Shur were fairly moderate in their testimony, but Shur was openly defiant, claiming that the Kishinev Court was not legally entitled to judge him and that the chief investigator in Moldavia had tried to bribe him by promising a release on probation if he admitted his guilt. "The Kishinev Court is not competent to try me," he declared; "I have never been to Kishinev; not a single witness to the items . . . relating to me is a resident of Kishinev. . . ." Witnesses who were called, including Butman, Korenblit, Dreizner, friends of the defendants, and Jews from Kishinev, were not helpful to the prosecution. Some refused to testify altogether. Six of the defendants were found guilty under Articles 67 and 69 of the Moldavian Criminal Code, corresponding to those in the Russian Code. Chernoglaz, Goldfeld, and Shur were charged under the Russian Code. All were sentenced on June 30 to prison terms ranging from one to five years. Shur conducted a hunger strike during the trial and wrote a strong complaint to the Supreme Soviet from prison (see Photo 30.4).

The activities of the defendants in the various trials of 1971 constituted extreme dissatisfaction and frustration with, and criticism of, the regime and the desire to emigrate—activities normally engaged in and familiar in the West—but suggesting alarming and dangerous challenges in the Soviet Union. A tiny, fragile movement of several dozen young Jews desiring to know something about Jewish history and literature, to study Hebrew, and to emigrate to a Jewish state were perceived and described as a criminal conspiracy aimed at undermining the Soviet state. Yet, concomitant with the trials, was a sudden upturn in emigration, beginning in March 1971, possibly prompted by the official hope that if the Jewish leadership were decapitated through emigration, the body would die.[92] Each spurt in emigration as well as imprisonment has surely robbed the Jewish movement of many of its most devoted and gifted leaders, but new cadres seem able to replace them after a time. The aftermath of the First Leningrad Trial was one of many baffling cycles to come: a depleted leadership, more trials, and increased, then decreased emigration. The great emigration surge was to take place from 1971 to 1973.

31

The Jewish Emigration Movement and Western Support, 1971–76

We are confronted with a paradox here. We are not wanted here, we are being forcibly oppressed, forcibly denationalized, and even publicly insulted in the press—while at the same time we are forcibly kept here. As the Lithuanian proverb goes, "He beats and he screams at the same time."

It has been decided not to make public the surnames of the twenty-six signers of this document. We know well how people who had protested against flourishing anti-Semitism in the Soviet Union at one time or another were dealt with summarily. The Party has taught us to be watchful, and we have to be watchful now as we write to the Central Committee of the Lithuanian Communist Party.

What painful irony.

> The first letter from twenty-six Jewish intellectuals
> of Vilnius, Lithuania, requesting permission to emigrate
> to Israel to reach the West, February 15, 1968.

Since you are the object of an obviously organized campaign in the Soviet press and in certain sections of the foreign press, we Jews who are struggling for their right to emigrate to Israel and are familiar from personal experience with the bitter pain of lawlessness, and are particularly sensitive to the main theme of your activities—the struggle for human rights—wish to assure you of our moral support and deep respect. Thank you for your great heart, for your clear understanding of reality, and for your honesty. Can one be grateful for your honesty? Yes, for in the world in which we live honesty frequently requires courage, which is not granted to all. Your courage is so immense that its radiance chases away some of the darkness around us, and enables us to hope that reason will prevail over folly, justice over lawlessness, and good over evil. God bless you.

> Message sent to Sakharov in early September 1973
> by thirty-five of the leading Jewish activists.

Following or overlapping the trials in Leningrad, Riga, and Kishinev, there were trials of individual Jews—Valery Kukuy in Sverdlovsk (June 17); the librarian Raiza Palatnik in Odessa (June 22–24); Yemilia Trakhtenberg in Samarkand (September); Boris Azernikov in Leningrad (October 6–8). Some cases, like that of Raiza Palatnik, aroused enormous interest and response from the West; others, for example, those of Lilia Ontman and Dr. Yury Rennert of Chernovtsy; Arnold Finger of Alma-Ata; Leopold Grinblat of Minsk, and countless, unnamed others in remote as well as in well-known centers suffered under a shroud of silence or absence of public information and, therefore, of Western intervention. Prisoners and those on trial became better known if they had champions in the West or if their friends who had already been allowed to emigrate to Israel could take up their cause.[1] In the early seventies, Jewish activists also received strong support from the unofficial Soviet Committee for Human Rights and liberal intellectuals.

The Committee for Human Rights was founded in November 1970 by three distinguished physicists, Andrei Sakharov and Valery Chalidze, both non-Jews, and Andrei Tverdokhlebov, a Jew. Because the regime had persecuted people for forming organizations, even when none existed, the group defined itself as "a creative association acting in accordance with the laws of the land," offering "consultative assistance" to the government and "creative assistance" to persons engaged in research and the study of human rights problems. In the course of his activity, Chalidze had become a legal expert, and when the Committee was warned that it was illegal, he wrote a detailed rejoinder, even challenging the regime to institute legal action. In time, many ordinary citizens as well as activists appealed to the Committee for help.

Just before the Riga Trial started, Chalidze wrote a letter[2] to the Presidium of the Supreme Soviet calling the charges of "anti-Soviet activities" "ridiculous," and attacking officials for their "unlawful" acts in refusing visa requests. He also differentiated the aim of the Jewish activists—that of emigration to Israel—from the broader aims of the human rights movement and challenged the official Soviet ideology on the issue of Zionism, which he defended as a movement of national liberation of a perennially persecuted people. Chalidze then described the right to emigrate as fundamental, and the blocking of this right as "illegitimate." He called for an end to the persecution and imprisonment of those Jews who had been victimized and pardons for those convicted. Sakharov and Tverdokhlebov signed a statement supporting and accompanying the letter.

On May 31, Chalidze wrote to Premier Kosygin urging that exit procedures be simplified and, in a letter to Premier Golda Meir of Israel, asked that she take steps to halt "extremist manifestations" by Jews outside the USSR against the Soviet government. He also suggested the establishment of "direct consular relations" between the two governments.

Sakharov personally was deeply involved in the group trials—sending letters of protest and "open appeals" to officials and providing information to Western correspondents. He also stressed the psychological torment suffered by Jews who were refused permission, lost their jobs, were ousted from universities, and faced a future of lost hopes and harsh prejudice.[3] A prominent Soviet author, Lydia Chukovskaya, whose widely hailed novel *Sofia Petrovna* (in English, published as *The Deserted House*) deals with the Stalin terror, spoke out sharply against the trial of Raiza Palatnik. Among other supporters of Jews was Roy Medvedev, a "liberal Marxist," who was openly critical of the regime's policy of forcible assimilation, cultural repression, open and secret discrimination, and deprivation of the right to emigrate.

Outside the RSFSR, some nationalist movements struggling against russification have spoken out against anti-Semitism and the regime's deprivation of Jewish cultural rights. Some spokesmen among Armenians, Latvians, Ukrainians, Lithuanians, and Georgians have expressed their sympathy with Jewish national-cultural aspirations,[4] but few have openly supported emigration rights. Insofar as they suffer from restrictions on their own national development, they envy Jews for having a state of their own outside the Soviet Union.[5] Moreover, official permission to allow some Jews to emigrate has been deeply resented by most Soviet citizens, either because they, too, would like to leave, but cannot, or because for loyal citizens emigration is considered the recourse of disloyal people. At the same time, the exodus of Jews from such places as Chernovtsy, Riga, Georgia, and Vilnius, where thousands left within a one-year period, meant apartments, jobs, openings in universities, and less competition generally. It is impossible to measure the elements in this variable picture that have been helpful to the Jewish activist cause, or the weight given them by the regime, but in a purely personal sense, some Jews have felt supported in their emigration efforts by certain individuals within the Soviet Union. However, massive support in recent years has come from the outside— from the West, and especially from Western Jewry.

The first dramatic expression of solidarity between world Jewry and the struggle of Soviet Jews to emigrate occurred at the historic Brussels Conference of February 23–25, 1971.[6] Many crosscurrents of individual and organizational conflict lay under the surface of ostensible unity, but the conference brought together for the first time Jews from thirty-eight countries all over the world—760 delegates from every continent, including prominent Jewish organizational leaders, and eminent world figures such as Elie Wiesel, André Schwarz-Bart, Arthur Goldberg, Albert Sabin, Gershom Scholem, and David Ben-Gurion. Most poignantly, four Soviet Jewish emigrés opened the conference: former Soviet Army Major Grisha Feigin, a hero of World War II who had returned his medals in protest against the Soviet treatment of Jews and had been committed to an insane asylum (he was finally released and allowed to leave just two weeks before the Brussels Conference); Vitaly Svechinsky, a forty-year-old architect-activist who had spent five years in the dread Kolyma camps; Dr. Mendel Gordin, a young biochemist from Riga; and Kreina Shur, the younger sister of Hillel, awaiting trial in Leningrad.

Worried about the publicity and worldwide attention the conference was arousing (an International Secretariat to plan the conference had begun to meet in November 1970), Tass, on February 15, 1971, condemned the forthcoming meeting as an "anti-Soviet provocation." Three days later, Aron Vergelis, editor of *Sovetish heymland,* and Col. Gen. David Dragunsky, a Soviet Jewish career officer, warned in an open letter to the Government of Belgium, published by Tass, that the purpose of the conference was to "smear the socialist system and . . . complicate relations between the Soviet Union and Belgium." *Pravda* declared that a Zionist band, "preparing for an international anti-Soviet Sabbath" could never speak for "Soviet citizens of Jewish parentage."[7] The culmination of these attacks was reached when a group of Soviet Jews, including Vergelis and Dragunsky, came to Brussels to meet with newsmen, denounce the meeting, and deny the existence of anti-Semitism in the Soviet Union.

From inside Russia, other voices were heard.[8] On February 17, the telex in the office of the Secretariat pounded out a cable addressed in

Russian to the "Djuish Kongress Bruxelles." It was a simple greeting from Raia and Karl Frusin from Orel: "We wish you success and unity." Later that day, a longer message in English came from six Jews in Moscow, including the writer Yosef Kerler. There was also a telephone call from Kharkov sending blessings to the conference. Later it was learned that similar cables had been intercepted by Soviet officials. On the second day of the conference there was a telephone message from Moscow reporting that thirty Jews had gone to the Presidium of the Supreme Soviet with a petition appealing for the right to emigrate.

Only one man was not accredited to the conference—Meir Kahane, head of the Jewish Defense League—because he was viewed as aiming to disrupt the conference and resort to violence in behalf of Soviet Jewry. Lawlessness and violence were rejected by the conference, while the public struggle, in Golda Meir's words, "must be determined and incessant," without resorting to Cold War polemics. Five commissions were created at the conference to report on the possible roles of governments, jurists, non-government bodies, mass media, youth, and campus in carrying forward the cause of Soviet Jewish activists.[9] There was a continuous flow of supportive messages from world renowned figures and press coverage by over 80 journalists, catapulting the issue of Soviet Jewry to a central news position, which Soviet officials tried to deflect. Their efforts, however, merely inflamed interest and coverage, and were almost immediately followed by a sharp rise in the number of permissions to leave.

No international structure for coordinating activity in behalf of Soviet Jews emerged, but most of the delegates were electrified by the high emotional pitch of the conference and the new bonds being forged with individual Soviet Jews. In the last hours of the conference a Brussels Declaration by the World Conference of Jewish Communities on Soviet Jewry was read, identifying world Jewry with "the heroic struggle" of Soviet Jews, expressing profound concern for their fate and future and denouncing Soviet repression of the Jewish cultural and religious heritage. At the end, a frail old man, David Ben-Gurion, said simply: "I am certain this gathering will not be in vain. May you be blessed for demanding respect for the honor of the Jewish people."

Despite the inevitable disappointments and frustrations of such a conference, most delegates were newly energized by their experience and left eager to intensify their work in their respective countries. The issue of Soviet Jewry was now on the world agenda; the Jews in the free world would not be silent. An unprecedented challenge had been flung down to Soviet Russia, an insistent demand that Jews have the right to emigrate. At the same time, there was no discussion of the predicament of those Jews remaining in the Soviet Union, who did not want to or could not emigrate and were possibly suffering from the backlash of the emigration movement. Nor were the cultural needs of such Jews analyzed or persistently pressed.[10] Cultural and religious rights were demanded in the final resolution, but there was no strategy for a campaign. This issue would arise later in some circles but was not an important priority of the supportive organizations.

Following the Brussels Conference, there was a sharp increase in exit visas. Whereas only 4,235 Jews had been allowed to leave between October 1968 and 1970, 1,000 left in March 1971 and over 1,300 in April, making a total of 13,022 for the year. This increase is generally attributed to the impact of the Brussels Conference and/or the desire of the regime to get rid of the "troublemakers," in the hope, perhaps, of eliminating the movement for good. However, the increased exodus and ongoing trials gave new strength to the movement. Leonard Schroeter has suggested that there was an official "quota" plan.[11] In November and December 1971, on some days, two planeloads left the Jewish Agency transit facility at Schönau Castle, near Vienna, for Israel.

The period 1972–73 also showed a marked increase in emigration, likely reflecting eager Soviet pursuit of détente and trade with the United States, to help bolster its faltering economy, and possible concern over Western public opinion.[12] In 1972, emigration figures jumped to 31,903,[13] with the rate of approximately 2,500 per month continuing throughout 1973, reaching a record high of 34,733 for the year.[14] Yet, typically, these gains were countered by new harsh measures. In August 1972, an education surtax (sometimes called a "diploma tax") was decreed, requiring emigrants to reimburse state costs for higher education and advanced degrees—a practice earlier imposed upon Jewish emigrants by Poland and Czechoslovakia. For graduates of universities and institutes, these charges were exorbitant, ranging from 4,500 to over 12,000 roubles. From all accounts, very few ethnic Germans or other ethnic groups were required to pay these taxes; they were primarily directed against Jews. Undoubtedly, Soviet officials hoped the tax would deter better educated Jews. It was also expected that American Jews would pay the fees.[15] However, there was widespread criticism of the education tax in the West, and just at this time there were ongoing Soviet-American negotiations for a comprehensive trade and credit agreement (see pp. 703–5). The tax was largely suspended at the beginning of 1973. Yet it remains on the books and may again be invoked, thereby, in the words of a legal expert, "perpetuating the uncertainty which seems a favourite Soviet technique in this sphere. The entire scene is steeped in legal ambiguity, when it is not just a legal waste-land. . . ."[16]

In its continuing effort to block contacts between Soviet Jews and Western visitors, a new Soviet law issued on December 25, 1972, made it illegal for Soviet citizens to meet with foreigners and disseminate "slanderous" information about the Soviet Union.[17] Sporadically, visitors have been searched, with certain articles confiscated, and occasionally detained and forced to return home. The effect of this law, which can be variously interpreted, was to intimidate non-activist Jews.

However, contacts multiplied and applications for emigration increased. By 1972–73, a number of outstanding Jewish scientists in the Soviet Union, who had not earlier been drawn to the Jewish national movement and had, indeed, considered themselves fully assimilated, came into the ranks of the activists and joined the few pioneering scientific figures—Dr. Alexander Lerner, Dr. Benjamin Levich, Dr. Alexander Voronel, and Dr. David Azbel who had applied early and had been refused. In 1972, Professor Voronel started the pioneering Sunday Scientific Seminar and the publication of the samizdat periodical *Evrei v SSSR* (Jews in the USSR), demonstrating a new leadership role among the scientists. In 1973, seven scientists staged a hunger strike, proving that "scientists could be courageous, prepared for personal risk, and willing to speak candidly."[18] Their first international conference of the Sunday Scientific Seminar took place in August 1973 and involved forty-one Western participants. The second in 1974 was blocked by the KGB, who arrested some of the organizers, but the Sunday Seminar became an extremely important rallying force among the scientist-dissidents, involving ever-widening circles in the Soviet Union and prestigious scientists in the West.[19] (After 1975, presentations were given in the humanities as well as in scientific fields.)

Scientists such as Lerner, Voronel, Levich, Azbel, Yuri Golfand, Nahum Meiman, Alexander Lunts, Mikhail Stern, Solomon Alber, Dina and Yosif Beilin, Vladimir and Maria Slepak, Vladimir Kislik, Yuri Orlov, Eitan Finkelshtein, Victor Polsky, and Victor Brailovsky have suffered particular harassment and persecution in their efforts to leave (see Photos 31.1, 31.2 and 31.3). However, they sustained their weekly seminars to keep abreast of scientific developments through material sent to them from the West, to maintain their intellectual interests and remain in contact with Western scientists. Sessions have dealt with such topics as: cybernetics, radio-physics, the chemistry of polymers, quantum mechanics, and solid state physics.

Many of these intellectuals have had close ties with leading dissidents who were not part of the Jewish national movement, but supported it. Persecution of any of their number deeply hurt the Jewish activists, just as suffering experienced by the Jewish activists was painful to the others. The loosening of emigration restrictions was in no way accompanied by a corresponding loosening in surveillance or harassment. Indeed, the elite of the general dissident movement, includ-

31.1 Left to right, Yuli Kosharovsky, Hebrew teacher, Vladimir Slepak, and Victor Polsky, physicist (extreme right), meeting with Joseph Smukler in Moscow, 1974. (Polsky was allowed to leave late in 1974 and the Slepaks in 1987). Mr. Smukler was then Chairman of the Philadelphia Soviet Jewry Council. Courtesy Connie Smukler.

31.2 Among the scientist-refuseniks involved in scientific seminars—Yuri Golfand. Courtesy Jewish Community Relations Council of Philadelphia.

31.3 Scientist-refusenik Dr. Victor Polsky. Courtesy Jewish Community Relations Council of Philadelphia.

ing Jews, were being hounded, arrested, or exiled to Siberia or the West. In late 1971, it was decided to crush the network of "correspondents" and couriers involved in the production of *Chronicle of Current Events*. Two special targets were Pyotr Yakir, the son of a celebrated Red Army general who had been executed in 1937, and his friend Viktor Krasin. Both had become important channels of information. Yakir's fourteen years in concentration camps, his fear of a new sentence and of his own death in captivity led him to break down under relentless grilling. "If they beat me, I will say anything," he confided before his arrest in June 1972. "I know that from my former experience."[20] Yakir's daughter Irina told friends after visiting him briefly in prison that her father was "not himself."[21] "Scores of intellectuals in several cities," according to Hedrick Smith, "perhaps as many as 200, were interrogated and some forced into soul-wrenching confrontations with

Yakir and Krasin, who urged them to admit activities, some real, some false, because the KGB 'already knows everything.' "[22] The effect on dissident morale was shattering, particularly since Yakir was regarded as absolutely incorruptible. The crackdown also accentuated the always present fear that one's small circle might be infiltrated, poisoning personal relations and heightening the nervous wariness of dissidents. Later, the government would further rob the dissident movement of inspiring figures by exiling them to the West: Solzhenitsyn, Valery Chalidze, Yosif Brodsky,[23] Pavel Litvinov, Viktor Nekrasov, Andrei Amalrik, and Sinyavsky. At least one—Litvinov—is known to have been asked to work for the KGB.

If some elements in the Soviet hierarchy accepted the new reality of limited emigration, it was certainly not true of the KGB. A new KGB directorate, known as the "Fifth Chief Directorate" was established in 1966 or 1967 to deal with the increasingly "dangerous" dissent and charged with responsibility for specific segments of the population— "religious groups, the intelligentsia, nationalist groups and former political prisoners."[24] Sometime in 1970–71 a "Jewish Department" was created to concentrate on individuals and individual localities where Jews were known to be involved in dissenting activities.[25] One correspondent in Moscow heard that the entire 1973 graduating class of the KGB Academy was assigned to this quickly growing department.[26]

The KGB has made it particularly painful and difficult for Jewish scientists to emigrate, but many others have felt the lash of KGB harassment and intimidation. Every known coercive tactic has been put to use: mail and telephone monitoring and interference, censorship, unannounced detention and interrogation, employment blacklisting, house arrest, conscription for military service, character assassination, torture, threats of reprisals against family members, and the accusation of espionage.

Persecution and terror punctuated the process of détente (see below pp. 705–8) in a bizarre juxtaposition. The Brezhnev visit to Washington in June 1973, which formed part of this process, was preceded by the closing of an episode in Minsk, known as "Case No. 97." This action was very frightening to Minsk activists and caused great emotional anguish to several dozen Jews who were interrogated, many of whom were arrested. The case, sometimes referred to as the "Jewish officers' plot," pivoted around Col. Yefim Davidovich, a highly decorated hero of World War II, and several other Jewish officers, who were accused of conspiring against the state once they had registered their intention of emigrating to Israel. Beginning in 1970, Minsk activists had signed collective letters and petitions and by the summer of 1972, about 1,000 had left, but about 4,000 applications were still being held by OVIR.[27] Among the leaders were a group of middle-aged military officers including Davidovich, his friend Col. Lev Ovsishcher, Lt. Col. Naum Alshansky, and a 67-year-old artist, Gedalia Kipnis, a former Red Army major. Increasingly enraged and pained by the "unrestrained anti-Semitic orgy in the press," Davidovich began protesting to various Soviet bodies and calling on the press to "join actively in the struggle against anti-Semitism."[28]

In the summer of 1972, the Minsk Regional Military Registration and Enlistment Office threatened to deprive Davidovich of his rank and pension if he persisted in his "slanderous" activities. (He remained a member of the Central Committee of the Belorussian Communist party until October.) Such a downgrading had already hurt Ovsishcher, a wounded hero of Stalingrad with fifteen orders and medals, and Alshansky. On November 29, Gedalia Kipnis and his wife, who had received exit permits and were traveling from Minsk to Vienna, were stopped at Brest-Litovsk, searched and forcibly removed, and brought back to Minsk. Copies of Davidovich's notes and letters and a rusty 1941 pistol were found. The next month, Davidovich's home was searched, he was interrogated continuously, and charged with "undermining the Soviet regime by spreading . . . slanderous fabrications vilifying the Soviet social and governmental system."[29]

In January 1973, Vladimir Begun, a notorious anti-Semitic writer, wrote a long monograph called "Invasion Without Arms" for the monthly writers' organ in Belorussia, accusing Zionists of cultural aggression against the nations in which they live, of an international conspiracy, and of cultural subversion. That same month, Davidovich wrote to war veterans all over the world describing his ordeal:

My complaints to the higher bodies of the Soviet Union have remained unanswered. . . . For forty days, scores of KGB agents have been keeping my house under siege. . . . I have committed no crimes. . . . An attempt is being made to present my implacable hatred for anti-Semites and anti-Semitism as anti-Soviet. I consider that the fight against anti-Semitism cannot "undermine the Soviet system"—it is in full accord with the testament of V.I. Lenin. . . . An honest person cannot stand by and ignore the numerous Trofim Kichkos, Bol-shakovs, Yuri Ivanovs and Ivan Shevtsovs who appear daily in the pages of newspapers, brochures and books. . . slandering the Jewish people, and vio-lating the testament of Lenin as well as Soviet laws.[30]

Meanwhile, other Minsk Jews who had been permitted to leave were being detained, questioned, and told that they would be allowed to go if they signed statements implicating Davidovich.[31] By May, this num-ber reached fifty. A number of times after exhausting interrogations, Davidovich, who had a serious heart condition, had to have medical treatment. At one time he had to remain in the hospital for twenty-four days. A trial was obviously being prepared.

Davidovich again wrote to Brezhnev, demanding that Begun be prosecuted under Article 123 of the Constitution for instigating na-tional antagonism. *"The Protocols of the Elders of Zion* are innocent bab-ble,"* he wrote, "compared with the Begun article. . . . Yet a trial is not being prepared for him. . . ."[32]

Meanwhile, Kipnis remained incommunicado in prison for six months, and Jews from Vilnius, Riga, Khabarovsk, and Mogilev were being coerced to act as witnesses against Davidovich. Closed trials of Lazar Lyubarsky in Rostov-on-the-Don, and of Isak Shkolnik in Vinnitsa were taking place during this time, with similar nerve-wracking interroga-tions and threats. But in the case of Davidovich, public opinion and the press in Israel and the West gave the case a great deal of publicity. On May 28, just before Brezhnev was due in Washington, Kipnis was released from prison and Davidovich was told by the KGB that the file on Case 97 had been closed. Kipnis and his wife were allowed to leave in June; the others were left behind but not imprisoned. Davidovich died of a fatal heart attack in April 1976. Ovsishcher, who had applied to leave in 1982, was finally permitted to in September 1987.

The ambiguities and capriciousness of emigration decisions continued throughout 1972–73. Selective emigration alternated with selective in-timidation, and each trend waxed and waned with the fluctuating for-tunes of détente and trade negotiations at the time, but showed no consistent pattern. The issue of human rights in the Soviet Union—particularly the right of emigration—was injected into American-Soviet commercial negotiations and became a dramatic two-year struggle over the so-called Jackson-Vanik Amendment. In October 1972, President

Nixon authorized a trade treaty with the Soviet Union granting most-favored-nation tariff treatment. A counterproposal was introduced by Senator Henry Jackson in the form of an amendment to the Trade Reform Act, stipulating that "no non-market economy country [i.e. the USSR and other Communist countries] shall be eligible to receive most-favored-nation treatment or to participate in any program of the Government of the United States which extends credits . . . directly or indirectly [as long as it] denies its citizens the right or opportunity to emigrate," or impedes emigration by imposing taxes, fines, and other charges.[33] A similar bill was introduced by Representative Charles Vanik in the House of Representatives. A long, drawn-out political struggle ensued, involving the Administration, Congress, and American Jewry.

The Administration argued that such an amendment would represent a "grave danger" for Soviet Jews by creating more anti-Semitism—a threat that was intimated by Soviet official G.A. Arbatov when he warned an American audience that such an amendment would give Soviet Jews "a special status and treatment." (Sakharov termed this threat "blackmail.")[34] Secretary of State William P. Rogers and National Security Adviser Henry Kissinger preferred quiet diplomacy to achieve the desired goal without endangering the trade bill. A conflict developed between the Administration on one side, and Congress and American Jewry, which was mobilized and became actively involved in the public debate, on the other. To the argument that such an amendment represented interference in the internal affairs of a sovereign state, Senator Jackson replied: "By acceding to the 'International Convention on the Elimination of All Forms of Racial Discrimination' in 1969, the Soviet Union acknowledged that emigration policy goes beyond the limits implied by the term 'internal affairs.' "[35] Minnesota's Senator Hubert Humphrey pointed out that "what we are seeking to do here is not to obstruct trade but to uphold the cause of human rights."

Nixon, meanwhile, had earlier tried to win over Jewish support for his approach to détente, using the suspension of the "diploma tax" and staunch American support for Israel as strong arguments. (In March 1973, a 200 million dollar loan to the Soviet Union from the Import-Export Bank was granted and was thought to have been a concession which helped keep the tax inactive.)[36] The divided American approach on Soviet trade and aid caused a serious dilemma for many American Jews, but opinion steadily shifted in favor of the Jackson-Vanik Amendment. A massive public relations campaign[37] was organized by several major Jewish national organizations and groups working on behalf of Soviet Jewry. Soviet Jewish activists also entered the debate. When news about "an apparent ambiguity" concerning Jewish support for the amendment reached Moscow, there was a quick reaction. On April 23, 1973, over 100 activists sent an emotionally loaded appeal to American Jewish leaders urging their support of the amendment. To accept the principle, they said, that the USSR could arbitrarily select who would or could not leave "would have a tragic, irreparable effect and would mean a complete collapse of all hopes of repatriation for many thousands of Soviet Jews."[38]

As summer began, harassment of activists intensified. Jackson held his ground, writing in the *New York Times* that the argument was not basically between supporters and detractors of détente but rather over the "progress toward individual liberty"[39] as a basis for "a genuine era of international accommodation." Sakharov echoed Jackson's views in a letter released in Moscow on September 14, pleading that the abandonment of principle would be a "betrayal of the thousands of Jews and non-Jews who want to emigrate . . . and would be tantamount to total capitulation in face of blackmail, deceit, and violence. . . ."[40]

The Yom Kippur War, which began on October 6, 1973, further complicated the situation. Kissinger, now secretary of state, argued that the American objective of a ceasefire required Soviet support and that passage of the amendment would jeopardize it. Some Jewish leaders appeared willing to yield, while popular Jewish opinion was not. Whether continued support of the amendment might undermine continued American support of Israel posed an extremely delicate and troubling question. The president of the National Conference on Soviet Jewry, Richard Maass, vigorously decried the attempt to use the Jewish leadership as the lever in this executive-legislative struggle.[41]

Congressional determination remained strong and Deputy Minister of Foreign Trade V.S. Alkhimov, who was head of the Soviet delegation in Washington, realized that "we were not going to get most-favored nation out of this Congress." A visit by George P. Shultz to Soviet leaders in March served to clarify the limits on presidential power over trade, and is thought to have led to the suspension of the "diploma tax." But Brezhnev himself came to Washington in June and tried to lobby for his position (see Photo 31.4). In moves to silence protests during the July 1974 visit of President Nixon to Moscow, many Jewish activists in Moscow, Leningrad, Odessa, Kiev, Kishinev, and

31.4 Rally in Washington, D.C., sponsored by the Greater New York Rally Conference for Soviet Jewry at the time of Brezhnev's visit in 1973. Courtesy Greater New York Conference for Soviet Jewry.

other cities were arrested.[42] Many Jews were also confined to their homes under militia guard.

The three-way deadlock on the Jackson-Vanik Amendment persisted through 1974 until Nixon's resignation and the early administration of President Gerald Ford, in which two critical elements dominated: continued harassments of applicants and a 40 percent drop in the level of emigration, as compared to the level in 1973. Jackson pressed his position tenaciously, rejecting job dismissals and other extreme forms of Soviet intimidation and asking for a three-year limit on "security clearance" cases. Informal assurances by Soviet officials were made public on October 18, 1974, in an exchange of letters between Kissinger and Jackson. In return, Jackson agreed to add a provision to his amendment giving the President the power for eighteen months to decide whether conditions stipulated in the amendment had been fulfilled. The amendment was then to be extended year by year, with congressional approval.[43] The new version passed both houses overwhelmingly in December 1974, but the Soviet reaction was plainly cold and angry. On December 18, Tass asserted that "leading circles" in the USSR "flatly reject as unacceptable" any attempt to attach conditions on trade arrangements or to otherwise "interfere in the internal affairs" of the USSR. The Tass communiqué further denied that any specific assurances had been given in return for trade concessions and credits and a letter from Foreign Minister Gromyko to Kissinger, dated October 26, 1974, was published, accusing him and Jackson of giving a "distorted image of our position." However, it may not have been so much the Jackson Amendment as such that angered Soviet officials, but a measure placing a very low ceiling on credits to the Soviet Union.

On the very same day as the Tass communiqué, the U.S. Senate had adopted a bill which would have placed a $300 million ceiling on credits for a four-year period—$75 million per year, which one State Department official called "peanuts in Soviet terms." The public airing of a deal—in crude terms, Jews for trade benefits—was bad enough for the Russians. But the added humiliation of being offered a pittance in credits was intolerable. Ambassador Dobrynin was dispatched to express Moscow's strong dissatisfaction with the credit limitation, and although the Administration tried to have the ceiling removed, Congress prevailed and the breakthrough in emigration was lost. Emigration for the year 1974 decreased to 20,628 as it would annually until 1980, when it virtually stopped. The increases in 1972–73, in retrospect, may have been calculated "to sweeten the climate before Nixon came to Moscow, Brezhnev went to America, or Congress was about to take up trade legislation."[44] The opportunity vanished as Moscow decided that the gains were not worth the cost. President Ford signed the amended Trade Reform Act in January 1975. The Jackson-Vanik Amendment still remains law, but the subsequent arrangements under President Carter gave much wider flexibility to the definition of "adequate" emigration levels than had been pressed earlier. The Soviet government remained adamant.

A massive Diaspora organizational effort had been involved for two years in the campaign to pass the Jackson-Vanik Amendment, and its failure to bring the hoped for Soviet response was a blow to the emotional and intellectual resources of the supportive movements. Groups floundered for a new strategy[45] while experiencing great frustration over the Soviet slowdown of emigration and increasing harassment of activists.

In Moscow on January 20, 1975, 14 Jewish activists told newsmen that they were "somewhat disappointed, but not depressed, angry or apprehensive" over the Soviet cancellation of the trade agreement, but many Soviet Jews hoping to emigrate and Jewish supporters in the West were extremely discouraged and anxious. The Soviet dissident historian Roy Medvedev was sharply critical of Senator Jackson's tactics, charging that he "worked hard to make humiliating the difficult compromise that was achieved" and made "pretentious personal publicity for himself."[46] At the same time, Dr. Nahum Goldmann, president of the World Jewish Congress, argued that the adoption of the Jackson-Vanik Amendment had caused the decrease in Jewish emigration and criticized American Jewry for antagonizing the Soviet Union over the emigration issue.[47]

Among many Jewish leaders and supporters of the Soviet Jewry movement there was also a reaction of disappointment and depression over *neshira*, the "drop-out" trend (see Chapter 32) for which there seemed no remedy. This negative term, from the Hebrew *nosher*, (to fall out) was applied to those emigrants who chose not to go to Israel, but "dropped out" in Vienna and went on to Rome to await papers and transportation to the United States or some other Western country.

The sources of emigration have changed over the years, with the result that in the early seventies most Soviet Jews who left went to Israel; by the middle seventies, the sources changed as did the destination. Fewer went to Israel; more chose Western countries, particularly the United States (see Table 31.1). The first large wave of migration in 1971 came primarily from the "peripheral areas"—the Baltic states and Georgia, where Jewish national and traditional feeling were strongest. In that year only small numbers came from Moscow, Leningrad, and eastern Ukraine. In 1972, Bukharan Jews were permitted to leave, the exodus from the Baltic countries decreased, and the numbers from the Ukraine

TABLE 31.1
Soviet Jewish Emigration to Israel and Other Countries, 1971–81†

	To Israel: Numbers	Percentage of Total	To USA and Elsewhere: Numbers	Percentage of Total	Total Number	Number of First Vyzovs Sent per Person*
1971	12,839	(99.6)	58	(0.4)	12,897	40,794
1972	31,652	(99.2)	251	(0.8)	31,903	67,895
1973	33,477	(95.8)	1,456	(4.2)	34,933	58,216
1974	16,816	(81.3)	3,879	(18.7)	20,695	42,843
1975	8,523	(63.4)	4,298	(36.6)	13,451	34,145
1976	7,321	(51.1)	7,004	(48.9)	14,325	36,104
1977	8,348	(49.6)	8,483	(50.4)	16,831	43,062
1978	12,126	(41.8)	16,867	(58.2)	28,993	107,212
1979	17,614	(34.2)	33,933	(65.8)	51,547	128,891
1980	7,516	(35.0)	13,956	(65.0)	21,471	32,335
1981	1,820	(19.4)	7,580	(80.6)	9,400	10,922
	158,051	(61.6)	98,395	(38.4)	256,446	591,497

Source: †R. J. Brym, "Soviet Emigration Policy: Internal Determinants—The Changing Rate of Jewish Emigration from the USSR: Some Lessons from the 1970s," Soviet Jewish Affairs, Vol. 15, No. 2, 1985, p. 32. Figures vary slightly from those of the National Conference on Soviet Jewry, Table 32.1

Note: *Vyzov figures from National Conference on Soviet Jewry, New York. A total of 38,917 vyzovs were sent from 1968–70, making a grand total of 630,414 first vyzovs sent between 1968 and 1981.

and large centers in the RSFSR increased. By 1973, the proportion from the Ukraine, Belorussia, and the RSFSR rose somewhat again.[48] The sources of *aliya*, or immigration to Israel, for the whole decade of the seventies have been stamped by this pattern: Georgian and Bukharan Jews, constituting only about 6 percent of Jews (about 120,000) in the Soviet Union, have provided 37 percent of emigrants, 97 percent of whom have gone to Israel. The annexed areas, Bessarabia and the Baltic states, in which there were about 270,000 Jews, have comprised 46 percent of emigrants, 80–90 percent of whom have gone to Israel. The most highly assimilated Jews from European Soviet Russia (about a million and a half in the large centers such as Moscow, Kiev, Leningrad, and Odessa) comprised only 17 percent of the emigration, and increasingly, they chose the West as against Israel (see Tables 31.2 and 31.3).[49]

In the second half of 1973, emigrants arriving in Vienna with visas for Israel began to make their destination the United States. By the end

TABLE 31.2
Jewish Emigration by Republic,
1968–80

Republic	Number of Visas
RSFSR	35,702
Ukraine	91,656
Belorussia	10,469
Uzbekistan	16,247
Moldavia	27,376
Georgia	32,926
Azerbaidzhan	7,244
Kazakhstan	375
Latvia	13,153
Lithuania	11,615
Tadzhikstan	2,981
Kirghizia	320
Estonia	551
Turkmen	113
Armenia	91

Source: Z. Alexander, "Jewish Emigration from the USSR in 1980," *Soviet Jewish Affairs*, Vol. 11, No. 2, 1981, p. 11.

of the year, 4.2 percent of the 34,933 emigrants went there or to some other Western country.[50] There were also some who reportedly wanted to return to the USSR, only a few of whom were re-admitted.[51]

The shift to the West became more pronounced in 1974, when 18.7 percent of the 20,695 emigrants chose not to go to Israel, 36.6 percent in 1975, and 48.9 percent in 1976.[52] This new pattern was a reflection of the shift in the source of emigrants and of practical problems confronting them in Israel. The absorption of Soviet Jews in Israel has generally been considered positive, effective, and relatively successful, but undoubtedly a number of newcomers have had severe difficulties.[53] These are enmeshed in the economic, military, social, and political problems facing Israel, which are reflected in a certain bureaucratic insensitivity and impatience with or lack of understanding of the varied cultural and psychological backgrounds of the newcomers. Especially difficult was the great gap between their soaring expectations and hopes before emigrating and the practical, sometimes painful, day by day adjustments involving language, climate, food, attitudes toward author-

TABLE 31.3
Percentage of Jewish Population
Receiving Visas, by Republic,
1968–81

Georgia	60.0
Lithuania	50.1
Latvia	36.4
Ukraine	12.0
Belorussia	7.4
RSFSR	5.0

Source: Z. Nezer, "The Emigration of Soviet Jews," Soviet Jewish Affairs, Vol. 15, No. 1, 1985, p. 23.

ity, transportation, employment, housing, and the very real confusions of freedom. Very little information about the real Israel had been available in the Soviet Union, and the postcards, maps, and stamps which had been so dearly cherished, and Israeli-beamed Russian language broadcasts aroused a highly romanticized image which no reality could possibly match. Israeli expectations, too, were unreasonably high, with many Israelis anticipating immediate gratitude and loyalty from the new immigrants after so many years of anti-Jewish repression.[54]

The shift away from Israel aroused much disappointment and considerable bitterness in official Israeli circles, among many "refuseniks," those whose applications to leave had been refused, and among a number of the Jewish organizations involved in support of emigration rights. Various proposals to stop the exodus to the West and redirect it to Israel became insistent and acrimonious by 1976 (see Chapter 32), but even earlier positions diverged.[55] Israel argued that the whole underpinning of the emigration movement had been: "Let my people go" to the Jewish homeland, that the deflection to the United States and other Western countries had caused a drop in numbers permitted by Soviet authorities and was hurting the movement generally. Others argued that the reasons for the decline were linked with Soviet national interests and internal factors, mainly the danger of a runaway emigration infecting other discontented national minorities and the loss of valuable Jewish manpower, especially in science, engineering, and mathematics.

Some Jews were also having second thoughts about the leverage of the Jackson-Vanik Amendment and raising questions about the reliance on public relations strategies to influence Soviet decisions (see Chapter 32). The fate of Soviet Jews seemed to have been pushed completely onto the tilting chessboard of American-Soviet diplomacy, making them counters in the global contest between the two superpowers and objects of trade-offs: American technology, long-term credits, and trade in return for increased emigration. However, the establishment organizations followed the pro-Israel policy of concentrating on emigration to Israel, and although the Union of Councils for Soviet Jews encouraged sending Jewish cultural materials to Soviet Jews through a "Right to Identity" campaign, such a program never took hold. Western Jews held demonstrations, met with their legislators, held public relations-oriented events, wrote to Soviet Jews, and encouraged visits to the Soviet Union to meet with activists. Visitors brought books, religious items, tapes of songs and traditional prayers, Jewish stars, vitamins for prisoners, and articles of clothing—especially denim slacks—that needy families could sell for food and other necessities. The visits sustained human bonds for the activists, reassured them that Jews in the free world cared deeply about them, and thereby let Soviet officials know about this interest and concern. Synagogues adopted refuseniks, and many Jews began writing to them, trying to keep their morale up, and letting Soviet authorities know that the outside world was concerned.[56]

Professional organizations were also drawn into the cause of Soviet Jewry. American scientific and academic communities formed a Committee of Concerned Scientists to undertake activities on behalf of Soviet intellectuals and scientists and keep its members informed of their status. The first newsletter of the Committee, called *Current*,[57] was issued in March 1973, protesting the "diploma tax" and reporting the many letters sent by large groups of distinguished mathematicians, urging its revocation. Five thousand academicians and scholars joined "in support of the efforts of Soviet scholars to overcome their government's repressive policy against emigration, and against those educated persons who seek to emigrate." There were also reports of actions taken by a Conference on Magnetism in Denver, the International Sixth Texas Symposium on Relativistic Astrophysics in New York City, the Dade County Medical Society, and the American Physical Society. There were strong protests against penalties suffered by Soviet scientists and the danger posed to continued international exchanges. A whole

31.5. Dr. Benjamin Levich and wife Tanya in Israel. Dr. Levich was a high-ranking scientist in the Soviet Union who was finally given permission to emigrate in 1976. He died in 1987.

section of the scientific community was devoted to the precise situation facing Soviet scientists: Boris Einbinder, David Azbel, Victor Polsky, Benjamin Levich, Alexander Lerner, Vladimir Roginski, Yevsey Ratner, Alexander Voronel, Benjamin Shapiro, and Victor Mandelzveig. Some had had their telephone lines cut, some had been in prison for "violating pubic order" and "parasitism"; all had lost their posts because of applications to emigrate (see Photo 31.5).

The newsletters grew in size from issue to issue, involving more individuals and professional societies, and adding more details about the beleaguered scientists and intellectuals in the Soviet Union, including their addresses and the lengthening list of "Prisoners of Conscience"— innocent individuals, many of them scientists, who had been subject to harsh prison sentences. The efforts of unemployed Soviet scientists to maintain their intellectual integrity and high standards of inquiry as well as make contributions to scientific knowledge were noted in a summary of work done by the Moscow Seminar. The Seminar was organized by Viktor Brailovsky and conducted weekly lectures in physics, biology, linguistics, and sociology. Reports of conferences involving Soviet scientists and invitations by American universities to Soviet scholars in the application limbo were also included.

American congressmen were also drawn into the struggle personally, in visits to refuseniks in connection with official missions and as adopters of individual families. In the mid-seventies there were frequent columns in the *Congressional Record* by interested congressmen such as Edward Kennedy, Millicent Fenwick, Joshua Eilberg, and Robert Drinan. A number, including Kennedy, Drinan, Pat Schroeder, Henry Waxman, Bob Carr, Margaret Holt, Charles Vanik, Elliott Levitas, and James H. Scheur (who was expelled from the Soviet Union in 1972 for ostensibly "inciting" Soviet Jews to emigrate to Israel), have visited with activists, bolstered their cause, "adopted" them, brought and taken materials to help publicize their situation, and undertaken "Congressional Vigils." (These actions have continued in recent years.) A number have also appeared at special conferences and workshops in Washington dealing with the Soviet Jewish problem and have met with Soviet officials to plead their case.

An astonishing variety of organizations all over the world has also become involved in the plight of Soviet Jewry: among others, the Dutch Academy of Sciences, the French Scientific Committee, the Physicians' Committee of the French National Council for the Protection of Soviet Jewish Rights, the Canadian Committee of Scientists and Scholars, the National Interreligious Task Force on Soviet Jewry, the British Council of Churches, the International Union of Pure and Applied Physics, Equity British Actors' Union, the International Association of Lawyers, as well as numerous governmental figures.

There was also an unusual project undertaken by Telford Taylor, law professor and member of the prosecution staff at the Nuremberg Trials in 1946, and a number of colleagues, who wanted to challenge the validity of Soviet criminal proceedings in the context of Soviet law. Several of them went to the Soviet Union beginning in 1967 and others in 1970, in the wake of the first Leningrad Trial. Interviews were carried on with relatives of the accused and with some of the accused themselves in Israel, after they had been released, to ascertain basic facts about Soviet legal procedures and violations. Dr. George P. Fletcher, a specialist in Soviet criminal law, and Professor Alan Dershowitz of Harvard subsequently drew up memoranda on Soviet criminal procedures. The team then began preparing petitions containing documentation of false indictments and irregular trial procedures, and pertinent affidavits for nineteen cases. Much material was focused on violations of the right to counsel, the meaning of the charge of anti-Soviet propaganda, conditions of confinement in the labor camps, and the definition of treason. Taylor tried to appeal personally to the Procurator General Roman Rudenko (who served with him at Nuremberg) to consider the documentation and review the cases, but to no avail. Instead, the story of the group's efforts and the documentation were published in 1976 in the book, *Courts of Terror*.[58] Taylor concluded that

the Soviet State had a strong interest in condemnation and punishment, and it applied pressures which badly fractured the rules for the conduct of trials and the confinement of prisoners. . . . It was State policy to discourage Jewish emigration without appearing to prohibit it. . . . Whatever the basis of the accusations, the State had a government interest not only to ensure conviction and punishment . . . but to warn other potential emigrants that they might meet a like fate.[59]

In the early seventies, during the fluctuating process of détente, despite these express and implied warnings, harassments, trials and imprisonment, as emigration waxed, so did the number of vyzovs and applications to emigrate, with the latter always far exceeding the number who left. From 1970 through 1976, 284,827 first-time vyzovs were received, while during the same period, 114,312 Jews left the Soviet Union.[60] Moreover, a large number of Jews, not included in these figures, had received several vyzovs by 1976. Besides the ongoing applications to emigrate, there continued to be demonstrations, protests, and petitions to Soviet institutions, Western and international bodies, and political leaders. A scientific and intellectual elite emerging in Moscow began to engage foreign correspondents and report these activities and official replies in detail.[61] For some of the activists, however, as the wait for exit permits stretched out, they realized their stay in the Soviet Union might be long, possibly forever. Recourse to protests and

31.6 A group of young Leningrad Jews celebrate Shabbat, 1976.

hunger strikes shifted to study, study of Hebrew, Jewish history, and religious literature as well as scientific material (see Photos 31.6 and 31.7). This shift was also influenced by the generally bleak cultural scene and by the crackdown on and emigration of renowned individuals.

During the early 1970s, Hedrick Smith, the *New York Times* correspondent in Moscow, reported that the general Russian cultural scene was impoverished: there was very little interesting writing; young writers were apprehensive; the deadening cultural conservatism drove writers into conformity or exile, and dancers such as Mikhail Baryshnikov and Valery Panov, to defect or apply to emigrate.[62] Voznesensky lamented the "fast of the spirit." Pasternak was still being read privately, and

31.7 Leningrad activists celebrate Purim, 1976.

there were forbidden pilgrimages to his gravesite. Nadezhda Mandelshtam had become a "living archive" of her husband's poetry, reciting lines from memory for hours to adoring listeners, fearing that the crackdown on *Chronile* would also trap her. Alexander Galich, the Jewish underground balladeer, who sang about canned propaganda, the labor camps, and anti-Semitism, was expelled from the Writers' Union late in 1971 for encouraging people to emigrate and was blacklisted. (Finally, as a result of an international campaign, he was allowed to emigrate in 1974.)

This was also the time of Solzhenitsyn's ordeal, of attacks on him as a traitor and renegade, his arrest and then forcible exile, and the harsh punishment of dissident Slav religious groups. In the fall of 1973, Sakharov was subjected to a barrage of denunciations and threatened with confinement in a mental institution. From 1968, when his paper, "Memorandum," (later published as *Progress, Peaceful Coexistence and Intellectual Freedom*) leaked out to the West, through the time of his marriage in 1971 to Elena Bonner, Sakharov had become more and more skeptical of socialism and the possibilities for reform within the Soviet Union. He took on the struggle of all who were persecuted and believed that only Western pressures could save them. Détente, he was convinced, without conditions and qualifications set upon the USSR, "would pose a serious threat to the world as a whole."[63] A shy, utterly unpretentious man, Sakharov is often considered a naive eccentric, but to hundreds who had been cast out of the Soviet system, he had become a lifeline. Day after day, while he still lived in his shabby two-room flat in Moscow, phone calls came from Ukrainian nationalists, religious dissenters, writers and artists being committed to mental institutions, dissidents and refuseniks. "For each, Sakharov sits down and painstakingly writes out a statement of support. . . . Or . . . he stands vigil outside a courtroom where a political prisoner is being tried." Of the usefulness of his activity he has said, ". . . even if what I am doing will not produce change in my lifetime, it is not useless because it is a moral act. It is being true to what I believe in and must do."[64]

During the officially inspired campaign and newspaper persecution against him in August-September, 1973, Jewish activist leaders rallied behind him: Drs. Benjamin Levich, Alexander Voronel, Boris Einbinder, Alexander Temkin, Mark Azbel, and Boris Orlov, among them, issued an open letter of support, and other Jews in Kiev and Novosibirsk publicly described Sakharov as "an example of true patriotism, humanity, and the highest moral principles." However, so effective were the regime's mechanisms of control that few of the most prominent scientists and intellectuals stood by him. One who did and suffered for it, Valentin Turchin, has testified to their collective vilification of Sakharov, cynicism, and posture of moral compromise so as not to lose favor themselves and the opportunities for travel to and contacts with the West.[65] Turchin himself was fired from his job at a prestigious computer institute. Chalidze, having been given permission to lecture in the United States late in 1972, was suddenly deprived of his Soviet citizenship and was forced into an exile that he did not want. Many lesser known men and women who had signed petitions in the past lost their jobs, and found themselves ostracized and economically blacklisted. Dissident morale had already been shattered by the KGB-instigated confessions of Yakir and Krasin and the arrests of many people linked or not necessarily linked to the *Chronicle* in 1972. (In November, the KGB used Yakir to say: "If Number 27 of the *Chronicle* comes out, a person not necessarily having any connection with it will be arrested.") The Yakir case involved his close connection with the *Chronicle*, its publication, distribution, and suspension for a short time after issue Number 27. The KGB had apparently succeeded in provoking fear that dissident groups were being infiltrated or corrupted. Older dissidents such as Sinyavsky, Daniel, Marchenko, Ginzburg, and Litvinov returned from prison or exile, subject to new fears and threats. Nor were new blows missing. Amalrik, for example, who was due to end his earlier three-year sentence on May 21, 1973, was sentenced to a further three years in a labor camp—later exile—for "defaming the Soviet state." The thirty-three-year old poet Yuri Galanskov died in the Potma labor camp, November 4, 1972. Another shattering loss was the suicide on October 20, 1973, of Ilya Gabay, a close friend of Yakir and active member of the human rights movement. Ginzburg was exiled April 4, 1974, and Tverdokhlebov was arrested a year later. In 1974–75, a deepening futility spread throughout the human rights community, broken only somewhat by the seeming protection of Sakharov by the West (see Photo 31.8).

In September 1973, the onslaught against Sakharov ended abruptly following protests from Western political leaders and a warning from the head of the U.S. National Academy of Science that continued harassment of Sakharov would seriously harm scientific exchange between the United States and the USSR. He continued, however, to be attacked, sometimes physically, for his courageous leadership of the Moscow Helsinki Group, and for his support of all persecuted dissidents and Jews struggling to leave the Soviet Union.[66]

The West seemed able for a time to protect Sakharov from the worst, (until his arrest and banishment to Gorky in January 1980), but it had arguable influence over the fate of hundreds of other dissidents and refuseniks. Yet their spokesmen perceived Western concern as having immense value to their cause, as being their vital lifeline, and kept urging that it be sustained and increased. The regime was just as determined to convince the dissidents and refuseniks that Western support had declined. Among others, the distinguished mathematician and refusenik Dr. Alexander Lunts, threatened with prosecution under treason charges, was told in 1975 that "the West has forgotten all about

31.8 Dr. Eleanor Holmes-Norton, then Chairperson, U.S. Equal Employment Opportunity Commission (standing right) and Philadelphia leaders in the Soviet Jewry Council; Enid Wurtman (standing left) and Connie Smukler (sitting), meet with Andrei Sakharov, Elena Bonner-Sakharov, and Anatoly Shcharansky, 1977, in Moscow. Courtesy Connie Smukler.

you." Lunts called 1975 "the black year," a year of intensified repression following the Soviet failure to prevent passage of the Jackson-Vanik Amendment and lowered credit ceilings (see Photo 31.9). He said the Soviets "felt themselves cheated and were not going to give their Jews away for nothing." They "were preparing for a compromise on emigration. But they had contingency plans to attempt to deal the aliya movement a death blow."[67] Yet emigration was not stopped. During the

31.9 Alexander Lunts, mathematician-refusenik, meeting with Joseph Smukler in Moscow, 1974. Courtesy Connie Smukler.

next three years, Jewish emigration averaged 15,000 per year.[68] More-over, on January 16, 1975, just two weeks after President Ford signed the Trade Reform Act, the USSR said that it wished to continue détente and maintain good commercial relations with the United States despite its rejection of the 1972 trade agreement. Officially, it also maintained, in the face of evidence to the contrary, that virtually all Jews who wanted to leave had received permission.[69]

The Jackson-Vanik Amendment had failed to change basic Soviet policy, and the gyrations of détente, the uncertain future of emigration and the mocking contradictions between Soviet words and deeds took their toll in activist ranks. Nerves became more frayed, hopes wore thin, personality differences rankled, and the loss of purposeful work for many eroded self-confidence and destroyed a crucial structure of life. At the same time, increasing numbers of seemingly assimilated, Russified, mature Jews with prestigious jobs were applying to leave because their children were suffering abusive anti-Semitic slurs and beatings[70] and because Soviet society no longer offered them a future.

Fear of a punitive military draft inhibited some families with older sons (between 17 and 30) from applying, and in many cases, this threat was carried out if the family applied, even though the men had been previously exempt. "It was difficult to explain the situation to Westerners," Lunts commented, "to make them understand that we were not out to break Soviet law. . . . We do not seek special privileges, but neither do we wish to become a target for discriminatory measures. Had the young men involved not applied to go to Israel, they would never have been called up."[71] The absence of consistent, predictable criteria for emigration and the maddening capriciousness of local officials left many applicants exasperated and exhausted. Petitions for consistent regulations and procedures were ignored. Yet Soviet officials insisted they existed.

"There are, of course, rules determining the emigration procedure of Soviet citizens," declared Boris Shumilin, deputy minister of internal affairs, in a special article in the *New York Times* of February 3, 1976. They derive from the International Covenant on Civil and Political Rights, adopted by the UN General Assembly in 1966 and can be restricted "in cases connected with the protection of state security, public order, health or moral standards of the population." Thus there can be delays if persons possess "state secrets"[72] or if they have recently undergone military training. However, according to Mr. Shumilin, as of January 1, 1976, decisions were postponed only in 1.6 percent of cases involving Jewish applicants. Reunification of families was and remains the basic principle associated with emigration, according to Mr. Shumilin, but activists cannot find consistent operative criteria they can rely on. Decisions vary from city to city, from official to official.

In 1975, there was a further dramatization of the Jewish emigration issue on a world stage in the discussions that led to the so-called "Helsinki Accords" on security and cooperation in Europe and human and minority rights. Thirty-five nations, including the Soviet Union and Eastern bloc countries, participated. On August 1, 1975, in Helsinki, the signatories reaffirmed their commitment to the principles in the UN Charter and the Universal Declaration of Human Rights. Special emphasis in the provisions of the Final Act was given to freedom of emigration, especially to those persons "who wish to be reunited with members of their family." Such applications were to be dealt with "as expeditiously as possible" and fees charged "at a moderate level." Re-applications were to be considered "at reasonably short intervals."[73]

The Helsinki Agreement is not legally binding, but was meant to carry "considerable moral and political persuasion."[74] Reunification of families and marriages between citizens of different states are chiefly stressed in defining the right of external travel. In response, the Soviet Union lowered the exit visa fee and the character reference was changed from local party leader to job supervisor. However, the gain for the Soviet Union at Helsinki was enormous, namely the recognition of her post World War II conquests in Eastern Europe, thus confirming the existing territorial status quo in Europe. A freer and wider dissemination and exchange of information and the right of national minorities to equality under the law and to various cultural activities were also included in the Final Act. These provisions were frequently invoked in the attempts to gain liberalization of emigration and cultural rights, but the Soviet Union was little moved to respond. A Public Group to Promote Soviet Implementation of the Helsinki Final Act was formed by activists in Moscow under the leadership of Yuri Orlov in May 1976, and they made their protests valiantly, but were made to suffer greatly for them (see Chapter 32). Other Watch Groups were formed in the Ukraine, Lithuania, Georgia, and Armenia,[75] to help persecuted churches such as Pentecostals, and a Working Commission to Investigate the Use of Psychiatry for Political Purposes was also formed (see Chapter 32). Sakharov, Ginzburg, General Pyotr Grigorenko, Lyuda Alexseva, Malva Landa, and Marchenko (in exile in Chuna) were the original members of the Moscow Group. Orlov then recruited a young activist, Anatoly Shcharansky, who knew many Western journalists, and Vitaly Rubin, an internationally known sinologist, a refusenik since 1972, to represent the Jewish emigration movement. These groups helped to reinvigorate the human rights movement in the Soviet Union. Moreover, they could act openly, sign their reports, and send their appeals directly to signatory governments. However, the regime had no intention of allowing the groups to function. Orlov was quickly picked up by the KGB and warned that his group was "illegal." The apartments of the monitors were searched; many were harassed; some were arrested. However, Soviet violations were publicized and in some instances the regime had to back down or change its tactics.[76]

Ironically, at the time of the signing of the Final Act, the Helsinki Agreement was hailed in the Communist world as the greatest event since the defeat of Hitler. The West was skeptical. However, in subsequent years, positions reversed, and by the time of the follow-up conference in Belgrade (October 1977), the Soviet Union had become uncomfortably defensive.[77] It had become clear that an immense gap existed between East and West on the meaning of the Helsinki Final Act and the approach of each side toward compliance. For the West, Helsinki "placed on the international agenda, for the first time, important issues affecting the daily lives of ordinary people [such as] freedom of movement, the reunification of families, the free availability and exchange of information . . . and . . . individual as well as institutional contacts in the field of culture and the sciences."[78] The Soviet Union, however, uses the rubric of "non-intervention" to prevent penetration of these regions. A new law of June 23, 1975 introduced serious curtailments of religious activity[79] and in the same month, Intourist announced that "tourist-Zionists" would be regarded as "interfering in Russia's internal affairs."[80]

Another large international conference on Soviet Jewry—the largest to date—was held in Brussels from February 17 to 19, 1976.[81] Twelve hundred delegates came to "Brussels II" from every Western country with an active Jewish community and Soviet Jewry movement—32 countries in all. The largest single delegation was from the United States—370 delegates, including distinguished non-Jews such as Telford Taylor and Bayard Rustin, and political leaders. There was also an impressive delegation of 40 Soviet Jews recently arrived in Israel. Out of the lengthy workshops, commissions, and speeches emerged a massive demonstration of world Jewish and non-Jewish solidarity with Soviet Jewry, large-scale publicity in the world press and mass media, and a resounding message to the Soviet Union. But there were also bureaucratic tangles, organizational disagreements, and conflicts between establishment organizations and more militant, younger movements and student groups,[82] such as the Student Struggle for Soviet Jewry and the 35's Women Campaign of London. Certain vital issues such as absorption problems in Israel and prospects for a resumption of diplomatic relations between Israel and the Soviet Union were not touched.

There was much talk of coordination, but, at the end, responsibility for programs in behalf of Soviet Jewry devolved upon numerous national, local, and grass roots organizations. The conference was a momentary morale-booster, but according to one observer, "the delegations returned home with no greater sense of direction . . . no clearer notion of how to lift the movement out of the doldroms than they had before Brussels." There was no doubt, moreover, that much of American Jewry's anxiety about Soviet Jewry had shifted to Israel in the wake of the trauma of the Yom Kippur War in 1973 and the succession of diplomatic setbacks suffered by Israel: the severance of diplomatic ties with many states during the war, the UN General Assembly invitation to PLO chief Yasser Arafat, and the admission of the PLO to observer status at the UN.[83] In 1975 came the shocking UN resolution defining Zionism "as a form of racism and racial discrimination," a phrase which rationalized a torrent of subsequent anti-Zionist and anti-Jewish attacks. The Arab oil weapon also loomed as a persistent threat to the West and there were justifiable fears that American official support for Israel and Soviet Jewry would suffer because of increased dependence on Arab oil. Graver security threats for Israel in turn influenced more and more Soviet Jews applying to emigrate to prefer Western countries, especially the United States, to Israel. By 1975, the pattern of emigration had markedly changed. More Jews were now leaving from the large cities of the Russian heartland: Moscow, Leningrad, Kiev, and especially Odessa, itself comprising 15 percent of all emigrants in 1975[84] (see Table 31.4). These shifts aroused disappointment and anger in certain Jewish circles in Israel and the West, and bitter controversy over the so-called drop-outs (see Chapter 32).

These problems represented serious setbacks for the Soviet Jewry emigration movement, but the Soviet government as well faced problems as a result of Jewish emigration. Not only were well-educated and skilled Jews and prominent intellectuals leaving, but the scarred fabric of Soviet life was being minutely scrutinized by the eyes of the world. There were also rumblings among other groups that wanted to emigrate, especially Volga Germans (see Table 31.5). In the early seventies, some had been allowed to leave quietly, but they became increasingly militant in their demands. In 1974 there were several demonstrations at party offices and the West German embassy, hunger strikes, and protests with placards—in the manner of the Jewish activists—and some were arrested.[85] During the year, some 40,000 applications for exit visas were reportedly made by Volga Germans and other non-Jews.[86] By 1980, more than 10,000 Soviet Armenians had emigrated.

The effect of public demonstrations and publicity, directed at the Brussels Conference and the Helsinki Final Act, on Soviet policy has

TABLE 31.4

Jewish Emigration from Twenty Cities in the USSR
and Percentages of Those Going to Countries other
than Israel, 1968–80*

Cities	Numbers Emigrating	Percentages
Moscow	14,494	62.9
Leningrad	13,872	74.1
Kiev	22,773	79.4
Odessa	24,385	82.7
Tashkent	6,846	34.4
Kishinev	15,482	19.3
Minsk	6,574	65.5
Chernovtsy	17,554	7.6
Riga	11,935	32.7
Lvov	7,942	56.5
Tbilisi	8,266	9.6
Vilnius	8,691	8.0
Samarkand	4,964	4.5
Dushanbe	2,789	8.0
Kaunas	2,089	5.2
Kutaisi	5,278	0.7
Sukhumi	3,229	1.7
Derbent	3,924	0.7
Kharkov	3,873	85.2
Mukachevo	1,079	5.3

Source: Z. Alexander, "Jewish Emigration from the USSR in 1980," *Soviet Jewish Affairs*, Vol. 11, No. 2, 1981, pp. 14, 17.

Note: *These include the United States, West Germany, Australia, Canada.

been and continues to be much debated, but in 1976–77, the Soviet government found it necessary for the first time to deal with some of the issues of emigration and human rights in its domestic press. In *Izvestiya*, November 10, 1976, for example, there was a long article on Soviet emigration policies, and an article, "Behind the Human Rights Hullabaloo," in *Pravda*, February 12, 1977, dealing with Charter 77 in Czechoslovakia and the Polish Workers' Defense Committee.[87] All Soviet positions could be justified and rationalized for domestic consumption, and Jews and Zionists blamed not only for the Jackson-Vanik Amendment, but for Washington's criticisms of Soviet violations. During a fresh period of harassment of Alexander Ginzburg (who was again arrested on February 3, 1977) and renewed threats to prosecute Sakharov early in 1977, before the Belgrade Conference, Tass charged that

TABLE 31.5

Emigration of Germans from the USSR, 1965–84

Year	Numbers
1965–70	4,495
1971	1,145
1972	3,426
1973	4,493
1974	6,541
1975	5,985
1976	9,704
1977	9,274
1978	8,455
1979	7,226
Total	56,249*
1980	6,954
1981	3,773
1982	2,071
1983	1,447
1984	913
Total	15,158†
Grand Total	71,407

Sources: Tabulation 1965–79 based on B. Pinkus, "The Emigration of National Minorities from the USSR in the Post-Stalin Era," *Soviet Jewish Affairs*, Vol. 13, No. 1, 1983, pp. 28, 30. †John L. Scherer, "A Note on Soviet Jewish Emigration, 1971–84," *Soviet Jewish Affairs*, Vol. 15, No. 2, 1985, p. 42.

Note: *B. Pinkus estimates that 1,000 additional Germans emigrated to the German Democratic Republic.

"Zionist organizations" were a major source of "anti-Soviet noise about the question of civil liberties in the USSR."[88] The steady reference to the Helsinki Final Act was hitting a raw Soviet nerve, but the Soviet Union refused to be the "whipping boy of Helsinki." Moreover, she would come to the conference well-armed with evidence of lack of compliance by the West—especially the United States.[89]

In a balance sheet of Soviet emigration from 1975 to the eve of the Belgrade Conference, the record was unquestionably a "dismal one."[90] The only improvement noted was very slight: the application fee was reduced from 900 to 800 roubles, re-application after a rejection could be made after six months instead of a year; and a certificate replaced a character reference from the place of work. Otherwise, the record was bleak. There were no improvements in the rate of reunification of families, postal contact, transmission of printed information, clarification of emigration regulations, or in abatement of anti-Semitic propaganda. Harassment of applicants had intensified, telephone contacts were increasingly disconnected, there were increased levies on gift parcels and cash remittances, and a deterioration of contacts in the field of religion. The very narrow range of cultural activities mocked the pledge given by the Soviet Union "to facilitate" the cultural contribution of national minorities.

As to contacts between non-governmental organizations, these never existed in the Jewish field except briefly during the war, and any prospect for them was crushed by the official position recently to "apply the designation 'Zionist' to practically every Jewish organization abroad."[91] On December 24, 1976, *Izvestiya* emphasized that "the establishment of direct and constant links between Jewish religious communities abroad . . . never was and never will be." Increasingly OVIR officials complained that relatives were not "close" enough to merit family reunification, but these decisions were arbitrary, in contrast to the liberal interpretation given for Polish and German applicants. Also, Jewish applicants were being refused if they left behind another family member, on the grounds that they were breaking up a family[92]—a wholly perverse interpretation.

The criterion of "national security" has also been used arbitrarily and frequently in denying emigration rights. At the beginning of 1976, Jewish activists made a survey[93] of 500 refusenik families and the reasons given for refusals. In 210 cases (42 percent) the reasons were "state security and secrecy considerations"; in another 22 cases (4.4 percent) it was "secrecy clearance of remaining relatives"; and in a further 160 cases (32 percent) it was past army service. Yet in Soviet legislation the meaning of national security is not clear. Officials maintain that "the secrets of a State are always its exclusive property," and that the matter is "an internal question." Only the state can decide "which specific works or information are to be considered secret."[94]

The full harsh lash of Soviet power and anger over public exposure of Helsinki violations before, during, and after Belgrade was felt in the form of several trials of a particularly destructive, shattering nature, involving leading activists in the late seventies. In reflecting on these events, the historian Roy Medvedev believed that a basic decision was taken by the Politburo in the fall of 1976 "to heighten dramatically the pressure on the activists and to cut off their contacts in the West, from which they draw moral support." Members of the Helsinki Watch Groups were the most vulnerable among these and the *Chronicle of Current Events* not only documented their harassment, but the far-flung net spread over the country involving the interrogation of former political prisoners, relatives, friends, and former employers of members.[95] In Sverdlovsk, Nizhny Tagil, Donetsk, Kaluga, Vladimir prison, Tarusa, Maikop, and dozens of towns and cities throughout the country there were interrogations, searches, and more arrests. People were grilled in hospitals, taken off trains, detained at metro stations, and summoned from work. Some members like Anatoly Shcharansky were at the hub of both human rights and Jewish emigration activism. His "case" and trial, overlapping preparations for and actual meetings of the Belgrade Conference, magnetized world attention in 1977–78.

32

Jewish Emigration, 1976–84: Trials, Achievements, Doubts, and Dilemmas

It is a hopeless task to defend myself facing such a . . . court. My fate has been predetermined.

SHCHARANSKY, at his trial, July 15, 1978

I had to adapt so that at the very least my throat would not constrict. . . . And so, gradually my memory proceeded to take me back to my past. I recalled each one of my friends and all of them together, and many other things . . . pictures from my past, thoughts concerning history and tradition, the Hebrew language and books that I had read, all that remained in my memory from my preoccupation with mathematics and chess.

SHCHARANSKY, letter to his mother, Chistopol Prison, May 6, 1984

T H E most shocking blow to the activist cause—and a very ominous one—was the Soviet accusation that several leading dissidents, all of them Jews, were working for the Central Intelligence Agency. By linking them with "treasonable" activities carried out on behalf of foreign intelligence, the movement, it was judged, could be discredited and destroyed. *Izvestiya,* on March 4, 1977, published the allegations in the form of an open letter "purportedly written by a former dissident Dr. Sanya L. Lipavsky, who contended that American diplomats responsible for reporting to Washington on the human rights movement were in fact CIA officers recruiting dissidents for the purpose of espionage."[1] The *New York Times* correspondent David K. Shipler commented that "it was the most serious charge yet in a series of recent Soviet attempts to portray dissidents as tools of Western subversion."[2]

These charges came amid the most severe crackdown on activists in several years and was aimed especially at an unofficial group monitoring Soviet violations of the 1975 East-West Helsinki Accords. Anatoly Shcharansky was a charter member of the group, two of whom were already in prison: Yuri Orlov and Alexander Ginzburg. In October 1976,[3] long-term refuseniks, while waiting at the Supreme Soviet for a response to their petition, were set upon by non-uniformed men. Their hands were tied and they were dragged into a bus. Several were badly injured; all were bloodied from beatings. Shcharansky telephoned several newspaper correspondents and an improvised press conference took place at Vladimir Slepak's home. A large delegation complained to the Interior Ministry, while others walked to the waiting room of the Central Committee of the party. The atmosphere became very tense as 200 police cordoned off access to the waiting room (see Photos 32.1 and 32.2). Again, several Jews were beaten up; a number, including Shcharansky, were arrested and two were placed in the "Sailor's Quiet," the sinister psychiatric hospital which the KGB used as a prison for dissidents. Thousands of protests poured in, including a letter from President Carter, and those arrested were released, but an anti-Semitic

32.1 Shcharansky and Slepak before their arrest. Courtesy Jewish Community Relations Council of Philadelphia.

32.2 Anatoly Shcharansky, Ida Nudel, and Dina Beilina before arrests of Shcharansky and Nudel. Courtesy Jewish Community Relations Council of Philadelphia.

baiting campaign began in the press, hinting or stating openly that the refuseniks were enemies of the Soviet Union. Shcharansky was referred to as a "gangster, prepared to take the law into his own hands."

The campaign culminated in the January 22, 1977 television showing of the film "Traders of Souls," designed to revile Jews applying to emigrate and cast them as "agents of world Zionism and Western secret services." The showing of names and addresses of activists including those of Shcharansky, Slepak, Yuli Kosharovsky and Yosif Begun, long-time refuseniks, figured prominently and was very frightening. Intensive KGB surveillance of Shcharansky began. All of the letters to his wife Avital were seized; the friend whose apartment he had used emigrated. Dr. Sanya Lipavsky, who had been a refusenik since 1974, and was well-liked and helpful within the activist circle in Moscow, asked Shcharansky to move in with him. He was about to when Lipavsky disappeared. On March 4, sudden searches were carried out in the apartments of seven Jewish families: the Lerners, Beilins, Slepaks, Ida Nudel, Chernobilsky, Mikhail Kremen, and Lipavsky. After the searches, Dina Beilina went out to get *Izvestiya* and saw the headline that numbed her with fear and disbelief: "To the Presidium of the Supreme Soviet, copy to the U.S. Congress and to the UN, Open Letter of Citizen of the USSR Lipavsky." In his letter of "confession," Lipavsky renounced his request to emigrate and accused his refusenik friends of being in the hire of the CIA. Specifically named were Vitaly Rubin, Dr. Alexander Lerner, David Azbel, Mark Azbel, Slepak, and Shcharansky. Lipavsky also accused two American diplomats, Melvin Levitsky and Joseph Pressel, of persuading dissidents to provide intelligence information.[4]

The entire sixth page of the newspaper was in the form of a supplement to Lipavsky's letter, entitled "The CIA, Spies and Human Rights," and included an attack on two former correspondents in Moscow, Alfred Friendly Jr. and George Krimsky, as CIA spies. (Mr. Friendly's tour ended in 1976; Krimsky was expelled.) The *New York Times* viewed the attack on the two diplomats as a "clear effort to sever contacts between the dissidents and the United States Government, just as efforts have been made to weaken contacts between dissidents and the Western press in recent months."[5]

The activists were stunned by these events; they had trusted Lipavsky and could not fathom his motives. Shcharansky and Slepak vehemently denied the charges, saying, "we never collected any illegal information, absolutely never, and never sent anything in an illegal way. . . . We never talked about espionage—nobody [from the U.S. embassy] ever made any approaches to get information."[6] Shcharansky speculated that the stepped-up drive against the activists was an effort by Moscow to convince the Carter Administration that its public outspokenness on human rights would be counterproductive, yet he believed that "Western pressure is the only possible way of saving the movement and of having real détente." President Carter vigorously denied the charges and the State Department described them as "preposterous."

A bright, lively young cyberneticist, Shcharansky, who speaks perfect English, had been trying to leave since 1974. He knew many Western visitors, talked with them freely, and was loved by Jewish as well as non-Jewish dissidents. He became the main interpreter of the activist community to the Western press and an important source of information for them. With the attack on him and the other leading activists, the prospect of new trials loomed. There were rising fears of a new "doctors' plot." Eight or nine men dogged Shcharansky's every move. His friends never let him out alone, but on March 15, someone came to the Slepak house to relay the news that Dr. Mikhail Stern, a friend of Shcharansky whom he had helped, had been released from prison. Shcharansky was so excited, he ran out of the house to phone the good news to others. Slepak ran after him, but was too late. The KGB had taken him.

For the next sixteen months, a relentless "investigation" was carried on while Shcharansky remained incommunicado and in solitary confinement in Lefortovo prison. Over one hundred persons in twenty cities, among them many refuseniks in Leningrad and Minsk who never knew Shcharansky, were interrogated and told, as was Shcharansky's mother Ida Milgrom, that he was charged with treason and with fabricating slanderous information about the Soviet Union and communicating it to the West for anti-Soviet ends. On June 14–15, Robert Toth, Moscow correspondent of the *Los Angeles Times*, was interrogated about his contacts with Shcharansky and the information he shared with him about obstacles to emigration, the special problems of refuseniks, and help he received from Shcharansky at press conferences. On July 12, Tass stated that Toth had used his position to receive and pass on secret information and that he was a spy.[7] However, no criminal charges were pressed and Toth was allowed to leave the Soviet Union.

On August 19, Arkady Mai, who conducted a seminar on Jewish culture and history, was shown a typewritten list of refuseniks compiled by Shcharansky. When Mai asked, "What does this list have to do with espionage?" the investigator said that the list was not espionage, but that secret information could have been communicated together with it.[8] At Shcharansky's subsequent trial in July 1978 (see below pp. 735–36) much was made of such lists and their connection with "state secrets." (In the autumn of 1976, a group of Jewish activists proposed that a list be started of those who were refused visas for reasons of state security. It was also decided to include some information about the institutions which served as grounds for refusal of those who had worked in them. The reasoning here was that if foreign firms were selling them complex technical equipment, there was no secret work and grounds for refusal were nonexistent.[9])

The existence of such lists was never kept secret and analogous lists were kept abroad by Jewish organizations interested in Jewish emigration. The list in question, including some names of workplaces, was begun in February 1977.[10] Shcharansky took no part in its preparation, but he occasionally read out the list in phone calls abroad and occasionally questioned applicants who were refused at the OVIR offices. Toth used some of this material in his article "Soviet Union Indirectly Reveals Centres of Secret Works" which had been published in the *Los Angeles Times* and the *International Herald Tribune*. The article stated that most refuseniks worked at places considered secret. Thus, Toth concluded, a list of such institutions would be a list of "centres of secret activity"—perhaps a harmless enough phrase in the West, but sinister to an already heightened paranoid leadership. Shcharansky was thus trapped in this web. Very likely, the regime had decided to punish and victimize Shcharansky in any case. Toth's poor judgment in slanting the article as he did, made it easier. Lipavsky, of course, had been planted all along[11] and wove a fabrication that provided the court with the "evidence" the court required to come to its predetermined verdict and sentence.

Early in October in Lvov, on the instructions of the Moscow KGB, the people interrogated were told that Shcharansky was head of a Moscow organization called "Aliya" [sic!], which had used him to turn over information used by Western secret services to harm the Soviet state.[12]

On October 28, Tass attacked "Zionist organizations in the West [which] have been going all out to blow up an anti-Soviet campaign around the case of the traitor Anatoly Shcharansky. . . . Commissioned by his masters he supplied the West with facts about Soviet enterprises and institutions. . . . The traitor to his country will be punished according to the full severity of Soviet law. . . ."[13] The predetermined guilt was also admitted by several of the interrogators. When the Beilins and Ida Nudel were interrogated on November 25, Investigator Skalov said that Shcharansky had *committed* a crime and called him a criminal.[14] In the interrogations in Riga, the investigator Kochetkov said that the investigation was being conducted "not in the interests of justice, but in the interests of the state."[15]

Shcharansky was scheduled to come to trial by December 15, but his pretrial imprisonment was extended by six months. Thus his official sentencing was postponed until after the Belgrade Conference, which opened on October 4, 1977, to review the Helsinki Accords. Meanwhile, Soviet lawyers approached by his relatives to take his case refused to do so unless he pleaded guilty.[16] Several French lawyers volunteered to represent him but officials refused to give them a visa.

On May 31, he was charged with espionage and with helping a foreign government carry out "hostile activities against the USSR," under Article 64 of the RSFSR Criminal Code. His trial[17] opened on July 10, 1978, a few weeks after the trials of Vladimir Slepak and Ida Nudel (see pp. 740–42 and Chapter 34), and on the same day as the trial for another member of the Helsinki Group, Alexander Ginzburg. In an unprepossessing courthouse in a back street not far from the Kremlin, Shcharansky's trial lasted five days. Although it was described as "open," militiamen and police stood behind iron barriers blocking entry to Western newspapermen, Shcharansky's friends, and even to his mother, Ida Milgrom. He rejected the lawyer assigned by the court and insisted on the right to his own self-defense. He had prepared a forty-page document supporting his innocence, but this material was ignored and he was prevented from calling any defense witnesses, or questioning government witnesses. In his summation he said,

It is a hopeless task to defend myself facing such a . . . court. My fate has been predetermined. . . . I hope that the absurd accusations against me and the entire Jewish emigration movement will not hinder the liberation of my people. . . .

The sentence was severe: three years in prison and ten in a "strict regime" labor camp. Meanwhile, his case was becoming an international *cause célèbre*, with distinguished figures from all fields in many parts of the world expressing their protests and appeals for redress, including President Carter.

Carter, who was inaugurated in January 1977, took up the cause of human rights passionately, rejecting the Soviet argument that actions involving its own citizens were its own business. He also, however, rejected linkage between rewards and punishments in reaction to human rights issues and détente, such as occurred when the Jackson-Vanik Amendment was passed. Carter's eloquent pronouncements and Administration responses to the waves of arrests in 1977–78 heartened the human rights activists—he even wrote open letters to Sakharov and Ginzburg—but did not ease their actual conditions.[18] Vladimir Bukovsky was released on December 18, 1976, but this was an unusual and expedient prisoner exchange for Chilean Communist leader Luis Corvalan Lepe. Bukovsky had served many years in camps and mental institutions, but had smuggled to the West documentation on psychiatric abuse in the Soviet Union (see below pp. 742–44). These abuses did not stop, nor did the continuing assaults on the remnants of the Helsinki Watch Group.

Western delegates to the Belgrade Conference were hopeful that the Helsinki provisions on human rights would be strengthened, but Soviet representatives proved intransigent, attacking Western proposals for creating an "unconstructive atmosphere."[19] Belgrade residents, watching sleek limousines go back and forth, and hearing of the seemingly interminable discussions and position papers, coined a new verb, *kebsovati,* which, roughly translated, means "talk endlessly to no effect," to describe the disillusioning effect produced after expectations had been raised quite high. After nine months, there was virtually no progress to report except that the pledges given at Helsinki had not been forgotten and that the review process would continue in Madrid in 1980. The disappointing outcome provoked searching arguments and debates on Western strategy and tactics. Would more have been achieved by a quieter approach, one that didn't hammer away at Soviet actions in the public glare? Did the American-led campaign to ease pressure on specific dissidents "poison" the atmosphere and "harden" positions and suspicions, as the Eastern bloc maintained? The most articulate and controversial of American spokesmen was Arthur Goldberg, former Supreme Court Justice, who detailed many specific Soviet violations but also said it was "unrealistic to expect the Soviets to allow a conference to dictate their internal situation," but that the arguments would not deter the process of détente or the SALT talks, and that the conference gave "hope to dissenters in Prague, the Soviet Union and others in Eastern Europe."[20]

There were serious rumblings at the time in Poland and Czechoslovakia, and even in Romania and East Germany some students, writers, and workers were issuing protests and appeals and invoking the Helsinki Accords, but in the Soviet Union the Watch Groups were suffering deeply and harsh ordeals and prison sentences were in store for their leaders and leaders of the Jewish emigration movement. Yet Jewish emigration rose both in 1977 and dramatically so in 1978—the period of the persecution and trials of leading activists and, partially, the period of the Belgrade Conference. It would seem that Soviet policy had two objectives: to assert absolutely its control over internal matters such as human rights activity, and yet to offer some concessions in terms of emigration to blunt some of the international criticism that showed no signs of abating, and gain favorable trading and credit treatment from the United States. However, one couldn't be sure how to interpret these varying signals—if signals there were—and no one on the outside could know for sure the weight of internal and external factors, their interplay, and the locus of decision-making. The correspondent David Shipler, who knew the Soviet scene well, said, during the nine-month long Belgrade Conference: "Nobody knows all that goes into a decision to arrest and try one dissident, to let another emigrate, and to ignore a third. Unpredictability seems a hallmark of high policy, probably intended to keep activists off balance."[21] And, also, their supporters in the West.

In 1977 Jewish emigration rose to 16,736, an increase of approximately 16 percent over 1976, with large numbers of urban professionals and skilled workers.[22] Moreover, according to Shumilin, deputy minister of internal affairs, during the first five months of 1977, 615 previously rejected applicants were allowed to leave.[23] During the first five months of 1978, about 9,507 Jews were allowed to leave, an increase of 66 percent over a similar period in 1977. Before the year ended, 28,864 Jews had left, the highest figure since 1973[24] (see Table 32.1). The Jewish Agency claimed that as of March 1977, there were still 180,000 Jews who had applied to emigrate. Nevertheless, the emigration increases were noteworthy.

At the same time, certain marked individuals inside the Soviet Union were suffering greatly and the human rights movement as a whole was being shattered. In the spring and summer of 1978, there were arbitrary, pro forma trials of Alexander Podrabinek, a member of the Working Commission to Investigate the Use of Psychiatry for Political Purposes, and author of *Punitive Medicine*, which had already cost Podrabinek five years' internal exile; Grigory Goldshtein, a member of the Georgian Helsinki Group; Pyotr Vins, Miroslav Marinovich, and Nikolai Matusevich, of the Ukrainian Helsinki Group; Yuri Orlov, founder of the Helsinki Watch Group; Shcharansky; Ginzburg; Viktoras Petkus, of the Lithuanian Helsinki Group; and Vladimir Slepak and Ida Nudel, Jewish emigration movement leaders.[25] Amnesty International and numerous Jewish as well as non-Jewish organizations abroad mobilized support for these soon-to-be well-known individuals, and varied governmental and unofficial representations were made on their behalf, but Soviet policy remained adamant.

The *Chronicle* continued its reportage and new figures emerged to

TABLE 32.1
Jewish Emigration from the
USSR, 1965–June 1987

1965–June 67	4,498
October 1968–70	4,235
1971	13,022
1972	31,681
1973	34,733
1974	20,628
1975	13,221
1976	14,261
1977	16,736
1978	28,864
1979	51,320
1980	21,471
1981	9,447
1982	2,688
1983	1,314
1984	896
1985	1,140
1986	914
1987 (first six months)	3,092

Source: National Conference on Soviet Jewry,
Soviet Jewry Research Bureau, New York.

take risks in providing information to the outside world, but the disappearance of the old leadership into frightening, brutal, and distant camps and exile[26] was an irrecoverable blow to those who still hoped for some measure of Soviet compliance with the Helsinki Accords as the West understood them. These trials were not only a new drive to crush the dissident movement, but the removal of a leadership that might provoke protests at the Moscow Olympics in 1980 and thus mar the spectacle. Some observers also speculated that the drive may have signalled a struggle among hard-liners to succeed Brezhnev. There were recurring rumors of a possible exchange of the Soviet spies Enger and Chernyavev held in the United States, but this never materialized.

For many prisoners and their families, the loss of Ida Nudel was especially great. She had applied to leave in 1971, and many times thereafter. Her husband and sister had been permitted to leave; she had not. An economist, she dealt mainly with maintaining hygienic standards in food stores and control of infectious material in foods, but officials claimed that her work involved "state secrets." Since 1971, Ida had become known as the "Guardian Angel of the Prisoners and Re-fuseniks" for her selfless, single-minded preoccupation with providing aid and comfort to those in prison and exile. One prisoner, Vladimir Markman, who had never seen her, recalled that "her letters gave me warmth, with an almost physical presence. . . . In her inscrutable way, she found methods of helping me in my captivity, which, unfortu-nately . . . one cannot recount."[27] These methods included cables to Soviet officials, packages of food, letters to the prisoners, saving some from isolation cells, and solace and material help for the families.

For seven long years, separated from her family, Ida continued her efforts to obtain a visa, meanwhile becoming more and more deeply involved in help for refuseniks in prison. Increasingly, she was subject to harassment and interrogation, including detentions in psychiatric fa-cilities. The climax came on June 1, 1978, when she was arrested on a charge of "malicious hooliganism." Ostensibly her crime was to hang a white sheet with a yellow star outside her apartment that read: "KGB Give Me My Visa!" But actually, as she was told in court, she was standing trial for her work over the previous years. She was sentenced to four years of Siberian exile. Her personal courage and indomitable spirit helped not only to sustain many prisoners, but her own experi-ence in exile in the Siberian village of Krivosheino (see Photo 32.3).

In October 1978, a former Prisoner of Conscience Sender Levinzon traveled to the remote Siberian marshlands where Ida was in exile and reported that she

is the only woman housed in a bleak barracks-like hut inhabited by 60 men considered so dangerous to society that they must spend the rest of their lives away from population centers. They are constantly drunk, quarrelling, brawl-ing, armed with knives and hatchets. "When I arrived at the barracks, I found the door to Ida's room broken. She told me of nightly breakins and attempted assaults. She is literally not safe and has gone so far as to keep a knife at hand—not to use it against anyone, but to take her own life if need be. . . . The barracks is located some four kilometers away from a backwoods hamlet in which the only provisions available are "moist half-baked bread and what they call milk twice a week." . . . For most of the year the entire area is snowed under and cut off altogether with temperatures of 50 below zero. Nudel works as a cleaning woman, is ill and unable to get the food she needs or medical attention. . . .[28]

After a year in the barracks she bought a log cabin with money bor-rowed from Moscow friends. Besides cleaning, she worked in the office of a swamp-draining crew and night guard. A steady barrage of pro-

32.3 Ida Nudel, known as the "Guardian Angel of the Prisoners," was herself arrested and exiled to Siberia from 1978 to 1982. Unable to return to her home in Moscow, she lived in exile in Bendery, Moldavian SSR until 1987. Photo taken in 1974. Courtesy Philadelphia Soviet Jewry Council.

tests, petitions, and attempted interventions from the West pressed the government to release her, but she was forced to serve the full four-year sentence minus pretrial detention time. She was released late in March 1982 but was unable to emigrate or regain residence rights in Moscow and finally gained permission to live in Bendery, Moldavian SSR. In a sudden turnabout, on October 2, 1987, Moscow OVIR announced that she had permission to leave.

In the late seventies, harsh repressive measures also worsened conditions in prisons and mental institutions. A decree of the Ministry of Internal Affairs that went into effect on March 15, 1978, increased time in punishment cells and the cooler, restricted the number of books a prisoner might have, prohibited any intercession on behalf of a prisoner, and gave the camp administration the right to destroy any confiscated letters. The new rules, moreover, could not be examined by the prisoners; only excerpts were read out.[29]

Chilling reports about the use of psychiatric internment and mind-bending drugs to suppress dissidents appeared frequently in the West during this period, although unethical practices had started earlier. The case of General Pyotr Grigorenko, a much-decorated war hero, has probably done more than anything else to dramatize the Soviet abuse of psychiatry. Grigorenko had urged reforms after Khrushchev's speech in 1956 and formed an organization called the Union of Struggle for Revival of Leninism. He was arrested in 1964 and was sent to a mental hospital for the first time for a year, then again in 1969, when he was confined for three years in solitary confinement in the Chernyakhovsk Special Psychiatric Hospital. In 1973 he was transferred to a psychiatric hospital about 60 miles from Moscow and confined to a large ward of mentally disturbed patients. He was diagnosed as having "pathological paranoid development of the personality with reformist ideas."[30] A young Soviet Jewish psychiatrist Dr. Semyon Gluzman was outraged at the treatment of Grigorenko and after studying the available data, published an anonymous essay called "A Forensic-Psychiatric Diagnosis on the Case of Grigorenko, made in the Examinee's Absence," which argued that he was indeed sane.[31] Grigorenko was eventually released and even permitted to visit his son in the United States in 1977, but was stripped of his citizenship early in 1978 and was unable to return.

One of the first of the Jewish refuseniks to be interned in a mental institution was Major Girsh Feygin of Riga who had applied many times so as to join his mother and sister in Israel. He protested several refusals and publicly renounced the military decorations he had won during the war. On December 18, 1970, he was placed in a psychiatric institution because "normal people do not renounce government decorations," but was released within a month and allowed to emigrate.

Gluzman received much harsher treatment. He refused to head a hospital for political cases and was himself imprisoned for "anti-Soviet agitation" in 1972. In the Perm labor camp he met Vladimir Bukovsky, a long imprisoned dissident who had also suffered psychiatric abuse. The two coauthored a book called *A Manual on Psychiatry for Dissenters* and smuggled it to friends. After seven years in a labor camp and in very poor health, Gluzman was sent into exile in May 1979 (see Photo 32.4). In 1977, *Scientists Bulletin* reported that two refuseniks, Lazard

32.4 Dr. Semyon Gluzman, psychiatrist, co-authored with Vladimir Bukovsky, *A Manual on Psychiatry for Dissenters* while in Perm prison camp. He did much to expose psychiatric abuses. Courtesy of National Conference on Soviet Jewry.

Brusilovsky of Rostov-on-the-Don and Yefim Pergamnik of Kiev, had also been committed to psychiatric institutions.[32]

Generally it is the refusenik leadership that is punished in this way with repeated detentions or long-term confinement. The dissidents are subject to sudden surprise visits by the police, arrests, detention, and referral to obliging psychiatrists who respond to the requirements of "communist morality."[33] It remains unclear why some dissidents are sent to labor camps and others to mental hospitals. Bloch and Reddaway estimate the ratio as one to four, in favor of the camps, with the hospital "the fate of the most determined, resilient and respected of the dissenters,"[34] including those who could be expected to defend themselves.

The first Western protests were made by the American Psychiatric Association and the American Psychoanalytic Association in 1973–74, and in 1976 the Medical Mobilization for Soviet Jewry organized lay support and health professionals to publicize abuses and pressure for changes. The World Psychiatric Congress in Honolulu in 1977 condemned the punitive and abusive recourse to psychiatry in the Soviet Union. Medical doctors, too, have taken an increasingly firm stand. In July 1980, the British Medical Association passed a resolution strongly condemning Soviet practices, which was then unanimously endorsed by the World Medical Association. On November 20, the British Royal College of Psychiatrists called on the World Psychiatric Association to expel the Soviet Union until such time as it "can show that the political abuse of psychiatry has been brought to an end."[35]

In some cases, outside pressures seemed to work; in others, these exertions were fruitless. The fate of refuseniks seesawed. By 1977–78, some of the leading refuseniks had been allowed to leave: Vitaly Rubin, Alexander Voronel, Dina Beilina, Mark Azbel, Benjamin Levich, Mikhail Shtern. Many others were languishing in camps and prisons, threatened by warnings of "parasitism," suffering beatings, or living in limbo. Western supporters kept struggling to find the key to Soviet decision-making on the chronic refuseniks, but it was either nonexistent or deliberately kept secret. The *Chronicle* periodically reported cases in which specific refuseniks were informed by OVIR and Internal Ministry officials that they would never be told why they couldn't leave, but both outside and inside the country, in certain circles the need to find the formula persisted.

Non-refuseniks, however, were leaving quite steadily in the late seventies with relative ease (the average wait was from three to six months), but their destination shifted from Israel to the West, particularly to the United States and caused serious policy differences and conflicts among supportive organizations.[36] The shift away from Israel was noticed in 1974, when 18.7 percent left for other countries. By 1977, it was over 50 percent, and higher each year thereafter (see Table 31.1). Some were also leaving Israel.[37] There were many reasons for the shift: perceptions of greater economic opportunities in the United States; the volatile military situation in the Middle East; and Israel's inflation and absorption difficulties communicated to emigrants in letters and in Soviet propaganda; the larger numbers of nonnational and nonreligious Jews leaving the Soviet Union for whom Israel had no strong appeal; the pervasive anti-Semitic and anti-Zionist atmosphere which poisoned life for many assimilated Jews and cut off opportunities for their children[38] (see Photo 32.5).

The reasons may have been understandable, but the reality of the statistics threw Western Jews and Israelis into intense debate. On one side were the government of Israel and the Jewish Agency and their supporters, insisting that all emigrants with Israeli invitations come to Israel, even to the point of wanting direct flights from Moscow. On the other were HIAS (Hebrew Immigrant Aid Society) and the J.D.C., which gave financial help for the transportation and resettlement of Soviet Jews in the United States and other Western countries, and their supporters.[39] In 1976 a "Committee of Eight" and then a "Committee of Ten" made up of representatives of the Israeli government, the Jewish Agency, and American Jewish organizations, tried to resolve the controversy on several occasions. Soviet activists in Israel also have become involved in arguments and proposals, and often the debates have been very acrimonious. Israel, in the throes of recurring crises and losing thousands of her own people in a reverse emigration, but also the land of Zionist fulfillment, insisted on the centrality of aliya to Israel, i.e., repatriation to the Jewish homeland, which had been the basis of Soviet permission to leave and the main thrust of the Jewish emigration movement. Israeli leaders and some Soviet Jews in Israel attacked HIAS and other agencies for giving assistance to emigrants choosing

32.5 David Shvartzman, 13, had to celebrate his Bar Mitzvah privately January 7, 1979. Courtesy Jewish Community Relations Council of Philadelphia.

the West while in transit in Vienna. They also argued that the shift in emigration might endanger the whole emigration movement and cause the Soviet government to stop the process altogether.[40]

Opponents argued for "freedom of choice" for Soviet Jews and objected to Israel's effort to control their destination and destiny. They also argued that Soviet policy-making cannot be penetrated—it is often arbitrary and capricious and impossible to gauge or predict by ordinary criteria except that at bottom national self-interest had to be served, however it was defined. Moreover, several hundred non-Jews have left the Soviet Union on the basis of Israeli invitations, including the dissidents Valentin Turchin, Andrei Amalrik, and several Russian Orthodox leaders who were pressed into doing so, even though the government knew they had no intention of going to Israel.[41]

There was further apprehension among American Jews because of the stated opposition of the American government to Israel's position. The government had been contributing large sums of money to Israel to help in the resettlement of Soviet Jews, and began to aid local welfare federations with matching grants as their communities began to receive Soviet Jews. (This aid was part of a total government program on behalf of refugees from Southeast Asia, Africa, Cuba, and Haiti.) The aid began in 1975 when 600–700 exit visas to the United States were given to Soviet Jews by the Soviet government, based on about 1,000 letters of invitation from relatives in the United States. It was then hoped that in the spirit of détente and the Helsinki Accords, the Soviet government would be more responsive as greater numbers of letters were sent. In 1978, about 3,000 such letters were sent, but only 518 were permitted to leave with American visas. Nevertheless, as the numbers of emigrants without such letters grew, the financial burdens became greater and American governmental aid increased.[42] However, in August 1981, the Jewish Agency instituted a new policy, aimed at channeling emigration to Israel, which drew official American criticism and created new channels for governmental funds.

At that time, the Jewish Agency decided to refer to HIAS for help in and from Vienna only those emigrés with first degree relatives in the West; others would be required to go to Israel or seek help, not from HIAS, to which Jews had been referred by the Jewish Agency, but elsewhere.[43] Among the latter were those who sought help from non-Jewish agencies such as the Catholic Migration Committee, the Church World Service, the Tolstoy Foundation, the International Rescue Committee, and the anti-Zionist Satmar Hasidic organization named Rav Tov—all of which could now call on official American help.

On January 11, 1982, in response to a personal appeal from the then Prime Minister of Israel Menakhem Begin, HIAS agreed on a three-month trial basis to assist Soviet Jews only if they have first-degree relatives in the United States or other Western countries. This decision, which broke a long tradition of HIAS to give unqualified help to Jews trying to find new homes, disappointed many American Jews and was opposed by the Union of Councils for Soviet Jewry, but there was general organizational acquiescence in the Israeli position in order to prevent a break in Jewish ranks.

The Israeli argument that the shift of emigration to the West would endanger the entire emigration movement collapsed in the face of a continued surge in emigration: 28,864 in 1978, and a record high of 51,320 in 1979 (these tabulations vary slightly)—when Israeli pressures to redirect the emigration flow were great—but ironically, the argument was later used by the Soviet government to justify its virtual stoppage of emigration (see Table 32.1). Western diplomatic sources and Jewish spokesmen believed that the sharp upturn in exit permits related directly to two major Kremlin goals, in which renewed Jewish emigration flow could serve as leverage: ratification in 1980 of a new Soviet-American strategic arms agreement, and easing or repeal of the Jackson-Vanik Amendment. Both goals were seen as linked with the need for the Soviet Union to improve its image by relaxing emigration controls. Some observers also suggested that the changed emigration policy was a response to the ongoing American interest in re-establishing diplomatic relations with China—even a possible American-Chinese alliance—and to China's emergence as a potentially successful Western trading partner.[44] (Official diplomatic relations were re-established in January 1979.) Moreover, by granting more permits to Jews who would not be going to Israel, Soviet leaders were showing the Arabs that they were not helping to increase Israel's military potential.

However, theories explaining fluctuations in emigration figures solely in terms of Soviet-American relations ignore internal forces such as fear of the spread of the desire to emigrate to other nationalities, the impact of emigration of Jews on Soviet science, medicine, and industry, and the uncertainties in Soviet leadership that began in Brezhnev's declining leadership and continued through 1984.[45] A sociologist has also suggested the factor of "elite integration"—that is, the removal of Jews from certain positions in the professional and administrative classes in order to provide jobs in those categories for other national groups.[46] Moreover, if there are emigration quotas, as has often been mentioned, these quotas may have been influenced by policy considerations involving particular republics or cities.[47]

The drop in emigration figures in 1980 to 21,471 after the great surge of 1979 is generally attributed to President Carter's sharp curtailment of trade (including a wheat embargo) after the Soviet invasion of Afghanistan in December 1979, the American boycott of the Moscow Olympic Games, and the failure to ratify Salt II, yet these were stiff actions which might be expected to draw very drastic Soviet reactions, including severe reductions in emigration. The drop from over 50,000 emigrants in 1979 to under 22,000 in 1980 was very substantial, but, especially in light of emigration figures for years before 1979, hardly a severe response to Carter's vigorous measures away from détente.

It seems probable that many complex factors influence Soviet emigration policy. However, the alleged patterns, nonpatterns, correlations, and noncorrelations exhibit so many contradictions and inconsistencies, we may never be able to unravel them. If domestic and specifically inside problems of republics have helped to shape emigration policies in recent years, then a new restriction introduced in the summer of 1979 may be seen as foreshadowing drastic changes. At that time, in Odessa first and then in other cities in the Ukraine, OVIR officials began to insist on vyzovs only from "first-degree" relatives in Israel.[48] "Family kinship" was deemed insufficient, thus at one stroke excluding many applicants. Detailed questions were being asked about relatives in Israel and the frequency of correspondence, and pressure was being exerted on the non-Jewish partners in mixed marriages to resist applying and on children to resist their parents' decision to apply.[49]

There may, indeed, have been serious economic consequences following the huge Jewish emigration—almost a quarter of a million— from 1968 through 1980, many of them well-educated men and women from the heartland cities of the Soviet Union. If their emigration has now served the varied external and internal interests that may have been involved, and if, as is often reported, the Soviet Union is now facing a period of labor shortage,[50] the loss of more highly trained Jews through emigration may have been extremely costly to the economy. A number of Jews, including some activists, reported official efforts to prevail on them to stay. Also, in 1979, the *Chronicle of Current Events* reported on the admitted need to make admission to universities and professional jobs easier for Jews, while, at the same time, stepping up anti-Zionist propaganda and making emigration more difficult.[51] In June 1980, it was reported that "prominent Soviet citizens visit Jewish applicants for emigration in Kiev offering employment and good housing. In Moscow meetings are held at workplaces on the Jewish question; speakers praise Jews but criticize those who emigrate."[52] At the Twenty-Sixth Congress of the Communist party, Brezhnev described "exaggerated national feelings" as characteristic of "politically immature people," and Zionism and anti-Semitism as undesirable examples of nationalism and chauvinism. At this same Congress, several Jews had been "demonstratively promoted in the Party hierarchy, while Jews who had asked for exit visas in 1981 and 1982 [were] told to 'go home and live a normal life.' "[53]

Whatever the causes, there was a radical drop in emigration in the first half of the eighties: 9,447 in 1981; 2,688 in 1982; 1,314 in 1983; 893 in 1984 (figures vary slightly); and fewer than 500 in the first five months of 1985. This precipitous decline reinforced the tendency of mainline Jewish organizations to view Jewish emigration as a counter in American-Soviet policy, this time, of President Reagan's harsh, anti-Soviet line. Western Jewish strategy thus did not change. Protest meetings, attempted interventions on behalf of refuseniks and the activists who had been imprisoned—"Prisoners of Zion"—and massive letter-writing campaigns continued. Although there had been and continued to be dissenting voices, organizational emphasis was still largely concentrated on Jewish activists seeking to emigrate, and hopes were pinned on the various conferences to review the Helsinki Accords. The first after Belgrade was held in Madrid in November 1980.

The year 1980 was an extremely grim one for Soviet dissenters, by no means just limited to Jews, but involving editors of unofficial literary and political journals, the surviving Helsinki monitors,[54] religious activists, and leaders of Ukrainian, Lithuanian, Estonian, and other nationalist movements. The crackdowns came as the Soviet Union hardened its policy in anticipation of the Moscow Olympics, which the United States boycotted, and in parallel with the invasion of Afghanistan. The "promises" that had been made to Mr. Robert Hawke in 1979, in his talks with the Central Committee of the Communist Party, namely, the

release of "Prisoners of Zion" and the granting of exit visas to all refuseniks who had been waiting for five years, did not materialize, but
all Soviet dissidents clung to Helsinki like a lifeline and at protest meetings in major cities invoked the principles of the Helsinki Accords. A
month before the conference, 7,900 prominent scientists and engineers
from forty-four nations suspended scientific relations with the Soviet
Union to protest the imprisonment and oppression of dissident Soviet
scientists. Linkage of the moratorium with the review was not expected
to change Soviet policy, but withdrawal from cooperative exchanges
and visits was viewed as "an immensely powerful weapon because
Soviet scientists understand its force."[55] However, this rupture had no
observable effect.

In the preparatory sessions, the Soviet Union attempted to curtail the
amount of time the conference would devote to the subject of human
rights, and filibustered at those sessions until after the U.S. presidential election. Certain procedural concessions were made to the Soviet
Union, including agreement to reduce the length of review. The CSCE
(Conference on Security and Cooperation in Europe) countries of Western Europe and the United States conducted "a relatively thorough,
honest, hard-hitting review during the first six weeks of the meeting."[56] The American delegation alone cited sixty individual cases of
human rights violations in the USSR and Czechoslovakia. However,
the Soviet Union rarely responded to the substance of the accusations,
but used the argument of noninterference in internal affairs. Serious
deficiencies in implementation of the accords remained.

There also loomed the possibility of Soviet intervention in Poland
and seasoned diplomats were "openly asking whether the Soviet Union
may see it in its interest to end a process that was supposedly to open
and relax East-West ties gradually."[57] There was also speculation that
the election of Ronald Reagan would sharpen doubts about the usefulness of the Helsinki Agreements. On the third day of the conference,
the Jewish activist-scientist Viktor Brailovsky was arrested and during
the Christmas recess, nine new Helsinki monitors were arrested or tried.

The conference was scheduled to end on March 15, 1981, but talks
dragged on. The treatment of Soviet Jewry occupied an important place
in the presentations, and the Western and even nonaligned countries
were more forthright than they had been at Belgrade, but the Soviet
hard line on human rights did not budge. Soviet negotiators, claiming
they had already conceded as much as they could, varied their tactics

between stony silence and refusal even to discuss Western proposals and a counteroffensive of tabling the question. After nearly three years of wrangling, reflecting a deterioration in East-West relations, the Conference ended in September 1983. The Soviet Union was preoccupied with the crisis in Poland, "military détente," and disarmament, while the West emphasized the human rights content of Helsinki[58] (see Chapter 34 for reference to the Vienna Helsinki Review in 1986).

President Reagan and Republican party leaders have regularly insisted that the fate of Soviet Jews and emigration rights would continue to be on the American agenda in any negotiations with the Soviet Union, but relations between the superpowers have become mutually hostile in recent years and in their antagonisms American Jews actually have had little power. However, they have been seen by the Soviet Union as having immense influence over the course of American policy. The United States in fact is viewed as a tool of world Jewry. In this wildly exaggerated conception, the Soviet Union attempts to use emigration as a device for turning American Jews against the Reagan Administration and for persuading them to adopt a more pro-Soviet attitude. Soviet Jews have become, in the words of Richard Pipes, "pawns in this game."[59] Thus, American Jews for the most part see themselves in lockstep with Washington in their efforts to break the virtual stoppage of emigration after 1981. But was this reliance, indeed dependence, on American official goodwill, the only or the best strategy for Jewish supportive movements? Was there no other way to find slits in Soviet armor-plated decisions?

Dr. Nahum Goldmann and Moshe Decter, among others, had already in the early seventies appealed for more independence and for broadening the range of Western concerns. Professor Hans J. Morgenthau, an international relations expert, urged that attention focus on the religious and cultural rights of Soviet Jews remaining in the Soviet Union. Goldmann faulted the emphasis on emigration and the use of Soviet Jewry as a "tool for mobilizing the young Jews of the United States." He also warned against "treating the USSR as if it were some minor country. This does not improve anything, and confirms the Russians in their attitude of distrust and even of hostility." The Soviet state, he believed, "is on its way to liberalizing itself," but if it feels threatened, "does not hesitate to assert its power."[60] He rejected as unjustified "unfounded attacks and exaggerated charges" against the Soviet Union, but believed that the Soviet Jewish policy was itself unjust and would be harmful to it. However, he favored quiet diplomacy and direct personal contacts instead of loud public protests and confrontational tactics. He also believed that a neutral Israel would best serve Jewish interests, instead of complete identification with one superpower, and that Israel's way to peace "leads more through Moscow than Washington."[61] Goldmann, moreover, felt that his friendship with Willy Brandt, who had cultivated an *Ostpolitik* for West Germany, would prove helpful to Soviet Jews. "One might tremble for the fate of Russian Jews," he wrote in 1979, "if another cold war sets in."[62] Some Western Jews—but not many—tended to agree.

The scientific community was also reconsidering its policies. The arrest of Brailovsky in 1980[63] and the periodic crackdowns and closures of scientific and cultural seminars led some Western scientists to question the wisdom of their decision to break off contacts. In 1980, officially sponsored contacts were only at 25 percent of their 1979 level, yet the fate of Sakharov, Shcharansky, and Orlov, over whom the scientists had exerted immense pressure, had not changed. The organizer of Scientists for Orlov and Shcharansky, Kurt Gottfried, admitted having second thoughts: "We have to re-examine what we should do. It is not clear we are making any progress on the dissidents. There must be some minimum level of contact before we can influence them." Dr. D. Allan Bromley, president of the American Association for the Advancement of Science, said: "The message has gotten through, but it's clear now that we are playing into [the hands of] the hard-liners in the Kremlin by a total close-down. We are making life incredibly difficult for the good guys there."

After the struggle to pass the Jackson-Vanik Amendment in 1974, there were also lingering troubled second thoughts about its consequences, about the insulation of the Jewish activist movement from the general human rights struggle in the Soviet Union, about having placed the whole stress on emigration and having yielded to Israel on policy, and having neglected the Jews who remained in the Soviet Union. Moshe Decter had written eloquently of the need for a more independent leadership, "largeness of imagination," and greater vision in dealing with the Soviet Jewry issue. He proposed an assertive political struggle for the survival of Soviet Jewry that would: expose the USSR "as the fountainhead of world anti-Semitism," and demand "authentic and viable institutions of learning, education, culture and religion," including a rabbinical seminary, a network of schools in which Hebrew and Yiddish would be taught, a Jewish publishing house, Jewish social-cultural centers, and a major translation program to make the totality of the Jewish heritage available to Soviet Jews in Russian.[64]

A suggestion that there were broader aspects to the Soviet Jewish predicament than emigration had emerged at a symposium of Soviet Jewish and Israeli scholars and intellectuals held in Jerusalem in January 1972.[65] Boris Tsukerman, Mikhail Zand, Yosef Kerler, and David Garber voiced the prevailing view that there is no future for Jewish culture in the Soviet Union, that all Jews who can must emigrate to Israel. But the Yiddish poet Rachel Boymvol stressed the importance of considering those who remained. Dr. Shmuel Ettinger saw a Jewish culture already existent in the Soviet Union—within the synagogue, samizdat, poetry, and approved literature, and deplored the singular emphasis on "catastrophic nationalism" and "catastrophic aliya." Through the middle seventies certain activists—Alexander Lerner, Vitaly Rubin, Vladimir Slepak, Vladimir Prestin, Ida Nudel, and Dina Beilina—had appealed for greater emphasis on the cultural needs of Jews inside the Soviet Union: "Our aim is to fill the enormous void created by the absence of Jewish cultural material in the Soviet Union. . . . Soviet Jews are completely deprived of the opportunity of any kind of contact with their own culture, customs and traditions. But the desire for such contacts not only exists but is growing all the time. . . ."[66]

An Israeli broadcasting specialist, Eli Eyal, prepared a detailed analysis[67] of the Jewish cultural wasteland in the Soviet Union for the Copenhagen meeting of the Presidium of the Brussels Conference in 1980 to serve as a guideline for the Madrid Conference. In it Eyal spelled out the "dry facts and figures which tell the sad story of the suppression of Jewish culture in the Soviet Union." Of the 119 different nationalities in the Soviet Union, 118 have their own schools and instruction in their own language. Only in the case of Soviet Jews is this denied. Even the Germans, Eyal pointed out, who are also a nonterritorial nationality, have their own schools, printing houses, radio and television services in German. The same is true of the Polish minority.

In the first six months of 1980, according to Eyal, 350 Russian-language books on various aspects of Jewish culture, free of any anti-Soviet nuance, were sent to 350 Soviet Jews by registered mail, but not a single one reached its destination or was returned. Persistent violations of Article 27 of the International Covenant on Civil and Political Rights, guaranteeing minority cultural rights, were cited, including the constant and consistent jamming of Israeli radio broadcasts (in Yiddish, Hebrew, Georgian, and Bukharian, or Judeo-Persian) by 6,000 Soviet transmitters. Eyal also stressed the absence of any Jewish periodical, newspaper, or literary review in Russian, in a society where 93 percent of Jews know Russian, and the regime's untenable persecution of Hebrew and Hebrew teachers.

The dominant thrust of Jewish organizational activity continued to be emigration to Israel, but serious questions were being raised about the strategy and tactics of their leaders and even the primacy accorded to emigration. Were there, for example, possibly disproportionate efforts being made on behalf of a comparatively small number of refuseniks and prisoners while the fate of three million Soviet Jews was being neglected in the preoccupation with emigration? In the light of increasingly punitive measures against Jewish activists, the virtual wiping out of the leadership, and the harsh prison sentences, had Western/Jewish leverage reached its limits in extracting concessions? Had anything been gained in separating the Jewish emigration issue from the human rights movement?[68] Whatever the carefully formulated framework for Jewish work on behalf of Soviet Jews, it was clear that from the Soviet point of view, Jews were indeed part of the simmering political discontent and were, if anything, particularly vulnerable. If it had been possible in the early period to delimit the Jewish struggle and differentiate it from the general human rights struggle, it had not been possible to delimit its consequences. The Jewish activists, whether inside or outside the human rights movement, had become in the Soviet view, the greatest enemies of the regime.

From time to time, and increasingly as they learned the uses of freedom in freedom, there were also vigorous expressions of dissatisfaction among Soviet Jews in Israel over policy decisions as well as absorption processes, over the issue of support or not for non-Jewish dissidents, and over the need for Jewish cultural institutions and activity in the Soviet Union. Especially vocal were emigrants who had been in the forefront of the Jewish activist struggle in the Soviet Union such as Leah Slovin, Dr. Benjamin Fain, Victor Polsky, and Alexander Voronel. They believed that action must urgently be taken to strengthen relations between Jews in the Soviet Union and in Israel through an international political struggle for the legalization of Jewish culture in the USSR. There were also Israeli scientists and several leading academicians from the USSR who not only wanted a massive action on the cultural issue, but the establishment of diplomatic contacts between Israel and the Soviet Union at a senior level, and freedom for "Prisoners of Zion" and refuseniks imprisoned for more than five years. There were angry debates over the "drop-out" issue and introspective analyses of the psychological and spiritual journeys the new emigrants had taken in their exodus from the Soviet Union.[69]

The absence of diplomatic relations between the Soviet Union and Israel and the Western emphasis on publicity seemed to foreclose quiet diplomacy.[70] American supportive organizations as well as the State of Israel also lacked flexibility in formulating a strategy vis-à-vis the Soviet Union because they were both interlocked with American interests and policy and have been viewed as agents of American imperialism. Meanwhile, throughout the seventies and early eighties some Soviet Jews were seeking alternatives to emigration. As the wait for vyzovs stretched out, or as fear to apply constrained them, they realized that their stay in the Soviet Union would be long—perhaps forever. The recourse to protest demonstration, petition, and hunger strike shifted to study—study of Hebrew, Jewish history, and literature. Their discussions and adaptations sharpened attention on the problems of Jews who wanted or had to remain in the Soviet Union and did not want to disappear as Jews.

33

Permitted Margins of Jewish Life, 1970–85

People literally pleaded for any small symbol of Jewish identity, a Star of David, a Jewish calendar, a Hebrew alphabet chart. . . . One man came every day to read Gershom Scholem's book on Kabbalah.

B. SHARFSTEIN, Second International Book Fair
in Moscow, September 4–10, 1979

THE exodus of over a quarter of a million Jews from the Soviet Union since 1968 is a remarkable, wholly unanticipated phenomenon in both Jewish and Soviet history and will have influences and reverberations in the years to come that we cannot yet measure. There are possibly another quarter of a million Jews or more[1] who have requested and received vyzovs, indicating a desire to leave and join relatives. A number of these presumably have some degree of Jewish consciousness; in many cases, however, their situation may have been undermined by the emigration of relatives and they may now be considered an "unreliable element" by Soviet security agencies. Some in the seventies who had not applied waited for their children to finish university, or delayed until they had time to assess the experiences of friends who had left.[2] Others hoped that things might get better in the Soviet Union, or at least not worse, or were relatively satisfied with their professional position or retirement benefits. Still others hoped that by becoming "more Russian than Ivan" they would somehow avoid the pain of anti-Semitism.

Such Jews, for different reasons, have chosen not to apply to leave, but we do not know to what extent they wish to live as Jews within the Soviet Union, nor do we know how many among them still cling to any of the fragile possibilities for living Jewishly: study circles, worship and religious observance, access to books, commemorative events, and attendance at Jewish cultural programs. Relatives and friends of those who have successfully emigrated plus the relatives and friends of those with vyzovs have been affected by the emigration phenomenon—some positively, some negatively—but some undoubtedly have been sufficiently affected to want to find some channels for expression of their sense of Jewishness. Still others feel themselves to be Jews by virtue of the rampant anti-Semitism in Soviet society and internalize a deep pain and consciousness of being "other." The rest, identified as Jews in the census, probably constitute a majority of the Jewish population and remain anonymous, dispersed, and problematic.

In the last official census, taken in 1979, there were 1,811,000 Jews, most of whom seem to have refused, or been alienated from, an active, articulated, or overt Jewish identity, either through emigration or an attempt to retain any aspects of a Jewish religious or secular culture. One scholar refers to this group as the "silent majority."[3] The 1979 Census figures show a decline from 2,151,000 in 1970, and 2,268,000 in 1959—declines attributed to emigration, a declining birth rate, and a high percentage of mixed marriages in which many offspring select a non-Jewish national identity (see Table 33.1).[4] It is generally believed that there are more Jews numerically than declare themselves as such in the census-taking, but greater numbers do not change the generally agreed upon perception that most of these Jews are melding into Russian Soviet society, and losing their cultural identity and consciousness through the force of circumstances, cultural and religious deprivation, official and environmental pressures, and the heavy cost of living a Jewish life. The postwar Jewish demographic profile projects a bleak future for Jewish survival. Huge war losses, a declining birth rate, russification, emigration, and intermarriage[5] have taken a great toll on the biological substance of Soviet Jews remaining in the country. Moreover, the Jewish population is aging and uncounted numbers of them still suffer from the scars of war, decimated families, prison, fear, anti-Semitism, and the backlash of hostility aroused by waves of Jewish emigration. There is no Jewish community structure or leadership to help buffer these traumas. Israel no longer serves to secretly fill such Jews with national pride, and the refuseniks, for all their great courage and strength, do not share the world of the Jewish "silent majority,"

TABLE 33.1
Jewish Population Decline, 1959–70

Republic (SSR)	1959	1970
RSFSR	875,307	807,915 (incl. 11,452 in Birobidzhan)
Ukraine	840,314	777,126
Belorussia	150,084	148,011
Uzbek	94,344	102,855
Georgia	51,582	55,382
Moldavia	95,107	98,072
Lithuania	24,672	23,564
Latvia	36,592	36,680
Estonia	5,436	5,288
Azerbaidzhan	40,204	41,288
Armenia	1,024	1,048
Kazakh	28,048	27,689
Tadzhik	12,414	14,615
Kirghiz	8,610	7,680
Turkmen	4,078	3,494
Total Jewish Population	2,267,814	2,150,728
Total USSR Population	208,826,650	241,720,134

Source: Figures from Council of Ministers, *Soviet Census of 1959, 1970*, in Thomas E. Sawyer, *The Jewish Minority in the Soviet Union*, 1979, p. 245.

many of whom have been frightened by the do-or-die activism and defiance of the refuseniks.

We cannot plumb the complex adjustments of this large mass or the fluctuations in their thinking and behavior as they try to survive in the hostile and unpredictable world of Soviet life, nor can we know how they truly feel about being Jewish. What is observable is that they choose not to emphasize their Jewish identity. One scholar has put it well:

Neither exodus nor overt Jewish protest are their response. Instead, they choose a combination of adaptation and inertia, the desire to avoid as much as possible the changing of familiar habits and surroundings, and the desire to believe that with a little patience, ingenuity and help, one can hold out until the storm blows over and a new favorable cycle of development sets in. In short, these are all the familiar responses of Jewish communities in many places at many different times.[6]

He also points out that "diligent and loyal" Soviet Jews can still make their way. For example, as of 1976, 294,774[7] members of the Communist party, with a membership of sixteen million, were identified as Jews—one out of every six or seven Jews eligible by age to join (see Table 33.2). In the same year, two more Jews were added to the party's four Jews on the Central Committee, including General David Dragunsky, who became chairman of the Anti-Zionist Committee of the Soviet Public (see Chapter 34) in 1983, and is "used both domestically and abroad to personify the loyal Soviet Jew."[8] In the economic and educational fields, Jews still represent a high percentage of "specialists in the national economy" and scientific workers, although the percentage has been dropping.[9] The numbers and percentages of Jews with higher education in the work force are also dropping, but, as of December 1984, there were still 395,000 Jews in this category—3.7 percent of the total number (about 10,700,000).[10] Brezhnev's call to Jews to "stay home" (see Chapter 32) also resulted in certain blandishments, token concessions, and acknowledgments of Jewish achievements, which some Jews have taken as an incremental easing of their situation, or, at least a few

TABLE 33.2

Jews in the Communist Party (Estimated Number except for 1922 and 1927)

Date	Number of Jews	Percentage of Jews to Total Number
1922	27,500	5.2 (members and probationers)
1927	52,000	4.3 (members and probationers)
1940	Between 146,000 and 166,000	4.3 to 4.9
1961	Between 260,000 and 269,000	2.8 to 2.9
1965	Between 176,000 and 200,000	1.5 to 1.7
	275,700*	2.3
1969	⎰210,000⎱	1.5
	⎱282,500⎰	2.1
January 1976	294,774	1.9
January 1977	296,424	1.85
January 1982	260,000	1.4

Sources: Figures based on T. H. Rigby, *Communist Party Membership in the U.S.S.R., 1917–1967*, Princeton, Princeton University Press, 1968, pp. 332, 373, 380–381, 387; Everett M. Jacobs, "A Note on Jewish Membership of the Soviet Communist Party," *Soviet Jewish Affairs*, Vol. 6, No. 2, 1976, pp. 114–115; Zev Katz, "After the Six-Day War," in Lionel Kochan, ed., *The Jews in Soviet Russia since 1917*, 3rd ed., 1978, p. 345; E. M. Jacobs, "Further Considerations on Jewish Representation in Local Soviets and in the CPSU," *Soviet Jewish Affairs*, Vol. 8, No. 1, 1978, p. 32; and Radio Moscow English Broadcast, January 1, 1982, quoted by L. Hirszowicz, "Anti-Jewish Discrimination in Education and Employment," *Soviet Jewish Affairs*, Vol. 15, No. 1, February 1985, p. 26.

Note: *These slightly higher figures are used by Jacobs.

signs that if they remain passive and conform, they may remain unharmed.

Much about the life of Jews making up the "silent majority" remains concealed, unspoken, and perhaps unknowable to Western outsiders. They are not a homogeneous group, but a few generalizations about them can be made.[11] About 75 percent live in the heartland of Russia—in those areas which have been under Soviet rule for more than two generations. They are overwhelmingly urban, have a higher educational level than non-Jews, and are concentrated in technical-cultural-scientific occupations, described as upper socioeconomic levels in Soviet terms. More than half a million live in the largest cities: Moscow, Kiev, and Leningrad, constituting 26 percent of all of the Jews counted in the 1970 Census. About 50,000 are in rural communities but the rest are scattered throughout other cities of the Soviet heartland. The largest single concentration is in Moscow, with about a quarter of a million. Socially and psychologically, their values, it is believed, center on the personal and professional gratification derived from interesting and challenging work. This also provides the greatest source of ego-strength for Jews who are especially vulnerable in today's Soviet society. However, the competition for jobs in high-level scientific and cultural fields has grown very fierce in recent years, and university-age Jewish students who apply to universities are often rejected or face discriminatory practices. Scientists in recent years have migrated to Yakutsk, Siberia, where new scientific institutions have been established, and students, to Novosibirsk, where there are greater opportunities for Jews.

Some insight into this large "silent majority" was contributed by Dr. Vitaly Rubin in 1975, before his emigration to Israel. After first describing the morally ambiguous, even duplicitous society which conditions the behavior of all Russians, including Russian Jews, and stressing the great differences between Russian Jews and other Jews in the Soviet Union,[12] Rubin characterized several groups among the former: the middle-aged living fairly comfortably and the elderly on pensions and in their own apartments, weary of life's struggles, neither willing nor able to begin life anew in a new setting. Then, there were Jews still in high positions, interested in their own careers and material affluence. Some of these may have identified with the emigration movement but were "filled with utter hopelessness in estimating their chances of achieving it . . . [and] frightened off by the example of the distinguished Jewish scientists and scholars who found the courage to take the desperate step . . . only to be denied permission to leave." There were also middle-level Jews engaged in "classified" work, including virtually all engineers. Rubin also penetrated to a central truth about specialists in humanistic disciplines, such as history, economics, philosophy, and law—those whose chances of receiving exit visas were better, but who have generally been forced to make compromises in their professional work and could not make the struggle to emigrate. He also described the active Communists who serve the regime and either still believe the clichés and slogans drilled out by the party, or behave as if they do. Besides those who have intermarried, some have changed their names and identified themselves as Russians, not Jews, and are so identified on their internal passports. Still others have converted.[13] An uncounted number who had lived in exile, remain in the distant eastern provinces, having lost touch with old friends and family, and can scarcely be concerned about a Jewish life unless there are nostalgic memories or accessible companions, books, and music.

Felix Kandel and Alexander Voronel, refuseniks who eventually emigrated to Israel, agreed with Rubin that activists through their cultural work and samizdat could penetrate the consciousness of the more passive Jews and raise the level of their Jewish awareness.[14] Some were undoubtedly affected, as indicated by an informal survey made by Benjamin Fain, a pioneering figure in Jewish cultural activity, who emigrated to Israel where he became a professor of physics.

In 1976, while still in Moscow, Fain, with the help of 100 volunteers, conducted an unusual public opinion poll among Soviet Jews in homes, trains, public gardens, cafés, and even at a wedding. The survey[15] involved 1,215 interviews and a 34-item questionnaire dealing with questions about Jewish culture. So as not to skew the findings, any Jew who had decided to go to Israel or felt himself to have Zionist leanings was excluded. The results indicate that most Jews polled wanted to be identified as Jews and know more about Jewish culture. A large majority preferred that their sons or grandsons be given a Jewish name. Over 77 percent either preferred that their close relatives marry Jews or opposed intermarriage. A surprising 85 percent would want their children or grandchildren to know Hebrew or Yiddish. Eighty-six percent wanted their children to go to Jewish schools. About half polled said that they observed some Jewish holidays and would attend synagogue services "sometimes" if it were possible. After news of the survey was reported on the BBC and the Voice of America, Soviet officials seized the data, but Fain had saved an extra copy of the interviews and was able to get it to Israel. How could those expressed needs be met?

One result of the appeal of seventy-seven activists in April 1976 for cultural opportunities was the plan for a December 21–23, 1976 symposium.[16] Fain and a small organizing committee that included Pavel Abramovich, Mark Azbel, Brailovsky, Kandel, and Arkady Mai, planned a symposium in Moscow to address the question of Jewish culture in the USSR and ways in which it could be strengthened. "Besides emigration, as significant in the national rebirth," Fain said, is "the ever-growing need of Soviet Jews for sharing in the cultural heritage and traditions of their people." A detailed agenda was prepared in two parts: one, an analysis of the present situation of Jewish culture in the USSR (characteristics of Jewish national self-consciousness; social, ethnic, and language characteristics of Soviet Jewry; the role of religion in the life of Soviet Jewry; problems of preserving traditional Jewish institutions; present state of Jewish literature, art, and music; the experience of Jewish life in other socialist countries; and world development of Jewish culture in the Diaspora); and part two: future prospects (forms of further development; mechanisms of transfer and preservation of Jewish national heritage; principles and methods of mass sharing in national values where Jews are a minority; efficiency of traditional elements of Jewish culture in contemporary Soviet society; the role of Bible and Talmud in the spiritual enrichment of Soviet Jewry; youth and national progress in the USSR; Soviet Jewry as part of world Jewry; influence of Israel and Western Jewish communities on Soviet Jewry; language as an element of national culture; and international and Soviet declarations and documents concerning national rights and culture).

The comprehensive and careful planning can be seen in the full agenda, while the full commitment of the organizers to the concept is revealed in Professor Fain's statement to the October 15 London *Jewish Chronicle*: "We have recognized for a long time that while emigration to Israel is important for the Jews who wish to leave, the cultural awareness of the mass of Soviet Jewry is even more important." In the invitation to foreign scholars, Fain wrote: "The task of preserving and reviving Soviet Jewry, the task of its salvation from total spiritual destruction is the noble cause in which all those who want to be Jews must take part. Concrete steps for achieving this end come into being as a result of the creative work of those who will be engaged in this noble mission."

Papers were invited in Russian, Hebrew, Yiddish, or English. Fifty-four papers were submitted, but the symposium was disrupted by officials. Fain and his associates were continually harassed, and visas to scholars abroad, including four from the United States, were denied. Most of the organizers were arrested or detained in their homes on December 21. Nevertheless, a truncated symposium was held for one day in the apartment of Grigory Rosenshtein, one of the detained speakers.[17] Only seven papers were read; most of the others had been seized by the police.

The thrust of the seminar was quite clearly to help pave the way for Jewish cultural possibilities for those unable or unwilling to leave. Undoubtedly, the harsh police action frightened off the more ambivalent Jews and those dreading any association with unsanctioned activities. However, although it is very difficult to measure the extent of interest in Jewish culture among these silent Jews, there has been one indication of a very lively interest partly nourished and partly frustrated, namely, the crowds pouring over books of Jewish interest at the Moscow International Book Fairs, the sixth of which was held in 1987. The first one was held in September 1977, immediately before talks were to begin in Belgrade to assess the Helsinki Accords. Twenty-five American publishers displayed about 5,000 volumes in a huge exhibit of 80,000 titles representing 1,500 publishers from 63 countries.[18]

One representative of the Association of Jewish Book Publishers in the United States, Joseph S. Drew, was subjected to a careful scrutiny of his bags, including books and booklists, and at their display hall, Jewish representatives found over twenty-five books, including Moshe Dayan's *Diary of the Sinai Campaign*, books on the kibbutz movement, Jewish philosophy, and heroes of Israeli independence, on the "questionable pile," getting severe scrutiny.[19] Eventually, however, all were approved.

No books could be purchased by individuals and officials had no interest or desire to purchase and distribute any. But there were vivid scenes of intense interest at both the American and Israeli Jewish Book booths. "People would stand . . . and read endlessly. Literally hundreds of them asked for copies . . . Some just came and cried. . . ." Many were desperate to talk to the Jewish representatives and asked about

Jewish life elsewhere and begged to be allowed to buy some books. One Soviet Jew said, "They don't allow us to read anything. There are more books here on Jewish subjects than I have seen in my whole life. Please let me take a souvenir. I promise I will pass the book on to someone else."[20] There was great interest in a hanging Jewish calendar and in gold pins from Israel.

Inevitably books began to disappear. Often the police trailed suspects, sometimes following them for several miles. Numerous books were confiscated at the door of the main pavilion. By the last day of the fair, only about sixty of the 350 books brought by the Association of Jewish Book Publishers remained on the shelves.

At the Russian exhibit, there were eleven books in Yiddish, but not a single copy of any of the well-known anti-Zionist and anti-Semitic books that have been published.[21]

The Second Moscow International Book Fair was held from September 4 to 10, 1979. This time, the Association of Jewish Book Publishers in the United States brought 750 books, 4,000 recordings of Yiddish, Hebrew, and liturgical music and 8,000–9,000 Russian-language catalogues that contained descriptions of Jewish holidays and a five-year calendar.[22] Bernard Sharfstein, president of Ktav Publishing House, commented: "People literally pleaded for any small symbol of Jewish identity, a Star of David, a Jewish calendar, a Hebrew alphabet chart." Two young girls spent an entire afternoon copying the music and lyrics of "Hatikvah," the Jewish national anthem. One man came every day to read Gershom Scholem's book on cabala. An elderly man copied down the names of all the Jewish Nobel Prize winners.[23] Another man, wearing ribbons showing him to be a much-decorated veteran of World War II, asked several times, "Has our government ordered any books from you?" and left very upset.[24] According to one observer: "The curiosity about Jewish life in America and in Israel was intense, the misconceptions, revealing. . . . Among the many visitors to our booth were Jewish soldiers, Jewish translators, Jewish novelists who cannot get their work published, activists, refuseniks, and members of the KGB."[25] The activists and refuseniks spoke in Hebrew; the middle-aged and older in Yiddish.

The Educational Director of the Workmen's Circle, Joseph Mlotek, also observed the avid interest in books on Jewish topics:

No sooner had the Book Fair opened, than our pavilion was beseiged by thousands of Russian Jews. With great interest and curiosity, they viewed the Yiddish, English, and Hebrew books on Jewish themes. They leafed through the books, looked at them, read them. Some sat and copied entire pages, because . . . the people could look at the books but could not buy them. . . . Many of them, however, couldn't resist the temptation, and on the first day many of the books "disappeared." This happened every day and by the end of the fair we were left with very few books on the shelves. . . . They brought cameras and photographed the alphabet so that they could use it to learn Yiddish and Hebrew.

We did have two items which we were permitted to give to the visitors. . . . : One was a catalogue of our books, which also included, in Russian, a Jewish calendar listing all the Jewish holidays and their significance. The second was a thin plastic record, containing several Yiddish songs . . . as well as a number of Israeli songs and one cantorial. The demand of the visitors . . . for these two items was so great, the crowds so large, that the Red Army guards ordered us, on several occasions, to stop distributing them.[26]

Alexander Hoffman, Board Chairman of the Association of Jewish Book Publishers, reported that he was "torn apart" at the Fair when a young Jewish man asked him if he could keep a book on Old Testament philosophy. He apologized for asking but explained that he was teaching Bible classes to friends at night and could not get such books.[27]

Israel's participation was also considered a "success despite some harassment by Soviet authorities."[28] There were about 700 books in Hebrew, Russian, and English, all printed in Israel. Four titles were banned and fourteen Israeli publishers were denied visas. One positive result was the acquisition of Hebrew translation rights to the highly acclaimed book *Heavy Sand* by Anatoly Rybakov.

At the Third Moscow International Book Fair held from September 2 to 8, 1981, 2,300 publishers from 80 countries were represented, including Israel. There were 800 titles from the Association of Jewish Book Publishers in the United States in English, Hebrew, and Yiddish. As in the past, the Israeli and other Jewish exhibits were very popular. Customs agents seized copies of the 1981 *American Jewish Yearbook*, a children's version of Abba Eban's history of the Jews, and Shmuel Ettinger's Russian-language history of the Jews. At the fourth and fifth fairs (September, 1983 and 1985), there were again enthusiastic and curious crowds, with some Jews coming from cities 1,200 miles from Moscow. In 1983, 49 books of Jewish content were banned; in 1985, there were fewer, but at the end of the fair in 1985 many books "disappeared"; some were given to the Lenin Library and some to the American embassy in Moscow.[29] In 1987, 18,000 catalogs of Jewish book titles and many of the 3,000 books exhibited were snapped up. Religious texts were especially popular. Many refuseniks were seen, including two who traveled 1,000 miles from Yerevan.

Contacts between the Jewish "silent majority" and Western visitors have been generally minimal or non-existent. Relatives have not been particularly welcome because of official disapproval and fear of punitive consequences.[30] Thus, if there are such visits they are conducted very discreetly, and no Jewish cultural materials are brought in, as happens when Westerners visit activists. The official position is that Jews have assimilated and merged and no longer need specialized materials. However, there are officially permitted cultural morsels for Soviet Jews, meagerly spooned out, but much publicized. Many Soviet Jews eagerly respond. Yet, just as one cannot be absolutely sure of the causes of the dips and rises in emigration, one cannot be sure why there have been occasional, official concessions to Jewish cultural activity. They may be signals to the West, bargaining chips, or ways of deflecting criticism and charges of Soviet anti-Semitism, but whatever the reason, Jews who participate do so with joy subdued by wariness. The rationed offerings have been chiefly dramatic and musical programs, sporadically scheduled. Groups are formed and closed down and permissions are granted and withdrawn in an uncertain, teasing, carrot-and-stick manner, but Soviet officials seem eager to publicize these programs. Their spokesmen frequently claim in defense of official Jewish culture that "about half a million people frequent shows and concerts in the Jewish language each year."[31] All of the groups except the Musical-Dramatic People's Theater (re-named the Jewish Chamber Theater) and the Moscow Jewish Dramatic Ensemble in Birobidzhan are amateur. Most of the presentations are in Yiddish and consist mainly of revivals of old, pre-Revolution works, thus appealing to nostalgic feelings still alive among Jews. Often, local groups are required to use non-Jewish performers and devote part of the program to non-Jewish works.

One of the earliest groups that formed during the post-Stalin thaw was the Jewish Choir and Drama Group in Riga (see Chapter 27), starting in 1957, but forced to close down in 1963. In the same year, the Vilnius Jewish People's Theater was started, offering programs of music, dance, and drama. When the Theater celebrated its twentieth anniversary, it was said to have given a total of 450 performances to a combined audience of 500,000.[32] The group lost a number of its members to emigration, but a core of veterans has remained and some young Jews have recently joined. This group has been permitted to perform elsewhere—in Kaunas, Borisov, Gomel, and several Lithuanian resorts. In June 1983 it was joined by an amateur group from Kaunas for a concert commemorating the fortieth anniversary of the Warsaw Ghetto Uprising.[33] The group also presented a new play "Towards Life" in June 1981 to coincide with the fortieth anniversary of the German invasion of the Soviet Union. Of special interest—in view of the immense official propaganda alleging that Jews helped Nazis during the war and merit no special acknowledgment of their suffering—was the fact that the play contains dramatic stories dealing with their tragic struggle under Nazi occupation.[34] In Kaunas itself Yaacov Beltser, the former director of the Zhitomir Yiddish Theater, led an amateur group of Yiddish players for several years until his death in March 1979.[35]

At times, apparently, the response of the audience overflows the line officials have drawn and the effort is shut down. In Tallin, Estonia, for example, where there are about 15,000 Jews, there had been a Jewish theater and dance company and choir for ten years until 1973. One of the actresses, Anna Krutchek, now in Israel, recalled that "Every performance was an experience, everyone looked forward to it, sang and danced, each time it was like a Jewish holiday." Why were the activities stopped? Perhaps, Anna thinks, "because aliya to Israel assumed serious proportions. . . . [There was] a massive re-awakening, the authorities began to place difficult obstacles in their paths."[36] Their last program dealt with the story of Anne Frank.

Elsewhere, small groups of individual actors and musicians or small dramatic groups have performed in various parts of the country. Anna Guzik, for example, the popular actress and singer and daughter of the well-known Jewish actor Yakov Guzik, created and directed an ensemble in Leningrad until she emigrated in 1973. There was also a variety group in Chernovtsy, led by the aging actress Sidi Tal, and a theater group in Kishinev, but these groups were no longer heard from or performing after the early and middle seventies.[37] Requests from a group of distinguished actors in Kiev to form a theater have been rebuffed. It has generally been believed that there have been no musical or dramatic groups in the Ukraine or White Russia. However, the Jewish activist Ilya Goldin, after his emigration to Israel, when he urged support of both official and unofficial culture, pointed to official permission granted in Minsk to form a Yiddish theater in 1979. He said, "It is impossible to have a large non-official cultural movement, and having it official is better than not having it at all." The aim of cultural efforts would be "to build a wall against assimilation. . . . It's a first step."[38] (At the time there were four *ulpanim* [Hebrew-language groups] in Minsk and a cultural seminar—all unofficial.) In the spring of 1980 a chorus organized by Leonid Zubarev was given permission to hold a concert of Hebrew and Yiddish songs but was not permitted to call itself a Jewish Chorus.

A group of Jewish actors began to perform in Moscow in 1961, eventually becoming known as the Moscow Jewish Dramatic Ensemble, directed by the veteran actor Venyamin Shvartser, but it has no home of its own, and has traveled to the far reaches of the country, often to places with few Jews and seldom to cities with large Jewish populations.[39] In October 1980, this small Jewish theatrical group created a stir in Moscow by presenting a poignant work dealing with the massacre of Jews at Babi Yar in September 1941. The play, written by a little-known playwright Alexander Borshchagovsky, is called "Ladies' Tailor" and, in sharp contrast to the conventional stereotype of the Soviet Jew, describes a courageous and patriotic Jewish working class family "capable of nobility to one another and generosity to their Russian neighbors, one of whom, a tortured anti-Semite, undermines the official fiction that there is no significant anti-Semitism in the Soviet Union." The central role of the ladies' tailor was played by Zinovy Kaminsky, the nephew of the famous Yiddish actress Ida Kaminska. Two cuts were ordered by the censors: the lifting of the skirt of a young girl showing the nakedness of Jews, ordered by the Germans to disrobe before they were shot; and a scene in which a Russian woman sings a Russian Orthodox prayer over Jewish friends. The play was sold out for all performances.[40]

For over eighteen years, the Jewish Drama Ensemble was on tour in Yiddish plays, but "Ladies' Tailor" was played in Russian—apparently a manifestation of the trend toward creation and translation of Jewish works into Russian. However, a Yiddish translation of the play under the title, "The Night Before Babi Yar" was made by the noted Yiddish writer Note Lurye and published in *Sovetish heymland* Number 9 in 1981, together with an introduction by the author, who heard an account of the horrors at Babi Yar when he entered liberated Kiev with the Russian army. "Why," it may be asked, "have the authorities permitted such a positive picture of Soviet Jews and so frank an acceptance of the solace of Judaism"? As with the novel *Heavy Sand*, published in 1978, such surprises "cannot all be neatly explained by changes, real or supposed, of Soviet policy. They are among the things that make Russia so unpredictable," observed a seasoned correspondent Anthony Austin.[41] "Ladies' Tailor" was performed again in Moscow in June 1981[42] and continues to be performed as of 1987.

A Yiddish People's Theater was started in Birobidzhan in 1965 and has been directed by several of Mikhoels' students. Its repertoire includes old favorites of Sholem Aleikhem, Goldfaden, and Buzi Miller, and Yiddish versions of selected Russian plays, including "Invasion" by Leonid Leonov. In October 1984, in line with the intense Soviet anti-Zionist policy, it performed Tsezar Solodar's play "The Scales," which dramatizes problems experienced by Soviet Jewish families in Israel.[43]

In 1979 the Jewish Chamber Music Theater was founded in Birobidzhan by Yuri Sherling, a young composer. This group is the first permanent Yiddish troupe in the Soviet Union since Stalin closed the Moscow State Theater in 1949. In a three-day stand in Khabarovsk in May 1979, the group performed a "rousing Yiddish rock musicale" called "A Black Bridle for a White Mare," with sets by Ilya Glazunov, the popular and controversial Russian nationalist artist, who is not Jewish. The show, based on an imaginary nineteenth-century shtetl named Mirazhnya, combines folklore, dance, rock music, and ballet (see Photo 33.1). It received "rave" reviews and was apparently enjoyed by mixed audiences in Vladivostok, Moscow, cities in the Baltic republics, and in Minsk.[44]

This Theater has its working base in Moscow; only half of the sixty employees are Jewish. The program content is strictly controlled, and although it is a touring company, it has not been permitted to perform in certain centers where there is a large Jewish population—in Leningrad and Kiev, for example.[45] In November 1983 it staged a premiere of "Tevye from Anatevka" based on "Fiddler on the Roof" in Tbilisi. Where it has performed, the Theater has played to packed houses. It went on tour in Czechoslovakia in October 1985.

There are also numerous concerts featuring Jewish music and soloists, and musical and literary soirées on the premises of *Sovetish heymland*. Among others, a special concert of the music of Max Goldin, musicologist and composer, was performed in 1976 in Riga by the Riga State Philharmonic, and in 1981–82, Ada Svetlova presented a program

33.1 Scene from the opera *A Black Bridle for a White Mare*, by Yuri Sherling. Performed by the Moscow-Birobidzhan Jewish Chamber Music Theater on a visit to Vilnius, 1978. Courtesy Boris Feldblyum.

of twenty-seven Yiddish folksongs in Goldin's settings in Riga, Chernovtsy, the Donetsk and Vinnitsa regions, and Moscow.[46] In December 1979, during the Russian Winter Festival, the Academic State Symphony Orchestra conducted an exclusively "Jewish" concert, including "Rhapsody on Jewish Themes" by Zinovy Kampaneets,[47] a leading Jewish composer in the early years of the Revolution and who, according to a prominent music critic, "had an unexpressed urge for Jewish music throughout his life."[48] He collected and composed Yiddish folksongs and those of Eastern peoples and in 1970 edited a collection in Yiddish. A number of lesser-known Jewish composers and singers appear from time to time in *Sovetish heymland* and, as further evidence of official dispensation, the Soviet recording company *Melodiya* began making recordings of Jewish music in 1982.[49]

In the field of visual art, innovative Soviet artists, including many Jews, formed an oppositionist, experimental movement in the early 1960s, as had happened in literature. Among the leading Jewish figures were Ernst Neizvestny and Oskar Rabin, both of whom emigrated. One of the most original of the Jewish painters was Alexander Tishler, whose work customarily was called "decadent" or "morbid," but whose studio in Leningrad in the last years of his life (he died in 1980) became a place of pilgrimage for many young painters. The Soviet art historian Igor Golomstock writes of his "specific artistic style . . . in which the exoticism of the Jewish way of life was expressed in bizarre images . . . which bore the imprint of biblical spirituality." But his experiences as a soldier in the Red Army witnessing traces of pogroms and the horrors of the Civil War created grotesque images of cruelty and violence. Tyshler also designed sets for the State Jewish Theater and various national theaters, which were highly acclaimed.[50] Natan Altman was another avant-garde painter who lived in Paris for several years; he returned to the Soviet Union in 1935, working as a stage and theater designer. "In his last works" a critic has written, "the images of his childhood seemed to return—the Chagall-like fantastic life of the Jewish shtetl."[51] Exhibitions of his works have been held in Leningrad in recent years as have been exhibitions of paintings and sculpture on Jewish themes featuring the works of Shloime Gershov, Meir Axelrod, and Shloime Iudovich.[52] There are also frequent exhibits of Jewish artists in the offices of *Sovetish heymland.* In August 1987, in Lvov, new works by the Soviet Jewish painter Mikhail Lishiner were shown, depicting Nazi war atrocities.

In December 1979, there was great excitement in Tbilisi, Georgia, because of an unprecedented Jewish program on television.[53] It was a fifty-minute program, at prime evening viewing time, on medieval Jewish poetry. An actress recited in Georgian a poem about the love of Zion by the great poet Yehuda Halevy, who lived in Spain in the eleventh century. Other poems followed against a backdrop of a painting of Old Jerusalem years ago, the ruined Temple, and one of Marc Chagall's stained glass windows. A cantor's voice chanted against a picture of the Western Wall. Why such a program? There was speculation that a Helsinki monitor and long-time refusenik Isai Goldshtein, had challenged Georgian authorities to follow their own doctrines on encouraging minority cultures. The television program may have been one result.

Jewish religious activities in the Soviet Union are technically legal, but severely limited and frowned upon, suspected, or condemned, depending upon the official climate at the time. Many Jews undoubtedly observe some private, unreported, and unrecorded form of religious ritual, celebration, or prayer, such as *Kaddish* (traditional prayer for the dead). However, official information deals primarily with synagogue attendance. In 1980 Iosif Shapiro, an official in the Council of Religious Affairs of the USSR Council of Ministers, reported that "the concrete sociological research conducted in individual towns and regions leads one to conclude that there are now in our country approximately 60,000 adherents to Judaism. These are for the most part elderly people, 70–75 years or older." Shapiro went on to say that the Georgian, Bukharan, and Mountain Jews "cling more fervently to religious customs and rites" than do Ashkenazi Jews, and that among the religiously observant of the former are middle-aged and young people. He claimed that there were ninety-one synagogues (twenty-two in Georgia alone) and seventy *minyanim*. In answering "foreign defenders of Judaism," who say that there are few synagogues in the Soviet Union, Shapiro calls this charge a "lie," arguing that "there are quite sufficient synagogues in existence to satisfy the religious needs of believers," and that "there are almost no rabbis" because of "the unpopularity of a religious career among the Jewish populations."[54] There is still no central Jewish religious body nor facilities for religious training or education.[55] Moreover, "in the hostile Soviet atmosphere, it is not a simple matter to organize a *dvadtsatka* . . . nor is it easy to rent premises for prayer."[56] Most of the members of the *dvadtsatka* are pensioners who have little to fear from the authorities; others are and would be much more at risk.

In April 1972, there were reports that the Moscow yeshiva Kol Yaacov was reopened after six years. Later, in the summer of 1974, Rabbi Yaacov Fishman, who had been appointed Rabbi of the Moscow Central Synagogue in June 1972, informed Ashkenazi Chief Rabbi Shlomo Goren of Israel that the yeshiva had eighteen adult and ten younger students. One of the students, Yaacov Ryklin, was reported to be spending one year at Yeshiva University in New York.[57] In May 1975, Rabbi Moses Rosen of Romania visited Moscow and "it was agreed that two more students would be sent to the Bucharest Yeshiva [there were then two in Budapest] and that there would be an exchange of visits between Dr. Rosen and the Moscow synagogue leaders."[58] In an apparent nod to Western protests, two graduates of Soviet universities were reportedly permitted to leave the Soviet Union in 1979 to train for rabbinate service by taking stepped-up courses at Yeshiva University in New York City.[59]

Novosti, the Soviet news agency, characteristically goes out of its way to present the image of Jews enjoying religious freedom. In November 1980, for example, it reported[60] that "all 92 Soviet synagogues held Rosh Hashanah services, with 5,000 attending the newly-renovated Moscow Choral Synagogue," and that all synagogues held Simchat Torah services, but the number of synagogues is believed to be about sixty. At the recently renovated Odessa Synagogue, it was reported that a *sukkah* (outdoor booth) was built. Outside the Leningrad Synagogue, there were large crowds. A banner was displayed reading, "Allow Us to Study Hebrew," and listing the names and addresses of Leningrad Hebrew teachers. This time the police did not interfere. In December 1980, Novosti published an article called "Weddings at the Moscow Choral Synagogue," in which it was reported that Rabbi Fishman in nine years had married "several hundreds of believing Jews" as well as "non-believing Jews" who "are moved by a desire to perform the wedding rites in keeping with purely national traditions."[61] Other articles report on the tons of matzos baked for Passover.

There have been sporadic reports about houses of prayer, minyanim, and even yeshivas established by the Habad and Bratzlav Hasidic movements, but these are unregistered and the extent of their influence and existence can only be guessed. It is generally thought to be quite considerable. In July 1981, 45 Bratzlaver Hasidim arrived in Moscow on their way to the grave of the mystic Rabbi Nahman of Bratzlav in Uman. Permission for the pilgrimage was secured by Rabbi Pinchas Teitz of Elizabeth, New Jersey, from Soviet authorities.[62] The officially recognized and appointed rabbis are often required to make pronouncements echoing official policies, attend conferences on international peace, "relations between the nations," and disarmament, and participate in meetings of "Friendship Societies." Most recently, they have been called upon to join the Anti-Zionist Committee of the Soviet Public (see Chapter 34) to attack "Western centers of Zionism and their emissaries" and declare that emigration of Jews has been completed.

The involvement of such Jews in a World Conference of Religious Leaders "For Lasting Peace, Disarmament and Just Relations between Peoples" held in Moscow in June 1977 is described in an interesting 200-page volume called *Jewish Religious Calendar for 5739/1978–79* (in

Russian), viewed as "the most substantial of its type to emerge from the Moscow religious community for a very long time . . . a veritable treasure-trove of information."[63] The work was edited by Solomon Kleynman, former president of the Moscow religious community and later cantor, and includes information on the significance of religious events during each month of the Jewish year; a table of festivals, fasts, and other important dates; a section on the history of prayers and excerpts from certain liturgical texts in Russian translation; essays on Maimonides and the Baal Shem Tov; a literary section, including several short stories by Peretz and several pages of biblical sayings and sayings of the Hebrew sages; and a section on religious customs and practices in Yiddish. There are also forty-nine pages of photographs, not only of elderly people in the synagogue, but also of youthful crowds celebrating Simchat Torah in the streets outside the synagogue. Thus, "there is a great amount of factual material of Jewish interest . . . and much to offer those Jews seeking their Jewish identity."[64]

One doesn't know how many such Jews there are or how accessible this publication is, but the fact that it has been published under official aegis represents a considerable shift from earlier constraints and gives at least some Jews who may be groping for some Jewish content in their lives a stronger grip on permissible sources of Jewish religious life.

In the November 1983 issue of a Czech monthly, Daniel Meyer, a graduate of the Budapest Rabbinical Seminary, who was inducted as Rabbi in Prague in June 1984, wrote an idealized report on the state of Jewish religious life in the USSR.[65] By that time thirty-six-year-old Boris Gramm had become chairman of the "Jewish religious community" in Moscow, and forty-one-year-old Adolph Shayevich from Birobidzhan, and thirty-year-old Menachem Nidel, had graduated from the Budapest Seminary. Shayevich succeeded Rabbi Fishman, who died in June 1983, as Chief Rabbi of the Moscow Choral Synagogue, and Nidel became Rabbi in Riga. Meyer stressed the point that young people were now in charge of the Moscow religious community and that "the Moscow community is not only the spiritual center of the Jewish population of Moscow, [but] also has a function similar to that exercised by our Council of Jewish Religious Communities." Meyer reported that at the time there were six students at the Moscow Yeshiva, where they were studying traditional religious texts and learning *shekhita* (ritual slaughter). Much was made of the daily and Sabbath services and attendance during the high holidays. "This year," he wrote, "there were inside and in front of the synagogue over eight thousand believers, of whom about forty percent were young people." Special note was also made of Hasidim "of several tendencies and highly observant young believers, who wear *peyot* [side curls] and *tsitsit* [a small fringed shawl]."

Such an article was obviously approved by Soviet authorities and may simply be one face of a dual or triple-faced policy, with basic intent and direction concealed. However, the official recognition of Jewish religious influences on young people represents a marked departure from previous public statements and may be an acknowledgment of a new reality in Soviet Jewish life. The inner migration of considerable numbers of young activist Jews toward a religious life-style when emigration is indefinitely postponed or abandoned has been realized for some time. It can be assumed that some among the silent majority have also moved toward this orientation.

As has been frequently pointed out, the synagogue remains the principal physical central address of Soviet Jews, a place where Jews can come together, even for those Jews who are not religiously minded, but want to meet with other Jews and, in this way, bespeak their Jewish consciousness. Another form of collective expression has been assembling for a commemorative service at a site where large numbers of Jews were murdered during the war. These experiences have met with an erratic, frequently repressive course. Many such events in the past ten years, especially those involving refuseniks, have been disrupted or barred, but some have been sanctioned and even arranged by authorities. At times it seems that official permission has been connected with some foreign intervention or quid pro quo. In the early and middle 1970s numerous memorial meetings at the sites of Nazi atrocities—Babi Yar, Rumbuli, Salispils in Latvia, Kaunas, and Ponary—were broken up. In July 1976, at Babi Yar, the simple stone slab that had marked the site was replaced by a huge monument designed by Ukrainian sculptors, bearing the inscription that 200,000 Soviet citizens of various nationalities had been murdered, but with no mention of Jews. In 1976, the KGB threatened three Kiev Jews with long prison sentences as punishment for holding a memorial rite at Babi Yar, but a number of congressmen intervened and sent a cable to Brezhnev.[66] Three hundred Soviet Jews came to Babi Yar on September 29 and were unmolested, but several Moscow, Riga, and Kiev activists were detained.

In the summer of 1979, an Israeli delegation to the International Political Science Association Congress in Moscow was permitted to go to Babi Yar and hold a memorial service there.[67] They were surprised to learn that, contrary to most past experiences, Intourist provided several luxury tourist buses for all Congress participants. The official guide spoke briefly about the history of the Babi Yar massacre, stressing that many Soviet citizens were killed here by the Nazis, including the Jews of Kiev.

In April 1979, over 3,000 Jews from Minsk and surrounding towns participated in a service commemorating the 40,000 Jews murdered there by the Nazis in 1942. A memorial slab carrying an inscription in Yiddish was erected through contributions made by thousands of widows and former soldiers and partisans, but there has been persistent fear that authorities will replace it with an official obelisk. Later in the year, a group of Minsk activists petitioned the Belorussian SSR Central Committee not to remove it: "The removal of this memorial will certainly offend the most sacred feelings of every honest person, of every Jew, because this place is literally permeated with the blood of our brothers and sisters and is the only reminder of that monstrous tragedy. . . . In whose interest is it to make impersonal the place where this terrible tragedy took place?" (see Photo 33.2).[68]

In December 1979, there was a commemorative meeting for the victims of fascism, including the 200,000 Jews of Lithuania, at the Ninth Fort in Kaunas.[69] On May 2, 1980, about 100 Jews from Riga gathered at the Rumbuli cemetery to commemorate the victims of the destruction of the ghetto. These meetings continue and help to provide an intermittent sense of solidarity for those Jews who participate. Often they are broken up, but from time to time they are permitted. There was also an unusual official recognition of *Kristallnacht*, when Rabbi Shayevich and Boris Gramm of Moscow Synagogue participated in a memorial ceremony held in the GDR, November 6–9, 1985. In February 1987, the USSR participated in a conference on non-Jewish Nazi victims held in Washington.

Additional officially permitted expressions of Jewishness involve increased activity in Yiddish, with initiatives taken generally by *Sovetish heymland*, and a marked trend to make certain Yiddish works available

33.2 Memorial to Jewish victims of Ponary in Vilna during World War II—an exception to Soviet policy of not identifying the Jewish victims of mass murder. The inscription was in Yiddish and Russian, but the monument was demolished in 1952.

in Russian, Ukrainian, and other languages, which makes it possible for a younger generation of Jews who do not know Yiddish to read the classics and certain modern works. For example, M. S. Belenky has translated and compiled material on Sholem Aleikhem in Russian (1984), and in 1985, Vergelis's selected poems by 48 Soviet Yiddish poets, which were translated into Russian by foremost Russian poets.

Many of the older, gifted Yiddish writers who survived the Stalin period have emigrated to Israel, among them Boymvol, Kerler, Osherovich, Shekhtman, and Telesin, thus robbing Soviet Yiddish literature of seasoned and creative figures. Their works are generally not published in the Soviet Union, but the works of Bergelson, Der Nister, Markish, Feffer, and others who perished, are. These Yiddish masters of another generation cannot be replaced, of course, but we are in a much contracted period when Jewish cultural survival remains problematical, and a few signs of activity in Yiddish offer a spark of hope since they are approved and seemingly encouraged by the government. Another possible sign of official support of Yiddish came in the summer of 1986 at the Soviet Writers' Congress when, for the first time since 1949, a Yiddish writer, Vergelis, was elected to the governing board.

Lessons in Yiddish, mentioned earlier, have continued in *Sovetish heymland*. Moreover, there seems to be evidence that interest in reading a Yiddish journal such as the *Sovetish heymland* has been increasing. Letters to the editor, articles, and reported conversations with readers indicate the great pleasure the journal provides in reawakening the joys of Yiddish. In the June 1976 issue, the Yiddish alphabet was published in bold letters under the heading "Fulfilling a Request." In its June 1977 issue, an "important conference" of its editorial board was reported at which it was admitted that "many Jews who cannot read and write Yiddish—adolescents and adults alike—would like to acquire a knowledge of the language."

The Yiddish writing pool at the present time is small—there are about sixty to seventy writers—most of them contributors to *Sovetish heymland* or the Warsaw *Folkshtimme*, but among them are several new talented figures, including Vladimir Danko, Alexander Lizen, Yosif Gegerman, Boris Sandler, and Yosif Rabin. A remarkable figure, a non-Jew, Alexander Belousov, appeared for the first time in 1969. Belousov is from Kuibyshev and studied both Hebrew and Yiddish by taking private lessons from Jewish neighbors. His deep interest in Jewish life and culture was stirred by his grandfather, the Russian writer Alexei Kompasov, who worked in the Russian section of the Jewish Antifascist Committee and had close relations with the Yiddish writers on the committee. "Yiddish is not a foreign language to me," Belousov told the Yiddish journalist S. L. Shneiderman. "It seems to me that anyone who comes to know the two languages of the Jewish people and their literature, must fall in love with this people and their culture. . . . And so, all the suffering and joys of the Jewish people are my own. . . ."[70] The Holocaust is a dominant theme in Belousov's poetry. He mourns over the Jews and their shtetlach that have perished, the synagogues and books that were desecrated, and promises to keep their memories alive.

The Yiddish literary past is slowly unfolding for middle-aged and young readers who can now not only read full critical analyses of classical Yiddish writers such as Sholem Aleikhem and Mendele, but also the works and critical reviews of the great writers who perished during the years 1948–52. Moishe Litvakov, the brilliant but much feared literary commissar and editor of *Der emes*, who was killed in 1937 during the purges, is now quoted[71] and the eminent literary critics and scholars of the 1920s and 1930s, Max Erik and Meir Wiener, are identified as pioneering figures in their understanding and appreciation of eighteenth- and nineteenth-century Yiddish literature. One can also find articles by Gorky on the Habimah Theater and Vakhtangov, letters from the literary critic Yehezkel Dobrushin to the literary historian Israel Tsinberg, and chapters from an unfinished work by Bergelson called "Alexander Barash" as well as memoirs by his sister. Readers can also now begin to understand the great excitement and fervor that animated the 1908 conference in Czernowitz (Chernovtsy) to establish Yiddish as *the* Jewish language throughout the world.[72]

Interest and fluency in Yiddish in the Soviet Union, although generally discounted by advocates of Hebrew, may still be quite strong. It is unlikely that Hebrew will ever be legitimated, given Soviet ideological conditioning and the long and vehement history of the regime's war against the language. Yiddish, on the other hand, *is* legitimate and seems to have conspicuously, if sparingly, the renewed support of the government. This support has been further demonstrated by the publication in 1984 of a new, monumental Russian-Yiddish dictionary. The dictionary had been long in coming to birth, having been started in 1935 in Kiev at the Institute of Yiddish Culture, but was interrupted by arrests, exacting demands, and then the deaths of its chief compilers, Eliahu Spivak, Chaim Loytsker, Moyshe Maydansky, and Moyshe Shapiro, all highly qualified Yiddish linguists and lexicographers.[73]

The dictionary was recovered and published under the initiative and stimulus of the editorial circle of *Sovetish heymland*[74] which has been concerned to enlarge readership by "reviving the vestigial awareness of the Yiddish language among the Jewish Ashkenazi population of the USSR," to impress Western Jewry and to counter the interest in Hebrew among certain young Soviet Jews.[75] *Sovetish heymland* established the initial contacts between the editors and publisher (Russky yazyk, Moscow), arranged meetings and conferences dealing with the dictionary, and published relevant articles and discussion materials.[76] Whether meant to be merely a showcase or an indication of an official shift toward a more serious view of Jewish needs, the publication of the dictionary is a major Yiddish cultural development, comparable, for those Jews interested in Hebrew, to Felix Shapiro's compilation of the Hebrew-Russian dictionary of 1963. It is also undoubtedly a propagandistic coup. Interestingly, the five final Hebrew letters which were restored by *Sovetish heymland* in 1961 (but not by *Birobidzhaner shtern*) are also used in the dictionary, but many words related to traditional Jewish life (for example, kosher, Haggadah, Chanukah) are omitted.

For those interested in theoretical and technical questions, Moyshe Shapiro himself contributed a number of articles to the journal between 1966 and 1973, in which he emphasized the unity of standard literary Yiddish. Yet, overall, as a linguistics scholar has pointed out, the new dictionary is "a dictionary of modern Soviet Yiddish and not of general literary Yiddish."[77] A Yiddish-Russian dictionary is now also being prepared.

To repeated requests for a dialogue between Soviet Jewish writers and those living elsewhere, Vergelis has replied that writers abroad "could not rise above their class depravity," and has attacked Yiddish literature in the West.[78] Only Soviet Yiddish writers and their "progressive" counterparts in the West, he maintains, are the rightful heirs of the Yiddish classics; the others represent a break in the *Goldene Keyt* (Golden Chain). Curiously, he accepts the Hebrew of Israeli anti-Zionist Communist writers, thus conceding that Hebrew is a living language in the state that the Soviet Union wishes to survive. Readers may also, indirectly, be picking up a little Hebrew from the numerous Hebraisms in Yiddish literature which are transliterated. They must also digest the irony of reading about "work in Hebrew in the Russian institutes of advanced study,"[79] which are off limits to Jews.

Although circumscribed ideologically and lacking in imaginative literary brilliance, *Sovetish heymland* is considered one of the best Yiddish literary journals in the world.[80] The circulation is disappointingly low—in 1979, it was estimated at only 7,000, but undoubtedly copies are made and passed from hand to hand. Meanwhile, Vergelis seems to be trying to broaden the scope of his activities and the range of material in the journal. He has been cooperating with Jewish painters, sculptors, and composers, and the journal has included memoirs, letters, and interesting references to Jewish composers, song writers (Leib Yampolsky, Zinovy Kampaneets, Shike Driz, and Shmuel Senderey),[81] and artists. The journal has close ties with the Moscow Jewish Dramatic Ensemble and has published a Yiddish translation of "The Ladies' Tailor" by Alexander Borshchagovsky (see pp. 769–70 this chapter).[82] *Sovetish heymland* sometimes sends a representative to accompany the ensemble on its tours and may even host a performance on its premises.[83] It also publishes reproductions of the work of Jewish painters and sponsors art exhibits.

Beginning in 1980, it published Yiddish book supplements to add to the few Yiddish books published each year: nine in 1979; twenty in 1980; twenty-two in 1981. (From 1956 to 1976, only fifty Yiddish books were published.) In 1982, as a means of stimulating new writers to replace the aging ones, *Sovetish heymland* prepared teaching materials including short stories, verse, and critical articles by four contemporary Jewish writers, for the two-year courses for Yiddish writers which opened at Moscow's Gorky Literary Institute.[84] In July 1982, it was reported that Note Lurye, a leading Yiddish writer and member of the *Sovetish heymland* editorial board, had met students of the Literary Faculty of the Odessa State University and discussed his own work, the literary and social activities of other Yiddish writers, and future plans of the journal.[85]

In the May 1983 issue, Vergelis critically reviewed a Yiddish primer (*Alefbeys*) published in 1982 with much fanfare but limited for use in Birobidzhan only. This was the first Yiddish primer published in the Soviet Union since 1947 and presumably would be used in elementary school classrooms in Birobidzhan. It is skewed to create the impression that Jews are no more than a Soviet nationality confined to Birobidzhan,[86] but without a history on Soviet soil, or any connection with Jews elsewhere in the world, or without a long history going back centuries. Vergelis "finds it amazing that the compilers drew only five lines from Sholem Aleikhem's writings," that important Yiddish writers such as Itzik Kipnis and Der Nister are not represented, and that "instead of the classical models, the clumsy lines of the primer's compilers were included."[87] Is Vergelis toying with his readers, giving them the impression that he has the "freedom" to be critical of a work, in which his deputy editor at *Sovetish heymland* (one of the compilers, who had to have the approval of Soviet authorities) is guilty of "clumsy lines"? Or is he quite genuinely critical and groping for ways to enlarge the substance and outreach of Yiddish? One cannot be certain. Yet he seems to be either the initiator or spokesman for the acknowledged greater support for Yiddish by the regime in recent years.[88] Whether this is another double-faced policy—one for public consumption masking the basic policy and another hidden one, concealing the basic policy—remains to be seen.

It is often said that there is no future for Yiddish in the Soviet Union, and that what is available is so controlled and disfigured as to be essentially worthless. Any comparison to the situation in the United States is overstretched, but in terms of reawakened interest, it is worth noting that although Yiddish was completely written off as a source of Jewish cultural experiences for fourth and fifth generation American Jews, it is witnessing reawakened interest and study through the work of the Yiddish Book Center in Amherst, Massachusetts, the Oxford University Summer Program in Yiddish, and the unexpected interest of wholly Americanized young Jews in learning Yiddish in order to know more about the Jewish past.[89] Conceivably, this may happen to some young Soviet Jews as long as Yiddish remains legitimate and as long as it is officially sanctioned. It is admittedly a very frail reed. A sudden familiar gust may blow it away, but while it exists, its significance in helping Jewish culture survive should not be gainsaid. Besides, Yiddish still has great meaning for some Soviet Jews.

In the meantime, not only is Yiddish receiving greater official encouragement, but there is a notable trend to make certain Yiddish works available in Russian, Ukrainian, and other languages, which makes it possible for a younger generation of Jews who do not know Yiddish to read Yiddish classics and certain modern works. In keeping with this trend, in January 1985, *Soviet Weekly* reported that beginning in 1985, *Sovetish heymland* would publish each year an anthology of selected works from past issues in English, French, and Russian as well as Yiddish.[90]

For some observers such announcements are so much overblown rhetoric to impress foreign opinion, or, at best, a doomed effort to artificially give life to a language and culture the Soviet Union itself has all but destroyed. It has also been pointed out that it has been Hebrew rather than Yiddish which has aroused the most heightened Jewish consciousness in recent years and which has been studied and mastered by many hundreds, possibly thousands of young Jews. Yet both are completely authentic *Jewish* languages. The regime, however, recognizes only Yiddish. One cannot help speculating that if Western Jewry had invested as much effort in the cultural needs of those Jews who want to or have to remain in the Soviet Union as it has in Hebrew and the needs of those emigrating, Yiddish might have become as highly esteemed as Hebrew, or at least, been deemed valuable and worthy of study.[91] At the same time, since Russian is the primary language for most Jews in the Soviet Union, it is in translation that most Jews will find reading matter on Jewish themes if they are at all interested. There were numerous translations of works from the Yiddish, especially in the years 1929–30 and 1939. In 1955–56, some of the surviving Yiddish writers did some work in Russian and after 1961, when *Sovetish heymland* began publication, most of the Yiddish writers who contributed were translated into Russian. After the "thaw," between 1957 and 1967, fifteen books on Jewish history were published in Russian, eight of them dealing with the Dead Sea Scrolls.[92] The emphasis, however, was on the importance of the Scrolls as a source of the beginnings of Christianity, rather than as a source for Jewish history. Moreover, because of official policy to eliminate all Jewish national content from writing about and by Jews, and because most of the Jewish writers today have not had a Jewish education, the translated material is somewhat problematical. For example, Leib Kvitko's children's poetry became very popular in Russian translation, but the Jewish names of children disappeared. "This policy of obscuring basic national feelings within Soviet Yiddish literature," which Mordechai Altshuler noted in 1970, "still continues to influence translations from Yiddish to Russian."[93]

In the post-Stalin period from 1958 to 1979, there were 713 items in Soviet journals dealing with Jewish literature, most in Russian but almost 300 in languages of national minorities. In the 22-year period, there were 444 Yiddish books translated, of which 313 were translated into Russian. The most popular author by far among the Yiddish classical writers is Sholem Aleikhem, but large editions of Mendele and Peretz have also been published. Among the Soviet Yiddish writers, Bergelson, Feffer, Halkin, Hofshteyn, Markish, Ovsey Driz, Iosif Rabin, and Lurye have been translated, but Der Nister and Nusinov have not. Hirszowicz, who made a detailed survey of this period, has also noted that many works of contemporary Yiddish writers and children's literature have been translated and published. However, studies in Jewish history and the history of Jewish literature are almost entirely absent.[94] Most significantly, and disappointingly, there is still no Russian-language journal of Jewish affairs comparable to the many that flourished in tsarist times and that many Soviet Jews have petitioned for.[95] More encouraging was the dedication at the Sixth Book Fair in September 1987, of a small Jewish public library in Moscow. Located in the apartment of Yuri Sokol, a Jewish war hero, the library consists of 500 books in Russian, Hebrew, English, and Yiddish, donated by private individuals.

The meager ration of permitted Jewish material and activity has been overwhelmed by the wholly negative, abusive propaganda and plain disinformation being spread through Soviet society and harming all Jews. The reverberations of the emigration struggle and the stigma attached to Jews who leave or apply to leave have also affected most Jews remaining in the large centers of Jewish concentration, causing acute personal self-consciousness and defensive or apologetic complexes. These Jews have little or none of the religious or spiritual armor that strengthened their parents and grandparents in tsarist Russia and almost no cultural supports that could help buffer or make more tolerable the insults and demeaning attacks they must endure. Nor is there the solidarity of a "community of fate" in which Jews in former times could find some measure of comfort and security. Whether the meager officially sanctioned and high-risk unsanctioned Jewish cultural activity can withstand the barrage of anti-Jewish assaults in present-day Soviet Russia is a moot question, but the possibilities should not be foreclosed. Nor should Western efforts to press these possibilities be dampened.[96]

34

A People in Limbo: The Continuing Soviet Jewish Predicament

I once had a Jewess in my life. . . . She spoke Russian like a Russian . . . and the only Jewish word she knew was *tsores,* which in their language means sorrow or trouble, or a kind of prickly sadness littering the heart. There was a grain of this *tsores* buried in her like a raisin you could never dig out—immured in her as it were, mixed into the very composition of her soul.

SINYAVSKY, *The Makepeace Experiment*

THE contradictions and inconsistencies in Soviet policies toward its Jewish population have not prompted its leaders or ideologues to undertake a review or extension of Leninist ideas regarding the nature of anti-Semitism, minority cultural rights, and the dangers of Great Russian chauvinism. Instead, the regime has used and continues to use its Jews as foils in East-West trade-offs and as a lightning rod to absorb and discharge domestic grievances. The anti-Zionist, anti-Semitic campaign has blazed across the whole of Soviet society, giving it an enemy and a perennially effective means of unifying a nation suffering from divisions, deferred hopes, and discontents. Soviet recourse to the crude anti-Semitism of tsarist Purishkeviches and Black Hundreds, whom Lenin excoriated, is a certain sign that the Soviet Union is far from a wholesome or satisfied society, and the escalating shrillness of its anti-Jewish spokesmen in the 1970s and 1980s is a way of shouting down chronically unresolved social and economic problems. Soviet Jews, meanwhile, have been severely hurt and endangered.

A host of authors—V. Bolshakov, R. Brodsky, B. Antonov, I. Shulmeister, M. Mayatsky, I. Mints, E. Kolesnikov, E. Yevseev and L. Korneev—have joined the specialists Ivanov, Begun, and Kichko and been given wide coverage and official endorsement in the daily press and periodicals, especially in the Ukraine. "Despite official denials," it is now widely believed, "anti-semitism has become an organic part of Soviet society, at both the bottom and top of the social ladder," even appearing in some "respectable underground publications of *samizdat*, like *Veche*."[1] Anti-Zionist and anti-Jewish indoctrination is also pervasive in Soviet military training, according to Dr. William Korey, and is conducted at all levels, from the 161 officer training schools to high-school teenagers, as well as the army, navy, and air force, which induct two million youths every year.[2]

Articles and books with inflammatory phrases such as "world Jewish power," "Jewish international intelligence center," and "Jewish millionaires' conspiracy" had already saturated the media after the 1967 Six-Day War, reaching a climax in 1971 during the first political trials. Zionism was labelled "an enemy of the Soviet people," engaged in subversive operations aimed at destroying the Soviet Union. Bolshakov then added the equation of Zionism and Fascism. This propaganda offensive ran into sharp criticism within Western Communist circles in 1972–73 and Vergelis himself, the editor of *Sovetish heymland*, published articles condemning anti-Semitic slurs under the guise of anti-Zionism, particularly the books *Fascism Under the Blue Star* by Yevseev and *Zionism—Theory and Practice*, edited by Mints.[3]

Moscow has also supplied voluminous anti-Semitic materials for dissemination abroad. One such article released by the Soviet press agency Novosti and published on September 22, 1972, in *U.R.S.S.*, the official newsletter of the Soviet embassy in Paris, moved the International League Against Antisemitism in Paris to bring a civil suit against Novosti. On March 26, 1973, a French court found the managing directors of *U.R.S.S.* guilty of defamation and incitement to racial hatred and violence.[4]

The torrent of abusive material momentarily declined until 1974, when Begun's *The Creeping Counter-Revolution* was published. Begun portrays Judaism as the principal source of Zionism and describes the Torah as "an unsurpassed textbook of bloodthirstiness, hypocrisy, treason, perfidy and moral degeneracy. . . ." Zionist plans for "world domination and enslavement of nations" are an outgrowth of the Torah and are seen to have existed even during the later tsarist period. Begun also justifies anti-Semitic outbreaks as part of the class struggle of the oppressed against Jewish exploitation—an old theme used by early Russian radicals in 1881–82 during the pogroms. In 1974, too, there appeared another anti-Zionist book *The Secret Front*, by the KGB first deputy chairman, Semyon K. Tsigun, and the extensive showing of the film, "Beware Zionism."

In the following year (1975) Begun's book was officially sanctioned in a long review article in *Moskva*, by the well-known critic Dmitri Zhukov.[5] Much is made of Judaism's alleged desire to master the world, "formulated" in the Holy Writings and "reflected in prayers." Zhukov then concludes that Hitler "borrowed" his own racist concepts directly from the Zionists. The strong endorsement of Begun's book signaled a return to the anti-Zionist and anti-Jewish fulminations of an earlier period, including articles in scholarly publications such as *Voprosy Istorii*,[6] the journal of the historical profession.

The crescendo in propaganda paralleled the movement in the UN, leading to the adoption of the resolution on November 10, 1975 equating Zionism with racism. All stops were pulled out in the enthusiastic Soviet welcome to and support of the resolution. On October 24, while the debate unfolded, Sakharov rightly understood that the resolution "can only contribute to anti-Semitic tendencies in many countries by giving them the appearance of international legality."[7] In the next month, Daniel Patrick Moynihan, who was U.S. ambassador to the United Nations when the resolution passed, predicted that "the terrible lie that has been told here will have terrible consequences. . . . There will be new forces, some of them arising now, new prophets and new despots, who will justify their actions with the help of just such distortions of words as we have sanctioned here today."[8] The Arab world and the Third World as well as the countries in the Eastern bloc in Europe, already conditioned by the Soviet ideological assault on Zionism after the Six-Day War, responded enthusiastically to UN resolution 3379. Moynihan spoke of it as a "watershed in Soviet-inspired anti-Semitism"[9] upon which later attacks were built.

The film "Traders of Souls" shown on prime time television on January 22, and again on March 11, 1977 clearly aimed at intimidating would-be emigrants and closing the vise around Shcharanky. Immigrants arriving in Israel were shown being forced to sign documents in a language they did not understand. When Israel was mentioned, screeching jets zoomed across the screen, followed by close-ups of bandaged Arab children. An obese man with an evil face was shown paying off hired demonstrators with five-pound sterling notes at the

Soviet embassy in London. Names and addresses of a number of activists were flashed on the screen. Their activities were shown as financed from overseas, by Western Zionists, who maintained ties with the CIA. Prisoners of conscience were presented as speculators, drunks, and hooligans. Former activists in Israel were "particularly alarmed" about the screening of names and addresses, "a fact which can in a very real sense endanger the safety of the people involved." Moreover, the program "appealed to the basest instincts of the most ignorant elements in the population . . . sufficient to trigger off pogroms. . . ."[10]

On a visit to Israel in 1978, Andrei Sinyavsky was extremely pessimistic about the future of Soviet political life and especially about the future of Soviet Jews:

Until now, anti-Semitism was not considered acceptable in intelligentsia circles. If an educated man was an anti-Semite, he would try to mask it in public, venting his feelings privately among a small circle of friends. But now, more and more, one can hear publicly an entire ideological elaboration of anti-Semitism, cunningly reasoned and shamelessly expounded. This not only harms the Jews, but is also a warning signal of the debasement of Russian social and political thinking, a symptom of serious social illness in the Russian people. . . .[11]

An exceptionally bold summation of the venomous anti-Semitism in Soviet Russia was presented to President Brezhnev in the form of a letter and accompanying findings after a two-year study of anti-Semitic publications made by Ruth Y. Okuneva in the spring of 1980. Mrs. Okuneva, a former student and scientific worker at the USSR Academy of Pedagogical Sciences, undertook a two-year study of this material and declared that

V. Begun, Y. [E.] Yevseev, V. Emelyanov, Y. Ivanov, L. Korneev, V. Pikul and V. Skurlatov, among others, have been violating the ideals of socialist internationalism that form the basis of the Communist Party's national policy. Their works are full of savage hatred, not of Zionism but of the Jews. . . . They present the Jews as the enemies of the Soviet state, as counterrevolutionaries, spies, accomplices of Hitlerism. Nowhere in their works do we find an objective evaluation of the Jews' role in the revolutionary movement, the heroic deeds of Jews during the Great October Socialist Revolution and the Civil and Great Patriotic Wars, the role of Jews in Soviet leadership and their participation in Socialist construction. . . . And how blasphemously is the tragedy of the Jews during World War II presented in these so-called 'anti-Zionist' pamphlets? . . . ."[12]

Recent official glorification of Russian history, concern for the physical survival of the past and emphasis on "roots" have been easily exploited in thrusting the Jew out of normative society and putting him at the very center of conspiracy theories. Right-wing dissidents and the KGB have been thought to be behind this version of conspiracy.[13] But there is also increasing rejection of the Jew because some have left the Soviet Motherland; the center of this "conspiracy" is Zionism. An emigré has become a traitor; the Jew, a foreigner. The Israeli invasion of Lebanon added new venom to the anti-Zionist campaign with two of the most anti-Semitic of Soviet authors, B. Kravtsov and Korneev, openly and widely publishing canards reminiscent of the "Protocols of the Elders of Zion." Korneev currently sees international Zionism as a mortal threat to the very existence of the Soviet Union and seems to be voicing the ideas of the most extreme Jew-hating elements in the Soviet leadership.[14] As in the past, in April 1983, prominent Jews in the Soviet Union were called upon to serve as instruments of government policy—this time intensified anti-Zionism.

On March 31, 1983, Tass announced that eight prominent Jews had appealed for the creation of a "Soviet Public Anti-Zionist Committee" to expose the "anti-people and anti-humanitarian nature of diversionary propaganda and policy of Zionism."[15] The Committee was created on April 21, and although it was planned to draw on both Jews and non-Jews, it remained essentially an all-Jewish operation, headed by the highly decorated Colonel General David Dragunsky, virtually the last of the Jewish ranking army officials, with law professor Samuil Zivs as his first deputy chairman. The primary aims of the Committee were to denounce the United States, international Zionism, and Israel and end the internal and foreign clamor over emigration. At the outset, ambitious plans for the Committee were projected, including the setting up of branches, the production of literary works, films, and scholarly research into the ideology and "aggressive character" of Zionism. However, differences arose within the Committee, shading from rabid Stalinist attacks to somewhat more moderate views. At a press conference on June 6, 1983, for Soviet and foreign journalists, Zivs, a "moderate," differentiated between those emigrants who left for reasons of family reunification (a process he called "basically completed") and those "lured by Zionist propaganda" who have committed "antipatriotic" acts. Zivs also stressed firm Soviet support for Israel's right to exist and support for an Arab Palestine state. Several times he argued against Lev Korneev's and Yuri Kolesnikov's fierce attacks on Zionists (see below) saying that the Committee would "struggle against improper expositions."

At the same time, articles appeared in local papers, referring to activists by name (Grigory Vasserman, Abba Taratuta, and Yaacov Gorodetsky in Leningrad; Vladimir Raiz and Eytan Finkelshteyn in Vilnius; and Yaacov Mesh, Yehudit Neopomnyashchy, and Zev Boguslavsky in Odessa), warning them against Zionist and unofficial cultural activities. The Committee has been condemned by Jewish activists generally, but others have been frightened. One was quoted as saying, "Even people with first-degree relatives in Israel are not going to OVIR offices in case something happens to them."

Since 1983, it is thought that the Committee has been steadily downgraded, possibly reflecting the slight easing of East-West relations by the end of 1984. Many of the proclaimed activities of the Committee did not materialize and representation from the only three Soviet Jewish elements still permitted—the synagogue, Yiddish, and Birobidzhan—was absent.

However, if Soviet authorities were hesitant or divided about promoting the Committee because of possible harm to a revival of détente, there was no lack of venomous output even as the Committee's activity dimmed. In the January 1984 issue of *Pravda*, Vladimir Bolshakov, a regular contributor to the paper on international affairs, published an article entitled "Fascism and Zionism: the Roots of Kinship," in which he repeats the stock Soviet arguments, adding the disturbing implication that there exists a Zionist "fifth column" in the countries of the world.[16] In 1984 Yuri Kolesnikov's virulently anti-Semitic book *The Curtain Rises* (published in 1979, serialized in a literary weekly in 1983) was translated into several foreign languages, including English, and lavishly praised by the Soviet press.[17] On January 17, 1985, Tass published the text of an interview with Lev Korneev, in which he accused Zionist-Jewish bankers and industrialists of financing the Nazis, and Zionists of sharing responsibility for the Nazi extermination of Jews during the Holocaust.[18] (In 1982 he had questioned the actual number of Jewish victims, viewing the figures as grossly exaggerated.)

The gradations of ferocity in the use of anti-Zionism and anti-Semitism may reflect variable patronage in the central leadership and aspects of the political succession struggle,[19] (Yuri Andropov succeeded Brezhnev in November 1982, and Konstantin Chernenko succeeded Andropov in February 1984. Chernenko died in March 1985, at which time Mikhail Gorbachev became the new general secretary of the party.) In the midst of the torrent of anti-Zionist and anti-Jewish material and the political changes, Ivan Martynov, a non-Jewish historian, like Ruth

Okuneva earlier, took the unusually courageous step of attacking the derogation of Jews and Jewish scholars in Soviet journals and confessing that in the past he had plagiarized works published by Jews and claimed them as his own. Martynov,[20] from Leningrad, together with his Jewish wife has tried repeatedly to emigrate. The prime target of his attacks has been Lev Korneev, the notorious anti-Zionist and anti-Semitic writer, who is also a member of the Institute of Oriental Studies of the USSR Academy of Sciences. His campaign against Korneev consisted of an "open letter" to the Presidium of the Academy in September 1983, a 48-page analysis of his works, and a file of correspondence and notes involving Soviet officials, publishers, and editors. Instead of Korneev's allegations that Jews are hostile to all things Russian, Martynov described those he knows as having profound respect for the Russian people and Russian history. He also deplored the withdrawal from circulation of publications by Jewish emigrants. In 1983, he and his wife and several refuseniks attempted to bring a lawsuit against Korneev and signed a protest, together with forty-four Leningrad Jews, against anti-Semitic articles in the Soviet press. In January 1985 he was given a one-and-a-half year suspended sentence on charges of fraud.

Since 1987, the emergence of *Pamyat* (Memory), an intensely chauvinistic organization, with an openly anti-Jewish agenda, and with close ties to Soviet officials and academic centers, has been causing increased anxiety among Jews.

The new regime of Gorbachev shows no sign of stopping or muting down the anti-Zionist and anti-Semitic onslaught and it is problematical whether the coming rounds of East-West talks can make it an important priority. Meanwhile, Soviet Jews suffer from the libels and lies,[21] yet only the Jewish activists can openly condemn them. The others must either remain silent or be used by the regime to deny them. The absence of a full-scale serious Western or Israeli counterdrive has been a grave miscalculation and lost opportunity. Dr. Alexander Lunts, speaking for many activists, has expressed his regret that the anti-Jewish vilification "is often dismissed as mere counterpropaganda on the part of the Soviets, but it is far more than that. It is a potent instrument of intimidation. It can create a dangerous atmosphere for Jews. It, in fact, invites the lower echelon authorities to oppress simple Jews and to instill fear in their hearts."[22] He also described relatives of Jews who emigrated as hostages. As Professor Ettinger has pointed out, the regime has been unwilling "to explain the roots of anti-Semitism by means of Marxist analysis," such as was done during the educational campaign against anti-Semitism in the 1920s and early 1930s, and instead has relied on dredging up and fostering negative stereotypes of Jews.[23]

It is sometimes suggested that a resumption of diplomatic relations between the Soviet Union and Israel, which were broken in 1967, might diminish or possibly eliminate the surge of this type of literature, and/ or ease the situation of Jews in the Soviet Union, but, if the past is any guide, such hopes seem fanciful. It will be recalled that during the most cordial relations in 1947–48, a great wave of persecution descended upon Jews inside the Soviet Union. Nor have levels of Soviet Jewish emigration been related to the status of Israeli-Soviet diplomatic relations. More Jews were allowed to leave after the breaking of relations in 1967 than before, and many left during the period of intensified Soviet hostility. Soviet-Israel relations seem to be determined by the superpower relationship in the world arena and in the Middle East specifically, and by the state of the Arab-Israeli conflict.[24] It has frequently been said that the Soviet Union regrets the rupture, making it harder for it to have any credibility in any Middle East peace conference. Constructive participation would also enhance the Soviet effort to relax tensions with the United States and improve its own economy. A full resumption of relations may be distant, but intermittent official and unofficial contacts have continued throughout the seventies and eighties.

Israel was blamed for the Yom Kippur War in 1973 and the Kremlin promised total support for the "just Arab cause" and the creation of a Palestinian state. Yet there were curious chinks that seemed to suggest a slit in the monolithic supportive wall. For example, in September 1973, Radio Moscow pointed out that "the USSR should not be blamed for permitting Jewish emigration to Israel in light of the fact that some 800,000 Jews from Arab countries [had] been permitted to go there."[25] *Sovetish heymland* was host to an Israeli delegation visiting Moscow in 1975 at the invitation of *Pravda*, and to representatives of the Soviet-Israel Friendship Society. "Both Israeli groups emphasized the need to establish closer contacts between Soviet Yiddish writers and Israeli 'progressive' circles."[26] In April 1975, two Soviet representatives visited Jerusalem and made contact with Israeli leaders. Five left-wing Israelis, including three from Mapam, visited the Soviet Union in September at the invitation of the Soviet Peace Committee and later reported a more "understanding attitude" on the part of the Committee.[27] In 1978, Israeli members of the Knesset were invited to visit the Soviet Union by the Soviet Peace Committee, at the behest of the government.[28] This was the first political delegation to be so invited since 1967 and included two Labor MK's and a member of the National Religious party. One member, Yossi Sarid, believed the invitation had come because the Soviet Union wanted to become involved again in Middle East negotiations and felt completely divorced from Israel, which represents half of the conflict. He also believed that interpower cooperation, not confrontation, was needed for a Middle East settlement. The delegation met with Soviet personalities of the highest rank who stressed that when there would be a significant political turn of events in the Middle East, such as the reconvening of the Geneva Conference, they would be able to reconsider resuming diplomatic relations. The Camp David agreements were viewed as part of an American plan to establish an anti-Soviet axis, a matter of "treating symptoms instead of the illness."

Discussion of the Jewish question, according to Sarid, "caused a good deal of tension . . . their attitude is extremely emotional." The Russians "are making an absolute exception to their emigration policy in the case of Jews," and still insisted that "98½ percent of those who ask for exit permits received them without any difficulties." The group showed their hosts a list of names of persons who had been refused an exit permit, including that of Ida Nudel. "Presenting the lists caused quite a stir, and even threatened to explode the whole visit," but, according to Sarid, "the matter was settled." No details were revealed, but Sarid believed that the discussions were valuable and that future dialogue "is important to both sides."

Chaim Herzog, President of Israel and Israel's former ambassador at the UN, has also argued for improved relations between Israel and the Soviet Union,[29] stressing the point that nations do not have permanent friends, or permanent enemies—only permanent interests. Herzog believes that the Begin government did not take advantage of signals sent by Moscow, such as the one in March 1977 when Brezhnev, for the first time, called for direct negotiations in the Middle East. He also thinks that the Begin policy, forbidding any Israeli initiative and permitting only a reaction to Soviet initiatives, must be changed.

In December 1981, another Israeli delegation was invited by the Soviet Peace Committee to come to the Soviet Union[30] and returned with "most important findings . . . that the Soviet Union is truly eager for peace around the world, not least in the Middle East, that it fully recognizes Israel's right to statehood, and would dearly wish to improve ties with it." However, there was at least one unpleasant moment, when one of the Labor party delegates, Ora Namir, was asked, apropos the understanding on strategic cooperation worked out by Reagan and Begin, if the Soviet Union would be interested in supplying Soviet citizens to Israel, "to become soldiers in any army pledged to fight the Soviet Union." Namir, nevertheless, "came away with the feeling that their initiative . . . was . . . motivated by a desire not to burn all their bridges to Israel. . . ."[31] The unpleasant experience of hearing "official Jews" trumpet the party dogma against teaching Hebrew was somewhat offset by meetings with groups of Hebrew teachers and their students. On other visits, Soviet officials generally have tried to stop such contacts.

There have been subsequent contacts and, since 1979, improved economic and cultural relations between Israel and several nations in the Soviet bloc, and international conferences and meetings where Soviet and Israeli representatives meet.[32] In the Israeli delegations to the Soviet Union there are always members of the Israeli Communist party. Significantly, there is no Soviet counterpart to the Soviet Israeli Friendship Society in Israel, which actively supports a resumption of relations. Moreover, Soviet-Israel relations lack contacts on Jewish historical and cultural topics, which do exist between Israel and Poland, Hungary, and Romania.

The first visit of a Soviet delegation to Israel after the Lebanon invasion took place in May 1983, marking the commemoration of the anniversary of VE Day in the Forest of the Red Army near Jerusalem. The Soviet guests toured the country and had a chance to speak to Israelis. Special significance was given to the presence of two top-flight Soviet political commentators who "were eager to speak to the Israeli media . . . [and] were able to report on their impressions back home."[33] Hopes were raised during the effective and relatively flexible regime of Shimon Peres, prime minister of Israel, particularly in the easing of emigration. It is doubtful, however, that improved relations will affect the condition of Jews within the Soviet Union.[34] As Yaacov R'oi has emphasized, "the Soviet Union has always sought to separate Israel: policy from its attitude to the Soviet Jewish question," insisting that the problem has been solved and that any remaining questions are a do-mestic matter of solely Soviet concern.[35] Moreover, despite Washing-ton's pledges of support for the relief of Soviet Jewry and its efforts to keep the subject alive in discussions, American media no longer give the issue the prominent coverage they once did, and, inasmuch as Moscow pays close attention to such publicity, this lack of interest "is considered a signal to the Kremlin that Soviet Jewry is not important despite all the pledges."[36]

As if to consolidate the current line that the Jewish issue has been resolved, there has been renewed publicity about Birobidzhan in the 1970s and 1980s aimed at refuting criticism of Soviet treatment of Jews and insisting on Birobidzhan as an alternative to emigration. Besides conspicuous coverage in the Soviet press, various issues of *Moscow News*, a paper published in Moscow for English readers, featured articles praising Birobidzhan as the Jewish Autonomous Region. The Moscow bureau chief of the North American Newspaper Alliance, Albert Axel-bank, visited Birobidzhan in 1976 where he found many Jews there extolling the system and their life: the fifty-member Jewish People's Amateur Theater, the friendliness of the city, the high productivity of the Dalselmash factory, which is managed by Jews and employs a number of Jews, the "Legacy of Lenin" collective, which contains over 350 Jews and twelve different nationalities. Axelbank, however, saw a culture "beginning to wilt, with no real possibility for rebirth. Inter-marriage is brisk today among the relatively small number of Jews. Yiddish is not taught . . . and religious education and culture are non-existent."[37]

Jewish life is, indeed, minimal, with Jews numbering only 10,000 or so—about 7 percent—in a population of 175,000. An amateur Yiddish Folk Theater functioned in the seventies and there were some Yiddish radio broadcasts. But young Jews did not—and do not—know Yiddish and, according to the census of 1970, only 2,000 persons in the area indicated Yiddish as their mother tongue. For about 1,700, it was the second language. Yet a Jewish reality was contrived and pumped up in the late 1970s and 1980s. A new professional Jewish Musical Cham-ber Theater that was started in May 1978 under Yuri Shperling held its premiere in Birobidzhan in December with a performance of Shper-ling's "Black Bridle for a White Mare."[38] During the school year 1979–

80, the teaching of Yiddish was introduced as an optional subject in several Birobidzhan schools.[39] In April 1980 a color documentary film about Birobidzhan, "On the Banks of the Bira and Bidzhan," was released by Soviet authorities.[40] Then, in a portentous gesture, on December 2, 1981, the RSFSR promulgated the "RSFSR Law of the Jewish Autonomous Region," i.e., the Constitution of Birobidzhan.[41] In 1982, 5,000 copies of a new Yiddish primer—the first since the *Alefbeys* of 1947—were published and conspicuously designed for use only in Birobidzhan. Hirszowicz notes that the primer "is clearly designed for children whose first language is Russian." Soviet holidays and values, especially "homeland" are emphasized and "some effort is made to arouse pride in the area and in its Jewish heroes. [However,] the concept of the Jews as a Soviet nationality, with a history on Soviet soil and a heroic revolutionary tradition, is not presented. . . ." Nor is Israel or the Diaspora mentioned. The primer suggests that "Jews are no more than a Soviet nationality confined to Birobidzhan."[42]

Whether cynical or perverse, the restriction of such a primer to Birobidzhan, while the principal centers of the Jewish population are in the large cities of Western Russia, is another in a multitude of contradictions in Soviet Jewish policy. If Yiddish is to be once more encouraged, why limit the use of such a primer at the same time that *Sovetish heymland* and the 1984 Russian-Yiddish dictionary are available to the Jews in the large cities?

There were other dramatic efforts to keep Birobidzhan publicly alive in June 1984, which marked the fiftieth anniversary of the designation of Birobidzhan as the JAR. Television programs, rallies, book exhibits, and the conferring of the Badge of Honor on the city of Birobidzhan by the Presidium of the USSR Supreme Soviet were yet new, bizarre and extremely strained efforts to resuscitate a quite moribund artifact of the Jewish past. There is no likelihood that Birobidzhan can ever be revived, except in these rhetorical flourishes, but it is interesting that such a non-reality can be promoted as if real. It is, of course, not taken seriously by Soviet Jews, but serves to answer arguments that Soviet Jewish life is being destroyed and that the only genuine option for them is emigration.

Far removed from the public relations gyrations surrounding Birobidzhan have been the experiences of the activists, including the refuseniks. They have undergone many traumas, confusions, and inner struggles that supportive Westerners often ignore or simply cannot grasp in *their* enthusiasm over establishing bonds with heroically cast figures. Such support has created a Western subculture of intense, exhilarating, and often fulfilling activity, but oversimplifies complex Soviet Jewish realities and tends to push dissidents and refuseniks into molds familiar to the West with its open-ended, free-ranging ideas and opinions, and capacity to absorb untidy, unregulated disharmonies and disorders. Just as the Soviet Union has projected its world onto the West, Westerners project their attitudes and conceptions onto the Soviet Union and think of dissidents and refuseniks as if they were displaced liberal democrats. There is very little appreciation of "the actual consequences of living within the monolithic and bureaucratic atmosphere that permeates every corner of the USSR and that drives its citizens to both exceptional aggressiveness and passivity, while creating different levels of relationships between individuals and between individuals and officialdom."[43]

In the early period of "refusal," Jewish activists experienced the joys of freedom, contacts with the West, and the thrill of participating in a struggle against oppression. As one of the activists has written, "How unexpected, joyful and vexingly late it was to discover what spiritual wealth there is in the world—not only in the Western world but in Russia itself—in the past and even present."[44] But later there were gnawing anxieties, pariah roles, loss of jobs, and a hectic, stress-filled round of days and nights. The refusenik's changed life has plunged him into patterns outside the framework of usual Soviet behavior: he meets with foreigners, corresponds with Jews overseas and possibly American Congressmen and other public officials, signs protests and sends copies overseas. Connections with people in the West are often defended as a kind of insurance protection for the refusenik—so long as someone is concerned and voices his concern publicly, it is thought the refusenik has a shield, that his lot would be much worse without it. However, it is a double-faced shield. Western "protectiveness" may buffer the isolation and fear but cannot remove it. Moreover, in recent years, Western interest has stigmatized and isolated refuseniks, causing many of them to be helpless and in great jeopardy.

The heavy mental and physical toll exacted was confirmed by Dr. Howard Shevrin of the University of Michigan Psychiatry Department, in extended talks with a Dr. Axelrod, a psychiatrist-refusenik, in October 1980.[45] Dr. Axelrod had traveled to a number of cities overnight from Moscow and spoken to a number of refuseniks about their situation. He found a "high incidence of . . . stress reactions—physical and mental disorders attributable to social, economic and psychological trauma." He concluded that there was "more than the normal incidence of various physical and psychosomatic disorders—cardiovascular disease, asthma, digestive ailments, depression, crippling obsessions, and phobias." None was exempt; both young and old, men and women were suffering. A young teenage girl, for example, had become obsessed with the irrational need to stand at her apartment window taking note of every car that stopped. If she failed to mark a particular car she was overcome by panic. This compulsion started when a car did stop near the apartment building, with several KGB agents who took her father away. After Isai Goldberg, another activist, was taken away for questioning, his son suffered repeated nightmares and hid under the bed when someone knocked on the door.

Dr. Axelrod also reported that many Jewish teenage boys "overreact to their sudden social isolation by involving themselves in dangerous and ineffectual shows of bravado . . . [finding] it hard to tolerate the passivity and helplessness they are required to endure for years." Teenage girls, facing a severe identity crisis when their parents apply for a visa, sometimes fall in love with Russian boys, creating great conflict within the family. Young children often suffer sudden temper outbursts and strike out at their parents because they "no longer feel secure in [their] parents' ability to protect [them.]"[46] Thus, a large group of people, having lost their usual social supports—families, jobs, schools, neighbors, and professional contacts—were being further penalized and placed in physical and emotional jeopardy. For those like Dr. Lerner, Brailovsky, the Slepaks, some of the Hebrew teachers and participants in study circles, who were able to channel the frustrations and isolation into substitute activity, the damage may not have been so great, but even for many of those, there later came the suffering in prison or exile. The suffering and isolation of Ida Nudel, who first applied to leave in 1971 and who was virtually alone in Bendery, had been very acute.[47]

Compounding these emotional stresses is the continuing influence of past Soviet conditioning, which is all but impossible to shake off. The essence of individual liberty, democracy, and the clash of ideas as the West understands them are poorly or not at all understood by the dissidents themselves, who, according to the correspondent Shipler, "rarely rid themselves of the deeply ingrained Soviet intolerance toward pluralism, toward the multiplicity of outlooks and opinions, which forms the central Western ideal of free thought. Many are political absolutists themselves [and] dogmatic . . . [seeing] themselves in ideological combat with the authorities. . . ."[48] Shipler was also disheartened by the inner conflicts and antagonisms within the dissident community itself and among refuseniks, which some Western visitors have also regretfully had to acknowledge. However, this fact aside, refuseniks are doubly or triply alienated from mainstream Soviet society and cannot have any sense of "home-ness" except in fleeting moments of emotional and intellectual equilibrium. The social and official persecution and rising then dimming hopes for emigration have played havoc with their lives, causing near-intolerable psychological stresses, extreme fluctuations in emotional mood from exhilaration to depression verging on despair, an agitated restlessness, and aching emptiness as leaders and comrades leave or are sent to prison and exile.

Occasionally there is a letter from prisoners far away giving the taste of life in exile. Volodya and Maria Slepak, for example, wrote sometime in the winter of 1979:

> Everything we did wasn't for nought. Now our sons are free. Our dream has come true. If it's God's will we'll see them again; if not, then. . . . After so many years, the pain has deadened. Ten years of refusals and stress have told on us both.
>
> Here in Siberia, our daily life consists of waiting for the 5 P.M. radio news broadcast. Every morning we visit the post office; letters are the main link with the world. Our life here resembles science fiction. We are so far away, more than 6000 km from Moscow. We two are so alien to the environment here. . . .
>
> Time slips away. Heat, dust, stuffy air, flies, foul smells. . . . In the winter the sewer pipe fell off. . . . After it thawed out, the stuff flows to a pit through the gutter.
>
> In front of our apartment is a "public convenience", which hasn't been cleaned since last September. . . . No water. Forty-one months are left to go for us without a water supply. . . . We'll have to carry it in buckets from a source 300 meters from our building.[49]

Halfway through their five-year term they were ordered to a dilapidated hut on the outskirts of the collective farm Tsokto-Khangil, where Maria later said, "Not a bird, not a dog, nothing is heard" (see Photo 34.1).

Once in a while there is heartening news. On April 19, 1979, five of

34.1 Vladimir and Maria Slepak in exile, 1979. Courtesy Jewish Community Relations Council of Philadelphia

the prisoners involved in the "Leningrad Hijacking Trial"—Anatoly Altman, Hillel Butman, Leib Knokh, Boris Penson, and Wolf Zalmanson—were freed and a few days later, on April 27, came the announcement that five political and religious dissidents, including Edward Kuznetsov and Mark Dymshits, had been freed in exchange for two Soviet spies being held in the United States. Looking pale, gaunt, and bone-weary, the first five prisoners and then Kuznetzov and Dymshits arrived in Israel to a tremulous welcome. On February 18, 1981, Yosif Mendelevich, the last of the Jewish prisoners involved in the "hijacking" trial was released, leaving Yuri Fedorov and Alexei Murzhenko the two non-Jews, still suffering in prison. Fedorov was released on

July 4, 1985; Murzhenko was released in June 1984, but was sentenced in August 1984 in Kiev to two years in a special regime camp for "malicious violation of the rules of administrative surveillance." Ida Nudel was released in March 1982 and returned to her home in Moscow only to go through a bureaucratic maze related to the technicality of a new residence permit, without which she cannot re-apply to emigrate. In one official questioning in April, she was told, "we are not going to give you permission [to leave]" and that she was expected to "behave herself."[50] In July she was told by the KGB to leave Moscow immediately and was finally allowed to register in Bendery in the Moldavian Republic in December 1983 where she lived, depressed and isolated until October 2, 1987, when she was allowed to leave. In September 1987, Vilnius refusenik Eytan Finkelshteyn arrived in Israel after a thirteen-year wait for permission to emigrate. In March 1984 Victor Brailovsky was released after five years of exile in Kazakhstan and was finally allowed to emigrate in September 1987.

The journey to exile in Russia has been and continues to be an experience filled with dread, cruelty, and great suffering,[51] marked by *etap*, or a stage at a time. Many political prisoners, common criminals, dissidents, and some refuseniks have endured five-thousand or more mile transports to the icy wastes of Siberia. Yosif Begun, for one, a Jewish engineer activist, lost his job when he applied to emigrate and was then arrested in 1977 as a parasite. He traveled for sixty-eight days, crammed into airless cubicles on ten different trains and nine prisons on the way to Burkandya, a gold-mining village of 3,000, where he was completely isolated.[52] He returned to Moscow within a few months but was re-arrested three times thereafter. In 1982 he was sentenced to seven years' strict regime imprisonment and an additional five years' exile. On April 3, 1985, he was sent to Chistopol prison in the Tatar Republic following a decision of the Perm labor camp that he serve three years of his twelve-year sentence there. On June 7, 1985, Evgeny Ayzenberg was sentenced to two-and-a-half years in a labor camp for "slandering the Soviet state." The former secretary of the Moscow chapter of Amnesty International, Andrei Tverdokhlebov, was exiled to Nyurbachan, a state farm where he spent two years shoveling coal into a heating plant's furnace, but living in a wooden dormitory heated only by a wooden stove. Anything left on the floor would freeze. There was no indoor plumbing and the wells froze, so water had to be trucked from twelve miles away in the wintertime (see Map 24.1).

The Jewish "Prisoners of Conscience" (or Zion) have been the focus of special concern to Western supportive movements. As of December 1986, there were twenty-one such prisoners,[53] some suffering in isolation cells, some from severe illness, and others from beatings. A few were released in 1986: Boris Vainerman, Vladimir Brodsky, and Nadezda Fradkova. A few long-term refuseniks were also allowed to leave in 1985–1986; Ilya Essas, Boris Kalendarov, Isai and Grigory Goldstein, Felix Kochubievsky, Stanislaw Zubko, Mark Nashpits, Yakov Gorodetsky and David Goldfarb. There was immense rejoicing throughout the human rights and Jewish emigration movements when Shcharansky was released in a spy-prisoner exchange (February 11, 1985), and when soon afterward the Soviet dissident Yuri Orlov, one of the original members of the Moscow Helsinki Watch Group, was also allowed to leave the Soviet Union.

Many of the refuseniks, even after they have been released from prison or returned from exile, still cannot emigrate and some, as was the case of Ida Nudel, cannot receive permission to return to their home cities and so live in a limbo, disconnected from friends and family, familiar work, and intellectual interests. Until 1987, they formed part of a growing number of long-term refuseniks. As of January 1982, the number of refuseniks of over ten years' standing was seventy; the number of five years' standing and over was 221.[54] Most, if they were not in prison or exile, lost their jobs and struggled to subsist. Their children have been generally dismissed from universities, sometimes even from secondary school, and thus automatically subject to army draft. Yet, despite their suffering, the worsening condition of applicants, and the debilitating uncertainty of the future of emigration, the number of refuseniks has increased even as the number of permits to long-standing refuseniks has diminished. At the end of 1980, there were 4,741 known refuseniks—a growth of 58.8 percent in one year. A year later, the number was about 7,040, and in June 1982, the figure reached 8,075—almost three times as many refuseniks as in December 1979.[55] In addition there are thousands of families who have not been able to apply because of "insufficient family kinship."

Moreover, a new leadership has evolved which is carrying on the tradition of cultural activities, Hebrew and religious studies, efforts to hold commemorative events, petitions, contacts with the West, and hunger strikes.[56] An innovative Women's Group in Moscow was organized in October 1977, proclaiming their right, as women, to be reunited with their families in Israel. The group also started a kindergarten in the flat of Boris Chernobilsky. Children of refuseniks, up to the age of seven, were welcome, and received lessons in general subjects as well as Hebrew. There was no charge, and the teachers were not paid, thus the group believed the school could not be considered illegal under Soviet terms. There had been little news of the school for a time, but visitors in 1987 reported that it was flourishing (see Photo 34.2).

A Legal Seminar was also started in 1977 in Moscow, devoted to helping Jews who apply for exit visas with various legal issues, including job dismissals, police searches of apartments, divorce and separations, and probing the caprices of Soviet law and its interpreters. The

34.2 Moscow *Gan* (nursery) for children of Jewish activists. Courtesy Soviet Jewry Council of Philadelphia.

Seminar met biweekly and issued a bulletin called *Emigration to Israel—Law and Practice* and was led for a time by a young refusenik-mathematician Mark Berenfield, who attracted large numbers to the meetings. By July 1980, Berenfield was warned by the KGB to stop the seminar and told that he and his family would never be allowed to leave the country.[57]

On October 21, 1979, there was an unusual uninterrupted event at Orashki,[58] a village about forty miles outside of Moscow. Three hundred Jews gathered there for a competition of Hebrew songs. Nearly all of the competitors and audience were young, but five of the ten judges were veteran refuseniks: Vladimir Prestin, Pavel Abramovich, Ilya Essas, Yuly Kosharovsky, and Mila Volvovsky. Old songs as well as new compositions were sung. "For those of us who are long-term refuseniks," one of them said later, "it is essential that we keep ourselves busy in a constructive way." Prestin added: "Perhaps the most constructive thing we can do is to let interested people hear the Hebrew language spoken and hear the beauty of it in ancient and Biblical songs."

Abramovich and Kosharovsky have been refuseniks since 1971. Both became foremost Hebrew teachers in the Jewish national movement and have been subject to harsh and vindictive harassment, grilling, and imprisonment. Early in 1981, Abramovich was told by KGB that he could have no hope of ever leaving. "If you don't care about yourself," they said, "have some consideration for your wife and son. They can be made to suffer too."[59] Both men signed an appeal to the Twenty-Sixth Communist Party Congress in 1981, outlining breaches in party commitments to national minority rights and specific actions taken against Jews.

Dr. Alexander Lerner, a long-term refusenik-scientist, who had conducted over 200 sessions of a seminar "Mathematical Methods in Medicine and Biology" by 1980, and Victor Brailovsky's wife Irina, a mathematician, who led a seminar on "Collective Phenomena" in the early 1980s, were periodically blocked by the KGB and warned not to meet with visitors from the West. In the fall of 1981, there was a severe crackdown on dozens of Hebrew teachers in Moscow, Leningrad, and the larger Ukrainian cities. On October 12, about a hundred teachers and students from Moscow went to the Supreme Soviet to present a letter protesting the systematic persecution, but they were not acknowledged.[60] It was noted that several who were questioned and warned by the KGB were not refuseniks. Moreover, with the sharp drop in emigration permits, there was a marked upturn in the number of refusals and reports that invitation affidavits were not being delivered. General Semyon K. Tsvigun, a top career officer of the KGB, declared during this period that the political dissent movement in the Soviet Union had been crushed, but warned that new forms of "Western-backed subversion," including reports on Soviet consumer shortages, Jews, fundamentalist Muslims, and pop music, were increasing.[61] Thus, all dissent from official dogma was and would be perceived as instigated by Western "agents" or subject to exploitation by them. President Reagan, nevertheless, decided to step up grain sales to the Soviet Union, undercutting previous American efforts to gain concessions on human rights and military matters through the leverage of trade, but obviously responding to the American farm crisis.

In the summer of 1982, during the Israeli occupation of southern Lebanon, two Israeli delegates to a conference on cardiology in Moscow reported hundreds of anti-Israel workers' meetings and a "hostile attitude on the part of the man on the street" when they toured wearing their Israeli tags on their lapels.[62] During this period, there was also a sharpened attack on Zionist "benefactors" who use postal channels "for direct ideological diversions." This was a reference to parcels sent to refuseniks who have lost their jobs and are in material need. The Soviet writers refer to these actions as a "crafty" tactic of Zionists who are trying to "erode the moral foundations of [Soviet] society." The charge that refuseniks lose their jobs is described as an absurd "fabrication."[63] Such reactions multiplied the following year to synchronize with the formation of the Anti-Zionist Committee. Human rights activists and members of the various Helsinki Watch Groups were also subject to increased harassment and arrest, and in September 1982, Elena Bonner Sakharov announced the dissolution of the Moscow Group. However, Jewish activism did not stop.

Throughout 1983 and 1984 and later, there were numerous reports of severe beatings of Jewish activists and prisoners and quite primitively contrived pretexts for arrests. A particularly severe crackdown on Hebrew teachers and students took a heavy toll. In 1984 the Ukrainian Criminal Code (Article 187/1) was amended to include the "teaching of Jewish subjects or possession of Jewish books." Observers noted a trend toward religious study and observance on the part of some of the younger Jewish activists, which also brought confiscations, beatings, and arrests. However, either from desperation or defiance, repression drove many of the refuseniks to extreme acts of protest. There were numerous long-term hunger strikes, militant statements, press conferences, and demands addressed to Soviet officials. There were more moderate requests, as well. For example, on February 20, 1986, seventy refuseniks gathered outside the Ministry of Interior building and delivered a petition to a high OVIR official appealing to the Twenty-seventh party Congress to release "Prisoners of Zion," to fix a maximum five-year waiting period for refuseniks and to publish emigration regulations. There have also been religious and cultural activities and occasional expressions of group solidarity such as Elie Wiesel's visit to Moscow during Simchat Torah in October 1986, when thousands of Jews rejoiced with him in and around the synagogue. In November 1986, observant Jews in Moscow requested a new cemetery. The old Jewish cemetery in Vostrayakova is closed and the one in Malakova, 30 kilometers outside of Moscow, is virtually filled.[64]

There was also an important resumption of cultural seminars on February 15, 1986, when the 850th anniversary of Maimonides was commemorated in the home of a Moscow refusenik, involving forty-two refusenik scientists and two Western scientists—the largest gathering of refusenik scientists since 1980. At the end of September 1986, three scientific seminars were held in biology, computer science, and physics, with about twenty refuseniks attending.

Emigration had slowed to a trickle (896 in 1984, and 1,140 in 1985) but did not stop entirely, giving some ground for guarded hope that if Gorbachev meant to embark on society-wide reforms and took a pragmatic course, Jewish emigration may be allowed to increase somewhat. There was also some cautious optimism expressed over the appointment of Eduard Shevardnadze, succeeding Andrei Gromyko, as Soviet foreign minister. Shevardnadze was first secretary of the Communist party in Georgia and has been described by Georgian Jews as helpful in their emigration quest and sympathetic to minority national rights. Emigration dropped to 914 for the year 1986, but in the first six months of 1987 rose to 3,092.

There is general agreement that Western economic and technical advances have left the Soviet Union far behind, but there is a limit to how much the Soviet Union is willing to bargain away for Western goods and technology. Moreover, a good deal has been available without any bargaining,[65] and the serious problems of Soviet food production, housing, and medical service chiefly require internal reforms, not Western imports. There may be some short-term negotiations possible on the issue of emigration, but the brain drain and contagious nature of emigration rights make fundamental change very problematic. All of the more basic human rights guarantees would threaten the very foundation of the Soviet system. It is illusory to expect Gorbachev or any other Soviet leader to take the 1975 Helsinki pledges on human rights literally, or to expect that they be granted the importance or understanding that prevails in the West.

Yet the country is going through severe crises, not only affecting the economy but also social relations and health.[66] The nation has paid a heavy price for its Revolution,[67] which the Soviet peoples have had to endure. Solzhenitsyn shocked the world when he put the price at sixty-six million people as well as the appalling suffering of millions more. Every Soviet family has experienced bereavement, fear, deprivation, cultural isolation, and the baleful consequences of party control of information and ideology. The immense propaganda efforts to mobilize Soviet citizens to hate Jews and close ranks in support of peace may, indeed, be desperate measures to stitch up the tensions and frustrations that lie close to the surface of Soviet society and rally the country to identify the "enemy" and unite to save the world from nuclear war. Gorbachev may grasp the opportunity to ease some of the frustrations and, in the process, some concessions may be granted to minorities, including Jews.

Hirszowicz considers the discussions at the Twenty-seventh CPSU Congress in February–March 1986, as "a turning point in Soviet history," with the economy as the "core of all Soviet problems."[68] In the projected growth up to the year 2000, there will have to be a total restructuring of the technical base of the economy and the development of a services industry in order to satisfy pent-up social needs. In turn, such changes involve serious manpower problems, especially in the fields of education, health, and other social services. Although the Jewish population has been declining, the particular occupational distribution and educational level of the Jewish work force may play a role in fulfilling some of the manpower needs. Brezhnev had alluded to its importance earlier, but Gorbachev has staked much of the success of his administration on economic reform, and thus the potential contribution of the Jewish work force may have to be taken even more seriously.

In terms of education, the number of Jews with special secondary and advanced education was 566,000 in 1975 (4.1 percent of the whole category), the last year for which figures are available. Jews also account for about 5.3 percent of research workers, 6 percent in art, culture, literature, and the press, 3.4 percent in the medical field, and 6 percent in law—numbers which in Hirszowicz' view, "though by no means crucial . . . [are] not easily expendable." Discriminatory practices and emigration have diminished the numbers in science, but the figure of 64,800 Jewish scientific workers was published in 1982, 4.5 percent of the total number, and four times the percentage of Jews in the population. Thus, Hirszowicz believes, "in conditions of dwindling manpower resources, the demand for the educated and skilled labour force that Soviet Jewry is still able to provide, should be relatively stronger than in the 1970s." This assumption, combined with the reality of reduced Jewish emigration since 1980, and the repeated advice of OVIR officials to Jewish applicants to give up their plans to emigrate strongly suggests that the period of large-scale Jewish emigration has been closed.

Hirszowicz further sees "important differences" between the Khrushchev and Gorbachev programs regarding the nationalities question. Khrushchev believed that the question had been essentially solved; Gorbachev, in his report to the Congress, said that "our achievements must not create the impression that national processes are without problems. *Contradictions* are inherent in any development [process] and are *unavoidable* in this sphere too." Moreover, the complete obliteration of national distinctions was not mentioned, as had been the party aim earlier. Nor was "the leading role" of the Russian nation among the Soviet nationalities. "The new tone," according to Hirszowicz, "is noticeable for its inclusion of the statement that 'The CPSU takes account in all respects of the multi-national character of Soviet society.' " However, lest this statement be stretched too far, Gorbachev denounced "national narrow-mindedness and arrogance . . . national isolation, localism, and parasitism," and called upon each republic to contribute to "the development of an integrated national economic complex." What these words will mean for the Jewish and other nationalities in the Soviet Union can easily be interpreted too far toward flexibility as well as toward repression. One cannot know. However, if the "vestiges of official Jewish culture," are permitted to continue and possibly expand, and if manpower needs in technical and professional life weaken discrimination against Jews in these fields, Jewish life under Gorbachev may be less painful than it has been.

At this Congress, Gorbachev supported the Helsinki Accords as the Soviet Union interprets them, and reaffirmed the Soviet position in July 1986 in a speech greeting French President François Mitterand. However, as always, in the Communist approach, human rights are a matter of domestic concern and jurisdiction, and this position prevailed at the Third Helsinki Review Conference, which was held in Vienna beginning November 4, 1986. An unheard-of six press conferences were held and Western journalists were sought out and impressed with the new conciliatory approach. Soviet delegates responded to almost every request for a meeting (except with Sakharov's step-son Aleksei Semyenov) and courteously listened to pleas about emigration restrictions and refuseniks. Promises were made to look into individual cases, and it was announced that new rules covering exit visas would be published on January 1, 1987.[69]

Despite the strongly held Soviet positions, Western supporters of the refuseniks and other Jews desiring to emigrate were very hopeful of a shift in Soviet policy at the much-publicized Reagan-Gorbachev summit in Reykjavik, Iceland, October 11–12, 1986. A great deal of cordiality between the two men and sophisticated public relations on the part of Soviet media representatives were reported. The Soviet effort stressed Gorbachev's campaign for *glasnost*, or openness, and Soviet spokesmen talked of "the process of democratization and reform that is taking place now in the Soviet Union," suggesting some room for dissent. However, the mask of affability began to slip a bit when Georgi Arbatov, the Soviet expert on America, became caustic and admitted that the summit was "not a symptom of improved relations but a test for worsening relations." When someone from the Committee for Soviet Jewry in Stockholm attempted to ask him a question, he snapped, "No, it is the Committee for anti-Soviet Jewry."[70] The summit, moreover, had been called primarily to discuss nuclear arms reduction, but ended in a stalemate.

Toward the end of December 1986, there was the long hoped for news that Sakharov was released from internal exile in Gorky and that his wife Elena Bonner, who had been convicted of slandering the Soviet state (but had been allowed to go to the United States for several months for medical treatment) had been pardoned. These decisions were, of course, greatly welcomed and seemed momentarily to signify a softer line under Gorbachev. However, there were many other darkening signs and growing fears that these actions were meant to mask a basically unchanging policy or blunt very harsh realities. For example, Orlov believed that Sakharov's release was meant to offset news of the death of long-suffering Anatoly Marchenko in Chistopol prison during a hunger strike on December 8. Sakharov's release was also interpreted as a way of undercutting Elie Wiesel's intention to visit Moscow and appeal directly to Gorbachev for his release. There were continuing reports of severe beatings of Alexei Magarik and harassment and intimidation of Jewish self-study efforts.[71] The National Conference on Soviet Jewry spoke of the Gorbachev shift as "merely tactical and cosmetic for Soviet Jews," and reported that only 914 Jews had left the Soviet Union in 1986, a 20 percent drop from 1,140 in 1985. It also noted that nearly half of the Prisoners of Zion were sentenced to prison or labor camps since Gorbachev came to power.[72]

The much-publicized new emigration regulations, called Codification of Emigration Decree, went into effect January 1, 1987 and strengthened the perception that large-scale Jewish emigration is finished. The new rules stipulate that visa applications will be considered only on grounds of reunification with immediate family members (parents, children, brothers, and sisters), not collateral relatives, and provide technical loopholes through which such applications can be denied. Refuseniks and Western Jewish supporters of the emigration movement attacked the new law and made efforts to obtain official and unofficial opposition in Washington to the new restrictions. There were also pressures to retain the Jackson-Vanik Amendment and the Stevenson Amendments of 1974 to the Trade Act, which some American political leaders and journals would like modified or dropped.

Shcharansky, who soon after his arrival in Israel began a whirlwind speaking tour, vehemently attacked the new rules, arguing that "90 percent of the 400,000 Jews who have already asked for invitations [to join relatives] cannot leave." He also passionately urged the West, the United States especially, to restrict trade and scientific exchanges until the Soviet Union eases emigration and improves its record on human rights. Linkage, even to the extent of an economic boycott of the Soviet Union, and continuing exposure of the Soviet human rights record were

Shcharansky's solutions.[73] However, there was considerable disagreement over his analysis in Congress, among Western political leaders and, to some degree, among Jewish organizational leaders, who realize that European companies, including American subsidies, have been supplying the technical expertise and equipment the Soviet Union wants, considerably diminishing the economic leverage the United States had in the 1970s. When he spoke at numerous meetings in England in November 1986, Shcharansky explained that in order for linkage to work, Western public opinion must be able to see the Soviet Jewry issues "as their own," that "in defending Soviet Jews they are defending their own interests," and helping "to strengthen the position of democracy all over the world." This line of argument, however, has not been shared by others.

On the frequently raised question, why so much attention is given to Jews, but not to non-Jews, Shcharansky explained that individual Jews like himself *had* championed their rights and would continue to do so, but that there was a relatively small number of prisoners and activists among non-Jewish Soviet dissident groups as compared to the large scale of the Jewish movement. He also stressed the point that in the past the Soviet government had accepted Israel as the goal of Jewish emigration, as opposed to the unacceptable goal of general emigration, or internal change.[74] However, these principles seem now to have been superseded if not nullified under Gorbachev. In the future, there may be responses on a case by case basis—Armand Hammer, Edward Bronfman, Senators Edward Kennedy and Gary Hart, for example, are known to have raised particular cases with Soviet officials and gained some concessions. Mass Jewish emigration seems no longer negotiable unless Israel insists on it in return for Soviet participation in the Middle East political process.[75]

If the time for certain economic and social reforms is at hand because of years of undue strain and demoralization in Soviet society, if the information revolution is allowed to trickle in, and if the arbitrary legal system is changed, dissidents and national minorities such as Jews would benefit by the greater relaxation. However, it seems to this writer that the springs for such change have to come from within. Western leverage has had little or no effect on these issues. Nor has outside pressure had any substantial effect on internal cultural or religious rights for

Jews or other minorities. Western Jewish efforts have concentrated on emigration rights, a priority which, in the long run, may prove to have been of limited value to the ultimate cause of Jewish survival in the Soviet Union. Western Jewish resistance to developing alliances with supporters of non-Jewish activist movements may also prove to have been ill-advised. The dependence on American official support, moreover, has created a seemingly total identity of interests between American foreign policy and Jewish concerns about Soviet Jewry, a position which has muffled or made very difficult independent Jewish voices that offer alternative courses of action, different tactics, and fresh approaches.[76]

Assuming that an opportunistic deal can be struck by Gorbachev whereby some Jews are allowed to leave, the Soviet Union, after almost seventy years, still has its unresolved "Jewish problem." Large and serious questions remain: What will happen to those Jews who remain in the Soviet Union? Do they have a future as Jews? Can those who want to feel and live as Jews find the strength to absorb the anti-Semitism that is bound to last in Soviet society for the forseeable future? Can the meager ration of permitted Jewish culture in Yiddish be enlarged, increment by increment? Will some circles be able to sustain underground study? Will some Jews have sufficient energy and inner drive to seek out sources of information on Jewish history, literature, and religion, which have been officially erased or condemned? One may respond to all these questions with a hesitant "yes," unless a fully brutal physical or cultural genocide is carried out, or unless all contacts with Western Jewry are closed off, which would mean a stoppage of letters, visits, and literature.

Yet, as a result of talks between world Jewish leaders and high Soviet officials in March 1987, there were several fairly reassuring Soviet statements to review previous visa denials to refuseniks, to allow Jewish religious books to be imported, and to evaluate the teaching of Hebrew in schools and synagogues. Implementation remains to be seen.

There is also the faint possibility that Lenin's belated cautionaries about the dangers of Russian ethnic dominance and the subjugation of cultural minorities may at least become known. The great reservoir of Jewish memory will also be tapped by some who remain. They will say Kaddish, attend Holocaust commemorative services, reflect upon Yom Kippur, celebrate Passover—perhaps even buy matzo, if it is available—learn a smattering or more of Yiddish and Hebrew, stand near a

34.3 Hebrew study group, Moscow, 1982. Richard Sobel, photographer. Courtesy Union of Councils for Soviet Jews.

synagogue at Simchat Torah, talk to another Jew about a book, or letter, or essay that touches on some aspect of Jewish life (see Photo 34.3). There is also the thus far untapped past history of Soviet Jews who formed the transition generation—those who were familiar with the old Jewish life and were catapulted into the revolutionary age. Curiosity about their own origins may drive fourth and fifth generation Jews to talk to their great-grandparents and older relatives to find out about *their* personal pasts. Several visitors have reported the beginnings of oral history projects among such young Jews. Efforts are also being made to collect records of medieval Jewish life, synagogues, cemeteries, Jewish life in St. Petersburg before it became Leningrad, and documentation of the Holocaust, including the efforts of "Righteous Gentiles" to save Jews.[77] Family letters, photographs, and diaries as well as the substantial samizdat literature provide openings to a Jewish past. There also exists a large, if censored, Jewish literature in Russian for curious and searching Jews.

Aside from anti-Jewish persecution, which historically has driven Jews either toward assimilation/conversion or to a stronger sense of Jewish identity, survival of Soviet Jewry will depend upon the individual Jewish will to survive. This will have to be tested in a harsh environment, without the community supports that other Jewries have had, under a regime hostile to Jewish survival and, except for brief periods, taking extreme measures to crush any effort to sustain it. Yet, Jewish history is full of unexpected turns, adaptations, and resiliency and, although Soviet Jewry faces a cramped and confined future, without much hope for a full-bodied culture, it would be foolhardy to write it off.

Notes

1. Pre-Bolshevik Jewish Parties and Lenin's View of Jewish Nationality

1. Quoted in Zosa Szajkowski, *Jews, Wars, and Communism*, Vol. I. New York, Ktav, 1972, p. 121.

   The great change in the Jewish mood can also be seen in a special appendix attached to the weekly *Ha-Am*, February 24, 1917, welcoming February 27 as "a great historic day for Russia and its people. The yoke of the previous regime did not burden any nation and group in the country as it did us. The wicked cruelty and crudeness of wild despotism selected us, of all the peoples of this country, as the objective of its poisoned darts. Now we will rest from our cruel suffering." Quoted in Yehoshua A. Gilboa, *A Language Silenced: The Suppression of Hebrew Literature and Culture in the Soviet Union*. London, Associated University Presses, 1982, p. 19.

2. Zvi Y. Gitelman, *Jewish Nationality and Soviet Politics: The Jewish Sections of the CPSU, 1971–1930*. Princeton, Princeton University Press, 1972, p. 74.

3. Fully described in Harold Shukman, "The Relations between the Jewish Bund and the RSDRP, 1897–1903," doctoral dissertation, Oxford University, 1961 and Henry J. Tobias, *The Jewish Bund from Its Origins to 1905*. Stanford, Stanford University Press, 1972.

   Lenin's arguments against the Bund may be found in the English translation of his *Collected Works*. Moscow, Progress Publishers and Foreign Languages Publishing House, 1961–1970, Vol. 6, pp. 319–25, 330–35, 486–88, 518–21; Vol. 7, pp. 59–65, 92–103; Vol. 11, pp. 195–96; and Vol. 19, pp. 503–8. There is also a convenient collection of Lenin's speeches and essays on the Bund and Jews in Hyman Lumer, ed., *Lenin on the Jewish Question*. New York, International Publishers, 1974. Lumer is completely sympathetic to Soviet Communism and believes that Lenin's predictions regarding the ultimate "amalgamation" of all religious and national minorities, including Jews, are historically correct.

4. Joseph B. Schechtman, "The U.S.S.R., Zionism, and Israel," in Lionel Kochan, ed., *The Jews in Soviet Russia since 1917*, 3d ed. Oxford, Oxford University Press, 1978, p. 107.

5. For a full analysis of these ideas, see Ber Borokhov, in Moshe Cohen, ed., *Nationalism and the Class Struggle: A Marxian Approach to the Jewish Problem*.

Selected Writings. Introduction by Abraham G. Duker. New York, Poale Zion, Zeire Zion of America, and Young Poale Zion Alliance of America, 1937.

6. Gitelman, op. cit., p. 79.
7. Schechtman, op. cit., p. 108.
8. From stenographic transcript of Proceedings of Constituent Assembly, quoted in Solomon M. Schwarz, *The Jews in the Soviet Union.* Syracuse, Syracuse University Press, 1951, p. 92.
9. Quoted in Salo W. Baron, *The Russian Jew under Tsars and Soviets,* 2d ed. New York, Macmillan, 1976, pp. 168–69. Elections were held in the autumn of 1917, but the Congress never met.
10. Large numbers of Jews in German-occupied provinces could not vote in the elections to the Constituent Assembly, but of the 498,198 votes cast for Jewish parties, the "nationalist" parties (Zionist, and to some extent, religious parties) polled 417,215, further augmented by 20,538 for Poale Zion. See Oliver Radkey, *The Elections to the Russian Constituent Assembly of 1917.* Cambridge, Harvard University Press, 1950, p. 17.
11. In May 1917, at an All-Russian Zionist Convention in Petrograd, 552 delegates represented 140,000 shekel holders (as against 26,000 in 1913) in 700 Jewish communities. Schechtman, op. cit., p. 108.
12. Leon Trotsky, *My Life: An Attempt at an Autobiography.* New York, Scribners, 1930, pp. 84–92. At first Trotsky believed that anti-Semitism was a product of decaying capitalism, but by 1926 he realized that the Soviet efforts at large-scale Jewish assimilation had failed and opposed the Evsektsiya excesses at what seemed to be forced assimilation. Later, during the war, he was deeply agitated by the anti-Jewish persecution in Europe and changed his thinking toward a recognition of the need for Palestine as a refuge for Jews. See Joseph Nedava, *Trotsky and the Jews.* Philadelphia, Jewish Publication Society of America, 1972, pp. 106–7, 221–26, 231–32.
13. Leonard B. Schapiro, *The Communist Party of the Soviet Union.* New York, Random House, 1960, p. 172.
14. Lenin's fierce opposition to separatist parties can be seen in his "angry, even rude polemic" against Lev Yurkevich, publisher of the Ukrainian Social Democratic journal *Dzvin* (Bell), in which he pressed for a separate Ukrainian Social Democratic party. In his attacks, in 1914, Lenin even resorted "to falsification and published in the name of an alleged group of Ukrainian Social-Democrats an appeal written by himself and directed against Yurkevich." Israel Kleiner, "National Movements: On Lenin's Attitude toward the Right of Nations to Self Determination," *Crossroads* (Jerusalem, Israel Research Institute of Contemporary Society), No. 5, Winter 1980, pp. 178–79.
    See also Lenin's "Critical Remarks on the National Question," Vol. 20, op. cit., pp. 17–51; and "The Right of Nations to Self-Determination," ibid., pp. 393–454. Yurkevich in turn attacked the Russian Social-Democrats for their admiration of "large states" and for centralism, which was killing their ability to view the nationalities question from a sincerely internation-

alist point of view and was being guided by the "Great-Russian chauvinist" tradition. Kleiner, op. cit., pp. 188–89, 190.

There is an expanding literature on Lenin's views of Jewish nationality, which were to condition and then control Soviet policy toward Jewish cultural aspirations. Among those who argue that Lenin would have followed a different nationality policy from that of Stalin are: Norman Levine, "Lenin on Jewish Nationalism," *Weiner Library Bulletin*, Vol. XXXIII, Nos. 51–52, 1980 new series, pp. 42–55; Moshe Lewin, *Lenin's Last Struggle*. London, Faber, 1969; Marcel Liebman, *Leninism under Lenin*. London, Jonathan Cape, 1975; and Ben Joseph [A. B. Magil], "Lenin and the Jewish Question," *Jewish Currents*, December 1970, pp. 4–9, 28–31, 33.

15. Gitelman, op. cit., pp. 105, 106. The exact number of delegates in 1907 could not be determined because of changes in accreditation rules. Nedava, op. cit., p. 145, records fifty-one Bundists.

16. Richard Pipes, *The Formation of the Soviet Union: Communism and Nationalism, 1917–1923*. Cambridge, Harvard University Press, 1964.

17. Harold Shukman, "Lenin's Nationalities Policy and the Jewish Question," *Bulletin on Soviet and East European Jewish Affairs*, No. 5, May 1970, p. 48.

18. Lenin, "Separatists in Russia and Separatists in Austria," Vol. 19, op. cit., pp. 87–88 and Vol. 20, op. cit., pp. 37–51.

19. Robert C. Tucker, "Stalin's Revolutionary Career before 1917," in Alexander and Janet Rabinowitch, eds., *Revolution and Politics in Russia*. Bloomington, Indiana University Press, 1972, pp. 168.

20. Ibid., p. 169.

21. Joseph Stalin, *Marxism and the National and Colonial Question*. London, Martin Lawrence, n.d., p. 8. Benjamin Pinkus points out that this sentence is omitted from the definition of "Jews" in the 1972 edition of the *Large Soviet Encyclopaedia*. Benjamin Pinkus, *The Soviet Government and the Jews, 1948–1967: A Documented Study*. Cambridge, Cambridge University Press, 1984, p. 473, note 56. However, the absence of a compact mass living in a common territory has been the determining Soviet criterion in rejecting the concept that Jews are a nation. Pinkus includes an excerpt from an essay by S. A. Tokarev, "Problems of Types of Ethnic Communities," published in 1964, which grants that Jews, among other peoples, have a common religion, which at one time gave them an "ethnic unity," but only in "the era of capitalism." Ibid., pp. 35–36.

22. Stalin, op. cit., p. 10.

23. Ibid., p. 36.

24. Ibid., p. 60ff.

25. Trotsky believed that this essay was wholly inspired by Lenin and written and edited under his careful supervision. Isaac Deutscher, Boris Souvaine, Bertram Wolfe, and Solomon M. Schwarz see it as a reflection of Lenin's thinking, but Tucker, op. cit., and Pipes, op. cit., disagree.

26. Lenin, "The Position of the Bund in the Party," Vol. 7, op. cit., pp. 100–101.

27. Besides *Iskra*, articles appeared in *Pravda*, *Proletarskaya Pravda*, and *Put Pravda*, among others.
28. Lenin, Vol. 19, op. cit., pp. 110–18, 505–7.
29. Ibid., p. 248. The full text appears on pp. 238–51. These *Theses* were not published until 1925.
30. Lenin, Vol. 20, op. cit., p. 26.
31. Ibid.
32. English translation of "Zur Judenfrage," in H. J. Stennig, *Selected Essays by Karl Marx*. New York, International Publishers, 1926, pp. 40–97.
33. Lenin, Vol. 20, op. cit., p. 43.
34. Ibid., p. 24.
35. Ibid., p. 34.
36. Ibid., p. 35.
37. P. Liebman, "A naye oyflage fun altn toes," *Tsayt*, September 17, 1913. Reproduced in Lenin, Vol. 20, op. cit., pp. 23–24.
38. Lenin, ibid., pp. 25–26.
39. Ibid., pp. 172, 173.
40. Nora Levin, *Jewish Socialist Movements, 1871–1917*. New York, Oxford University Press, 1978, p. 367.
41. Lenin, Vol. 20, op. cit., p. 224.
42. Ibid., Vol. 19, pp. 307–8 and 354–57.
43. Levine, op. cit., p. 44.
44. Ibid.
45. Quoted in Thomas E. Sawyer, *The Jewish Minority in the Soviet Union*. Boulder, Colo., Westview Press, 1979, p. 124.
46. Lenin assumed power precisely at a time when numerous separatist movements threatened the emergent Soviet state and at the time of the Balfour Declaration, which promised Jews a homeland in Palestine.
47. Baron, op. cit., p. 172.
48. Shukman, "Lenin's Nationalities Policy," op. cit., pp. 48–49.
49. David Shub, *Lenin: A Biography*. New York, New American Library, 1948, pp. 178–83.
50. Edward H. Carr, *The Bolshevik Revolution, 1917–1923*, Vol. I. Harmondsworth, Penguin, 1966, p. 281.
51. Gitelman, op. cit., p. 122, note 43.

2. Jews in the Cross Fire of War and the Bolshevik Struggle for Power, 1914–21

1. Mordechai Altshuler, "Russia and Her Jews—The Impact of the 1914 War," *Weiner Library Bulletin*, Vol. XXVII, Nos. 30–31, 1973–74, new series, p. 12.
2. Maxim Gorky, "Anti-Semitism" (1929), in his collection of essays, *Culture and the People*. New York, International Publishers, 1939, p. 67.
3. Quoted in Howard Morley Sachar, *The Course of Modern Jewish History*. New York, Delta Books, 1958, p. 298.
4. Altshuler, op. cit., p. 14.

5. Nora Levin, *Jewish Socialist Movements, 1871–1917*. New York, Oxford University Press, 1978, p. 369.
6. Raphael Abramovich, *In tsvay revolutsias: Di geshikhte fun a dor*, Vol. 2. New York, Arbeter Ring, 1944, pp. 47–53.
7. J.S. Hertz and Gregory Aaronson, et al., eds., *Di geshikhte fun bund*, Vol. 2. New York, Unser Tsayt, 1962, p. 95.
8. *Di arbeter shtimme*, August 20, 1917, quoted in Zvi Y. Gitelman, *Jewish Nationality and Soviet Politics*. Princeton, Princeton University Press, 1972, p. 88.
9. Ibid., pp. 88–90.
10. See Sir Stuart Samuel, *Report on My Mission to Poland*. London, His Majesty's Stationery Office, 1920, for a description of excesses committed by Polish troops in occupied territories.
11. Fritz Fischer, *Germany's Aims in the First World War*. New York, Norton, 1967, pp. 150–51.
12. Quoted in Alan Moorehead, *The Russian Revolution*. New York, Harper and Row. 1965, p. 183.
13. Ibid.
14. Leonard B. Schapiro, in his *The Russian Revolutions of 1917: The Origins of Modern Communism*. New York, Basic Books, 1984, deals at length with the importance of the Petrograd Soviet in the ultimate Bolshevik conquest of power.
15. The city was known as St. Petersburg from 1700 to 1914, Petrograd from 1914 to 1924, and Leningrad since 1924.
16. Edward H, Carr, *The Bolshevik Revolution, 1917–1923*, Vol. I. Harmondsworth, Penguin, 1966, p. 96.
17. Mikhail Frenkin, "Some Observations on Russian Jewry and Russia's Political Parties (1917–1921)," *Crossroads*, (Jerusalem, Israel Research Institute of Contemporary Society), No. 3, Spring 1979, p. 110.
18. Carr, op. cit., p. 100.
19. Frenkin, op. cit., pp. 107,111.
20. Ibid., p. 112.
21. This shift is described in detail in Alexander Rabinowitch, "The Petrograd Garrison and the Bolshevik Seizure of Power," in Alexander and Janet Rabinowitch, eds., *Revolution and Politics in Russia*. Bloomington, Indiana University Press, 1972, pp. 172–91.
22. Ibid., p. 191.
23. Quoted in Robert C. Tucker, "Stalin's Revolutionary Career Before 1917," in ibid., p. 375, note 32.
24. On November 3, 1917, several leading Bolsheviks—Lev Kamenev, Grigori Zinoviev, Alexei Rykov, V. Nogin, and Vladimir Milyutin—resigned from the Bolshevik Central Committee, protesting against terrorist methods and demanding a coalition with other socialists. Carr, op. cit., p. 119. New style dates, replacing the old Julian calendar, will be used hereafter.
25. Quoted in Carr, op. cit., p. 123.
26. See Israel Getzler. "Marxist Revolutionaries and the Dilemma of Power," in Rabinowitch, op. cit., pp. 88–112.

27. Joseph B. Schechtman, "Jewish Community Life in the Ukraine," in Gregory Aaronson, et al., eds., *Russian Jewry, 1917–1967.* New York, Thomas Yoseloff, 1969, pp. 41–43.
28. Printed in *Razsvet,* September 6, 1917, and quoted by Elias Tcherikover in his *Antisemitizm un pogromen in Ukraine 1917–18.* Berlin, Yidisher Literarisher Farlag, 1923, p. 52.
29. Schechtman, in Aaronson, et al., eds., op. cit., pp. 45–46.
30. Ibid., pp. 50–51.
31. N. Gergel, "The Pogroms in the Ukraine in 1918–21," *YIVO Annual of Jewish Social Science,* Vol. VI. New York, 1951, p. 239.
32. Ilya Trotsky, "Jewish Pogroms in the Ukraine and Byelorussia (1918–1920)" in Aaronson, et al., eds., op. cit., p. 73.
    An unusual and interesting account of these turbulent changes in the Ukraine by a Jewish lawyer and diplomat who served in the Ukrainian People's Republic can be found in Arnold Margolin, *Ukraine and Policy of the Entente.* Tr. from Russian by V. P. Sokoloff. Temple Hill, Md., McDonald and Eudy, 1977. In connection with the Skoropadsky regime, he noted that at first all of the Ukrainian political parties boycotted it, leading Skoropadsky and the Germans to look for support among Russian parties (p. 40). By July 1918, the parties united and elected the Directory. In November he observed that the Directory had posted proclamations appealing for order and respect for human life and property. The words "Jews are our brothers," appeared (p. 54). On December 14, Skoropadsky resigned and the forces of the Directory occupied Kiev where they were welcomed by Nachman Syrkin, on behalf of the Jewish Community (p. 62). Eagerly awaited representatives of the Entente to help avoid civil war never came.
33. Gitelman, op. cit., p. 168.
34. Ibid., pp. 167–70.
35. Some details of the atrocities are described in Saul S. Friedman, *Pogromchik: The Assassination of Simon Petlyura.* New York, Hart Publishing, 1976, p. 1–26. See also Ilya Trotsky, "Jewish Pogroms in the Ukraine . . . (1918–1920)," in Aaronson, *Russian Jewry,* op. cit., pp. 77–87. Petlyura was assassinated by Samuel Schwartzbard in 1926. Schwartzbard's trial (1927) in Paris revealed the complicity of the regime in the massacres. See Friedman, op. cit., pp. 99–101, 148–85, 267–78, 285–99.
36. Gergel, op. cit., p. 241.
37. *Folkstsaytung,* February 19, 1919, quoted in Gitelman, op. cit., p. 170. Many Bundists had been deeply impressed and stirred by revolutionary outbreaks in Germany in November 1918, which they believed heralded world revolution.
38. Gitelman, op. cit., p. 171.
39. Ibid., p. 175. Their vaunted independence, however, was shortlived.
40. *Folkstsaytung,* February 15, 1918, quoted in Gitelman, op. cit., p. 175.
41. A. Revutski, *In di shvere teg oyf Ukraine.* Berlin, 1924, p. 290, quoted in Gitelman, ibid., p. 161.
42. By contrast there were few pogroms perpetrated by the army of Alexander Kolchak.

43. Friedman, op. cit., p. 28.

44. Ibid., p. 283–84.

45. Ibid., p. 284.

46. Peter Kenez, "White Pogroms in the Ukraine 1919," *Weiner Library Bulletin*, Vol. XXX, 1977, new series, p. 3.

47. Ibid.

48. The Jewish socialist parties and the *Folkspartai* were not enthusiastic about such units, fearing they would arouse anti-Semitism, but groups were formed generally at the initiative of Jewish soldiers. The most powerful group, consisting of 400–600 well-armed regulars, was formed in Odessa and saved the Jews of Odessa from pogroms. Gitelman, op. cit., p. 158, note 25.

49. Kenez, op. cit., p. 7.

50. Salo W. Baron, *The Russian Jew under Tsars and Soviets.* 2d ed. New York, Macmillan, 1976, p. 184.

51. *Jewish Chronicle*, (London) January 23, 1920, p. 14.

52. Yaacov Lestschinsky, "Tsu der frage vegn di pogromen fun der roiter armai in Ukraine," *Di tsukunft*, Vol. XXIX, No. 10, October 1921, cited in Gitelman, op. cit., p. 164.

53. Elias Tcherikover, "Di ratnmakht un yidishe pogromen," in *In der tkufe fun revolutsie: memoirn, materialn, dokumentn*, Vol. I. Berlin, Yidisher Literarisher Farlag, 1924, pp. 377–80, cited in Gitelman, op. cit., p. 165.

54. Gitelman, op. cit., pp. 165–66.

55. Tcherikover, *Di Ukrainer pogromen in yor 1919.* New York, YIVO Yiddish Scientific Institute, 1965, p. 327.

    In Khmelnik, the Bolsheviks dropped arms that enabled 300 Jews to defend the town (Interview with Mark Goddis, Philadelphia, February 27, 1985). In the shtetl of Gritzev, near Constantine in Volynia, the coming of the Bolsheviks was hailed as the coming of "di groyser"—the big ones. They raced through the town but left some guns for the defenseless Jews (Interview with Ben Shamus, Philadelphia, March 23, 1985).

56. Under the terms of this controversial and complicated treaty, Germany and Soviet Russia ended hostilities. The Soviet government also gave up claims to Georgia, the Ukraine, and Finland, and recognized German control over Poland, Lithuania, Latvia, and Estonia. The treaty was annulled, however, by the collapse of Germany in November 1918.

57. Relations were poisoned by suspicion, distrust, and popular violence. As soon as the Germans withdrew from Warsaw, signs calling for a boycott of Jewish stores appeared throughout the capital. A mission from Britain collected documents showing that pogroms and anti-Jewish actions were carried out in one hundred towns and villages in three months from November 1918 through January 1919. See Israel Cohen, "Documents—My Mission to Poland (1918–19)," *Jewish Social Studies*, Vol. 13, April 1951, pp. 149–72.

58. Zosa Szajkowski, *Jews, Wars, and Communism*, Vol. I. New York, Ktav, 1972, p. xvii.

3. The Collapse of Jewish Political Parties and the Rise of the Evsektsiya

1. Roger Pethybridge, *The Social Prelude to Stalinism*. London, Macmillan, 1974, p. 8.
2. See ibid., pp. 1–72 for fuller elaboration of these unanticipated problems.
3. Ibid., pp. 73–131.
4. *Bleter far yidishe demografye, statistik un ekonomik*, No. 4 (June 1924), p. 289; Zvi Halevy, "Jewish Students in Soviet Universities in the 1920's," *Soviet Jewish Affairs*, Vol. 6., no. 1, 1976, p. 57.
5. Halevy, op. cit.
6. T. H. Rigby, *Communist Party Membership in the USSR, 1917–1967*. Princeton, Princeton University Press, 1968, p. 366. See Table 33.1 of present work.
7. Halevy, op. cit., p. 58.
8. Some sources cite five. Kamenev was a half-Jew.
9. Zvi Y. Gitelman, *Jewish Nationality and Soviet Politics*. Princeton, Princeton University Press, 1972, p. 106.
10. Ibid., p. 120.
11. Ibid.
12. Hirsh Smoliar, *Fun eynevaynik: zikhronos vegn der "Evsektsiya."* Tel Aviv, Peretz, 1978, p. 94. In ibid., pp. 23–91, passim, Smoliar describes the evolution of his political career from the time he smuggled his way over the frontier from Poland (Zambrow) to Russia in 1921 when he was twenty-one, through the various stages of his work in the Communist Party: as a member of the Kiev state youth office, secretary of the Jewish office of the Uman area Komsomol committee, member of the main office of the Jewish Section of the Komsomol in Kharkov and Moscow, and on the staff of *Der emes*. He has omitted his experiences during the period 1928 to 1939. In the latter year he went to work on a new paper in Bialystok and during the war led Jewish resistance in the Minsk Ghetto (see Chapter 18). After the war Smoliar returned to Poland where he edited the newspaper *Folkshtimme* and later emigrated to Israel. (He remained a committed Communist until the outbreak of the war and, despite misgivings over the party's shabby, even sordid practices and betrayals, he stubbornly clung to the promise of a solution to Jewish insecurity in a secular socialist society. The second and third parts of his autobiography describe his remarkable odyssey: *Vu bistu, khaver Sidorov?* Tel Aviv, 1973, and *Oyf der letzter pozitsye—mit der letzer hofenung*. Tel Aviv, 1982. Both published by Peretz.) Smoliar came to know many of the Evsektsiya activists, members of the Jewish socialist parties who opposed Bolshevism, and frequently used the materials in the Kultur-Lige Library and the writings of journalists and historians such as Abram Yuditsky, Tevye Heylikman, Israel Sosis, and Asher Margolis.
13. Samuil Agursky, *Der idisher arbeter in der kommunistisher bavegung*. Minsk, Melukhe-farlag fun veisrusland, 1925, pp. 5–6.
14. Quoted in Solomon M. Schwarz, *The Jews in the Soviet Union*. Syracuse, Syracuse University Press, 1951, p. 93. According to Smoliar, op. cit., pp.

92, 94, in 1919, Dimanshtain admitted that "those who had begun the work of the Commissariat often knew nothing about the life of the Jewish worker, and didn't even know any Yiddish." This statement, however, was not published until 1928. A few years later, he said that "the Russian Bolshevik party had not conducted any activity among the Jewish masses, and published only the party program and a few leaflets in poor Yiddish."

15. Samuil Agursky, ed., *Di oktiabr revolutsie in Veisrusland*, p. 304, cited in Gitelman, op. cit., p. 137.
16. Daniel Charney, *A yortsendlick aza*. New York, CYCO, 1943, p. 221. Cited in Gitelman, ibid., p. 135.
17. Gregory Aaronson, "The Jewish Question during the Stalin Era," in Gregory Aaronson, et al., eds., *Russian Jewry, 1917–1967*. New York, Thomas Yoseloff, 1969, p. 173.
18. Agursky, *Der idisher arbeter*, op. cit., p. 7. An archive kept by Leib Abram, secretary of the Kiev regional party committee, contained "much about the helplessness and continuous struggles among leftist Jewish socialists who insisted that the October Revolution must prepare the Jewish masses. But how? What kind of program is required?" Smoliar, *Fun eynevanik*, op. cit., pp. 94, 95, 96, 104. Abram was a former Bundist from Shavli who later became an active Evsek in Odessa, Kiev, and Vitebsk. He is referred to often in Smoliar's work and was an important influence in his political development. According to Smoliar (p. 91), Abram was one of the first to say that the October Revolution necessitated a fundamental revision in the ideological and technical foundation of the Jewish workers' movement.
19. Agursky, *Di oktiabr revolutsie*, op. cit., p. 292, quoted in Schwarz, op. cit., p. 108.
20. Agursky, *Der idisher arbeter*, op. cit., p. 21 ff.
21. Agursky, *Di oktiabr revolutsie*, op. cit., p. 294, quoted in Schwarz, op. cit., p. 108.
22. Ibid., p. 242.
23. Ibid.
24. Ibid. See Chapter 4 for a fuller treatment of this kind of resistance.
25. Ibid., p. 306, quoted in Schwarz, op. cit., p. 110.
26. Agursky, *Der idisher arbeter*, op. cit., p. 23 ff.
27. Gitelman, op. cit., p. 129, note 60.
28. Charney, op. cit., pp. 224–26, cited in Gitelman, p. 130.
29. *Di varheit*, June 2, 1918. Quoted in Gitelman, op. cit., p. 125.
30. Gitelman, op. cit., p. 124. Other nationality sections existed as early as August 1917.
31. Ibid.
32. Ibid., p. 144. Smoliar (op. cit., p. 105) heard that at the October 20 meeting, a number of the Bolshevik activists had no doubt that in the interparty and intraparty conflicts, the Bolsheviks would ultimately triumph. Among the most confident was Yolis (Julius) Shimolevich who predicted that "the left-Bundists will be our true comrades and will help us build a great Jewish party . . . when they come together with us . . . as part of the united

party." Dimanshtain, recalling earlier conflicts with the Bund, agreed, adding that the "Jewish party's position must not be as part of a federated party, but an autonomous one." The word "autonomous" itself was to become a subject of tormenting dispute and hair-splitting.

33. Gitelman, op. cit., pp. 145, 146.
34. Agursky, *Der idisher arbeter*, op. cit., p. 48 ff.
35. Gitelman, op. cit., p. 147.
36. See Gitelman, op. cit., pp. 167–230, for an extended treatment of the splitting, fragmentation, and ultimate dissolution of the non-Bolshevik socialist parties, on which I have drawn greatly. Smoliar, op. cit., pp. 106–10, also describes the splitting process, noting that the question of self-determination of each party was the crucial, central issue for each one.
37. Stephen F. Cohen, "In Praise of War Communism: Bukharin's 'The Economics of the Transition Period,' " in Alexander and Janet Rabinowitch, eds., *Revolution and Politics in Russia*. Bloomington, Indiana University Press, 1972, p. 193.
38. Ibid.
39. The theoretical analysis and rationale of these policies was made by Bukharin in his essay, "The Economics of the Transition Period," which appeared in May 1920, and is analyzed in ibid., pp. 192–203. War communism lasted until March 1921, when it was replaced by the New Economic Policy (NEP).
40. Ibid., pp. 198–201.
41. Dzerzhinsky was appointed Commissar of Internal Affairs in March 1919, thus "the tsarist connection between the two bodies was established." Pethybridge, op. cit., p. 94. The Cheka was abolished in February 1922 and replaced by the State Political Administration (GPU), which was formally attached to the Commissariat of Internal Affairs.
42. Quoted in Wiktor Sukiennicki, "An Abortive Attempt at International Unity of the Workers' Movement," in Rabinowitch, ed., op. cit., p. 207.
43. Ibid.
44. Schwarz, op. cit., p. 98.
45. Ibid.
46. According to Smoliar, Esther Frumkin, a Bundist leader, told him in 1927 that there was a Bolshevik group within the Bund even before the Bolshevik Revolution. This fact was confirmed twenty years later by the ex-left Bundist leader Chaim Vaser when Smoliar went to visit Treblinka with him. Smoliar, op. cit., 94.
47. Ibid., p. 99.
48. Ibid. The reference to Gedali is to the old Jew by that name in Isaac Babel's evocative story, "Gedali." In the dying Jewish life in Zhitomir, battered by violent changes, Gedali laments: "And now you're firing because you're the Revolution. But surely, the Revolution means joy, and having orphans in the house doesn't contribute to joy. A good person does good deeds and the Revolution is a good deed of good people. But good people don't kill. Then Revolution is made by wicked people. . . . Who, then, will explain to Gedali where Revolution is and where Counterrevolution is? . . .

And now, all of us learned people, we fall upon our faces and shout in one voice: 'Woe to us, where is she, the sweet Revolution?' " From "Gedali," in Isaac Babel, *Lyubka the Cossack and Other Stories*. New York, New American Library, 1963, p. 125.

49. Joseph Nedava, *Trotsky and the Jews*. Philadelphia, Jewish Publication Society of America, 1972, pp. 110–11.

50. Smoliar, op. cit., p. 98.

51. Ibid., pp. 97–98. According to Nedava, op. cit., p. 106, Trotsky was opposed to the Evsektsiya (it was under Stalin's jurisdiction, and the two were already antagonists), but he would generally not intercede on behalf of other Jews.

52. Smoliar, op. cit., p. 99.

53. Schwarz, op. cit., p. 98.

54. Samuil Agursky, *Di yidishe komisariatn un di yidishe komunistishe sekties*. Minsk, Party History Department, Central Committee of the Communist Party of White Russia, 1928, p. 187. Smoliar, op. cit., pp. 101, 102, and ff., frequently refers to the discussions and arguments he had with Shmeun (Shimoni) Dobin regarding the party splits and their significance. Dobin had been one of the founders together with Borokhov of Paole Tsion, but joined the Bund in 1911. After the Revolution, he was active in Gezerd and Jewish cultural work in the Ukraine. In his talks with Smoliar, he said that "what tsarism couldn't do to liquidate Bundism through hard labor, exile and death sentences was achieved when a ban no longer existed . . . first because of the formation of the Komfarband in 1919 and then, March 1, 1921, at a special conference of the Bund when a majority voted for a Comintern resolution stating that there was no basis for the existence of the Bund as a separate party." Dobin was especially bitter when he recalled Esther Frumkin's pledge at the time that "Bundism will live and struggle." He was also extremely skeptical about the Evsektsiya, seeing it as a bureaucracy, "doing work for Jews, but not with them."

55. Agursky, *Der idisher arbeter*, op. cit., p. 86.

56. Gitelman, op. cit., p. 220.

57. Ibid., p. 177.

58. Ibid., pp. 183–93.

59. *Folkstsaytung*, April 2, 1919, quoted in Gitelman, ibid., p. 187.

60. Gitelman, op. cit., p. 190.

61. Nedava, op. cit., pp. 114, 115.

62. Gitelman, op. cit., pp. 192–93.

63. Ibid., p. 195.

64. *Der veker*, July 15, 1920, quoted in ibid., p. 205.

65. Gitelman, op. cit., p. 207.

66. Quoted in Agursky, *Di yidishe komisariatn*, op. cit., p. 382.

67. *Der veker*, February 18, 1921, in Gitelman, op. cit., p. 211.

68. *Der veker*, March 7, 1921, in Gitelman, op. cit., p. 213.

69. Quoted in Gitelman, op. cit., p. 213. The entire text appears in Agursky, *Der idisher arbeter*, op. cit., pp. 166–70.

70. Gitelman, op. cit., p. 214.

71. Agursky, *Di yidishe komisariatn*, op. cit., 415 (note).
72. Schwarz, op. cit., p. 100. Schapiro concluded that up to the beginning of 1922, 136,386 members of the party had been expelled and that the purge and defections between March 1921 and January 1922 caused a drop in membership from 730,000 to 515,000. Leonard Schapiro, *The Communist Party of the Soviet Union*. New York, Random House, 1960, p. 232, 233.
73. Schwarz, op. cit., p. 100.
74. Gitelman, op. cit., 223, 227, 230.
75. Ibid., p. 227.
76. See Chapter 5 for a description of Hekhalutz activities until 1928.
77. Gitelman, op. cit., p. 263.

4. The Campaign against Traditional Jewish Life, 1917–29

1. Bohdan R. Bociurkiw, "Soviet Religious Policy and the Status of Judaism in the USSR," *Bulletin on Soviet and East European Jewish Affairs*, No. 6, December 1970, p. 13.
2. Michael Bourdeaux, "A Basic Work on Judaism in the USSR," *Soviet Jewish Affairs*, No. 3, May 1972, p. 129.
3. Bociurkiw, op. cit., p. 13. Political expediency has often dictated policy. The Tatars in Crimea suffered severely at the hands of the Bolsheviks, possibly because they had no connections, or very slight ones, with their fellow Mohammedans in the other countries. By contrast, the Mohammedans in the Caucasus and Siberian republics who had strong bonds abroad were interfered with to a much lesser degree. They have even been accorded a privilege no other religious group has, namely admission to religious seminaries at age fourteen instead of eighteen. This was explained on the grounds that a knowledge of Arabic was an essential prerequisite to the study of Koran. (Zosa Szajkowski, *Jews, Wars, and Communism*, Vol. I. New York, Ktav, 1972, pp. 395–96.) If religious sects can serve Soviet interests they are left alone to publish their magazines and conduct prayer meetings. In recent years the regime's accommodations with the Russian Orthodox Church have been interpreted as part of its massive peace offensive. In October 1986, Konstantin Kharchev, Chairman of the Soviet Council of Religious Affairs, on a visit to the United States, promised an expansion of religious rights and an increase in religious books (*Jewish Exponent*, Philadelphia, October 31, 1986). Recently, traveling groups from the National Council of Churches to the Soviet Union have been especially active in reaching out to church leaders there to contribute to Soviet-American dialogue, to the cause of peace, and better understanding. However, persecution of hundreds of thousands of believers among numerous religious sects and denominations, Jews among them, continues, and the promised "expansion" of rights has yet to materialize. Except for the period during World War II and détente in the early 1970s, foreign Jewish concern about Jewish religious life in the Soviet Union has mattered very little. For possible changes under Gorbachev, see Chapter 34.

4. Joshua Rothenberg, *The Jewish Religion in the Soviet Union*. New York, Ktav, 1971, p. 6.
5. Ibid., pp. 6–7.
6. Aryeh Y. Yodfat, "The Closure of Synagogues in the Soviet Union," *Soviet Jewish Affairs*, Vol. 3, No. 1, 1973, pp. 48–49. A personalized survey of religious life in Moscow from 1922 to 1972 was published in 1986 in Emanuel Michlin, *Ha-Gahelet*. Jerusalem, Shamir.
7. Rothenberg, op. cit., p. 10.
8. Zvi Y. Gitelman, *Jewish Nationality and Soviet Politics*. Princeton, Princeton University Press, 1972, p. 311.
9. Ibid., pp. 309–10.
10. Quoted in Boris D. Bogen, *Born a Jew*. New York, Macmillan, 1930, p. 329. However, according to Dr. Boris D. Bogen, representing the JDC in Hoover's American Relief Administration in Russia at the time, Trotsky's new book, *Problems of Life*, published in 1923, helped to quiet Esther's "turbulent spirit." Trotsky "counseled moderation in the methods of anti-religious propaganda" and advised "a milder and even respectful attitude toward those who, because of their background, cannot lift their minds to an understanding of modern ideas." Joseph Nedava, *Trotsky and the Jews*. Philadelphia, Jewish Publication Society of America, 1972, pp. 107–8.
11. Letter written on May 9, 1922, printed in *Novoe russkoe slovo* (New York), December 3, 1954. Quoted in Gitelman, op. cit., p. 298.
12. Aryeh Y. Yodfat, "The Closure of Synagogues in the Soviet Union," op. cit., p. 49.
13. Ibid.
14. M. Litvakov, "Di anti-religieze kampanie," *Der emes*, October 18, 1922. In Gitelman, op. cit., pp. 312–13.
15. Yodfat, "The Closure of Synagogues in the Soviet Union," op. cit., p. 50.
16. Ibid.
17. Ibid., p. 51.
18. Petition from 2,000 Jewish citizens of the city of Kherson (untitled, in Russian), Rosen Archives, Box I, File 98, YIVO Institute for Jewish Research, New York,.
19. In Vitebsk, in 1920, there were about 10,000 Jewish workers, but only 100 Jewish Communists and only 10 Evsektsiya activists. Gitelman, op. cit., p. 265.
20. The trial is described by the Evsektsiya agents in L. Abram, *Der mishpet ibern kheder*. Vitebsk, 1922.
21. Y. D. K., "Der mishpet iber der yidisher religie," in E. Tcherikover, ed., *In der tkufe fun revolutsie*. Berlin, 1924, p. 385 ff. In Gitelman, op. cit., p. 301–2.
22. Gitelman, op. cit., p. 313.
23. *Der veker*, March 6, 1924, in ibid., p. 359.
24. Excerpts from the sovietized passages appear in Yosef Hayim Yerushalmi, *Haggadah and History*. Philadelphia, Jewish Publication Society of America, 1975, Plate 144.

25. Abba Lev, *Religie un klaikoidesh in kamf kegn der idisher arbeter-bavegung*. Moscow, 1928, p. 3. Quoted in Gitelman, op. cit., p. 303.

William Henry Chamberlin noted that "While Russian Orthodox Judaism has never been actively counter-revolutionary in the sense that many bishops and priests of the Russian Orthodox Church were counter-revolutionary . . . Judaism is also 'opium for the people' in the eyes of the Communists and is exposed to much the same forms of hostile agitation and pressure." In his *Soviet Russia: A Living Record and a History*. Boston, Little, Brown, 1931, p. 322.

26. Samuil Agursky, *Der idisher arbeter in der komunistisher bavegung*. Minsk, Melukhe-farlag fun veisrusland, 1925, pp. 88–89. Quoted in Gitelman, op. cit., p. 272.

27. Aryeh Y. Yodfat, "Jewish Religious Communities in the USSR," *Soviet Jewish Affairs*, No. 2, November 1971, p. 62.

28. Ibid.

29. Ibid.

30. Avraham Yarmolinsky, *The Jews and Other Nationalities under the Soviets*. New York, Vanguard, 1928, p. 121, quoted in ibid., p. 67.

31. Yaacov Lestschinsky, *Dos sovetish idntum*. New York, Yidisher kemfer, 1941, p. 321, also notes that many Jews were still observing religious laws and rituals and that it was clear from the press that Jews were struggling to save Judaism. "Hundreds and hundreds of rabbis, cantors, and mohalim have been sent to Siberia," he wrote. "But the Jewish masses did not go under. Their faith is stuck in their bones. . . . The Evseks have made war against the children. . . . What is left is our private, intimate life" (pp. 314, 319, 322).

32. M. M. Sheinman, *O ravinakh i sinagogakh* (About Rabbis and Synagogues). Moscow, *Bezbozhnik*, (1929), p. 3. Quoted in Yodfat, "The Closure of Synagogues," op. cit., p. 52.

33. Yodfat, "Jewish Religious Communities in the USSR," op. cit., p. 52.

34. Ibid.

35. Ibid., p. 52.

36. Ibid., pp. 52–53.

37. Joshua Rothenberg, op. cit., pp. 11, 15.

38. J. Rothenberg, "Jewish Religion in the Soviet Union," in Lionel Kochan, ed., *The Jews in Soviet Russia Since 1917*, 3d ed. Oxford, Oxford University Press, p. 174. The Constitution of 1936 theoretically restored the right to vote to the clergy, thus eliminating the category of lishentsy that had been adopted in 1918.

39. Salo W. Baron, *The Russian Jew under Tsars and Soviets*, 2d ed. New York, Macmillan, 1976, pp. 246–47. Many instances of the fierce resistance to antireligious measures are described in A.A. Gershuni, *Yahadut Be-Rusiya Ha-Sovietit*. Jerusalem, Mosad Ha-Rav Kook, 1961.

40. Gershon Swet, "The Jewish Religion in Soviet Russia," in Gregory Aaronson, et al. eds., *Russian Jewry, 1917–1967*. New York, Thomas Yoseloff, 1969, p. 214.

41. Some of these reactions are discussed in Zosa Szajkowski, *Jews, Wars, and Communism*, Vol. I. New York, Ktav, 1972, pp. 392–402.
42. Hayim Hazaz, *Gates of Bronze*, G. Gershon Levi, tr. Philadelphia, Jewish Publication Society of America, 1975.

5. The Campaign against Zionism and Hebrew Culture

1. Ran Marom, "The Bolsheviks and the Balfour Declaration, 1917–1920," *Weiner Library Bulletin*, Vol. XXIX, Nos. 37–38, new series, 1976, p. 22.
2. P. Lipovetzky, *Joseph Trumpeldor: Life and Works*. Jerusalem, Youth and Hekhalutz Department, World Zionist Organization, 1953, pp. 66–67.
3. Joseph B. Schechtman, "The U.S.S.R., Zionism, and Israel," in Lionel Kochan, ed., *The Jews in Soviet Russia since 1917*, 3d ed. Oxford, Oxford University Press, 1978, p. 108.
4. Ibid., p. 109.
5. Guido G. Goldman, *Zionism under Soviet Rule (1917–1928)*. New York, Herzl Press, 1960, p. 39.
6. *Zionist Review*, May 1919, pp. 9–11.
7. Goldman, op. cit., p. 54.
8. Text of resolution in ibid., p. 41. Goldman notes (p. 42) that the Evsektsiya "did not feel sufficiently strong [in 1919] to initiate a massive campaign against the well-organized Zionists until the Bund had been annihilated, a process which was to swell the ranks of the Sections" with anti-Zionists.
9. Joseph B. Schechtman, "Soviet Russia, Zionism, and Israel," in Gregory Aaronson, et al., eds., *Russian Jewry, 1917–1967*. New York, Thomas Yoseloff, 1969, p. 410.
10. *Kommunistishe Fon*, July 8, 1919, quoted in Goldman, op. cit., p. 47.
11. Schechtman, in Kochan, ed., op. cit., p. 110. Ironically, during this period, in Ukrainian cities still outside Bolshevik control (Kamenetz-Podolsk, Mogilev-Podolsk, and Berdichev), Jewish parties, including Zionists, were supporting the principle of an independent Ukrainian state and struggling to press Ukrainian authorities, especially Petlyura, to stop the pogroms. Some counterpogrom actions taken by the Ukrainian government are described in Arnold Margolin, *Ukraine and the Policy of the Entente*. Temple Hill, Md., McDonald and Eudy, 1977, pp. 201–13, passim.
12. Aryeh L. Tsentsiper, *Eser Sh'not Redifot*. Tel Aviv, Akhdut, 1930, p. 51.
13. Schechtman, in Kochan, ed., op. cit., p. 111.
14. Aaronson, et al., eds., op. cit., p. 413.
15. The amnesty was granted because Evkom was eager at the time to have the JDC become part of the newly conceived Idgezkom, an overall Jewish relief organization. JDC aid in securing the release of the imprisoned Zionists was widely regarded in Russian Zionist circles as a damaging and compromising blow to their cause. Tsentsiper, op. cit., p. 85 ff. Harry M. Fischer, a Chicago municipal judge, and Max Pine, secretary of the United Hebrew Trades, represented the JDC in these efforts in 1920. On his return, Fischer lamented the state of the Soviet judicial system: "It is not a

832 5. The Campaign against Zionism and Hebrew Culture

[judicial] system at all. It is something that has grown up since the Revolution, subject to no restraint, to no particular laws, and it is a power exercised by men wholly unrestrained, many of them illiterate and responsible only to what they call their 'revolutionary conscience'. . . . The same man may be the arresting officer, the prosecutor, the judge who renders the decree and who with his own hands executes the offender. . . ." Zosa Szajkowski, *Jews, Wars, and Communism*, Vol. I. New York, Ktav, 1972, p. 404.

16. Goldman, op. cit., p. 61. Among the interventions at the time was the effort of Solomon Gepstein, a Zionist activist, who knew that Gorky was also sympathetic to Zionism. Gorky went to Lenin, but Lenin was negative, making a speech about the reactionary nature of national movements. S. Gepstein, "Russian Zionists in the Struggle for Palestine," in Aaronson, et al., eds., op. cit., p. 512. Gepstein was among the Zionists arrested in September 1919. At the interrogation, Gepstein who knew no English and had no cellar in his house was told: "I know that you transmit military information every day from the cellar of your house to London."

17. Samuil Agursky, *Di yidishe komisariatn un di yidishe komunistishe sekties*. Minsk, Party History Department, Central Committee of the Communist Party of White Russia, 1928, p. 352, quoted in Goldman, op. cit. p. 56.

18. Goldman, op. cit., p. 69.

19. *The Jewish Chronicle* (London), March 11, 1921. The dilemmas and vicissitudes of Poale Tsion's survival until 1928 are described in Baruch Gurevitz, *National Communism in the Soviet Union, 1918–28*. Pittsburgh, University of Pittsburgh Press, 1980.

20. Goldman, op. cit., p. 75. The trial is reported in Tsentsiper, op. cit., pp. 99–103. See also Goldman, op. cit., pp. 74–77.

21. Goldman, op. cit., p. 75.

22. Schechtman, in Aaronson, et al., eds., op. cit., p. 418.

23. Judd Teller, *The Kremlin, the Jews, and the Middle East*. New York, Thomas Yoseloff, 1957, pp. 44–45.

24. I. N. Shteinberg, "Di naye heroishe idishe yugent," *Di tsukunft*, May 1928, quoted in Gitelman, op. cit., p. 288.

25. Teller, op. cit., p. 51.

26. *Der emes*, October 22, 1924, quoted in Goldman, op. cit., p. 84.

27. Ibid.

28. Goldman, op. cit., p. 86.

29. The number of Jews who emigrated to Palestine or had to leave cannot be determined with complete accuracy. Estimates vary. Goldman (using statistics from the American Jewish Committee) states that about 15,800 emigrated during the period 1919–23, and about 15,500 between 1925 and 1931 (op. cit., p. 82). Schechtman (in Kochan, ed., op. cit., p. 118) notes 21,157 in 1925–26; 1,197 for 1927–30; and 1,848 between 1931 and 1936. S. Gepstein (in Aaronson, et al., eds., op. cit., p. 514) estimates that over 18,000 left between 1919 and 1921; Margolin (in Aaronson, ibid., p. 544), using statistics from the Jewish Agency ("Aliyah" Anthology No. 3) states that 30,134 Jews emigrated from Soviet Russia between 1925 and 1936.

30. Jewish Telegraphic Agency, *Daily News Bulletin*, October 30, 1923, quoted in Schechtman, "The U.S.S.R., Zionism and Israel," in Kochan, ed., op. cit., p. 117.
31. *Gecholuts* (Moscow), June 1924, Nos. 1–2. The address of the paper's editorial staff, printed in small letters under the title is Sretenka, 15 Lukov Street, Apartment 2. This is not even a street in the customary sense, but a tiny narrow lane (*pereulok* in Russian). This leads one to believe that someone donated his own apartment for the Hekhalutz staff writers, typists, and members when they met, and that the apartment belonged to one of the members. (This information was provided by Dr. Minna Shore, who at one time lived in Moscow.) A number of issues are in the Joseph Rosen Archives, File 83, YIVO Institute for Jewish Research. The last issue of *Gecholuts* appeared in 1928.
32. Ibid., July–August, Nos. 4–5.
33. Ibid. See also Yehuda Slutsky's essay "Gecholuts" in *Shvut*, Vol. I, 1973, pp. 131–37.
34. *Der emes*, May 7, 1927, quoted in Goldman, op. cit., p. 111.
35. Schechtman, in Kochan, ed., op. cit., p. 111.
36. Quoted in Yehoshua A. Gilboa, *A Language Silenced: The Suppression of Hebrew Literature and Culture in the Soviet Union*. New York, Associated University Presses, 1982, p. 117.
37. See especially ibid., pp. 54, 55, 63, 65, 66–98.
38. Alfred A. Greenbaum, "Hebrew Literature in Soviet Russia." *Jewish Social Studies*, Vol. XXX, 1968, p. 135.
39. Zvi Y. Gitelman, *Jewish Nationality and Soviet Politics*. Princeton, Princeton University Press, 1972, pp. 277, 279.
40. Jehuda Slutski [Yehuda Slutsky], "The Fate of Hebrew in Soviet Russia," in Aaronson, et al., eds., op. cit., p. 397.
41. Quoted in Salo W. Baron, *The Russian Jew under Tsars and Soviets*, 2d ed. New York, Macmillan, 1976, p. 230.
42. Slutski, op. cit., p. 402.
43. Zvi Halevy, *Jewish Schools under Czarism and Communism: A Struggle for Cultural Identity*. New York, Springer, 1976, p. 129.
44. Gitelman, op. cit., pp. 278, 279.
45. Quoted in Halevy, op. cit., p. 402.
46. The visit with Lunacharsky is described by Jacob Mase [Mazeh], "In the Wake of the Russian Revolution," in Leo W. Schwarz, *Memoirs of My People*. Philadelphia, Jewish Publication Society of America, 1945, pp. 523–528. Lunacharsky's remarks in ibid., p. 527, tr. by Maurice T. Galpern from Mazeh's *Zikhronot*, Vol. IV, Tel Aviv, 1936, p. 13.
47. There is another aspect based on Lunacharsky's talk with Professor Solomon Zeitlin of Dropsie College, Philadelphia, as reported by Zeitlin to Cyrus Adler. In the interview Zeitlin noted that the fight of the Jewish Communists against Hebrew seemed to justify their existence as a Jewish Communist party. They are "more fanatic in their fight against the Hebrew language than the Russian Communists," he added. Lunacharsky agreed, alleging that the central government was against their "fanaticism" and

"has nothing against the teaching of the Hebrew language and Jewish history," adding that "if there were any initiative on the part of the Jewish people to organize schools" for their study he—as Commissar of Education—"would satisfy their demands." Lunacharsky permitted Zeitlin to make the statement public but he was warned not to, especially by Dr. Joseph Rosen of Agro-Joint who believed it "would not help our cause." Dr. Bernard Kahn, European Director of JDC, said that "one cannot and should not rely upon such declarations and promises. . . ." Professor Zeitlin had hardly left Russia, when, according to Kahn, "Lunacharsky officially stated his hostility towards the Hebrew language and [said] that he would not tolerate schools with Hebrew as the language of instruction." Szajkowski, op. cit., pp. 397–98, and notes 10, 11, 12, p. 604.

48. Tsentsiper, op. cit., p. 34.
49. Gilboa, op. cit., p. 113.
50. Ibid., pp. 42–44.
51. Ibid., p. 120.
52. Quoted from Yehuda Livrov, "Minaftulei Ha-Tarbut Ha-Ivrit B'Rusia Ha-Bolshevit," *Bekhaf Hakele*, Tel Aviv, August 2, 1935, in Gilboa, ibid,. pp. 121–22. See also Aryeh L. Tsentsiper, *B'Maavak L'Geulah: Sefer Ha-Tsionut Ha-Russi (From Dust to Redemption: The Book of Zionism in Russia.)* Tel Aviv, Akhdut, 1956, p. 179.
53. Avraham Kariv [Krivoruchka], "Seminar Lemorim Ivriim B'moskva," in Benjamin West, ed., *Naftulei Dor.* Tel Aviv, Foreign Delegation of Tseirei Tsion, 1946, p. 312, and Tsentsiper, *B'Maavak*, op. cit., p. 180.

    Dr. Meir Gelfond, who was born in Moscow in 1930 and arrested for Zionist activity in 1949 (he emigrated to Israel in 1971) refers to several other later influences in "Illegal Zionist Activity . . . ," in David Prital, ed., *In Search of Self: The Soviet Jewish Intelligentsia and the Exodus.* Jerusalem, Mt. Scopus Pubs., 1982, p. 36.

    The agricultural school "Hekhalutz" existed in Malakhovka until 1928; the Russian-language newspaper *Hashomer Hatzair* was published illegally until 1934; labor and religious Zionist movements existed until the early thirties; and the underground central committee of the united Zionist party functioned until 1940.

54. Letter to Voyslavsky, January 4, 1928, quoted in Gilboa, op. cit, p. 248.
55. Quoted in Gilboa, ibid., p. 245.
56. Baron, op. cit., p. 234.
57. Gilboa, op. cit., p. 120.
58. Ibid., pp. 168–69.
59. Ibid., pp. 179–80. Steinman, together with other contributors to the paper, soon left the Soviet Union. "Perhaps," he wrote in his journal, "I lack the physical strength to withstand the great storm." Ibid., p. 174.
60. Ibid., p. 180.
61. David Ben-Gurion, "Bi-shlikhut Ha-histadrut L'moskva," *Mibifnim*, June 10, 1944, pp. 94–95, quoted in ibid., pp. 180–81.
62. Yehoshua A. Gilboa, ed., *Gekhalim Lokhashot.* Tel Aviv, M. Neuman, 1954,

pp. 378–80, quoted in Gilboa, "Hebrew Literature in the U.S.S.R.," in Kochan, ed., op. cit., pp. 229–30. *Gekhalim Lokhashot* (Glowing Embers) contains excerpts from the Hebrew writings of Lensky, Friman, Preygerzon, Bat Hama, Novak, Hyog, and Rodin and translations of the Yiddish works of Markish, Halkin, Kvitko, and Kipnis, among others, into Hebrew.

63. The struggle to publish *Bereshit* is described in Gilboa, *A Language Silenced*, op. cit., pp. 186–92.

64. Of the twelve contributors (including Babel), six later emigrated to Israel, Cohen in 1976, after many years in prison. Hyog, too, became disillusioned and wanted to go to Palestine, but was refused. He was arrested in 1948 and suffered many years of hard labor at a prison camp. Haboneh was arrested and exiled several times; Babel and Tsfatman were arrested in the thirties and exiled. The latter five all died in the Soviet Union. Bat Hama was still alive in the Soviet Union as of 1984. Details of the fate of these writers are described in Gilboa, *A Language Silenced*, op. cit., pp. 193–200.

In 1927, Ben Zion Fradkin managed to publish in Kharkov a few Hebrew poems celebrating the tenth anniversary of the Revolution, but the atmosphere was so dismal that some had proposed that the Moscow collection be called *Akharit* (End) instead of *Bereshit*. See Wolf Blattberg, *The Story of the Hebrew and Yiddish Writers in the Soviet Union*. New York, Institute of Jewish Affairs, 1953, p. 5, cited in Greenbaum, "Hebrew Literature," op. cit., p. 138.

65. Sh. Rusi, in *Davar Supplement*, March 1927. Quoted in Gilboa, "Hebrew Literature," in Kochan, ed., op. cit., p. 233.

66. Tsentsiper, *B'Maavak*, op. cit., p. 242.

67. Tsentsiper, *B'Maavak*, op. cit., p. 179.

68. Greenbaum, "Hebrew Literature," op. cit., p. 139.

69. Tsentsiper, *B'Maavak*, op. cit., p. 179.

70. Zvi Preygerzon, *Yoman Hazikhronot, 1949–1955*. Tel Aviv, 1976, p. 49. Quoted in Gilboa, *A Language Silenced*, op. cit., p. 226.

71. Friman suffered greatly in the Soviet Union, living close to starvation by giving Hebrew lessons. He did, however, learn that his book would be published in Palestine. In 1934, just before his arrest, he met the writer Yosef Opatoshu, then visiting the Soviet Union, and lamenting the absence of Hebrew books told him, "Jewish life is dying here." Gilboa, *A Language Silenced*, op. cit., p. 255.

72. Yosef Opatoshu, "Drei Hebraier," *Zamlbikher*, No. 8 (New York, 1952), quoted in Gitelman, op. cit., p. 282.

73. Letter to Daniel Charney, undated [1925], quoted in Gitelman, op. cit., p. 283.

74. Alfred A. Greenbaum, *Jewish Scholarship and Scholarly Institutions in Soviet Russia, 1918–1953*. Jerusalem, Center for Research and Documentation of East European Jewry, Hebrew University, 1978, p. 4.

75. Ibid.

76. Ibid., p. 6.

77. Ibid., pp. 59, 168, 169.

78. In a letter to the author dated August 14, 1984, from Hayim Y. Sheynin, a Semitology scholar who worked in the Oriental Institute, University of Leningrad, from 1966 to 1971, and who follows the Hebrew manuscript bibliography continuously, he states that "he never found any record of this [Gintsburg] catalog," but that it may have appeared without his knowledge. Mr. Sheynin himself completed the catalog of the Friedland Collection in *Kohelet Mosheh*, begun in 1893 by Samuel Weiner. This was, in Mr. Sheynin's words, "a very copious job," and he doubts that his catalog will ever be published. For later work on the cataloging of Hebrew manuscripts in Leningrad, see Chimen Abramsky, "Hebrew *Incunabula* in Leningrad," *Soviet Jewish Affairs*, Vol. 17, No. 1, Spring 1987, pp. 53–60.

    Korey, however, finds that despite "a systematic pattern of discrimination against the use and teaching of Hebrew," the U.S.S.R. "currently accords in a variety of ways official recognition of the Hebrew language as a vital and living language, intimately linked to the culture of the Jewish people." He cites the program of the Communist party adopted by the 22d Congress in October 1961, which affirms the right of every citizen "to speak and write any language," and an article in *Izvestiya*, December 24, 1976, which declared that "no one in the Soviet Union is forbidden to study any language, including Hebrew or Yiddish." He also notes that Hebrew is taught at the Institute of Oriental Studies of Tbilisi State University, the Institute of Asian and African Countries of Moscow State University, and at the Russian Orthodox theological academies in Leningrad and Zagorsk. See William Korey, "International Law and the Right to Study Hebrew in the USSR," *Soviet Jewish Affairs*, Vol. 11, February 1981, pp. 3, 8, 10. The struggling to legitimize their right to teach and learn Hebrew, except in Baku.

79. Greenbaum, *Jewish Scholarship*, op. cit., pp. 131, 168–69. Semitic studies generally suffered an almost total eclipse under Stalin, even including the closing of the Chair of Assyriologic-Hebraistic Studies at Leningrad University in 1950. Some guarded optimism as to the future development of Hebraic studies, "regardless of the future of Soviet relations with the State of Israel" has been expressed by Greenbaum. See ibid., pp. 132–33. See also Yehuda Slutsky's bibliographical study, "Hebrew Publications in the Soviet Union," in Hebrew, in Chone Shmeruk, ed., *Pirsumim Yehudiim Be-Brit Ha-Moatsot, 1917–1960* (Jewish Publications in the Soviet Union, 1917–1960), compiled by Y. Y. Cohen and M. Piekarz. Jerusalem, Historical Society of Israel, 1961, pp. 19–54.

    Sheynin (note 78) has noted with interest a substantial section on "Old Hebrew Literature" (Biblical literature including Apocrypha and Pseudo-Epigraphs) in *Istoriia Vsemirnoi Literatury* (Moscow), Vol. 1, 1983, pp. 271–302, and a short sketch of medieval Hebrew literature in Vol. 2, 1984, pp. 209–10. Conversation of author with Mr. Sheynin, January 12, 1987.

80. Benjamin Pinkus, *The Soviet Government and the Jews, 1948–1967: A Documented Study*. Cambridge, Cambridge University Press, 1984, pp. 452–53. See also Halevy, op. cit., pp. 135–36.

81. Mikhail Zand, "Bukharan Jewish Culture under Soviet Rule," *Soviet Jewish Affairs*, Vol. 9, No. 2, 1979, p. 17. Since 1938 Cyrillic has been used.

82. Mendel Kohansky, *The Hebrew Theatre: Its First Fifty Years.* New York, Ktav, 1969, p. 19.

83. Gershon Swet, "The Jewish Theater in Soviet Russia," in Aaronson, et al., eds., op. cit., pp. 295–96. See also Kohansky, op. cit., pp. 19–54, for a dramatic account of this and other struggles.

84. In a recent book in Russian called *Essays and Portraits: Articles on Yiddish Writers*, Moscow, Sovetsky Pisatel, 1975, p. 10, the author G. Remenik takes surprising issue with Lenin's well-known view that Hebrew was used only for works of a religious nature. He argues that:

> Pre-revolutionary Yiddish literature was developed in close links with the best traditions of world literature and, in the first place, Russian literature. The new Yiddish literature has an old tradition, covering many epochs of the ancient Hebrew culture. This was not only a national, but an international factor, because the ancient Jewish culture outgrew [its] narrow national boundaries.

Quoted in Chimen Abramsky, " 'Literary Portraits of a Bygone Age': Review of Ocherki i Portrety, by G. Remenik, Moscow, 1975." In *Soviet Jewish Affairs*, Vol. 7, No. 1, 1977, p. 85.

85. Abraham Itai, *Korot Hashomer Hatzair be-S.S.S.R. (Noar Tsofi Khalutsi-N.Ts.H.)* (The Saga of Hashomer Hatzair in the U.S.S.R.). Jerusalem, Society for Research on Jewish Communities, 1981, pp. 284 ff. See also Benjamin West, *Ben Yayesh L'tikva* (Between Despair and Hope). Tel Aviv, Flame Pub., 1973 and West, ed., *Naftulei Dor*, op. cit., passim.

86. Tsentsiper, *B'Maavak*, op. cit., p. 191.

87. Ibid.

88. Ibid.

89. Interviews with Nelly Vortmann (April 1981) and Uri Shalon (January 1984) in Haifa.

90. Itai, op. cit., p. 284.

91. Described in ibid., pp. 286–87.

92. In 1938 the Peshkova agency was eliminated. Vinaver was imprisoned and sentenced to ten years' forced labor and died. Peshkova was rescued from imprisonment, perhaps thanks to her reputation. On her eightieth birthday, after Stalin's death, she was recognized by the Soviet regime. From Israel she received blessings and best wishes and eighty trees were planted in Herzl Forest by "Magen"—the organization for the aid of Soviet Prisoners of Zion. Peshkova died in 1965. Ibid., p. 287. In Lubyanka, a prisoner named Anatoly Fastenko told Solzhenitsyn about Peshkova, about her personal immunity and generous help to prisoners, but when he asked Fastenko if her help extended to all prisoners, Fastenko explained that the so-called "Counter-revolutionaries"— engineers and priests, for example, were not included, only members of "former political parties." Aleksandr I. Solzhenitsyn, *The Gulag Archipelago, 1918–1956.* New York, Harper and Row, 1973, p. 227.

93. Teller, op. cit., pp. 52–53.
94. Ibid., p. 53.

6. Uprooting and Resettlement on the Land, 1922–28

1. During the early and mid-1800s, several agricultural experiments had been undertaken, with varying degrees of official cynicism and seriousness, and colonies were established in the Ukraine and the Crimea (see Michael Stanislawski, *Tsar Nicholas I and the Jews.* Philadelphia, Jewish Publication Society of America, 1983, pp. 155, 156, 158, 164). The census of 1897 revealed that 190,000 Jews were gainfully employed in farming, about half in 300 farm colonies, mainly in the provinces of Kherson, Ekaterinoslav, and Kiev. The figure dropped to 55,000 toward the end of the tsarist period.
2. Jewish Colonization Association, *Rapport de la direction generale pour l'année 1923.* Paris, 1925, p. 197.
3. Solomon Bloom, "ORT: Fifty Years of Jewish Relief in Eastern Europe," *ORT Economic Review,* Vol. 2, December 1945, p. 9.
4. Yaacov Lestschinsky, *Dos sovetishe idntum.* New York, Yidisher kemfer, 1941, pp. 92–93.
5. In the period from 1914 through 1920, JDC spent $5,750,000 for "purely palliative relief" with the cooperation of the American Red Cross and other organizations. During the famine period, from August 1921 through December 1922, JDC spent $3,827,000 toward nonsectarian relief, in cooperation with ARA, the American Friends Service Committee, and other organizations. (The JDC report states that during this period "upwards of 10 million people in Russia were saved from starvation through installation of 15,000 food kitchens.") "Statement of Russian Activities," compiled by J. C. Hyman, March 16, 1934. Rosen Archive, ARA–JDC Files, YIVO Institute for Jewish Research, New York.

   Intense debates among Jewish organizations regarding the Communist demand for "non-sectarian relief" are discussed in Boris D. Bogen, *Born a Jew.* New York, Macmillan, 1930, pp. 272–76, 281, 289–91, and in Zosa Szajkowski, *Jews, Wars, and Communism,* Vol. 1. New York, Ktav, 1972, pp. 88–97, 396. According to Bogen (pp. 289–90), Zionists in Russia organized for separate relief of Jews in Odessa and refused to help those who had caused pogroms and suffering earlier. These Zionists were later arrested and their food confiscated.
6. Letter from Bogen to JDC, New York, January 24, 1923. Rosen Archive, Box I, Folder 12. YIVO Archives.
7. Ibid. See also Bogen, op. cit., pp. 272–350.
8. Zvi Y. Gitelman, *Jewish Nationality and Soviet Politics.* Princeton, Princeton University Press, 1972, p. 238.
9. According to Daniel Charney (*A yortsendlik aza.* New York, CYCO, 1943, p. 285), a $10.00 food package could feed a family of four or five for an entire month. One dollar could buy three poods of corn and 30 poods

6. UPROOTING AND RESETTLEMENT ON THE LAND, 1922–28 839

could buy a "good prewar house in town." Quoted in Gitelman, ibid., p. 238.

10. Gitelman, op. cit., p. 237.
11. Up to the fall of 1924, JDC expended $4,500,000 on "independent relief and reconstructive work through Dr. Rosen and Dr. Bogen . . . for feeding, clothing, medical activities, etc.," of which $1,290,000 was allocated for "experimental reconstructive agricultural activities." "Statement of Russian Activities," by J. C. Hyman, op. cit.
12. Solomon M. Schwarz, *The Jews in the Soviet Union.* Syracuse, Syracuse University Press, 1951, p. 160.
13. Merle Fainsod, *Smolensk under Soviet Rule.* Cambridge, Harvard University Press, 1952, p. 442. The Smolensk archive, which Fainsod used, contains more than 500 files of party and government documents dealing with the Smolensk province, covering the period 1917–38 (about 200,000 pages). The files were shipped to Germany during the war and fell into American hands at the end of the conflict.
14. Salo W. Baron, *The Russian Jew under Tsars and Soviets,* 2d ed. New York, Macmillan, 1976, p. 219.
15. Chone Shmeruk, "Ha-Kibutz Ha-Yehudi Ve Ha-Hityashvut Ha-Klaklait Be-Byelorusia Ha-Sovietit 1918–1932" (The Jewish Community and Jewish Agricultural Settlement in Soviet Belorussia 1918–1932). Doctoral thesis, Hebrew University, Jerusalem, 1961, p. xiii.
16. *Der emes,* December 20, 1923.
17. Quoted from Yaacov Lestschinsky in *Der emes vegn di idn in rusland.* Berlin, Jalkut, 1925, pp. 19–21.
18. According to a report in *Der emes,* December 1924, a large majority of the colonists consisted of former farmers, artisans, and workers.
19. Leon Shapiro, *The History of ORT.* New York, Schocken, 1980, pp. 134–35.
20. Chone Shmeruk, "Yiddish Literature in the U.S.S.R.," in Lionel Kochan, ed., *The Jews in Soviet Russia Since 1917,* 3d ed. Oxford, Oxford University Press, 1978, p. 247.
21. Gitelman, op. cit., pp. 383–84.
22. Schwarz, op. cit., pp. 117, 161.
23. A possible explanation for Kalinin's ardent support of Jews and his numerous speeches on the importance of preserving Jewish national identity is suggested in Jack Miller, "Kalinin and the Jews: A Possible Explanation," *Soviet Jewish Affairs,* Vol. 4, No. 1, 1974, pp. 61–65.
24. Avraham Yarmolinsky, *The Jews and Other Minor Nationalities under the Soviets.* New York, Vanguard, 1928, pp. 82–83.
25. Bogen, op. cit., p. 315. See also note 11.
26. The agreement was signed by K. Lander for the government and Rosen for JDC. Rosen Archive, Box I, Folder 2.
27. Rosen Archive, Box I, Folder 11.
28. Ibid.
29. Dr. Rosen's report to JDC, 1922. Rosen Archive, Box I, Folder 11.

30. Ibid.
31. Rosen Archive, Box 1, Folder 11.
32. M. Kamenshtein, *Sovetskaya vlast', yevreiskoye zemleustroyeniye i OZET* (The Soviet Government, Jewish Land Settlement, and OZET). Moscow, OZET Publications, 1928, p. 48. Quoted in Schwarz, op. cit., p. 268.
33. Maurice Hindus, *Humanity Uprooted*. Westport, Conn., Greenwood, 1972 (reprint of 1929 ed.), p. 269.
34. Quoted in appendix of Yaakov Lvavi (Babitzky). *Ha-Hityashvut Ha-Yehudit Be-Birobijan* (Jewish Settlement in Birobidzhan). Jerusalem, Historical Society of Israel, 1965.
35. GEZERD included leading figures in the Evsektsiya and the Soviet state apparatus. The well-known economist Yuri Larin was chairman. Among the non-Jewish members were Kalinin; Chicherin, the Commissar for Foreign Affairs; Leonid Krassin, Commissar for Foreign Trade; and Peter Smidovich, Vice-President of the Supreme Soviet.
36. Text of agreement in Rosen Archive, Box I, Folder 11.
37. Report by Bogen to JDC, April 10, 1923. Rosen Archive, Box I, Folder 12.
38. Ibid.
39. Evelyn Morrissey, *Jewish Workers and Farmers in the Crimea and Ukraine*. New York, privately printed, 1937, p. 122.
40. Ibid., p. 125.
41. The article is undated. Rosen Archive, Box L, File 19.
42. Letter from Rosen to James Rosenberg, March 27, 1925. Rosen Archive, Box I, Folder 18.
43. Bogen, op. cit., p. 345.
44. Ibid., p. 352.
45. Bernard Kahn, "My Trip to Russia," June–July, 1925. Rosen Archive, Box I, Folder 21.
46. Report by Rosen to Conference of UJA Campaign, Philadelphia, September 12–13, 1925. Rosen Archive, Box I, Folder 20.
47. Markoosha Fisher, *My Lives in Russia*. New York, Harper and Bros., 1944, p. 25.
48. Rosen Archive, Box I, Folder 19.
49. Report by Moscowitz to David Brown, October 1925. Rosen Archive, Box I, Folder 21.
50. *Jewish Daily Forward* article, 1925 (undated). Rosen Archive, Box I, Folder 19.
51. Kahn, "My Trip to Russia," op. cit.
52. The negative attitude of the native population was largely rooted in the strong desire of Crimean leaders of Tatar origin to give the Crimean ASSR, set up in 1921, a Tatar character. This feeling was in conflict with Soviet authorities, and in 1928 some of these leaders were shot. However, the Crimean Tatars still hoped for the repatriation of hundreds of thousands of Tatars who had left during the tsarist period, and when KOMZET decided to settle 1,000 Jewish families in the Crimea in 1925 on 40,000 desiatins (one desiatina is equivalent to 2.7 acres), the Crimean authorities gave

the Jews only about 13,000 of poor quality. However, the central Soviet authorities overrode this decision, restoring the planned acreage but leaving the Tatars angry and resentful. Yaakov Lvavi (Babitzky), " 'Ibrahimism' and the Jewish Colonization in the Crimea" (Hebrew), *Shvut*, Vol. 3, 1975, pp. 35–39.

53. Yarmolinksy, op. cit., p. 92. In his "Statement of Russian Activities," op. cit., J. C. Hyman tabulated Agro-Joint expenditures as follows: From 1924 to the spring of 1928, JDC spent $5,880,000 for land-settlement activities, which included settling 7,500 new families by Agro-Joint; substantially aiding 10,000 in old Jewish colonies; and giving 7,000 families initial assistance in colonies outside Agro-Joint districts. Over 100,000 Jews were settled in Agro-Joint colonies in this period, on over one million acres in 215 settlements. In addition, 15,000 non-Jewish peasant families (neighbors of Jewish colonists) were aided by Agro-Joint.

54. Yaakov Lvavi, "Jewish Agricultural Settlement in the USSR," tr. from *Bekhinot* (Tel Aviv), No. 1, 1970. *Soviet Jewish Affairs*, No. 1, June 1971, p. 94.

55. Gitelman, op. cit., p. 290.

56. Shmeruk, op. cit., p. xii.

57. Ibid.

58. Ibid., p. xiv. These conflicts are described in Hirsh Smoliar, *Fun eineveynik: zichronos vegn der "Evsektsiya."* Tel Aviv, Peretz, 1978, pp. 307–8, 314, 317.

59. Shmeruk, op. cit., pp. xiv, xv.

60. Ibid., p. xv.

61. Ibid., p. xvii.

62. Zosa Szajkowski, in commenting on the immense output of books, reports, and articles on the "miracle" of Jewish colonization, labels it "well-controlled propaganda, carefully prepared so as not to shock anti-Communists." (*Jews, Wars, and Communism*, Vol. I. New York, Ktav, 1972, p. 410.) A number of the more enthusiastic writers and their articles are listed in op. cit., p. 607. Some writers, however, criticized Agro-Joint for not helping more of the *lishentsy* into the colonies, and for "blindly following the demands of the Evsektsiya program and giving up relief for 'productivization.' " In this sense, Agro-Joint fell in with the widespread notion that middlemen's activities were ipso facto unproductive or parasitic. Countering this is Bauer's statement that between 1924 and 1928, 5,446 families were settled on the land, "most of them *lishentsy*." Yehuda Bauer, "The Relations between the American Joint Distribution Committee and the Soviet Government, 1924–38," in Bela Vago and George L. Mosse, eds., *Jews and Non-Jews in Eastern Europe 1918–1945*. New York, Wiley, 1984, p. 273. See also Chapter 7 of the present work.

63. Schwarz, op. cit., p. 164.

64. Baron, op. cit., p. 222.

65. Schwarz, op. cit., p. 165, based on figures compiled by L. Zinger and B. Engel, *Idishe Bafelkerung fun FSSR in Tabeles un Diagrames*, tables I–2, II–7, III–8, and VII–15.

66. Gitelman, op. cit., p. 407.

67. Ibid., p. 408.
68. Ibid.
69. *Ershter alfarbandisher tsuzamenfor fun GEZERD, Moskve, 15–20 November 1926—stenografisher barikht.* Moscow, GEZERD, 1927, pp. 28–29. Quoted in Gitelman, op. cit., p. 412.
70. Lvavi, op. cit., p. 99.
71. *Ershter alfarbandisher,* op. cit. Quoted in Gitelman, op. cit., p. 413.
72. Ibid., pp. 84–85. Quoted in Gitelman, p. 413.
73. Smoliar, op. cit., p. 360.
74. A. Chemerisky, *Di alfarbandishe kommunistishe partai (bolshevikes) un di idishe masn.* Moscow, Shul un bukh, 1926, p. 17. Quoted in Schwarz, op. cit., p. 163.
75. Schwarz, op. cit., p. 119.
76. Ibid.
77. *Ershter alfarbandisher,* op. cit., p. 31. Cited in Gitelman, op. cit., p. 415.
78. Shmeruk, op. cit., p. xviii.
79. Gitelman, op. cit., p. 403.
80. Ibid., p. 436.
81. Yehoshua A. Gilboa, *The Black Years of Soviet Jewry, 1935–1953.* Boston, Little, Brown, 1971, p. 229.
82. *Jewish Daily Forward* article, 1925 (undated). Rosen Archive, Box I, Folder 19.
83. Described in vivid detail in Smoliar, op. cit., pp. 332–73.
84. Alfred A. Greenbaum, "Soviet Jewry during the Lenin-Stalin period," *Soviet Studies,* Vol. XVI, No. 4, April 1965, p. 413. Smoliar also describes Kalinin's ardent support for Jewish national reconstruction in his *Fun eine-vaynik,* op. cit., pp. 351, 352, 353, 355, 356, 357.
85. Gitelman, op. cit., p. 420.
86. *Alfarbandisher baratung fun di idishe sektsies fun der Al.K.P.(B).* Moscow, Shul un bukh, 1927, pp. 105ff. Quoted in Schwarz, op. cit., p. 124.
87. M. Vishnitser, "Di GEZERD konferents in Moskve," *Di tsukunft,* February 1927. Quoted in Gitelman, op. cit., p. 420.
88. Smoliar, op. cit., passim, pp. 332–73.
89. Ibid., pp. 359–60.
90. Ibid., p. 361.
91. Gitelman, op. cit., p. 420.
92. *Alfarbandishe baratung . . . ,* p. 47, cited in Schwarz, op. cit., pp. 163–64. The touchy, even dangerous possibility of a Jewish national substance developing as a result of the resettlement project can be traced in the changes in the GEZERD journal *Tribuna.* This monthly appeared in March 1927, and was published and edited by Dimanshtain. The editorial staff included Golde, the Jewish Communists David Zaslavsky, Moshe Kats, and Yaakov Levin and Bragin. For several years, Shlomo Niepomniashchi, an Evsek who loved Hebrew, was secretary of the board. "*Tribuna*'s character was determined by OZET's policy, the general lines of which were set out by the Communist Party." In its first two years (1927–28), which were the final years of

NEP, the journal bore the title "Tribune of the Soviet Jewish People," and described OZET as an "organization in which participate elements not belonging to the toilers . . . men of differing ideologies." The "Soviet Jewish public" was called upon to help the government "with the overwhelming task of re-arranging the economic and cultural life of the Jewish masses." The first issue, reporting on the national conference of the Evsektsiya, stressed the number of Jewish members of the Communist party (48,000), Jewish members of the Komsomol (100,000), and children attending Jewish schools (115,000), but the Evsektsiya secretary Chemerisky warned against notions of preserving Jewish nationality or creation of a Jewish republic. But other opinions were also permitted and Jewish events outside Soviet Russia were noted, including the deaths of Ahad Ha'am and the poet Yehoash. Much space was devoted to OZET's problems of organization, finance, propaganda, and youth work, especially with non-Jews, directed toward rooting out anti-Semitism and stressing Jewish involvement in agricultural labor.

By 1929, with the onset of the First Five Year Plan, *Tribuna* became an outright Communist organ, "expressing faithfully the line of the party and the Soviet authorities and serving as a tool for the internationalist education of the masses." It continued to devote space to the achievements of Jewish farmers in the old as well as new colonies, but increasingly emphasized the importance of Birobidzhan. Information on *Tribuna* based on Y. Slutsky, "*Tribuna*—A Soviet Jewish Russian Journal, 1927-1937," *Soviet Jewish Affairs*, Vol. 12., No., 1, February 1982, pp. 45-53.

93. The subtle shadings and shifts in Esther's views are elaborated in Gitelman, op. cit., pp. 420-25.

7. Jews under the New Economic Policy (NEP), 1921-27

1. *Der shtern*, August 29, 1925.
2. Yehuda Bauer, "The Relations between the American Jewish Joint Distribution Committee and the Soviet Government, 1924-1938," in Bela Vago and George L. Mosse, eds., *Jews and Non-Jews in Eastern Europe*. New York, Wiley, 1974, p. 273.
3. Yaacov Kantor, *Ratnboyung in der idisher suive*. Kiev, Kultur-Lige, 1928, pp. 38-39.
4. Ibid.
5. Lev Zinger, *Dos banayte folk*. Moscow, Der Emes Publishing House, 1948, p. 40.
6. Merle Fainsod, *Smolensk under Soviet Rule*. Cambridge, Harvard University Press, 1952, p. 441.
7. Quoted in George Vernadsky, *A History of Russia*. New Haven, Yale University Press, 1944, p. 294.
8. Basil Dmytryshyn, *USSR: A Concise History*, 3d ed. New York, Scribners, 1978, p. 120.

9. Zvi Y. Gitelman, *Jewish Nationality and Soviet Politics.* Princeton, Princeton University Press, 1972, p. 355. Hirsh Smoliar, however, blames the Evseks for being late in instituting NEP policies for Jews. See his *Fun eynevaynik: Zikhronos vegn der "Evsektsiya."* Tel Aviv, Peretz, 1978, pp. 199–200. Yaacov Lestschinsky described the uneven, puzzling nature of the program. In Vitebsk, for example, while some Jews are planning clandestine night trips to sell some wares in Moscow, Cheka men arrive and say that blackmarketing is over. There will be no more arrests. Now people are free to open shops and sell whatever they wish. But some of the Jews are frankly skeptical. Everything is too smooth. The Bolsheviks must be trying to win over the people with this sweet talk. See his *Dos sovetishe idntum*, New York, Idisher kemfer, 1941, pp. 99–100.

10. "Dos shtetl vi es iz," *Der shtern*, March 14, 16, 17, 1926. Cited in Gitelman, op. cit., pp. 357–58. Kiper also revealed that the shtetlach in the Ukraine and White Russia were "far poorer than in wartime" or under the tsars, that poverty is taking "extraordinary forms." *Der emes*, July 16, 1924.

11. Bogen letter to JDC (New York), April 27, 1923. Rosen Archive, File I, No. 12, YIVO Archives, New York. Lestschinsky notes the decline in the number of tailors in various tailors' associations in the large cities: for example, in Odessa, a drop from 3,328 members in 1920 to 1,282 in 1923; and in Kiev, a drop from 4,350 members in 1920 to 1,699 in 1923. In cities such as Retshitze and Mogilev in 1924, unemployment was 70 to 80 percent. Those tainted with the stigma of "bourgeois" worked at home at sweated labor 16 to 18 hours a day "for more groshen" in order to survive. See Yaacov Lestschinsky, op. cit., pp. 109, 110. By mid-summer 1924, Kiper reports that hunger "is driving many Jews to flee to the land," that many people are walking barefoot, and working from 4 A.M. to 9 P.M. Lestschinsky, ibid., pp. 105, 106.

12. Bogen, letter to JDC, op. cit.

13. Ibid.

14. Avraham A. Yarmolinsky, *The Jews and Other Minor Nationalities under the Soviets.* New York, Vanguard, 1928, p. 64.

15. Ibid., p. 66. See also Lestschinsky, op. cit., p. 104, for other examples of severe taxation.

16. Boris D. Bogen, *Born a Jew.* New York, Macmillan, 1930, pp. 299–300.

17. Louis Fischer, article in *The Jewish Daily Forward*, n.d., 1925. Rosen Archive, File I, No. 19. There is an interesting account of Fischer's changing attitude toward NEP in James W. Crowl, *Angels in Stalin's Paradise: Western Reporters in Soviet Russia, 1917 to 1937.* Washington, D.C., University Press of America, 1982, pp. 77–78.

18. Fischer, op. cit.

19. JTA cable, Warsaw, November 27, 1929. Rosen Archive, File II, No. 28A. Lestschinsky speaks of the kustars as being in the "worst possible condition." See Lestschinsky, op. cit., p. 105.

20. JTA cable, Warsaw, November 27, 1929. Rosen Archive, File II, No. 28A, op. cit.

21. JTA cable, Moscow, December 3, 1929. Ibid.
22. JTA cable, Moscow, November 29, 1929. Ibid.
23. Fainsod, op. cit., p. 444.
24. Evelyn Morrissey, *Jewish Workers and Farmers in the Crimea and Ukraine*. New York, privately printed, 1937, p. 69.

    In a cable dated January 1, 1930, Dr. Rosen stressed the point that there were actually few Jewish kulaks, but many lishentsy. The Agro-Joint presence is "extremely important" in spite of difficulties, and differences must be tided over, but that this was "not the proper time for entering new agreements extending over a period of time." He proposed appropriating $300,000 for industrial purposes, covered by government bonds, and increased importation of raw materials to help industrialization by working with Jewish mutual aid societies. Rosen Archive, File II, No. 29.
25. Gitelman, op. cit., p. 360.
26. *Der veker*, May 24, 1924.
27. Salo W. Baron, *The Russian Jew under Tsars and Soviets*, 2d ed. New York, Macmillan, 1976, p. 211.
28. Quoted in ibid.
29. Shmuel Ettinger, "Russian-Jewish Relations Before and After the October Revolution," in Richard Cohen, ed., *Let My People Go*. New York, Popular Library, 1971, p. 157. Essay adapted from paper delivered at World Conference of Jewish Communities, Brussels, February 23–25, 1971.
30. Baron, op. cit., p. 212.
31. *Oktyabr*, February 3, 1927. Quoted in Smoliar, op. cit., p. 211.
32. Yaacov Lestschinsky, *Der emes vegn di idn in rusland*. Berlin, Jalkut, 1925, pp. 34ff.
33. Lev Zinger, *Di idishe bafelkerung in Sovet-rusland*. Moscow, 1932, p. 34, cited in Lestschinsky, *Dos sovetishe idntum*, op. cit., p. 114.
34. Smoliar, op. cit., p. 210.
35. Ibid.
36. Ibid., p. 211.
37. Ibid., p. 215.
38. Boris Smolar, "The Jewish Artisan Has Fallen from Favor in Russia," Rosen Archive, File II, No. 28A. JDC also established kustar artels, beginning in 1924, to productivize artisans. In 1929, at Rosen's urging, JDC began to negotiate with the government on a plan to put Jewish workers in state factories. The government reaction, according to Rosen, was favorable and negotiations proceeded throughout 1930 but were terminated because of the deepening depression in the United States and skepticism among Agro-Joint subscribers in New York over the future of their relations with the Soviet Union. Even so, in 1930 and 1931 JDC was still helping kassy, artels, and medical societies. See Bauer, op. cit., p. 277.
39. Smoliar, op. cit., p. 213.
40. Ibid., pp. 199–200.
41. Gitelman, op. cit., p. 494.
42. Ibid. p. 493.

43. Maurice Friedberg, "Jewish Themes in Soviet Russian Literature," in Lionel Kochan, ed., *The Jews in Soviet Russia since 1917*, 3d ed. New York, Oxford University Press, 1978, pp. 96–97. For a fuller analysis of anti-Semitism in the proletarian literature of the 1920s, see Joshua Kunitz, *Russian Literature and the Jew*. New York, Columbia University Press, 1929.

The 1920s also witnessed a widespread campaign against anti-Semitism, trials against some accused of anti-Semitism, and violent attacks against another of Kozakov's books called *The Man who Prostrates Himself* (1929), which suggested that anti-Semitism still lingered in Soviet life among officials as well as workers and that some Soviet Jews found it wiser and safer to conceal their identity. Maxim Gorky and several other writers wrote articles deploring the anti-Jewish expressions of some of their colleagues. Friedberg, op. cit., pp. 96–97. See Chapters 6 and 10 of present work for other manifestations of anti-Semitism in the 1920s.

44. Solomon M. Schwarz, *The Jews in the Soviet Union*. Syracuse, Syracuse University Press, 1951, p. 258.

45. Bogen, op. cit., p. 341.

46. Yuri Larin, *Yevrei i Antisemitizm v SSSR* (Jews and Anti-Semitism in the USSR). Moscow, Government Printing House, 1929, pp. 124f. Quoted in Schwarz, op. cit., p. 258.

47. Bogen, op. cit., pp. 299–300.

48. *Der emes*, June 24, 1937.

8. Yiddish Culture in the Soviet Mold: Soviets, Courts, Schools, and Scholarship

1. See Chapter 1 for a discussion of Leninist-Communist nationality policy.

2. Basil Dmytryshyn, *USSR: A Concise History*, 3d. New York, Scribners, 1978, p. 123.

3. Ibid.

4. Ibid.

5. Solomon M. Schwarz, *The Jews in the Soviet Union*. Syracuse, Syracuse University Press, 1951, p. 80.

6. Mordechai Altshuler, "The Attitude of the Communist Party of Russia to Jewish National Survival, 1918–1930," in *YIVO Annual of Jewish Social Science*, Vol. XIV, 1969, pp. 77–78.

7. Ibid., p. 78.

8. Zvi Y. Gitelman, *Jewish Nationality and Soviet Politics*. Princeton, Princeton University Press, 1972, p. 352.

9. Yaacov Kantor, *Ratnboyung tvishn di yidishe massn*. Moscow, 1932, p. 62. Quoted in ibid.

10. Schwarz, op. cit., p. 150.

11. Gitelman, op. cit., p. 353.

12. Schwarz, op. cit., p. 152.

13. *Der emes*, July 3, 1927. Yarmolinsky mentions a figure of 115.

14. Altshuler, op. cit., p. 79–80.

15. Avraham Yarmolinsky, *The Jews and Other Minor Nationalities under the So-viets.* New York, Vanguard, 1928, p. 106.
16. Schwarz, op. cit., p. 152.
17. *Der emes,* July 12, 1937.
18. Quoted in Schwarz, op. cit., p. 155–56.
19. Benjamin Pinkus, "Yiddish-Language Courts and Nationalities Policy in the Soviet Union," *Soviet Jewish Affairs,* No. 2, November 1971, p. 48. Because of special circumstances in Vitebsk, trials were conducted in Yiddish as early as May 1922, but this decision did not result in a network of Yiddish courts. Pinkus, ibid., pp. 44–46.
20. Ibid., p. 50.
21. Schwarz, op. cit., p. 157.
22. The process of organizing the courts and the description of the court procedures is based on Pinkus, op. cit., pp. 51–60.
23. Lucy S. Dawidowicz, "What Future for Judaism in Russia?" *Commentary,* November 1956, p. 405.
24. Esther Frumkin, "Eynike bamerkungen vegn natsionaler dertsiung," *Tsayt fragn* (Vilna), No. 1, 1909.
25. *A yor-arbet fun der russlender kommunistisher partai in der yidisher suive.* Moscow, Central Board of Jewish Sections of the Russian Communist Party, 1924, pp. 40–44.
26. Ibid., pp. 44–48.
27. Gitelman, op. cit., p. 338.
28. Ibid., p. 350.
29. Ibid.
30. The account of the "complex system" is based on Zvi Halevy, *Jewish Schools under Czarism and Communism: A Struggle for Cultural Identity.* New York, Springer, 1976, pp. 216–20.
31. Ibid., p. 218.
32. E. Schulman, *A History of Jewish Education in the Soviet Union.* New York, Ktav, 1971, p. 70.
33. Boris D. Bogen, *Born a Jew.* New York, Macmillan, 1930, p. 330.
34. Schulman, op. cit., p. 80.
35. Ibid., p. 77.
36. Ibid., p. 78.
37. This judgment on the Jewish labor movement is made even more strongly by Chone Shmeruk in his "Yiddish Literature in the U.S.S.R." in Lionel Kochan, ed., *The Jews in Soviet Russia since 1917,* 3d. ed. Oxford, Oxford University Press, 1978, p. 246.
38. Schulman, op. cit., p. 140.
39. Ibid., p. 125.
40. Ibid., p. 139.
41. Ibid.
42. Rachel Erlich, "Politics and Linguistics in the Standardization of Soviet Yiddish," *Soviet Jewish Affairs,* Vol. 3, No. 1, 1973, p. 74.
43. Quoted in Zvi Lipset, "Yiddish Schools in the Soviet Union," *Bulletin on Soviet and East European Jewish Affairs,* Vol. B5, 1970, p. 73.

44. Gitelman, op. cit., p. 343.
45. It was not until 1923–24 that the total number of students in the country reached the 1914–15 levels. Lipset, op. cit., p. 72.
46. Schwarz, op. cit., p. 131.
47. Halevy, op. cit., pp. 176–78.
48. Ibid., p. 177. Schulman, op. cit., p. 163, estimates that only 20 percent of the Jewish school population (about 75,000) attended Yiddish schools as of October 1939, after the Western Ukraine was annexed. Later annexations included centers with Jewish schools, but these centers were diminished by the flight and exile of many Jews in 1939–41. These centers were later destroyed by the Nazis.
49. Schwarz, op. cit., p. 136.
50. S. Klitenik, *Di kultur arbet tsvishn di yidishe arbetndike inem ratn farband.* Moscow, Central Publishing House, 1931, p. 10. Quoted in Halevy, ibid., p. 179.
51. Merle Fainsod, *Smolensk under Soviet Rule.* Cambridge, Harvard University Press, 1952, p. 442.
52. Ibid., p. 443.
53. Lipset, op. cit., p. 73.
54. The full curricula are presented in Schulman, op. cit., pp. 114–17.
55. Halevy, op. cit., p. 170, and interview of author with Shimon Kipnis, November 3, 1983, Philadelphia.
56. Schulman, op. cit., p. 123.
57. Halevy, op. cit., p. 224. See Louise I. Shelley's *History Without Jews: The Vanishing Jew in Soviet History Textbooks.* Washington, D.C., B'nai B'rith International Council, 1977, for documentation of the virtual elimination of Jewish history from recently published Soviet textbooks.
58. Quoted in Schwarz, op. cit., p. 131.
59. See detailed tables in Halevy, op. cit., p. 181.
60. Schwarz, op. cit., p. 136.
61. Schulman, op. cit., pp. 103–5.
62. Lipset, op. cit., p. 72.
63. Ibid., p. 73.
64. Schwarz, op. cit., pp. 135–37.
65. Halevy, op. cit., pp. 196, 198–99.
66. B. Z. Goldberg, *The Jewish Problem in the Soviet Union.* New York, Crown, 1961, p. 253.
67. Benjamin Pinkus, *The Soviet Government and the Jews, 1948–1967: A Documented Study.* Cambridge, Cambridge University Press, 1984, pp. 260–61.
68. Lipset, op. cit., p. 73.
69. The fullest treatment in English is Alfred A. Greenbaum, *Jewish Scholarship and Scholarly Institutions in Soviet Russia, 1918–1953.* Jerusalem, Center for Research and Documentation of East European Jewry, Hebrew University, 1978. The author has made extensive use of this work.
70. Alfred A. Greenbaum, "Jewish Historiography in Soviet Russia," *Proceedings of the American Academy for Jewish Research,* Vol. XXVIII, 1959, p. 63.

71. Ibid.
72. See Greenbaum's measured analysis, ibid., pp. 66–71, and his *Jewish Scholarship*, op. cit., pp. 94–97, 101–4, 168–69.
73. Greenbaum, "Jewish Historiography . . . ," op. cit., pp. 70–71.
74. Ibid. p. 64.
75. Greenbaum, *Jewish Scholarship*, op. cit., p. 27.
76. Ibid., p. 39.
77. Ibid., p. 47.
78. Ibid., pp. 53–54.

9. Yiddish Literature and Theater, 1917–30

1. Yudel Mark, "Yiddish Literature in Soviet Russia," in Gregory Aaronson, et al., eds., *Russian Jewry, 1917–1967*. New York, Thomas Yoseloff, 1969, p. 224. A number of letters in *Briv fun idishe sovetish shribers* (Letters of the Soviet Yiddish Writers), compiled and annotated with an introduction by E. Lifschutz and M. Altshuler, ed. by Mordechai Altshuler, Jerusalem, Center for Research and Documentation of East European Jewry, Hebrew University, 1979, contain expressions of this great enthusiasm and hope.
2. James H. Billington, *The Icon and the Axe: An Interpretive History of Russian Culture*. New York, Vintage, 1970, p. 492.
3. Introduction to Chone Shmeruk, ed., *A shpigl af a shteyn*. Tel Aviv, *Di goldene keyt* and Peretz, 1964.
4. Quoted in Max Eastman, *Artists in Uniform: A Study of Literature and Bureaucratism*. New York, Knopf, 1934, pp. 137, 223.
5. See Vyacheslav Polonsky, "Lenin's Views of Art and Culture," in ibid., pp. 217–52.
6. Billington, op. cit., p. 521.
7. Ibid.
8. Ibid., pp. 488–90.
9. Chone Shmeruk, "Yiddish Literature in the U.S.S.R.," in Lionel Kochan, ed., *The Jews in Soviet Russia since 1917*, 3d ed. Oxford, Oxford University Press, 1978, p. 254.
10. Salo W. Baron, *The Russian Jew under Tsars and Soviets*, 2d ed. New York, Macmillan, 1976, p. 237. Bergelson's enthusiasm over the future of Yiddish literature in the Soviet Union is expressed in his "Dray tsentrn" (Three Centers), *In shpan*, No. 1, April 1926, pp. 84–96, cited in Shmeruk, "Yiddish Literature," in Kochan, ed., op. cit., p. 255.
11. Solomon M. Schwarz, *The Jews in the Soviet Union*. Syracuse, Syracuse University Press, 1951, p. 139. Based on the work of N. Rubinshtain, who was the director of the Yiddish section of the Belorussian State Library, and who published bibliographies of Yiddish books published in the years 1932–1935, Shmeruk notes that 668 books and pamphlets in Yiddish were published in 1932 (the peak year of Yiddish publishing in the USSR); 391 in 1933; and 348 in 1934 (incomplete because of the purges). Chone Shmeruk,

"Yiddish Publications in the U.S.S.R. from the Late Thirties to 1948," *Yad Vashem Studies*, Vol. IV, Jerusalem, 1960, pp. 99. 100.

12. Quoted in Chone Shmeruk, "Destruction of a Literature," tr. by H. H. Paper, *Judaism*, Vol. 82, No. 2. Spring 1972, p. 199.

13. See the interesting article by H. Remenik, "Tsu der frage vegn di onheyb fun der yidisher sovetisher literatur," *Sovetish heymland*, No. 11, 1966.

14. Shmeruk, "Yiddish literature in the USSR," in Kochan, ed., op. cit., p. 248. See also an analysis of the varying approaches to literature in Seth Wolitz, "The Kiev-Grupe (1918–1920) Debate: The Function of Literature," *Modern Jewish Studies Annual*, II, 1978, pp. 97–106.

   Jewish culture in Kiev had also been given a fresh lease on life by the March Revolution of 1917. Daily Yiddish newspapers appeared and two literary presses competed for readers. Under the new Ukrainian government, the Rada, autonomy for all national minorities including Jews seemed promising. The central element of Jewish life in Kiev was the *Idishe Kultur-Lige* (League for Jewish Culture), created early in 1918 and soon involving a network of schools, including a teacher's college, a publishing house, and facilities devoted to literature, theater, and music. The League blossomed during the first Soviet occupation of the city from February to August 1919, a period in which the future of Yiddish literature was mooted.

15. Shmeruk, "Yiddish Literature," in Kochan, ed., op. cit., pp. 250, 251.

16. Ibid., p. 250.

17. Altshuler, ed., op. cit., intro., pp. vii–viii.

18. Ibid., p. viii.

19. Irving Howe, ed., *Ashes Out of Hope: Fiction by Soviet-Yiddish Writers*. New York, Schocken, 1978, pp. 8–9.

20. Shmeruk, "Yiddish Literature," in Kochan, ed., op. cit., p. 252.

21. Charles A. Madison, *Yiddish Literature: Its Scope and Major Writers*. New York, Schocken, 1971, p. 412.

22. Ibid., p. 413.

23. Ibid.

24. Among these were Oyslender, Dobrushin, Hofshteyn, Markish, Nusinov, David Volkenshteyn, Ezra Fininberg, and Kvitko.

25. Altshuler, ed., op. cit., p. xi.

26. Hofshteyn to Niger, May 2, 1933, in ibid., pp. 159–61. Hofshteyn to Charney, 1922, pp. 91–93.

27. *Der emes*, February 3 and 12, 1924, cited in Altshuler, op. cit., p. 79.

28. Altshuler, ed., op. cit., p. 132.

29. *Der emes*, April 28, 1926, cited in ibid., p. 80.

30. Altshuler, ed., op. cit., pp. 103–4.

31. Ibid., pp. 81, 107, 141–42.

32. *Der emes*, October 22, 1929.

33. Yehoshua A. Gilboa, *The Black Years of Soviet Jewry: 1939–1953*. Boston, Little, Brown, 1971, p. 133.

34. Translated into English by Bernard Martin. Columbus, Ohio State University Press, 1977. Summaries of Bergelson's major works appear in Madi-

son, op. cit., pp. 426–33. English translations of three short fictional works ("Joseph Schur," "The Hole through Which Life Slips," and "Civil War" can be found in Howe, op. cit., pp. 29–123. See Yekiel Hofer, "Dovid Bergelson," in *Di goldene keyt*, No. 25, 1956, for a critical review in Yiddish; and in English, Susan A. Slotnick, "David Bergelson and the Metamorphosis of Tradition," *Jewish Book Annual*, Vol. 41, 1983–84, pp. 122–32.

35. Slotnick, op. cit., pp. 128–29.
36. "Dray tsentren," *In shpan*, No. 1., April 1926, pp. 84–96. See Note 10.
37. Howe, op. cit., p. 24. *Birger-milkhome* was included in a collection called *Shturem-teg* (Storm Days), published in 1928. (In an official Soviet anthology of selected works by Bergelson published in 1961, the interpretation of *Shturem-teg* is much more along orthodox Soviet lines. *Dovid Bergelson, Oysgevaylte verk*. Moscow, State Publishing House for Creative Literature, 1961, p. 12.)
38. Quoted in Madison, op. cit., p. 443.
39. Quoted in Gilboa, op. cit., p. 99.
40. Ibid.
41. Ibid., p. 97.
42. Letter from Markish to Opatoshu, March 27, 1929, in Altshuler, op. cit., p. 270. The story, however, was never published.
43. Howe, op. cit., p. 10.
44. Ibid.
45. A. Abtshuk, "Af fremde vegn," *Prolit*, Nos. 8–9, 1928, p. 78. Quoted in Shmeruk, op. cit., p. 259.
46. Howe, op. cit., p. 10.
47. Shmeruk, "Yiddish Literature," in Kochan, ed., op. cit., pp. 259–60.
48. On September 4, 1929, Reisin, Leivick, Boraisha, Raboy, and Leon Feinberg severed their connections with *Morgen freiheit* over the Commun·.t party support for the Arab cause at the time of the 1929 riots in Palestine, in which Jews were murdered. Altshuler, ed., op. cit., p. 276, note 61. In Markish's letter to Opatoshu (October 25, 1929), he refers to the departure of *"Freiheit* comrades," and an especially harsh attack on Leivick at a meeting in Kharkov (Altshuler, ed., p. 275). Toward the end of the 1920s, there was also a marked shift from an earlier trend in the Soviet Union to publish Yiddish writers from abroad who did not hew to the Communist line. Books by Leivick, Opatoshu, and Raboy did not appear after 1929, or appeared with highly critical forewords and afterwords.
49. Shmeruk, "Yiddish Literature," in Kochan, ed., op. cit., p. 261. See also Markish's letter to Opatoshu, October 25, 1929, and Altshuler, ed., op. cit., pp. 275–76, note 60. Also, in Kvitko's book *Gerangel* (Conflict) there were "Portraits and Exaggerations," including the satirical poem on Litvakov called *Der shtinkfoygel moyli* (The Stinkbird Moy[she] Li[tvakov]). The main bureau of the Evsektsiya in the Ukraine also attacked Hofshteyn for defending Kvitko and continuing his "petty bourgeois inclinations." Leivick maintained that Litvakov's bitter personal hostility toward Kvitko began in 1925, at a special evening for Kvitko in Moscow when he returned to Rus-

sia, by which time Litvakov saw Kvitko as a symbol of the "sins of exaggeration," of "disobedience," and of other wrongs. Kvitko, moreover, did
not remain silent. (*Di voch*, November 1, 1929, quoted in Altshuler, ed.,
op. cit., p. 276, note 60.)

50. Altshuler, ed., op. cit., p. 275. Pilnyak had already been attacked for his
"The Tale of the Unextinguished Moon" which exposed the callous, inhumane actions of party men. In 1929 his short novel *Mahogany* was published in Germany, having been sent there in order to obtain international
copyright protection, unavailable in the Soviet Union.

51. The proletarian writers argued that Kvitko's "exaggerations were an open
attack on the Communist party and an expression of a right-wing attack
on literature." (*Der emes*, September 10, 1929). In Markish's letter to Opatoshu (October 25, 1929), he writes that "the last few months have been
full of arguing," and that the issue of Kvitko has "cost us a lot of hear-
tache." Altshuler, ed., op. cit., p. 275 and note 60.

52. Translated into English by Nathan Halper in Howe, op. cit., pp. 124–92.

53. Translated into English by Seymour Levitan in ibid., pp. 193–218.

54. *Prolit*, No. 5, May 1929, pp. 73–67, cited in Altshuler, ed., op. cit., Introduction, p. [27]. Markish's retort appeared in *Der emes*, May 30, 1929.

55. Shmeruk, "Yiddish Literature," in Kochan, ed., op. cit., p. 260.

56. Ibid.

57. Altshuler, ed., op. cit., 283.

58. Shmeruk, "Yiddish Literature," in Kochan, ed., op. cit., p. 264.

59. Altshuler, ed., op. cit., pp. 141–42.

60. Letter from Hofshteyn to Charney, August 10, 1928. Altshuler, ed., op.
cit., p. 107, and *Prolit*, No. 3, June 1928, quoted in ibid., note 51.

61. Quoted in Shmeruk, "Yiddish Literature," in Kochan, ed., op. cit.,
p. 264.

62. Ibid., pp. 264, 265.

63. Gilboa, op. cit., p. 135.

64. Ibid.

65. Volume 2 was published in New York in 1948, and one chapter of Volume
3 was published in *Sovetish heymland*, No. 2, 1967. In his introduction, Der
Nister writes that he wants "to acquaint the young generation with the
extraordinary distance which we have traveled . . . which separates our
reality from that one. . . . Depicting these characters, already gone physically and spiritually, I have tried not to 'fight' them but to let them go,
quietly and slowly, to their distinct fate. . . ." He wanted to show "those
secret powers" of the Jewish poor tragically destroyed. See also Chapter
33, note 87.

66. Yosef Kerler, *12 August 1952* (Yiddish). Jerusalem, Eygns Verlag 1978, p.
71.

67. In Altshuler, ed., op. cit., Dobrushin to Leivick, pp. 60, 67; Kvitko to Yaacov Lestschinsky, p. 461; Oyslander to Leivick, p. 20; Hofshteyn to Niger,
pp. 166–67; Markish to Opatoshu, pp. 251, 256; Hofshteyn to Charney, p.
99; Volkenshteyn to Leivick, p. 182; Hofshteyn to Niger, pp. 159–60; Dobrushin to Leivick, pp. 55, 59.

68. Ibid., Dobrushin to Leivick, pp. 46, 54, 58, 60–61.

69. Gleb Struve, "Soviet Literature in Perspective," in Max Hayward, ed., *Soviet Literature in the Sixties: An International Symposium*. London, Methuen, 1965, p. 135.

70. E. Podriachik, "Genizah-shafungen in der idish-sovetisher literature." *Di goldene keyt*, No. 77, 1972, pp. 40–60. (Part I of *Fun finftn yor* was published in *Sovetish heymland*, January–February, 1964, pp. 3–73 and "Nakhvort un Forvort" in No. 2, 1967, pp. 97–123.)

71. Ibid., p. 42.

72. Edward J. Brown, *Russian Literature since the Revolution*. Cambridge, Harvard University Press, 1982, p. 84.

73. Struve, op. cit., p. 130.

74. Nahma Sandrow, *Vagabond Stars: A World History of Yiddish Theater*. New York, Harper and Row, 1977, p. 222.

75. Chagall's work for the Jewish theater, including superb reproductions of his sets and costumes, is described in the encyclopaedic *Chagall: Life and Work* by Franz Meyer, translated by Robert Allen and published by Harry N. Abrams, New York, n.d., pp. 265–313.

76. Ibid., p. 294.

77. Ibid.

78. Sandrow, op. cit., p. 230.

79. Reproduced in Meyer, op. cit., pp. 284–85.

80. Sandrow, op. cit., p. 232.

81. Ibid., p. 235. See Zeev Raviv, "Bay Nakht Oyfn Altn Mark," *Yiddish* (New York), Vol. 4, No. 2, 1980, pp. 70–81 for a study of Granovsky's staging of this work.

82. Sandrow, op. cit., p. 240.

83. Schwarz, op. cit., p. 141.

84. Described in S. Mikhoels, "Yidishe teatr-kultur in ratnfarband," S. Dimanshtain, ed., *Yidn in FSSR*. Moscow, Der Emes Publishing House, 1935, pp. 156–62.

10. Proletarianization: Collectivization of Agriculture and the End of the Jewish Colonies

1. Lenin is generally thought to have been not only more cultivated, reasonable, and comradely in his relations, but devoid of the spitefulness, malice, and vengefulness of Stalin. Lenin belonged to the cosmopolitan, emigré European branch of the party, whereas Stalin was part of what Kennan calls the "criminal-defiant wing . . . who has accepted society as an enemy . . . part of the seething, savage underworld of the Transcaucasus." Even in his early years in the party he was known as a troublemaker—fond of "stirring up resentments and suspicions among others, for provoking others into quarrels and acts of violence, and in this way, getting his revenge on people who had in some way offended him or stood in his path." George F. Kennan, *Russia and the West Under Lenin and Stalin*. Boston, Little, Brown, 1960, p. 231. Kennan also notes that there was a document in the tsarist

police archives showing that between 1906 and 1912 Stalin may have been a police informer (published in *Life*, April 23, 1956). Ibid., p. 232.

A good introduction to this question of "discontinuity" is Stephen F. Cohen's "Bolshevism and Stalinism," in Robert C. Tucker, ed., *Stalinism: Essays in Historical Interpretation.* New York, Norton, 1977, pp. 3–29. Older historians who saw no discontinuity as well as newer scholars who do are discussed. Cohen also deals with the complexities of this kind of historical analysis.

Among those scholars who see greater continuity are Marc Jansen, *A Show Trial Under Lenin: The Trial of the Socialist Revolutionaries, Moscow 1922.* Amsterdam, Nijhoff, 1982; Lennard D. Gerson, *The Secret Police in Lenin's Russia.* Philadelphia, Temple University Press, 1976; and Alan Besancon, *The Rise of the Gulag: Intellectual Origins of Leninism*, Sara Matthews, tr. New York, Continuum Books, 1980.

Edward Crankshaw, a prolific writer on the Soviet Union and a member of the British Military Mission in Moscow during World War II saw Lenin's rule as a "contemptuous dictatorship, a disaster for Russia and mankind," among other very strong attacks. See his *Putting Up with the Russians: Commentary and Criticism, 1947–84.* London, Macmillan, 1984.

2. Among the standard biographies of Stalin are: Isaac Deutscher, *Stalin: A Political Biography.* New York, Oxford University Press, 1949; Adam B. Ulam, *Stalin: The Man and His Era.* New York, Viking, 1973; and Robert C. Tucker, *Stalin as Revolutionary, 1879–1929.* New York, Norton 1973.

3. Robert Conquest, *The Great Terror: Stalin's Purge of the 30's.* New York, Macmillan, 1968, p. 77.

Once in power, these habits dominated his behavior and for almost thirty years, Russia was in the grip of a man jealous of the gifts of others, vindictive, unable "ever to forget an insult or a slight, but [with] great patience and power of dissimulation . . . a master of . . . the art of 'dosage' . . . of the art of playing people and forces off against each other for his own benefit." He particularly hated and feared Trotsky, the brilliant and popular Bolshevik orator, theoretician, and organizer of the Red Army, and the other cosmopolitan leaders in the early movement, many of whom were Jews, after he consolidated his power and felt threatened by their opposition. His tactic was invariably to set one against another, to keep them fighting. As these conflicts and factional disputes became more intense, Stalin became particularly ruthless toward those who had been close to him. Not wanting any witnesses to those who shared in his crimes, he disposed of them. Kennan, op. cit., p. 235.

4. Raphael R. Abramovitch, *The Soviet Revolution, 1917–1939.* New York, International Universities Press, 1962, p. 285.

5. The struggle between Stalin and Trotsky, Zinoviev and Kamenev was generally regarded in nonparty circles as a "struggle for power at the top," of little concern to the ordinary Soviet citizen. Occasionally, reactions to this intraparty contest "took on distinct anti-Semitic overtones." A fairly typical peasant remark is quoted in a party report in the Smolensk archives:

Our good master, Vladimir Ilich had only just passed away when our Commissars began to fight among themselves, and all this is due to the fact that the Jews became very numerous, and our Russians do not let them have their way, but there is nobody to suppress them, and each one considers himself more intelligent than the others.

Merle Fainsod, *Smolensk under Soviet Rule*. Cambridge, Harvard University Press, 1952, p. 48.

In a document found in the archives of a veteran Bolshevik, E. P. Frolov, called "The Antisemitism of J. V. Stalin," there are numerous statements alleging that there were many Jews in the opposition groups and an attempt to represent the "united opposition of Trotsky, Kamenev and Zinoviev as a conspiracy of three dissatisfied Jewish intellectuals." Cited in Roy A. Medvedev, *Let History Judge: The Origins and Consequences of Stalinism*. New York, Knopf, 1971, pp. 495ff.

6. Abramovitch, op. cit., p. 315.
7. Cohen, "Bolshevism and Stalinism," op. cit., p. 23.
8. Abramovitch, op. cit., pp. 331–32. Schapiro believed that, in view of the "course of his political maneuvers during 1928," that Stalin "had already formed this decision by the time of the Fifteenth Congress, while taking every precaution to conceal it. It is certain that the decision was formed outside the councils of the Politburo, since the support upon which he relied on in his conflicts with the left opposition depended upon complete acceptance of NEP." Leonard B. Schapiro, *The Communist Party of the Soviet Union*. New York, Random House, 1960, pp. 361–62.
9. Quoted in Basil Dmytryshyn, *USSR: A Concise History*. New York, Scribners, 1978, p. 167. The best single work on collectivization in English is M. Lewin, *Russian Peasants and Soviet Power: A Study of Collectivization*. New York, Norton, 1975.
10. Lewin, op. cit., p. 454.
11. Ibid., p. 455. A full description of these measures can be found in ibid., pp. 454–69.
12. Fainsod, op. cit., p. 444.
13. KOMZET meeting, August 13, 1929. Rosen Archive, File I, No. 119. YIVO Archives, New York.
14. JTA dispatches, October 16, 1929, November, 12, 1929. Rosen Archive, File II, 28A.
15. JTA cable, November 12, 1929. Ibid.
16. JTA cable, November 21, 1929. Ibid.
17. JTA cable, Moscow, December 4, 1929. Ibid.
18. JTA cable, Moscow, December 3, 1929. Ibid.
19. Articles by Boris Smolar, 1929–30. Rosen Archive, File II, 28A.
20. JTA cable, November 21, 1929. Ibid.
21. JTA cable, November 25, 1929. Ibid.
22. JTA cable, Warsaw, November 27, 1929. Ibid.
23. JTA cable, Moscow, December 4, 1929. Ibid.
24. JTA cable, November 21, 1929. Ibid.

25. JTA cable, November 25, 1929. Ibid.

26. JTA cable, November 21, 1929. Ibid.

27. *Tribuna*, 1929, No. 15, p. 25, quoted in Y. Slutsky, "*Tribuna*—A Soviet Jewish Russian Journal, 1927–1937," *Soviet Jewish Affairs*, Vol. 12, No. 1, February 1982, p. 51.

28. Ibid.

29. JTA cable, November 21, 1929. Rosen Archive, File II, 28A.

30. Statement by Leo M. Glassman, at a conference of the American Jewish Congress, December 8, 1929. Quoted in Zosa Szajkowski, *Jews, Wars, and Communism*, Vol. I. New York, Ktav, 1972, p. 389.

31. Ibid., p. 410.

32. Rosen Archive, File II, 29.

33. Rosenberg's notes, 1930. Rosen Archive, File II, 30.

34. Rosenberg's notes, op. cit. As of 1931, the Soviet Jewish demographer Y. Kantor estimated the number of Jews on the land at 255,000 (including 5,000 in Birobidzhan), but Lestschinsky believed that this figure was overstated by 35 percent. Yaacov Lestschinsky, *Dos sovetishe idntum*. New York, Yiddisher kemfer, 1941, p. 209. See also Note 58.

35. Thelma Nurenberg, *This New Red Freedom*. New York, Wadsworth, 1932, pp. 179–80.

36. Ibid., p. 181.

37. Ibid., pp. 185–86.

38. Ibid., p. 195.

39. Rosenberg's notes, op. cit.

40. A. A. Gershuni, *Yahadut Be-Russia Ha-Sovietit: Le-Korot Redifot Ha-Dat*. Jerusalem, Mosad Ha-Rav Kook, 1961, p. 103. Quoted in Joshua Rothenberg, "Jewish Religion in the Soviet Union," in Lionel Kochan, ed., *The Jews in Soviet Russia Since 1917*, 3d ed. Oxford, Oxford University Press, 1978, p. 75.

41. JTA cable, December 5, 1929. Rosen Archive, File II, 28A.

42. Nurenberg, op. cit., p. 194.

43. Ibid.

44. Ibid., pp. 196, 199.

45. Quoted in Rothenberg, op. cit., p. 75.

46. Quoted in Szajkowski, op. cit., p. 396.

47. Quoted in Roy A. Medvedev, "New Pages from the Political Biography of Stalin," in Tucker, ed., op. cit., p. 212. Fainsod mentions orders to Jewish kolkhoz families in the Western Oblast to move to the Ukraine to help replenish the depopulated kolkhozes there. *Smolensk under Soviet Rule*, op. cit., p. 444. Isaac Babel, too, wrote a story about the life of a village during collectivization, called "Kolivushka," translated into Hebrew by Arieh Aharoni in *Shvut*, Vol. 3, 1975, pp. 125–27. Antonov-Ovseyenko estimated that as many as three million kulak families were deported to camps and prisons where large numbers perished. Children of these families, if they survived, were severely penalized and stigmatized. No grain whatsoever was sent by the government to the stricken areas, yet exports of grain

continued during the famine. Anton Antonov–Ovseysenko, *The Time of Stalin: Portait of a Tyranny*. New York, Harper and Row, 1986. The horrors of the famine of 1932–34 are described in Robert Conquest, *The Harvest of Sorrow: Soviet Collectivization and the Terror-Famine*. New York, Oxford University Press, 1986. There are also accounts in Dana Dalrymple, "The Soviet Famine of 1932–34," *Soviet Studies*, Vol. XV, 1963–64, pp. 250–84, and Vol. XVI, 1964–1965, pp. 471–74; and in Ewald Ammende, *Human Life in Russia*, first published in 1936 and reprinted in 1984 by the Foundation to Commemorate the 1933 Ukrainian Famine, Montreal. The Soviet Government has never acknowledged the immense suffering the famine caused, with some estimates running as high as seven million deaths by starvation.

Official Soviet histories of the period omit all reference to the famine, but according to Alex Nove, "some Soviet historians, during the years 1964–70, did try to tell some of the real story, but the hard-liners stopped them." Nove adds that "a devastating picture of man-made famine on the Lower Volga by Dimitri Alekseyev appeared in 1985 and was favorably reviewed . . . in the literary monthly *Nasha sovremennik*. There are also uncensored samizdat written in Russia and memoirs published abroad." Nove, "When the Head is Off . . . ," *New Republic*. November 3, 1986, p. 35.

48. Rosen Archive, File I, No. 127; File II, Nos. 236, 238, 277, 289.
49. Evelyn Morrissey, *Jewish Workers and Farmers in the Crimea and Ukraine*. New York, privately printed, 1937, pp. 30, 41, 42.

Through the early and middle thirties, Agro-Joint aid continued, but on a declining slide: to industrial and credit cooperatives, factories (through its Industrial Department), Jewish vocational schools (see next chapter), health care societies, as well as agro-technical help to newly established collectives.
50. Ibid., p. 55.
51. Ibid., pp. 47–48.
52. Ibid., pp. 31–32.
53. "Ten Years' Work of Agro-Joint in the USSR," Report to National Conference on Jewish Welfare by Joseph Rosen, June 3, 1935. Rosen Archive, File II, No. 34.
54. *Jewish Daily Bulletin*, February 1, 1935.
55. Memo from Rosen, September 9, 1937. Rosen Archive, File II, No. 35. It was significant, too, that in an anthology published by the Emes Publishing House in 1935, called *Yidn in FSSR: Zamlbukh*, S. Dimanshtain, ed., there are glowing accounts of the economic and social reconstruction of Jewish life in the Soviet Union up to that time, but the introduction, p. 7, emphasized that the book was issued "at the initiative of GEZERD, with the historic designation of the Soviet regime regarding the transformation of Birobidzhan into a Jewish autonomous region." Many of the articles and photographs stress the achivements in Birobidzhan, and GEZERD and KOMERD are pointedly mentioned as participating in the upbuilding of the region.
56. Morrissey, op. cit., p. 129.

57. Minutes of meeting, January 21, 1937. Rosen Archive, File II, No. 35.

58. Lev Zinger, *Dos banayte folk.* Moscow, Der Emes Publishing House, 1941, p. 89. Lestschinsky, *Dos sovetishe idntum,* op. cit., p. 219, estimated a figure of 130,000 Jews still on the land. He believed that some Jews may have viewed resettlement on the land as "temporary." Besides, "millions of non-Jews had fled from the land. Why not Jews?" Ibid. He seems to have used different data for tables on pp. 170–71, called "Social classifications among economically active Jews in Soviet Russia," in which 100,000 Jews are in "farm employment"—7.1 percent of "economically active" Jews.

The last days of Jewish agriculture were tragic. Kolkhozes and villages in which most Jews lived and worked were under German occupation; most Jews were massacred. Those few who survived came out of hiding and tried to reconstruct their lives in their old villages, but the government, instead, encouraged them to go to Birobidzhan in 1946–48. The Jewish administrative districts were never revived. In 1965, at a meeting of the editorial committee of *Sovetish heymland,* when Jewish agriculture was mentioned as a subject for prose writing, these writers confirmed that the Jewish village no longer existed and that there were very few Jewish kolkhoz members. Yaacov Lvavi, *Ha-Hityashvut Ha-Yehudit Be-Birobijan* (Jewish Settlement in Birobidzhan). Jerusalem, Historical Society of Israel, 1965, p. 97.

11. Proletarianization: The First Five Year Plan and Industrialization, 1928–39

1. Alec Nove, *An Economic History of the U.S.S.R.* Harmondsworth, Penguin, 1969, p. 136.

2. Ibid.

3. Ibid., p. 187.

4. Ibid., p. 188.

5. Among other strategies, there was a massive Soviet effort to sell art abroad to help finance the Five-Year Plan. Andrew Mellon, U.S. secretary of the treasury at the time, was the most famous buyer, but only one of many foreigners who bought great art treasures from Soviet Russia. The Commissar of Foreign Trade, Anastas Mikoyan, was the principal Soviet agent handling foreign art sales. Exhibits and sales featured paintings, icons, rugs, textiles, toys, and gold and silver pieces. In 1929, income from such sales amounted to over one million dollars, and in 1930–31, twenty-one Hermitage paintings sold to Mellon totaled over six million dollars. Dr. Armand Hammer, the American industrialist who had obtained mining and manufacturing concessions in Russia in the early 1920s, also became an avid purchaser. See Robert C. Williams, "The Quiet Trade: Russian Art and American Money," *The Wilson Quarterly,* Winter 1979, pp. 162–75.

6. "Bukharin-Kamenev Meeting, 1928," by George Saunders, tr.; annotations by Stephen F. Cohen, *Dissent,* Winter 1979, p. 78.

7. Ibid., p. 79.

8. Ibid., pp. 83, 85, 86.

9. Solomon M. Schwarz, *The Jews in the Soviet Union*. Syracuse, Syracuse University Press, 1951, p. 169.

10. Yaacov Lestschinsky, *Dos sovetishe idntum*. New York, Yidisher kemfer, 1941, p. 246. Schwarz, ibid., p. 265, basing his figures on Zinger, noted that there were 153,000 Jewish wage earners (manual workers) in 1926.

11. Schwarz, op. cit., p. 265.

12. Lev Zinger, *Dos banayte folk*. Moscow, Der Emes Publishing House, 1941, pp. 33–35.

13. Lestschinsky, op. cit., p. 248.

14. Zinger, op. cit., pp. 109–11.

15. Lestschinsky, op. cit., p. 249.

16. Ibid., p. 248.

17. Schwarz, op. cit., p. 168.

18. Ibid.

19. Zinger, op. cit., pp. 109ff.

20. Schwarz, op. cit., p. 168.

21. Yaacov Lestschinsky, "Economic and Social Development," in *The Jewish People Past and Present*, Vol. 1. New York, Jewish Encyclopaedic Handbooks, 1946, p. 385.

22. Ibid.

23. Lestschinsky, *Dos sovetishe idntum*, op. cit., p. 253.

24. Boris Smolar, "The Jewish Artisan has Fallen from Favor in Russia." Rosen Archive, File II, No. 28A. YIVO Archives, New York.

    JDC also established kustar artels, beginning in 1924 to productivize artisans. In 1929, at Rosen's urging, JDC began to neogotiate with the government on a plan to put Jewish workers in state factories. The government reaction, according to Rosen, was favorable and negotiations proceeded throughout 1930 but were terminated. See Chapter 7, Note 38.

25. Rosen Archive, File II, No. 29.

26. Rosen statements to press, February 19, 1930. Rosen Archive, File 25.

27. [Report,] June 7, 1930. Rosen Archive, File 8.

28. JTA cable, June 6, 1930. Rosen Archive, File 8, No. 92.

29. Minutes of meeting of Agro-Joint staff in Moscow, August 16–20, 1930. Rosen Archive, File 25.

30. Ibid.

31. Ibid.

32. Report of Inspector for Technical Assistance of Agro-Joint, January 28, 1932. Rosen Archive, File 25.

33. Rosen Archive, File 25.

34. Zvi Halevy, "Jewish Students in the Soviet Universities in the 1920's," *Soviet Jewish Affairs*, Vol. 1, 1976, pp. 57, 58.

35. Ibid., p. 59.

36. Ibid., p. 63.

37. Ibid., p. 60.

38. Schwarz, op. cit., p. 265.

39. Halevy, op. cit., p. 65.

40. Ibid., p. 61.
41. Ibid., p. 58.
42. Ibid., p. 66.
43. Markoosha Fischer, *My Lives in Russia*. New York, Harper and Bros., 1944, p. 33. Mrs. Fischer, neé Bertha Mark, was born in Latvia, worked on the European staff of Soviet Foreign Minister George Chicherin, and married the American correspondent in Moscow, Louis Fischer. Fischer became disillusioned with the Bolshevik experiment after the purge trials, but wrote enthusiastically about improved living conditions in 1931. Walter Duranty was even more enthusiastic. For a critical evaluation of both journalists, see James W. Crowd, *Angels in Stalin's Paradise*. Washington, D.C., University Press of America, 1982.
44. Ibid., p. 37.
45. Interview of author with Naomi Tamarkin (December 16, 1984) in Philadelphia.
46. Schwarz, op. cit., p. 169.
47. Ibid.
48. Ibid., p. 266.
49. Lestschinsky, *Dos sovetishe idntum*, op. cit., p. 250.
50. Genrikh I. Neiman, *Vnutrennaia torgoviliia SSSR* (The Soviet Union's Internal Trade), E. I. Kviring, ed. Moscow, 1935, pp. 145f., in Salo W. Baron, *The Russian Jew under Tsars and Soviets*, 2d ed. New York, Macmillan, 1976, p. 210. According to the census figures of 1926, there were only 125,000 Jews in the commercial class, or 11.8 percent of all gainfully employed Jews. Possibly another 7.3 percent in "indefinite occupations" included "commercially active persons." Baron, op. cit., p. 210.
51. Ibid.
52. Baron, op. cit., p. 210.
53. Based on Schwarz, op. cit., p. 265, who used data from Zinger.
54. Baron, op. cit., p. 217.
55. Schwarz, op. cit., p. 170. It is estimated that by 1935, of the 250,000 young Jews between 18 and 23, 30 percent had received a higher education, seven times greater than the percentage of Russians of comparable age, eight times greater that White Russians, and ten times greater than Ukrainians, The numbers increased subsequently, but the percentage of Jews in relation to non-Jews in subsequent years dropped markedly. Lestschinsky, *Dos sovetishe idntum*, op. cit., p. 167.
56. Baron, op. cit., pp. 206, 208.
57. Schwarz, op. cit., pp. 169, 170.
58. Lestschinsky, op. cit., p. 166.
59. Baron, op. cit., p. 217, based on Zinger, op. cit., p. 103ff.
60. Bernard J. Choseed, "The Soviet Jew in Literature," *Jewish Social Studies*, Vol. XI, 1949, p. 274.
61. These themes are analyzed in ibid., pp. 259–82. There was immense pride in showcase projects such as the Dnieper Dam, the Magnitogorsk steel complex and the Kharkov tractor factory.

62. H. Orland, *Aglomerat*. Kiev, 1935. Discussed in Choseed, op. cit., pp. 272–73.
63. Peretz Markish, *Der finfter horizont*. Moscow, 1933. Discussed in Choseed, op. cit., p. 266.
64. Ibid., p. 262.
65. Lestschinsky, op. cit., pp. 161, 162.
66. Choseed, op. cit., p. 279.
67. Baron, op. cit., 207, 208.
68. *Der emes*, October 22, 1930, June 4, 1934, August 3, 1935, quoted in Lestschinsky, *Dos sovetishe idntum*. op. cit., pp. 269, 270, 273.
69. Lestschinsky, ibid., p. 245.

12. Stalin's Iron Age: New Controls, Repression, and Anti-Semitism, 1929–34

1. Quoted in Solomon M. Schwarz, "The New Anti-Semitism of the Soviet Union," *Commentary*, June 1949, p. 537.
2. Ibid., p. 538.
3. Ibid.
4. Yaacov Lestschinsky, *Dos sovetishe idntum*. New York, Yidisher kemfer, 1941, p. 258.
5. Bernard J. Choseed, "The Soviet Jew in Literature," *Jewish Social Studies*, Vol. XI, 1949, p. 264.
6. Ibid., p. 265.
7. Ibid.
8. Solomon M. Schwarz, *The Jews in the Soviet Union*. Syracuse, Syracuse University Press, 1951, p. 295.
9. Ibid., p. 243.
10. Lestschinsky, op. cit., p. 263.
11. Schwarz, *The Jews in the Soviet Union*, op. cit., p. 247.
12. Ibid., p. 245.
13. Merle Fainsod, *Smolensk under Soviet Rule*. Cambridge, Harvard University Press, 1958, p. 361.
14. Letter from Zalman Venutov, dated June 18, 1929, to relative in Philadelphia (courtesy of Max Rosenfeld).
15. Schwarz, *The Jews in the Soviet Union*, op. cit., p. 248.
16. Freda Utley, *The Dream We Lost*. New York, John Day, 1940, pp. 102–3.
17. Ibid., p. 102.
18. Marshall papers, quoted in Zosa Szajkowski, *Jews, Wars, and Communism*, Vol. 1. New York, Ktav, 1972, p. 384.
19. Ibid., p. 385.
20. Leon Fram, "A Jew Looks at Russia," Detroit *News*, June 1, 1930. Quoted in ibid., p. 385.
21. Szajkowski, op. cit., pp. 388, 390, 391.
22. Zvi Y. Gitelman, *Jewish Nationality and Soviet Politics*. Princeton, Princeton University Press, 1972, p. 456.
23. Mordechai Altshuler, ed., *Pirsumim Rusiim Bi-Brit Ha-Moatsat al Yehudim Ve-*

Yahadut, 1917–1967 (Russian Publications on Jews and Judaism in the Soviet Union, 1917–1967), B. Pinkus and A. A. Greenbaum, compilers. Jerusalem, Society for Research on Jewish Communities, 1970, p. xi.

24. R. Beermann, "Russian and Soviet Passport Laws," *Bulletin on Soviet and East European Jewish Affairs*, No. 2, July 1968, p. VI/3.
25. Hedrick Smith, *The Russians*. New York, Ballantine, 1976, p. 354–55.
26. A new internal passport law called the "Statute on Passports" was passed by the Council of Ministers on October 21, 1953, under which the whole population was divided into two categories: collective farmers and the rest of the population. Only the latter (except for convicts, the military, and those confined in institutions) have the privilege of having a passport. The passports are issued by the local authority or militia at the place of a person's permanent residence. Passports are the only acceptable form of identification in the Soviet Union, and all individuals over sixteen must have one. However, a passport does not mean freedom to settle anywhere one wants to. Residence visas *(propiskas)* are required for residence rights, but in order to obtain these, employment is a prerequisite. The statement regarding one's nationality is still retained from the original law of 1932. If both parents are Jewish, the child must also be identified as *Evrei*. In the case of a mixed marriage, the child may choose either national identity. The governments refusal to issue internal passports to collective farmers had been felt as a humiliating stigma and has embittered them. "Technically, without them, the peasantry [was] almost as tied to the land as serfs used to be." See Beermann, op. cit., pp. VI/3–VI/4. Passports were finally given to them in 1976–77.
27. Alec Nove and J. A. Newth, "The Jewish Population: Demographic Trends and Occupational Patterns," in Lionel Kochan, ed., *The Jews in Soviet Russia since 1917*, 3d ed. Oxford, Oxford University Press, 1978, p. 155.
28. Ibid., p. 136.
29. The definitions of nationality and nation have not been consistent, and, when used, vary from group to group. In the 1926 census, the word *narodnost'* (subnationality) was used to determine the ethnic composition of the population. In the census of 1939, the concept of *natsional'nost'* (nationality) was introduced, but not every Soviet ethnic group has acquired this status. To prevent confusion, it had been suggested for the 1970 census that both terms be used, but this was not done. (Thomas E. Sawyer, *The Jewish Minority of the Soviet Union*. Boulder, Colo., Westview Press, 1979, pp. 32–33). More important, however, than these argued nuances is the principle of absolute equality of all nationality groups, "that the different levels of statehood or political importance should not be taken as affecting this principle." However, the Jewish nationality is excluded from this principle, despite numerous efforts by Soviet officals to proclaim it. The theoretical principles, inconsistencies, and contradictions as they affect Jews are examined throughout this work in different periods of Soviet history. See also Benjamin Pinkus, *The Soviet Government and the Jews, 1948–1967: A Documented Study*. Cambridge, Cambridge University Press, 1984, pp. 1, 3–4, 13–14, 35–38, 77–78.

In the absence of a "uniquely correct" definition of nationality, respondent self-identification has been used in most of the censuses (Sawyer, op. cit., p. 32). In a recent 190-page book by Galina Sdobnikova (1983) called *The Nationalities Question: Lenin's Approach,* translated by S. Gililov and published by Progress Publishers (Moscow), there is no reference at all to Jews or the Jewish nationality except a reference to "the propaganda of Zionism," which "serves the interests of imperialism" and "divert[s] the working people from class positions." (pp. 168–69).

The demise of Birobidzhan is discussed in Chapters 13 and 22. See Jacob Miller, "Soviet Theory on Jews," in Kochan, ed., op. cit., pp. 60–62, for a further discussion of the Jewish exception. Quotation is from Miller, p. 61.

30. Miller, op. cit., p. 62.
31. James H. Billington, *The Icon and the Axe: An Interpretive History of Russian Culture.* New York, Vintage, 1970, p. 522.
32. Sheila Fitzpatrick, *Cultural Revolution in Russia, 1928–1931.* Bloomington, Indiana University Press, 1978, p. 32.
33. Ibid., pp. 198–99.
34. Ibid., especially the essay by Fitzpatrick, "Cultural Revolution as Class War," pp. 8–40.
35. Ibid., p. 10.
36. Roy A. Medvedev, *Let History Judge: The Origins and Consequences of Stalinism.* New York, Knopf, 1971, p. 112.
37. Fitzpatrick, op. cit., p. 192.
38. Mark Slonim, *Soviet Russian Literature: Writers and Problems, 1917–1977,* 2d ed. New York, Oxford University Press, 1977, p. 160.
39. Ibid., p. 162.
40. Edward J. Brown, *Russian Literature since the Revolution.* Cambridge, Harvard University Press, 1982, p. 172.

In 1937, Averbakh was "unmasked" as an agent of Trotsky, one whose errors formed "a pattern of subversion in Soviet literature." In keeping with the atmosphere, which was heavily saturated with accusations of treason and denunciations, Averbakh was attacked as well "with snarling caricatures of . . . speech, gestures, and manner of movement. The accent of anti-Semitism could hardly be missed." Ibid., p. 173.

41. Ibid., p. 42.
42. Ibid., p. 85.
43. Fitzpatrick, op. cit., p. 34.
44. Slonim, op. cit., p. 163.
45. Summarized from Yehuda Slutsky, "Jews at the First Congress of Soviet Writers," *Soviet Jewish Affairs,* Vol. 2, No. 2, 1972, pp. 62, 63.
46. Slonim, op. cit., p. 165.
47. Slutsky, op. cit., p. 62.
48. Ronald Hingley, *Nightingale Fever: Russian Poets in Revolution.* New York, Knopf, 1981, pp. 195–96.
49. Slutsky, op. cit., p. 67. At this time, Israel Tsinberg was writing his ten-volume *Geshikte fun der literatur bay yidn.*
50. Isaac Babel, *Lyubka the Cossack and Other Stories.* Tr., with an afterword by

Andrew R. MacAndrew. New York, New American Library, 1963. This edition includes *Red Cavalry* and *Old Odessa*. Avraham Yarmolinsky has also edited *Benya Krik, the Gangster and Other Stories* (including several from *Red Cavalry*). New York, Schocken, 1969. In the same year Max Hayward translated a potpourri of twenty-five stories, sketches, and articles called *You Must Know Everthing*, published by Farrar, Straus and Giroux in New York, and sensitively reviewed by Elsie Levitan, in "The Towers of Babel," *Jewish Currents*, November 1969, pp. 24–27. See also Brown, op. cit., pp. 87–94; Lionel Trilling's introduction to Babel's *Collected Stories*. New York, Meridian, 1955; and Patricia Carden's *The Art of Isaac Babel*. Ithaca, Cornell University Press, 1972.

51. MacAndrew, afterword, in *Lyubka the Cossack*, op. cit., p. 281.
52. Slonim, op. cit., p. 74. The Yiddish writers at the Congress were able to cling to the slippery slope of socialist realism for a time, but a number of them perished in the Great Terror of 1936–38 or died in prison: Litvakov, Kulbak, Bronshteyn, Dunyets, Kharik, and Khashin. Many other leading figures in the Evsektsiya, in Jewish scholarship, and in Birobidzhan would also become victims of the purges (see Chapter 14).
53. See the works by his wife, Nadezhda Mandelstam, *Hope Against Hope: A Memoir*, Max Hayward, tr. Harmondsworth, Penguin, 1975, and *Hope Abandoned*, Max Hayward, tr. New York, Atheneum, 1974. Some of Mandelstam's poetry in English can be found in *Osip Mandelstam, Poems*, chosen and tr. by James Greene. London, Elek, 1979. Many have also been translated by Hingley in his *Nightingale Fever*, op. cit., passim.
54. Yudel Mark, "Jewish Schools in Soviet Russia," in Gregory Aaronson, et al., eds., *Russian Jewry 1917–1967*. New York, Thomas Yoseloff, 1969. p. 256.
55. Ibid., p. 257.
56. Interviews with Chayele Ash (April 1984) and Shimon Kipnis (June 1984), Philadelphia.
57. Alfred A. Greenbaum, *Jewish Scholarship and Scholarly Institutions in Soviet Russia, 1918–1953*. Jerusalem, Hebrew University Center for Research and Documentation of East European Jewry, 1978, p. 16.
58. Ibid., p. 19.
59. Ibid., pp. 22–23.
60. Ibid., pp. 104–5.
61. Ibid., p. 106.
62. Aryeh Y. Yodfat, "The Closure of the Synagogues in the Soviet Union," *Soviet Jewish Affairs*, Vol. 3, No. 1, 1973, p. 53.
63. Ibid., p. 54.
64. Joshua Rothenberg, "Jewish Religion in the Soviet Union," in Kochan, ed., op. cit., p. 177.
65. Szajkowski, op. cit., pp. 399, 401, citing Schneersohn's *Di yesurim fun lubavitsher rebn in sovetrusland*. Riga, 1930.
66. Lucy S. Dawidowicz, "What Future for Judaism in Russia?" *Commentary*, November 1956, p. 405.
67. For examples of these views, see Szajkowski, op. cit., pp. 392–402.

68. *Jewish Tribune,* New York City, March 7, 1930.
69. Mordechai Altshuler, "The Attitude of the Communist Party to Jewish National Survival, 1918–1930," YIVO *Annual,* Vol. XIV, 1969, p. 84.
70. Litvakov, Esther Frumkin, Rakhmiel Veinshtain, and Rafes were specifically attacked in Samuil Agursky, "Der kamf kegn opnoign afn historishn front," *Der shtern,* Vol. V, No. 11, November 1929. Agursky also wrote a whole work on "idealization" of the Bund: *Afn historishn front kegn der idealizirung fun "bund,"* Moscow, Tsentraler-farlag far di felker fun FSRR, 1930. Cited in Gitelman, op. cit., pp. 458–59.
71. Ibid., p. 466.
72. Ibid., pp. 452–53.
73. Ibid., p. 455.
74. Letter to Joseph Opatoshu, November 25, 1929. Quoted in ibid., p. 471. See also pp. 471–475 for Gitelman's summary of Evsektsiya "malaise".
75. Ibid., p. 476.
76. Ibid., p. 370.
77. Ibid.
78. Quoted in E. Schulman, *A History of Jewish Education in the Soviet Union.* New York, Ktav, 1971, p. 146.
79. Alfred A. Greenbaum, "Soviet Jewry under Lenin and Stalin," *Soviet Studies,* Vol. XVI, No. 4, April 1965, p. 409.
80. Schwarz, op. cit., p. 103.
81. Gitelman, op. cit., p. 480. See also his "Conclusion" and "Epilogue," pp. 485–523.
82. Gregory Aaronson, "The Jewish Question during the Stalin Era," in Aaronson, et al. eds., op. cit., p. 180.
83. Gitelman, op. cit., pp. 519, 520.

13. Birobidzhan, 1928–40

1. *Pravda,* November 26, 1926, quoted in Solomon M. Schwartz, *The Jews in the Soviet Union.* Syracuse, Syracuse University Press, 1951, p. 174. (Schwarz' chapter on Birobidzhan, ibid., pp. 174–94, is one of the best summaries in English.)
2. The perception of such a threat may have come at different times. Merezhin warned against Chinese incursions in July 1928. Baron stresses the alarm over the Japanese invasion of Manchuria in 1931. Esther Rozenthal-Shneiderman, who was a teacher in Birobidzhan for a number of years, mentions this threat several times in *Birobidzhan fun der noent.* Tel Aviv, H. Leivik, 1983, p. 41 and passim.
3. Chimen Abramsky, "The Biro-Bidzhan Project, 1927–68," in Lionel Kochan, ed., *The Jews in Soviet Russia Since 1917.* Oxford, Oxford University Press, 1978, p. 70.
4. Solomon M. Schwarz, "Birobidzhan: An Experiment in Jewish Colonization," in Gregory Aaronson, et al., eds., *Russian Jewry 1917–1967.* New York, Thomas Yoseloff, 1969, pp. 350–52.
   A. Kirhznitz writes of GEZERD developing several experimental sites,

then "going over the material collected" and deciding on Birobidzhan. He also describes subsequent discussions of this decision "at many meetings, in many towns, and the rightness of the KAMERD (sic!) decision." His article, "Idishe autonomie gegnt," in S. Dimanshtain, ed., *Yidn in F.S.S.R.* Moscow, Der Emes Publishing Co., 1935, pp. 74, 77. The act of March 28, 1928, giving Birobidzhan over to KOMERD (KOMZET) appears in ibid., p. 177.

5. Schwarz, "Birobidzhan," op. cit., pp. 354–55.
6. Zvi Y. Gitelman, *Jewish Nationality and Soviet Politics*. Princeton, Princeton University Press, 1972, p. 435. Kirhznitz, op. cit., p. 75, wrote that "broad Jewish masses undertook the decision with the greatest joy and passed many resolutions expressing great enthusiasm." According to him, 1,000 Jews originally agreed to go to Birobidzhan, but only 650 left in 1928.
7. Melech Epstein, "Pages from My Stormy Life," *American Jewish Archives*, Vol. XIV, No. 2, November 1962, p. 148.
8. Gitelman, op. cit., p. 431. The leaders of the Evsektsiya were, in fact, somewhat embarrassed by Kalinin's enthusiasm and by nationalist feeling in OZET, which considered the Jewish Communists to be working in a national cause without admitting it.
9. Described in Yaacov Lvavi, *Ha-Hityashvut Ha-Yehudit Be-Birobijan*. Jerusalem, Historical Society of Israel, 1965, pp. 141–42.
10. Ibid., p. 143.
11. Quoted in Schwarz, "Birobidzhan," op. cit., 356–57. In the Kirhznitz account, there is an "unpublished memoir" by one of the original group describing a small unit of seven who wanted to settle in the thick woods, 10 km. from Tikhonkaya. They finally received permission and began cutting trees but were plagued by tiny flies. Twenty-five new settlers joined them, but most left, greatly demoralized. (Kirhznitz, op. cit., pp. 81–82). IKOR is mentioned as "being actively involved in the Birobidzhan project from the beginning." Ibid., p. 77.
12. H. Smoliar, *Fun eynevaynik: zikhronos vegn der "Evsektsiya."* Tel Aviv, Peretz, 1978, pp. 4–6.
13. Ibid., p. 407.
14. Quoted in Lvavi, op. cit., p. 237. In the mid-thirties, Mrs. Rozenthal-Shneiderman observed some hostility toward Jews, who were looked upon as newcomers, among the deported kulaks and Cossacks in kolkhozes. Some Jews complained that "things here are like things at home: they don't like us." Rozenthal-Shneiderman, op. cit., pp. 89–90.
15. Ibid., p. 238.
16. Ibid.
17. A. P. Nechayev, et al., eds., *Voprosy geografi Priamurya: Yevreiskaya autonomnaya oblast* (Aspects of the Geography of the Amur Region: The Jewish Autonomous province). Khabarovsk, 1968. Summarized by J. A. Newth in *Bulletin on Soviet and East European Jewish Affairs*, No. 4, December 1969, pp. 80–81.
18. Abramsky, op. cit., p. 71. Kirhznitz never mentions the numbers who re-

turned but lists "1,000 new settlers" in 1929, 1,500 in 1930, and 3,000 in 1931 (Kirhznitz, op. cit., pp. 83–84). Four new farm colonies—Waldheim, Birofeld, IKOR, and Red October—are mentioned as 1930 achievements. Ibid., p. 83.

19. Schwarz, "Birobidzhan," op. cit., p. 359.
20. Abramsky, op. cit., p. 71. According to Kirhznitz, 25,000 new settlers were needed in 1932. Kirhznitz, op. cit., p. 85.
21. Newth, op. cit., p. 81.
22. Lvavi, op. cit., p. 240.
23. Ibid., p. 245.
24. Ibid., p. 125.
25. *Der shtern,* December 20, 1928.
26. Quoted in Abramsky, op. cit., p. 69.
27. President Harris was urged to go to Birobidzhan by Benjamin Brown, the brother of the famous Yiddish singer Sidor Belársky, and a farmer in the Jewish cooperative colony "Clarion" in Utah. Brown was also a member of IKOR. The expedition was filmed and Joshua Waletzky, curator of films at YIVO, recently edited the film, which was shown at YIVO on April 10, 1984. *News of YIVO,* No. 167, 1984–85.
28. Schwarz, *The Jews in the Soviet Union,* op. cit., p. 191.
29. B. Z. Goldberg, *The Jewish Problem in the Soviet Union.* New York, Crown, 1961, pp. 177–88.
30. Esther Markish, *The Long Return.* New York, Ballantine, 1978, pp. 33–34. Markish and other noted Jewish writers had visited Birobidzhan in December 1934. Kirhznitz, op. cit., p. 95.
31. Salo W. Baron, *The Russian Jew under Tsars and Soviets,* 2d ed. New York, Macmillan, 1976, pp. 197–98. Dr. Rosen of Agro-Joint was especially hopeful that Birobidzhan might become a refuge for Jews from Eastern Europe in the mid-thirties when their situation was becoming "precarious," and in January 1935 it was reported that the Soviet government "ha[d] opened negotiations with Poland to permit Jews from that country to cross the Russian frontier and settle in Birobidzhan." Interest in Birobidzhan among Jews in White Russia and the Ukraine was also noted, and a link made between this interest and the visit of Goering to Poland at the time. (The Russian press was interpreting this visit as a "clear indication of a possible war on Polish frontiers bordering these sections.") JTA cable, January 29, 1935. Rosen Archive, File 8, No. 92. YIVO Archives, New York.
32. Baron, op. cit., p. 198.
33. *Der emes,* August 8, 1936 and April 2, 1937.
34. Lvavi, op. cit., p. 253.
35. Ibid.
36. Ibid.
37. Yaacov Lestschinsky, *Dos sovetishe idntum.* New York, Yidisher kemfer, 1941, p. 242.
38. Schwarz, "Birobidzhan," op. cit., p. 376 and Rozenthal-Shneiderman, op. cit., pp. 79–80.

39. Lvavi, op. cit., p. 250.
40. Ibid.
41. Ibid.
42. Ibid. p. 251.
43. Ibid. p. 252.
44. Ibid. p. 241.
45. Ibid. p. 242.
46. David Bergelson, *Birobidzhaner*. Moscow, Der Emes Publishing Co., 1934.
47. Yehuda Slutsky, "Jews at the First Congress of Soviet Writers," *Soviet Jewish Affairs*, Vol. 2, No. 2, 1972, p. 65.
48. Schwarz, *The Jews in Soviet Russia*. op. cit., p. 178.
49. Lvavi, op. cit., p. 126.
50. Quoted in Schwarz, "Birobidzhan," op. cit., p. 64.
51. The entire speech is reproduced in S. Dimanshtain, ed., op. cit., pp. 31–38.
52. Figures from Hayim Sloves, *Sovetishe idishe malukhishkeit*. Paris, Imprimerie S.I.P.E., 1979, pp. 239–40. See also Abramsky, op. cit., pp. 73–74. In 1934 Mrs. Esther Rozenthal-Shneiderman, who had been working at the Institute for Jewish Culture in Kiev, joined Liberberg and other Kiev personnel who had gone to Birobidzhan. From the time of the liquidation of the Evsektsiya in 1930, she and other Jewish activists were stunned by this decision. "For a long time," she recalled, "we couldn't come to ourselves . . . it smelled like the end." They realized there would now be a marked movement of Jewish youth away from Yiddish schools and special institutes and Jewish culture generally, and a shift to Russification. What and where would be the future of Jewish culture in the Soviet Union? Birobidzhan provided them with the answer. "Here, in a Jewish territory, Jews could be saved from assimilation. There a new Jewish culture could develop." Rozenthal-Shneiderman, op. cit., pp. 10–12. After Liberberg left for Birobidzhan, others from the Kiev Institute followed. Liberberg himself had ambitious plans for creating Birobidzhan as a center for Jewish scholarly research.
53. Goldberg, op. cit., p. 197.
54. Lestschinsky, op. cit., p. 232.
55. Quoted in Schwarz, *The Jews in the Soviet Union*, op. cit., p. 181.
56. Lestschinsky, op. cit., p. 236.
57. Sloves, op. cit., p. 241. Kirhznitz' fulsome description of a "colossal gathering" of people from "proletarian and socialist masses—not just Jewish masses," December 18–21, 1934, may also have portended changes, Kirhznitz, op. cit., pp. 94–95.
58. The ambivalence or hesitancy about continued foreign help for Birobidzhan in the mid-thirties, when the Polish government was eager to get rid of its Jews, may be seen in the following episode: Dr. Charles Rosen, Director of Agro-Joint and founder of a private fundraising arm called the American Society for Jewish Farm Settlements (ASJFS), had met with representatives from Poland who had pledged free transport of a number of Polish Jews

into Russia. At sessions of the Administrative Committee of the ASJFS in January and February 1935, Rosen's idea to use Society bonds to finance the transfer of 1,000 Jews was adopted in principle. The committee empowered him to continue "the investigation of possibilities," but the impression left was that "many leaders of the society, including Dr. Rosen himself, wanted to diminish their efforts in Birobidzhan." Soviet powers also "hesitated to permit an additional immigration into Birobidzhan" at the time. Lvavi, op. cit., p. 130. (Agro-Joint, which served as the operating agency for ASJFS, closed down its work in the Soviet Union in 1938.) Ambijan distributed releases alleging that "100,000 Jews in Poland have signified their desire to emigrate to Birobidzhan," but as Baron concluded, "this clearly was but a propaganda and fund-raising gimmick." Baron, op. cit., p. 198. In a letter from James McDonald, High Commissioner for Refugees, to Felix Warburg, September 9, 1935, he noted that the suggestion to send Jewish refugees to Birobidzhan "was rejected by the Soviet authorities." Henry L. Feingold. "Roosevelt and the Resettlement Question," in *Rescue Attempts during the Holocaust*. Proceedings of the Second Yad Vashem International Historical Conference, April 1974. Jerusalem, Yad Vashem, 1977, p. 131.

59. Schwarz, *The Jews in the Soviet Union*, op. cit., p. 180.
60. Schwarz, "Birobidzhan," op. cit., p. 369.
61. Sloves, op. cit., p. 244. According to Rozenthal-Shneiderman, "Economic possiblities at times seemed glowing: apples were being grown in the cold climate. The water resources and fisheries in the Amur and the abundance of cedar and cork trees were impressive." Rozenthal-Shneiderman, op. cit., p. 40.
62. Ibid.
63. *Der emes*, March 26, 1938.
64. Schwarz, "Birobidzhan," op. cit., p. 371.
65. Ibid., p. 372. Estimates vary. The November 7, 1937 issue of *Der emes* estimated the Jewish population to be 29,000.
66. Sloves, op. cit., p. 240. The schools and cultural institutions are described in pp. 231–37.
67. Ibid., p. 245.
68. The visit is described in Sloves, ibid., pp. 245–47.
69. *Forpost* 1, 1936, p. 27.
70. Ibid., 129.
71. Sloves, op. cit., p. 275.
72. Schwarz, *The Jews in the Soviet Union*, op. cit., p. 192.
73. Lvavi, op. cit., p. 242.
74. Abramsky, op. cit., p. 72. Sloves noted that 9,357 Jews left Birobidzhan in 1937 and that about 3,000 arrived, among whom were many non-Jews, leaving about 19,000 Jews in the JAR at the end of 1937. Sloves, op. cit., p. 265.
75. Lvavi, op. cit., p. 66.
76. *American Jewish Yearbook*, 1941–42, Vol. 43, 1941, pp. 314–18.

77. Lvavi, op. cit., pp. 66, 100.
78. *Morgen Freiheit*, April 20, 1941.

14. The Great Purges, 1936–38, and the Hitler-Stalin Pact, 1939–41

1. Robert Conquest, *The Great Terror: Stalin's Purge of the 30's*. New York, Macmillan, 1968, p. xi.
2. Khrushchev's extensive and detailed exposure of Stalin's crimes is found in "Khrushchev's De-Stalinization Speech," February 24–25, 1956, in Basil Dmytryshyn, *USSR: A Concise History*, 3d ed. New York, Scribners, 1978, pp. 494–537. See further discussion in Chapter 26 and related notes.
3. Esther Rozenthal-Shneiderman heard the speech in school. See her "Jewish Communists in the USSR, 1926–1958: A Memoir," *Bulletin on Soviet and East European Jewish Affairs*, No. 5, May 1970, p. 57.
4. The U.S. State Department published the complete text of the speech in June 1956. It was published in the *New York Times*, June 5, 1956, and was reprinted in the *Congressional Record*, 84th Congr., 2d Sess., Vol. 102, Pt. 7, pp. 9389–9402. Eleven pages devoted to the speech appeared in *Pravda*, February 15, 1956.
5. Robert C. Tucker, *The Soviet Political Mind: Stalinism and post-Stalin Change*, rev. ed. New York, Norton, 1971, pp. 69, 72. In Robert C. Tucker and Stephen F. Cohen, eds., *The Great Purge Trial*. New York, Grosset and Dunlap. 1965, pp. xxxiv–xxxvi, Tucker noted Stalin's interest in a deal with Hitler as early as June 30, 1934, when Roehm's S.A. force was purged, and a more "hardened resolve" after Hitler's occupation of the Rhineland in March 1936. The advantages, purposes, and rationale for such a deal are analyzed in ibid., pp. xxxiv–xl.

   Ideological differences, moreover, did not prevent Stalin from coming to an understanding with Hitler. As early as 1934, at the Seventeenth Party Congress, January 26–February 10, 1934, he put out feelers for such an understanding: "Of course we are far from enthusiastic about the Fascist regime in Germany. But Fascism is beside the point if only because Fascism in Italy, for example, has not kept the USSR from establishing the best relations with that country." Conquest, op. cit., p. 217.
6. These events which foreshadowed the massive purges are discussed in Conquest, op. cit., Appendix F; Roy A. Medvedev, *Let History Judge: The Origins and Consequences of Stalinism*, Colleen Taylor, tr. New York, Knopf, 1971, pp. 112–13; Anton Antonov-Ovseyenko, *The Time of Stalin: Portrait of a Tyranny*. New York, Harper and Row, 1981, pp. 69–213 and passim., and Aleksander I. Solzhenitsyn, *The Gulag Archipelago, 1918–1956*. New York, Harper and Row, 1973, pp. 60–76, 93–98 and passim.
7. George F. Kennan noted that the provisions of the German-Soviet Treaty of 1925 dealing with the arrest and detention of German nationals in the Soviet Union were "wholly inadequate for the protection of the foreign interests involved." For example, it was specifically stated that "officials of

the courts or prisons" might *not* be required to withdraw when the visiting consul meets with the prisoner, thus allowing for the easy intimidation of the prisoner. See his *Memoirs: 1925–1950.* Boston, Little, Brown, 1967, p. 50. Kennan also describes the long-time tradition of most Russian rulers to view foreign influences with fear and suspicion. See pp. 73–76.

Antonov-Ovseyenko, op. cit., pp. 75–76, described the Trial of the Industrial Party as a diversion from defective planning and harsh realities requiring the "sacrifice of the technical specialists." He also described it as "the first frame-up trial," involving the first use of torture and the first executions. For analyses of subsequent trials, see Alexander Orlov, *The Secret History of Stalin's Crimes.* New York, Random House, 1953; F. Beck and W. Godin, *Russian Purge and the Extraction of Confession.* New York, Viking, 1951; and references in note 6.

8. Seweryn Bialer, *Stalin's Successors: Leadership, Stability, and Change in the Soviet Union.* Cambridge, Cambridge University Press, 1980, p. 40. The reemergence of Bukharin (by 1930, he, Rykov, and Tomsky had been removed from the Politburo) into public life at the Seventeenth Party Congress and his leading role in preparing the new constitution were also viewed as signs of a more benign and moderate time. See Roy A. Medvedev, *Nikolai Bukharin: The Last Years.* New York, Norton, 1980, pp. 37–69.

9. "Khrushchev's De-Stalinization Speech," February 24–25, 1956, Dmytryshyn, op. cit., p. 498. Khrushchev also admitted that in inventing the concept of "enemy of the people," Stalin totally destroyed the process of proving ideological errors in a controversy, thus leading to "most cruel repression, violating all norms of revolutionary legality, against anyone who in any way disagreed with . . . [him], against those who were only suspected of hostile intent, against those who had bad reputations. . . . In the main, and in actuality, the only proof of guilt used . . . was the confession of the accused himself, and, as subsequent probing proved, confessions were acquired through physical pressures against the accused." Antonov-Ovseyenko, op. cit., p. 80, revealed that 292 delegates at the congress— one-fourth of the total—voted against retaining Stalin as General Secretary, but that he had 289 ballots burned. Of the 139 members and candidates of the party Central Committee elected at the Seventeenth Congress, 98 persons—70 percent—were arrested and shot and in 1937–38, of the 1,966 delegates, 1,108 were arrested. After Kirov's murder, Stalin issued decrees ordering death sentences for those charged with the "preparation or execution of acts of terror." "Khrushchev's De-Stalinization Speech," Dmytryshyn, op. cit., pp. 499, 505.

10. Ibid., p. 505. See Antonov-Ovseyenko, op. cit., pp. 84–104, for a penetrating analysis of Kirov's assassination and Stalin's sinister role in plotting it and falsifying the facts of his death. Leonid Nikolaev, an embittered low-level bureaucrat who hated Kirov, was the assassin. Solzhenitsyn, op. cit., pp. 58–59, stated that "one-quarter of Leningrad was purged" and that Esperantists, members of the Free Philosophical Society and the Red Cross were likewise victims after Kirov's murder.

11. Bialer, op. cit., pp. 40–41.
12. George F. Kennan, *Russia and the West under Lenin and Stalin*. Boston, Little Brown, 1960, p. 283.
13. Roy A. Medvedev, "New Pages from the Political Biography of Stalin," in Robert C. Tucker, ed., *Stalinism: Essays in Historical Interpretation*. New York, Norton, 1977, p. 212.
14. Kennan, *Russia and the West*, op. cit., pp. 284, 287–88. Tucker also agrees: "Finally, the view that the Great Purge and the trials were preparation for a coming conflict with Hitler collides with evidence that Stalin at this time was *not in fact preparing for conflict with Hitler but for collaboration with him*. He was preparing the diplomacy of the Soviet-Nazi Pact that was finally concluded, on Stalin's initiative, in August 1939" (author's italics). *The Great Purge Trial*, op. cit., p. xxxiv, and further elaborated pp. xxxv–xl.

    Clear evidence of Stalin's willingness to help bring Hitler to power lies in his instructions to German Communists to refrain from active opposition to him and to fight the Social Democrats as the chief enemy.
15. Kennan, *Russia and the West*, op. cit., p. 289.
16. "Khrushchev's De-Stalinization Speech," Dmytryshyn, op. cit., p. 511.
17. While Tukhachevsky was being tried, General Jan Gamarnik, chief of the Political Administration of the Army, a Jew, committed suicide. Franz Borkenau, a penetrating political analyst, has suggested the possiblity that the Gestapo had a hand in the Tukhachevsky trial. It has also been said that Hitler as well as Heydrich boasted to Nazi party leaders of having deceived the GPU with planted evidence encompassing the destruction of the Soviet high command. Franz Borkenau, "Stalin's Political Contribution," *Commentary*, January 1950, pp. 97, 98. Nazi-planted evidence is also suggested by Leopold Trepper in his *The Great Game: Memoirs of the Spy Hitler Couldn't Silence*. New York, McGraw Hill, 1977, pp. 66–67.

    At the February–March Central Committee plenum in 1937, Stalin introduced a new concept, namely, that as the nation moves forward toward socialism, class war becomes intensified, the more enemies the country faces, and, thus, as Khruschev admitted, providing the pretext for ever greater mass repression. Ibid., p. 506. Among other doomed old Bolsheviks, Bukharin and Rykov were expelled from the party on February 27, 1937.

    Stalin, throughout these shattering events "contrived to hold himself aloof and in the background so that people would not understand his true role. . . . Even in the fateful Central Committee session of March 3–5, 1937 . . . he carefully posed as a force for moderation by cautioning . . . against 'a heartless attitude toward people.' " *The Great Purge Trial*, op. cit., p. xiv. The transcript of the March 1938 trial is reproduced in ibid.
18. Bialer, op. cit., pp. 34, 35.
19. Medvedev, *Let History Judge*, op. cit., p. 169. There is much evidence for this belief, including the memoirs of Ilya Ehrenburg, Eugenia Ginzberg and other camp prisoners, many of whom said "if only Stalin knew!" Dr. Aron

Katsenelinboigen, who lived in the Soviet Union during this time, confirmed the fact that he and many other Russians were unaware of the extent of the purges. Conversation with author, Philadelphia, May 6, 1983.

20. Medvedev, ibid. Tucker, however, believes that "in a brilliant display of Aesopean language," Bukharin condemned Stalin "before the court of history," by showing "what Stalin was doing to Bolshevism." *The Great Purge Trial*, op. cit., pp. xlv, xlvii.

21. Conquest, op. cit., p. 428.

22. Ibid.

23. Autobiographical essay by Arthur Koestler in *The God That Failed*, Richard Crossman, ed. New York, Bantam, 1952, pp. 61–62.

24. Kennan, *Russia and the West*, op. cit., p. 293.

25. Esther Markish, *The Long Return*. New York, Ballantine, 1978, pp. 80–83.

26. See Shmuel Ettinger, "Historical Roots of Anti-Semitism in the USSR," *Anti-Semitism in the Soviet Union: Its Roots and Consequences. Proceedings of the Seminar on Soviet Anti-Semitism*, April 7–8, 1978. Vol. 1. Jerusalem, Hebrew University, Center for Research and Documentation of East European Jewry, 1979, p. 20.

27. Quoted in Marie Syrkin, "The Moscow Trials, 1936" in *Jewish Frontier*, June 1971, p. 22. At the March 1938 trial, Vyshinsky denounced Bukharin in the same way: "How many times has Buhkarin kissed the great teacher with the kiss of Judas the traitor! Bukharin reminds us of Vasily Shuisky [a Russian tsar depicted in dramatizations of Boris Godunov as a Judas figure] and Judas Iscariot, who betrayed with a kiss." *The Great Purge Trial*, op. cit., p. 545.

In his 1956 speech, Khrushchev himself admitted that the mass terror under the slogan of a fight against the Trotskyites had no validity whatsoever: "Did the Trotskyites at this time actually constitute such a danger to our party and to the Soviet state? We should recall that in 1927 . . . only some 4,000 votes were cast for the Trotskyite-Zinovievite opposition while there were 724,000 for the party line." During the next ten years, "Trotskyism was completely disarmed. . . . It is clear that in the situation of socialist victory there was no basis for mass terror in the country." "Khrushchev's De-Stalinization Speech," in Dmytryshyn, op. cit., p. 506.

The elimination of the opposition and its connection with conspiracy and terrorism had already been anticipated by Trotsky as far back as 1927. Moreover, the anti-Semitic strains in the Moscow Trials were elaborated in his essay, "Thermidor and anti-Semitism," written in February 1937: "Sometimes Moscow is constrained to resort to demonstration trials. In all such trials the Jews inevitably comprise a significant percentage, in part because they make up a great part of the bureaucracy and are branded with its odium, partly because . . . the leading cadre of the bureaucracy . . . strives to divert the indignation of the working masses from itself to the Jews. This fact was well known to every critical observer in the USSR as far back as ten years ago." Trotsky also noted the deliberate use of the

Jewish-sounding names of Radomislyski and Rozenfeld—of Zinoviev and Kamenev respectively. Joseph Nedava, *Trotsky and the Jews*. Philadelphia, Jewish Publication Society of America, 1972, pp. 184–85.

28. Gregory Aaronson, "The Jewish Question during the Stalin Era," in Aaronson, et al., eds., *Russian Jewry, 1917–1967*. New York, Thomas Yoseloff, 1969, p. 181.

29. Esther Frumkin died in 1943 from a lack of insulin, after being imprisoned in a camp in Karaganda. Zvi Y. Gitelman, *Jewish Nationality and Soviet Politics*. Princeton, Princeton University Press, 1972, p. 517.

30. Alfred A. Greenbaum, *Jewish Scholarship and Scholarly Institutions in Soviet Russia, 1918–1953*. Jerusalem, Hebrew University Center for Research and Documentation of East European Jewry, 1978, p. 66.

31. Esther Rozenthal-Shneiderman, *Af vegn un umvegn*, Vol. 2. Tel Aviv, Verlag Ha-Menorah, 1978, pp. 227, 228, 233–36. Mrs. Rozenthal-Shneiderman was active in the Jewish secular school movement in Poland, joined the Communist party there, and in 1926 settled in the Soviet Union. At first she worked in the Institute for Jewish Proletarian Culture in Kiev preparing school textbooks, helping to train teachers for the Yiddish schools, and editing journals for children *(Der pionyer* and *Oktyaberl)*. In 1934 she went to Birobidzhan, but the growing oppression of the Stalinist state and the crushing of the Jewish intelligentsia and Jewish culture in the mid-thirties turned her into a disillusioned opponent of the regime. She returned to Poland in 1958 and later emigrated to Israel.

32. Interview with Shimon Kipnis (December 12, 1984) in Philadelphia, and his unpublished essay, "When the Soviet-Yiddish Press Was Closed Down," tr. from Yiddish by Max Rosenfeld.

33. B. Z. Goldberg, *The Jewish Problem in the Soviet Union*. New York, Crown, 1961, p. 255.

34. Solomon M. Schwarz, "Birobidzhan: An Experiment in Jewish Colonization," in Aaronson, et al., eds., *Russian Jewry*, op. cit., p. 379.

35. Quoted in Zosa Szajkowski, *Jews, Wars, and Communism*, Vol. I. New York, Ktav, 1972, p. 391.

36. Letter and account in Lukasz Hirszowicz, "The Great Terror and the Jews," *Soviet Jewish Affairs*, Vol. 4, No. 2, 1974, pp. 80–86.

37. Mikhail Agursky, "My Father and the Great Terror," *Soviet Jewish Affairs*, Vol. 5, No. 2, 1975, pp. 90–93.

38. Varlam Shalamov, *Kolyma Tales*. New York, Norton, 1982; Solzhenitsyn, op. cit.; E. Ginzburg, *Journey into the Whirlwind*. New York, Harcourt Brace and World, 1967, and *Within the Whirlwind*. New York, Harcourt Brace Jovanovich, 1981.

39. Tucker, *The Soviet Political Mind*, op. cit., p. 31, and *The Great Purge Trial*, op. cit., pp. xxx–xxxii.

40. Irving Howe, *Leon Trotsky*. New York, Penguin, 1978, p. 128.

41. Winston Churchill, *The Second World War*, Vol. I. Boston, Houghton Mifflin, 1948, p. 393.

42. Department of State, *Documents on German Foreign Policy, 1918–1945*. Series

D (1937–1945). Washington, D.C., Government Printing Office, 1956. VII, p. 247.

43. Andrei Sakharov, *Progress, Coexistence, and Intellectual Freedom.* New York, Norton, 1968, pp. 65–66.

44. Quoted in Nora Levin, *The Holocaust: The Destruction of European Jewry, 1933–1945.* New York, Schocken, 1973, p. 118.

45. Arnold Goldberg, *Ilya Ehrenburg, Revolutionary, Novelist, Poet, War Correspondent, Propagandist: The Extraordinary Epic of a Russian Survivor.* New York, Viking, 1984, p. 175. See also I. Ehrenburg, *Memoirs: 1921–1941.* Cleveland World Publishing, 1963, pp. 502, 504.

46. Ben-Cion Pinchuk, "Soviet Media on the Fate of Jews in Nazi-Occupied Territory (1939–41)," *Yad Vashem Studies,* XI. Jerusalem, Yad Vashem, 1976, p. 226.

   On September 7, *Jewish Morning Journal* reported arrests of Jews for criticizing the Nazi-Soviet Pact. On March 14, 1940, it reported that the organ of Soviet youth, *Molodaya gvardya,* had praised friendship with Germany and that the USSR had much to learn regarding the racial question. The journal of the Red Army *Krasnaya zvezda* reprinted the article. On April 14, the *New York Times* reported that Andrei Zhdanov, Leningrad party leader who had succeeded Kirov, had forced the "Aryanization" of the Soviet Embassy in Berlin as early as 1938.

47. Maurice Friedberg, "Jewish Themes in Soviet Russian Literature," in Lionel Kochan, ed., *The Jews in Soviet Russia since 1917,* 3d ed. Oxford, Oxford University Press, footnote, p. 207.

48. B. Z. Goldberg, op. cit., p. 306.

49. *American Jewish Yearbook,* Vol. 43, 1941–1942, p. 315.

   During the period of the pact, there were rumors that some Soviet officials in their desire to cooperate closely with Nazi Germany, were ready to discriminate against Jews and had removed some Jews from official posts. These rumors were later confirmed. Zhdanov, for example, Stalin's right-hand man and head of the party in Leningrad, was thought to be responsible for Litvinov's removal as foreign minister in 1939. (Litvinov was also expelled from the Central Committee of the party in February 1941.) He was also mentioned in connection with the removal of Lazar M. Kaganovich, his political archenemy, as commissar of the oil industry by the Presidium of the Supreme Soviet.

50. M. Michaelis, "Stalin, Ribbentrop and the Jews," *Bulletin of Soviet and East European Jewish Affairs,* No. 5, May 1970, p. 91.

51. Ibid.

52. Ibid., p. 92.

53. The swift military advance of the German army took the Soviet government "by surprise," according to Friedrich Schulenburg, the German ambassador to the Soviet Union, in another cable on September 10. The Red Army "had counted on several weeks, which had now shrunk to a few days." The intervention of the Soviet Union would be rationalized by a declaration that "Poland was falling apart and that it was necessary for the

Soviet Union, in consequence, to come to the aid of the Ukranians and the White Russians 'threatened' by Germany." *Schulenberg to the German Foreign Office*, No. 317, September 10, in R. J. Sontag and J. S. Beddie, eds., *Nazi-Soviet Relations, 1939–1941: Documents from the Archives of the German Foreign Office*. Washington, D.C., Department of State, 1948, p. 91.

54. General Wladyslaw Sikorski later became prime minister of the Polish government-in-exile. Quotations are from *Pravda* and *Izvestia* in Pinchuk, op. cit., pp. 224–25.

   In Anatoly Rybakov's highly acclaimed novel of the Holocaust, *Tiazhelyi pesok* (Heavy Sand) published in *Oktyabr* (nos. 7, 8, and 9) 1978, the narrator comments on what Russians surmised at the time of the pact. He speaks of hearing from a Polish Jewish refugee about the anti-Jewish horrors, of not being able to believe them, and of his interpretation of the phrase "final solution of the Jewish question." At the time, he says, "it sounded like a promise to end the excesses and restore order. It even occurred to me that maybe this had been brought about by pressure from us, that in signing the pact we had made it a condition that the anti-semitic antics must cease." *Heavy Sand*, Harold Shukman, tr. New York, Viking, 1981, p. 229.

55. *The German Ambassador in the Soviet Union (Schulenburg) to the German Foreign Office*, September 6, 1939. Documents from the Archives of the German Foreign Office, Pol. V8924, No. 279. In R. J. Sontag and J. S. Beddie, eds., op. cit., p. 88.

15. Jews in the Soviet-Annexed Territories, September 1939–June 1941

1. Shimon Redlich, "The Jews in the Soviet Annexed Territories, 1939–41," *Soviet Jewish Affairs*, No. 1, June 1971, p. 82.
2. Nora Levin, *The Holocaust: The Destruction of European Jewry, 1933–1945*. New York, Schocken, 1973, pp. 269–70.
3. Redlich, op. cit., p. 84.
4. Quoted from *Megiles Gline* [Documents of Gliniana], New York, 1950, pp. 219–23, in Redlich, op. cit., p. 84.
5. *Jewish Telegraphic Agency News*, February 25, 1940, quoted in Redlich, op. cit., p. 85.
6. Ben-Cion Pinchuk, "Jewish Refugees in Soviet Poland, 1939–1941," *Jewish Social Studies*, Vol. 40, No. 2, Spring 1978, p. 146.
7. Ibid., p. 143.
8. Account by Julius Margolin, "When the Red Army Liberated Pinsk," *Commentary*, December 1952, pp. 517–28.
9. D. Grodner, "In Soviet Poland and Lithuania," *Contemporary Jewish Record*, April 1941, p. 140.
10. Ibid., p. 139. See also Pinchuk, op. cit., pp. 146–47 and Shimon Redlich, "The Jews under Soviet Rule during World War II." Doctoral dissertation, New York University, 1968, pp. 44–45.
11. Grodner, op. cit., p. 139.

12. Ibid.
13. Reports in *Contemporary Jewish Record*. January–February, 1940, p. 74, and May–June, 1940, p. 307. See also Pinchuk, op. cit., p. 146–47.
14. The following true story capsulates the tragedy: At Biala Podlaska, the first station on the German side of the border, the train carrying refugees east encountered the train moving West: "When the Jews coming from Brisk saw Jews going there, they shouted: 'You are insane, where are you going?' Those coming from Warsaw answered with astonishment: 'You are insane, where are you going?!'" Quoted from Moishe Grossman, *In far-kisheftn land fun legendern Dzhugoshvili.* 2 vols. Paris, 1950, Vol. I, p. 94, in Pinchuk, op. cit., p. 153.
15. Grodner, op. cit., p. 137.
16. Taped interview with Meyer Adler (November 10, 1982). Gratz College Holocaust Oral History Archive, Philadelphia.
17. Grodner, op. cit., pp. 137–38.
18. Abraham I. Katsh, tr. and ed., *Scroll of Agony: The Warsaw Diary of Chaim A. Kaplan.* New York, Macmillan, 1964, pp. 89–90.
19. Ibid., pp. 96–97.
20. *Contemporary Jewish Record*, January–February 1940, p. 70.
21. *Morning Journal*, December 21, 1939; January 26, 1940.

Shayne Broderzon's *Mayn laydns veg mit Moshe Broderzon*, Buenos Aires, Union Central Israelita Polaca en la Argentina, 1960, pp. 17–18, describes friendly actions of Soviet soldiers at border points.

On November 11, a Kremlin decree prohibiting all further immigration from the conquered territory was reported, and border patrols were reinforced, but irregular crossings continued. On December 21, the *Morning Journal* reported that twelve Soviet officers and 160 soldiers had been convicted on charges of accepting bribes to help Jewish refugees enter the Soviet area. A later report from Polish sources (December 29) indicated that the frontier may have been temporarily reopened. Thusands of Jews were reported massing at certain points along the border. Forty to fifty thousand Jews were said to have congregated on the Soviet side of Przemysl, in "pitiful condition." *Contemporary Jewish Record*, January–February, 1940, p. 74.
22. Ibid., p. 64.
23. Peter Meyer, et al., eds., *The Jews in the Soviet Satellites.* Syracuse, Syracuse University Press, 1953, p. 330.
24. Pinchuk, op. cit., p. 144.
25. Yehoshua A. Gilboa, *The Black Years of Soviet Jewry, 1939–1953.* Boston, Little, Brown, 1971, p. 18.
26. Grodner, op. cit., p. 142.
27. Ben Zion Goldberg, *The Jewish Problem in the Soviet Union.* New York, Crown, 1961, pp. 52–53.
28. Pinchuk, op. cit., p. 148.
29. Gilboa, op. cit., p. 24; for example, during Passover, 1940, a Soviet Jewish officer from Gomel visited a synagogue in Bialystok and attended a seder—

altogether new but memorable experiences for him. Described in Jacob Ben-Shlomo, "Sufferings of Polish Zionists," in Benjamin West, ed., *Struggles of a Generation*. Tel Aviv, Massadah, 1969, pp. 71–72.

30. Gilboa, op. cit., p. 24. See also Pinchuk, op. cit., p. 148 and various issues of *Bialystoker shtern* cited by him, p. 157.

31. Gilboa, op. cit., p. 24.

    Hashomer Hatzair delegates met in Rovno in the western Ukraine in December 1939 and again in Lvov in March 1940. They issued a newsletter called *Mimaamakim* (From the Depths) describing their activities. They also hoped to initiate contacts with Soviet Jewish youth, but their plans did not materialize. Most of their leaders were arrested in October 1940 and sentenced at a public trial. Redlich, dissertation, op. cit., p. 41, and Grodner, op. cit., p. 147.

32. Moshe Grossman, in *Heimish* (Tel Aviv), February–March, 1960, cited in Gilboa, p. 24.

33. Salo W. Baron, *The Russian Jew under Tsars and Soviets*, 2d ed. New York, Macmillan, 1976, p. 264. See also Gilboa, op. cit., p. 26. When the Russians evacuated Minsk in 1941, Akselrod was shot and killed by his jailers. He was 57. Kahan was released, joined the army, and was killed in action.

34. Esther Markish, *The Long Return*, New York, Ballantine, 1978, p. 101. See also Pinchuk, op. cit., pp. 148–49.

35. Pinchuk, op. cit., p. 157 (note 52) mentions Broderzon's article, "On Our Trip Through the Soviet Union," published in the *Vilner emes*, December 8, 1940, in which he admits that he will have to adopt a Soviet repertoire. Later the theater collective promised to prepare performances adapted "to Soviet reality."

36. Goldberg, op. cit., p. 60.

37. Grodner, op. cit., p. 143.

38. Redlich, "The Jews in the Soviet Annexed Territories," op. cit., p. 89.

39. Pinchuk, op. cit., p. 148.

40. *Jewish Chronicle*, December 15, 1939, January 3, 1941, and other sources cited in Redlich, dissertation, op. cit., p. 32.

41. *Jewish Chronicle*, January 19, 1940, cited in ibid., p. 33.

42. *Jewish Chronicle*, December 27, 1940, cited in ibid., p. 39.

43. Grodner, op. cit., p. 145.

44. Taped interview with Avraham Shnaper (August 26, 1981). Gratz College Holocaust Oral History Archive, Philadelphia. The cultural, social, and political importance of Vilna and its special significance as a gathering place for leaders of youth movements and underground resistance organizations that came into being during the Holocaust are described in Dov Levin, "1930–1941: The Intermediate Period and Its Implications for the Holocaust," *Forum*, Vol. 37, Spring 1980, pp. 108–9.

45. *Jewish Daily Forward*, October 19, 1939.

46. Redlich, dissertation, op. cit., pp. 53–54.

47. *Morning Journal*, December 27, 1939. Lists of those to be arrested were pre-

pared with the help of local Communists and included those who had relatives in Palestine and those who had received mail from Palestine. Jacob Ben-Shlomo, op. cit., p. 71.

48. Grodner, op. cit., p. 141.
49. Some Polish Jews have told of hearing from Jewish Communists who had gone to the Soviet Union and returned disappointed; and of Jewish community leaders who told Jews not to accept Soviet passports. Taped interview with Frieda Kaplan (April 30, 1981), in Haifa. Deposited in Gratz College Holocaust Oral History Archive, Philadelphia. See also Pinchuk, op. cit., p. 151.
50. Ibid., p. 152.
51. On March 19, 1940, an agreement for the exchange of refugees between German and Soviet-occupied Poland was announced in Crakow. This agreement involved the transfer of over 60,000 Poles and Jews to the Nazi-held territories, and 14,000 to the Soviet area. On March 13, it was reported that the Soviet Commission in Warsaw rejected the petitions of 1,200 Jews who were born in the Soviet Union, allowing only sixteen of them to return. *Contemporary Jewish Record*, May–June, 1940, p. 307. The Germans, however, according to Pinchuk (p. 152) refused to register any Jews.
52. Redlich, dissertation, op. cit., pp. 46–47. Stalin was bent on limiting or, whenever possible, eliminating identification of Polish citizens in the USSR with the Polish Government-in Exile. This could hardly be denied to Polish nationals, but was often denied to Jews, Belorussians, and Ukrainians who had lived in Poland prior to the war. Instead, it was claimed that they "had strong bonds with people living outside the USSR." Many Jews, indeed, had relatives in the United States, Palestine, and England, which were considered hostile by the USSR until June 1941. Redlich, p. 47.
53. B. D. Weinryb, "Polish Jews under Soviet Rule," in Meyer, et al., eds., *The Jews in the Soviet Satellites*, op. cit., p. 342, estimates a figure of 300,000. Avraham Pechenik (in his *Yidn un yidishkayt in sovet rusland*. New York, 1943, pp. 59–60, cited in Ben-Cion Pinchuk, "Jewish Refugees," op. cit., p. 145) estimated the figure at one million.
54. Z. Kaplan, "Jewish Refugees from Poland in the USSR." Manuscript in Yiddish. Cited in Redlich dissertation, op. cit., p. 47.
55. Redlich, dissertation, ibid., p. 47 and Pinchuk, op. cit., pp. 153–55.
56. Grodner, op. cit., p. 143.
57. Interview with Frieda Kaplan, op. cit.
58. Redlich, dissertation, op. cit., p. 58.
59. Ibid.
60. Redlich estimated that the death rate ranged between 30 and 50 percent, Ibid., p. 60.
61. Yehoshua A. Gilboa, *Keep Forever* (Hebrew). Tel Aviv, n.d., p. 45. cited in ibid.
62. Taped interview with Dr. Leon Friedman (April 7, 1981). Gratz College Holocaust Oral History Archive, Philadelphia.

63. See Chapter 16 for several accounts of experiences of Jews in Central Asia.
64. *Jewish Chronicle*, October 27, 1939, cited in Redlich, dissertation, op. cit,. p. 52.
65. *Contemporary Jewish Record*, January–February, 1940, p. 74.
66. One report mentions 360 from Kishinev. *Jewish Chronicle*, September 13, 1940.
67. *Contemporary Jewish Record*, April 1941, p. 192.
68. This figure includes about 15,000 refugees from Poland.
69. Redlich, "The Jews in the Soviet Annexed Territories," op. cit., p. 82.
70. A. Shochat, "The Beginnings of Anti-Semitism in Independent Lithuania," *Yad Vashem Studies*, Vol. II, 1958, pp. 7–48.
71. See Yehuda Bauer, "Rescue Operations through Vilna," *Yad Vashem Studies*, Vol. IX, 1973, pp. 216–19, for a discussion of various local and foreign aid organizations and efforts of the Lithuanian authorities to control aid to Jewish refugees. Shnaper recalls that food especially was plentiful. Taped interview, op. cit.
72. Yitzhak Arad, "Concentration of Refugees in Vilna on the Eve of the Holocaust," *Yad Vashem Studies*, Vol. IX, 1973, pp. 201–14.
73. Yehuda Bauer, "Rescue Operations through Vilna," op. cit., p. 222. Between 18,000 and 20,000 Jews from Germany, Austria, and Poland fled to Shanghai in 1938–39. See David Kranzler, *Japanese, Nazis and Jews: The Jewish Refugees of Shanghai, 1938–1945*. New York, Yeshiva University Press, 1976.
74. In his "The 'Final Solution' in Lithuania in the Light of German Documentation," Yitzhak Arad concluded that between 220,000 and 225,000 Jews remained in Lithuania after the German occupation. *Yad Vashem Studies*, Vol. XI, 1976, p. 234.
75. Menakhem Begin, a Revisionist Zionist leader in Poland and later Prime Minister of Israel, was interrogated by the NKVD for several months beginning September 1940, accused of being an agent of British imperialism and a counterrevolutionist. From the Lukishki prison in Vilna, he was taken to Kotlas camp, then Pechora, near the Barents Sea, where he met a diverse prison population, many of whom were arrested for fictitious crimes. The prisoners were to build the Kotlas-Vorkuta railway and Begin offloaded iron sleepers that supported the railway lines. They worked sixteen hours a day.
76. Azriel Shochat, "Jews, Lithuanians, and Russians, 1939–1941," in Bela Vago and George L. Mosse, eds., *Jews and Non-Jews in Eastern Europe*. New York, Wiley, 1974, p. 308.
77. Redlich, "The Jews in the Soviet Annexed Territories," op. cit., p. 85.
78. Shochat, op. cit., p. 308.
79. The amnesty of August 1941 did not apply to Lithuanian or Latvian prisoners and they remained in camps or rural settlements.
80. About a week before the invasion, a few thousand Lithuanian Jews were evacuated to farms in Soviet Mongolia and eastern Siberia. Some of the Baltic Jewish leaders previously arrested by Soviet officials were released,

including Mordecai Dubin, former president of the Jewish community in Riga and ex-deputy in the Latvian Parliament. There is a poignant memoir, "Latvian Halutzim Face Extinction," in West, op. cit., pp. 101–7.

81. Largely based on Dov Levin, "Estonian Jews in the U.S.S.R. (1941–1945)," *Yad Vashem Studies,* Vol. XI, 1976, pp. 273–97.

82. Quoted in Dov Levin, "The Jews and the Inception of Soviet Rule in Bukovina," *Soviet Jewish Affairs,* Vol. 6, No. 2, 1976, p. 52.

83. Stephen Fischer-Galati, "Fascism, Communism, and the Jewish Question in Romania," in Vago and Mosse, eds., op. cit., pp. 158, 159.

84. Ibid., pp. 162, 163.

85. *Contemporary Jewish Record,* July–August, 1940, p. 427 and April 1941, p. 192. Because of fears that their movement would be crushed by the Russians, Zionist youths tried to flee to Bucharest but were blocked. M. Friedman, "Bessarabia," in West, op. cit., p. 108.

86. D. Levin, "The Jews and the Inception of Soviet Rule in Bukovina," op. cit., pp. 52, 53.

87. Ibid., p. 55.

88. Ibid., p. 64. See also Avraham Ben Yona, "Bucovina: The Story of a Zionist Prisoner," in West, op. cit., pp. 130–33.

89. Dov Levin, "The Jews and the Inception of Soviet Rule in Bukovina," op. cit., p. 64.

90. Ibid., p. 55.

91. Ibid., p. 59.

92. Redlich, dissertation, op. cit., p. 28.

93. M. Friedman, "Bessarabia," in West, op. cit., pp. 112–13, 114, 118–21.

94. Ibid., p. 117.

95. Dov Levin estimates that 25,000 Jews were expelled from these areas, including 8,000 from Bessarabia, 3,000 from northern Bukovina, 7,000 from Lithuania, 6,000 from Latvia, and 500 from Estonia. See his "Attitude of the Soviet Union to the Rescue of Jews," in *Rescue Attempts During the Holocaust. Proceedings of the Second Yad Vashem International Historical Conference.* Jerusalem, April 8–11, 1974. Jerusalem, Yad Vashem, 1977, p. 230.

96. Dov Levin also argues that Soviet nationalization measures in the annexed areas made economic spoliation of Jews easier for the Nazis, while imprisonment and exile of local leaders caused a leadership vacuum. On the other hand, many Jews under proletarianization learned carpentry and other useful trades that enabled some to survive. See his "1939–1941: The Intermediate Period and Its Implications for the Holocaust," *Forum,* Vol. 37, Spring 1980, pp. 104–5.

16. Jews as Pawns in Polish-Soviet Relations, 1941–46

1. The number of Jews deported to the Soviet interior has not been definitely determined, but some estimates are as high as 400,000. Flight and evacuations involved several hundred thousand more (see note 53 in Chapter 15). One scholar estimates that of approximately 1.8 million former Polish citi-

zens in the Soviet Union at the time, about one-third were Jews. See Klemens Nussbaum, "Jews in the Polish Army in the USSR, 1943–44," *Soviet Jewish Affairs*, No. 3, May 1972, p. 95. Dov Levin analyzes the difficulties in determining accurate figures in his "The Attitude of the Soviet Union to the Rescue of Jews," in *Rescue Attempts during the Holocaust. Proceedings of the Second Yad Vashem International Historical Conference*, Jerusalem; April 8–11, 1974. Jerusalem, 1977, pp. 227–36.

2. These phases are outlined in Shimon Redlich, "The Jews Under Soviet Rule During World War II." Doctoral dissertation, New York University, 1968, p. 76.

3. Shimon Redlich, "Jewish Refugees from Poland as a Factor in the Relations between the Polish and Soviet Governments during World War II," *Yad Vashem Bulletin*, No. 14, March 1964, p. 33.

4. Redlich, dissertation, op. cit., pp. 75, 76.

5. Stanislaw Kot, *Conversations with the Kremlin and Dispatches from Russia*. London, Oxford University Press, 1963, p. 62, quoted in ibid., p. 77.

6. Redlich, "Jewish Refugees from Poland. . . ," op. cit., p. 33.

7. Kot, op. cit., p. 226, quoted in Redlich dissertation, op. cit., p. 78.

8. Quoted in Redlich, dissertation, op. cit., pp. 77–78.

9. Account based on Shimon Redlich, *Propaganda and Nationalism in Wartime Russia: The Jewish Antifascist Committee in the USSR, 1941–1948*, East European Monographs No. CVIII, *East European Quarterly*, 1982, pp. 15–31. See also Leonard Schapiro, "The Jewish Anti-Fascist Committee and Phases of Soviet Anti-Semitic Policy during and after World War II," in Bela Vago and George L. Mosse, eds., *Jews and Non-Jews in Eastern Europe, 1918–1945*. New York, Wiley, 1974, pp. 284–88. Schapiro records some details supplied by Lucjan Blit, who shared a room in Kuibyshev with Erlich and Alter for five weeks. These details are elaborated in *The Case of Henryk Erlich and Victor Alter*. London, Liberty Pubs., 1943.

10. Redlich believes that the improved military situation and Soviet suspicion of Poles as well as the old hostility, destroyed any possible Soviet-Bundist cooperation. Redlich, *Propaganda and Nationalism*, op cit., pp. 27–29. In his "The Jewish Antifascist Committee in the Soviet Union," *Jewish Social Studies*, Vol. 31, 1969, pp. 26–28, he noted that Erlich and Alter realized that their objectives diverged from those of the Soviet leaders, but believed that Stalin would allow socialists to dominate the work of the committee. Their most serious miscalculation "was their belief that the Soviets would allow the existence of an independent or even a semi-independent Jewish body in the USSR merely for some foreign policy objectives." According to *Contemporary Jewish Record*, February 1942, p. 94, as late as December 3, from Kuibyshev, they appealed to all Polish Jews in the Soviet Union to join the newly formed Polish army to help fight Nazism. Then suddenly, on December 5, they were arrested again and shot under Stalin's personal orders. For months afterward there were protests and inquiries about the fate of the men, but Soviet officials reassured correspondents that they would soon be free. Not until January 1943 were letters sent to the American

Federation of Labor and to Albert Einstein, admitting their execution on the grounds that they had "incited" Soviet soldiers and the Soviet people to make peace.

Gilboa emphasized Stalin's deep-seated hatred of the Bund and the two Bundists, their criticism of the Moscow Trials, their contacts with the West, and efforts to get Polish prisoners in the USSR freed. See Yehoshua A. Gilboa, *The Black Years of Soviet Jewry, 1939–1953*. Boston, Little, Brown, 1971, p. 45.

11. Kot, op. cit., p. 159, quoted in Redlich, dissertation, ibid., p. 72.
12. Zosa Szajkowski, *Jews, Wars, and Communism*, Vol. I. New York, Ktav, 1972, p. 629. Quoted from Waldman Papers (American Jewish Archives, Cincinnati, Ohio) n.d., p. 642.
13. "General W. Sikorski's Memorandum March 5, 1942, to Churchill," *British Foreign Office Documents*, Ref. No. FO371/31079. Quoted in "Documents: The Soviet Union and the Jews during World War II," annotated by Lukasz Hirszowicz, *Soviet Jewish Affairs*, Vol. 3, No. 2, 1973, p. 80.
14. Ibid.
15. Ibid., p. 81.
16. For discussion of this issue, see Yisrael Gutman, "Jews in General Anders' Army in the Soviet Union," *Yad Vashem Studies*, Vol. XII, 1977, pp. 236–48, on which I have based my account.
17. *Documents on Polish-Soviet Relations, 1935–1945*, Vol. II. London, 1961, Document No. 160, p. 244, quoted in Gutman, op. cit., p. 248.
18. Quoted in Menachem Begin, *White Nights: The Story of a Prisoner in Russia*, Katie Kaplan, tr. New York, Harper and Row, 1977, p. 216.
19. Redlich, dissertation, op. cit., pp. 86–87.
20. According to Redlich, it reached somewhat over 30 percent. Ibid., p. 88.
21. Gutman, op. cit., p. 253.
22. Ibid.
23. Ibid., p. 242. A Polish Jewish survivor of Soviet exile, Dr. Leon Friedman of Philadelphia has reported that two of his brothers were in the Anders army. One changed his name from Friedman to Fried and may not have been considered Jewish; he became a captain. The other, a chemical engineer (who would normally have been an officer), who did not change his name, was given a job loading ammunition instead of work in a laboratory. Taped interview (April 7, 1981). Gratz College Holocaust Oral History Archive, Philadelphia.
24. Gutman, op. cit., p. 243.
25. "General W. Sikorski's Memorandum of March 5, 1942 to Churchill" op. cit., pp. 79–82.
26. Gutman, op. cit., p. 253.
27. Ibid., p. 254.
28. Szajkowski, op. cit., p. 461.
29. Waldman to Jos. M. Proskauer, October 18, 1943, quoted in ibid., p. 625.
30. Ibid., p. 626.
31. Ibid., p. 627.

32. "Emigration to Palestine from Soviet-Controlled Territories, 1940," *British Foreign Office Documents*, Ref. No. FO371/25243. Quoted in *Soviet Jewish Affairs*, op. cit., p. 74.
33. "Exchange of Letters between M. L. Perlzweig and Lord Halifax, and Comments by M. L. Perlzweig," *British Foreign Office Documents*, Ref. No. FO371/27128, ibid., p. 77.
34. Ibid.
35. "Minutes by F. K. Roberts," *British Foreign Office Documents*, Ref. No. FO371/31079, ibid., p. 83.
36. Redlich, dissertation, op. cit., p. 79.
37. Kot, op. cit., p. 184.
38. Ibid., p. 246.
39. *Foreign Relations of the United States: Diplomatic Papers 1942*, Vol. III (Europe). Washington D.C., Government Printing Office, 1961. 861.02/213.
40. Begin, op. cit., pp. 189–218.
41. Ibid., p. 214.
42. Ibid., p. 216.
43. Alexander Werth, *Russia At War, 1941–1945*. New York, Dutton, 1964, pp. 586–87. Cited in Redlich, dissertation, op. cit., p. 97.
44. Redlich, dissertation, op. cit., p. 80 and taped interview with Frieda Kaplan (April 30, 1981) in Haifa.
45. Redlich, dissertation. op. cit., p. 92. Late in 1942, the Polish Ministry of Social Welfare decided to grant a permanent monthly allowance of four pounds per child to over 1,000 orphaned Jewish children evacuated to Teheran. *Contemporary Jewish Record*, December 1942, p. 642.
46. Conversations with Dr. Tikva Natan and Mrs. Mina Rogozik Ben Zvi (May 1981) in Haifa.
47. *Report on the Relief Accorded by the Polish Embassy in the U.S.S.R.* Teheran, 1943, p. 6. Cited in Redlich, op. cit., p. 82.
48. Redlich, dissertation, op. cit., p. 83. See also Joachim Schoenfeld, *Holocaust Memoirs: Jews in the Lwow Ghetto, the Janowska Concentration Camp and as Deportees in Siberia*. New York, Ktav, 1986.
49. Ibid.
50. Dr. Jerzy G. Glicksman, a Warsaw lawyer who spent a number of years in the Soviet Union, observed considerable anti-Jewish feeling among Russians, Ukrainians, and Tatars in Soviet Central Asia: "While working with Jews they tried to inconvenience their work, and molest them as much as they could. The comparatively poor output of the Jewish deportees—caused by physical exhaustion and lack of previous experience in physical work—was ascribed to their unwillingness for physical labor, which the local population took as a typically Jewish characteristic. The high-ranking functionaries . . . sometimes also comported themselves with undisguised unfriendliness toward the Jews, assigning them the hardest tasks." J. G. Glicksman, "Jewish Exiles in Soviet Russia, 1939–1943" (unpublished manuscript in Library of American Jewish Committee, New York), quoted in Redlich, dissertation, op. cit., p. 80.

51. Taped interview with Chayale Ash-Fuhrman (September 21, 1981). Gratz College Holocaust Oral History Archive, Philadelphia.
52. Taped interview with Meyer Adler (November 10, 1982). Gratz College Holocaust Oral History Archive, Philadelphia.
53. Taped interview with Frieda Kaplan (April 30, 1981) in Haifa. Gratz College Holocaust Oral History Archive, Philadelphia.
54. Taped interview with Dr. Leon Friedman, op. cit.
55. Ibid.
56. Klemens Nussbaum, op. cit. p. 96.
57. Ibid., p. 97.
58. Redlich, dissertation, op. cit., p. 98.
59. Nussbaum, op. cit., p. 100.
60. Ibid., pp. 101–2.
61. Redlich, dissertation, op. cit., p. 99.
62. B. Mark, "Di Badaytung fun Lenino," *Dos naye lebn*, October 12, 1947, quoted in ibid., p. 100.
63. Nussbaum, op. cit., p. 102.
64. In August 1941, it was reported that the names of hundreds of Jews exiled in Soviet Russia were submitted to the Polish Government-in-Exile to expedite their release under the terms of the Soviet-Polish amnesty. There were also some reports about the efforts of Jews to join the Polish army, in special Jewish units and in units together with other Poles. *Contemporary Jewish Record*, October 1941, pp. 558, 559; February 1942, pp. 92, 94; December 1942, p. 641.
65. The composition and functions of the committee are described in Redlich, *Propaganda and Nationalism*, op. cit., pp. 64–65.
66. Ibid.
67. Mordechai Altshuler, *Soviet Jewry in the Mirror of the Yiddish Press in Poland.* Jerusalem, 1975, p. ix.
68. Redlich, dissertation, op. cit., p. 105. Bernard D. Weinryb, "Polish Jews under Soviet Rule," in Peter Meyer, et al., eds., *The Jews in the Soviet Satellites.* Syracuse, Syracuse University Press, 1953, p. 241, estimates the figure at 170,000.
69. Ida Kaminska, "My Wartime Flight Through the Soviet Union," *Midstream*, October 1973, p. 39.
70. Taped interview with Chayele Ash-Fuhrman, op. cit.
71. According to a report submitted to a conference of JDC officials in Cairo on May 9, 1944, there were then more than 300,000 Jewish refugees still in Asiatic Russia, a great number of whom were Polish Jews. See *Contemporary Jewish Record*, August 1944, p. 416.

17. The Jewish Antifascist Committee and Other Illusions, 1942–43

1. Salo W. Baron, *The Russian Jew under Tsars and Soviets*, 2d ed. New York, Macmillan, 1976, p. 261 and Shimon Redlich, *Propaganda and Naitonalism in*

Wartime Russia: The Jewish Antifascist Committee in the USSR, 1941–1948, Eastern European Monographs No. CVIII, *East European Quarterly,* 1982, p. 39.

2. Redlich, ibid.
3. Ibid.
4. Baron, op. cit., p. 261. See Chapter 16 for details of their plan.
5. Ibid.
6. Yehoshua A. Gilboa, *The Black Years of Soviet Jewry, 1939–1945.* Boston, Little, Brown, 1971, p. 43.
7. Ibid.
8. *Pravda,* August 25, 1941, according to Gilboa, ibid., p. 359, note 3.
9. Themes and speakers are described in Redlich, *Propaganda and Nationalism,* op. cit., pp. 40–41.
10. Gilboa noted that the appointment of Mikhoels as chairman in August 1941, is mentioned in an anthology in Russian entitled *Mikhoels,* K. L. Rutnitsky, ed., Moscow, 1965, p. 606. Gilboa, op. cit., p. 359, note 4.
11. The various speeches and appeals were published in Yiddish by Der Emes Publishing House in a brochure, *Brider yidn fun der gantser velt,* Moscow, 1941. Quotation from Reuben Ainsztein, "Soviet Jewry in the Second World War," in Lionel Kochan, ed., *The Jews in Soviet Russia since 1917,* 3d ed. Oxford, Oxford University Press, 1978, p. 284.
12. Gilboa, op. cit., p. 47.
13. Quoted in *American Jewish Yearbook,* Vol. 44, 1942–43, p. 238.
14. Ibid.
15. Redlich, *Propaganda and Nationalism,* op. cit., p. 41. Feuchtwanger had visited the Soviet Union in 1937 and written optimistically about the future of the USSR in *Moscow, 1937.*
16. Ibid., note 7, p. 194, and p. 42.
17. Shimon Redlich, "The Jews under Soviet Rule during World War II." Doctoral dissertation, New York University, 1968, p. 148.
18. Redlich, *Propaganda and Nationalism,* op. cit., pp. 175–77, contains the names of the members from 1941 to 1948.
19. Chone Shmeruk, "Yiddish Publications in the USSR from the Late 30's to 1948," *Yad Vashem Studies,* Vol. IV, 1960, p. 120.
20. See S. Levin, "Shakne Epshteyn." *Morgen Freiheit,* July 30, 1970, for a sympathetic essay. Epshteyn died in 1945.
21. Redlich, dissertation, op. cit., p. 149.
22. Ibid., p. 150.
23. It was published three times a week from early 1945 to November 20, 1948, when publication was stopped. See Shmeruk, op. cit., pp. 162–63 for details of its publishing history.
24. Redlich, *Propaganda and Nationalism,* op. cit., pp. 46–49.
25. Ibid., pp. 48, 49.
26. Shmeruk, op. cit., p. 121. Schwarz, op. cit., p. 205 and Baron, op. cit. pp. 263–64 disagree.
27. Shmeruk, op. cit., p. 112.

28. Ibid., p. 123.
29. Ibid. and Avraham Ben-Yosef, "Bibliography of Yiddish Publications in the USSR During 1941–48," *Yad Vashem Studies,* Vol. IV, 1960, pp. 135–66.
30. Shmeruk, op. cit., p. 122.
31. Ibid.
32. Elaborated in Redlich, *Propaganda and Nationalism,* op. cit., pp. 43–46.
33. Gilboa, op. cit., p. 51.
34. Redlich, *Propaganda and Nationalism,* op. cit., p. 32.
35. Solomon M. Schwarz, *The Jews in the Soviet Union.* Syracuse, Syracuse University Press, 1951, p. 203.
36. Ben Zion Goldberg, *The Jewish Problem in the Soviet Union.* New York, Crown, 1961, p. 47.
37. Quoted in Schwarz, op. cit., p. 217.
38. Quoted in Zosa Szajkowski, *Jews, Wars, and Communism,* Vol. I. New York, Ktav, 1972, p. 459.

   In the pro-Soviet *Yidishe kultur,* No. 6–7, June–July 1943, pp. 63–65, the first address of Mikhoels is reproduced, in which he speaks to the audience as "Brothers! Brothers from our folk, brothers of those buried in Hitler's death-prisons, those burned in the ghettos!" He spoke with intense emotion about the persecution and atrocities, named Jewish heroes who had fallen, and called upon American Jews to join in the mighty struggle in the ultimate triumph over fascism. Feffer also dwelt on the suffering and murder of Jewish victims during the past two years, in his speech, then moved to the resistance against the Nazis on the part of the partisans and the Allied armies. "We have come to the United States," he declared, "at a time when the Red Army, under Marshal Stalin, is struggling against the greatest enemy of mankind . . . when this enemy still vents his hatred of the Jewish masses. . . . Let us answer back in military action . . . with concrete actions that will speed the end of our bitter enemy and save our people from annihilation!"

39. Redlich, *Propaganda and Nationalism,* op. cit., p. 116.
40. Gilboa, op. cit., p. 53. In November 1942, a group of distinguished American Jews formed the "American Committee of Jewish Writers, Artists and Scientists" to support the Soviet Union in its struggle against Hitler, with Albert Einstein as honorary chairman. Among the members were Ben Zion Goldberg, Thomas Mann, and Eleanor Roosevelt. This committee was in contact with the JAC and had received substantial material dealing with Nazi atrocities against Soviet Jews collected by Ehrenburg and others. An English version of part of this material was published by the Jewish Committee for the Publication of *The Black Book* in 1946 under the title: *The Black Book: The Nazi Crime Against the Jewish People.* See Chapter 20 for a discussion of the fate of all of the material collected by Ehrenburg and others.
41. *Contemporary Jewish Record,* December, 1942, p. 643.
42. Ibid.
43. Ibid.
44. *Contemporary Jewish Record,* December 1943, pp. 653–54.

45. Gilboa, op. cit., p. 55. Emiot was the pseudonym of Israel Yanovsky-Gold-wasser, who became a well-known poet in Poland, fled to Bialystok in 1939, and joined the ranks of the Soviet writers there, developing great admiration for the new Soviet society envisioned by many Yiddish writers. He settled in 1944 in Birobidzhan as a newspaper correspondent, was arrested in 1948, and spent eight years in Siberian labor camps.

46. Gilboa, op. cit., p. 54.

47. Leonard Schapiro, "The Jewish Anti-Fascist Committee and Phases of Soviet Anti-Semitic Policy during and after World War II," in Bela Vago and George L. Mosse, eds., *Jews and Non-Jews in Eastern Europe*. New York, Wiley, 1974, pp. 288–89.

48. These differences are dealt with in great detail in Szajkowski, op. cit., pp. 456–62.

49. A. Sutzkever, "Mit Shloyme Mikhoels," *Di goldene keyt*, Vol. 43, 1962, p. 165.

50. Quoted in Gilboa, op. cit., p. 60.

51. My account is based on Jacob Hen-Tov, "Contacts between Soviet Ambassador Maisky and Zionist Leaders during World War II," *Soviet Jewish Affairs*, Vol. 8, No. 1, 1978, pp. 47–55.

52. "Documents: The Soviet Union and the Jews during World War II," introduced and annotated by Lukasz Hirszowicz, *Soviet Jewish Affairs*, Vol. 4, No. 1, 1974, p. 73.

53. Y. Klinov to M. Shertok. August 30, 1942 (excerpt from Zionist Archives, Jerusalem), ibid., p. 77.

54. Ibid., pp. 77–78.

55. Ibid., p. 75.

56. Ibid., p. 76.

57. Ibid., pp. 79–80, quoted from Ben-Zvi's diary.

58. Ibid., p. 85.

59. Ibid., pp. 81, 85.

60. "Notes by Sir Harold MacMichael on his Conversations with S. S. Mikhaylov," August 27, 1942, *British Colonial Office Documents*, Ref. No. CO733/437, in ibid., pp. 87, 88, 89.

61. Hen-Tov, op. cit., p. 51.

62. Ibid., pp. 52–53.

63. Bartley Crum, *Behind the Silken Curtain*. New York, Simon and Schuster, 1947, p. 64.

64. Ibid.

18. Jews and the War

1. Halder affidavit at Nuremburg, November 22, 1945. *Nazi Conspiracy and Aggression*. Washington, D.C., 1946, Vol. VIII, pp. 645–46. Quoted in Nora Levin, *The Holocaust: The Destruction of European Jewry, 1933–1945*. New York, Schocken, 1973, p. 238.

2. Ibid.

3. Raul Hilberg, *The Destruction of the European Jews*. Chicago, Quadrangle Books, 1961, p. 196. Jürgen Förster's "The Wehrmacht and the War of Extermination against the Soviet Union" in *Yad Vashem Studies*, Vol. XIV, 1981, pp. 7–34 describes the obliteration of international law, the burning of villages, mass shootings of civilians, and other excesses committed by the German army.

Until recently, it was generally believed that a report sent by the Jewish Bund underground to the Polish Government-in-Exile in May 1942 was the first documentation of the Einsatzgruppen massacres to reach the West. However, Walter Laqueur, *The Terrible Secret: Suppression of the Truth about Hitler's "Final Solution"* (Boston, Little, Brown, 1980, pp. 81–82) mentions an earlier source, namely, Alexander Lados, the Polish diplomatic representative in Bern, presumably through a Polish courier, to the British legation in Switzerland sometime in November 1941. There is also the possibility, according to Laqueur, that the British, who had broken the SS code by late 1941, could also read the Einstazgruppen wireless reports (p. 83).

The most comprehensive compilation of Einsatzgruppen reports in English is Yitzhak Arad, Shmuel Krakowski, and Shmuel Spector, eds., *The Einsatzgruppen Reports: Selections from the Official Dispatches of the Nazi Death Squads' Campaign against the Jews*. New York, Holocaust Library, 1986.

See Azriel Eisenberg, *Witness to the Holocaust*. New York, Pilgrim Press, 1981; and Martin Gilbert, *The Holocaust: A History of the Jews of Europe during the Second World War*. New York, Holt, Rinehart and Winston, 1985, for numerous eyewitness and personal accounts of the Nazi massacres of Jews in the Soviet Union. The most extensive documentation in English can be found in Ilya Ehrenburg and Vasily Grossman, eds., tr. by John Glad and James S. Levine, *The Black Book: The Ruthless Murder of Jews by German-Fascist Invaders Throughout the Temporarily Occupied Regions of the Soviet Union and in the Death Camps of Poland during the War of 1941–1945*. New York, Holocaust Library, 1981.

4. The poet David Hofshteyn told the journalist Ben Zion Goldberg that his uncle in Korosten, near Kiev, along with a few other elders of the town, went forth to meet the invading Nazis with the traditional bread and salt. They were shot on the spot. This ignorance of Nazi intentions is confirmed in many accounts. In some cases, families whose fathers had been prisoners of war in Germany (in November 1918, there were over one million Russian POWs in Germany), or who had been political emigrés, remained in Germany until 1933. Soon after Hitler came to power they were expelled and brought back to their families in the Soviet Union with some understanding of what Nazism portended for Jews. Some Soviet Jews had also seen the film *Professor Mamlock*, and were aware that the Nazi invasion would be a catastrophe for Jews. Most, however, were completely unaware.

5. Report enclosed in *Reichskommissar Ostland to Generalkommissar White Russia*, August 4, 1941. Quoted in Hilberg, op. cit., p. 207.

6. Dov Levin, "The Attitude of the Soviet Union to the Rescue of the Jews,"

in *Rescue Attempts during the Holocaust; Proceedings of the Second Yad Vashem International Conference,* Jerusalem, April 8–11, 1974. Jerusalem, Yad Vashem, 1977, p. 226.

7. Ibid. A survivor from Soviet-annexed Poland has described the situation in Kovel (Kowle), Volynhia, where he was a school inspector at the time of the Nazi invasion. On June 23, the evacuation of families of Soviet military and civilian officials began. Very few of the teachers who were natives of Kovel wanted to leave and the head of the Jewish orphanage was utterly opposed to the evacuation of the orphans, arguing that "she remembered the Germans during World War I. . . . Similar illusions were widespread." After a time, the children were forcibly evacuated, but the head and most of the staff stayed behind. Contrary to statements attributed to some that Kalinin issued an order evacuating Jews as a first priority, Michael Mirsky, the survivor, denies that such an order was ever given. He explains the survival of Polish and Soviet Jews "not as a result of a definite, special action on the part of the Soviet government to save them, but rather as a consequence of a general policy." He further states that, like other *zapadniki* (Westerners), western peoples originally from Poland and the western Ukraine and Belorussia who were evacuated, "were discriminated against and refused admission into the ranks of the Red Army in accordance with a special order from the highest military command, and were transferred to the so-called *Trudfront* or workfront in the hinterland. Michael Mirski, "Soviet Evacuations in World War II," *Jewish Currents,* July–August, 1980, pp. 15–17.

8. Ibid., p. 235 and E. Kulisher, *The Displacement of Populations in Europe.* Montreal, International Labor Office, 1943, p. 53. See also M. Minski, op. cit., p. 16.

9. *Einikayt,* October 15, 1942 and September 13, 1945.

10. *Jewish Chronicle,* April 17, 1942, cited by Shimon Redlich, "The Jews under Soviet Rule during World War II." Doctoral dissertation, New York University, 1968, p. 41.

11. *Einikayt,* July 3, 1945, cited in ibid., p. 119.

12. Ibid., p. 120.

13. See Yehoshua A. Gilboa, *The Black Years of Soviet Jewry, 1939–1953.* Boston, Little, Brown, 1971, pp. 27–28 for a number of such publications.

14. Ben-Cion Pinchuk, "Soviet Media on the Fate of Jews", *Yad Vashem Studies,* Vol. XI, 1976, pp. 230–33. Laqueur concludes that "little would be gained if the Soviet Union publicized this fact [the murder of Jews]. For the murder of Jews may well have been quite popular in some sections of the population: Ukrainians, Lithuanians, and Latvians had played a prominent part in the massacres. If the German invaders . . . rapidly became unpopular in the occupied areas, it was not because of their behavior towards the Jews." Walter Laqueur, op. cit., p. 71.

15. William W. Orbach, "The Destruction of the Jews in the Nazi-Occupied Territories of the USSR," *Soviet Jewish Affairs,* Vol. 6, No. 2, 1976, p. 15.

16. *The Black Book: The Nazi Crime Against the Jewish People.* New York, Duell, Sloan, and Pearce, 1946, p. 363.

17. Orbach, op. cit., p. 18.

18. Ibid., p. 16.

19. Nora Levin, op. cit., pp. 241–44, 258.

20. William Korey, "Babi Yar Remembered," *Midstream*, March 1969, p. 26. A list of the names of 2,000 victims, photographs, and memoirs written by relatives and friends of the victims have been assembled in Joseph Vinocur, Shimon Kipnis, and Nora Levin, eds., *The Babi Yar Book of Remembrance.* Philadelphia Committee for the Babi Yar Book of Remembrance, 1983. The text is in Russian, Yiddish, and English.

21. Quoted in Korey, op. cit., p. 26.

22. Kuznetsov's book was first published in a three-part serialization in *Yunost,* a "liberal" literary journal, beginning August 1966. He had experienced Nazi rule as a child in Kiev and accumulated a thick notebook on Babi Yar filled with clippings, documents, and eyewitness accounts. The first edition was published in 1967 and was heavily censored; the second version appeared in 1970 after the author had defected to England and contains new material and the uncensored sections. A reprint of the 1970 edition was published by Bentley in London in 1979. Kuznetsov's name was changed to A. Anatoli in England.

23. Nora Levin, op. cit., pp. 256–57.

24. Ibid., p. 572.

25. *Contemporary Jewish Record,* February 1942, p. 93. Hilberg reports the figure of 19,000. Hilberg, op. cit., p. 201.

26. Hilberg, op. cit., p. 493.

27. Ibid.

28. Nora Levin, op. cit., pp. 575–76. See Julius S. Fisher, *Transnistria: The Forgotten Cemetery.* New York, A. S. Barnes, 1969, for a full account of the camp. There is also an excellent study in Yiddish by Joseph Shechtman, "Transnistria," *YIVO Bleter,* Vol. XXXVII, YIVO-Yiddish Scientific Institute, 1953, pp. 37–57.

29. Hilberg, op. cit., p. 494.

30. These camp ghettos are described in Orbach, op. cit.; in Martin Gilbert, *The Holocaust,* op. cit., pp. 183–84, 217, 287; and in Ehrenburg and Grossman, eds., *The Black Book,* op. cit., pp. 28, 29, 30, 183, 198, 363–64, 505.

31. Orbach, op. cit., p. 22.

32. Ibid.

33. Ibid.

34. Abba Kovner, "The Mission of the Survivors," in Yisrael Gutman, ed., *The Catastrophe of European Jewry.* Jerusalem, Yad Vashem, 1976, p. 67.

35. See "The History of the Minsk Ghetto," prepared for publication by Vasily Grossman, in Ehrenburg and Grossman, eds., *The Black Book,* op. cit., pp. 139–81.

36. Shalom Cholawsky, "The Judenrat in Minsk," in *Patterns of Jewish Leader-*

ship in Nazi Europe, 1933–1945. Proceedings of the Third Yad Vashem International Historical Conference, Jerusalem, April 1977, pp. 115–20. See also Hirsh Smoliar, Resistance in Minsk. Oakland, Judah L. Magnes Memorial Museum, 1966, for a detailed account of the resistance movement.

37. Smoliar, ibid., p. 25.

38. A. Z. Braun and Dov Levin, "Factors and Motivations in Jewish Resistance," Yad Vashem Bulletin, No. 2, 1957, p. 4. See also Dov Levin, Fighting Back: Lithuanian Jewry's Armed Resistance to the Nazis, 1941–1945, M. Kohn and D. Cohen, trs. New York, Holmes and Meier, 1985.

39. Smoliar, op. cit., pp. 65–67.

40. Yitzhak Arad, "The Judenräte in the Lithuanian Ghettoes of Kovno and Vilna," in Patterns of Jewish Leadership, op. cit., p. 93.

41. Ibid.

42. Ibid., p. 104.

43. The author has an undated memoir called "The Escape from the Ninth Fort," by Abraham Golub, which describes the escape of sixty-four Jewish prisoners from the notorious Ninth Fort, where 25,000 Jews from Kovno and 20,000 others were tortured and executed. The breakout was led by a Captain Vassilienko, a Russian Jewish prisoner of war.

44. Shmuel Kaczerginski's Khurban Vilne. New York, CYCO Publishing, 1947, describes the destruction of the Vilna Ghetto. The resistance efforts of the FPO are described in a number of books, including Abraham H. Foxman, "The Resistance Movement of the Vilna Ghetto," in Yuri Suhl, ed. and tr., They Fought Back: The Story of the Jewish Resistance in Nazi Europe. New York, Schocken, 1967, pp. 148–59; Meyer Barkai, ed., The Fighting Ghettos. Philadelphia, Lippincott, 1962; and Reuben Ainsztein, Jewish Resistance in Nazi-Occupied Europe. New York, Harper and Row, 1974. A great deal of documentary material on the United Partisan Organization in Vilna can be found in Isaac Kowalski, A Secret Press in Nazi Europe: The Story of a Jewish United Partisan Organization, rev. ed. New York, Jewish Combatants House, 1978.

45. Chowalsky, op. cit., p. 115. Also mentioned by Isaiah Trunk in his Jewish Responses to Nazi Persecution: Collective and Individual Behavior in Extremis. New York, Stein and Day, 1982, p. 38. See Chapter 34, Note 77 for Latvian aid in Kaunas.

46. American Jewish Yearbook, Vol. 43, 1941–42, p. 320.

47. Ibid., p. 321.

48. Ibid. Before the German attack on Russia, Germans began recruiting young Ukrainians and forming so-called "labor divisions" where they received full military training. After the invasion, some of these formations, "Roland" and "Nachtigall," were sent to fight partisans in the White Russian forests, and many Ukrainian organizations, especially police formations and the Ukrainian SS units, were involved in mass executions of Jews. See Phillip Friedman, "Ukrainian-Jewish Relations during the Nazi Occupation," in his Roads to Extinction: Essays on the Holocaust, by Ada June Friedman, ed. Philadelphia, Jewish Publication Society of America, 1980, pp. 176–208.

49. John A. Armstrong, ed., *Soviet Partisans in World War II*. Madison, University of Wisconsin Press, 1964, p. 668. Trunk, op. cit., pp. 38–40; Gilbert, op. cit., passim; and Friedman, op. cit., passim, describe similar episodes.

50. Armstrong, ed., op. cit., p. 668.

51. "Why Are there No Jews at the Front?" Speech delivered at the second meeting of the JAC in Moscow, February 20, 1943. Published originally in *Einikayt* and translated in *Davar*, May 21, 1943. English translation included in "Memo to Dr. Wise, Dr. Goldmann, Dr. Kubowitzki, et al. from Dr. Robinson," June 30, 1943. World Jewish Congress Archives, New York.

52. Friedman, op. cit., pp. 179–80.

53. Ibid., p. 184. Friedman also noted a "dearth of data from non-Jewish sources." Ibid.

54. Ibid., p. 186.

55. Orbach, op. cit., p. 64.

56. Kovner, op. cit., p. 676. The absence of help is also marked in the taped testimony of Rachel Lieberman, who was a child in the Minsk Ghetto for three years. Interview by Lenora Berson, April 1983. Gratz College Holocaust Oral History Archive, Philadelphia. On the other hand, the survival of a Jewish couple and three friends who escaped from the Minsk Ghetto and hid in a nearby village protected by a peasant, torn between fear and greed, is described in Leyb Rochman, *The Pit and the Trap*. New York, Holocaust Library, 1986.

   Among the Jewish writers, in Pinkus' view, Grossman observed that generally only a minority collaborated with the enemy but Saava Golovanivsky, the poet, found the local population guilty of "gross apathy" as the Jews were lead to slaughter in his poem "Abraham." On the other hand, Boris Gorbatov in *The Undefeated*, described acts of heroism by the Russian population to aid Jews. In 1946–47, non-Jewish writers, such as P. Vershigora, V. Nekrasov, Fadeyev, I. Kozlov, and Tatyana Valednitskaya "stressed the fact that those who collaborated with the Nazis were a small group. . . . The majority of the population was moved by the tragedy of its Jewish neighbors but lacked the means to save them." Benjamin Pinkus, *The Soviet Government and the Jews, 1948–1967: A Documented Study*. Cambridge, Cambridge University Press, 1984, pp. 387–88.

57. Ilya Ehrenburg, *Merder fun felker* (2d collection). Moscow, Der Emes Publishing House, 1945. (The first collection appeared in 1944.) Ehrenburg and Grossman, eds. *The Black Book*, op. cit., pp. 355–82.

58. *Einikayt*, June 25, 1943, quoted by Redlich, dissertation, op. cit., p. 125.

59. Gilboa, op. cit., p. 8.

60. *Einikayt*, November 25, 1943 and December 2, 1943, cited in ibid, p. 354, note 21. See also Orbach, op. cit., note 78, p. 31.

61. Solomon M. Schwarz, "The New Anti-Semitism of the Soviet Union," *Commentary*, June 1949, p. 542.

62. Orbach, op. cit., pp. 25–26; Ehrenburg and Grossman, eds., *The Black Book*, op. cit., passim; and Trunk, op. cit., passim.

63. Ibid., p. 26.

64. Moshe Kaganovich, *Der idisher ontayl in der partizaner-bavegung fun Sovet-Rusland*. Rome, Central Historical Commission of the Partisan Federation PAKHAKH in Italy, 1948, p. 165.

65. The literature on Jews in partisan units is considerable. Besides Kaganovich, ibid., there is his massive two-volume work, *Di milkhome fun di yidishe partizaner in mizrakh—eyrope*, 2 vols. Buenos Aires, Central Union of Polish Jews in Argentina, 1956. In English, there are numerous accounts of Jewish partisan activity in Ainsztein, op. cit.; in Suhl, op. cit.; and *Jewish Resistance During the Holocaust. Proceedings of the Conference on Manifestations of Jewish Resistance*, Jerusalem, April 7–11, 1968. Jerusalem, Yad Vashem, 1970, passim. See also Jack Nusan Porter, ed., *Jewish Partisans: A Documentary of Jewish Resistance in the Soviet Union during World War II*, 2 vols. Washington, D.C., University Press of America, 1982. (See Chapter 19, note 21 for information about the origin of this work.)

In Hebrew, there is a collection of memoirs of Jewish partisans in the Soviet Union during the war written by non-Jews (from which Vol. 1 of the Porter work was translated): Benjamin West, ed., *Heym Hayu Rabim: Partizaner Yehudim B'brit Hamoatsot B'milkhemet-Haolam*. Tel Aviv, Labor Archives Press, 1968. There is also a great deal of material (in Yiddish and Hebrew) on Jews who fought in the partisan movements in eastern Poland, Belorussia, Lithuania, the western Ukraine, and the USSR in the so-called "Memorial" or "Yiskor Books." See Abraham Wein, " 'Memorial Books' as a Source for Research into the History of Jewish Communities in Europe," *Yad Vashem Studies*, Vol. IX, 1973, pp. 269, 271, 272, 277–79, 318–21.

Additional references are cited in Chapter 19, note 18.

19. Jewish War Losses, Traumas, and Ominous Signs, 1944–1946

1. Shimon Kipnis, "A kristal vaz funm erd fun Babi Yar," *Fraye naye prese* (Paris), September 29, 1973.

2. Jewish Black Book Committee, *The Black Book: The Nazi Crime against the Jewish People*. New York, Duell, Sloan, and Pearce, 1946, p. 69.

3. Ibid. pp. 133–34.

4. Ruth Turkow-Kaminska, *I Don't Want to Be Brave Anymore*. Washington, D.C., New Republic Books, 1978, p. 70.

5. *Contemporary Jewish Record*, December 1944, p. 639.

6. *Information Bulletin*, Embassy of the USSR, Washington, D.C., January 12, 1942.

7. *Soviet Government Statements on Nazi Atrocities*, Embassy of the USSR, London, 1946, p. 258.

8. *Soviet War News*, Embassy of the USSR, London, May 7, 1942.

Walter Laqueur also documents the paucity of Soviet reports in *The Terrible Secret: Suppression of the Truth about Hitler's "Final Solution."* Boston, Little, Brown, 1980. In discussing reports of the annihilation of the Riga

Ghetto and Lithuanian Jewry, he writes: "From Soviet sources there was very little information. A detailed report from Borisov was an exception (p. 69). Regarding Molotov's three notes (January 6, April 27, and October 14, 1942) to all governments with which the USSR had diplomatic relations, describing German atrocities, Jews are either not mentioned or mentioned together with other victims (pp. 69–70). He also cites an OSS Department of Research and Analysis memorandum of December 12, 1943, entitled "Gaps in the Moscow Statement of Atrocities [in the Ukraine]" which stressed that "non-Aryans" were not mentioned (p. 69, note). However, on December 19, 1942, the Soviet Foreign Ministry Information Bureau distributed a short document (reproduced in *Pravda* and *Izvestiya* on the same date), referring to the Nazi plan to concentrate millions of Jews from all parts of Europe "for the purpose of murdering them" (p. 70). See note 9. This was published eighteen months after the invasion and after the start of the Einsatzgruppen massacres.

Schwarz mentions a leaflet (in the YIVO Archives) issued by a strongly nationalist Lithuanian group and captured by the Germans in January 1942, protesting against the use of Lithuanian auxiliary police detachments to murder Jews, but he adds, "it is significant that no such documents issued by the far more numerous pro-Soviet or Soviet-inspired groups came into the possession of the Germans," with one exception: a declaration of the "League for the Liberation of Lithuania" (June 1, 1943) urging Lithuanian police and soldiers to resist German attempts to enlist them in the extermination of Jews and other peoples. S. M. Schwarz, *The Jews in the Soviet Union.* Syracuse, Syracuse University Press, 1951, pp. 319, 320, 332 note 25.

9. *Soviet Government Statements on Nazi Atrocities*, op. cit., pp. 57–62.
10. *Contemporary Jewish Record*, December 1943, p. 654.
11. *Contemporary Jewish Record*, August 1944, p. 416.
12. *Documenty Obvinyayut: Sbornik dokumentov* (The Documents Accuse: Collections of Documents), Vol. 1. Moscow, Gospolitizdat, 1943, pp. 140–46, and Vol. 2. Moscow, Gospolitizdat, 1945, pp. 160, 292. Cited in Shimon Redlich, "The Jews under Soviet Rule during World War II." Doctoral dissertation, New York University, 1968, p. 123. B. Pinkus also adds pp. 17, 23, 140–43, 151 to Vol. 2 references. See full citation in this chapter, note 14. See also Joseph Guri, "The Jewish Holocaust in Soviet Writings," *Yad Vashem Bulletin*, No. 18, April 1966, p. 4.
13. Guri, op. cit. There were a few exceptions, as reported by the *American Jewish Yearbook*. For example, in September 1943, the Russian press featured the heroism of a Captain Moishe Landsun, commander of an artillery unit which destroyed fourteen tanks and fifty-one cannons, and annihilated more than 1,700 Germans. In October the story was told of a Sarah Maisel, a twenty-three-year-old Jewish girl who saved Russian units from destruction by maintaining telegraph contact where she worked at great risk; of a nurse who dropped with Red parachutists behind German lines, and of Jewish heroes in embattled Stalingrad. *American Jewish Yearbook*, Vol. 45, 1943, p. 302.

14. For an analysis of the works of non-Jewish writers that deal with the Holocaust in the field of belles-lettres, during and after the war, see Benjamin Pinkus, *The Soviet Government and the Jews, 1948–1967: A Documented Study*. Cambridge, Cambridge University Press, 1984, pp. 392–93, 398–401, and related notes 83–104 (pp. 553–54), and note 45 of present chapter.

15. Guri, op. cit., pp. 8–9.

16. Ibid., p. 11.

17. Dov Levin, "Jews in Soviet Lithuanian Forces in WWII: The Nationality Factor," *Soviet Jewish Affairs*, Vol. 3, No. 1, 1973, pp. 57–64.

18. Moshe Kaganovich, *Der idisher ontayl in der partizaner-bavegung fun Sovet-Rusland*. Rome, Central Historical Commission of the Partisan Federation PAKHAKH in Italy, 1948, pp. 119, 123, 125. Additional material in English on Jewish partisan activity in the Soviet Union may be found in Reuben Ainsztein, *Jewish Resistance in Nazi-Occupied Eastern Europe*. New York, Harper and Row, 1974, pp. 353–60, 389–93; Isaac Kowalski, ed. and comp., *Anthology on Armed Jewish Resistance, 1939–1945*, 3 vols. Brooklyn, Jewish Combatants Publishers House, 1984, 1986 (a number of articles contain eyewitness or first-hand testimony); Yitzhak Arad, *The Partisan: From the Valley of Death to Mount Zion*, New York, Holocaust Library, 1979; and Nahum Kohn and Howard Roiter, *A Voice from the Forest: Memoirs of a Jewish Partisan*. New York, Holocaust Library, 1986.

19. Judd Teller, *The Kremlin, the Jews, and the Middle East*. New York, Thomas Yoseloff, 1957, pp. 69–72.

20. *Einikayt*, July 13 and August 31, 1944. Cited by Redlich, dissertation, op. cit., p. 134.

21. In describing the book, Dr. Porter wrote that the Russian work was published "at a time when anti-Semitism was being stimulated by Stalin, with Jews made to appear as dubious citizens of the state—even traitors—and often depicted as collaborators with the Nazis. Thus, the materials in this first edition were gathered by Russian-Jewish editors eager to demonstrate the involvement of Jews in the fight against fascism." The book appeared in Russian, entitled *Partizanska druzhba* (Partisan Brotherhood), very probably the last publication effort of the JAC and Der Emes Publishing House. It was prepared for printing on October 9, 1948 and a few copies apparently were distributed before the press and all other Jewish cultural institutions were closed or purged. A copy was preserved in the Lenin Library in Moscow and fifteen years later Israeli journalist Benjamin West was allowed to purchase a microfiche copy which he translated into Hebrew (*Heym Hayu Rabim: Partizaner Yehudim B'brit Hamoatsot B'milkhemet Haolam*). The English translation was made by the Magal Translation Institute, Ltd., and edited with an introduction by Jack Nusan Porter. From *Prospectus* to and Introduction, *Jewish Partisans*, Vol. 1. See Chapter 18, Note 65 for full citation.

Dr. Porter's parents were both active in a partisan group called the Kruk Division, which fought in the vicinity of Rovno and Volynhia in the western Ukraine, between 1942 and 1944. The English translation of the book is the first documentary account of the Jewish partisan movement in the Soviet Union to appear in English. Letter from Dr. Porter, November 10, 1979. A reevaluation of Jewish resistance may result from the recent recognition that the first person publically hanged by the Nazis in the USSR was the seventeen-year-old partisan Masha Bruskina—a Jewess from Minsk. *New York Times*, September 15, 1987.

22. The account is told in D. Levin, op. cit., pp. 58–60 and in David Sonin, "For Our Fathers and Mothers," *Hadassah Magazine*, February 1980, pp. 13, 35, 39.

23. According to J. Litvak, ("Hadivazya Halitait," *Gesher*, No. 2–3, 1960, pp. 95–102), in the years 1942–43, the division consisted of 15,000 soldiers, about 12,000 of whom were Jewish. Cited by Redlich, op. cit., p. 131.

24. Taped interview with Alexander Bogen (May 1982). Courtesy of Mary Costanza. See also Boris Green, "Wilejka Near Vilna," in Kowalski, ed., *Anthology*, Vol. I, op. cit., pp. 537–45.

25. Sonin, op. cit,. p. 39.

26. D. Levin, op. cit., p. 60.

27. Shimon Redlich, "Jewish Anti-Nazi Resistance in Lithuania," *Soviet Jewish Affairs*, Vol. 6, No. 1, 1976, p. 88.

28. See Reuben Ainsztein, "The War Record of Soviet Jewry," *Jewish Social Studies*, January 1966, pp. 3–24 and Joseph Guri, "Jewish Participation in the Red Army in World War II: Sources for Research," *Yad Vashem Bulletin*, No. 16, February 1965, pp. 6–13, for insight into the scale of Jewish participation and the difficulties of researching the material.

29. Ainsztein, "The War Record," op. cit., p. 7.

30. Ibid., p. 8.

31. Kantor computed the figures 160, 772, and 121, respectively, in his article "Yidn oif dem grestn un vikhtikstn front," in *Folkshtimme* (Warsaw), April 18, 1963.

32. Ainsztein, "The War Record," op. cit., p. 7. According to Ainsztein, *Pravda* did not publicize the Jewish Heroes until May 6, 1965, when it listed 107 Jews so designated. Ibid., p. 8. Redlich, in his dissertation, op. cit., p. 130, suggests that the percentage of Jews in the Soviet armed forces may have been lower than that of other nationality groups because some occupied positions in industry and lower levels of administration and were therefore not mobilized.

33. Ainsztein, op. cit., p. 8.

34. Nora Levin, *The Holocaust: The Destruction of European Jewry, 1933–1945*. New York, Schocken, 1973, p. 279.

35. Redlich, dissertation, op. cit., p. 126.

36. The Jewish Black Book Committee, *The Black Book: The Nazi Crime Against the Jewish People*, op. cit.

Philip Friedman noted that information about Soviet documentation is "very scarce," but that "an enormous number of documents, eyewitness records, and depositions of war crimes' trial defendants have been collected by the Russian War Crimes Commission and in the numerous local war crimes trials in various Russian cities. A considerable quantity of material was also stored with the Jewish Antifascist Committee in Moscow, and with the Organization Committee of the Polish Jews in Moscow. But neither of these institutions exists any longer." Information about the fate of these archives was not available to Dr. Friedman or to subsequent researchers. Philip Friedman, "European Jewish Research on the Holocaust," in Ada June Friedman, ed., *Roads to Extinction: Essays on the Holocaust.* Philadelphia, Jewish Publication Society of America, 1980, p. 501.

37. Joseph Kermish, The History of the Manuscript of *The Black Book,* in Ilya Ehrenburg and Vasily Grossman, eds., *The Black Book: The Ruthless Murder of Jews . . . During the War of 1941–1945.* Tr. from the Russian by John Glad and James S. Levine. New York, Holocaust Publications, 1981, p. xxiv.

38. The Jewish Black Book Committee, *The Black Book,* op. cit., pp. 306–14, 313–16, 324–28, 338–40, 342–43, 344–45, 346–48, 349, 352, 353–55, 355–56, 356–57, 357–58.

39. Ibid., p. 364.

40. Ibid., pp. 364–65.

41. Ibid., pp. 369–70.

42. Ibid., pp. 434–52. In early 1945, the JAC began sending abroad lists of Jewish survivors found in various towns and cities liberated by Soviet armies. Among the decimated communities were Lublin with 685 survivors; Bialystok, 113; Riga, 158; Radun, 46; Grodno, 146; Jezno, 3; and Osteryn, 1. "Memo to Dr. Wise, Dr. Goldman, Dr. Perlzweig, et al., from Chaim Finkelstein," February 5, 1945. World Jewish Congress Archives, New York.

43. Chone Shmeruk, "Yiddish Publications in the U.S.S.R. from the Late Thirties to 1948," *Yad Vashem Studies,* Vol. IV, 1960, pp. 118–20, 122, 123. Shmeruk tabulated twenty-one books and pamphlets about Jews during World War II out of seventy-nine Yiddish works published in the Soviet Union from 1941 (pre-invasion) to 1945. Ibid., p. 122.

44. Benjamin Pinkus, op. cit., 1984, p. 389.

45. Shmeruk, op. cit., p. 126. These works are listed in Avraham Ben-Yosef, "Bibliography of Yiddish Publications in the U.S.S.R. during 1941–48," *Yad Vashem Studies,* Vol. IV, 1960, pp. 145–47.

In the field of belle-lettres, some non-Jewish Soviet writers and poets dealt with the Jewish Holocaust and Jewish heroism, among them Fadeyev, Surkov, Polevoi, Simonov, Korneichuk, Vasilevskaya, Kochura, Tychna, and Mavr but it remained with the writers of Jewish origin to plumb the depths of pain and outrage: Pavel Antokolsky, Margarita Aliger, Lev Ozerov, Ehrenburg, and Markish, among others. After Zhdanov's speech of August 1946, however, the singularity of the Jewish tragedy was no longer a permitted theme. See Pinkus, op. cit., pp. 388–93 and notes 5–56, inclusive, pp. 549–52, for extended comments on Jewish and non-Jewish writers who dealt with Holocaust themes.

Gilboa mentions several stories describing tragic events suffered by Jews during the war by Der Nister: "Vidervukhs" (Regrowth) and "Flora," written in 1946, which were sent abroad and published by *Yidishe kultur,* Nos. 6 and 7, 1946, and Nos. 4, 5, 6, and 7, 1949. Gilboa, op. cit., pp. 136–39.

46. Ehrenburg pursued the issue of publication in the United States during his visit in 1946. In May he visited Albert Einstein at Princeton and showed him some of the material and photographs that had been gathered. Einstein was deeply moved and was later asked to write a preface for the projected *Black Book*, which Ehrenburg believed would appear at the end of 1948. Some of this material did appear in 1946 in an English-language volume called *The Black Book: The Nazi Crime Against the Jewish People* and its publication was marked by a mass meeting of some 15,000 people at Madison Square Garden. The American edition included parts that had been compiled and edited in Moscow but eliminated Einstein's preface out of deference to Moscow, which apparently thought it was too "Zionist." (Einstein had urged protection of national minorities within all countries, and "special consideration in the organization of peace" to the Jewish people, who had lost more proportionally than any other during the war. Palestine, he said, must now "be thrown open to Jewish immigration.")

Part of the *Black Book* was also translated into Romanian and published under the title, *Cartea Neagra, A supra uciderilor evreilor de catre fascisti germani . . . dela 1941–1945, in Uniunea Sovetica si in lagărele . . . Polonei*, Vol. I. Bucharest, Editura Institul Roman de Documentare, 1947.

47. Paul Novick, editor of *Morgen Frieheit*, saw some of these letters during a visit to Ehrenburg on November 6, 1964, described in his article "Ehrenburg un dos 'Shvarze Bukh' " in *Morgen Freiheit*, December 28, 1980.

48. Kermish, op. cit., p. xx. See also his "Tsu der geshikhte fun shvarz bukh," *Di goldene keyt*, No. 102, 1980, pp. 125–26.

49. Vilna was liberated by the Russians in the summer of 1944. After the German retreat, Ehrenburg met with a group of Jewish partisans who had survived in nearby forests and was captivated by their gallantry. He returned in 1947 and spoke at the Jewish Museum, the center of Yiddish literary culture in Vilna after the war and of hopes for a revived Jewish cultural life. Certain high-ranking Jewish army officers personally intervened with party officials and helped to establish a Jewish school and orphanage, but the official policy toward a substantial renewal was negative. See Shmerl Kaczerginski, *Tvishn hamer un serp*. Paris, Gohar, 1949, p. 74 and passim.

50. Novick, "Ehrenburg un dos 'Shvarze Bukh,' " op. cit.

51. Kermish, op. cit., p. xxi.

52. Ibid.

53. Ibid., xxiv.

54. See Chapter 20 for further details about the aborting of the Soviet edition and S. L. Schneiderman, "The Black Book of Soviet Jewry," *Midstream*, December 1981, pp. 50–60.

55. The Nazi massacres of Jews received only "fleeting mention in Soviet literature published during the war" according to Maurice Friedberg, "Jewish Themes in Soviet Russian Literature," in Lionel Kochan, ed., *The Jews in Soviet Russia since 1917*, 3d ed. Oxford, Oxford University Press, 1978, p. 207. Reuben Ainsztein concludes that Soviet war literature, while Stalin was still alive, was unable "to deal with Jewish martyrdom and heroism in the war . . . and in a manner worthy of the subject and the literary tradi-

tions established by Gorky" and others. See his "Jewish Tragedy and Heroism in Soviet War Literature," *Jewish Social Studies*, Vol. 23, No. 2, April 1961, pp. 77–78. However, in the detailed analyses made by Pinkus, op. cit., (notes 14 and 45, this chapter), there were some notable exceptions in the literature published during and immediately after the war.

Vasily Grossman's novel *Za pravoe delo* (For a Just Cause), based on his experiences as a war correspondent, was severely criticized during the Stalin terror, but was reprinted after 1953. His novel (he died in 1963), *Zhizn i sudba* (Life and Fate) written in 1960, could not be published in the Soviet Union, but some copies reached the West and were edited by Peretz Markish's son Simon and Efim Etkind and published in Lausanne by L'Age d'Homme in 1980. The work deals intensively with life in and behind the front lines in Russia in 1942–43 and includes details of Maidanek, one of the Nazi death camps, a Ukrainian ghetto (perhaps similar to the ghetto in Berdichev where Grossman's mother perished), and bitter recollections of the Stalin terror. A. Nove, "A Courageous Achievement," *Soviet Jewish Affairs*, Vol. 15, No. 2, May 1985, pp. 60–64. (The English edition was published by Collins Harvill, London, 1985.

56. Redlich, dissertation, op. cit., pp. 133–34.
57. Kaczerginski, op. cit., pp. 165ff. and Y. Granatsztein, *Ich hob gevolt lebn.* Paris, A. B. Cerata, 1950, pp. 88, 193–94.
58. Teller, op. cit., p. 69. Schwarz, op. cit., pp. 332–33, note 48, also refers to a number of affidavits of expartisans collected by the Jewish Historical Commission in Poland that corroborate Kaganovich's observations.
59. *Commentary*, February 1948, pp. 132–33.
60. *British Foreign Office Documents*, Ref. No. FO371/43406. Cited in "Documents: The Soviet Union and the Jews during World War II," annotated by Lukasz Hirszowicz, *Soviet Jewish Affairs*, Vol. 3, No. 1, 1973, p. 115.
61. The visitor was a Lt. Penn, the bilingual interpreter at Archangel. *British Foreign Office Documents*, Ref. No. FO371/43406, in op. cit.
62. Redlich, dissertation op. cit., p. 135.
63. Yehoshua A. Gilboa, *The Black Years of Soviet Jewry 1939–1953.* Boston, Little, Brown, 1971, p. 86.
64. Teller, op. cit., p. 74.
65. Taped interview with Leonid Sherman (May 2, 1981). Gratz College Holocaust Oral History Archive, Philadelphia.
66. Igor Gouzenko, *The Iron Curtain.* New York, Dutton, 1948, pp. 157–58. Gouzenko, who was on the Soviet diplomatic staff in Canada, said that in 1939 people at the Architectural Institute in Moscow were "warned" that Jews in general were in "disfavor". They were told of a "confidential" decree of the Central Committee of the All-Union Communist party setting up secret quotas of admission of Jews to educational institutions. Ibid.

It has been alleged that in 1942 Soviet authorities also disseminated a "secret" order establishing quotas for Jews in particular positions. John Armstrong, "Soviet Foreign Policy and Anti-Semitism," in Nathan Glazer, ed., *Perspectives on Soviet Jewry.* New York, Columbia, University Press, 1971, pp. 62–75.

67. Alec Nove and J. A. Newth, "The Jewish Population: Demographic Trends and Occupational Patterns," in Kochan, ed., op. cit., p. 154.

Besides the widespread anti-Semitism in the country that had developed during the war, Pinkus observed that "the local population which had cooperated with the Nazis feared that the Jews returning . . . would denounce them to the authorities . . . [and/or] demand the return of their property. And, again, those who had occupied the various posts which Jews had held before the outbreak of war—especially at institutions of higher education, art, and science—were similarly afraid of being replaced." Pinkus, op. cit., p. 85.

68. Kaczerginski, *Tvishn hamer un serp*, op. cit., p. 70.
69. Zvi Halevy, *Jewish Schools under Czars and Communism: A Struggle for Cultural Identity*. New York, Springer, 1976, pp. 268–69. Halevy notes that in a 1967 published study (Harvey Lipset, "The Status of National Minority Languages in Soviet Education," *Soviet Studies*, XIX, 1967, pp. 183–84), Soviet schools had fifty-four languages of instruction. Ibid., p. 269.
70. Based on Hirsh Smoliar, "Why Do They Hate Us?" *Jewish Currents*, July–August 1975, pp. 4–11. This material comprises two chapters of Smoliar's *Vu bistu, khaver Sidorov?* Max Rosenfeld, tr. Tel Aviv, Peretz, 1975.
71. Soon after this episode, Smoliar, who was at the time working in the editorial offices of a Belorussian periodical, met an old friend Gregory Beryozken, a scholar in Belorussian and Yiddish literature who had fought gallantly in the war, and learned that he was being sought by the police.
72. Smoliar, op. cit., p. 11.
73. Ibid.
74. Ehrenburg's disappointment refers to the continued delay and ultimte cancellation of the publication of the *Black Book* in the Soviet Union. See Chapter 20.
75. Smoliar, op. cit., p. 11.

20. Collapse of JAC Projects and Signs of the Cold War, 1944–47

1. Shimon Redlich, "The Jews under Soviet Rule during World War II." Doctoral dissertation, New York University, 1968, p. 184. A report on the third plenary session and meeting of other representatives of Soviet Jews associated with the plenary session was published under the title: *The Jewish People in Its Struggle Against Fascism* (in Russian, *Evreiskii narod v bor'be protiv fashizma*, and in Yiddish, *Dos yidishe folk in zayn amf kegn fashizm*) in 1945.
2. Redlich, op. cit., pp. 184–86.
3. A. Sutzkever, "Mit Shloyme Mikhoels," *Di goldene keyt*, Vol. 43, 1962, p. 156.
4. *Contemporary Jewish Record*, September 1944, pp. 639–40.
5. Cables dated February 4, March 27, April 25, August 23, September 22, and December 26, 1944, and February 28, 1945, from Executive Board of the World Jewish Congress to JAC. World Jewish Congress Archives, New York. See below notes 9–15, 17, 18.

6. *Contemporary Jewish Record*, April 1944, pp. 188–89.
7. Ibid., p. 189.
8. Ibid.
9. Cable from Rabbi Irving Miller to JAC, February 4, 1944. World Jewish Congress Archives, New York.
10. Ibid.
11. Cable from Goldmann/Perlzweig, September 22, 1944. World Jewish Congress Archives, New York.
12. Telegram from Nahum Goldmann, ibid.
13. Minute of conversation with Ambassador Gromyko, ibid. Letter from Goldmann to Gromyko, ibid.
14. Ibid.
15. Report on conversation with the Russian Ambassador, ibid.
16. *British Foreign Office Documents*, Ref. No. FO371/43406, Enclosure. Cited in "Documents: The Soviet Union and the Jews During World War II," annotated by Lukasz Hirszowicz, *Soviet Jewish Affairs*, Vol. 3, No. 1, 1973, pp. 116–17.
17. "Memo to Dr. Wise, Dr. Goldmann, Dr. Perlzweig, et al. from Chaim Finkelstein," February 5, 1945. World Jewish Congress Archives, New York.
18. Cables dated May 14, 1945, from JAC to World Jewish Congress, ibid.
19. Yitzhak Rosenberg, "Meetings with Soviet Jewish Leaders, 1944–45," *Soviet Jewish Affairs*, Vol. 3, No. 1, 1973, p. 65.
20. Ibid.
21. Ibid.
22. Ibid.
23. Ibid., p. 67.
24. Ibid., p. 68.
25. Ibid., note 12, p. 70.
26. Ibid., p. 69.
27. Ibid., p. 70.
28. Quoted in Yehoshua A. Gilboa, *The Black Years of Soviet Jewry, 1939–1953*. Boston, Little Brown, 1971, p. 236.
29. Ibid., p. 237.
30. Joseph Rubinstein, *Megilas Russland*. New York, CYCO, 1960, pp. 215–17. This meeting is also mentioned in Israel Emiot, *The Birobidzhan Affair*. Philadelphia, Jewish Publication Society of America, 1981, p. 3, according to whom there was a revival of the "old debate"—Birobidzhan or the Crimea. Israel Goldmacher, Leah Lishniansky, and Shlomo Kushner came as delegates from Birobidzhan. See also Redlich, *Propaganda and Nationalism in Wartime Russia: The Jewish Antifascist Committee in the USSR, 1941–1948*, East European Monographs No. CVIII. Boulder, Colo., East European Quarterly, 1982, pp. 53–57.
31. A. Sutzkever, "Ilya Ehrenburg: A kapitel zikhronos fun di yorn 1944–1964," *Di goldene keyt*, No. 61, 1967, p. 32.
32. Quoted in Gilboa, op. cit., p. 239.
33. Redlich, *Propaganda and Nationalism*, op. cit., pp. 54, 55.
34. Ibid., pp. 55, 56.

35. Esther Markish, *The Long Return*. New York, Ballantine, 1978, p. 143.
36. The journalist was Menachem Flakser. Gilboa, op. cit., p. 240.
37. Boris Smolar, *Soviet Jewry Today and Tomorrow*. New York, Macmillan, 1971, p. 98.
38. From "History of the Manuscript of *The Black Book*," by Joseph Kermish, in I. Ehrenburg and V. Grossman, *The Black Book: The Ruthless Murder of Jews by German-Fascist Invaders Throughout the Temporarily Occupied Regions of the Soviet Union and in the Death Camps of Poland during the War of 1941–1945*. New York, Holocaust Publications, 1981, p. xxii.
39. Ibid., p. xxiii.
40. However, nothing appeared in Palestine or Israel for many years, much to the mystification of many people. Mr. Shlomo Tzirulnikov, a member of the Friendship League with the Soviet Union, who had gone to Palestine in 1928, has explained the urgency of the JAC messages and time lapse before anything was published in Palestine:

> During the visit of the first Soviet delegation which came from Ankara in 1942, we reached an agreement which was not to be publicized . . . concerning the creation of a Publishing Society which would allow us to maintain direct contacts with the Jewish Anti-Fascist Committee in Moscow. Since that time I had systematic contacts with the Moscow Committee and received from them regularly material in Yiddish and sometimes Hebrew (works of Hebrew poets who could not be published in the Soviet Union).
>
> When rumors started about the pogrom in Kiev after the liberation of this city, I sent them a cable and received an appeasing answer. At the same time, I have never had information about the internal discussions within the Committee and have no knowledge about it. I received the material on the "Black Book" from the J.A.C. with the request to do everything in my power to have it translated into Hebrew and published here, as urgently as possible.

Letter to the author from Shlomo Tzirulnikov, December 7, 1981.
41. Ehrenburg continued to do everything in his power to have the work published, but wrote: "When the Jewish Anti-Fascist Committee was shut down at the end of 1948, the book was destroyed." Quoted in Kermish, op. cit., p. xxiii.

In Palestine, according to Tzirulnikov, "when we heard that the publication of this book was stopped in Moscow, we stopped the translation work in Eretz Israel." Included in the version that had been sent to Palestine were accounts of the murder of Jews that had been assembled to the end of 1944, the defeat of the Nazis in May 1945, and the Nuremburg trials in 1945. Letter from Tzirulnikov, op. cit.

According to S. L. Shneiderman, Tzirulnikov gave the manuscript to Yad Vashem in 1965. Some scholars in Israel apparently opposed the publication of the book on the grounds that "very little was new." Others disliked Ehrenburg. Still others in the Israeli Foreign Ministry apparently believed that such a book, in Hebrew, might have an "adverse effect on Soviet-Israeli relations." When Soviet Jewish researchers began coming to Israel in the early 1970s, there was a hue and cry raised against these rationalizations and work on translating and editing was finally resumed. See S. L. Shneiderman, "The Black Book of Soviet Jewry," *Midstream*, December 1981, p. 52.

42. Paul Novick, "Ehrenburg un dos 'Shvarze Bukh,' " *Morgen Freiheit*, December 28, 1980.

43. Shneiderman, op. cit,. p. 50.

44. Ben Zion Goldberg, *The Jewish Problem in the Soviet Union*. New York, Crown, 1961, p. 59.

45. Ibid.

46. Conversation with Shimon Kipnis (June 1980) in Philadelphia.

47. Goldberg, op. cit., p. 67.

48. Ibid.

49. Ibid., pp. 80–81.

50. Ibid., p. 84.

51. Ibid., p. 86.

52. Paul Novick, the editor of the pro-Communist *Morgen Freiheit*, also visited the Soviet Union about this time and met with key Jewish writers and Communist officials. During his visit to the Ukrainian Academy of Science, he met with heads of the divisions of Yiddish language, literature, and folklore. One evening together with Hofshteyn, Oyslander, singers, and folkore specialists, they discussed two expeditions that had been made to the Ukraine to collect ghetto songs and stories. Over 7,000 songs were already collected in the archive prior to the war and several books of songs were printed. In 1944 an expedition had gone to Czernowitz in Transnistria to collect camp songs and brought back seventy. Two were played for Novick, which "tore his heart." Little girls sang "I'm leaving my mother's heart" at a camp called Karlovka. Many stories were collected in Bershad and Chistopol about nearby concentration camps. Writers were planning to write the history of Babi Yar and to write monographs on various towns in the Ukraine. Paul Novick, *Eyrope tvishn milkhome un sholem*. New York, YKUF, 1948, pp. 268–70.

53. Goldberg, op. cit., p. 92. This was a reference to news about the Crimea.

54. Redlich, *Propaganda and Nationalism*, op. cit., p. 152.

55. Solomon M. Schwarz, *The Jews in the Soviet Union*. Syracuse, Syracuse University Press, 1951, p. 205.

56. Bernard J. Choseed, "Jews in Soviet Literature," in E. J. Simmons, ed., *Through the Glass of Soviet Literature*. New York, Columbia University Press, 1963, p. 143.

57. Franz Borkenau, "Was Malenkov Behind the Anti-Semitic Plot?" *Commentary*, May 1953, p. 439. W. Averell Harriman describes a number of earlier occasions during the war when the alliance was severely strained and Stalin's suspicions were aroused, e.g., over the frequent postponements of the opening of the second front, the suspending of Arctic convoys, and the liberation of Rome. See his *Special Envoy to Churchill and Stalin, 1941–1946*. New York, Random House, 1975, pp. 199, 213, 251.

58. Benjamin Pinkus, "Soviet Campaigns against Jewish Nationalism and Cosmopolitanism, 1946–1953," *Soviet Jewish Affairs*, Vol. 4, No. 2, 1974, p. 54.
59. Hélène Carrère d'Encausse, *Decline of an Empire: The Soviet Socialist Republics in Revolt*. New York, Newsweek Books, 1970, p. 33.
60. Ibid.
61. Quoted in ibid., p. 34.
62. Ibid., p. 35.
63. Pinkus, op. cit., p. 54.
64. Ibid., p. 71.
65. Ibid., p. 60.
66. Ibid.
67. See Mark Slonim, *Soviet Russian Literature: Writers and Problems, 1917–1977*, 2d ed. New York, Oxford University Press, 1977, pp. 305–7, 308.
68. Dina Spechler, "Zhdanovism, Eurocommunism, and the Cultural Reaction in the USSR," Research Paper No. 34, March 1979, p. 4. Hebrew University of Jerusalem, Soviet and East European Research Center.
69. Ibid., p. 161.
70. Pinkus, op. cit., p. 60.
71. Ibid., p. 61.
72. Ibid.
73. Ibid.
74. Chone Shmeruk, "Yiddish Publications in the U.S.S.R. from the Late Thirties to 1948," *Yad Vashem Studies*, Vol. IV, 1960, p. 132.
75. *Einikayt*, February 1, 1947, cited in ibid., p. 127. Yet the plans for 1949 were substantial and ambitious. See Chapter 22, note 54.
76. Shmeruk, op. cit., p. 126.
77. Ibid., p. 124.
78. Ibid., p. 129.
79. Ibid., pp. 126, 127, and Benjamin Pinkus, *The Soviet Government and the Jews: A Documented Study, 1948–1967*. Cambridge, Cambridge University Press, 1984, pp. 264–65.
80. Redlich, dissertation, op. cit., pp. 198–99.
81. Alfred A. Greenbaum, *Jewish Scholarship and Scholarly Institutions in Soviet Russia, 1918–1953*. Jerusalem, Center for Research and Documentation of East European Jewry, Hebrew University, 1978, pp. 81, 82, 83.

During his visit to Kiev in the winter of 1946, Novick (See note 52, present chapter) was deeply stirred by the cordiality of Ukrainian writers, attended several evenings of readings by Yiddish and Ukrainian poets and heard pledges of Ukrainian-Jewish friendship. He was told that the Institute (Office) of Jewish Culture of the Ukrainian Academy of Sciences was collecting documentation of the Holocaust. Later, at the end of December, in his walks through the streets of Vilna, he sensed that there would be a revival of the Yiddish theater, museum, synagogue, and a children's Yiddish school, which soldiers from the Red Army had helped to clean up so that children returning from wandering and hiding could be housed. He also met with Lithuanian writers and party officials together with the Yid-dish writers Kushnirov and Osherovich and all talked optimistically about the recovery of the museum, the school, and Jewish culture generally. However, the theme of the question of American friendship for the Soviet Union dominated. Novick, op. cit., pp. 262–63, 322–25.

82. Gleb Struve, *Soviet Russian Literature, 1917–1950*. Norman, University of Oklahoma Press, 1951, pp. 338–39.

83. Ibid., p. 339.

84. *Oktyabr*, 1947, No. 7, pp. 154–55, quoted in Pinkus, *The Soviet Government and the Jews*, op. cit., p. 153.

85. Ibid.

86. Esther Markish, op. cit., p. 137. Earlier, as Sutzkever remembered it, Markish had a premonition of dark days ahead. In recalling a meeting he had with Markish in Vilnius in 1944, Sutzkever perceived that Markish and the other Yiddish writers, "deep in their hearts . . . knew that the time did not belong to them." The political line kept shifting and "fear of an unclear tomorrow continually compelled Markish to erase the uncertain and write in a manner that would please the rulers." Markish himself seems to have had a prevision of his future arrest. See "Sutzkever on Markish's last days" (from "Perets Markish un zayn svive," *Di goldene keyt*, 1962, No. 43, pp. 36–38, 44–47), in Pinkus, *The Soviet Government and the Jews*, pp. 290–93.

87. In a book describing Soviet impressions of the Nuremburg Trial by Boris Polevoi, called *The Final Reckoning* (Moscow, Progress Publishers, 1978), Sutzkever is described as "a city of Vilnius and a poet, well known in Europe. His face, which was continuously twitching, bore the tormented expression of a martyr from an old Russian icon" (p. 159).

88. A. Sutzkever, "Mit Shloyme Mikhoels," op. cit., pp. 167–68.

89. S. Rabinovich, "In krumen shpigl," *Einikayt*, October 10, 1946; Y. Dobrushin, "Vos darfen mir bahandlen," *Einikayt*, October 12, 1946, cited in Pinkus, *The Soviet Government and the Jews*, op. cit., pp. 148–49.

90. *Einikayt*, March 20, June 10, 1947.

91. Struve, op. cit., p. 336. Similar attacks were made against Ukrainian and Belorussian writers and artists.

92. Pinkus, "Soviet Campaigns," op. cit., p. 70. It appeared in *Dos naye lebn*, May 19, 1947.

93. Quoted in Y. Gilboa, op. cit., p. 144.

94. Pinkus, "Soviet Campaigns," op. cit., p. 55.

21. Soviet Policy toward the Jewish State and Hebrew Stirrings, 1946–49

1. Yaacov Ro'i, *From Encroachment to Involvement: A Documentary Study of Soviet Policy in the Middle East, 1945–1973*. New York, Wiley, 1974, p. 37.

2. Yaacov Ro'i, *Soviet Decision-Making in Practice; The USSR and Israel, 1947–1954*. New Brunswick, N.J., Transaction Books, 1980, p. 76.

3. Quoted in Ro'i, *From Encroachment to Involvement*, op. cit., p. 38. The En-

glish text of Gromyko's speech was distributed by the press department of the Soviet Embassy in London. See the *Zionist Review*, May 23, 1947.

4. "The Gromyko Declaration," in *Commentary*, June 1947, p. 561.

5. Ro'i, *Soviet Decision-Making*, op. cit., p. 49.

6. Quoted in ibid., p. 75.

7. Ibid.,, p. 76.

8. Ro'i, *From Encroachment to Involvement*, op. cit., p. 49.

9. Avigdor Dagan, *Moscow and Jerusalem: Twenty Years of Relations between Israel and the Soviet Union*. New York, Abelard-Shuman, 1970, p. 23. In 1947 Egypt was still ruled by King Farouk, and Iraq and Jordan, by the Hashemite regimes, which were still linked to Britain.

10. An account of these deals—first with the Jewish *Yishuv* in Palestine and then with the State of Israel—is given in Arnold Krammer, *The Forgotten Friendship: Israel and the Soviet Bloc, 1947–53*. Urbana, University of Illinois Press, 1974; Leonard Slater, *The Pledge*. New York, Pocket Books, 1971; and an unpublished autobiography furnished to the author by David Ha-Cohen.

11. Y. Ro'i, "Soviet Policies and Attitudes toward Israel, 1948–1978: An Overview," *Soviet Jewish Affairs*, Vol. 8, No. 1, 1979, p. 36.

12. Ibid., p. 45.

13. Ro'i, *Soviet Decision-Making*, op. cit., p. 201.

14. Mordecai Namir, *Shelikhut B'moskva*. Tel Aviv, Am Oved, 1951, pp. 39, 71, 125–26. In 1949, a Soviet Jew told the Israel legation in Moscow that the courts were especially harsh with Jews showing any sympathy with Israel, or wanting to emigrate. Ibid., pp. 307–8. Pinkus notes that "Many immigrants who arrived in Israel in recent years were imprisoned for Zionism in this period, for example, Meir Gelfond, Vitaly Svechinsky, Mikhail Margolis." Benjamin Pinkus, *The Soviet Government and the Jews: A Documented Study*. Cambridge, Cambridge University Press, 1984, p. 506, note 5.

15. Ibid., p. 224.

16. Holocaust survivors from Hungary have told of intense interest in Palestine on the part of some Jewish soldiers in the Red Army, during the advance of the army into Hungary in 1944. Taped interview with Pearl Elfant (March 16, 1981). Gratz College Holocaust Oral History Archive, Philadelphia.

17. *Einikayt*, December 11, 1947.

18. *Einikayt*, October 6, 1948.

19. *Kol Ha-Am*, January 29, 1948, quoted in Ro'i, *Soviet Decision-Making*, op. cit., p. 186.

20. Judd Teller, *The Jews, the Kremlin and the Middle East*. New York, Thomas Yoseloff, 1957, p. 106. It is now known that at least one Evsektsiya activist, Barukh Vaisman, who worked at the Kiev Institute of Jewish Culture, also rejoiced in the creation of the Jewish state. He apparently started a diary-letter, *To My Brothers in the State of Israel* in November 1952. The manuscript, sent anonymously, reached Israel at the end of 1955 and a selection of letters was edited by B. Eliav and published in 1957 in Jerusalem. A November 1953 entry reads: "The greatest event in the history of our peo-

ple has taken place: The state of Israel has been reborn. And this great miracle has displayed new wonders from day to day. . . . The Jewish writers and the rest of those active in Jewish culture . . . have found it necessary to conceal the exultation in their hearts." Pinkus, op. cit., p. 474 note 61.

21. Golda Meir, *My Life*. New York, Putnam, 1975, pp. 246–50.
22. Ibid., p. 250.
23. Ibid., p. 251.
24. Quoted in Marie Syrkin, *Golda Meir: Israel's Leader*. New York, Putnam, 1969, p. 227.
25. Yehoshua A. Gilboa, "Hebrew Literature in the Soviet Union," typescript supplied to author, p. 288.
26. Described in ibid., pp. 288–90.
27. Ibid., pp. 323–35.
28. Published in Israel in 1966 under the title *Esh Ha-Tamid* (The Eternal Flame) by A. Tsfoni, a pseudonym.
29. *Yoman Ha-Zikhronot, 1949–1955*. Tel Aviv, Am Oved, 1976.
30. Gilboa, *Hebrew Literature*, typescript, op. cit.
31. Account based on Yehoshua A. Gilboa, "Tsvi Preygerzon—A Hebrew Writer in the USSR," *Soviet Jewish Affairs*, Vol. 7, No. 2, 1977, pp. 62–68, and Gilboa, "Hebrew Literature," typescript, op. cit.
32. Svetlana Alliluyeva, *Only One Year*. New York, Harper and Row, 1969, p. 168.
33. Ibid.
34. Ibid., p. 175.
35. Quoted in Thomas E. Sawyer, *The Jewish Minority in the Soviet Union*. Boulder, Colo., Westview Press, 1979, p. 159.
36. Bernard D. Weinryb, "Antisemitism in Soviet Russia," in Lionel Kochan, ed., *The Jews in Soviet Russia since 1917*, 3d ed. Oxford, Oxford University Press, 1978, p. 320.
37. Dagan, op. cit., p. 37.
38. Quoted in Shimon Redlich, "The Jews under Soviet Rule during World War II." Doctoral dissertation, New York University, 1968, p. 210.
39. Ro'i, *From Encroachment to Involvement*, op. cit., p. 38.
40. Ibid. In an unconfirmed aspect of Mrs. Meir's mission, Lev Navrazov stated that she "was asked by Stalin in 1948–49 to draw up a list of all those Soviet Jews who wished to volunteer to serve in the Israeli War of Independence. A Soviet-Jewish volunteer army, so to speak. Mrs. Meir complied, and Stalin duly handed the lists over to his secret police, who arrested the proposed volunteer army and sent the volunteers off to concentration camps for extermination by hunger, labor, and frost." Navrazov does not cite his source. "Notes on American Innocence," *Commentary*, August 1974, p. 39.
41. Ro'i, *Soviet Decision-Making*, op. cit., p. 204.
42. Marie Syrkin, *Golda Meir, Woman With a Cause: An Authorized Biography*. New York, Putnam, 1963, pp. 230–31.

43. Ro'i, *Soviet Decision-Making,* op. cit., p. 279.
44. Krammer, op. cit., p. 142, calls the results a "shattering failure for the USSR."
45. Ro'i, *Soviet Decision-Making,* op. cit., p. 273.
46. Ibid., pp. 214–15.
47. Dagan, op. cit., p. 41.
48. Ibid.

22. Birobidzhan Diversion and Onset of the Black Years, 1946–49

1. Yaacov Lvavi, *Ha-Hityashvut Ha-Yehudit Be-Birobidzhan.* (Jewish Settlement in Birobidzhan). Jerusalem, Historical Society of Israel, 1965, p. 68, and Shimon Redlich, "The Jews under Soviet Rule during World War II." Doctoral dissertation, New York University, 1968, p. 205.
2. Lvavi, op. cit., p. 101. Moishe Zilbershtain later reported that 3,500 orphans were actually transferred and that five orphanages were erected for them, but the superintendent of the education department in one of the orphanages said "there was no substance to these reports." He added that "many hundreds of trainees benefited from Ambijan," but only ten were Jews. Ibid.
3. In 1940, the Immigration Committee of the Soviet Nationalities was instructed to develop a comprehensive plan for settling the region and a special committee was sent there. The eventual plan called for resettling 45,000 people from Poland, Romania, and the Baltic countries. Ibid., p. 100, and *American Jewish Yearbook,* 1941–42, p. 318.
4. Lvavi, op. cit., p. 68.
5. *Einikayt,* March 21, 1946.
6. Lvavi, op. cit. p. 69.
7. Ibid., p. 70. By the end of 1947, more than 1,000 Jews had been moved from Vinnitsa province to Birobidzhan. In view of the then existing labor shortage, this shift probably reflected Jewish-Ukrainian strains and conflicts. *Commentary,* February 1948, p. 134.
8. Hayim Sloves, *Sovetishe idishe malukhishkeit.* Paris, Imprimerie S.I.P.E., 1979, p. 310.
9. Lvavi, op. cit., p. 103.
10. Ibid.
11. Solomon M. Schwarz, "Birobidzhan: An Experiment in Jewish Colonization," in Gregory Aaronson, et al., eds., *Russian Jewry 1917–1967.* New York, Thomas Yoseloff, 1969, p. 337.
12. His journey is described in *Heymland,* No. 1, October 1947, pp. 108–18.
13. Sloves, op. cit., p. 315.
14. Ibid.
15. Ibid.
16. These activities are described in Ben Zion Goldberg, *The Jewish Problem in the Soviet Union.* New York, Crown, 1961, pp. 202–4. Some writers, how-

910   22. Birobidzhan Diversion

ever, like Ehrenburg and David Zaslasky, who wrote for *Pravda*, were hostile. The sudden renewal of Birobidzhan, however, was official party policy and had to be respected. Ehrenburg apparently wanted wartime Jewish national feelings put to rest. He referred to Birobidzhan as a "new ghetto."

17. Ibid., p. 204.
18. *Einikayt*, July 22, 1948, cited in Yehoshua A. Gilboa, *The Black Years of Soviet Jewry, 1939–1953*, Boston, Little Brown, 1971, p. 193.
19. Goldberg, op. cit., p. 204.
20. Ibid., p. 205.
21. Sloves, op. cit., p. 325.
22. Ibid. Up to July 1948, 1,770 families were brought to Birobidzhan and employable adults distributed among the following categories: 830 to kolkhozes, 125 to light industry, 180 to local industry, 100 to cooperative factories, 165 to building operations, 50 to trade, 25 to railroading, 32 to health, 35 to education, and 203 to miscellaneous jobs. Lvavi, op. cit. p. 106.
23. Lvavi's figure (p. 107) is 6,326 for the period from December 1946 through September 1948.
24. *Einikayt*, October 12, 1948.
25. Esther Markish, *The Long Return*. New York, Ballatine, 1978, pp. 142–44.
26. "A yor fun rumfule tsign," *Einikayt*, January 1, 1948.
27. Markish, op. cit., pp. 144–45. He was "chief *Einikayt* commentator on Jewish affairs abroad," and "throughout 1947 and 1948 *Einikayt* published criticism and attacks in accordance with Party directives." Moreover, Feffer denied an all-encompassing Jewish unity principle and "never approved of any kind of 'unity' 'if it was not based on a positive attitude toward the Soviet Union.' " See Redlich, *Propaganda and Nationalism in Wartime Russia: The Jewish Antifascist Committee in the USSR, 1941–1948*. East European Monographs No. CVIII. Boulder, Colo., *East European Quarterly*, 1982, p. 160. Feffer also was the chief advocate of the changing Soviet line on Yiddish writers and attacked Hofshteyn, Kipnis, and others for their strongly national Jewish themes. Ibid. Mrs. Markish wrote that Feffer "disdained neither intrigue nor denunciation to make his way to the top." *The Long Return*, op. cit., p. 140.
28. Ibid.
29. Gilboa, op. cit., p. 81. According to Mrs. Markish, (*The Long Return*, op. cit., p. 146) while Zbarsky worked on Mikhoel's crushed skull, in a backstage dressing room, her husband composed the first two quatrains of his ode "To Mikhoels—An Eternal Light at His Casket." ("Sh. Mikhoelsn—A ner tomed baym orn"). Parts 1 and 7 appeared in *Einikayt*, January 17, 1948, and Parts 1–6 in *Tog-morgen zhurnal*, March 31, 1957. In the line,

> "I want to come, Eternity, before your dishonored threshold,
> With hurt and murder-scars upon my face, . . ."

Markish understands that Mikhoels has been murdered. Quotation from C. R. Saivert and S. L. Woods, eds., *August 12, 1952: The Night of the Murdered Poets*. New York, National Conference on Soviet Jewry, 1973, p. 26.

30. Leon Leneman, *La tragedie des juifs en URSS*. Paris, Desclée de Brouwer, 1959, p. 133.
31. Sh. M. Broderzon, *Mayn laydnsveg mit Moyshe Broderzon*. Buenos Aires, Union Central Israelita Polaca en la Argentina, 1960, p. 41. Cited in Redlich, dissertation, op. cit., p. 218.
32. Ibid.
33. Gilboa, op. cit., p. 85.
34. Ibid., p. 82.
35. Ibid., p. 83.
36. Ilya Ehrenburg, "People, Years, Life," *Novy Mir*, No. 2, 1965, p. 51, quoted in ibid., p. 84. Ehrenburg also believed that Mikhoels was killed by Beria's agents.
37. Redlich, dissertation, op. cit., p. 193. See also *Commentary*, February 1948, p. 134.
38. Khaim Loytzker, "Far idisher raynkayt fun unzer literature," *Der shtern*, No. 2, 1948, pp. 105–12.
39. Described in Michael Mirski and Hirsh Smoliar, "Commemoration of the Warsaw Ghetto Uprising: Reminiscences," *Soviet Jewish Affairs*, Vol. 3, No. 1, 1973, pp. 100–101.
40. Jacob Sonntag, "Yiddish Writers and Jewish Culture: 20 Years After," *Soviet Jewish Affairs*, Vol. 2, No. 2, 1972, p. 38.
41. Ibid. Sonntag gives no specific date.
42. Ibid. Sonntag considers this article an act of great courage on Feffer's part, but this writer is more inclined to agree with Redlich who emphasizes that Feffer echoed the party line.
43. Redlich, *Propaganda and Nationalism*, op. cit., p. 165.
44. Ibid., pp. 162–63.
45. *Einikayt*, August 19, 1948, cited in ibid., p. 165. Pinkus finds that, although "the worsening attitude toward Zionism . . . began in 1946 . . . after Zhdanov's speech," there followed a period of "probing in terms of the Soviet attitude towards the *yishuv* and the Arab world," which included a brief pause "in what was essentially a permanent anti-Zionist and anti-Israel line." In analyzing the evolution of these shifts, he comments that "the first signs of an imminent change in the 'neutral' attitude towards Zionism were apparent as early as August 1948." This was in the form of a new pamphlet based on a lecture by Vladimir Lutsky, an orientalist, who had a negative view of Israel and Zionism, attacking "bourgeois Jewish nationalists" supported by England and the United States. Benjamin Pinkus, *The Soviet Government and the Jews, 1948–1967: A Documented Study*. Cambridge, Cambridge University Press, 1984, pp. 234, 235, 245, 521 note 68. Feffer's assigned role in speaking for the regime's new line is documented in ibid., pp. 234 and 518 notes 22 and 23.
46. Also translated into Yiddish in *Einikayt*, September 21 and 23, 1948 and reprinted in *Morgen Freiheit*, October 2–3, 1948.
47. Ilya Ehrenburg, *Post-War Years, 1945–1954*, Tatiana Shebunina, tr. Cleveland, World Publishing, 1967, p. 126.

48. In the memoirs noted above, Ehrenburg comments that Zionist theories "have never had any appeal for me. The State of Israel, however, exists. . . ." But the *Pravda* article was not as neutral.

49. The background of the *Pravda* article was explained by Ehrenburg to Menachem Flasker, who had translated some of Ehrenburg's works into Yiddish. Ehrenburg reminded Flasker of the atmosphere in the Soviet Union in the summer of 1948 when the article was conceived. Kaganovich and Malenkov asked him "to do something" about Soviet Jewish enthusiasm over the establishment of the State of Israel and the tumultuous welcome given to Mrs. Meir [formerly Meyerson]. They said the time had come to explain to Soviet Jews that their fate was bound up with the Soviet Union. Ehrenburg's article was the result of that conversation.

S. L. M. Shneiderman, "Ilya Ehrenburg Reconsidered," *Midstream*, October 1971, p. 53. Shneiderman believes that "directly or indirectly, Ehrenburg did permit himself to become part of the Soviet propaganda campaign directed toward the assimilation of Soviet Jewry," but that the charge of fomenting hatred against Israel is "a gross exaggeration." Nor does he accept the charge that anything in the *Pravda* article "provided the theoretical basis, the signal for the liquidation of Jewish culture." Rather, he considers it "a statement of the beliefs of an assimilated Soviet Jew who felt himself deeply rooted in Russian culture and wished to protest against a new anti-Semitic campaign whipped up under the guise of fighting 'cosmopolitans' ". Ibid., pp. 52, 53.

Shlomo Tzirulnikov, who had been actively involved in Palestine mobilizing support for the Soviet war effort and who was an important contact during the Mikhailov-Petrenko visit (see Chapter 17), has a similar opinion:

I have no first source information about the article of Ehrenburg in 1948. I can only say that from the conversations with the Soviet representatives who visited Israel, I learned that the problem of the attachment of Soviet Jews to Israel was for them a very delicate one. When they supported the creation of the State of Israel, they emphasized that the Jewish State was necessary for the Jews of the capitalist world, but not for the Jews of the Soviet Union—a homeland for all its peoples— therefore for the Jews, too.

Letter to author, December 7, 1981

When Paul Novick, editor of *Morgen Freiheit*, saw Ehrenburg in January 1959 and asked him about the article, Ehrenburg told him "that this was his last chance of publishing something in *Pravda* against anti-Semitism. Ehrenburg had his faults, he was a complicated personality, but he was most viciously slandered for a number of things and particularly for the *Pravda* article." (Letter from Novick to author, December 3, 1980.) Novick subsequently wrote a sympathetic analysis called "Ehrenburg un dos 'Shvartze Bukh' " in *Morgen Freiheit*, December 28, 1980. See also Novick's article, "Ehrenburg: Der assimilator un der yid," in *Morgen Freiheit*, January 18, 1981.

Several newspapers and journals wrote about this charge which Ehren-

burg denounced as a "calumny," based solely on the accident of his survival, with survival considered proof of his betrayal. Ehrenburg, op. cit.,
p. 133, in Pinkus, op. cit., p. 514, note 88. Ehrenburg's biographer Anatol
Goldberg admits that "a dark cloud hangs over Ehrenburg's activities" from
the time of the *Pravda* article (September 21, 1948) to 1954, and that he lied
when asked about the fate of Bergelson and Feffer at a press conference in
London in 1950, when he said that he hadn't seen them for two years, but
that "if anything unpleasant had happened to them, he surely would have
known about it." Further, that "in the early fifties, there . . . began a
period of servility [including an extravagant tribute to Stalin in January
1951], punctuated by sporadic flashes of independence." Goldberg's view
is that Ehrenburg served as a "living refutation of any charge of anti-Semitism that might be levelled against the Soviet regime . . . [and that] officially recognized writers were obliged to play a more or less disgraceful
role in some form or another." In his *Ilya Ehrenburg: Revolutionary, Novelist,
Poet, War Correspondent, Propagandist: The Extraordinary Epic of a Russian Survivor*. New York, Viking, 1984, pp. 238, 239, 240.

Even Akhmatova was reduced to writing a panegyric to Stalin in 1950.
Her son was arrested for the third time in 1949. Hoping to save him, she
wrote fifteen lyrics called *Glory and Peace*, in which grateful people proclaim
that

> Where Stalin is, there too are Freedom,
> Peace, and Earth's Grandeur.

Her attempt was in vain.

Mrs. Markish was particularly bitter about Ehrenburg since he considered himself one of Markish's genuine admirers. According to her account, she had tried to talk to him "about the rumors that connected him
with the loss of Markish and other members of the Jewish Antifascist Committee. He denied them, of course, and said that he knew nothing about
the fate of our loved ones." But Mrs. Markish believed that he "was too
intelligent not to understand the role of *shirmach* [a blind person who dis-
tracts passersby while the victim is being robbed]. *The Long Return*, op. cit.,
p. 327. (See Chapter 25 for Soviet official admission of the death, but not
murder, of the writers.)

Regarding the murder of Jewish writers in 1948–49, in 1956, a correspondent in the USSR, Bernard Turner, who had been a prisoner in the Soviet
Union, wrote an account of the piteous condition in which he found Feffer
and Bergelson in Bratsk, near Irkutsk, in March 1949. Feffer "looked haggard and dried up—skin and bones, and a bundle of nerves. He trembled
all over . . . [and] was covered with rags." Bergelson was "the old bar-
rack-sweep," who told Turner that "an ill wind was blowing from the
Kremlin and that the anti-Semitic line in the internal policy of the Soviet
Union was fully sanctioned by Stalin and the Politburo." Lozovsky had
told Bergelson that Wanda Wasilewska, member of the Supreme Soviet
and wife of the Deputy Foreign Minister A. Korneichuk, had played a great

part in the anti-Semitic policy, according to Turner. Lozovsky himself was also imprisoned, and he, Bergelson, and Feffer were tortured. As Turner reported it, Bergelson and Feffer blamed Ehrenburg for the arrest of the Jewish writers. B. Turner, "Meyn bagegenish mit Dovid Bergelson un Itsik Feffer in Sovetishn arbet-lager Bratsk," *Di goldene keyt,* No. 25, 1956, pp. 33–37. In Pinkus, op. cit., pp. 214–17.

50. There was a noticeable fear of war in the country during this period and apprehension over Stalin's rupture with Tito in June 1948. On August 22, 1949, Harrison Salisbury wrote a dispatch to the *New York Times* speculating about "security jitters." "In mid-June, several thousand persons of foreign origin were moved out of Baku and surrounding area, presumably to Central Asia and Siberia. . . . There is a report that Jews with relatives in the United States and Britain have been removed from Odessa; that persons of Greek origin have been removed from Georgia." He could find no confirmation of reports "originating apparently in Jewish circles in America . . . of large-scale Jewish transfers from White Russia." Harrison Salisbury, *Moscow Journal: The End of Stalin.* Chicago, University of Chicago Press, 1961, p. 56.

51. Shneiderman, op. cit., pp. 52–53.

52. Ehrenburg, *Post-War Years,* op. cit., p. 135.

53. Despite his luck or apparent gifts of survival, even Ehrenburg was baffled by Stalin's unpredictability. In 1948, a few months after he had completed the novel *The Storm,* Fadeyev, the chairman of the committee which awarded the Stalin Prizes, told him that Stalin wanted to know why the novel received only a second prize. When Fadeyev explained that it suffered from certain defects, for example, that there were no real heroes and that a Soviet citizen falls in love with a Frenchwoman, Stalin is alleged to have said, "But I like this French-woman, she's a nice girl." Soon afterward he decreed a ban on marriage between Soviet citizens and foreigners! "Stalin's deeds," Ehrenburg remarked, "so often contradicted his words that I ask myself whether by any chance my novel could have given him the idea of promulgating this inhumane decree." Ibid., p. 46.

54. Markish, op. cit., p. 149. The publishing plans of Der Emes Publishing House for 1949 were extremely ambitious and reveal the great hopes of Yiddish editors and editors for Jewish cultural expression, as late as midsummer 1948. Besides the prescribed works of Marx, Lenin, Engels, and Stalin, there were plans to publish the collected works of Hofshteyn, Kushnirov, and Kvitko, the great epic poem of Markish *War,* Der Nister's *Mashber Family,* new works by Bergelson, Kipnis, and Feffer, among numerous others. Many of the writers mentioned were soon to be arrested and murdered in 1952. The detailed plans were published in L. Strongin and M. Belenky, "Bafridikn dem nokhfreg afn yidishn bukh," *Einikayt,* August 10, 1948. Translated as "Publishing Plans of 'Der Emes' for 1949 (August 1948)," Pinkus, op. cit., pp. 286–88.

55. Gilboa, op. cit., p. 187.

56. Conversation with Menachem Furlander (May 1981) in Haifa.

57. Account based on Markish, *The Long Return,* op. cit., pp. 155–63.
58. In 1955 Mrs. Markish first learned that her husband had died and had never received the money.
59. Yosef Kerler, *August 12, 1952* (Yiddish). Jerusalem, Eygns Verlag, 1978, p. 102.
60. Ibid. Kerler states that Kushnirov died of a heart attack. Other sources say that he died of throat cancer.
61. Ibid., p. 42–43.
62. Ibid., p. 76.
63. Paul Robeson, Jr., "How My Father Last Met Itzik Feffer," *Jewish Currents,* November 1981, pp. 4–8.
64. The party in Leningrad, the traditional "window to the West" and, in Communist times, the center of international culture and intellectual and artistic ferment, was one of the chief victims of the 1948–49 assault. The key purges of that time are referred to as "the Leningrad case" in Soviet literature. Such a preceived threat to Stalin was punctured in the massive decimations and the sudden mysterious death on August 31, 1948, of Zhdanov, who had been head of the party in Leningrad and Kirov's successor.
65. Gilboa, op. cit., p. 189.
66. Ibid.
67. Ibid., p. 190.
68. Greenbaum notes that the only work published by the scholars in this "office" after the war was a pamphlet on Soviet Yiddish by the Jewish philologist E. Spivak, in which he bravely "does his best to break the barrier" against mentioning the specific nature of Jewish suffering, commenting, for example, that "nekomenemer" (revenge-taker) is a new word, even though Jews have "with what and from whom to take revenge." Alfred A. Greenbaum, *Jewish Scholarship and Scholarly Institutions in Soviet Russia, 1918–1953.* Jerusalem, Hebrew University Center for Research and Documentation of East European Jewry, 1978, p. 124.
69. Israel Emiot, *The Birobidzhan Affair,* tr. by Max Rosenfeld, Philadelphia, Jewish Publication Society of America, 1981, p. 34. See pp. 535–41, 559–60, 564–67 for the fate of some of these, including the writers and intellectuals who were executed on August 12, 1952.
70. Gilboa, op. cit., p. 159.
71. Benjamin Pinkus, "Soviet Campaigns Against 'Jewish Nationalism' and 'Cosmopolitanism', 1946–1953," *Bulletin on Soviet and East European Jewish Affairs,* Vol. IV, No. 2, December 1969, p. 64.
72. Ibid.
73. Ibid., p. 67. Translations of articles from *Izvestia,* February 18, 1949, on "rootless cosmopolitans," and "anti-patriotic" drama critics, described as "conspicuous followers of the Yuzovskys, and Gurviches," and a review of Aleksander Isbakh's "loathsome book" *Years of My Life,* in *Vechernaya Moskva,* March 14, 1949, appear in S. Ettinger, ed., *Anti-Semitism in the Soviet Union: Its Roots and Consequences.* Jerusalem, Hebrew University Cen-

ter for Research and Documentation of East European Jewry, 1983, pp. 205–13. Isbakh was the pseudonym of Isaac Bakhrakh. The central character's fundamental trait is shiftless cowardliness.

74. See Mark Slonim, *Soviet Russian Literature: Writers and Problems, 1917–77*, 2d ed. New York, Oxford University Press, 1977, pp. 98, 304–19.

75. Pinkus, op. cit., p. 65.

76. Ibid., p. 68.

77. Ibid.

78. Ehrenburg, *Post-War Years*, op. cit., p. 133.

79. Ibid.

80. Edward Crankshaw, *Khrushchev, A Career*. New York, Viking, 1966, pp. 236, 265.

81. Anon., "The Road Home: A Russian Jew Discovers His Identity," *Bulletin on Soviet and East European Jewish Affairs*, No. 4, December 1969, p. 74.

82. Ibid., p. 4.

83. Sloves, op. cit., pp. 320, 321, 326. In 1948, a number of foreign visitors came to the Soviet Union but were not permitted to visit Birobidzhan. Henry Wallace, for example, Roosevelt's special envoy to China, was allowed to visit such exotic places as Magadan, Yakutsk, Chita, and Novosibirsk, but could not go to Birobidzhan. The excuse was that it was too close to Manchuria and that his presence might cause an incident and thus a premature war with Japan. Lvavi, op. cit., pp. 67, 68.

84. Gilboa, op. cit., p. 194
Ber Slutsky, who had been in charge of the regional geographic museum in Birobidzhan, and was also well-known for his Yiddish translations of Russian classics and, in the United States, as the Kiev correspondent for the *Jewish Daily Forward*, was also accused of working for a foreign espionage service. He was sent to the notorious prison Alexandrovka near Irkutsk where he died in 1954, two years before his scheduled release and "rehabilitation." Emiot, op. cit., pp. 73–75.

85. Goldberg, op. cit., p. 206.

86. Zev Katz, "The Anomaly of the Jewish Autonomous Region in Birobidzhan—Some Recent Figures," *Bulletin on Soviet Jewish Affairs*, No. 2, July 1968 [Chapter V], p. 3.

87. Ibid., p. 7.

88. Hayim Maltinsky, "Der mishpat iber di Birobidzhaner in Moskva," *Yidishe Kultur*, No. 4, July–August 1980, p. 32.

89. Ibid.

90. Ibid., p. 33.

91. Ibid.

92. Ibid., p. 38.

93. Ibid.

94. Ibid., pp. 32, 33.

95. Pinkus, op. cit., p. 65.

96. Ibid.

97. The *New York Times* Moscow correspondent Harrison Salisbury wrote in

his journal entry for January 19, 1950: "There was a spate of anti-Semitism; they did use the cosmopolitanism campaign to put a crimp into most of the surviving Jewish organizations and to knock off a certain number of Jewish critics and intelligentsia. But the roots of the drive were wider and deeper than merely the Jews." Salisbury, op. cit., p. 156.

98. Gilboa, op. cit., p. 199.

23. Power Struggles, the Cold War, Trials, and Purges, 1949–52

1. Franz Borkenau, "Getting at the Facts Behind the Soviet Facade," *Commentary*, April 1954, p. 394.
2. Franz Borkenau, "Was Malenkov Behind the Anti-Semitic Plot?" *Commentary*, May 1953, p. 439.
3. Ibid.
4. Edward Crankshaw, *Khrushchev, A Career*. New York, Viking, 1966, p. 161.
5. According to Salisbury, the drive against cosmopolitanism "almost disappeared from the press" by May 1949. By this time, he noted, "all Jewish cultural institutions in the Soviet Union had been closed down and scores of leading Jewish intellectuals were being held in prison, but nothing of this was known in the diplomatic or newspaper colony in Moscow at the time." *Moscow Journal: The End of Stalin*. Chicago, University of Chicago Press, 1961, p. 29. In his April 2, 1949 dispatch to the *New York Times*, he touched on Malenkov's apparent bid for party leadership. Ibid., p. 21.
6. Ibid.
7. L. Leneman, *La tragédie des juifs en URSS*. Paris, Desclée de Brouwer, 1959, p. 113.
8. Borkenau, "Malenkov" op. cit., p. 440.
9. Crankshaw, op. cit., p. 161.
10. Borkenau, "Malenkov," op. cit., p. 442.
11. Ibid., p. 441.
12. Martin Ebon, *Malenkov: Stalin's Successor*. New York, McGraw-Hill, 1953, p. 30.
13. Ibid., p. 101.
14. Crankshaw, op. cit., p. 160.
15. Milovan Djilas, *Conversations with Stalin*. New York, Harcourt, Brace and World, 1962, p. 154.
16. Ibid.
17. Isaac Deutscher, *Russia in Transition*. New York, Coward-McCann, 1957, pp. 37, 38.
18. Arnold Krammer, *The Forgotten Friendship: Israel and the Soviet Bloc, 1947–53*. Urbana, University of Illinois Press, 1974, p. 184.
19. Peter Meyer, "The Jewish Purge in the Satellite Countries," *Commentary*, September 1952, pp. 213, 214.
20. Ibid., p. 214.
21. Ibid., p. 215.

22. Yaacov Ro'i, *From Encroachment to Involvement: A Documentary Study of Soviet Policy in the Middle East, 1945–1973.* New York, Wiley, 1974, p. 71.
23. Ibid.
24. Ibid., p. 78.
25. Ibid.
26. Avigdor Dagan, *Moscow and Jerusalem: Twenty Years of Relations between Israel and the Soviet Union.* New York, Abelard-Shuman, 1970, p. 49.
27. Ibid.
28. Ibid., p. 60.
29. Ibid.
30. Ibid., p. 65.
31. N. Kantorowitz, "Israel Through Soviet Eyes," *Jewish Frontier,* November, 1951, pp. 9–11.
32. Quoted from Eugene Loebl, *Sentenced and Tried: The Stalinist Purges in Czechoslovakia* (Maurice Michael, tr. London, Elek, 1969), in a review article by Lucjan Blit, *Bulletin on Soviet and East European Jewish Affairs,* No. 4, December 1969, p. 77.
33. Yehoshua A. Gilboa, *The Black Years of Soviet Jewry, 1933–1953.* Boston, Little, Brown, 1971, p. 258.
34. Ibid., p. 259.
35. In May 1952, the Jewish Communist leader in Romania, Ana Pauker shared Slansky's fate and many Romanian Jews as well were arrested in massive purges. See Peter Meyer, "The Jewish Purge in the Satellite Countries," *Commentary,* September 1952, pp. 212–18.
36. Ibid. and Peter Meyer, *The Jews in the Soviet Satellites.* Syracuse, Syracuse University Press, 1953, pp. 153–91.
37. Gilboa, op. cit., p. 273.
38. Ibid., p. 380 notes 16–18, p. 38.
39. Ibid., p. 279.
40. Otto Arie, "Czech Study of the Slansky Trial and Antisemitism," *Bulletin on Soviet and East European Jewish Affairs,* No. 4, December 1969, p. 61.
41. Ibid.
42. Ibid., p. 60.
43. Ibid., p. 61.
44. Artur London, *The Confession,* tr. from French by Alastair Hamilton. New York, Morrow, 1970.
45. Morris Schappes in *Jewish Currents,* April 1971, p. 24.

In April 1968, before the fall of the Dubcek regime, the Central Committee of the Czechoslovak Communist party set up a commission to reexamine the trials of the 1950s and the reasons why "every move to redress the wrongs was sidetracked long after [they] were known to have been rigged from beginning to end." The report revealed that many of the victims were Jews and that the trials "were more than a violation of the law, they inaugurated a state of misrule throughout our society," and that "legal proceedings were converted into a monstrous farce staged by the secret police" (p. 138). However, these revelations were never published in

Czechoslovakia and some of the members of the commission were expelled from the party and punished. The report was first published in Vienna in 1970. Jiri Pelikan, ed., *The Czechoslovak Political Trials, 1950–1954: The Suppressed Report of the Dubcek Government's Commission of Inquiry, 1968.* London, Macdonald, 1970. See also a critical review of the book by Otto Arie, "The Authentic Story of the Czechoslovak Trials in the 1950s," *Soviet Jewish Affairs,* Vol. 2, No. 2, 1972, pp. 114–18.

46. Quoted in Gregory Aaronson, "The Jewish Question during the Stalin Era," in Gregory Aaronson, et al., eds., *Russian Jewry, 1917–1967.* New York, Thomas Yoseloff, 1969, p. 201.

47. It should be noted, however, that after the death of Stalin, relations between Israel and the Soviet Union improved and were officially restored on July 21, 1953 (see Chapter 25) until 1967.

24. Intensified Persecution: Anti-Semitism Becomes Official Policy, 1952–54

1. Esther Markish, *The Long Return.* New York, Ballantine, 1978, p. 243.

2. Yehoshua A. Gilboa, *The Black Years of Soviet Jewry, 1939–1953.* Boston, Little Brown, 1971, p. 202.

   The prosecutor demanded prison terms of twenty-five years for all the defendants, but the final decision was referred to the Military Collegium of the Supreme Court for review and there they were condemned to death. For Mrs. Markish's efforts for many years to determine what happened to her husband, see *The Long Return,* op. cit., pp. 158–243, passim.

3. This account of Dr. Shtern's remarks appears in Markish, op. cit., pp. 243–44. In 1957, Sheine-Miriam Broderzon, the widow of the Polish Jewish writer Moshe, who died after serving in a Soviet prison camp, wrote a series of articles on the trial, which were published in Paris. According to her account, all of the accused appeared in court with signs of having been tortured. All denied the charges except one whose name she refused to disclose for the sake of relatives in Russia. In her account, the twenty-fourth figure, Zuskin was not shot, but went mad and died in a mental asylum. Mrs. Broderzon accused the Writer's Union, and particularly Konstantin Simonov, the chairman, of having cooperated with the MVD. Her articles appeared in *Unzer shtimme* (Paris), May–December 1957.

4. The randomness of arrests during this period has been noted by many victims. Like countless thousands, one survivor Yosef Kerler, a Yiddish writer, now in Israel, has no explanation to this day. He had spent his boyhood in a kolkhoz in the Crimea and joined the Communist party in 1942. He served in the Soviet army during World War II. Suddenly in 1950 he was sent to a forced labor camp and worked in a mine. "I don't know why I was arrested," he said in an interview in 1972. "There was no real reason, except for the fact that Stalin decided to liquidate Jewish culture. So they made up reasons. I was accused of disseminating propaganda harmful to the Soviet Union, and of being a bourgeois nationalist. What

this means, I don't know. . . . For me, it was easier than for many of the others in the camp. Not the work: that was hard for everybody. But the fact that I was not married . . . only my sister. . . . You see, there were no visits allowed in these camps; and letters came only twice a year. Also, you never knew what would be the end."

When he was asked about the nature of Russian anti-Semitism and the problematic of Jewish culture, he said:

In the Soviet Union, one feels this anti-Semitism every day and everywhere—in the stores, the streets, and among one's neighbors. The Russian people are filled with this disease, but what makes it all the worse is that the government encourages them. . . . And do not believe that just because a few books are published in Yiddish, the Soviets are interested in supporting Jewish culture. It is a bluff. Even the rehabilitations of some our dead literary giants means nothing in the context of Soviet society—you can rehabilitate individuals, yes, but it is quite another thing to rehabilitate a culture. This they will never do.

Michael Gorkin, "Interviews with Soviet Yiddish Writers in Israel," *Midstream*, August–September 1972, pp. 37, 38.

5. Hayim Greenberg, "What is Happening to Soviet Jewry? An Open Letter to the Soviet Ambassador to the U.S.," *Jewish Frontier*, February 1951, pp. 5–8.
6. *Jewish Daily Forward*, March 7, 1956, and Gilboa, op. cit., p. 372 note 34.
7. Gilboa, op. cit., p. 283.
8. Ibid., pp. 284–92.
9. Joseph B. Schechtman, *Star in Eclipse: Russian Jewry Revisited*. New York, Thomas Yoseloff, 1961, p. 53.
10. Ibid.
11. Milovan Djilas, *Conversations with Stalin*. New York, Harcourt, Brace and World, 1962, p. 170.
12. Gilboa, op. cit., p. 250.
13. Salo W. Baron, *The Russian Jew under Tsars and Soviets*, 2d ed. New York, Macmillan, 1976, p. 324.
14. Anon., "The Road Home: A Russian Jew Discovers His Identity," *Bulletin on Soviet and East European Jewish Affairs*, No. 4, December 1969, p. 9. Pinkus noted that the number of Jewish "scientific workers—those employed at the academic level at universities, research institutes, academies of science, and affiliated institutions—dropped from 25,125 (15.46 percent) to 24,620 (11.04 percent) by 1955. Benjamin Pinkus, *The Soviet Government and the Jews, 1948–1967: A Documented Study*. Cambridge, Cambridge University Press, 1984, p. 33.
15. Anon. "The Road Home," op. cit., p. 10.
16. Ibid.
17. Ibid.
18. Aron Katsenelenboigen, "Jews in Soviet Economic Science," *Soviet Jewish Affairs*, Vol. 11, No. 1, 1981, pp. 31–32.
19. Ibid., pp. 39–40.

20. Anon., "The Road Home," op. cit., p. 7.
21. Gilboa, op. cit., p. 252.
22. Ibid., p. 256.
23. Ibid., pp. 209, 212. Vol. 53, 2d. ed. (1958) has entries on the murdered writers.
24. Ibid., pp. 215–19. See also Baron, op. cit., pp. 275–77, 424 note 16.
25. Harrison Salisbury, *Moscow Journal: The End of Stalin.* Chicago, University of Chicago Press, 1961, pp. 254–55.
26. Gilboa, op. cit., pp. 219, 220.
27. Account based on Khaim Maltinsky, "Der mishpat iber birobidzhaner in moskva," Part 1, *Yidishe kultur,* May–June 1980, pp. 6–16.
28. In a letter from Paul Novick in *Yidishe kultur,* July–August, pp. 59–60, he takes exception to the way Maltinsky involved him in the prosecution of the Birobidzhan leaders, in ibid. Novick writes: "Even though my corrections are of negligible value compared to the shattering nightmare of . . . Maltinsky's historic report . . . nevertheless, I would like to be permitted to correct the points in the document where I am mentioned." Specifically, he denies that he was in Moscow and Minsk at the beginning of the winter of 1947; that he, in any way, aided in Maltinsky's prosecution.
29. Maltinsky, "Der mishpat iber birobidzhaner in moskva," Part 2, *Yidishe kultur,* July–August, 1980, pp. 28–38.
30. Israel Emiot, *The Birodidzhan Affair: A Yiddish Writer in Siberia,* Max Rosenfeld, tr. Philadelphia, Jewish Publication Society of America, 1981.
31. Ibid, p. 18.
32. Ibid., p. 22.
33. Ibid., pp. 23, 24.
34. Ibid., p. 48.
35. Ibid.
36. Emiot returned to Birobidzhan for a time, suffering greatly, and was finally expatriated to Poland in 1964. See also Chapter 26, note 64.
37. The Jewish doctors were Professors M. S. Vovsi, B. B. Kogan, M. B. Kogan, A. M. Grinshtein, Y. G. Etinger, and A. I. Feldman. The first official report gave the number of doctors as nine, but this was later increased to eleven, then thirteen, and finally fifteen. After Stalin's death, when the doctors were cleared and released, officials said that twelve had been rehabilitated. Throughout the pretrial propaganda, the names of the non-Jewish doctors were not revealed, but the names of the Jewish doctors were given frequently. Communiqué quoted in Isaac London, "Days of Anxiety: A Chapter in the History of Soviet Jewry," *Jewish Social Studies,* Vol. 15, 1953, p. 278.
38. Ibid., p. 277.
39. Ibid., p. 278.
40. Ibid., p. 279.
41. Ibid.
42. Ibid., pp. 279–80.
43. Gilboa, op. cit., p. 296.
44. A. Hiram, "Soviet 'Medical Murder' Trials," *Jewish Frontier,* March 1953,

pp. 14–15. This article describes several Soviet medical murder trials. One such case is described in the famous story "The Moon did Not Go Down" by Boris Pilnyak.

45. Cited in Judd Teller, *The Kremlin, the Jews, and the Middle East*. New York, Thomas Yoseloff, 1957, pp. 112–13. The widespread dismissal of doctors, even in Soviet Asia, was confirmed by Dr. Ella Torpeda, a Jewish physician in Novosibirsk during this period. Interview with Dr. Torpeda (May 1981) in Haifa.

46. *The Jewish Situation in the Soviet Sphere*. Institute of Jewish Affairs, New York, 1953.

47. Anon., "The Road Home," op. cit., p. 10.

48. Ibid., p. 12.

49. Ibid., p. 11.

50. Ibid.

51. Gilboa, op. cit., pp. 295–96.

52. Quoted in Bertram D. Wolfe, *Khrushchev and Stalin's Ghost*. New York, Praeger, 1957, pp. 202–4.

53. Hugh Trevor-Roper, "Medicine in Politics," *The American Scholar*, Winter 1981–82, pp. 32–33. Borkenau also draws the same conclusion. See his "Was Malenkov Behind the Anti-Semitic Plot?" *Commentary*, May 1953, p. 444.

54. Borkenau, ibid., p. 442. The confession to the murder of Zhdanov was also motivated by the anti-Semitic faction in the Kremlin that wanted to make a bid to the army officers protected and favored by Zhdanov. According to Borkenau's interpretation, these machinations were set in motion by Malenkov, using anti-Semitism as a political weapon to win over army support and ultimately supreme power—which he gained briefly a few months after Stalin's death. This support, he gambled, was necessary in his struggle with the Beria-Molotov faction, which was aiming to bring him down— possibly with Stalin's help. Moreover, as Stalin had raised men like Kirov and Zhdanov, only to have them murdered, so Malenkov, too, may have been Stalin's intended victim. Borkenau, ibid., p. 444.

55. Ibid.

56. Boris I. Nicolaevsky, who directed the Historico-Revolutionary Archives in Moscow from 1919 to 1921, and was a distinguished critic of Soviet Russia, also believed that Malenkov may have taken steps to hasten Stalin's death and saw the announcement of the doctors' plot as evidence of this interest. Martin Ebon, *Malenkov: Stalin's Successor*. New York, McGraw Hill, 1953, p. 103. Ebon also speculates (pp. 100–101) that "Malenkov had instigated the purges that were sweeping Communist parties in the satellite nations, with Jewish officals prominent among the accused."

57. Borkenau, op. cit., p. 444.

58. Teller, op. cit., pp. 114, 115, 116.

In the second prison memoir of Eugenia Ginzburg, a loyal Communist, who was arrested in 1937 and suffered eighteen years of prisons, camps, and exile, wrote that the "doctors' plot" even penetrated desolate Magadan:

The sequel was unlike anything Kolyma had yet experienced. It was the first time this pestilence had penetrated our distant planet. . . . Even the "cosmopolitan" campaign of '49 had somehow passed us by . . . It was only in 1953 that the administrators pulled themselves together and started to "regularize the nationality mix." The head of the Medical Administration Shcherbakov . . . rushed around the hospital courtyard as if he had suddenly gone out of his mind, exclaiming: "Isn't Gorin a Jew? Isn't Walter a Jew? Well, where are the Jews around here?"

Eugenia [Evgenia] Ginzburg, *Within the Whirlwind*, tr. by Ian Boland. New York, Harcourt Brace Jovanovich, 1980, p. 345.
59. James H. Billington, *The Icon and the Axe: An Interpretive History of Russian Culture*. New York, Vintage, 1970, p. 542.
60. Ibid.
61. Ibid.
62. Anon., "The Road Home," op. cit., p. 4.
63. Ibid.
64. Goldberg, op. cit., pp. 148–49.
65. Quoted in Thomas E. Sawyer, *The Jewish Minority in the Soviet Union*. Boulder, Colo., Westview Press, 1979, p. 100. According to A. Antonov-Ovseyenko's version, Stalin appeared at a meeting of the Politburo and said that there was a danger of pogroms, requiring protective measures, including relocation of Jews from Moscow and Leningrad to a safe place. Lists were drawn up, and in early 1953, "the MVD publishing house issued a pamphlet by Dmitry Chesnokov . . . called *Why Jews Must Be Resettled from the Industrial Regions of the Country*." He also reported that Olga Goloborodka, who worked in the Ministry of Social Security, heard at an official meeting that "there were empty buildings in Birobidzhan intended for the deported Jews." See *The Time of Stalin: Portrait of a Tyranny*. New York, Harper and Row, 1981, pp. 290, 291.
66. Taped interview with Leon Sherman (May 2, 1981). Gratz College Holocaust Oral History Archive, Philadelphia.
67. Ibid.
68. Isaac Deutscher, *Stalin: A Political Biography*, 2d ed. New York, Oxford University Press, 1967, p. 627.
69. Dr. Aron Katsenelenboigen believes that Stalin's plan to deport Soviet Jews was a gesture made to "give the people a great gift" before some large-scale action, perhaps of a military nature, and that the climactic anti-Jewish persecutions of the "Black Years" were merely more of what he started to do in the 1920s. Furthermore, Stalin's anti-Semitism in Dr. Katsenelenboigen's view, was entwined with his highly charged Russian chauvinism, which also began to be stressed in the 1920s. Taped interview (July 13, 1981), Philadelphia.

Dr. Katsenelenboigen, a Soviet-born Professor of Economics at the Universtiy of Pennsylvania, had a Jewish friend who was a professor in the Institute of National Economy in Moscow and who together with his wife shared a communal apartment with a member of the Central Committee of the party in the early fifties. The professor and his wife who were childless became very much attached to the party man's child. One day sometime in early January or February 1953, the little girl visited them and began to cry. When asked why she was crying, she said, "My father talked to my mother and told her that trains are being prepared for you. You will be going into exile." In Philadelphia, a woman who is afraid to identify herself told Dr. Katsenelenboigen that her uncle was the chief engineer in charge of building the barracks in Siberia that Jews were to be housed in. Interview, ibid.

In the more relaxed atmosphere following Khrushchev's speech at the Twentieth Party Congress, a number of Russians acknowledged that the MVD had received orders to prepare camps for 600,000 Jews in Siberia. Some Jews are known to have started packing.

70. Zeev Ben-Shlomo, "The Khrushchev Apochrypha," *Soviet Jewish Affairs*, No. 1, June 1971, p. 67.

71. Franz Borkenau, "Getting at the Facts Behind the Soviet Facade," *Commentary*, April 1954, p. 393.

25. The Heirs of Stalin, 1953–56: Restricted Thaw

1. Borkenau analyzed the feuding as follows: "While Zhdanov was alive, Beria was one of his most determined opponents, and so was Bulganin. But after he died, they both got together with Molotov, who until then had sided with Zdanov, to form a 'left' bloc in order to frustrate Malenkov's bid for supreme power." Borkenau, "Was Malenkov Behind the Anti-Semitic Plot?" *Commentary*, April 1954, p. 443. The attack on the Soviet security system after the announcement of the "doctors' plot" was thus an attack on Beria and Molotov.

2. H. Gordon Skilling, "Interest Groups and Communist Politics,: in H. Gordon Skilling and Franklyn Griffiths, eds., *Interest Groups in Soviet Politics*. Princeton, Princeton University Press, 1971, p. 8.

3. Carl Linden, ed., "Khrushchev and the Party Battle," in *Problems of Communism*, Vol. XII, No. 5 (September–October) 1963, pp. 27–35 and No. 6 (November–December) 1963, pp. 56–58.

4. Among others, Roger Pethybridge, *A Key to Soviet Politics: The Crisis of the 'Anti-Party' Group*. London, Allen and Unwin, 1962.

5. Edward Crankshaw, *Khrushchev, A Career*. New York, Viking, 1966, p. 181.

6. Ibid.

7. Zeev Ben-Shlomo, "The Khrushchev Apocrypha," *Soviet Jewish Affairs*, No. 1, June 1971, p. 63.

8. Ibid.

9. Thomas E. Sawyer, *The Jewish Minority in the Soviet Union*. Boulder Colo., Westview Press, 1979, p. 153.

10. This is quoted in Ben-Shlomo, op. cit., p. 63, from a very early Jewish samizdat document recorded in the 1950s and published anonymously later in Israel, which describes some of the interrogations of surviving Yiddish writers between 1953 and 1956, before their release. The entry referring to Beria was made in August 1956.

11. Judd Teller, *The Kremlin, the Jews, and the Middle East.* New York, Thomas Yoseloff, 1957, pp. 124, 125.

12. Basil Dmytryshyn, *USSR: A Concise History,* 3d ed. New York, Scribners, 1978, p. 266.

13. Ibid., p. 270.

14. Crankshaw, op. cit., p. 60.

15. Ibid.

16. Roman Kolkowicz, "The Military," in Skilling, *Interest Groups,* op. cit., pp. 155–56, 158.

17. Teller, op. cit., pp. 120, 121. The official announcement of the doctors' release, in the form of a communiqué from the Ministry of Internal Affairs, appeared in *Pravda,* April 4, 1953 and is reproduced in Benjamin Pinkus, *The Soviet Government and the Jews, 1948–1967: A Documented Study.* Cambridge, Cambridge University Press, 1984, pp. 21–22. Khrushchev, in his "secret speech" at the 20th party Congress, blames Beria for playing a "very base role," but accuses Stalin of setting up the "ignominious case" of the "doctors' plot". He also discusses the case in *Khrushchev Remembers: The Last Testament.* Boston, Little, Brown, 1974, pp. 283–87.

18. Teller, op. cit., p. 125.

19. Ibid., p. 126. Ryumin was the sadistic deputy minister of state security deeply implicated in the "doctors' plot".

20. Joseph B. Shechtman, *Star in Eclipse: Russian Jewry Revisited.* New York, Thomas Yoseloff, 1961, p. 43.

21. Harrison Salisbury, *To Moscow and Beyond.* New York, Harper Brothers, 1960, p. 72.

22. Ibid.

23. Peter Meyer, "Has Soviet Anti-Semitism Halted? The Record since Stalin's Death," *Commentary,* July 1954, p. 8.

24. Ibid., pp. 1–8.

25. *Neue Zürcher Zeitung,* April 27, 28, 1954, quoted in Meyer, op. cit., p. 3.

26. Walter Laqueur, "Soviet Policy and Jewish Fate," *Commentary,* October 1956, p. 303.

27. Michael Gorkin, "Interview with Soviet Yiddish Writers in Israel," *Midstream,* August–September, 1972, p. 37. The Yiddish press in Poland, which later revealed much that was happening to Jews in the Soviet Union in the period of the Black Years, did not mention the liquidation of Jewish culture there or the anti-Jewish horrors of the "doctors' plot," but published articles from the Soviet press and generally defensive material. However, after Stalin's death, there was a change. For example, a number of poems by Kvitko, one of the writers executed in 1952, and works by Soviet Jewish writers released from the camps appeared in Poland, but not until 1955.

Mordechai Altschuler, ed., *Yahadut Brit Ha-Moatsot Be-Aspaklariah Shel Itonut Yidish Be-Polin; Bibliografia, 1945–70*. (Soviet Jewry in the Mirror of the Yiddish Press in Poland; Bibliography, 1945–70) Jerusalem, Hebrew University, 1975, pp. x, xi, xii.

28. Ibid.

29. Ben Zion Goldberg, *The Jewish Problem in the Soviet Union*. New York, Crown, 1961, p. 112.

30. Ibid.

31. Ibid., pp. 112, 113.

32. Ibid., p. 113.

33. Warsaw *Folkshtimme*, April 4, 1956. Reprinted in *Morgen Freiheit*, April 11, 1956. Tr. by Max Rosenfeld in *Jewish Life*, May 1956, pp. 3–7, 8, 27.

    After Ponamorenko's threatening warnings (see Chapter 19), Smoliar, still unable or unwilling to give up his illusions about communism, decided to return to Poland, where he hoped to organize an autonomous secular Jewish life after the war. In 1946 he left for Warsaw and there carried on a losing struggle against the Communist party's liquidation of Jewish organizations and intensifying anti-Semitism. Finally, in March 1968, with both sons in prison and some 25,000 Polish Jewish survivors forced to leave Poland, Smoliar managed to get his sons released and to obtain passports. He emigrated to Israel, his sons to Western Europe. His struggle in Poland is described in his *Oyf der letzter pozitsye—mit der letzter hofenung*. Tel Aviv, Peretz, 1982.

34. *Jewish Life*, op. cit., p. 8.

35. Ibid., pp. 3–4.

36. Ibid., p. 5.

37. Ibid., pp. 6–7.

38. Ibid., p. 7.

39. *Jewish Life*, June 1956, pp. 34–37.

40. Joel Cang, *The Silent Millions: A History of the Jews in the Soviet Union*. London, Rapp and Whiting, 1969, p. 130. Cang, ibid., also mentions "documentation of the executions . . . provided by Polish citizens who had returned from the Soviet Union where they had been imprisoned together with the Jewish writers."

41. From the interview with Furtseva: T. Petran, "Why Khrushchev Spoke," *National Guardian*, June 25, 1956, quoted in Benjamin Pinkus, op. cit., pp. 58–59. Ilyichev's remarks were made in an "Interview with a Soviet Spokesman on Anti-Semitism," *National Guardian*, September 3, 1956, Pinkus, ibid., pp. 59–61.

42. Cang, op. cit., p. 132.

43. Laqueur, op. cit., pp. 303, 304, is highly critical of Western and Israeli Jews for not protesting energetically enough against the first signs of "anti-Semitic opportunism" in the Soviet Union. Both in its "treatment of Russian Jewry and . . . its hostile policy toward Israel, Moscow has been able to pull the wool over the eyes of Jews outside the Communist world."

44. Jewish Culture Congress, "Decade of Destruction," n.d., as described by

the wife of Moshe Broderzon, p. 29. This pamphlet notes that 238 Yiddish writers, 87 Jewish artists, 94 Yiddish actors, and 19 Jewish musicians disappeared (pp. 12–14).

45. Described in Esther Markish, *The Long Return*. New York, Ballantine, 1978, pp. 169–231.

46. Ibid., pp. 169–70. Ryumin, who had also helped to prepare the case against the doctors, was executed in 1953.

47. Ibid., p. 200.

48. Ibid., pp. 232–34. According to Mrs. Markish, "later evidence suggested that the letter concerned the well-known appeal, subscribed to by the poet Yevgeny Dolmatovsky . . . for the application of the death penalty against the 'Jewish doctor-assassins.' " Ibid., p. 235. This so-called "letter of the fifty-two" is also described by Teller, op. cit., pp. 118–20. In his account, based on an unverified source, Ehrenburg and Kaganovich, among others, signed the letter after police hunted them down and delivered them to the editors of *Pravda*, whose invitations they had evaded previously. According to his own memoirs, Ehrenburg first read about the "doctors' plot" in the January 13, 1953 issue of *Pravda*.

Tass reported that the nine doctors (six of whom were Jewish) had been responsible for the deaths of Zhdanov and Shcherbakov, that most of them were agents of "the international Jewish bourgeois-nationalistic organization 'Joint' who had received instructions through Doctor Shimelovich and the Jewish bourgeois nationalist Mikhoels." Everywhere people reported chaos in the hospitals; many patients regarded doctors as dangerous and refused to take medicine. Later that month, Ehrenburg was to have been awarded a prize and was asked to speak about "the criminal doctors," but he refused. Instead, at the prize-awarding ceremonies, he made a courageous reference to Beria's victims: "On this solemn and festive occasion . . . I want to pay tribute to those fighters for peace who are being persecuted, tortured, and hounded; I want to call to mind the dark night of prisons, of interrogations, of trials, and the courage of so many." Ehrenburg, *Post-War Years, 1945–1954*, tr. by Tatiana Shebunina. Cleveland, World Publishing, 1967, p. 298, 299.

49. Markish, op. cit., p. 242.

50. Ibid., p. 247.

51. Eugenia Ginzburg, *Within the Whirlwind*, tr. by Ian Boland. New York, Harcourt Brace Jovanovich, 1981, p. 385. See also ibid., pp. 354–423 for a powerfully written evocation of the experiences of prisoners after they received news of Stalin's death through the liberation and rehabilitation process. See also excerpts from prison memoirs of returnees in Stephen F. Cohen, ed., *An End to Silence: Uncensored Opinion in the Soviet Union*. New York, Norton, 1982; Varlam Shalamov, *Kolyma Tales*, John Glad, tr. New York, Norton, 1982; Aleksandr I. Solzhenitsyn, *The Gulag Archipelago, Three*, Harry Willetts, tr. New York, Harper and Row, 1978.

52. Esther Rozenthal-Shneiderman, "Jewish Communists in the USSR, 1926–1958: A Memoir," *Bulletin on Soviet and East European Jewish Affairs*, No. 5,

May 1970, pp. 58–59, Bertram Wolfe attributes the release of prisoners to the need to make up for the depleted labor force required for the Sixth Five-Year Plan. See his *Six Keys to the Soviet System.* Boston, Beacon, 1956, pp. 146–47. Documents announcing the rehabilitation of Markish (December 29, 1955), Bergelson, and Kvitko (January 24, 1956), Feffer (May 15, 1956), and Hofshteyn (August 23, 1956) may be found in Benjamin Pinkus, op. cit., pp. 293, 295.

53. Ibid., p. 60.
54. Ibid.
55. Ibid., p. 63.
56. Ibid.
57. Ilya Zilberberg, "From Russia to Israel: A Personal Case-History," *Soviet Jewish Affairs,* No. 3, May 1972, p. 49.
58. Ibid.
59. Yehoshua A. Gilboa, "Tsvi Preygerzon—A Hebrew Writer in the USSR," *Soviet Jewish Affairs,* Vol. 7, No. 2, 1977, p. 65.
60. Ibid.
61. Described in Pyotr Yakir, *A Childhood in Prison,* ed. with an intro. by Robert Conquest. New York, Coward, McCann and Geoghegan, 1973.
62. For example, Israel Emiot, *The Birobidzhan Affair,* tr. by Max Rosenfeld. Philadelphia, Jewish Publication Society, 1981. Abraham Shifrin, however, reported that in "the uprisings in Kingir, Norilsk, [and] . . . on the Vorkuta River, . . . the rebelling inmates were shot by firing squads." See his *The First Guidebook to Prisons and Concentration Camps of the Soviet Union.* New York, Bantam, 1982, p. 108.
63. Ibid., p. 135.
64. Ibid., pp. 177–79.
    Israel Emiot was the pseudonym of Israel Yanofsky-Goldwasser, a Polish-born Jewish poet who fled to Bialystok in Soviet-occupied Poland after the Nazi invasion and joined Soviet Yiddish writers there. He became an enthusiastic supporter of Soviet communism and its future promise. In 1941 he was evacuated to Alma-Ata, Kazakhstan, where he wrote reports on Jewish refugees in the Soviet Far East, published in the Moscow Yiddish press and sent abroad by the JAC. In February 1944, at a meeting of the JAC, he was persuaded to go to Birobidzhan and become a regular correspondent. When he arrived in July 1944, he found the Jewish cultural situation there "lamentable," but encouraging signs of a "revival" in the next few years. However, he was swept up in the arrests of 1948–49 and spent seven years in prison camps in Khabarovsk, Taishet, Norilsk, and Molotov. He was eligible for release under the amnesty of March 27, 1953, but was not freed until February 1956. He was repatriated to Poland, joined his wife and two children in America, and settled in Rochester, N.Y. He died in 1978. Emiot, op. cit., pp. 2–6.
65. Quoted in Goldberg, op. cit., p. 208.
66. Emiot, op. cit., p. 196.
67. Bertram D. Wolfe, "Stalinism versus Stalin: Exorcising a Stubborn Ghost," *Commentary,* June 1956, pp. 523–24.

26. "We Have No Intention of Reviving a Dead Culture": Jewish Policy under Khrushchev in the 1950s

1. *Khrushchev Remembers*, Strobe Talbott, ed. and tr. Boston, Little, Brown, 1970, pp. 347–48. For a careful analysis of the materials, sources, and authenticity of this book, about which there has been considerable controversy, see Zeev Ben-Shlomo, "The Khrushchev Apocrypha," *Soviet Jewish Affairs*, No. 1, June 1971, pp. 52–73. The author (Z. B.) considers the text to be "substantially authentic" (p. 53).

2. The speech is often referred to as "secret" but, in fact, it was reproduced in thousands of copies and read at meetings, institutes, and universities. However, it was never published in the mass media. The text of Khrushchev's speech with commentary and analysis can be found in Bertram D. Wolfe, *Khrushchev and Stalin's Ghost*. New York, Praeger, 1957. It was translated and published by the U.S. State Department, June 4, 1956. It was also published by the U.S. Congress. *Congressional Record*, 84th Congr., 2d Sess., Vol. 102, Part 7, pp. 9389–9402. The unprecedented charges against Stalin received most of the world's startled attention, but Bertram Wolfe has reminded us that "nine-tenths of the 'debates' were on how to maintain the Stalinist line of 'priority for heavy industry' and continue thereby to deprive the Russian people of even a modest reward for their unremitting toil. . . ." Similarly, the push for collectivization at the expense of small private peasant parcels of land was pressed. Larger and larger kolkhozes were planned, and most had party units. Pronouncements on an "alternative peaceful . . . road to socialism" (e.g. Czechoslovakia, Bulgaria, Romania, and the Baltic countries) meant transforming parliament "into an organ of the people's will," led by a "vanguard party, the Communist Party," and establishing "a one-party dictatorship in the name of the proletariat." (The forcible repressions in East Germany, Hungary later in 1956, and Poland showed how this neo-Stalinist policy would be implemented.) Moreover, centralized planning and ever-larger defense appropriations continued in an essentially Stalinist line. See Bertram D. Wolfe, "Stalinism versus Stalin: Exorcising a Stubborn Ghost," *Commentary*, June 1956, pp. 527, 528.

3. David K. Shipler, *Russia: Broken Idols, Solemn Dreams*. New York, Viking 1983, p. 312.

4. Esther Rozenthal-Shneiderman, "Jewish Communists in the USSR, 1926–1958: A Memoir," *Bulletin on Soviet and East European Jewish Affairs*, No. 5, May 1970, p. 57.

5. Quoted by S. H. Shneiderman in *"Sovetish Heimland* and its Editor, Aron Vergelis," *Midstream*, October 1971, p. 42.

6. Quoted in Zeev Ben-Shlomo, "The Khrushchev Apocrypha," op. cit., p. 59.

7. Edward Crankshaw, *Khrushchev, A Career*. New York, Viking, 1966.

8. Joel Cang, *The Silent Millions: A History of Jews in the Soviet Union*. London, Rapp and Whiting, 1969, pp. 122–23.

930   26. "We Have No Intention of Reviving a Dead Culture"

9. Ibid., p. 122. Regarding the mass destruction of Soviet Jews during the war, in contrast to his official silence, Khrushchev privately, after his resignation, admitted a number of times that he was aware of Nazi annihilation plans and their implementation. There is a dramatic description of the mass murder of Kiev Jews in his memoirs. *Khrushchev Remembers*, op. cit., pp. 216, 259–60.
10. Ben-Shlomo, op. cit., p. 67.
11. Ibid.
12. Ibid., p. 61.
13. Shimon Redlich, "Khrushchev and the Jews," *Jewish Social Studies*, Vol. XXIV, No. 4, October 1972, p. 352.
14. *Khrushchev Remembers*, op. cit., p. 269.
15. Ibid.
16. Bernard D. Weinryb, "The Concept of 'Anti-Semitism' and Its Meaning in Soviet Russia: A Study in Soviet Semantics," *Gratz College Annual of Jewish Studies*, I, Philadelphia, 1972, p. 92.
17. Ben-Shlomo, op. cit., p. 59. There were also interviews with Henry Shapiro, a veteran American correspondent in Moscow, in November 1957, in which Khrushchev spoke about "types without ethnic roots and ties"; and with Serge Groussard, correspondent of *Le Figaro*, in March 1958, in which he attributed the failure of Birobidzhan to Jewish "individualism," their dislike of collective work and discipline, and incapacity for a "genuine Jewish cultural . . . and political community." Benjamin Pinkus, *The Soviet Government and the Jews, 1948–1967: A Documented Study.* Cambridge, Cambridge University Press, 1984, pp. 51, 61–63, 289–90, 480 note 50.
18. Josef Cywiak, "Why the Jews left Poland," *Bulletin on Soviet and East European Jewish Affairs*, No. 5, May 1970, pp. 64–67.
19. Ibid., p. 67.
20. Anon. [Checinski], "USSR and the Politics of Polish Antisemitism, 1956–68," *Soviet Jewish Affairs*, No. 1, June 1971, p. 19.
21. Cywiak, op. cit., p. 68.
22. Ibid.
23. Quoted from *Les Réalités*, 1957, no. 136, pp. 103–4, in Pinkus, op. cit., p. 58. See ibid., pp. 54–59 for entire interview.
24. Ibid., p. 58.
25. Quoted from Roy A. Medvedev in a Moscow samizdat document, May 1970, in Thomas E. Sawyer, *The Jewish Minority in the Soviet Union.* Boulder, Colo., Westview Press, 1979, p. 160. For Jews in the party Central Committee, Supreme Soviet and other party and government structures in the middle and late 1950s, see Pinkus, op. cit., pp. 342–63.
26. Judd Teller, *The Kremlin, the Jews, and the Middle East.* New York, Thomas Yoseloff, 1957, p. 96.
27. Aron Katsenelenboigen, "Jews in Soviet Economic Science," *Soviet Jewish Affairs*, Vol. 11, no. 1, 1981, pp. 42–46.
28. Ibid., p. 48.
29. Yaacov Ro'i, *Soviet Decision-Making in Practice: The USSR and Israel, 1947–1954.* New Brunswick, N.J., Transaction Books, 1980, pp. 475–76.

30. Ibid., pp. 476, 477.
31. Avigdor Dagan, *Moscow and Jerusalem: Twenty Years of Relations between Israel and the Soviet Union*. New York, Abelard-Shuman, 1970, p. 75–76.
32. Ro'i, op. cit., p. 490.
33. Ibid.
34. Joseph B. Schechtman, *Star in Eclipse: Russian Jewry Revisited*. New York, Thomas Yoseloff, 1961, pp. 186–87.
35. Ibid., p. 188.
36. Ibid., p. 190.
37. Ibid., pp. 190, 191, 192.
38. William Korey, *The Soviet Cage: Anti-Semitism in Russia*. New York, Viking, 1973, p. 193.
39. *New York Times*, September 25, 1959.
40. Quoted in William Korey, "The 'Right to Leave' for Soviet Jews: Legal and Moral Aspects," *Soviet Jewish Affairs*, No. 1, 1971, p. 11. Schechtman, op. cit., p. 199, estimates that between July 1953 and September 1955, 125 Jews, mostly from the annexed territories, and all of them old, reached Israel. From January to April, 1956, there were 118 emigrants from various parts of the country. In 1958, 1,120 left for Israel.
41. Korey, "The 'Right to Leave,' " op. cit., p. 11.
42. Ibid.
43. *New York Times*, August 9, 1960.
44. Korey, *Soviet Cage*, op. cit., p. 193.
45. Ibid., p. 191.
46. Korey, "The 'Right to Leave,' " op. cit., p. 10.
47. Meir Gelfond, "Illegal Zionist Activity in the Soviet Union in the 1950's–1960's," in David Prital, ed., *In Search of Self: The Soviet Jewish Intelligentsia and the Exodus*. Jerusalem, Mt. Scopus Pubs., 1982, p. 39.
48. Quoted in "The Soviet Definition of Judaism," *Jewish Frontier*, November 1954, pp. 19–20.
49. Joshua Rothenberg, "Jewish Religion in the Soviet Union," in Kochan, ed., *The Jews in Soviet Russia Since 1917*, op. cit., p. 165.
50. Andrew Meisels, "The Rabbi of Minsk," *Commentary*, October 1955, pp. 353–56.
    The journalist Ben Zion Goldberg was particularly saddened by his visit to the synagogue in Kiev in 1959, where the external, well-dressed appearance of the congregants contrasted with the general tone. "The spirits were lower, and the fear greater [than in 1946]." After the service the congregants stared at him sadly and mumbled "Gut Shabbes" (A good sabbath to you) but none spoke to him. However, he found considerably less fear in the synagogues of the new territories: the Baltic republics, Moldavia, and eastern Ukraine. A determination to hold on to the old traditions was noticeable and ceremonies such as Bar Mitzvahs were still celebrated there. This was even more striking in the non-Slavic republics of Central Asia and the Caucasus where young and old filled the synagogues and all traditional customs and rituals were sustained. Ben Zion Goldberg, *The Jewish Problem in the Soviet Union*. New York, Crown, 1961, pp. 159–60.

There are numerous magazine articles describing visits to the Soviet Union in the middle and late 1950s by those who found much repression of Jews and officially sanctioned anti-Semitism, as well as articles (particularly in issues of *Jewish Life*) that are defensive of Soviet policy in Randolph L. Braham, *Jews in the Communist World: A Bibliography, 1945–1960*. New York, Twayne, 1961, pp. 33–48, 53–59.

51. Salo W. Baron, *The Russian Jew under Tsars and Soviets*, 2d ed. New York, Macmillan, 1976, p. 340.

52. Bohdan R. Bociurkiw, "Soviet Religious Policy and the Status of Judaism in the USSR," *Bulletin on Soviet and East European Jewish Affairs*, No. 6, December 1970, p. 17.

53. Kevin Devlin, "Western Communist Parties and the Soviet Jewish Question," *Bulletin on Soviet and East European Jewish Affairs*, No. 6, December 1970, p. 6. It should be noted that there are at least some legally registered synagogues, whereas Eastern Rite Catholics, Pentecostals, Jehovah's Witnesses, and some Baptist groups have no independent legal existence. In 1960, Rabbi Yehuda Levin of Moscow stated that in "private conversations" with authorities, Jewish spokesmen have "already brought up the question of creating a religious center" without success. Bociurkiw, op. cit., p. 17.

54. Sawyer, op. cit., p. 76. An even more intemperate attack on Judaism would erupt in the sixties (see Chapter 28).

55. Pinkus, op. cit., p. 96. Soviet acknowledgment appears in ibid., pp. 140–41. The leaflets contain such phrases as "Throw the Jews out of commerce, where they damage socialist property and the people's wealth. . . . Catch hold of them and pluck out their sinful deeds. . . . They can be pushed under and will crawl up; like an excrescence it will befoul the clean and pure soul of the Russian people." Ibid., pp. 139–40.

In connection with greater freedom for writers in 1956, Ehrenburg is frequently praised for making available to Soviet youth for the first time during this period, a fuller history of Russian literature in the twentieth century than had been available. See also Hugh McClean and Walter Vickery, eds., *The Year of Protest, 1956*, Westport, Conn., Greenwood, 1974.

56. Schechtman, op. cit., p. 169.

57. Ibid.

58. Solomon M. Schwarz, *The Jews in the Soviet Union*. Syracuse, Syracuse University Press, 1951, pp. 139–41.

59. Schechtman, op. cit., p. 166.

60. Quoted in ibid., p. 122. The first head was at the time the rabbi of the Moscow Synagogue, Rabbi Solomon Shlieffer, who had petitioned for a yeshivah. Rabbi Shlieffer died within a few months, and Rabbi Yehuda Leib Levin succeeded him and became head of the yeshivah.

61. Rothenberg, op. cit., pp. 185, 186, 187, 189.

62. From all evidence, the yeshivah has been closed.

63. Schechtman, op. cit., p. 137.

64. Described in Arie L. Eliav, *Between Hammer and Sickle*. New York, Signet, 1969, pp. 40–44.

65. Sloves is a Polish-born lawyer, now living in Paris. He was once a member of the Communist party, fought in the French resistance during the war, and is a playwright of some renown. For many years he was editor of *Naye prese* (Paris) and legal adviser to the Soviet Embassy in France. The manuscript from which I have quoted is called "Concerning Yiddish Culture in the Soviet Union," ("Vegn der yidisher kultur in sovetnfarband", tr. by Max Rosenfeld), p. 19–36. The paper was first circulated in manuscript form in Left Jewish circles in the United States, Europe, and South America, and stands as one of the early voices of an anguished Jew, once deeply faithful and attached to Soviet communism, shaken by the murder of Jewish culture, but still left with a fragile hope of some healing and restorative redress. (Manuscript supplied through the courtesy of Max Rosenfeld.) An expanded version of Sloves' efforts has been published in Sloves, *A shlikhes kayn moskve. Dokumentn, komentarn un intermetso—mayses.* New York YKUF, 1985, which explains that Sloves was a member of a French Communist party delegation sent to the USSR in 1958 to discuss problems affecting Soviet Jews and Jewish culture.

66. Quoted in Schechtman, op. cit., p. 178.

67. The post-Stalin policy of locking Yiddish out of Soviet culture and stressing Jewish assimilation has shifted to making original Yiddish works available in translation. (According to Soviet sources, between 1955 and 1970, 466 such books were published in fifteen Soviet languages, totaling more than 46 million copies.) Only two dozen books in Yiddish appeared between 1959 and 1970. See Sawyer, op. cit., pp. 81–82. Sholem Aleikhem has been particularly favored, but his identity is being obliterated. A plaque in front of his home in Kiev, which originally read, "Jewish writer Sholem Aleikhem lived in this house," has been changed—the word "Jewish" has been removed. A 40-kopek stamp honoring him does not identify him as a Jewish writer. However, this policy may change under Gorbachev.

    In an analysis of translations available to minority peoples, Maurice Friedberg notes that ethnic minorities such as Latvians, Lithuanians, Armenians, Georgians, and others have been supplied with translations of Russian classics and foreign literatures, but that "the most blatant case of discrimination against a particular ethnic group is, of course, that of Soviet Jews: although in the 1960 census almost a half million of them declared Yiddish to be their native tongue, *not a single* translation from any language into Yiddish appeared between 1956 and 1962, the most clearcut case of cultural discrimination encountered." See Maurice Friedberg "Literary Output: 1956–1962," in Max Hayward and Edward Crowley, eds., *Soviet Literature in the Sixties: An International Symposium.* London, Methuen, 1965, p. 167.

68. *A Decade of Destruction: Jewish Culture in the USSR, 1948–1958.* New York, Congress for Jewish Culture, 1958.

69. Ibid. In 1955, Walter Laqueur reported that the Jewish Antifascist Committee in Moscow "might be resurrected," but nothing materialized. Later, there were reports that representatives of Jewries from the satellite countries wanted to join the World Jewish Congress, but Soviet Jewry was not

included. Walter Laqueur, "Soviet Policy and Jewish Fate," *Commentary*, October 1956, p. 307.

70. Goldberg, op. cit., p. 151.
71. Ibid., pp. 154, 155.
72. Ibid., p. 156.
73. Maurice Hindus, *House Without a Roof*. New York, Doubleday, 1961, p. 321 and passim.
74. Laqueur, op. cit., p. 305.

27. The Literary "Thaw," 1956–62, and the First Jewish National Stirrings, 1958–63

1. Ernest J. Simmons, "The Writers," in H. Gordon Skilling and Franklyn Griffiths, eds., *Interest Groups in Soviet Politics*. Princeton, Princeton University Press, pp. 263–64.
2. Ibid., p. 264.
3. Mark Slonim, *Soviet Russian Literature: Writers and Problems, 1917–1977*. 2d ed. New York, Oxford University Press, 1977, p. 321.
4. Ibid., p. 324. For fuller treatment of dissident literature in the late fifties, see A. Gaev, "The Decade Since Stalin," in Max Hayward and E. L. Crowley, eds., *Soviet Literature in the Sixties*. London, Methuen, 1965, pp. 18–54.
5. Ibid., pp. 21–22.
   A remarkable document of the traumatic and divisive consequences of Khrushchev's revelations among party members of the Soviet Writers' Union who met in March 1956 appeared in Roy Medvedev's samizdat monthly *Political Diary*, in March 1967. It is a partial transcript of the discussions involving well-known authors and literary critics, some of whom were victims, others, accomplices of the terror. See Stephen F. Cohen, ed., *An End to Silence: Uncensored Opinion in the Soviet Union* from Roy Medvedev's Underground Magazine *Political Diary*. New York, Norton, 1982, pp. 105–16. For more details of the 1956 "thaw," see Hugh McClean and Walter N. Vickery, eds., *The Year of Protest, 1956: An Anthology of Soviet Literary Materials*. Westport, Conn., Greenwood, 1974; L. G. Churchward, *The Soviet Intelligentsia: An Essay on the Social Structure and Roles of Soviet Intellectuals during the 1960s*. London, Routledge, 1973; and Maurice Friedberg, "Literary Output: 1956–62," in Max Hayward and E. L. Crowley, eds., op. cit., pp. 150–77.
6. Stephen F. Cohen, "The Stalin Question since Stalin," in Stephen F. Cohen, ed., op. cit., p. 35. Between 1954 and 1956 possibly as many as eight million people returned from prison and exile, many of whom had been rearrested after having served full sentences.
7. Meir Gelfond, "Illegal Zionist Activity in the Soviet Union in the 1950's and 1960's," in David Prital, ed., *In Search of Self: The Soviet Jewish Intelligentsia and the Exodus*. Jerusalem, Mt. Scopus Publications, 1982, p. 37.
8. Ibid.
9. Ibid., p. 37–38.

10. Ibid., p. 38.
11. *Samizdat* is a Soviet term coined by post-Stalin dissidents for the old Russian revolutionary practice of circulating uncensored material privately— usually in manuscript form. (The word parodies official acronyms such as "Gosizdat,"which stands for State Publishers.) However, the practice was also used by the so-called Left Opposition in the late twenties and early thirties. Especially important in the latter literature are "Memoirs of a Bolshevik-Leninist," an anonymous account by a survivor of Stalin's camps who had been in the Left Opposition, and the "Memoirs of Aleksandra Chumakova," which became known in 1970 and was translated into English and edited by George Saunders in *Voices of the Soviet Opposition*. New York, Monad Press, 1974, pp. 61–188, 189–205. According to Zyame Telesin, a Jewish writer who emigrated to Israel in 1970, the word samizdat first occurs in the late fifties when a Moscow poet, exasperated with the operation of the censorship system, bound together typewritten sheets of his poems and wrote *Samsebiaizdat* ("Publishing House for Oneself") in the place where the name of the publisher would normally appear. See J. [Julius—anglicized from Zyame] Telesin, "Inside 'Samizdat' ", *Encounter*, Vol. 15, No. 2, 1973, pp. 25–33.
12. Ibid.
13. See, for example, Ludmilla Dymerskaia-Tsigelman, "The Ideological Motivation of Soviet Aliya" and Maia Kaganskaia, "Where is Our Promised Land," in ibid., pp. 52, 53, 184.
14. Experiences of Riga Jews based on Leonard Schrocter, *The Last Exodus*. New York, Universe Books, 1974, pp. 76–79, 62, 63, 64.
15. Ibid., p. 64.
16. Quoted from Mendel Gordin, a physician, who did not reveal his identification with the Jewish movement until 1968. Ibid., p. 75.
17. Gershon Tsitsuashvili, "We Wanted to Produce a Large Aliyah," in Prital, ed., op. cit., p. 77.
18. Ibid., pp. 78–80.
19. Recounted in Alla Rusinek, *Like a Song, Like a Dream: A Soviet Girl's Quest for Freedom*. New York, Scribners, 1973, pp. 251–56.

There is some controversy about the earliest beginnings of Jewish samizdat but often the Russian translation of Leon Uris' novel *Exodus* is mentioned by Jewish activists in the Soviet Union and emigrants to Israel as their first and most influential piece of underground literature. There are several versions of its beginnings. One involves Yaakov Sharett, son of the late prime minister of Israel, who in the summer of 1961 was employed at the Israeli embassy in Moscow and went to Riga on official business. The local KGB accused him of espionage and he was compelled to leave the city. Several weeks later he had to leave the Soviet Union altogether. At the railway station he realized that he had one English-language copy of *Exodus* in his pocket. Glancing around he noticed a man who seemed Jewish to him and he hurriedly slipped him the book. Many years later Sharett learned that this man was a Latvian Jew who gave the book to another

Jew, saying, "Listen, this is a very good book about the Jews." It was possibly from this copy that the first Russian translation of *Exodus* began its remarkable march through the Soviet Union. Based on Vladimir Lazaris, "The Saga of the Jewish Samizdat," *Soviet Jewish Affairs,* Vol. 9, No. 1, 1979, pp. 6–7, and Schroeter, op. cit., p. 65. Schroeter also recounts the story of another translation of *Exodus* from English to Russian inside the Dubrovlag concentration camp in Soviet Mordovia in 1963 by Avram Shifrin and Alexander Guzman, who translated over 600 pages in two months. The first copy was for circulation inside the camp; a second copy for outside use was made by giving trusted prisoners twenty pages each to rewrite in one day. Ibid., p. 67. Alla Rusinek's father-in-law Ezra recounts the struggle to have the manuscript typed and to buy carbon paper without being suspected. See his "The Saga of the Samizdat," *Hadassah Magazine,* December 1972, pp. 8–9.

Cecil Roth's *The History of the Jews from Ancient Times to the Six-Day War,* has also influenced a number of young Jews to become interested in the Jewish past. Irene Roth, "Cecil Roth, Russian Jews, the Holy Mountain," *Moment,* September 1978, pp. 7–8.

20. Described in David Garber, "Choir and Drama in Riga," *Soviet Jewish Affairs,* Vol. 4, No. 1, 1974, pp. 39–44.
21. Ibid., p. 44.
22. Mordecai Lapid, "The Memorial at Rumbuli: A First-Hand Account," *Jewish Frontier,* June 1971, pp. 10–19. See also D. Garber, "Rumbuli ha babi yar shel Riga," *Davar,* May 4, 1970.
23. Ibid., p. 18.
24. Schroeter, op. cit., p. 71.
25. Ibid.
26. Ibid., p. 72.
27. Quoted in Cohen, "The Stalin Question since Stalin," op. cit., p. 36.
28. Quoted in the *Manchester Guardian Weekly,* September 12, 1957. In the August 1959 issue of *Literatura i zhizn,* Ehrenburg insisted that art deal not with the secrets of engineering, but with "the secrets of the human heart." A few weeks later, this same magazine denounced him and the courageous editor of *Novy mir* (New World) Alexander Tvardovsky, for violating the aesthetic principles of socialist realism, but they were defended by the sometimes liberal *Literaturnaya gazeta* and other writers, and Tvardovsky, by Khrushchev himself. See Peter Viereck, "The Split Personality of Soviet Literature." *The Reporter,* March 15, 1961, p. 27.
29. Joshua Rubenstein, *Soviet Dissidents: Their Struggle for Human Rights.* Boston, Beacon Press, 1980, pp. 19–20. See also Priscilla Johnson, "The 'New Men' of the Soviet Sixties," *The Reporter,* May 9, 1963, p. 20.
30. Ibid., pp. 21–22.

The early history of the dissident movement, the involvement of Soviet Jews, and the separate Jewish movement are discussed at varying length in Frederick G. Barghoorn, *Detente and the Democratic Movement in the USSR.* New York, Free Press, 1976; Rudolf L. Tokes, ed., *Dissent in the USSR:*

Politics, Ideology and People. Baltimore, Johns Hopkins University Press, 1975; Rubenstein, op. cit.; Peter Reddaway, "Dissent in the Soviet Union," *Dissent*, Vol. 23, No. 2, Spring 1976, pp. 136–54; Abram Rothberg, *Heirs of Stalin: Dissidence and the Soviet Regime (1953–1970).* Ithaca, Cornell University Press, 1972.

31. Sidney Monas, "Engineers or Martyrs: Dissent and the Intelligentsia," in Abraham Brumberg, ed., *In Quest of Justice: Protest and Dissent in the Soviet Union Today.* New York, Praeger, 1970, p. 26.

32. Burton Rubin, "Highlights of the 1962–63 Thaw," in Max Hayward and Edward L. Crowley, eds., op. cit., p. 94. Khrushchev's alternating flexibility and inflexibility regarding creative expression are examined in Priscilla Johnson and Leopold Labedz, eds., *Khrushchev and the Arts: The Politics of Soviet Culture, 1962–1964.* Cambridge, MIT Press, 1965.

33. Quoted in William Korey, "Babi Yar Remembered," *Midstream*, March 1969, p. 33. Nekrasov's demand for the monument ("Why is it Left Undone," *Literaturnaya gazeta,* October 10, 1959) and the various attacks on Evtushenko can be found in Benjamin Pinkus, *The Soviet Government and the Jews, 1948–1967: A Documented Study.* Cambridge, Cambridge University Press, 1984, pp. 436–37, 118–23.

34. William Korey, *The Soviet Cage: Anti-Semitism in Russia.* New York, Viking, 1973, pp. 112–13. Pinkus, op. cit., p. 401, states that "part of the virulently anti-Semitic literature dealing with the Holocaust period" of the Khrushchev period includes P. Gavrutto's *Clouds Over the City,* published in 1963, "under the clear influence of a speech by Khrushchev" accusing Kogan of treachery. Various documents dealing with the alleged charges against Kogan and his own account appear in ibid., pp. 127–33.

35. *Pravda,* March 8, 1963.

36. The full address is published as Document No. 38 in Brumberg, ed., op. cit., pp. 200–204.

37. See Korey, op. cit., pp. 115–19, the *New York Times,* August 22, 1971, and *Atlas,* Vol. 13, No. 2, February 1967, pp. 10–19 for discussions of this controversy. The original uncensored Russian version was published in West Germany and an English version was published in Great Britain in 1970 by Jonathan Cape. (Kuznetsov had changed his name to Anatoly.) The attack on Shostakovich appears in Pinkus, op. cit., pp. 123–25.

28. The Sixties: Renewed Attacks on Jews and Judaism and a Few Concessions

1. Described in Arie L. Eliav, *Between Hammer and Sickle.* New York, New American Library, 1969, pp. 121–22.

2. Robert G. Kaiser, *Russia: The People and the Power.* New York, Pocket Books, 1976, p. 370.

3. Ibid., pp. 370–72.

4. Hedrick Smith, *The Russians.* New York, Ballantine, 1977, p. 115.

5. Pinkus interprets these measures as follows: "The adoption of these de-

crees by the Supreme Soviet, followed by the relevant amendments in the criminal codes of the republics, had one important economic aim: to reduce the corruption, private commerce, and thefts of state property which had apparently reached intolerable levels in this period. And, since the Soviet leadership was not prepared to alter fundamentally the economic structure, it was compelled to take Draconian measures which resulted in a wave of economic trials that covered the entire Soviet Union." Benjamin Pinkus, *The Soviet Government and the Jews, 1948–1967: A Documented Study.* Cambridge, Cambridge University Press, 1984, p. 202.

6. Bernard D. Weinryb, "Antisemitism in the Soviet Union," in Lionel Kochan, ed., *The Jews in Soviet Russia since 1917*, 3d ed. Oxford, Oxford University Press, 1978, p. 326. A table of the number of economic trials involving Jewish defendants reported in the press, 1960–67, has been constructed in Table 8, Pinkus op. cit, p. 203. The number of Jews and non-Jews sentenced to death is shown in Table 9, ibid., p. 205.

7. Weinryb, op. cit., p. 326.

8. *Sovetskaya Litva*, April 4, 1962 and *Lvovskaya pravda*, March 16, 1962, quoted in William Korey, *The Soviet Cage: Anti-Semitism in Russia.* New York, Viking, 1973, p. 79.

9. *Izvestiya*, October 20, 1963, quoted in Pinkus, op. cit., p. 512 note 61.

10. Text in Gunther Lawrence, *Three Million More?* New York, Doubleday, 1970, p. 136.

11. Ibid., pp. 136–37.

12. Text in ibid., p. 139–41. In this connection, Pinkus, op. cit., p. 204, makes the important point that "the explanation that so high a percentage of Jews was sentenced to death because the Jews headed the groups engaged in theft, speculation, and the receiving of bribes may be correct. But it does not satisfactorily explain why the Soviet authorities gave so much publicity to those trials involving Jews. This is especially perplexing in view of the official claim that Jews accounted for the lowest percentage of crime in the Soviet Union both in absolute numbers and relative to other nationalities."

13. "Economic Crimes in the Soviet Union," *Journal of the International Commission of Jurists,* Summer 1964, pp. 3–47. See also Korey, op. cit., pp. 78–79.

14. Lawrence, op. cit., pp. 160–61.

15. Kevin Devlin, "Western Communist Parties and the Soviet Jewish Question," *Bulletin on Soviet and East European Jewish Affairs,* No. 6, December 1970, p. 5.

16. Quoted in ibid.

17. Quoted in ibid.

18. Ibid., p. 6.

19. Soviet travelers abroad, including scientists, were briefed on how to deal with anticipated questions regarding Kichko's book. See also Ronald I. Rubin, ed., *The Unredeemed: Anti-Semitism in the Soviet Union.* Chicago, Quadrangle Press, 1968.

20. *Pravda*, April 4, 1964, translated into English in Shmuel Ettinger, ed., *Anti-Semitism in the Soviet Union: Its Roots and Consequences,* Vol. 3. Jerusalem,

Hebrew University, Center for Research and Documentation of East European Jewry, 1983, pp. 253–55. See J. Miller's comments in, "The Kichko Affair: Additional Documents," *Soviet Jewish Affairs*, No. 1, 1971, pp. 109–13, which demolish Soviet arguments.

21. "A Book about the Reactionary Nature of Judaism," in *Radyanska kultura*, March 26, 1964. English text in *Jews in Eastern Europe*, July 1964. See also "How the Soviets Criticized Kichko," *Jewish Frontier*, March 1965, pp. 14–17, for a translation of the review. The *Jewish Frontier* concludes that "contrary to the impression given to world public opinion by Tass' choice of quotations, the reviewers actually endorsed the book" (p. 14).

22. Boris Smolar, *Soviet Jewry Today and Tomorrow*. New York, Macmillan, 1971, p. 30. Kichko attacked critics of his book in an article in the Ukrainian paper *Silski Visti*, September 28, 1971, attributing the "clamor" to anti-Soviet "Ukrainian bourgeois nationalists" and "Zionists." *Jewish Currents*, March 1972, p. 47. Pinkus, op. cit., pp. 85–86 note 85, has some revealing details about Kichko during the war and his compromising behavior during the Nazi occupation.

23. Suggested by Smolar, op. cit., p. 33.

24. Quoted in Korey, op. cit., p. 81. The recommendation of Osipov's book appears in the *Pravda* April 4, 1964 article cited in note 20 of this chapter.

25. Ibid., pp. 81–82.

26. This decision was reversed in 1979. See note 47 of present chapter. In the middle of September 1979, there was a puzzling announcement that "members of the Buddhist, Moslem, and Jewish religions attend[ed] a conference of Soviet religious leaders in Moscow, called to discuss the results of the 5th All-Christian (sic!) Peace Congress held in Prague during the summer." *Soviet Jewish Affairs*, Vol. 9,. No. 1, 1979, "Chronicle of Events," p. 97.

27. Bohdan R. Bociurkiw, "Soviet Religious Policy and the Status of Judaism in the USSR," *Bulletin on Soviet and East European Jewish Affairs*, No. 6, December 1970, p. 17.

28. JTA release, September 30, 1960. This figure would have to include *minyanim*.

29. Joshua Rothenberg, *The Jewish Religion in the Soviet Union*. New York, Ktav, 1971, p. 46.

30. Rubin, op. cit., pp. 308–12. Yaacov Ro'i, who visited several synagogues in 1979, believed there were "less than 60." See his "Jewish Religious Life in the Soviet Union: Some Impressions," *Soviet Jewish Affairs*, Vol. 10, No. 2, 1980, p. 41.

31. Lawrence, op. cit., p. 90. See Pinkus, op. cit., pp. 320–25 for several other examples of rabbis defending Soviet policies.

32. Eliav, op. cit., pp. 55, 56, 57.

33. Lawrence, op. cit., p. 90.

34. Rothenberg, op. cit., p. 86. The matzo issue, from 1959–1967, is also dealt with in Pinkus, op. cit., pp. 313, 317, 326–27.

35. Lawrence, op. cit.

36. *Pravda Vostoka,* March 17, 1964, quoted in Rothenberg, op. cit., p. 87.

37. Moscow Radio English transmission, August 21, 1969, as monitored by the BBC and *Zhurnal Moskovskoi Patriarkhii,* quoted in "Religious Conference in the USSR," *Bulletin on Soviet and East European Jewish Affairs,* No. 4, December 1969, pp. 56–57.

38. Rothenberg, op. cit., p. 129. The Moscow and Leningrad synagogues were given permission to mimeograph calendars intermittently after 1956.

39. *Yalkut Mogen,* August 1964, p. 14, quoted in ibid., p. 130. The ban on importing Bibles was lifted, as of 1987 (see Chapter 33).

40. In Hebrew, *Siddur Ha-Shalom,* edited by Rabbi Shleiffer, then the Chief Rabbi of Moscow. A new edition of the same prayerbook was photographed and reproduced in 1968 and edited by Rabbi Levin. This edition included the Hebrew alphabet with vowels and the original Kaddish prayer, with Russian transliteration.

41. Zvi Y. Gitelman, "What Future for a Jewish Culture in the Soviet Union," *Soviet Jewish Affairs,* Vol. 9, No. 1, 1979, p. 22.

42. Rothenberg, op. cit., p. 137. Shleiffer's son-in-law, Emanuel Michlin, has written an important biography of Schleiffer (*Ha-Gahelet.* Jerusalem, Shamir, 1986.) which also reveals much about Jewish religious life in Moscow from 1922 to 1972, when Michlin emigrated to Israel.

43. Zalman N. Kiselgof, *B'Meitzar Birkat Hazan. Hadranim V'Derashot.* Jerusalem, Mossad Ha-Rav Kook, 1970.

44. Quoted from ibid. in a review by Chimen Abramsky, *Soviet Jewish Affairs,* No. 3, 1972, pp. 131, 133.

45. Zalman Yefroikin, *A bazukh in sovet rusland.* New York, 1962, p. 102, quoted in Rothenberg, op. cit., p. 44.

46. Rothenberg, op. cit., p. 51.

47. *Inside Yeshiva University* (New York), Vol. 25, No. 1, September 1979, pp. 1, 3. The two young men were Boris Gramm and Isaak Fuchs, according to a Novosti Press Agency article, November 17, 1981. Gramm is mentioned as the "head of the congregation" of the Moscow Choral Synagogue and a graduate of the Moscow Yeshiva in *Jewish Currents,* January 1982, p. 47.

48. Itzhak Ben-Zvi cites a study, "The 1946 Expedition to Daghestan," by J. M. Shilling, published in 1948 and a short essay on the Mountain Jews of the Caucasus by J. J. Ichileff in 1950. See his *The Exiled and the Redeemed,* tr. from Hebrew by I. A. Abbady. Philadelphia, Jewish Publication Society, 1961, p. 263.

49. Ibid., p. 39.

50. Eliav, op. cit., pp. 147–76. Eliav, Russian-born, emigrated to Palestine in 1924. He served as first secretary to the Israeli embassy in Moscow from 1958 to 1960.

51. Ibid., p. 174.

52. Quoted in Rothenberg, op. cit., p. 192.

53. Reuben Ainsztein, "The Fate of Soviet Jewry," *Midstream,* Spring 1959, p. 16.

54. Abraham Brumberg, "Sovyetish Heymland and the Dilemmas of Jewish Life in the USSR," *Soviet Jewish Affairs*, No. 3, May 1972, p. 28. Yekaterina Furtseva, the Minister of Culture at the time, told André Blumel, the vice-chairman of the France-Soviet Friendship Society, that if the USSR "did anything at all [for Jewish culture] it would not be for domestic reasons, but to please our friends abroad."

55. S. L. Shneiderman, *"Sovietish Heimland and its Editor, Aron Vergelis," Mid-stream*, October 1971, p. 31.

56. Yet in the early seventies he criticized the more virulent purveyors of Soviet anti-Semitism, such as Yevseev, Begun, and Kichko and showed them to be ignorant of Lenin's views on Jews and Jewish culture. A. Vergelis, "Nit bloyz ameratses," *Sovetish heymland*, No. 6, 1973, p. 170; "Farvos di fayl dergreykht nit dem tsil," No. 12, 1973, pp. 148–49; "Leyenendik Leninen," No. 1, 1974, pp. 154–56.

57. Shneiderman, op. cit., p. 34.

58. Shekhtman's novel was translated into English by Joseph Singer and published by Crown, New York, in 1967.

59. Shneiderman, op. cit., p. 34. *Znamya*, however, has published some of Evtushenko's previously censored work.

60. Elias Schulman, "Soviet Yiddish Writing as Mirrored in Sovetish Heimland," *Jewish Book Annual*. Vol. 37, 1979–80, p. 54.

61. Brumberg, op. cit., p. 29.

62. Chaim Malamud, "Di shetlach fun undzer heylikaytn," *Sovetish heymland*, No. 5, 1971, p. 156. Quoted in ibid., p. 29–30.

63. Shneiderman, op. cit., p. 39.

64. Lukasz Hirszowicz, "Jewish Cultural Life in the USSR—A Survey," *Soviet Jewish Affairs*, Vol. 7, No. 2, 1977, p. 14. Other estimates indicate that most copies are sold overseas. By 1979, its circulation was reported to be only 7,000.

65. Hélène Carrère d'Encausse, *Decline of an Empire: The Soviet Socialist Republics in Revolt*. Martin Sokolinsky and Henry A. La Farge, trs. New York, Newsweek Books, 1979, p. 203.

66. Reported in Shneiderman, op. cit., pp. 36–37.

67. *Sovetish heymland*, No. 1, January 1965, noted in ibid., pp. 35–36. Of interest are later essays dealing with Hebrew, e.g., Alexandra Aykhenvold, "The Formation of Modern Hebrew as a Linguistic Experiment," *Sovetish heymland*, No. 7, 1986, pp. 122–25.

68. Raskin's contributions abruptly stopped after he applied to emigrate to Israel. Letter from his daughter Ruth Klugerman (Israel), October 23, 1981.

69. *New York Times*, May 27, 1974. The whole exchange appeared in *Commentary*, January 1965.

70. *Sovetish heymland*, No. 11, 1965.

71. Quoted in Brumberg, op. cit., p. 32.

72. Ibid.

29. The West, Dissidents, and the "Jews of Silence"
Protest Soviet Repression, 1960–1968

1. American Jewry's inhibitions and hesitancy are described by Judd Teller in "American Jews and Soviet Anti-Semitism," *Jewish Frontier*, April 1965, pp. 14–16.
2. Joseph B. Schechtman, *Star in Eclipse: Russian Jewry Revisited*. New York, Thomas Yoseloff, 1961, pp. 219, 220.
3. Moshe Decter, ed., "The Jews in the Soviet Union," *New Leader* (special issue), September 14, 1959, and "The Status of Jews in the Soviet Union," *Foreign Affairs*, Vol. 41, January 1963, pp. 420–30.
4. Richard Cohen, ed., *Let My People Go: Today's Documentary Story of Soviet Jewry's Struggle to Be Free*. New York, Popular Library, 1971, pp. 10–11.
5. William W. Orbach, *The American Movement to Aid Soviet Jews*. Amherst, University of Massachusetts Press, 1979, p. 20.
6. Ibid.
7. Interview with Richter, June 16, 1977, cited in Paul S. Applebaum, "U.S. Jews' Reaction to Soviet 'Anti-Zionism,' " *Patterns of Prejudice* (London), Vol. 12, No. 2, March-April, 1978, p. 27.
8. Cohen, op. cit., p. 12.
9. Between 1959 and 1966 only 13 titles in Yiddish were published.
10. Arie L. Eliav, *Between Hammer and Sickle*. New York, New American Library, 1969, p. 96.
11. Gunther Lawrence, *Three Million More?* New York, Doubleday, 1970, p. 74.
12. Ibid., p. 96.
13. Jacob Goldberg, "Rabbi Levin's Visit," *Congress Bi-Weekly*, September 16, 1968, p. 6.
14. S. L. Shneiderman, "Moscow Revisited," *Midstream*, February 1970, p. 52.
15. Ibid.
16. Ibid.
17. Goldberg, op. cit., p. 6.
18. Ibid.
19. Eliav, op. cit., p. 96.
20. Anon., "The Road Home: A Russian Jew Discovers His Identity," *Bulletin on Soviet and East European Jewish Affairs*, No. 4, December 1969, p. 6.
21. Eliav, op. cit., pp. 97–98.
22. Elie Wiesel, *The Jews of Silence: A Personal Report on Soviet Jewry*, Neal Kozodoy, tr. Toronto, Signet, 1966.
23. Ibid., p. 61.
24. Leonard Schroeter, *The Last Exodus*. New York, Universe Books, 1974, p. 70.
25. Ibid., p. 74.
26. Lawrence, op. cit., p. 136.
27. Schroeter, op. cit., pp. 38–39.
28. Ibid., p. 39.

29. Information based on letters to writer from Dina Beilina, dated February 20 and March 7, 1982 and *Rachel P. Margolina Yeyo Perepiska Korneyen Ivanovichem Chukovskum* (Rachel Pavlovna Margolina and Her Correspondence with K. I. Chukovsky). Jerusalem, 1978, p. 47. Courtesy of Mikhail Zand.

The well-known Moscow refusenik Vladimir Prestin was adopted by Shapiro after Prestin's father was killed during the war, and a Hebrew textbook Shapiro completed but was never allowed to publish, was confiscated from Prestin's apartment. Letter from D. Beilina, March 7, 1982.

30. Zand wrote an important analysis for samizdat circulation called "The Jewish Question in the USSR: Theses," (see Chapter 30) and emigrated to Israel where he is Professor of Indian, Iranian, and Armenian Studies at Hebrew University. Mrs. Ratner died in an automobile accident in 1971.

31. Salo W. Baron, *The Russian Jews under Tsars and Soviets*, 2d ed. New York, Macmillan, 1976, p. 325. See also A. A. Greenbaum, *Jewish Scholarship and Scholarly Institutions in Soviet Russia, 1918–1953*. Jerusalem, Hebrew University Center for Research and Documentation of East European Jewry, 1978, pp. 128, 129, 131, 132, for other references to Hebrew scholarship in the Soviet Union. See also the translation by Lukasz Hirszowicz of a survey of Judaica scholarship by Igor Krupnik (in *Sovetish heymland*, No. 11, 1986), "The Contribution of the Younger Generation of Soviet Scholars to Jewish Studies in the USSR," *Soviet Jewish Affairs*, Vol. 17, No. 2, 1987, pp. 35–48.

32. Baron, op. cit., p. 326.

33. Schroeter, op. cit., p. 55.

34. Ibid.

35. Moshe Decter, "Crisis in the Soviet Jewry Movement," *Moment*, April 1976, pp. 36, 37.

36. David McKenzie and Michael W. Curran, *A History of Russia and the Soviet Union*, rev. ed. Homewood, Ill., Dorsey Press, 1982, p. 622.

37. Ibid., 623.

38. Background information based on Abram Tertz (Andrei Sinyavsky), *A Voice from the Chorus*, Kyril Fitzly and Max Hayward, trs. New York, Farrar, Straus and Giroux, 1976. Intro. by Max Hayward, pp. viii–xii.

39. Helen Muchnic, "Light from Above," *New York Review of Books*, August 5, 1976, p. 5.

40. Tertz, op. cit., Intro., pp. xv–xvi.

41. Quoted in Maurice Friedberg, "Jewish Themes in Soviet Russian Literature," in Lionel Kochan, ed., *The Jews in Soviet Russia Since 1917*, 3d ed. Oxford, Oxford University Press, 1978, p. 214. The novel was published in English in 1965.

42. Tertz, op. cit., Intro., p. xvii.

43. Issue No. 12, September 1965.

44. Joshua Rubenstein, *Soviet Dissidents: Their Struggle for Human Rights*. Boston, Beacon, 1980, p. 37. Bukovsky was rearrested. See also Vladimir K. Bukovsky, "General Svetlichny: We Will Let Him Rot in the Insane Asylum," *New York Times*, May 3, 1977.

45. On Trial: The Soviet State versus "Abram Tertz" and "Nikolai Arzhak," tr. and ed., with an intro. by Max Hayward. New York, Harper and Row, 1966, p. 20.
46. Translations of both articles appear in ibid., pp. 212–32.
47. Ibid., p. 25.
48. Vladimir Bukovsky, the organizer of poetry readings and student demonstrations, who had been committed to a mental hospital in 1963 for refusing to repent and inform on those who helped him prepare photocopies of one of Djilas' books, had been released in February 1965, but was rearrested toward the end of the year for organizing the first human rights demonstration on December 5, in defense of Sinyavsky and Daniel. It was carried out with the slogan, "Respect Your Constitution."
49. Ibid., p. 1
50. See note 45 above. Most of the February and March 1966 issues of Political Diary were devoted to the trial, including statements by Sinyavsky and Daniel and letters.
51. See Roy Medvedev's 1966 essay, "The Danger of a Revival of Stalinism," in Stephen E. Cohen, ed., An End to Silence: Uncensored Opinions in the Soviet from Roy Medvedev's Underground Magazine Political Diary. New York, Norton, 1982, pp. 153–57.
52. Pavel Litvinov, ed. The Trial of the Four. English text ed. by Peter Reddaway. New York, Viking, 1972. See also Karel het van Reve, ed., Letters and Telegrams to Pavel M. Litvinov, December 1967–May 1968. Dordecht, Holland, Reidel, 1969.
53. Roman Rutman, "Jews and Dissenters: Connections and Divergencies," Soviet Jewish Affairs, Vol. 3, No. 2, 1973, p. 37.
54. Izvestiya, December 5, 1966, quoted in Schechtman, "The USSR, Zionism and Israel," op. cit., p. 129.
55. William Korey, The Soviet Cage: Anti-Semitism in Russia. New York, Viking, 1973, p. 126.
56. Quoted in Zev Katz, "The Aftermath of the June War: The Soviet Propaganda Offensive against Israel and World Jewry," Bulletin on Soviet and East European Jewish Affairs, No. 1, 1969, p. 27.
57. Shneiderman, op. cit., p. 47.
58. Described in Rebecca Rass, From Moscow to Jerusalem. New York, Shengold Pubs., 1976, pp. 9–12.
59. Ibid., p. 15.
60. Cohen, ed., op. cit., pp. 34–35, 37–38.
61. Rass, op. cit., p. 71.

30. The Jewish National Movement: Trials, Tests, and Affirmations, 1968–71

1. Kochubievsky's case is described in "Documents," Bulletin on Soviet and East European Jewish Affairs, No. 4, December 1969, pp. 46–47.
2. Moshe Dector, "Silence Means Death," in Richard Cohen, ed., Let My Peo-

ple Go: Today's Documentary Story of Soviet Jewry's Struggle to Be Free. New York, Popular Library, 1971, pp. 57–58.

3. Quoted in ibid., pp. 57–58.

4. "Documents," *Bulletin on Soviet and East European Jewish Affairs,* No. 4, December 1969, p. 46.

5. Ibid., p. 47.

6. An account of Kochubievsky's trial appears in Moshe Decter, ed., *A Hero for Our Time,* published jointly by the Conference on the Status of Soviet Jewry and the Academic Committee on Soviet Jewry. New York, April 1970. This pamphlet is based on samizdat materials (*Khronika,* Nos. 8 and 9).

7. Joshua Rubenstein, *Soviet Dissidents: Their Struggle for Human Rights.* Boston, Beacon, 1980, p. 160.

8. An account of the Ryazan trial appears in *Jews in Eastern Europe,* Vol. IV, No. 7, November 1971, pp. 205–8.

9. Leonard Schroeter, *The Last Exodus.* New York, Universe Books, 1974, p. 91.

10. Ibid.

11. Ibid., p. 92.

12. Quoted in Letter of D. C. Drabkin, April 18, 1969, in "Documents," *Bulletin on Soviet and East European Jewish Affairs,* December 1969, p. 47.

13. Cohen, ed., op. cit., p. 32.

14. Ibid., p. 33.

15. Full text can be found in "Documents," *Bulletin on Soviet and East European Jewish Affairs,* No. 4, December 1969, pp. 48–49.

16. There were detailed accounts of the arrests of Jews in connection with the hijack attempt (Nos. 14 and 15) and the First Leningrad Trial was described in No. 17 (December 1970).

17. Preface by Amnesty International to *A Chronicle of Current Events,* No. 16, February 1971. Nos. 1–11 (April 30, 1968 to December 31, 1969) appeared in full, with annotations and seventy-six photographs in Peter Reddaway, ed., *Uncensored Russia: Protest and Dissent in the Soviet Union.* New York, American Heritage Press, 1972. Amnesty International began publishing English translations of the *Chronicles* as they appeared, beginning with No. 16 in February 1971. Publication ceased temporarily after No. 27, dated October 1972, as a result of a KGB effort to suppress the journal in the USSR, but it reappeared in the spring of 1974, when Nos. 28–31, covering the period from October 1972 to May 1974, were distributed. Since that time publication has continued without interruption. As of 1987, Amnesty International was still publishing English translations.

18. In his Introduction to *Uncensored Russia,* op. cit., pp. 15–40, Reddaway describes the aims and structures of the so-called "Democratic Movement," the ways in which it illuminates other aspects of Soviet life, and historical traditions that nourished it. The Foreword, pp. 43–51, by Julius Telesin, noted mathematician and early human rights activist, pays tribute to pioneering figures such as Bukovsky, Litvinov, Grigorenko, and Amalrik—"who had nothing in common with Zionism"—from whom he "learned

how to struggle for my legal right to live in my historic homeland." Telesin emigrated to Israel in 1970. Many others such as Vitaly Rubin, Shcharansky, and Vladimir Slepak were deeply involved in both movements.

19. Schroeter, op. cit., p. 139. Extracts from *Iton Aleph* and *Iton Bet* were translated in *Jews in Eastern Europe*, Vol. IV, No. 7, November 1971.

20. Quoted in Vladimir Lazaris, "The Saga of the Jewish Samizdat," *Soviet Jewish Affairs*, Vol. 9, No. 1, 1979, p. 7.

21. Ibid., Yosef Kerler, the Yiddish writer, has an interesting critique of these first efforts in "Jewish Russian Samizdat in the USSR," in David Prital, ed., *In Search of Self: The Soviet Jewish Intelligentsia and the Exodus.* Jerusalem, Mt. Scopus Pubs., 1982, pp. 241–47. Kerler notes the courageous efforts "to escape the spiritual wilderness in which Soviet Jews have been wandering for decades," but also laments the gaps in knowledge of the Jewish past and the contempt for Yiddish culture.

22. Schroeter, op. cit., pp. 95–96.

23. Account based on Philip Gillon, "Exodus '71," *Jerusalem Post*, April 13, 1971.

24. Schroeter, op. cit., p. 80.

25. Account based on Leonard Schroeter, "Samizdat and the Struggle of Soviet Jewry," *Jerusalem Post*, March 28, 1972. Fedoseyev edited the first four issues of *Exodus* until he emigrated to Israel in February 1971. In the summer of 1971, *Exodus* was replaced by *Exodus Herald*, published by Boris Orlov, Vadim Meniker and Yury Breytbart, but none of the names of the editors appeared. Ludmilla Alexeyeva, *Soviet Dissent: Contemporary Movements for National, Religious, and Human Rights.* Carol Pearce and John Glad, trs. Middletown, Wesleyan University Press, 1985, p. 183.

26. Documents from *Exodus, Bulletin on Soviet and East European Jewish Affairs*, No. 6, December, 1970, p. 61. This issue contains a translation of the entire issue of *Exodus* No. 2 (pp. 51–69) and the contents table of No. 1 (p. 70). Many letters were reproduced for the first time in the United States in Moshe Decter, ed. *Redemption: Jewish Freedom Letters from Russia.* New York, American Jewish Conference on Soviet Jewry, May 1970. Some were also published in *Jews in Eastern Europe*, July 1969, pp. 51–55 and August 1970, pp. 16–18, 90–92.

27. Documents from *Exodus*, ibid.

28. Text in ibid., p. 57. Schroeter, "Samizdat," op. cit.

29. Schroeter, *The Last Exodus*, op. cit., p. 104.

30. Ibid.

31. Ibid., p. 101.

32. Schroeter, "Samizdat," op. cit.

33. During the second half of 1969, emigration averaged about 100 people per month. It remained at that level throughout 1970 until early 1971 when it leaped, in March, to about 1,000 per month. *New York Times*, September 16, 1970, cited in Jonathan Frankel, "The Anti-Zionist Press Campaign in the USSR, 1969–1971: An Internal Dialogue?" *Soviet Jewish Affairs*, No. 3, May 1972, p. 6.

34. "Documents of the Campaign" [from *Pravda, Izvestiya, Sovetish Heymland, Vechernaya Moskva,* and *Sovetskaya Latvia,* 1969–1970], *Bulletin on Soviet and Eastern European Jewish Affairs,* No. 5, May 1970, pp. 15–17.

35. Quoted from M. Meerson-Aksenov and B. Shragin, eds., *The Political and Religious Thought of Russian Samizdat,* Belmont, Mass., 1977, p. 586, in Stephan F. Cohen, ed., *An End to Silence: Uncensored Opinion in the Soviet Union.* New York, Norton, 1982, p. 245.

36. Received by the Institute of Jewish Affairs in May 1970 and translated and published in the *Bulletin on Soviet and East European Jewish Affairs,* No. 6, December 1970, pp. 49–50. (It was also published in No. 67, April 1970, of *Political Diary,* and appears in English in Cohen, ed., *An End to Silence,* op. cit., pp. 245–49.)

37. Ibid., p. 49.

38. Tat is a Persian dialect spoken in certain parts of the Caucasus.

39. [Mikhail Zand], "The Jewish Question in the USSR (Theses)," *Bulletin on Soviet and East European Jewish Affairs,* No. 6, December 1970, p. 50.

40. "They Want to Rule the World," by V. Vysotsky, in *Sovetskaya Belorossia,* May 31, 1969, translated in "Documents," *Bulletin on Soviet and East European Jewish Affairs,* No. 4, December 1969, p. 55.

41. Frankel, op. cit., p. 3.

42. Ibid., p. 7.

43. "Documents of the Campaign," op. cit., p. 22.

44. Ibid., pp. 17–18.

45. Ibid., pp. 18–21. Lest there be any doubt about Dragunsky's Jewish origins, instead of Dimitry, his Jewish names "David Abramovich" are used in his autobiography, *A Soldier's Life,* tr. from Russian by K. Russell and Y. Sviridov. Moscow, Progress Publishers, 1977. The book is filled with stock Soviet attacks on Israel, Zionism, and Jewish "radicalism." See also Chapter 34 for Dragunsky's involvement in an official Soviet anti-Zionist committee.

46. Frankel, op. cit., p. 8.

47. Zeev Ben-Shlomo, "The Current Anti-Zionist Campaign in the USSR," *Bulletin on Soviet and East European Jewish Affairs,* No. 5, May 1970, pp. 8–9.

48. For the "press conference" and extracts from the letter, see ibid., pp. 14–35.

49. Ilya Zilberberg, "An Open Letter of 12 March 1970," *Soviet Jewish Affairs,* No. 3, May 1972, p. 64. In the spring of 1970, there appeared two "viciously anti-Semitic novels by Ivan Shevtsov . . . published in scores of thousands of copies, and under the imprimatur of powerful state agencies," which were considered a "radical break" with Soviet fiction in the past, which had generally been free of anti-Semitism. In one of the novels, *Love and Hate,* the archvillain is a Jew described as a pervert, sadist, dope-peddler, and killer. The other novel, *In the Name of the Father and the Son,* "recalls the propaganda of *Der Stürmer.*" The tone and language were so venomous that even *Pravda* (July 12, 1970) felt impelled to criticize it as

"ideologically and artistically weak." See William Korey, *The Soviet Cage: Anti Semitism in Russia*, New York, Viking, 1973, pp. 155–58 for further comments.

50. Frankel, op. cit., p. 10.

51. Philippa Lewis, "The 'Jewish Question' in the Open," in Lionel Kochan, ed., *The Jews in Soviet Russia since 1917*, 3d ed. Oxford, Oxford University Press, 1978, p. 353.

52. Peter Reddaway believes that emigration in 1970 was permitted on a "significant scale . . . less because of pressure from abroad . . . than because the example given by the militancy and skillful coordination of the Jewish movement to other discontented groups was simply intolerable to the autocratic regime." Peter Reddaway, "The Resistance in Russia," *New York Review of Books*, December 12, 1974, p. 37. In emphasizing the reciprocally helpful benefits to both movements, Reddaway (*Uncensored Russia*, op. cit., pp. 300–301) comments: "Those Jews anxious only to reach Israel can . . . scarcely be seen as part of the Democratic Movement proper. They have, however, already contributed to its development both by the force of their example regarding tactics, organization and general bravery, and by their success in compelling the regime to establish a solid body of precedent for the right to emigrate to a noncommunist country, if only on the condition that a person's relatives live in that country and invite him to join them." The "loss of the old ruthlessness" in the leadership is credited with establishing this precedent.

53. Frankel, op. cit., pp. 14–16.

54. Quoted in Korey, op. cit., p. 201.

55. Edward Crankshaw, "The Heroism of Leningrad," *Jerusalem Post*, March 9, 1971.

56. Translated from *Iskhod* (Exodus) No. 2, *Bulletin on Soviet and East European Jewish Affairs*, No. 6, December 1970, pp. 68–69.

57. Ibid., pp. 74–75.

58. Frankel, op. cit., p. 21.

59. Ibid., pp. 23–24.

60. Dina Spechler, "Zhdanovism, Eurocommunism, and Cultural Reaction in the USSR," Research Paper No. 34, the Soviet and East European Research Center, Hebrew University, Jerusalem, March 1979, p. 34.

61. Schroeter, *The Last Exodus*, op. cit., p. 155.

62. After the initial announcement of the trial, Soviet officials tried to impose a strict news blackout and rebuffed inquiries by those seeking information, but the trial and sentences brought worldwide condemnation from the press and public opinion, including western Communist parties.

63. An informal transcript of the trial proceedings was published in *Iskhod*, No. 4, translated and published by the Institute of Jewish Affairs (London) as *Exodus*, No. 4 (supplement to the *Journal of Soviet Jewish Affairs*, June 1971). An edited transcript of the trial also appears in Cohen, ed., op. cit., pp. 81–109 and a summarization based on a transcript of taped testimony in

Schroeter, *The Last Exodus*, op. cit., pp. 157–70. See also *Jews in Eastern Europe*, 1971 and Rene Beerman, "The 1970–1971 Soviet Trials of Zionists: Some Legal Aspects," *Soviet Jewish Affairs*, No. 2, November 1971, pp. 3–8.

64. Korey, op. cit., p. 210. Among several documents received by the Institute of Jewish Affairs in October 1970 were a number of biographies of arrested persons and the statement: "In Leningrad there is no authenticated information as to whether a plane hijacking was in fact attempted. However, if it did take place, it was done by a handful of irresponsible people. . . . The attempted hijacking was without any doubt a provocation thoroughly prepared by the KGB." *Bulletin on Soviet and East European Jewish Affairs*, No. 6, December 1970, p. 71. Later, subsequent trials in 1971 were linked to the hijacking attempt. A number of defendants and families of defendants who ultimately went to Israel were certain that the hijack attempt was a KGB provocation. See Schroeter, op. cit., pp. 179–81. It has also been noted that many searches and arrests were made of people who were not in Leningrad on June 15, indicating that the KGB was waiting for some pretext—the "hijacking"—to act against them.

65. Schroeter, *The Last Exodus* op. cit., p. 179.

66. Ibid., pp. 182–83. For reasons why the "Testament" was not introduced at the trial, see ibid., pp. 183–86.

67. Korey, op. cit., p. 214.

68. Schroeter, op. cit., p. 166.

69. Crankshaw, op. cit.

70. Ibid.

71. Korey, op. cit., p. 224.

72. Cohen, ed., op. cit., p. 109.

73. In the "liberal" wing were Premier Kosygin, Aleksei Rumyantsev (Vice-President, USSR Academy of Sciences); KGB Chairman Yuri Andropov; former trade union chief Alexander Shelepin; and Marshal of the Soviet Army Ivan Yakubobsky. Identified as hardliners and particularly anti-Semitic were former Deputy Premier Dmitri Polyansky; former Ukrainian party chief P. Shelest; and party theoretician Mikhail Suslov. See Thomas E. Sawyer, *The Jewish Minority in the Soviet Union*. Boulder, Colo., Westview Press, p. 186 and Lukasz Hirszowicz, "The Soviet-Jewish Problem: Internal and International Developments, 1972–1976," in Kochan, ed., op. cit., p. 367. Zand's paper, "Yevreiskii vopros v S.S.S.R. (Tezisy)" (The Jewish Question in the U.S.S.R.) was issued in samizdat form May 1970, and was translated and published in *Bulletin on Soviet and East European Jewish Affairs*, December 1970, pp. 49–50.

74. Sawyer, op. cit., p. 189.

75. George Ginsburgs, "Soviet Law and the Emigration of Soviet Jews," *Soviet Jewish Affairs*, No. 3, 1973, pp. 14–15.

76. This is a very serious step, emphasizing the finality of the break with the homeland, motivated by purely political considerations and leaving an in-

dividual in a legal limbo. By contrast, both Jewish and non-Jewish immigrants to the United States receive regular passports and retain their Soviet citizenship.

77. A. S. Karlikow, "What It Takes to Leave the Soviet Union," in Cohen, ed., op. cit., pp. 212–17 and Ginsburgs, op. cit., pp. 3–13.

78. George Ginsburgs, "Current Legal Problems of Jewish Emmigration from the USSR," *Soviet Jewish Affairs*, Vol. 6, No. 2, 1976, p. 4. See Chapter 34 for 1986 changes in emigration regulations under Gorbachev.

79. Karlikow, op. cit., pp. 215–16.

80. Schroeter, *The Last Exodus*, op. cit., pp. 252–53.

81. Sawyer, op. cit., pp. 193–94.

82. See Schroeter, *The Last Exodus*, op. cit., pp. 195–212.

83. Ibid., p. 198. See also reports on the Second Leningrad Trial in *Jews in Eastern Europe*, Vol. IV, No. 7, November 1971, and Beermann, op. cit., pp. 8–16.

84. Schroeter, *The Last Exodus*, op. cit., p. 204, and Beermann, op. cit., p. 9. Korenblit was born to an observant Jewish family and, having spent the first eighteen years of his life in Romanian Bessarabia, knew Hebrew and felt responsible for teaching it to others who didn't have his background. During the war, he had lost almost his entire family (Beermann, p. 9).

85. Some of this reassessment was analyzed by Korenblit's wife, Poline. Many of the reevaluations are described in Schroeter, op. cit., pp. 179–94. Beermann expresses surprise that neither the prosecution nor defense made enough of Butman's and Korenblit's withdrawal from the project as early as April 1970, or earlier, and apparently had persuaded Dymshits and the others to give it up as well. The court and prosecution interrupted Korenblit and had him rushed out of the courtroom at a very important point in his testimony, namely, when he was "startled and shocked" during a visit to Dymshits' flat on June 13, 1970. Did he see "some known *stukach* (informer) or some disguised KGB officer?" (Beermann, p. 15).

86. See Beermann, ibid., pp. 16–17, 21–22; Korey, op. cit., pp. 250–75; and Schroeter, *The Last Exodus*, op. cit., pp. 225–38.

87. Schroeter, *The Last Exodus*, op. cit., p. 227.

88. Ibid., pp. 234, 237.

89. Korey, op. cit., pp. 266–67.

90. Beermann, op. cit., p. 21.

91. Ibid., pp. 18–22. Some details of the Kishinev trial can also be found in *Jews in Eastern Europe*, Vol. IV, No. 7, November 1971, and Schroeter, op. cit., 213–24.

92. If, as has been also suggested, Soviet pro-Arab policies dictate the restrictions on Jewish emigration, it can be argued that "the easing of . . . policies in 1971 coincided with developments in Egypt after Nasser's death, which were unwelcome to the Soviet government." However, Soviet interests in the Middle East may not be the decisive factor in general, but rather, national self-interest, however that is perceived at any given time. See Hirszowicz, op. cit., p. 368.

31. The Jewish Emigration Movement and Western Support, 1971–76

1. Joshua Rubenstein, *Soviet Dissidents: Their Struggle for Human Rights*. Boston, Beacon, 1980, p. 131.
2. Ibid., p. 132.
3. Sakharov's protests and interventions on behalf of Jews have been numerous, frequent, and forthright. See, for example, "Jewish Aspects of the Sakharov Memorandum," Institute of Jewish Affairs, Research Report, U.S.S.R./3, December 1968; his letter to the Chairman of the USSR Supreme Soviet Presidium, December 28, 1970, protesting the charge of treason against those charged with hijacking a plane, and criticizing the Soviet restriction on the right to emigrate, *Exodus*, No. 4, 1971, p. 42; protesting the arrest of Yosif Begun, May 18, 1978, *Chronicle of Current Events*, No. 50, 1979, p. 17. See also note 66.
4. Victor Swoboda, "Ukrainian 'Unpublished' Literature on the Jews," *Bulletin on Soviet and East European Jewish Affairs*, No. 4, December 1969, pp. 39–43. A number of Ukrainian artists were expelled from their union for protesting against violations of Soviet law in trials of Jewish activists.
5. Zev Katz, "The New Nationalism in the USSR," *Midstream*, February 1973, pp. 12–13.
6. A summary of the work of the Brussels Conference and the text of the Brussels Declaration by the World Conference of Jewish Communities on Soviet Jewry can be found in Richard Cohen, ed., *Let My People Go: Today's Documentary Story of Soviet Jewry's Struggle to Be Free*. New York, Popular Library, 1971, pp. 119–42.
7. Ibid., p. 122.
8. Albert D. Chernin, "From the Inside: An Evaluation of the Goals and Accomplishments of the Brussels Conference on Soviet Jewry," *Jewish Exponent* (Fourth Friday), Philadelphia, June 25, 1971, p. 4.
9. William W. Orbach, *The American Movement to Aid Soviet Jews*. Amherst, University of Massachusetts Press, 1979, pp. 60–61.
10. Abraham S. Karlikow noted this neglect in his "The Brussels World Conference on Soviet Jewry: An Analysis," New York, American Jewish Committee, Foreign Affairs Department, 1971, pp. 2–3. See Chapter 32 for a further exploration of this issue.
11. Leonard Schroeter, *The Last Exodus*. New York, Universe Books, 1974, p. 353.
    Brezhnev maintained that OVIR had granted 95 percent of all applications, but Israeli sources countered by saying that from July 1968 through December 1970, 80,000 vyzovs had been issued, and another 80,000 new vyzovs as of August 1972. (No one knows at any given time how many Jews have applied or want to leave. It is generally believed that some, probably many, affidavits were and are not delivered.)
12. William Korey, "The Future of Soviet Jewry: Emigration and Assimilation," *Foreign Affairs*, Vol. 58, No. 1, Fall 1979, p. 75.

952 31. The Jewish Emigration Movement

13. In March 1972, Soviet officials, apparently wanting to minimize the out-flow, noted that two-thirds of the emigrants were "aged people and women," but Israeli sources indicated that over 50 percent were under forty-five. There are also differences in the reported occupational breakdown, with Israeli sources generally indicating a large proportion of professionals and skilled workers. Schroeter, op. cit., p. 358; Israel Public Council for Soviet Jewry, *News Bulletin*, No. 193/194, January–February, 1981, p. 8.

14. National Conference on Soviet Jewry, Soviet Jewry Research Bureau, "Soviet Jews: Emigration Statistics," New York, 1979. The figure was 31,652 according to certain Israeli sources and 31,681 according to Israel Public Council for Soviet Jewry, *News Bulletin*, No. 193/194, January–February, 1981.

15. For English-language translation of the "Educational Tax" decree and specified educational reimbursement costs, see Thomas E. Sawyer, *The Jewish Minority in the Soviet Union*. Boulder, Colo., Westview Press, 1979, pp. 310–14. See also "Soviet Publishes Fee for Emigration," *New York Times*, January 24, 1973.

    In helping to see the exorbitance of these fees, Mr. Hayim Sheynin, who emigrated in the early 1970s, pointed out that the average teacher in the Soviet Union at this time earned 60–70 roubles per month; a senior engineer earned about 700 roubles per month, while a middle-level engineer earned 120 roubles per month; an automobile designer might earn as much as 17,000 roubles per year. Conversation with Mr. Sheynin, February 17, 1987.

16. George Ginsburgs, "Soviet Law and the Emigration of Soviet Jews," *Soviet Jewish Affairs*, No. 3, 1973, p. 5. It was also noted that in the last minutes before leaving, often women are subjected to a gynecological examination, "a special form of humiliation . . . artificially prolonging [the] procedure [which] makes those leaving late for the plane and again places them and their relatives in a state of agonizing uncertainty." Ilya Zilberberg, "An Open Letter of 12 March 1970," *Soviet Jewish Affairs*, No. 3, May 1972, p. 60.

17. "Chronicle of Events," *Soviet Jewish Affairs*, Vol. 3, No. 2, 1973, p. 125. See also Vitaly Rubin, "Human Rights Are Indivisible," in David Prital, ed., *In Search of Self: The Soviet Jewish Intelligentsia and the Exodus*. Jerusalem, Mt. Scopus Pubs., 1982, pp. 113–15.

18. Mark Azbel, "Aliya of Scientists from the Soviet Union," Israel Public Council for Soviet Jewry, *News Bulletin*, No. 181/182, July 31, 1980, p. 17.

19. Voronel and Polsky were allowed to leave at the end of 1974. See *Current*, Newsletter of Committee of Concerned Scientists, Vol. 3, No. 1, March 1975, p. 2.

20. *Newsweek*, December 18, 1972, p. 50.

21. During this visit on November 4, 1972 in Lefortovo Prison, in the presence of two investigators, Yakir said that continued publication of the *Chronicle* would cause new arrests, that it had harmful effects and should be stopped. The KGB investigation was very intense and included forced confronta-

tions between Yakir and Krasin and with those who refused to agree with their accusations. Others succumbed. *Chronicle of Current Events in the USSR,* Nos. 28–31, 1975, pp. 14–15, 62–65.

22. Hedrick Smith, *The Russians.* New York, Ballantine, 1977, p. 617.

23. Brodsky is a Jew, but does not identify himself as such, nor does he have a firm ideological position. He is generally considered the most talented poet of his generation who merely wanted to be left alone to write as he pleased—a freedom the regime refused. His poetry is intensely personal and meditative, altogether apolitical, but the authorities described it as not "socially useful," and Brodsky as an "idler and parasite." In 1964 he was sentenced to two years in a labor camp north of the Arctic Circle. In June 1972 he was abruptly summoned by the minister of the interior and given ten days' notice to leave Russia for good. When asked why he was forced out, Brodsky told reporters; "They can take citizens in just two ways, either as slaves or as enemies. If you are not a slave, and yet not an enemy, they don't know what to do with you." *Newsweek,* March 5, 1973, p. 82.

24. Sawyer, op. cit., p. 169.

25. Ibid.

26. Robert G. Kaiser, *Russia: The People and the Power.* New York, Pocket Books, 1976, p. 453.

27. Schroeter, op. cit., p. 277.

28. Moshe Decter, ed., *Terror in Minsk: KGB Case Number 97: The Jewish Officers' "Plot".* New York, National Conference on Soviet Jewry, 1973, p. 17.

29. Ibid., p. 12.

30. Ibid., p. 22.

31. Ibid., p. 13.

32. Schroeter, op. cit., p. 283.

33. S. 16835–6, *Congressional Record,* October 4, 1972.

34. William Korey, "Rescuing Russian Jewry: Two Episodes Compared," *Soviet Jewish Affairs,* Vol. 5, No. 1, 1975, p. 6.

35. Orbach, op. cit., p. 121.

36. Ibid., p. 138. On April 18, 1973, Senator Hugh Scott announced that the Soviet Union had notified the United States of the suspension of the education tax in two oral communications to President Nixon (March 30 and April 10), *Soviet Jewish Affairs,* Vol. 3, No. 2, 1973, p. 124.

37. For a full account, see Orbach, op. cit., pp. 129–54 and Korey, "Rescuing Russian Jewry," op. cit., pp. 3–19.

38. Korey, ibid., p. 10.

39. *New York Times,* September 9, 1973.

40. Ibid.

41. Ibid.

42. "Chronicle of Events," *Soviet Jewish Affairs,* Vol. 4, No. 2, 1974, pp. 112, 113.

43. Text in *Congressional Record,* December 13, 1975, pp. 3–4. For a more extended treatment of the Jackson-Vanik Amendment debate, see Korey, "Rescuing Russian Jewry" op. cit.; "Politics and Trade: Trade Agreement

Linked to Soviet Emigration Policy," *Nation*, February 1, 1975, pp. 100–101; Joseph Albright, "Pact of Two Henrys: Trade Bill Linked to Russian Emigration," *New York Times Magazine*, January 5, 1975, pp. 16–17ff.; and "The Right to Emigrate Amendment," *Congress Bi-Weekly*, November 8, 1974, pp. 3–51. The official Soviet reaction can be found in translated excerpts of articles in *Pravda* and *Izvestiya*, December 19 and 20, 1974 in "Moscow Denies U.S. Trade-Emigration Link," *Current Digest of Soviet Press*, Vol. 26, No. 5, January 15, 1975. See also William Korey, "The Struggle Over Jackson-Mills-Vanik," *American Jewish Yearbook*, Vol. 75, 1974–75, pp. 199–234.

44. Smith, op. cit., p. 635.

45. For a few of the reassessments, see Phil Baum, "Rethinking Jackson-Vanik: New Approaches to Soviet Jewish Emigration," *Congress Monthly*, June 1976, pp. 7–9; Nora Levin, "Soviet Jewry: Problems and Policies," *Congress Monthly*, February 1977, pp. 11–13. Henry Kissinger, in his *Years of Upheaval* (Boston, Little Brown, 1982), pp. 985–98, deplored the lost opportunity to increase Jewish emigration to 45,000—agreed to by Brezhnev—if Jackson-Vanik were dropped.

46. Quoted in "Around the World," *Jewish Currents*, March 1975, p. 47.

47. "Soviet Jewish Cultural Stirrings," Editorial, *Jewish Currents*, February 1977, p. 3.

48. Sawyer, op. cit., p. 203.

49. National Conference on Soviet Jewry, *Fact Sheet*, New York, 1980.

50. *Insight*, Vol. 1, No. 2. See Table 31.1 (p. 709). These figures differ slightly from those of the Jewish Agency.

51. On December 3, 1974, it was reported that more than fifty Soviet Jews occupied the Soviet consulate in Vienna for several hours requesting or demanding reentry visas. (Forty families that had left Israel were reported to have been allowed to return to the Soviet Union since 1971, as of that date.) By December 26, the number had risen to 100. It is generally believed that there were some Soviet planted agents among those as well as disgruntled and disappointed people. "Chronology," *Soviet Jewish Affairs*, Vol. 4, No. 1, 1974, p. 124. According to *Soviet Weekly*, June 12, 1976, there were about 200 in 1972, 350 in 1973, and 808 in 1974. On December 30, 1986; the Soviet Foreign Ministry announced that over 1,000 Soviet emigrants in the U.S. had applied for permission to return to the USSR.

52. See Table 31.1. *Insight*, Vol. 1, No. 2, has slightly different percentages: In 1974, 18.8 percent of the 20,695 emigrants chose not to go to Israel, 37.2 percent in 1975, and 49.1 percent in 1976. In 1972–73 approximately 90 percent of the emigrants came from the Baltic republics, the Chernovtsy region, Lvov, and Georgia, where Jewish national feeling and tradition were still strong. By 1974, a greater proportion was coming from centers of Jewish population in pre-1939 USSR, such as Leningrad and Moscow.

53. Among numerous studies of absorption in Israel, the following are fairly representative: Tamar R. Horowitz, "Integration without Acculturation: The Absorption of Soviet Immigrants in Israel," *Soviet Jewish Affairs*, Vol. 12,

No. 3, November 1982, pp. 19–44. "Survey on Absorption of Immigrants Five Years after Immigration," Israel Ministry of Immigrant Absorption, Jewish Agency and Absorption Department, 1982 (in Hebrew); Judith T. Shuval, "Soviet Immigrant Physicians in Israel," *Soviet Jewish Affairs*, Vol. 14, No. 2, May 1984, pp. 19–39; Betsy Gidwitz, "Problems of Adjustment of Soviet Jewish Emigrés," *Soviet Jewish Affairs*, Vol. 6, No 1, 1976, pp. 27–42; and several segments of Zvi Y. Gitelman, *Becoming Israelis: Political Resocialization of Soviet and American Immigrants*. New York, Praeger, 1982.

54. The president of Ben-Gurion University Yosef Tekoah admitted that the "Israeli public does not recognize the importance of the Soviet Jewish immigration, does not understand its importance to the State, its strength and development." Israel Public Council for Soviet Jewry, *News Bulletin*, No. 195/196, March–April 1971, pp. 6–7.

Rabbi Mordecai Kirshblum, cochairman of the commission on immigration and absorption of the Jewish Agency, attributed the decline to letters of Soviet Jews in Israel describing their problems.

55. See, for example, Leonard Fein, "A Wooden Welcome to Soviet Jews," *Moment*, Vol. 1, October 1975, pp. 78–79; Emanuel Litvinoff, "Emigrants Who Turn Away from Israel," *Insight*, Vol. 1, April 1975, pp. 1–3; G. E. Johnson, "America Again the Promised Land," *National Jewish Monthly*, Vol. 89, November 1974, pp. 22–26.

56. A singularly devoted figure in the close bonding between activists and those in the West has been Michael Sherbourne, a retired London schoolteacher, who learned enough Russian to make the first telephone contact with dissidents in 1969. He has made thousands of calls since and has shared his news with key Soviet Jewry groups throughout the world. Sherbourne also translated a number of surveys in a series called "Message from Moscow," drawn up by Jewish activists including Anatoly Shcharansky, Slepak, Lerner, Dina Beilina, and Vitaly Rubin, detailing violations of the Helsinki Agreement (see below pp. 722–29). The material came out intermittently and documented "the full force of a totalitarian apparatus" to suppress emigration and intimidate potential emigrants, cut contacts, and spread anti-Jewish and anti-Zionist material in the press, television, films, and books.

57. *Current: Newsletter of the Committee of Concerned Scientists*, Vol. 1, No. 1, March 1973, p. 2.

58. Telford Taylor, *Courts of Terror: Soviet Criminal Justice and Jewish Emigration*. New York, Knopf, 1976.

59. Ibid., p. x.

60. See Table 4, "Emigration since the Six-Day War," in Z. Alexander, "Jewish Emigration from the USSR in 1980," *Soviet Jewish Affairs*, Vol. 11, No. 2, 1981, p. 11. This analysis shows the number of departures and vyzovs from each of the republics and from selected cities between 1968 and 1980 (pp. 3–21). The author reports 780 known refusenik families (2,001 persons), as of 1976 (p. 20). For later figures, see Chapter 34.

61. Some of these are reported in Lukasz Hirsowicz, "The Soviet-Jewish Prob-

lem: Internal and International Developments, 1972–1976," in Lionel Kochan, ed., *The Jews in Soviet Russia since 1917*, 3d ed. Oxford, Oxford University Press, 1978, pp. 397–98.

62. See Smith's *The Russians*, op. cit., pp. 531–56, for his first-hand account of the cultural scene.

63. Ibid., pp. 594–95.

64. *Newsweek*, October 20, 1975, p. 53. In October 1975, Sakharov's selfless devotion to the cause of human rights was finally acknowledged when he was awarded the Nobel Peace Prize. The citation lauded him for showing that "the inviolable rights of man can serve as the only sure foundation" for peace.

65. Smith, op. cit., pp. 605–10. Smith believed that, as the seventies wore on, "dissent among the liberal Russian intelligentsia was disintegrating," and that the loose coalition of a few hundred dissident intellectuals called the "Democratic Movement" had been "dispersed, deported and demoralized" (p. 607). *A Chronicle of Current Events* temporarily suspended publication after Issue No. 27, dated October 15, 1972 (see Chapter 30, note 17). Since 1974, issues have continued to be published in samizdat form and include texts of letters, trial proceedings, notices of arrests, reports from prison camps, official documents, and interviews with the Western press—all related to violations of human rights in the Soviet Union. English translations of the journal are made by Amnesty International Publications, London. Rubenstein (op. cit., pp. 151–52) believed that the periodic reports by Western observers of the "collapse of the Soviet human rights movement," is belied by the continuation of the *Chronicle* and the later activities of the Helsinki Watch Groups. By 1980, however, he felt that "Soviet dissidents find themselves more vulnerable and isolated than at any time since their movement began" (p. 275).

66. Sakharov's countless interventions, letters, and statements are cited in detail in *A Chronicle of Current Events*, beginning in 1968 (in English 1971). His commitment to individual human rights never flagged, but he, too, was arrested on January 22, 1980 and banished to Gorky, accused of divulging state secrets to foreign diplomats and journalists. William Korey has recently written a splendid essay describing Sakharov's numerous interventions on behalf of Jews: "Andrei Sakharov—The Soviet Jewish Perspective," *Soviet Jewish Affairs*, Vol. 16, No. 3, November 1986, pp. 17–28.

67. Sara Honig, "Luntz [Lunts] Assesses Soviet Jewish Plight," *Alert*, May–June, 1976, p. 7.

68. The precise figures were: 1975, 13,459; 1976, 14,216; 1977, 16,737. In January 1975, President Ford claimed that the reduced emigration rate was the result of the passage of the Jackson-Vanik Amendment. In signing the Trade Reform Act on January 3, he expressed "reservations about the wisdom of legislative language that can only be seen as objectionable and discriminatory by other sovereign states." Quoted in "Chronicle of Events," *Soviet Jewish Affairs*, Vol. 5, No. 1, 1975, p. 129.

69. A *Novosti* commentary, "Soul Hunters," cited official data showing that

98.4 percent of Soviet Jews applying to leave had been granted permission. Ibid.

70. These actions as well as official anti-Semitic propaganda were intensified after the passage of the Soviet-inspired U.N. Resolution defining Zionism "as a form of racism and racial discrimination" in the fall of 1975.

71. Honig, op. cit., p. 7.

72. The "state secrets" provision can be applied arbitrarily to anyone, without any consistency or standard. For example, Viktor Brailovsky was supposedly exposed to confidential data and not permitted to emigrate, though Lunts, his superior at the Institute for Electronic Control Computers in Moscow, was, in February 1976.

73. U.S. Department of State, Bureau of Public Affairs, *Conference on Security and Cooperation in Europe, Final Act.* Washington, D.C., 1975, pp. 75, 81.

74. Sawyer, op. cit., p. 138.

75. See *Chronicle,* Nos. 40, 43, 44, and later issues for reports on the organization of these groups. See also Ludmilla Alexeyeva, *Soviet Dissent: Contemporary Movements for National, Religious, and Human Rights.* Carol Pearce and John Glad, trs. Middletown, Wesleyan University Press, 1985.

76. Rubenstein, op. cit., pp. 213–50, wrote enthusiastically about the Helsinki Watch Groups, but as of 1980, saw the regime shifting its primary target from the *Chronicle* to the Watch Groups. Among many others, Orlov was arrested in 1977, sentenced to seven years in a labor camp and five years in internal exile. See *Chronicle,* No. 50, May 15–18, 1978, for a detailed account of Orlov's trial.

77. Stephen J. Roth, "Facing the Belgrade Meeting: Helsinki—Two Years After," *Soviet Jewish Affairs,* Vol. 7, No. 1, 1977, pp. 4–5.

78. Statement by Foreign Secretary Dr. David Owen, May 18, 1977, in the House of Commons. Quoted in ibid., p. 6.

79. Ibid., p. 9.

80. "Chronicle of Events," *Soviet Jewish Affairs,* Vol. 5, No. 2, 1975, p. 121.

81. Moshe Decter, "On Brussels," *Moment,* April 1976, p. 42. See also Richard Cohen, "Background to Brussels II," *Congress Monthly,* February 1976 and "Brussels II: A Documentary Note," *Soviet Jewish Affairs,* Vol. 6, No. 1, 1976, pp. 71–76, which includes the text of the Declaration of the Second Conference and official Soviet Jewish reactions to the conference.

82. There is a very critical review, "Reflecting on Brussels II," by Irene Manekovsky and David Nussbaum, *Exodus,* May 6, 1976, pp. 4,8. Dr. Nahum Goldmann, who decided not to attend the conference because "he was told he would not be given an opportunity to voice his views," was also very critical of the value of such a conference, maintaining that "Soviet authorities are more sensitive to behind-the-scene diplomacy than to the clarion blasts of public rallies. . . ." *Jerusalem Post Weekly,* February 24, 1976. Leonard Schroeter, author of *The Last Exodus* and a very knowledgeable figure, was virtually ignored by conveners of the conference.

83. William W. Orbach, "The Yom Kippur War and the Soviet Jewry Movement," *Crossroads,* Jerusalem, pp. 205–6.

Soviet involvement in the war and Soviet attempts to maintain their interests in the Middle East are analyzed in Galia Golan, *Yom Kippur and After.* Cambridge, Cambridge University Press, 1977.

84. Sawyer, op. cit., p. 205.

85. On February 11, May 26, and August 4, there were arrests of ethnic Germans, ("Chronicle of Events," *Soviet Jewish Affairs,* Vol. 4, Nos. 1 and 2, 1974). On May 20, 188 Soviet Pentecostals appealed to President Nixon to help them emigrate to the United States. Ibid., Vol. 4, No. 2, 1974.

86. *American Jewish Yearbook,* Vol. 76, 1975, p. 381. Most Soviet citizens of German origin are descendants of colonists who came after the Manifesto of 1763, issued by Catherine the Great, which extended special privileges to those willing to settle the empty steppes of the Lower Volga. Between 1763 and 1862, an estimated 100,000 German settlers came to Russia. In 1924 the Volga German Autonomous Republic was created, in which about one-third of the 1.2 million Germans lived. In August 1941, the Volga German Republic was dissolved and some 800,000 Germans were deported from European Russia to Asiatic Russia. They lived under the strict supervision of the KGB until 1955. Between 1958 and 1960, 14,000 were allowed to emigrate, and from 1971 to 1975, another 19,000 emigrated. An illuminating study of the similarities and differences between conditions of life and history of Volga Germans and Soviet Jews can be found in John W. Kiser, "Emigration from the Soviet Union: The Case of the Soviet Germans," Institute for Jewish Policy Planning and Research of the Synagogue Council of America, Washington, D.C., Analysis No. 57, June 1976. Experiences of Germans and others trying to emigrate in subsequent years are described in each issue of *Chronicle.*

87. Cited in Roth, op. cit., p. 6.

88. Quoted in "Dual Messages to Washington," *Time,* February 14, 1977.

89. Roth, op. cit., p. 5.

90. Ibid., p. 9. The specific failures are spelled out in pp. 9–10, and desired clarifications of certain issues in pp. 11–17.

91. Ibid., p. 10.

92. Ibid., p. 12.

93. Ibid. Based on "document signed by B. Fain and others addressed to the 215th CPSU Congress."

94. Ibid.

95. *Chronicle of Current Events,* Nos. 33, 41, 42, 44, 45, 46, 47, 48, 49.

32. Jewish Emigration, 1976–84: Trials, Achievements, Doubts, and Dilemmas

1. David K. Shipler, *New York Times,* March 5, 1977. Fuller details of this period can be found in *Chronicle,* No. 45.

2. *New York Times,* op. cit.

3. Events described in Avital Shcharansky, with Ilana Ben-Josef, *Next Year in Jerusalem,* tr. from Russian by Stefani Hoffman, New York, Morrow, 1979,

pp. 83–84; and *Chronicle*, No. 45. See also *Alert*, July 7, 1977 for biographies of the Shcharansky family and letters to the Soviet Procurator General protesting arrest and charges.

4. *Chronicle*, Nos. 45, 46, 47. The most comprehensive work on Shcharansky—his early life, involvement in the human rights and Jewish national movements, his trial, imprisonment, and remarkable prison letters—is Martin Gilbert, *Shcharansky: Hero of our Time*. New York, Viking, 1986. See ibid., pp. 167–72, 173–74, 246–48 and passim, for Lipavsky's role.

5. *New York Times*, March 5, 1977.

6. Ibid.

7. *Chronicle*, No. 46, pp. 26–28. Much of the prosecution's case hinged on Shcharansky's contacts with Robert Toth, who was named as the agent allegedly masquerading as a journalist to whom Shcharansky allegedly had given military secrets. Toth had been arrested in June in Moscow while a Soviet scientist handed him a paper on parapsychology. During four intimidating grillings, Toth denied receiving any sensitive material from Shcharansky, but was required to sign a protocol, or transcript of his interrogation, in Russian, which he could not read. This transcript was produced in court as evidence against Shcharansky, who, throughout, understood that he was being used as a victim of a show trial.

8. *Chronicle*, No. 47, p. 22.

9. *Chronicle*, No. 50, p. 51.

10. Ibid., p. 52.

11. Later, in December 1979, an illuminating footnote to the case was added. A former leading Soviet prosecutor, Boris Kamenetsky, who emigrated to Israel in 1977, offered a detailed account of how the government's key witness, Lipavsky, began working for the KGB in the early 1960s as provocateur and informer. Kamenetsky had been a senior aide to the chief prosecutor in Uzbekistan, where Lipavsky grew up. Kamenetsky explained that he had not told the story before because his youngest brother was still in the Soviet Union, but was now out. Lipavsky, according to Kamenetsky, offered himself to the KGB in 1962 in order to save his father, apparently accused of stealing state property, from the death sentence. After Lipavsky became a KGB agent, his father's sentence was commuted to thirteen years. *New York Times*, December 17, 1979.

12. *Chronicle* No. 47, p. 29.

13. Ibid., pp. 23–24.

14. Ibid., p. 26.

15. Ibid., p. 28.

16. One attorney, Dina Kaminskaya, was dismissed from her position and later ordered to leave the country. See Dina Kaminskaya, *Final Judgment: My Life as a Soviet Defense Attorney*, Michael Glenny, tr. New York, Simon and Schuster, 1982. The period awaiting trial is described in Gilbert, op. cit., pp. 216–29.

17. Described in detail in *Chronicle*, No. 50, pp. 42–69, and in Gilbert op. cit., pp. 231–76. Some information on the trial was also apparently obtained

from Shcharansky's brother Leonid, who was permitted to attend. See "The Moscow Trial," *Newsweek*, July 24, 1978, pp. 20–28; and "The Shcharansky Trial," *Time* July 24, 1978, pp. 24–31.

18. Some observers believed that these widely publicized statements might prove to be harmful. David Zilberman, in "Dissent in the Soviet Union," *Liberation*, Fall 1977, called them "counterproductive, if not disastrous" (p. 32). He also believed that after 1968, the dissident movement suffered a "dramatic loss of momentum and popularity within the country" and relied overmuch on international public opinion and support (p. 5).

19. Michael Dobbs, "Belgrade Meeting Near End," *Washington Post*, January 28, 1978.

20. Michael Getler, "Belgrade Meeting: Lost Hopes and Stalled Effort at Détente," *Washington Post*, February 23, 1978.

21. David K. Shipler, "Soviet Repression and U.S.: Both Sides in a Quandary," *New York Times*, December 7, 1977.

22. National Conference on Soviet Jewry, *News Bulletin*, No. 119, January 16, 1978, cited in Thomas E. Sawyer, *The Jewish Minority in the Soviet Union*. Boulder, Colo., Westview Press, 1979, p. 207.

23. Quoted in Sawyer, ibid.

24. National Conference on Soviet Jewry, Soviet Jewry Research Bureau, *Jewish Emigration from the USSR: Statistics*, n.d. As of November 1977, there were an estimated 2,000 refuseniks, but it was not clear if this figure also included children. See D. M. Jaffe, "Refusenik Life," *Soviet Jewish Affairs*, Vol. 8, No. 2, 1978, p. 25.

  On November 15, 1978, in speaking to a group of refuseniks in Moscow, Shumilin refused to show them reports from their places of work "on security grounds," and said that there was no maximum term for obtaining permission to leave and that no term would be fixed. He also intimated that there were people who would never be given permission to leave. *Chronicle*, No. 51, p. 156. The finality of this decision, however, has not been accepted by emigration supportive organizations.

25. Reports of their trials can be found in *Chronicle*, No. 48, pp. 5–8, 9–14, 23–25, 33–38; and No. 49, pp. 3–9, 14–17. A summary of *Punitive Medicine* and *The Silent Asylum* (accounts of prisoners in psychiatric hospitals, compiled by Podrabinek and V. Nekipelov) may be found in Harvey Fireside, *Soviet Psychoprisons*. New York, Norton, 1979, pp. 133–82. See also note 35 of present chapter.

26. Orlov was sentenced to seven years at hard labor and was sent to Labor Camp No. 35 in the Ural Mountains; Ginzburg who had already spent seven years in the Gulag was sentenced to eight years at hard labor. A fervent convert to the Russian Orthodox Church, Ginzburg was accused of using a fund set up by Solzhenitsyn to help prisoners and families pay for "sex orgies" and "hostile activities of criminal elements." He was sent to the squalid Sosnovka labor camp in the Mordovian Autonomous Republic. Shcharansky went to Vladimir and was transferred in October to Chistopol in the Tatar Republic.

27. V. Markman, "For Whom the Bell Tolls," published in Release from Detroit Committee for Soviet Jewry, n.d.
28. "Press Conference [with S. Levinzon], March 5, 1979," *News Bulletin*, Israel Public Council for Soviet Jewry, No. 151/152, March 31, 1979.
29. *Chronicle*, No. 51, p. 46.
30. Paul S. Appelbaum, "Law and Psychiatry, Soviet Style," *Alert*, September–October, 1981, p. 10. In 1979, Grigorenko was examined by a team of American psychiatrists and neurologists and found to be completely free of diagnosable mental illness.
31. Paul S. Appelbaum, "Gluzman Declines Offer from KGB," *Exodus*, Vol. 6, No. 3, May–June, 1976, p. 3. Published by Union of Councils for Soviet Jews. Grigorenko died in 1987.
32. *Scientists Bulletin*, Nos. 119, 122, cited in D. M. Jaffe, op cit., p. 32.
33. Robert Coles, "Victims of Soviet Psychiatry: A Report from Honolulu," *New York Review*, October 27, 1977, pp. 23, 26. In July 1980, another Jewish activist, Vladimir Kislik, was confined to a psychiatric hospital after being arrested on unfounded charges of "malicious hooliganism" two weeks before the start of the Moscow Olympics. A metallurgical engineer, Kislik had been trying to emigrate since 1973, when his wife and son were permitted to leave. When his prison term was extended without explanation, Kislik went on a hunger strike and was placed in a mental institution. *Alert*, August 14, 1980.
34. Peter Reddaway, "An Appeal to Psychiatrists," *New York Review*, March 18, 1982, p. 54.
35. Coles, op cit., p. 26. Alexander Podrabinek, a leading Soviet figure in the campaign against the abuse of psychiatry and one of the founders of the Working Commission, was brought to trial on December 3, 1980 in Yakutsk on charges of anti-Soviet slander but actually for smuggling out his book *Punitive Medicine* on his investigation of confinement of dissidents in mental hospitals. The manuscript was published by Amnesty International in London in 1980.

A bold appeal to world psychiatrists has recently been smuggled to the West from a Russian labor camp in the Urals, written by Dr. Anatoly Koryagin, himself a psychiatrist, who was sentenced in June 1981 to a twelve-year term in prison for opposing the use of political psychiatry. "Let there be no doubt," he writes, ". . . that the Soviet authorities have turned a most humane branch of medicine into an instrument for achieving a main aim of their internal policy—the suppression of dissent. Peter Reddaway, *Uncensored Russia: The Human Rights Movement in the Soviet Union*. New York, American Heritage, 1972, p. 54. Periodically, fears have been expressed about the condition of Dr. Koryagin, and most recently in the *New York Review of Books*, February 12, 1987 ("A Test Case"), pp. 3–4, David Satter expressed grave concern about his very survival. As a result of unsuccessful efforts to force him to recant, Dr. Koryagin spent three years in solitary confinement, two years on hunger strikes, during which he has been fed artificially, and six months in a punishment cell. When his wife saw him in September 1983, she said he was reduced to a "starving bag of water." Unexpectedly, Koryagin was released soon after Satter's letter appeared.

Continuous criticism from the West has forced authorities to intern fewer victims in central institutions such as the Serbsky Institute and send more of them to the provinces, where fewer foreign colleagues are apt to visit. Podrabinek deplored the continued professional contacts Western psychiatrists still maintained and urged a vigorous exposure of the shameful practices. The Working Commission has published numerous case histories in its *Information Bulletin* and news about those arrested and their trials appear in issues of *Chronicle of Current Events*. See *Chronicle* No. 50, pp. 81–89, for the trial of Podrabinek.

36. In the voluminous literature on these conflicts, the following are a few that analyze opposing positions or suggest possible solutions: Phil Baum, *Noshrim: The Current Dilemma*. Commission on International Affairs, American Jewish Congress, 1979; Avraham Schenker, "The Dropouts: A Zionist and Jewish Dilemma," *Israel Horizons*, December 1978, pp. 9–12; Leonard Fein, "Let My People Go . . . Where?" *Moment*, January 1977, pp. 7–12 and his "No Need to Apologize," in *Moment*, January–February 1980, pp. 22–47; "The Noshrim: A Jewish Tragedy," *The American Zionist*, February–March 1980, pp. 6–12; Leon Dulzin and Leonard Schroeter, "Whither Soviet Jews: The Debate Goes On," *Moment*, September 1979, pp. 7–14. By the early eighties, as emigration figures fell, the debate became more and more academic, until Israel's prime minister Yitzhak Shamir raised the issue of *noshrim* again in January 1987, insisting that the United States refuse the status of refugee to any Soviet Jews emigrating.

37. David K. Shipler reported in the *New York Times*, September 13, 1981, that the Israel Ministry of Labor and Social Welfare had reported that from 1969 to 1979, 510,528 Israelis had left the country—reason enough for Israeli anguish and bitterness over the failure to attract more Soviet Jews to help replenish this loss—only partially offset by 384,000 immigrants during this period.

38. Some of the earlier studies of resettlement in the United States, including reasons for preferring the United States, are: *Soviet Jewish Resettlement in North America*, Council of Jewish Federations and Welfare Funds, November 1975; Ethel Taft, "The Absorption of Soviet Jewish Immigrants," *Journal of Jewish Communal Service*, Winter 1977, p. 166–71; Zvi Y. Gitelman, "Soviet Immigrants and American Absorption Efforts: A Case Study in Detroit," *Journal of Jewish Communal Service*, Summer 1978, pp. 72–82.

39. By the end of 1977, 123,180 Soviet Jews had emigrated to Israel while 28,332 were assisted by HIAS to resettle in the United States, Canada, Australia, New Zealand, Latin America, and Western Europe (23,582 of whom settled in the United States). Gaynor I. Jacobsen, "Perspectives on the 'Dropout' Issue," *Journal of Jewish Communal Service*, Autumn 1978, p. 883. See also Sara Honig, "Plan to Stop Aid to Soviet Immigration Drop-outs in Vienna," *Jerusalem Post*, September 27, 1976. One suggestion was to deny

refugee status to any Jew leaving the USSR with an Israeli visa, which HIAS was trying to secure for them. Initially, and up to 1977, most Soviet immigrants to the United States came as conditional entrants, or, technically, refugees under old immigration laws. Between 1978 and 1980, they were accepted as parolees, a conditional admission involving the loss of two years from the usual naturalization requirement. This condition was removed by the passage of the Refugee Act of 1980.

40. Zvi Nezer, "Jewish Emigration from the USSR in 1981–82," felt that the reduction of exit permits in 1980 was "drastic," and interpreted this "as a sign of Soviet displeasure with the 'drop-out' phenomenon," seeing a correlation between the number of "drop-outs" and the scale of reduction in visas in 1980 and 1981. *Soviet Jewish Affairs*, Vol. 12, No. 3, November 1982, p. 16. Z. Alexander, "Jewish Emigration from the USSR in 1980," felt that the rise in the number of "drop-outs" might endanger the future of Jewish emigration from the USSR." *Soviet Jewish Affairs*, Vol. 11, No. 2, May 1981, p. 18.

Among others, Benjamin Pinkus not only rejects this idea but believes that it may have been "disinformation activity of the KGB with the aim of sowing dissension among the different organizations which handle the absorption of Soviet Jewish emigrants." See his "The Emigration of National Minorities from the USSR in the Post-Stalin Era," *Soviet Jewish Affairs*, Vol. 13, No. 1, 1983, pp. 31–32.

41. Shipler, *New York Times*, op. cit.

An American consul in the USSR noted that those Jews who, "in a different political climate" were designated as "Russians," not "Jews" in their internal passports were consistently being refused permits. This distinction, apparently, is of great importance because, according to Dr. Maurice Friedberg, a widely respected Russian scholar, "Soviet authorities insist on maintaining the fiction that anyone who chooses to leave the USSR must be both a Zionist and a Jew. . . . This pretense was observed even in the case of several Russian Orthodox leaders who were forced to leave Russia a few years ago, in effect, deported abroad." Maurice Friedberg, "From Moscow to Jerusalem—and Points West," *Commentary*, Vol. 65, No. 5, 1978, p. 63.

42. In 1978 this aid amounted to twenty million dollars. At the same time, the United Jewish Appeal allocated forty million dollars less in 1980 than in 1979 to Israel as a result of reduced resettlement needs there. Israel Public Council for Soviet Jewry, *News Bulletin*, Nos. 167/168, December 31, 1979.

43. Jewish Telegraph Agency, September 10, 1981.

44. *Jerusalem Post*, January 1, 1979.

45. D. A. Harris, "The Emigration Phenomenon: New Challenges" (a review of Robert O. Freedman, ed., *Soviet Jewry in the Decisive Decade, 1971–1980*. Durham, Duke University Press, 1984), *Soviet Jewish Affairs*, Vol. 14, No. 3, 1984, p. 59.

46. Robert J. Brym, "Soviet Emigration Policy: Internal Determinants," *Soviet Jewish Affairs*, Vol. 15, No. 2, 1985, p. 29. The author notes, for example,

that during the period between 1975 and 1977, when Soviet-American relations were "relatively good," and the incidence of refusals dropped
markedly, the emigration rate dropped from the 1972–74 levels. However,
he neglects to factor in the reaction to the passage of the Jackson-Vanik
Amendment. At the same time, although internal factors are very difficult
to appraise, they are generally ignored in analyses by Western organizational supporters. In the above cited reference, John L. Scherer also rejects
the theory of absolute linkage between emigration and the course of Soviet-American relations, although the Soviet Union has encouraged this
notion. He suggests that many holders of vyzovs (380,000, as of 1980) were
not fired from their jobs or allowed to emigrate because of the immense
economic loss to the state and that emigration for the rest of the decade
would probably not rise. Ibid., pp. 38–44.

Theodore H. Friedgut finds the bitter anti-Zionist campaign and attacks
on Israel's invasion of Lebanon related to the curtailment of emigration and
influenced by two domestic factors: "the disastrous state of the Soviet
economy, greatly aggravated by four successive harvest failures" and "the
protracted crisis of an elderly and ailing leadership." See his "Soviet Anti-
Zionism and Antisemitism—Another Cycle," *Soviet Jewish Affairs*, Vol. 14,
No. 1, February 1984, p. 4.

47. Nezer, op cit., p. 10. The author points to the very sharp decline in visas
from 1979 to 1980 in the Ukraine, the RSFSR, and Uzbekistan (see Table 2,
p. 12) and the sharp drop in certain cities, such as Kiev, Odessa, and Tashkent (Table 3, p. 13). In Odessa, according to the *New York Times* correspondent Craig R. Whitney, in mid-summer 1980 he heard that "people
are being told that the Jewish exodus was harming the well-being of the
city as a whole. If the West can use these people, so should we." *New York
Times*, July 11, 1980. Whitney also noted that there were a "surprising number
of Jewish names" among the prestigious Lenin Prizes.

48. Nezer, op cit., pp. 10–11. In the summer of 1980, it was reported that
many Jews in Chernovtsy, in the Ukraine, received confidential questionnaires, in which they were asked:

(1) What is your attitude to Jews who wish to leave the USSR?
(2) Do you have any relatives abroad and what contact do you maintain with them?
(3) What is your attitude to living in Birobidzhan where you would be offered a
good job in a large flat?

A protest by local Ukrainians against the "special privilege of emigration
being accorded Jews" was also reported. *Alert*, August 28, 1980, p. 3. Whitney also noted, ibid., that a record number of emigrating Armenians (7,000)
were being projected for 1980—all going to the United States. The number
of German emigrants also remained steady: 7,226 for 1979 and 6,954 for
1980. The figures dropped sharply thereafter until 1987.

49. Israel Public Council for Soviet Jewry, *News Bulletin*, No. 167/168, December 31, 1979, pp. 1–2.

50. Brym, op. cit. p. 32. In an analysis of Soviet policy toward Zionism at a

conference in the Academy of Sciences' Institute of Oriental Studies, in February 1976, academician B. G. Gafurov, in asking why so many Jews have already left the country, said that some left for religious reasons and that those who left from the Baltic States, Western Ukraine, and Western Belorussia had "only recently become part of the USSR and are therefore still contaminated by the spirit of petty private ownership." He was willing for the shopkeepers, writers, and artists to go, but said, "It's a pity when specialists in important branches of the economy and science go. They are lured away by the monopolies. . . ." Described in the samizdat journal *Evrei v SSSR* (Jews in the USSR), No. 14, Moscow, 1977 and cited by E. L. Solmar, "Protocols of the Anti-Zionists," *Soviet Jewish Affairs*, Vol. 8., No. 2, 1978, p. 61.

51. *Chronicle*, No. 52, p. 127, cited in ibid., p. 35.
52. "Chronicle of Events," *Soviet Jewish Affairs*, Vol. 10, No. 3, November 1980, p. 91.
53. Lukasz Hirszowicz, ed., *Proceedings of the Experts' Conference on Soviet Jewry*, London, January 4–6, 1983. London, Institute of Jewish Affairs, 1985, p. 34. See also Lukasz Hirszowicz, "Brezhnev's Speech to the 26th Congress of the Communist Party of the Soviet Union," Institute of Jewish Affairs *Research Report*, No. 4, April 1981.

There were two other indications of a slight, possibly significant, official turn of policy toward Jews at this time. One dealt with the dusty past— Birobidzhan—as if it still had meaning; the other—an increase in Yiddish cultural activities (see Chapter 33), has more substance, and holds out slender threads of hope for some identifiably Jewish life for those who remain.

54. At the time of the Conference, forty-three monitors were in prison or in exile. Prior to the Conference, the press carried statements by Western leaders underscoring numerous violations of human rights in the Soviet Union and Soviet bloc countries. In October 1980, Senator Frank Church reported that since 1978 "more than 280 Soviet human rights activists have been imprisoned. Just since January of this year, 57 persons have been imprisoned . . . for seeking to exercise the basic human rights guaranteed them under the Helsinki accords. Persecution of Soviet religious activists is increasing, with 180 jailed in 1979 and 264 in prisons this year." The "brutal military invervention in Afghanistan last December" was also condemned as a violation of five of the ten Helsinki principles. *Alert*, October 10, 1980. From his exile in Gorky, Sakharov urged the Western states "to coordinate their tactics with more determination and consistency than at Belgrade. . . . The whole point of the . . . accords is mutual monitoring, not mutual evasion of difficult problems." *Boston Globe*, September 16, 1980.
55. *Washington Post* editorial, October 19, 1980.
56. "Madrid—A Midterm Review," Madrid CSCE Review Meeting: An Interim Report by the CSCE Staff, January 6, 1981.
57. Joseph M. Markham, "Soviet Stalls Talks in Madrid on Rights," *New York Times*, November 2, 1980.
58. "Madrid Ends and Helsinki Continues: The Agreement at the CSCE [Con-

ference on Security and Cooperation in Europe] Follow-Up Conference," Institute of Jewish Affairs *Research Report*, 1983.

59. See Richard Pipes, "Soviet Relations with the USA," in the *Experts' Conference*, op. cit., p. 111.

60. Nahum Goldmann, "The Hammer and Sickle and Star of David," Israel Public Council for Soviet Jewry, *News Bulletin*, August 31, 1982, No. 225/226, pp. 7–8.

61. *The Autobiography of Nahum Goldmann: Sixty Years of Jewish Life*. New York, Holt, Rinehart, and Winston, 1969, pp. 301, 306.

62. Goldmann, "The Hammer and Sickle," op. cit., p. 8.

   In a letter to the author dated June 18, 1982, Goldmann spoke of his earlier interest in contacts between Soviet Jews and the World Jewish Congress, of which he was President, and his pessimism about the future: "I do not see any positive outcome in the near future, especially because of the Jewish agitation against the Soviet Union, giving the main importance to the question of emigration and not, as I insisted, on the right of Jews in the USSR to live as Jews. . . . Generally speaking, I regard the fact that the Jewish people in its majority is violently anti-Soviet as dangerous, because it will make Jewish life in the Soviet Union impossible in the long run." See also William W. Orbach, *The American Movement to Aid Soviet Jews*. Amherst, University of Massachusetts Press, 1979, pp. 59–60; Marshall Goldman, "The Case for Moderation," *Moment*, October 1977, pp. 49–50; and Nora Levin, "Soviet Jewry: Problems and Policies," *Congress Monthly*, February 1977, pp. 11–13, urging policies beyond emigration rights.

63. Brailovsky's arrest and trial aroused worldwide attention. Brailovsky was a well-known refusenik-scientist who took over the leadership of the Moscow Scientific Seminar in the spring of 1977 (after Mark Azbel emigrated) and who became coeditor of the samizdat journal *Jews in the USSR* (Russian) later that year. In a lecture by Azbel at Princeton University in November 1977, he reported that Brailovsky was told by authorities that he would be permitted to emigrate if he would testify against Shcharansky; if not, he too would be charged with spying. Both the journal and seminar were continuously harassed and interventions on behalf of both and Brailovsky personally were steady and persistent. In April 1980, Brailovsky was arrested and told that his articles "defamed the Soviet." He was released, then rearrested on November 13. There was a two-day trial on June 17–18, 1981, in a heavily guarded Moscow courthouse, in which the prosecution concentrated on the journal *Jews in the USSR*. Amid a loud outcry from the world scientific community, Brailovsky was sentenced to thirty-nine months in internal exile. He was released in 1984 and allowed to emigrate on September 7, 1987.

64. Moshe Decter, "Crisis in the Soviet Jewry Movement," *Moment*, April 1976, pp. 33–48.

65. *Tarbut Yehudit Bi-Brit Ha-Moatsot* (Jewish Culture in the Soviet Union), Cultural Department of the World Jewish Congress, Jerusalem, 1972, and

summary of conference in Lukasz Hirszowicz, "Jewish Culture and Survival in the USSR," *Soviet Jewish Affairs*, Vol. 3, No. 1, 1973, pp. 128–31.

66. Quoted in Decter, op. cit. p. 45.

67. Eli Eyal, "The Suppression of Jewish Cultural Rights in the Soviet Union." Presented at the Copenhagen meeting of the Presidium of the Brussels Conference. Department of Information, World Zionist Organization, December 1980.

68. See, for example, Vitaly Rubin's strong defense of the indivisibility of human rights ("Human Rights Are Indivisible," *Jerusalem Post*, August 1, 1978) as against Yermiahu Branover's advice to Soviet Jews to dissociate themselves completely from the human rights movement (interview published in *Jerusalem Post*, July 21, 1978), and Vladimir Lazaris' strong defense of Branover ("The Don Quixote Complex," *Jerusalem Post*, August 15, 1978).

69. Some appeared in Russian in the journal *Sion*. See also *Russian Aliya and Its Relationship to Russian Culture and to Israeli Culture*. Seminar on Humanitarian Problems, Jerusalem, 1977; and David Prital, ed., *In Search of Self: The Soviet Jewish Intelligentsia and the Exodus*. Jerusalem, Mt. Scopus Pubs., 1982. Within the Soviet Union, the samizdat journal *Evrei v S.S.S.R.* often dealt with the problematic future of Jewish culture and the journal *Tarbut*, which first appeared in Moscow in 1975, contained many reprints and translations of essays dealing with Jewish culture.

70. For intermittent contacts since the break in relations in 1967, see Chapter 34.

33. Permitted Margins of Jewish Life, 1970–85

1. Zvi Nezer, "Jewish Emigration from the USSR in 1981–82," *Soviet Jewish Affairs*, Vol. 14, No. 1, February 1984, p. 14, puts this figure at 381,700.

2. D. Harris, "A Note on the Problem of the 'Noshrim'," *Soviet Jewish Affairs*, Vol. 6, No. 2, 1976, p. 107.

3. Theodore H. Friedgut, "Soviet Jewry: The Silent Majority," *Soviet Jewish Affairs*, Vol. 10, No. 2, May 1980, pp. 3–19.

4. See Mordechai Altshuler, "The Jews in the 1979 Soviet Census," *Soviet Jewish Affairs*, Vol. 10, No. 3, November 1980, pp. 3–12; Lukasz Hirszowicz, "Further Data on the Jewish Population from the 1979 Census," *Soviet Jewish Affairs*, Vol. 11, No. 2, May 1981, pp. 53–61; and Yoel Florsheim, "Demographic Significance of Jewish Emigration from the USSR," *Soviet Jewish Affairs*, Vol. 10, No. 3, February 1980, pp. 5–22, for detailed analyses of the 1980 and 1979 Censuses. The 1979 decline from the 1980 figure of 2,151,000 was 15.9 percent—8.1 percent attributable to emigration and 7.7 percent to an excess of deaths over births and to a change from Jewish to another national identification. In nine of the eleven republics officially surveyed in 1979 (Kazakhstan, Kirgizia, Turkmen, and Armenia were omitted), there was a marked decline from 1970 in the percentage of Jews who declared a Jewish language as their mother tongue. (Even so, 257,000, or

14.2 percent declared Yiddish to be their mother tongue; and another 135,000 or 7.5 percent declared it to be their second language. Thus, almost one quarter of the Soviet Jewish population knows Yiddish. Most, of course, are older Jews, but undoubtedly a number of their children have heard Yiddish at home and have some familiarity with it.) In the Slavonic republics (RSFSR, the Ukraine, and Belorussia), the proportion of Jews who declared Russian as their first language was between 85 and 90 percent, and those who declared Russian as either their first or second language was 98 percent or higher. Hirszowicz, p. 55. These high percentages of linguistic Russification may be just a little higher than the use of English by Jews in the United States, where, however, there exist rich opportunities to be religiously and culturally Jewish in several languages.

5. Nearly one out of every two marriages among Soviet Jews involves a non-Jewish partner, according to a 1982 World Jewish Congress study. The study, based on official Soviet statistics from the 1960s to the mid-1970s, examined marriage patterns in four Soviet republics and three cities. The percentages ranged from a high of 76.7 percent in the Ukraine, to 27.7 percent in the city of Makhachkala bordering the Caspian Sea. After calculating the weighted average of these percentages, the rate of mixed marriages among Jews was determined to be between 40 and 50. Report of study in the *Jewish Exponent* (Philadelphia), January 29, 1982. The Soviet Jewish scholar, M. Chlenov notes a 50 percent rate in some regions (cited in Hirszowicz' "Uni-National and Mixed Marriages in the USSR," Institute of Jewish Affairs *Research Report*, No. 19, December 1983, p. 4, from "Jews in the USSR," *Sovetish heymland*, No. 7, 1982, pp. 102–3, 110). Hirszowicz' own findings are lower: 33 percent in the RSFSR, 19 percent in the Ukraine, and 14 percent in Belorussia. In 1979, 81.2 percent of Soviet Jewry lived in these three republics, the only republics for which data on Jewish families are available. These figures are lower than many other observers have assumed, according to Hirszowicz, who believes that a greater danger to the Jewish demographic decline lies in the dwindling size of the Jewish family. *Research Report*, op. cit., pp. 3–4.

Pinkus, however, although he noted the limited data on inter-marriage and its effect on Jewish identity, observed that "the test comes when the children of mixed couples reach the age of sixteen and must choose between the national identities of their parents." (In the Fain study, 93 percent declared that they would prefer not to register their children as Jewish; 60 percent said that they preferred that "nationality" be removed from passports. See note 15.) Benjamin Pinkus, "National Identity and Emigration Patterns among Soviet Jewry," *Soviet Jewish Affairs*, Vol. 15, No. 3, 1985, pp. 5, 6. The entire study, pp. 3–28, is an analysis of categories of Jewish emigrants, constituent elements in personal and public Jewish identity, motivations for emigration, and interrelationships between and among these elements.

6. Friedgut, op. cit., p. 13.

7. Ibid., p. 16. In Lukasz Hirszowicz, ed., *Proceedings of the Experts' Conference*

on Soviet Jewry, London, January 4–6, 1983. London, Institute of Jewish Affairs, 1985, Hirszowicz noted that in a Moscow Radio English broadcast in 1982, the number given was "close to 260,000" (p. 26).

8. Friedgut, op. cit., p. 16.

9. William W. Orbach, "A Periodization of Soviet Policy Towards Jews," *Soviet Jewish Affairs*, Vol. 12, No. 3, November 1982, p. 59.

10. Hirszowicz, *Proceedings*, op. cit., p. 30.

11. These generalizations are largely based on Friedgut, op. cit., pp. 6–9. The 1970 Census figures for Moscow, Leningrad, and Kiev should be adjusted for the emigration of 42,575 from those cities for the period 1976–81 (11,983 from Moscow, 11,913 from Leningrad, and 18,679 from Kiev). Florsheim, op. cit., p. 13 and Z. Alexander, "Jewish Emigration from the Soviet Union in 1980," *Soviet Jewish Affairs*, Vol. 11, No. 2, May 1981, p. 15.

12. Vitaly Rubin, "Moscow Testimony: Is There Any Hope for Those Who Choose To Stay?" *Present Tense*, Vol. 2, Spring 1975, pp. 54–55. (Dr. Rubin died in 1981.)

13. Ibid., pp. 58–59.

14. "A Message from Soviet Jewish Activists on How to Assist Jewish Identity and Culture in the USSR," tr. from the Russian. New York, National Jewish Community Relations Advisory Council, [1976]. See also [Alexander Voronel], "Culture Revival or Emigration: An Activist's View," *Jewish Week*, February 12–18, 1976, p. 16. In the mid-seventies, Voronel said that "Jewish *samizdat* materials are very popular in the Soviet Union not so much among young applicants for emigration, the so-called *refuseniks*, but among those who have no desire to emigrate, but are interested in things Jewish." See his "Search for Jewish Identity in Russia," *Soviet Jewish Affairs*, Vol. 5, No. 2, 1975, p. 74. The Jewish activists have continuously pressed for Jewish cultural rights. See *News Bulletin of the Scientists' Committee of the Israel Public Council for Soviet Jewry*, No. 18, March 15, 1976; statements published in *Insight* (London), Vol. 2, No. 10, October 1976, among others.

15. Described in Judy Siegel, "Search for Identity," *Jerusalem Post*, April 3, 1981, p. 9. Although the symposium was canceled, the survey was completed and most of the questionnaires were smuggled out of the Soviet Union to the West. The Center for Public Affairs in Jerusalem has analyzed the data and prepared a full report, *Jewishness in the Soviet Union: Report of an Empirical Study*, 1984. The questionnaire, which was developed by Michael Chlenkov, an anthropologist and Hebrew teacher in the Soviet Union, and a sociologist who wishes to remain anonymous, was tested in a pilot survey of 100 residents in Riga. Because of the problems involved in conducting surveys in the Soviet Union, sixty copies of the questionnaire had to be typed with several carbons each. Sympathetic interviewers then had to be obtained and from May to November 1976 when surveillance was fairly light, 1500 interviews were completed, of which 1215 were eventually brought to Israel.

Among the conclusions in such an admittedly limited survey are the following:

1. Men are more likely than women to express their Jewishness, both in public and private ways;
2. Age is not consistently related to Jewishness, although those over 60 years of age have higher levels of Jewish self-expression;
3. Jews living in the Caucasus and Central Asia and in regions annexed to the USSR in 1939–40 have higher levels of Jewish identity and commitment than do other Jews;
4. A high proportion of respondents expressed a desire for opportunities to enrich their knowledge of Jewish history and culture;
5. Some Jewish religious expression is correlated more strongly with a sense of Jewish identity than any other element.

Jewishness in the Soviet Union, op. cit., pp. 1–5, 43–44. Findings regarding Jewish education for children, official status of Jews, and attitudes toward Soviet Jewry's future were also analyzed (pp. 27–42).

16. Letter from Professor Benjamin Fain to author, dated June 2, 1976.
17. "Moscow Symposium on Jewish Culture in USSR," *Jewish Currents,* February 1977, p. 4.
18. Joseph S. Drew, "The Moscow Book Fair," *American Educator,* December 1977, p. 28. See also Joseph S. Drew, "At Moscow's Book Fair," *Nation,* January 28, 1978, pp. 78–82.
19. Drew, *American Educator,* op. cit., p. 28.
20. Ibid., p. 29.
21. Ibid.
22. Richard Yaffe, "Soviet Jews at the Fair," *Israel Horizons,* December 1979, p. 25.
23. Ibid.
24. Ruth Septee, "The Moscow Book Fair," *Reconstructionist,* January 1980, p. 23.
25. Ibid.
26. Joseph Mlotek, *Yiddish Studies and MJS Newsletter,* Vol. VI, No. 1, Winter 1979, pp. 11–12.
27. Ibid., p. 15.
28. Israel Public Council for Soviet Jewry, *News Bulletin,* No. 163/164, September 30, 1979, p. 10.
29. *Jewish Exponent* (Philadelphia), October 4, 1985. At the September 1983 Fair, the Soviet Foreign Language Publishing House, Raduga, signed options for the rights to two books of Jewish content: *Voices from the Holocaust,* edited by Sylvia Rothschild, and *Hebrew Ballads and Other Poems,* edited by E. Lasker-Schuler. (*Jewish Currents,* December 1983, p. 79.) The Association of Jewish Book Publishers distributed free 10,000 copies of a 52-page catalog of titles, a Hebrew-Yiddish alphabet chart, four pages in Russian on the Jewish holidays, a Jewish calendar through 1987, several prayers, and the Sabbath candle-lighting blessing. *Jewish Currents,* November 1983, p. 47. See also Elias Schulman, "Bringing Jewish Books to Russia," *The Book Peddler* (New York), Winter 1985, No. 5, p. 5.
30. On July 14, 1975, for example, Intourist announced that "tourist-Zionists"

would be regarded as "interfering in Russia's internal affairs." This announcement followed a similar warning in the Soviet weekly *Nedelya*. "Chronicle of Events," *Soviet Jewish Affairs*, Vol. 5, No. 2, 1975, p. 121.

31. V. P. Ruben, "Soyuz ravnykh" (Union of Equals), *Literaturnaya gazeta*, January 12, 1976, quoted in Lukasz Hirszowicz, "Jewish Cultural Life in the USSR—A Survey," *Soviet Jewish Affairs*, Vol. 7, No. 2, 1977, p. 15.

32. Hirszowicz, "Jewish Cultural Life," op. cit., p. 16.

33. "Chronicle of Events," *Soviet Jewish Affairs*, Vol. 13, No. 3, November 1983, p. 95.

34. "Chronicle of Events," *Soviet Jewish Affairs*, Vol. 11, No. 3, November 1981, p. 97.

35. "Chronicle of Events," *Soviet Jewish Affairs*, Vol. 9, No. 2, 1979, p. 96.

36. *Alert*, May 2, 1980, p. 4.

37. Hirszowicz, "Jewish Cultural Life," op. cit., p. 17.

38. *Alert*, October 31, 1979, p. 5.

39. Shvartser died in 1979; the Ensemble has recently been directed by Felix Berman.

40. Anthony Austin, "New Play in Moscow Exposes the Anti-Semitism of Babi Yar," *New York Times*, October 14, 1980.

41. Ibid. Two other quite exceptional works in Russian (besides the work of Evtushenko and Kuznetzov) dealing with the Holocaust and published after the war were Masha Rolnikaite's diary *Ya dolzhna rasskazat* (I Must Tell), Moscow, Politizat, 1965; and Anatoly Rybakov, *Tyazhely pesok* (Heavy Sand), first published in issues 7, 8, and 9 of *Oktyabr* (Moscow), 1978, and in book form by Sovetski pisatel in 1979.

In the same year there appeared an English translation of Boris Polevoi's *The Final Reckoning: Nuremberg Diaries* (Moscow, Progress Publishers). Polevoi had seen Babi Yar, Treblinka, Maidanek, and Auschwitz and had admitted to becoming "hardened" by the evidence, but was much shaken when Lev Smirnov, the Soviet Chief Prosecutor's assistant, read from Stroop's report of the destruction of the Warsaw Ghetto and from Hans Frank's diaries specifically detailing the mass murder of Jews. It is not known whether this material (pp. 108–14) appears in the Russian edition, which was published in 1968.

Jakub Blum deals with lesser-known Soviet writers in the 1960s and 1970s who depicted Jews in World War II: Fedor Grachev, I. Grekova, Ilya Konstantinovsky, as well as Kuznetzov and Evtushenko; and Vera Rich, with Jewish themes and characters in Belorussian literature. Jakub Blum, "Soviet Russian Literature," in *The Image of the Jew in Soviet Literature: The Post-Stalin Period*. New York, Ktav, 1985, pp. 39–97; and Vera Rich, "Jewish Themes and Characters in Belorussian Texts," in ibid., pp. 209–71.

42. "Chronicle of Events," *Soviet Jewish Affairs*, Vol. 11, No. 3, November 1981, p. 97.

43. "Chronicle of Events," *Soviet Jewish Affairs*, Vol. 15, No. 2, May 1985, p. 93.

44. "Chronicle of Events," *Soviet Jewish Affairs*, Vol. 9, No. 2, 1979, p. 96. Sher-

ling was pressured into becoming vice-chairman of the Anti-Zionist Committee (see Chapter 34), but refused and was dismissed from his theater position. *Jewish Currents,* October 1986, p. 47.

45. Israel Public Council for Soviet Jewry, *News Bulletin,* No. 181/182, July 31, 1980, p. 2.

46. Hirszowicz, "Jewish Cultural Life," op. cit., p. 18, and "Chronicle of Events," *Soviet Jewish Affairs,* Vol. 13, No. 2, May 1983, p. 100. Goldin did his doctoral disseration on Latvian folk music and devoted much time researching the field of Jewish folklore. He also wrote many instrumental pieces based on Jewish folk tunes. In 1972 he succeeded in having Jewish folk song transcriptions published in Russian. See Joachim Braun, "Jews in Soviet Music," in Jack Miller, ed., *Jews in Soviet Culture.* New Brunswick, N.J., Transaction Books, 1984, p. 90.

47. "Chronicle of Events." *Soviet Jewish Affairs,* Vol. 10, No. 2, May 1980, p. 97.

48. Braun, op. cit., p. 74.

49. Ibid.

50. Based on Igor Golomstok, "Aleksander Tyshler, 1898–1980," *Soviet Jewish Affairs,* Vol. 11, No. 3, November 1981, pp. 15–23.

51. Quoted by Igor Golomstok in "Jews in Soviet Art," in Miller, ed., *Jews in Soviet Culture,* op. cit., p. 50. See also Yuri Kuperman, " 'No Places!': The Jewish Outsider in the Soviet Union," *Soviet Jewish Affairs,* Vol. 3, No. 2, 1973, pp. 17–25 for a description of little-known Jewish artists.

52. *American Jewish Yearbook, 1974–1975,* Vol. 74, 1974, p. 503.

53. Anthony Austin, "Soviet Georgia Jews Win Prime Spot," *New York Times,* December 17, 1979, p. 6.

54. Data based on summary of article by Shapiro called "Judaism in the USSR" in the Soviet monthly *Nauka i religiya* (Science and Religion), No. 9, 1980, pp. 38–39, translated and published in *Soviet Jewish Affairs,* Vol. 11, No. 2, May 1981, pp. 62–64. The figure of 60,000 is up from 50,000 reported in 1976 (Moscow Radio English Broadcast, April 12, 13, 14, 1976, cited in Hirszowicz, "Jewish Cultural Life," op. cit., p. 21, note 21). Pinkus, however, warns that "these figures are suspect; indeed there are fewer than sixty known synagogues in the Soviet Union." On the various studies cited, he concludes that "we can estimate that 5–10 percent of Soviet Jews are observant." Pinkus, op. cit., p. 9.

55. Centers of large Jewish populations such as Kiev, Odessa, and Leningrad have no rabbis. Rabbi Israel Shvartsblatt was removed from his post as rabbi of Odessa's only synagogue in August 1972.

56. Hirszowicz, ibid., p. 11.

57. *American Jewish Yearbook, 1976,* Vol. 76, 1975, p. 378. In 1976, Rabbi Fishman and Iosif Shapiro reported that there were ten students at the yeshiva. Thomas E. Sawyer, *The Jewish Minority in the Soviet Union.* Boulder, Colo., Westview Press, 1979, pp. 77. However, in June 1982, Rabbi Fishman ordered the "Gemara study circle" closed. "Chronicle of Events," *Soviet Jewish Affairs,* Vol. 12, No. 3, 1982, p. 97.

58. Ibid. A visit which took place in August 1975 involved the president of the synagogue Mikhail Tandeytnik, Rosen, and Romanian church officials. The promise that "two more students" would be allowed to go to Budapest was repeated to Rabbi Schneier in September 1984. "Chronicle of Events," *Soviet Jewish Affairs,* Vol. 15, No. 2, May 1985, p. 92.

59. *Alert IV,* No. 5, October 31, 1979, p. 7. The students were Boris M. Gramm and Isaak V. Fuchs. The arrangement was made through the good offices of Rabbi Arthur Schneier, president of the Appeal of Conscience Foundation, which first proposed rabbinic training in the United States in 1965. Gramm's background is not altogether clear. He was graduated from Rostov University and "is said to have spent three years in the Moscow yeshiva." He became chairman of the Moscow religious community in 1979. See "Moscow's Choral Synagogue," document introduced and annotated by Hirszowicz, note 4, *Soviet Jewish Affairs,* Vol. 14, No. 2, May 1984, p. 65.

60. Soviet Embassy, Information Department. *Novosti Press Agency [Release],* November 17 and 25, 1980.

61. Quoted in *Jewish Currents,* June 1981, p. 47.

62. *Jewish Currents,* October 1981, p. 47.

63. Quoted from a review of the book, *Nastolny Iudeysky Kalendar Na 5739 God,* by Howard Spier, in *Soviet Jewish Affairs,* Vol. 9, No. 1, 1979, p. 75. The contents are described in pp. 75–76.

64. Ibid., p. 74. Spier notes that there is no way of knowing whether and to what extent the work is available to the Soviet Jewish public, nor how far it is intended for foreign consumption.

65. See Hirszowicz, "Moscow's Choral Synagogue," op. cit., pp. 63–66. The Czech journal is *Herald of the Jewish Religious Communities in Czechoslovakia.* Quotations are from Hirszowicz, pp. 64–65.

66. Release from Union of Councils for Soviet Jews, September 30, 1976. On May 9, 1985, it was reported that Rabbi Schneier led services and read Kaddish at the Babi Yar monument. Present were Rabbi Shayevich and representatives of the Russian Orthodox Church. "Chronicle of Events," *Soviet Jewish Affairs,* Vol. 15, No. 3, November 1985, pp. 95–96.

67. Ibid., p. 4.

68. Israel Public Council for Soviet Jewry, *News Bulletin,* No. 163/164, September 30, 1979, p. 12.

One other memorial to Jews who were murdered during the war has been reported in Pechora, 20 miles south of Nemirov, where 8,000 Jews were rounded up and buried alive. Morris Osterneck of Philadelphia, whose parents were among the victims, visited the Soviet Union in April 1976 and reported that his brother Israel, who lived in the Soviet Union, showed him a photograph of a monument which the authorities had agreed to erect with the help of funds raised by Morris. The inscription reads: "Here Are Buried 8,000 Soviet People—Jews Killed During the German Nazi Fascist Occupation, 1941–1944." Morris Osterneck himself later saw the monument. A. Einbinder, "Localite Wins Struggle for Soviet Shrine," *Jewish Exponent* (Philadelphia), July 9, 1976.

69. "Chronicle of Events," *Soviet Jewish Affairs*, Vol. 10, No. 2, May 1980, p. 97.
70. S. L. Shneiderman, *"Sovietish Heimland* and its Editor, Aron Vergelis," *Midstream*, October 1971, p. 38.
71. *Sovetish heymland*, 1973, No. 12, p. 131.
72. "Minutes from Forgotten Sources from Chernovtsy" (Yiddish), *Sovetish heymland*, August 1983, No. 8, pp. 71–77.
73. The complex history of the dictionary is described in Wolf Moscovich, "An Important Event in Soviet Yiddish Cultural Life: The New Russian-Yiddish Dictionary," *Soviet Jewish Affairs*, Vol. 14, No. 3, November 1984, pp. 31–49.
74. Ibid., p. 34.
75. Ibid., p. 35. The present dictionary was issued in 20,000 copies, more than half of which have been sold outside of the USSR.
76. Ibid., p. 38.
77. See also Rakhmiel Peltz' interesting essay, "The Dehebraization Controversy in Soviet Yiddish Language Planning: Standard or Symbol?" in Joshua A. Fishman, ed., *Readings in the Sociology of Jewish Languages.* Leiden, E. J. Brill, 1984, pp. 125–50.
78. Elias Schulman, "Soviet Yiddish Writing as Mirrored in Sovetish Heymland," *Jewish Book Annual*, Vol. 37, 1979–1980, p. 57.
79. Israel Kovelman, "Hebraistik in di rusishe lern-anshtaltn un visnshaftlekhe institutszes," *Sovetish heymland*, Vol. 3, 1975, pp. 158–62.
80. Moscovich, op. cit., p. 35.
81. *Sovetish heymland*, No. 1, 1976, p. 172.
82. *Sovetish heymland*, No. 9, 1981.
83. Hirszowicz, "Jewish Cultural Life," op. cit., p. 19.
84. "Chronicle of Events," *Soviet Jewish Affairs*, Vol. 10, No. 3, November 1982, p. 96. According to *Sovetish heymland*, No. 10, 1982, there were five students in the first group. See note 57 above.
85. "Chronicle of Events," *Soviet Jewish Affairs*, Vol. 13, No. 1, February 1983, p. 99.
86. According to the 1979 census, there were only 10,166 Jews in Birobidzhan, just 5 percent of the population, yet the area is still called the "Jewish Autonomous Region."
87. "As Jewish as Birobidzhan—A New Yiddish Primer," a review of *Alefbeys*, Kharbarovsk, 1982, by Lukasz Hirszowicz in *Soviet Jewish Affairs*, Vol. 14, No. 1, February 1984, pp. 85–86. Also noteworthy was the publication in Moscow of Der Nister's *Di Mishpokhe Mashber* in 1985, on the 100th anniversary of his birth.
88. See, for example, Theodore Shabad, "Study of Yiddish Given New Support in Soviet," *New York Times*, Section 1, March 20, 1983, p. 5.
89. One of the five lecturers in the Oxford program is Dov-Ber Kerler, son of the well-known Soviet Yiddish writer Yosef Kerler. He is also a doctoral student (1986) at Oxford preparing a thesis on Yiddish linguistics.

90. "Chronicle of Events," *Soviet Jewish Affairs*, Vol. 15, No. 2, May 1985, p. 95.
91. I have argued for the greater support of Yiddish in "Can Yiddish Be Revived in the Soviet Union?" *Present Tense*, May 1987, pp. 41–44, and enlarged possibilities through *Sovetish heymland* in "The Problematic of Sovetish Heymland," *Gratz College 90th Anniversary Annual*. Philadelphia, April 1987.
92. B. Pinkus, A. Greenbaum, and M. Altshuler, eds., *Pirsumim Rusiim Bi-Brit Ha-Moatsot al Yehudim Ve-Yahadut, 1967–1917*. Jerusalem, Society for Research on Jewish Communities, Historical Society of Israel, 1970, p. xiv.
93. Ibid., p. xvi.
94. Lukasz Hirszowicz, "Translations from Yiddish Published in the USSR, 1958–1979," *Soviet Jewish Affairs*, Vol. 12, No. 1, February 1982, pp. 20–21, 33–34. Detailed statistical and biographical analyses can be found in the appendixes, pp. 35–44. Hirszowicz also found a decline in the number of translations in the period 1971–1979 compared with 1958–1964. Ibid., p. 24.

As part of the "rehabilitation" process, a large anthology of Russian translations of the poetry of 48 Soviet Yiddish poets was published in 1985 (*Sovetskaya evreyskaya poeziya*, Moscow, Khudozhestvennaya literatura) in 10,000 copies. More than one-third of the volume contains poems by writers who, with the exception of Halkin, were killed in the war or in the purges. Among the translators were major Russian poets including Akhmatova, Antokolsky, and Evtushenko. "Books Received," *Soviet Jewish Affairs*, Vol. 16, No. 3, November 1986, p. 84.
95. For example, in 1976, Felix Dektor, who had been expelled from the Soviet Writers' Union, submitted a plan to the Union, urging that writings on Jewish thought and history and a Russian-language journal be permitted. *American Jewish Yearbook, 1977*, Vol. 77, 1976, p. 464.
96. For a survey of these permissible activities in the past ten years see "Jewish Culture in the USSR," *IJA Research Reports*, No. 10, Institute of Jewish Affairs (London), December 1985.

34. A People in Limbo: The Continuing Soviet Jewish Predicament

1. *American Jewish Yearbook, 1974–75*, Vol. 74, 1974, p. 498.
2. Israel Public Council for Soviet Jewry, *News Bulletin*, No. 181/182, July 31, 1980, p. 7.
3. *Sovetish heymland*, No. 6, 1973, p. 168, and No. 12, 1973, p. 144.
4. *American Jewish Yearbook, 1974–75*, op. cit., p. 500.
5. *Moskva*, No. 3, March 1975, cited by William W. Korey, "The Soviet Public Anti-Zionist Committee," *Midstream*, August–September, 1985, p. 12.
6. *Voprosy Istorii*, No. 7, July 1975, cited by Korey, op. cit., p. 13.
7. Quoted in Daniel P. Moynihan, "Z=R, Plus 9," *Forum*, No. 54/55, Spring 1985, p. 1.

8. Ibid., p. 2.
9. Ibid., p. 5.
10. Martin Gilbert, *Shcharansky: Hero of Our Time*. New York, Viking, 1986, pp. 161–68, 180; and Sara Honig, "A Warning to Activists," *Jerusalem Post*, International ed., February 8, 1977.
11. Israel Public Council for Soviet Jewry, *News Bulletin*, No. 145/146, December 31, 1978, p. 8.
12. *Jewish Currents*, February 1981, p. 47. The full text of the letter was published in *Present Tense*, Autumn 1980, p. 80, and in R. Okuneva, "Anti-Semitic Notions: Strange Analogies," Jacob M. Kelman, ed., *Anti-Semitism in the Soviet Union: Its Roots and Consequences*, Vol. 2. Jerusalem, Hebrew University Center for Research and Documentation of East European Jewry, 1980, p. 189–97. Her full study, showing similarities between statements by leaders of the Black Hundreds and Nazi ideologists on the one hand, and those of Soviet authors, is published in Kelman, pp. 198–313, and a bibliography of the works consulted, on pp. 324–36. This documentation must stand as one of the most exhaustive indictments of Soviet anti-Semitism, often masked as anti-Zionism. Dr. Okuneva's letter was also published in Yiddish in *Morgen Freiheit*, December 23, 1980. See also note 21.
13. John A. Armstrong, "Soviet Nationalities Policy," in Lukasz Hirszowicz, ed., *Proceedings of the Experts' Conference on Soviet Jewry*, London, January 4–6, 1983. London, Institute of Jewish Affairs, 1985, pp. 67, 68. Armstrong cites Soviet press reports of protests by Russian parents against their adult children accompanying "morally depraved" spouses who emigrated, p. 71, note 26. S. Lukin in the samizdat journal *Jews in the USSR*, No. 17, identified several leading officials of the All-Union Komsomol Central Committee, rightist dissidents and editors on the *Molodaya Gvardiya* publishing staff who are taking this line. Pamyat (Memory), organized in 1980, became militantly anti-Semitic in 1987.
14. Theodore H. Friedgut, "Soviet Anti-Zionism and Anti-Semitism—Another Cycle," *Soviet Jewish Affairs*, Vol. 14, No. 1, February 1984, p. 10. Friedgut cites several of the articles by Kravtsov and Korneev, showing how broad a platform they enjoy, p. 21.
15. The appeal was published in *Pravda* and *Izvestia* on April 1, 1983. An English translation of the full text and analysis was published in L. Hirszowicz and H. Spier, "Eight Soviet Jews Appeal for the Creation of an Anti-Zionist Committee," in Institute of Jewish Affairs *Research Report*, No. 6, 1983. Material on the Committee has been drawn from ibid.; Friedgut, "Soviet Anti-Zionism," op. cit.; Korey, op. cit., pp. 11–17; and Howard Spier, "The Soviet Anti-Zionist Committee—Bleak Prospects for Soviet Jewry," *Israel Horizons*, November–December, 1983, pp. 11–15. A translation of a press conference held by the Committee on June 22, 1983, appears in *Soviet Jewish Affairs*, Vol. 13, No. 3, November 1983, pp. 54–68.
16. "Pravda Equates Zionism with Fascism," Institute of Jewish Affairs *Research Report*, No. 2, 1984, p. 3. Translation of the text appears in *Soviet Jewish Affairs*, Vol. 14, No. 1, February 1984, pp. 71–75.

17. Korey, op. cit., p. 15. Kolesnikov, an obscure novelist, is a Jew by birth and a member of the anti-Zionist Committee.
18. Ibid., p. 16.
19. Friedgut makes this point, op. cit., pp. 9, 19.
20. Martynov's "open letter" is translated and annotated by Howard Spier in "Documents: Jews and Russian Culture," *Soviet Jewish Affairs,* Vol. 14, No. 2, May 1984, pp. 55–61.
21. The documentation of Soviet anti-Semitism in English is abundant. Besides material in journals such as *Soviet Jewish Affairs, Midstream, Moment, Present Tense, Insight,* and *Jewish Currents,* the Institute of Jewish Affairs in London has published *Soviet Antisemitic Propaganda: Evidence from Books, Press and Radio* (1978), and the Center for Research and Documentation of East European Jewry of the Hebrew University has published three important volumes called *Anti-Semitism in the Soviet Union: Its Roots and Causes.* Vol. 1 (1979) contains the Proceedings of the Seminar on Soviet Anti-Semitism held in Jerusalem, April 7–8, 1978, and includes a short list of anti-Semitic works published in the USSR in the 1960s and 1970s. Vol. 2 (1980) contains papers delivered at the International Colloquium on Anti-Semitism in the Soviet Union held in Paris, March 18–19, 1979. It also contains some material from samizdat and the following material from Ruth Okuneva: her letter to Brezhnev referred to above and a detailed tabulation described in note 12. Vol. 3 (1983) includes a long introduction by S. Ettinger, various special studies including one by Okuneva on the position of Jews in Soviet school syllabi, excerpts from Soviet publications and samizdat (including cartoons) from the 1940s through the 1970s, and a list of anti-Semitic and anti-Zionist books published in the USSR in 1979–81.
22. Sara Honig, "Luntz Assesses Soviet Jewish Plight," *Alert,* May–June, 1976, p. 7.
23. *Anti-Semitism in the Soviet Union,* Vol. 3, op. cit., p. x.
24. Yaacov Ro'i, "Soviet Policies and Attitudes toward Israel, 1948–1978," *Soviet Jewish Affairs,* Vol. 8, No. 1, 1978, p. 44.
25. *American Jewish Yearbook, 1974–75,* op. cit., p. 504.
26. *American Jewish Yearbook, 1976,* op. cit., p. 382.
27. *American Jewish Yearbook, 1977,* op. cit., pp. 458, 460.
28. Described in Yossi Sarid, "The Israeli Delegation to the USSR," *Jewish Frontier,* February 1979, pp. 8–12.
29. Chaim Herzog, "Talking to the Soviet Union," *Jerusalem Post,* September 25, 1981.
30. *Jerusalem Post,* December 29, 1981.
31. *Jerusalem Post,* International ed., January 3, 1982.
32. These contacts are described in Raphael Vago, "Soviet and East European Relations with Israel since Camp David," *Soviet Jewish Affairs,* Vol. 13, No. 3, November, 1983, pp. 7–26.
33. Ibid., p. 12.
34. Rita E. Hauser, "The Jerusalem–Moscow Avenue to Mideast Peace," *New York Times,* September 9, 1986.

35. Y. Ro'i, "Aliyah vs. Neshira," *Experts' Conference*, op. cit., pp. 143–45.
36. "Disinterest in Western Media Dampens Hopes Summit Will Help Soviet Union's Jews," *Forward* (English Section), October 4, 1985.
37. Albert Axelbank, "A 'Jewish National State'?" *Present Tense*, Autumn 1976, pp. 20–23. Earlier, there was a bizarre report of a new group called North American Jewry for Birobidzhan (NAJB) in 1972, which tried to recruit candidates for Birobidzhan in Boston on the ideological premise that Birobidzhan, not "Palestine" (the name "Israel" was not used) was the true homeland of Jews everywhere. A graduate student in Slavic and Russian studies, Claude Yevreysky [*sic!*] was interviewed by *Genesis II*, a Jewish student newspaper in the Boston area, and admitted looking for recruits in the United States and Canada. He refused to give any figures on membership and could not elucidate the group's "concrete program, as most of our proposals are classified," but said it would establish branches "in the very near future in Fargo, North Dakota and in Chicoutimi, Quebec," and a Birobidzhan agency in Cambridge. When the question of language in Birobidzhan was raised, Yevreysky said it would be Judeo-German. "Birobidzhan," he said, "is thirsting for workers to till the soil," and his group is "trying to convince the North American community that their homeland is in Birobidzhan," and that the Jews in Israel would also "see the light." When the interviewer raised the question of Soviet support for the State of Israel as a Jewish homeland, he said "the Soviet Union had no way of knowing that Israel would turn into a lackey of American imperialism." Described in *Genesis II* (Boston), November 16, 1972, p. 7.
38. Reported in "Chronicle of Events," *Soviet Jewish Affairs*, Vol. 9, No. 1, 1979, p. 98. See also "Soviet Jewry: A Review of Developments in 1978–79," in Institute of Jewish Affairs *Research Report*, 1980, for Soviet attempts to give new emphasis to the role of Birobidzhan in Soviet Jewish life.

William Mandel ("An Interview with Director Yuri Sherling: Rebuilding the Moscow Musical Theater," *Jewish Currents*, December 1983) wrote a highly exaggerated account of the theater, later realistically reviewed by the editor of *Jewish Currents* Morris U. Schappes. Schappes described Sherling as being in an "anomalous position . . . pathetically dangled by the authorities before carefully selected and carefully restricted parts of the Soviet theater public." (*Jewish Currents*, March 1984, p. 40.)
39. *Soviet Jewish Affairs*, Vol. 10, No. 2, May 1980, p. 98.
40. *Soviet Jewish Affairs*, Vol. 10, No. 3, November 1980, p. 89.
41. *Soviet Jewish Affairs*, Vol. 12, No. 2, May 1982, p. 87.
42. Lukasz Hirszowicz, "As Jewish as Birobidzhan—A New Yiddish Primer," *Soviet Jewish Affairs*, Vol. 14, No. 1, February 1984, pp. 82–83, 84, 85.
43. David Harris, "A Note on the Problem of the 'Noshrim'," "*Soviet Jewish Affairs*, Vol. 6, No. 2, 1976, p. 105.
44. Ilya Zilberberg, "From Russia to Israel: A Personal Case-History," *Soviet Jewish Affairs*, [Vol. 2], No. 3, May 1972, p. 49.
45. Dr. Howard Shevrin, "Refuseniks: The Internal Refugees of Russia," *Alert*, November–December 1981, pp. 3–4. Dr. Lev Goldfarb, a neurologist and

former refusenik, who formerly treated fellow-refuseniks for stress, has been lecturing in the United States on the problem and has formed an international committee of concerned physicians. *Forward*, October 24, 1986, p. 24.

46. *Alert*, op. cit., pp. 3, 4.

47. McGill University law professor Irwin Cotlar, who had been working on behalf of Ida Nudel for eight years, brought up the question of her banishment with the head of the Soviet delegation at the Helsinki Review Conference in Vienna in November 1986. He was told that there were "state reasons" which prevented her departure; this, despite Gorbachev's statement that no one can invoke state reasons after a lapse of more than ten years. In Nudel's case it had been fifteen years since she first applied to leave. "Soviet Public Relations on the Emigration Issue," *Forward* (English Section), January 16, 1987, pp. 13, 32. In October 1986, she was physically prevented from traveling to Moscow to meet Elie Wiesel. See Martin Gilbert, "Ida Nudel: An Appeal from Afar," *Forward* (English section), January 9, 1987, p. 11.

48. David K. Shipler, *Russia: Broken Idols, Solemn Dreams*. New York, Viking, 1983, pp. 370–71.

49. Published in *Alert*, November 16, 1979, p. 5. Slepak and his wife Masha completed their internal exile sentence in December 1982, but they were not allowed to emigrate until October 14, 1987. Particularly poignant and deeply introspective are the letters of Shcharansky to his parents and messages to his wife Avital published in Gilbert op. cit., p. 293–325, 349–408.

50. *Alert*, May 3, 1982, p. 3.

51. Avraham Shifrin has collected an immensely detailed body of material on the Soviet Gulag in his *The First Guidebook to Prisons and Concentrations Camps of the Soviet Union*, tr. from the Russian. New York, Bantam, 1982.

52. David K. Shipler, "Exiles Still Face and Adjust to Siberia's Inhumanity to Man," *New York Times*, April 30, 1978.

53. Based on information from the Student Struggle for Soviet Jewry, the Union of Councils of Soviet Jews, the National Conferences on Soviet Jewry and "Chronicle of Events," 1985–1986 issues of *Soviet Jewish Affairs*, the Prisoners of Zion (or Zion), as of January 1987, were as follows: Moshe Abramov, Evgeny Aizenberg, Iosif Berenshteyn, Iosif Begun, Alexander Chernyak, Yuly Edelshteyn, Evgeny Koifman, Yakov Levin, Mark Livshits, Alexei Magarik, Mark Nepomnyashchy, Yakov Rosenberg, Anatoly Virshuvsky, Leonid Volvovsky, Alexander Yakir, Vladimir Yelchin, Iosif Zisels, Roald Zelichenok, and Zakhar Zunshain. It was also reported in the *Jerusalem Post*, September 23, 1986, that Grigory Steshenko, a refusenik from Krivoy Rog was still in a psychiatric hospital. He was expelled from the Dnepropetrovsk Institute in January 1984 for attending synagogue services. This behavior was deemed "incompatible with the ideological and political image of a Soviet student." In the *Jerusalem Post*, September 9, 1986, seven of the Prisoners of Zion at the time were reported to be suffering from "serious health problems, aggravated by the harshness of prison conditions and

the stricter regimes often accorded to Jewish prisoners." However, in surprise Soviet concessions, all of the Prisoners of Zion were released as of
September 1987 and a number permitted to emigrate.

The latest full account of all Prisoners of Conscience, covering the period
from June 1975 to May 1979, was published by Amnesty International in
April 1980 (*Prisoners of Conscience in the USSR: Their Treatment and Conditions*, London), and among other details explains that only certain lawyers
are given official clearance to act as defense counsel in human rights cases.
These are compiled by the KGB in a confidential list given to each college
of advocates. As of May 1982, forty-eight of the seventy-one men and women
in the various Helsinki Watch groups were serving 443 years of imprisonment. *Alert*, May 24, 1982, p. 5. As of May 30, 1987, Keston College reported 296 religious prisoners. *Soviet Jewish Affairs*, Vol. 17, No. 2, Summer–Autumn 1987, p. 84.

54. Zvi Nezer, "Jewish Emigration from the USSR in 1981–82," *Soviet Jewish
Affairs*, Vol. 12, No. 3, November 1982, p. 15. The longest-term refusenik
is Benjamin Bogomolny from Moscow, who first applied to emigrate in
1966. He was finally allowed to leave October 1, 1986.

55. Ibid. Various sources reported 11,000 refuseniks as of January 1987. In Martin
Gilbert, *The Jews of Hope: The Plight of Soviet Jewry Today* (London, Macmillan, 1984, p. 78), the author estimates the number of refuseniks to be about
10,000. The book is based on the author's visit in early 1983 to several
major cities in western USSR, where he visited with a number of refuseniks.

56. For example, Alexander Lavout, a mathematician in Moscow, was involved
in monitoring alleged Soviet use of psychiatric hospitals to silence dissidents. Natalia Rosenshtein and Riva Feldman became active in the Moscow
Women's Group. Natasha Khassin of Moscow has looked to the needs of
prisoners in distant parts of the Soviet Union. Alexander Kholmyansky is
a Hebrew teacher and religious activist from Moscow whose courage during a five-month hunger strike and defiant testimony at his trial has made
him a hero among young activists. A gun had been planted in his apartment and he was arrested in July 1984 and tried early in 1985. Yuly Edelshteyn, another young Hebrew teacher, was arrested in September 1984
on trumped-up drug charges. The KGB claimed that they found opium;
actually it was tobacco. Iosif Zisels, a young physicist from Chernovtsy, a
prisoner in a strict regime camp in Sokiryany, was active in helping other
prisoners improve their conditions. Alexei Magarik, a young cellist and
Hebrew teacher was sent to a labor camp for allegedly possessing 6 grams
of hashish (which had been planted by the KGB). He made a stirring defense of his innocence.

57. *Alert*, August 28, 1980, p. 3.

58. *Alert*, November 16, 1979, p. 3. Ironically, while Jews struggle to have the
freedom to study Hebrew, an all-Union Conference on Linguistic Reconstruction and the Ancient History of the East was organized by the Soviet
Academy of Sciences' Oriental Institute in April 1985, at which time several

papers on the Hebrew Language were submitted. *Soviet Jewish Affairs*, Vol. 15, No. 3, November 1985, p. 95.

59. *Alert*, March 31, 1981, p. 4. In 1987, Prestin and Abramovich were granted permission to leave.

60. *Alert*, October 23, 1981, pp. 1–2. There was another heavy crack-down in August and September 1985. *Alert*, February 1985, pp. 1–2.

61. *New York Times*, October 7, 1981.

62. Israel Public Council for Soviet Jewry, *News Bulletin*, No. 225/226, August 31, 1982, p. 6.

63. Quoted from "Sovietskaya Moldavya" (n.d.) in ibid., pp. 7–8.

64. "Chronicle of Events," *Soviet Jewish Affairs*, Vol. 16, No. 2, May 1986, p. 99; *Jerusalem Post*, October 21, 1986; *Jerusalem Post*, November 4, 1986.

65. This includes large shipments of grain from the United States, chemicals and machinery from Western Europe, and the immense benefits being derived from the ongoing construction of a gas pipeline connecting Europe with the Soviet Union.

66. See Peter Reddaway's "Waiting for Gorbachev," *New York Review*, October 10, 1985, pp. 5–10, for a graphic description of some of these problems and Reddaway's cautious optimism about possibilities for change.

On October 4, 1986, the Soviet government announced a plan of legislation for the next five years to codify Gorbachev's blueprint for the reconstruction of Soviet society. Thirty-eight measures were listed, including laws on voting, referenda, economic incentives, the pricing system, intrusion on the rights of citizens, on the activities of the KGB. Gorbachev, however, has been meeting with considerable resistance and has complained that "his plans have become mired in red ink and bureaucracy." "Soviet to Codify Gorbachev Overhaul," *New York Times*, October 7, 1986.

67. Michael Heller in his "The Price of Revolution," *Midstream*, April 1982, pp. 7–11, describes the "demographic catastrophes" in Soviet history and the incomplete, often deliberately false, data published by official statisticians. "Each Soviet generation," he writes, "lived through a demographic shock and remembered the preceding one. Fear became the most important element of stability in the system. . . . Soviet society lives in the hope that tomorrow will not be worse than today or yesterday" (p. 10).

A samizdat study by an author who was imprisoned in 1980 estimates that Soviet population losses were between 43 and 52 million in the period covered. Iosif G. Dyadkin, *Unnatural Deaths in the USSR, 1928–1954*, Tania Deruguine, tr. New Brunswick, N.J., Transaction Books, 1983.

68. This summarization is based on Lukasz Hirszowicz, "The Twenty-Seventh Congress of the CPSU," *Soviet Jewish Affairs*, Vol. 16, No. 2, May 1986, pp. 3–27. A sound biography of Gorbachev is Christian Schmidt-Häuer, *Gorbachev: The Path to Power*, E. Osers and C. Romberg, trs. London, I. B. Tauris, 1986.

69. William W. Korey, "Mikhail Gorbachev's 'Potemkin Villages'," *Forward*, December 26, 1986, p. 3. However, S. J. Roth underscored the Soviet position by referring to Soviet statements at the 10th Anniversary Meeting of

the Signing of the Helsinki Final Act, July 30–August 1, 1985 at Helsinki, and at earlier meetings. These meetings "brought into sharp relief the differing concepts on human rights." At a meeting in Berne, April 15–May 27, 1986, the chief Soviet delegate Yuri Kashlev said, regarding emigration, "in the Soviet Union . . . there are neither social nor national causes for emigration . . . we have no unemployment and the Constitution . . . guarantees equal social, political, and cultural rights to all its citizens of every nationality." There was a very serious Soviet attempt at Berne to exclude the reunion of Soviet Jews with relatives in Israel from the scope of the Helsinki process. Roth, "From Madrid to Vienna: What Progress in the Helsinki Process," *Soviet Jewish Affairs*, Vol. 16, No. 3, November 1986, pp. 3–16.

70. "Soviet Spin Control," *Time*, October 20, 1986, p. 28.

71. "Release of Sakharovs Welcomed But Kremlin Reminded 'Reality' as Many Others Suffer," *Forward* (English Section), December 26, 1986, p. 25.

Marchenko's crusade on behalf of Soviet political prisoners virtually consumed his whole life. Since 1958, with few interludes, he had lived in labor camps, prisons, or exile, often in solitary confinement. His friendship with Yuli Daniel in a camp in Mordovia and later with other dissidents matured him politically, and challenged the regime through extreme actions—giving up his Soviet citizenship, wanting to emigrate to the United States, but refusing a visa to Israel. He engaged in numerous hunger strikes and resisted forced feeding. His book *Moi Pokazaniya* (My Testimony, translated by Michael Scammell, and published in 1969) was one of the first accounts of life in the prisons and camps, the suffering and degradation endured in the post-Stalin period. It also described the anti-Jewish abuse of Daniel by the other prisoners and some security guards. Shcharansky, when he visited Philadelphia on December 14, 1986 said that Marchenko had been on a hunger strike for three and a half months protesting a beating, suggested that Marchenko lacked the public support that had saved *him*, because of a new hesitancy about criticizing Soviet policies. "Public opinion is not ready [because of the deceptive Gorbachev style] to take such critical stands against the Soviet Union." *Jewish Exponent* (Philadelphia), December 19, 1986.

72. " 'Mere Words' When It Comes to Soviet Jews, Conference Says of Gorbachev's 'Glasnost'," *Forward* (English Section), January 16, 1987, p. 21.

73. "Shcharansky-Orlov Challenge USSR Trade Benefits," *Forward* (English Section), January 30, 1987, p. 18.

74. Martin Gilbert, "Sh[ch]aransky in London: Linkage Is the Key," *Jerusalem Post*, November 4, 1986.

75. Vice Premier and Foreign Minister Peres set the terms under which Israel would be willing to participate in such a conference in meetings with French leaders in January 1987. "Peres Says Israel Would Support International Conference," *Forward* (English Section), January 30, 1987, p. 11.

76. Earlier the proposals of Goldmann and Decter, among others, were rejected. In the 1980s, the approaches of Edgar M. Bronfman, president of

the World Jewish Congress; Rabbi Alexander M. Schindler, president of the American Hebrew Congregations, and local efforts to moderate Jewish dependence upon the American hardline in American-Soviet relations and lower the strident rhetoric have not been adopted. Professor Stephen F. Cohen of Princeton University has also been critical of mainstream American Jewish resort to public protest as the primary means of trying to change Soviet policy toward its Jews. In his *Rethinking the Soviet Experience* (Oxford, Oxford University Press, 1985), he blames the West for worsening the Cold War and for "misperceptions" of communism, arguing that the Soviet Union must be acknowledged as a full-fledged global power, coequal with the United States, and that the dissident and Jewish activist movements are being badly used by the West.

For various aspects of these differences, see "East-West Relations: A Jewish Perspective," address delivered by Rabbi Alexander M. Schindler at the January 1985 meeting of the World Jewish Congress; "Israel and Russia," *Boston Jewish Times,* July 25, 1985; Address of Bronfman to the Central Council of Jews in Germany in Munich, March 27, 1984; "Re-examining Strategies for Soviet Jewry Advocacy," paper delivered by Dr. Lawrence Rubin at the National Jewish Community Relations Advisory Council Plenum, February 28, 1984; and October 3, 1986, editorial in *Jewish Chronicle* (London). This author tends to agree with these analyses and approaches.

77. Minutes, Soviet Jewry Council of Philadelphia, October 24, 1985.

In February 1984, Yad Vashem honored Halina Musinskas, who rescued many Jews in Kaunas during the war. *Soviet Jewish Affairs,* Vol. 14, No. 2, 1984, p. 99.

Glossary

AGITPROP. Agitation-propaganda and departments devoted to agitation and propaganda within the Communist party of the Soviet Union.

AGRO-JOINT. American Jewish Joint Agricultural Corporation, which helped resettle Jews on the land, 1924–1938.

ARTEL. A producers' cooperative formed by artisans or peasants.

ASSR. Autonomous Soviet Socialist Republic.

BEZBOZHNIK (THE AETHEIST). The name of a Communist newspaper attacking religion, started in 1922, which became an organ of the League of Militant Aetheists in 1925.

BLACK HUNDREDS. Extreme rightist groups in Russia in the early 1900s, which disseminated anti-Jewish propaganda and instigated pogroms.

BREST-LITOVSK TREATY. Ended Russia's participation in World War I, signed March 1918 with the USSR, giving up the Baltic states, Poland, the Ukraine, Georgia, and Finland to Germany.

BUND. General League of Jewish Workers in Russia and Poland, organized in 1897. Helped to found Russian Social Democratic Workers' Party in 1898, but intense struggles with Lenin led to its withdrawal from the party in 1903 over the issues of federalism and national-cultural autonomy. Greatly influenced Jewish workers in early twentieth century through its ideology, political and economic program, and network of cultural and social institutions.

CHEKA. The All-Russian Commission for Suppression of Counterrevolution, Sabotage and Speculation, the first secret political police, 1917–22, succeeded by the GPU.

CHEVRAS. Voluntary associations or societies in the Pale of Settlement providing services to widows, orphans, indigent aged, unemployed and injured workers, burial for the deceased, and mutual aid exchanges. In some towns, the chevras were the forerunners of Jewish guilds and trade unions.

COLLECTIVIZATION. Forced nationalization of farms and farm colonies, 1928–33.

COMINFORM. Communist Information Bureau, started in 1947. It was dissolved in 1956.

COMINTERN. Acronym for Communist International, the world organization of Communist parties, 1919–43.

COMMISSARIAT FOR JEWISH NATIONAL AFFAIRS (known as Evkom). A central governmental organization with provincial bodies, set up in 1918, within the People's Commissariat for Nationality Affairs (Narkomnats), to win Jews over to Communism, to combat non-Bolshevik Jewish parties, and to create local Jewish Sections *(Evsektsii)*. Dissolved in 1924.

CONSTITUENT ASSEMBLY. Freely elected representative body which met in January 1918 and was dissolved by the Bolsheviks.

COSSACKS. Frontier warriors, particularly skillful as horsemen and scouts, who created a semi-military, semi-agricultural caste with its own head (hetman) in the Ukraine in the seventeenth century and often perpetrated massacres of Jews in tsarist Russia.

DVADSATKA. A group of twenty people requesting permission to hold religious services.

EKOPO. Acronym for Russian words meaning Committee for Jewish Relief, started in 1916 to aid Jewish war victims.

EVKOM. See Commissariat for Jewish National Affairs.

EVSEKTSII (EVREISKIE SEKTSII, popularly known as the EVSEKTSIYA). Jewish Sections of the Communist party (1918–30), created to bring the Communist message to the Jewish masses and create "the dictatorship of the proletariat on the Jewish street." Dissolved in 1930.

FARAYNIGTE. United Jewish Socialist Workers Party, at first anti-Bolshevik, divided into factions in 1919, with one joining the Kombund, another, the Komfarband, and ultimately being absorbed into the Communist party in the Ukraine and Belorussia.

GLAVLIT. Chief Administration for Literary and Publishing Affairs, i.e., the central censorship organ.

GOSPLAN. State planning agency, responsible for long-range planning.

GPU. Russian acronym for State Political Administration, i.e., the secret political police, which replaced the Cheka in 1922. In the same year when the USSR was formed, the official designation was changed to OGPU, the "O" standing for "united" in Russian.

GULAG. Russian acronym for Chief Administration of Corrective Labor Camps, a vast Soviet penal system.

HASKALAH. Movement of enlightenment or modernism, influenced by German Jews, aimed at introducing secular studies and reformist measures in Jewish life in the Pale of Settlement.

IKOR. Pro-Communist American Jewish organization that contributed money and equipment to agricultural colonies through OZET and to Birobidzhan.

JAC. Jewish Antifascist Committee. Organized in 1942 to rally Jewish support for war. It was an important Jewish organization and cultural agency. It dissolved in 1948.

JDC. American Joint Distribution Committee, founded in 1914, and offering worldwide relief to Jewish communities, including relief to Jews in the Soviet Union in the 1920s.

JTA. Jewish Telegraphic Agency.

KAHAL, or KEHILLAH. Self-governing body permitted Jews in tsarist Russia until 1844, embracing totality of Jewish communal life and used by the government for enforcement of laws and collection of taxes. After 1844, functions were absorbed by voluntary bodies and liquidated after the Bolshevik Revolution.

KGB. Russian acronym for State Security Committee, used to describe Soviet secret police since 1953.

KHEDER (pl. KHADARIM). Literally, room, in Hebrew; the name given to a traditional Jewish elementary school.

KOMBUND. The section of the Ukrainian Bund that split off to become a Communist Bund in 1918. In Belorussia the process took place in 1920.

KOMFARBAND. Short-lived merger of short-lived Kombund and pro-Bolshevik Socialist parties with Jewish Communist party in the Ukraine in 1919. After a few months it joined the Communist party of the Ukraine. In Belorussia the Komfarband was formed in 1920 and joined the Communist party in 1921 after arduous efforts to maintain organizational autonomy.

KOMSOMOL. Communist League of Youth in the USSR, controlled by the Communist party.

KOMZET. Committee for the Settlement of Jewish Toilers on the Land, 1924–38.

KUSTAR. Self-employed artisan.

LISHENTSY. So-called declassed persons of bourgeois or capitalist origins or occupation who were penalized in various ways after the Bolshevik Revolution.

MENSHEVIKS. Democratic faction of Russian Social Democratic Workers' Party, split away from Bolsheviks in 1903 and was repressed after the Bolshevik Revolution.

MGB. Russian acronym for Ministry of State Security (1946–1953), referring to Soviet secret police. Succeeded by KGB.

MOHEL. Ritual circumciser.

NARODNIK. Member of populist revolutionary movement in tsarist Russia.

NEP. Russian and English acronym for New Economic Policy, a period of limited private enterprise from 1921 to 1927.

NKGB. Acronym for People's Commissariat of State Security, served as Soviet secret police from 1943 to 1946.

NKVD. Acronym for People's Commissariat of Internal Affairs, which served as Soviet secret police from 1934 to 1943, succeeded by NKGB. The NKVD special boards became one of the most formidable weapons of repression under Stalin, exempted from all criminal procedural requirements. In the late 1930s and 1940s, their sentencing powers were increased from five- and ten-year to twenty-five-year terms. In 1941–42, NKVD had its own military units at the war fronts.

OGPU. Acronym for United State Political Administration, i.e., the secret political police, 1922–1934. In 1934, OGPU's juridical functions were transferred to NKVD's (q.v.) special boards. Administratively, OGPU was absorbed by NKVD.

OKHRANA. Tsarist secret police, from the Russian word meaning "guard."

ORT. Organization for Rehabilitation and Training, founded in St. Petersburg in 1880; for a time set up training programs in Jewish colonies and workshops in the Soviet Union until 1938. It still functions worldwide in surviving Jewish communities.

OVIR. (OTDEL VIZY I REGISTRATSII). Visa and Registration Department of the Ministry of Internal Affairs, which processes applications for permission to leave the Soviet Union through its local offices.

OZE. Acronym for Russian words meaning Society for the Preservation of the Health of the Jewish Population.

OZET. Society for the Settlement of Jewish Toilers on the Land, 1925–38.

PALE OF SETTLEMENT. Geographically restricted area of Jewish settlement in Russia, first defined after the Partitions of Poland (1772, 1793, 1795) and formalized in 1835.

POALE TSION. Socialist-Zionist party, formed in 1906 and basing its platform on the Zionist-Marxist synthesis of Ber Borokhov. Its extreme left wing was permitted to exist in the Soviet Union until 1928.

POLITBURO. All-powerful Political Bureau of the Central Committee of the Communist Party of the Soviet Union, known as the Presidium from 1952 to 1966; headed by party leader (the Secretary General), the Politburo is the supreme and only policy-making body in the USSR.

PROLETKULT. Abbreviated form for Proletarian Cultural and Educational Organization, 1917–1932.

PROVISIONAL GOVERNMENT. Coalition government in Russia after overthrow of tsarist regime in March 1917, under Prince Lvov and Kerensky; overthrown by Bolsheviks in October 1917.

RSFSR. Russian Soviet Federated Socialist Republic.

SHOCHET. Ritual slaughterer of animals who prepares meat for religiously observant Jews.

SHTETL (pl. SHTETLACH). Small Jewish town, characteristic locale of Jewish life in the Pale of Settlement under Russian tsars.

SOCIAL REVOLUTIONARY PARTY. Founded in 1901, peasant-oriented movement influenced by populist ideas, spreading agitation among peasantry and resorting to terror in response to increasing reaction in early 1900s. Called for end to autocracy, distribution of land to people and self-determination for minorities. At first the SR's cooperated with the Bolsheviks in overthrowing the Provisional Government, but soon became an opposition force which established separate regimes in western Siberia and at Samara and enjoyed great support in the Constituent Assembly (1918). Suppressed by Bolsheviks in 1921–22.

SOMINFORMBURO. Soviet information agency formed during World War II.

SOVIET. A council. In 1905, soviets of workers and soldiers demanded constitutional government and fundamental economic and social reforms. In 1917, the soviet in Petersburg became an important source of support for Lenin's plan to seize power.

VTsIK. Acronym for the All-Union Russian Central Executive Committee, the highest body of the Russian Soviet Federated Socialist Republic from 1917 to 1937, when it was succeeded by the Presidium of the RSFSR Supreme Soviet. The Central Committee of the USSR (TsIK) was the national equivalent of VTsIK and lasted from 1922 to 1938, to be succeeded by the Presidium of the national Supreme Soviet.

YESHIVAH (pl. YESHIVOT). Academy for advanced Talmudic studies.

Index